The Indignant Muse

The indignant Muse, with unrelenting hand,
Shall bind them pilloried to their thrones of shame

— *Roger Casement* (see p. 346)

Little pens, if tipped with fire,
Cause the Revolution's shock

— *John Fitz-Gerald* (see p. 41)

The Indignant Muse

Poetry and Songs of the
Irish Revolution
1887–1926

Compiled and edited by
Terry Moylan

THE LILLIPUT PRESS
MMXVI

First published 2016 by
THE LILLIPUT PRESS
62–63 Sitric Road, Arbour Hill
Dublin 7, Ireland
www.lilliputpress.ie

Foreword © Gearóid Ó Tuathaigh, 2016
Introduction and notes © Terry Moylan and Liam McNulty, 2016

ISBN 978 1 84351 664 4

1 3 5 7 9 10 8 6 4 2

A CIP record for this title is available
from The British Library.

Set in 9 pt on 12 pt Sabon by Terry Moylan
Printed in Navarre, Spain, by GraphyCems

Contents

Foreword

Few 'poets of one poem' are as frequently quoted as Arthur O'Shaughnessy, whose 'Ode' to the music makers – 'the movers and shakers' – includes the confident boast:

> One man with a dream, at pleasure,
> Shall go forth and conquer a crown;
> And three with a new song's measure
> Can trample an empire down.

Very different claims – but, in their way, no less extravagant – have been made by others for the historical role and significance of popular ballad and song. Terry Moylan is inclined to concur with Andrew Fletcher's view that 'if a man were permitted to make all the ballads he need not care who should make the laws of a nation.' The great collector and singer Frank Harte claimed that 'those in power write the history, those who suffer write the songs.' Yeats worried aloud that a play of his had 'sent out' men whom the English shot. Nor are such claims confined to the Irish historical experience: the myth that Verdi's 'Chorus of the Hebrew slaves' in *Nabucco* excited an Italian audience to launch a revolution has stubbornly resisted scholarly debunking.

The Irish revolutionary decade might seem a suitable episode for testing such claims. The lead-in to the revolutionary events of 1913 to 1923 was marked by an extraordinary cultural revival of many strands; with a literary renaissance in English (in various forms – poetry, prose and drama), and a movement to arrest and reverse the long-term decline of Irish as a spoken language and to develop it as a literary medium for the modern world. A proliferation of reviews, journals, magazines, and newspapers provided an outlet for literary effort of every kind and standard, and a lively culture of song performance (from street-singers to theatrical settings) ensured a steady demand for songs and ballads. The pre-war generation was the last before the explosion of radio, recordings and cinema transformed the ways and means by which popular culture would be produced and consumed.

Contemporary publications richly registered the responses of poets and songsters to the events of the revolutionary period, and, in the decades that followed, there were many collections of poetry, song and vernacular verse – compositions relating to the revolutionary period: by anthologists, partisan groups claiming descent from the rebels of 1916, editors catering for the variable demands of ballad singing (individual or in groups) in formal or popular venues. But Terry Moylan's compilation surpasses in scale, variety and historical interest anything that's been attempted to date.

There are more than five hundred and fifty verse compositions in this marvellous collection; roughly half of the more than a thousand relevant items located by Moylan in his long search through nearly three hundred sources. All earlier collections have been combed, but the glory of the collection is the large number of items published here for the first time, many of them seized by the authorities immediately, or soon after publication, and now deposited in the Samuels Collection in Trinity College Dublin. In addition to the helpful historical notes by Liam McNulty, more than half the items are accompanied by the musical score or attributed air, Moylan himself being the source for some of the airs and for particular versions and verses of various songs. Clearly this has been a herculean effort by a lifetime collector of songs with an encyclopædic knowledge of his material.

The collection includes verses by many of the notables of the literary canon: Yeats, Colum, Ledwidge, George Russell, Sean O'Casey (a larger selection than most readers may expect) and a host of lesser but clearly accomplished poets. The poets of the Rising and the independence struggle are well represented and, on the labour side, there is a heavy contribution from Connolly to put alongside Jim Connell's generous quota. The verses of Tom Kettle, Patrick Macgill and Winifred Mary Letts, among many others, give vivid testimony to the 'mood' and experience of the Great War. The long-popular repertoire of Peadar Kearney merits an entire section for itself. Scores of 'second order' versifiers are here, including the familiar and prolific Brian O'Higgins and the equally prolific but not so familiar Maeve Cavanagh. And, of course, the versatile 'Anon' is present throughout.

The performance 'life' in later decades of some of the more rousing of the songs and ballads pertaining to the revolutionary period merits a word of notice. Here a personal recollection may be allowed. During my youth and adolescence in the 1950s and early 1960s a regular feature of the 'day out' at the big hurling games in Thurles, Cork and Limerick was the presence of ballad singers and vendors selling single-sheet printed copies of ballads to patrons – and giving their own rendition of the repertoire to prime the demand. It was a mixed repertoire, but always included a selection of 'rebel' ballads: 'Kevin Barry', 'The Upton Ambush', 'The Valley of Knockanure' featured regularly.

Nor was it only on penny sheets or through being hoarsely belted out between cupped hands at hurling grounds that many of these 'patriotic' songs and ballads reached their audience. A core of dedicated programmes on Radio Éireann brought a popular selection of the repertoire to a wider audience: *Ballad-Makers' Saturday Night*, 'Din Joe' Fitzgibbon's *Take the Floor*, and the commercially-sponsored *Walton's Programme* – sellers of musical instruments and sheet music, with strong nationalist connections through the programme's host Leo Maguire – with its familiar closing exhortation: 'and remember, if you feel like singing, do sing an Irish song.' Likewise, for live performances, a selection of the ballads relating to the revolutionary era – together with 'rousing' numbers from an earlier Young Ireland repertoire and, invariably, Moore's *Melodies* – formed a staple element of the programme of variety and charity concerts in villages and towns throughout rural Ireland.

As with the general temper of Irish social life, the 1960s brought change to Irish popular culture and entertainment, and not only through the impact of television. Yet, as the success of the Clancy Brothers (and their imitators) demonstrated, neither the increased international dimension of the folk and ballad revival of the decade, nor the increased prominence of songs of social protest in the repertoire signalled the abandonment of the 'rebel' songs by popular ballad singers. A decisive shift in attitude across the broad nationalist community (certainly in the Republic) followed the outbreak of the conflict in Northern Ireland from the end of the 1960s.

The 'Troubles' generated their own store of new songs, adding to the traditional repertoire of the rival communities; within republican circles, including support groups overseas, these rebel songs (old and new) continued to be performed. But, after an early surge of solidarity with the embattled Northern nationalist minority, ignited by patriotic sentiment and the evidence of loyalist militancy and oppressive state security action, the public mood in the Republic changed as the conflict darkened and dragged on and as the death count mounted and the terror of the dirty war began to chill patriotic ardour. Outside the embattled enclaves of support for the 'armed struggle', the repertoire of 'rebel' songs fell into abeyance: abandoned voluntarily through a recoil from the valorization of the physical-force message or silenced through official disapproval, mediated through the national broadcaster. Increasingly – and decisively – the horror of the conflict allowed for no inflammatory popular song from earlier episodes of the independence struggle.

A changing historiography on the Irish revolution itself during recent decades – reflecting new sources and shifting perspectives – has shaped a more complex historical narrative (and popular understanding) of all phases of the revolutionary period: from the stirrings of cultural nationalism in the wake of Parnell's fall, through the emerging labour and women's struggles, the Home Rule Movement, the Ulster revolt and the widening militarization of Irish political confrontation, the Great War, the Rising and its aftermath, the war of independence, partition and the Civil War. Versions of the revolution cast in Manichaean terms (heroic/cowardly, glorious/shameful) have been substantially eclipsed by more research-based studies that draw out the invariably more complex and contradictory nature and conduct of all conflicts.

This is the ideological and cultural climate in which Terry Moylan's magnificent compilation will be read and appreciated. He honestly confesses to a lingering scruple that (as originally intended in some instances) certain songs and ballads may still carry an exhortatory (not to say inflammatory) charge. In the light of current global conflicts and concerns, and the prevailing state of public opinion in early twenty-first century Ireland regarding politics, identity and violence, such anxiety may be unfounded. It is hardly naïve or complacently Whiggish to suggest that the terms of discontent and conflict that sustained the rebel 'muse' of the revolutionary era now seem increasingly historical, their legacy demanding strategies of resolution clothed in more complex shades than the black and white legends that gave life to many of the songs and ballads collected here. What is incontestable, however, is the rich historical value of this material. Moylan writes: 'These pieces are offered solely for whatever pleasure they may deliver, or whatever historical interest they may satisfy.' He need have no anxieties whatever that they will achieve these objectives.

Gearóid Ó Tuathaigh
Bearna, Nollaig, 2015

Introduction

This book contains a selection of the thousands of songs and poems created during, or reflecting upon, the events of that extraordinary decade of Ireland's history that started with the Dublin labour dispute of 1913 and ended with the Civil War, and which embraced World War I, the Rising of 1916, and the War of Independence.

As no great events occur without cause, the previous decades have been scanned to hear the voices that gave some indication of the upheavals to come. Everyone will have their own idea of continuity. At National School we were taught that the 1916 Rising and the War of Independence were the final acts in an unbroken 700-year struggle against foreign oppression. This facile construction is no longer being peddled in the schools, but many citizens have failed to shed their unthinking acceptance of an interpretation of Irish history framed to suit a contemporary political purpose. It can be argued that all interpretations of history are slanted to suit some agenda, but that is simply a good reason for not investing exclusively in any single reading. Apparently, in Northern Irish schools, students were taught nothing at all of Irish history, but that's another story.

The fashion among nineteenth-century anthologists was to treat 1169 – the coming of the Normans – as the starting point of 'Ireland's struggle for independence', but we do not reach so far back. The year from which we begin to track the signs of turbulence which foreshadowed outright conflict is 1887, the year of Queen Victoria's Jubilee. Not just in Ireland, poems written around that date began to question the settled order of things, as if the act of taking stock of a monarch's reign had caused observers to reflect that certain things 'could have been done differently, or not at all.' At any rate, that date allows us to notice some of the preliminaries, including the cultural revival, the nationalist awakening, the Irish military involvement in, and widespread public opposition to, the Boer War, the campaign for Home Rule, and others, which affected the outcome of events in our target decade. As Conor Cruise O'Brien wrote in *The Shaping of Modern Ireland*:

> In the summary historical retrospect which we all acquire at school and probably never quite lose, this period, 1891 to 1916, forms, I think, a sort of crease in time, a featureless valley between the commanding chain of the Rising and the solitary enigmatic peak of Parnell. It was a time in which nothing happened; nothing except a revolution in land ownership, the beginning of a national quest for a lost language and culture and the preparation of the two successful rebellions which were, among other things, to tear Ireland in two.

What is of interest in the material presented here is simply that it is a response *in verse* to the events of that time. No viewpoints are favoured other than the viewpoints of the song-maker and poet. In a way that prose accounts do not, poems and songs condense experience and afford the reader an opportunity of sharing another's perceptions in a more or less pleasing way.

'Pleasing' is the crucial word. We are interested in verse because to read it, or to hear it spoken or sung, is to experience an aesthetic pleasure. This delight in verse can be – often is – combined with an interest in history, particularly the history of one's own spot on the earth. It can be also, and often is, combined with a narrow view of history and a political agenda, but that is not our intention here. These pieces are offered solely for whatever pleasure they may provide, or whatever historical interest they may satisfy.

Although they may often overlap, the concerns and intentions of the song-maker differ from those of the poet. The skill of the poet is (or was, just about up to the period we are dealing with) to marshal appropriate and/or insightful language in a disciplined way, according to various well-established conventions, in order to reveal the meaning or insights they wish to communicate. The conventional forms are all well known, and include micro-structures such as the metres in which lines are to be written, and macro-structures like the several verse-forms – ballad, sonnet, quatrain, heroic verse, etc. – that contain those lines. The song-maker is less concerned with such fine structure, being more focused on stresses than syllables. It is the melody that provides the scaffolding for a song, and irregular lines can be accommodated, depending on the skill of the singer, by allocating more notes to a syllable, or by sub-dividing notes to carry extra syllables. For comic effect, Bob Dylan can fit the following verse into the melodic structure of a standard twelve-bar blues:

> Well, you look so pretty in it, Honey, can I jump on it sometime?
> Yes, I just wanna see if it's really that expensive kind.
> You know it balances on your head just like a mattress balances on a bottle of wine.
> (Bob Dylan – 'Brand New Leopard-skin Pillbox Hat')

Each of those three lines occupies the same number of bars of music. A song-maker can do that, so the criteria for assessing songs must be different.

Lest it should be thought that the sins against discipline are all on one side, it should be noted that songs have conventions peculiar to themselves, which, in some cases, poets disregard. A readily recognizable example is contained in the well-known poem/song 'Raglan Road', written by Patrick Kavanagh and memorably sung by Luke Kelly. But Kelly had to modify one verse to make it singable, at least to his taste. Kavanagh wrote the nicely rhyming couplet:

> I gave her gifts of the mind, I gave her the secret sign that's known
> To the artists who have known the true gods of sound and stone.

Kelly sang:

> I gave her gifts of the mind, I gave her the secret sign
> That's known to the artists who have known the true gods of sound and stone.

which doesn't rhyme at all, but which also doesn't split a clause over the end of a line. Any singer of traditional song will recognize why Kelly made the change. The enjambment (as it's called) involved in splitting the clause 'that's known to the artists' is acceptable in poetry but sounds awkward when sung. Kelly preferred to sacrifice the rhyme and to deal, in the way described above, with the resulting irregular numbers of syllables in the re-arranged lines than to end a line on half a phrase. Every other singer I have since heard perform the song has followed Kelly's example.

All the material included here has some historical relevance. The reader will find that some of the pieces are very fine poems, and that is enough to justify their inclusion, while some combine their historical interest with well-crafted versification, and repay interest in two ways. Others are very poor poetry indeed (although they might work well as songs), and have only their historical significance to reward investigation. Lovers of good poetry may be inclined to damn such pieces as doggerel, but, if you are such a one, we suggest that you simply pass over these items, or approach them from a different perspective. If a text has an associated air, keeping that air in mind will add to the reading experience.

Often the most apparently banal set of verses will be found to contain some excellent phrases or lines that lift an otherwise indifferent song. The reader may feel like echoing

Dr Johnson's remark about the Giant's Causeway – 'worth seeing, but not worth going to see' – but as the journey has been made, the book opened, try all the material. Different tastes will find different rewards.

Then again, there seem to be many understandings of what is meant by doggerel. For a friend of mine, Noel Pocock, it is quite simple – 'doggerel' he says 'doesn't do drama,' unlike, say, the great ballads of the English-Scottish borders, which do. My own understanding of the term is more concerned with structure. Inspired by some dreadful event or powerful emotion, poems and songs are often written by people who have never before wielded a pen in anger. In such circumstances, it is not surprising if their models should be the only types of verse that they have encountered, which will probably have been the popular ballads and songs of their community. Remember, we are dealing with a period before the advent of mass media, and before the ascent of a music industry that was able to form public taste.

With no idea of technique, nor of possibilities, the urge to commemorate some person or event will inevitably find expression in the form most familiar to the writer – the 'ballad', with its alternating lines of four and three stresses. Aware of the need to rhyme but, it may be, equipped only with the word-store required for ordinary life and habitual pursuits, the writer may grasp any means to complete the line, the verse or the song. The use of banal or inappropriate words, wrenched rhythms, repeated use of hackneyed words and expressions, cliché – these, to me, constitute doggerel. It is a form where the adjective is all-important. In verse, adjectives can perform a function similar to that of illustrations in newspapers, where pictures are sized to neatly fill the space remaining after the text has been entered and arranged. In a similar fashion the amateur rhymester will reach for an adjective of a suitable length and stress-pattern (but not necessarily having an apposite meaning) to complete his or her line.

This is not necessarily something to sneer at; it is a very ancient practice in oral poetry. The American scholar Milman Parry (d. 1935) recognized and described the technique as one that goes back to the centuries of oral tradition culminating in the tales attributed to Homer. His insight is described by Bernard Knox in his introduction to Robert Fagle's translation of *The Odyssey*:

> Parry's achievment was to prove that Homer was a master of, and heir to, a tradition of oral epic poetry that reached back over many generations, perhaps even centuries. Parry drew attention to the so-called ornamental epithets, those long, high-sounding labels that accompany every appearance of a hero, a place, or even a familiar object. Odysseus, for example, is 'much-enduring', 'a man of many schemes', 'godlike' and 'great-hearted'; the island of Ithaca is 'rocky', 'seagirt' and 'clear-skied'; ships are 'hollow', 'swift' and 'well-benched', to list only some of the often polysyllabic epithets attached to them. These recurring epithets had of course been noticed before Parry, and their usefulness understood. They offer, for each god, hero or object, a choice of epithets, each one with a different metrical shape. In other words, the particular epithet chosen by the poet may have nothing to do with, for example, whether Achilles is 'brilliant' or 'swift-footed' at this particular point in the poem – the choice depends on which epithet fits the meter.
>
> Parry pursued this insight of the German analytical scholars to its logical end and demonstrated that in fact there was an intricate system of metrical alternatives for the recurring names of heroes, gods and objects. It was a system that was economical – hardly any unnecessary alternatives were used – but had great scope: there was a way to fit the names into the line in any of the usual grammatical forms they would assume. Parry demonstrated that the system was more extensive and highly organized than anyone had dreamed, and he also realized what it meant. It meant that this system had been developed by and for the use of oral poets who improvised. In Paris he met scholars who had studied such improvising illiterate bards still performing in Yugoslavia. He went there to study their operations himself.

The Homeric epithets were created to meet the demands of the meter of Greek poetry, the dactylic hexameter. They offer the improvising bard different ways of fitting the name of his god, hero, or object into whatever section of the line is left after he has, so to speak, filled up the first half (that too, quite possibly, with another formulaic phrase).

James Joyce was familiar enough with this Homeric practice to lampoon it in *Ulysses*. His 'snotgreen sea' and 'scrotum-tightening sea' were surely intended as comic echoes of the device.

Nor has the example of Homer's life and work been ignored by humble Irish rhymesters! When he was brought before the Magistrate in the Henry Street Police Office, and charged with 'obstruction and annoyance' caused by singing songs in the public street (in Cole's Lane Market, off Great Britain Street), the blind street-singer Michael Moran – aka 'Zozimus' – pleaded that he was doing nothing more than Homer, among others, had done:

> Your worship, I love me country. She's dear to me heart, an' am I to be prevented from writin' songs in her honour, like Tommy Moore, Walter Scott and Horace done for theirs, or from singin' them like the an-shent bards, on'y I haven't got me harp like them to accompany me aspirations! ... It is true that I can't see; but I can warble that which can rise the hearts ov me counthrymen; an' if crowds gother 'round me how can I help it? Homer sung the praises ov his country on the public highways; an' we are informed that dramatic performances wor performed in the streets, with nothin' else for a stage but a dust cart.
> (P.J. McCall, *In the Shadow of St Patrick's*, Irish National Literary Society, Dublin, 1894)

John Hand also appealed to the Greek precedent:

> Ireland owes much to her ballad poetry, and not a little to that portion of it which is associated with the streets. Most, if not all, nations owe more or less to poetry. The songs of Homer, even more than her banded might, preserved Greece independent for over a thousand years ... For Ireland the ballad and the song have done more than for even Spain or Greece ...When English laws put the ban of outlawry on her bards, and finally destroyed them, did England even then succeed in her nefarious design? No! – the song lived, though the lips that first chaunted it were silent for ever. The ballad never lost its significance or its power.
> (John Hand, *Irish Street Ballads*, John Denvir, London, 1903)

One final observation on what we might agree to call 'vernacular poetry' must be made. When in search of rhymes, the writers of many of the later songs contained in this collection took full advantage of two facts – the number and variety of the names of the leaders of the 1916 Rising, and the fact that their flag was a tricolor.

As well as some rhymes, the names of the executed could be arranged in many different orders to satisfy different rhythmical requirements and, as Georges-Denis Zimmermann has remarked, to repeat 'strings of names ... in a litany like names of saints' had already become a feature of political song. (Zimmermann, 1967, p. 66)

As for the colours of the flag, they provided three different rhymes, notwithstanding the well-known fact that there is no rhyme for 'orange' in the English language. It is astonishing how often self-professed republicans disregard the republican symbolism embodied in the green, white and orange of the tricolor, and refer to the third colour as 'gold', or even 'yellow'. It could be politically motivated contempt for the strand of Irish life represented by the colour; it could be that the need to come up with a rhyme trumped the writers' incompletely grasped republican ideology; it could be pure, bloody, ignorance. It would be interesting to know, but we probably never will.

Whatever about their literary value, the songs and poems written by unsophisticated versifiers provide one more reason for reading them – the insight which they provide into the political outlook of the writers and their communities. When, as here, they can be examined in some numbers, they reveal a certain consistency of perception and belief. One of the things revealed is the attitude of self-righteous certainty, and the tendency to see all matters in absolute terms. No shades of grey here! The persistent (sometimes idiotic) glorification of 'our' side and the simultaneous (sometimes vicious) vilification of the foe are far more tedious than any literary shortcomings. Irish heroes or victims are invariably virtuous, proud, bold, brave, gallant etc., while their opponents can be nothing but treacherous, savage, knaves (if British) or slaves (if Irish). Any who oppose 'the movement', or at any rate who disagree with it, are not to be given the benefit of any doubt for there is no possibility that they act from honourable motives. On the contrary, they cannot be other than malevolent or unfit.

Earlier compilations of 'party songs' have been published, containing the poems and songs occasioned by earlier conflicts, and several carried disclaimers by the editors. Thomas Crofton Croker appealed to the indulgence of his readers in his introduction to *The Historical Songs of Ireland Illustrative of the Revolutionary Struggle between James II and William III* (1841), and in his Introduction to *The Ballads of Ireland* (1855) Edward Hayes noted:

> The excitement before or after a nation's struggle is the hot-bed of poetry. When peace is restored, then triumph is chanted, or defeat mourned, in national song; and the daily increasing means of education will quicken Ireland's acknowledged poetical genius, hitherto prostrated by adversity, and shed a glory around the land and the language which it celebrates and adorns.

R.R. Madden, in the preface to his *Literary Remains of the United Irishmen* (1887), wrote:

> I can see no good reason why the Jacobite relics of Scotch song should be in high repute with loyal men throughout the kingdom, and the old songs of '98 and the other Tyrtæan lyrics of the people called 'United Irishmen' should be held unworthy of the attention of literary curiosity. It is very possible to be gratified at hearing an old song, however political its tendencies, well sung, or to find it rescued from oblivion in a modern collection, without having one's spirit excited to the frenzy of a passion for rebellion by the poetry, which stimulated the souls of our fathers and grandfathers to acts of violence and desperation.
>
> The sense of wrong which breathed in it, died with the oppressors and the oppressed. Our wrongs spring not from Protestant ascendancy, from Penal laws, or an un-reformed Parliament. Every age has its proper grievances – and a befitting expression for them.

I am not so hopeful that the songs in this collection have lost their power to inflame. I am more inclined to agree with Andrew Fletcher's (1653–1716) remark: 'if a man were permitted to make all the ballads he need not care who should make the laws of a nation.' A more recent commemtator has remarked:

> We may admit that the political street ballads had some influence on the attitude of the Irish people, and therefore on the course of Irish history, although we cannot say precisely to what extent. They were effect and cause at the same time: expressing strong collective emotions, they could profoundly affect the climate of opinion. They were effective in shaping a common memory of some events and in binding the Irish together. In every period before an expected rising, nationalist movements published violent songs which must have helped to raise the public to a high pitch of excitement and to prepare the minds for coming disturbances. Through them the desire was born in some young men to conform to the popular idea of a national hero and perhaps to die a martyr's death. More than in initiating action, however, they seem to have been effective in confirming people in their own already existing attitudes; they excited deeply only those who were already convinced.
>
> (Georges-Denis Zimmermann, *Songs of Irish Rebellion*, Allen Figgis, Dublin, 1967)

I do hope, however, that any supporters of armed struggle resorting to this collection for entertainment or moral support may discover here some differing outlooks that they may not have encountered before.

Many readers will be curious as to the provenance of the material in this collection. The bibliography will answer most questions, but there are many pieces here that are contemporary with the events described, but which vanished almost immediately. In many cases they were simply seized and suppressed by the authorities. The bulk of such material may be found in the online collections of Trinity College, Dublin, in the Samuels Collection, which

> consists of printed ephemera of the 1916 Rebellion, World War I, the War of Independence and the Civil War. It was gathered in part by the Royal Irish Constabulary, and collected by Arthur Warren Samuels, Solicitor General for Ireland (1917–1918) and Attorney General (1918–1919). It was presented to the Library in the 1960s.
>
> (TCD website)

Previously published collections of 1916-related songs are remarkable for the small number of items that they contain, which are repeated from collection to collection. It seems that the civil and military powers were assiduous and successful in suppressing most of the dissident verse that was being published. Scores of items printed at the time will not have been seen again until their inclusion in the present volume. I have used over seventy such items from the Samuels Collection here (around one eighth of the total), none of which have re-appeared in print in the last century. In some cases the TCD copies have explicit notes, such as

> Found at 46 Mount Eden Road, Ranelagh between 2 & 3pm 10th February 1917
> – George Love

on the TCD copies of both *Songs & Poems – The Rebels Who Fought and Died for Ireland in Easter Week, 1916*, and *Songs of Freedom, Easter 1916*; or the eight-page songster *Ballads and Marching Songs of Ireland*, which has the note 'Seized by Police 14/10/16'. A typed sheet in the Samuels Collection, entitled 'List of copies of seditious documents seized at Fergus O'Connor's, 44, Eccles St., on 15th December, 1917', lists sixteen items, including postcards, song sheets and booklets, all but two of which were 'destroyed by order of the G.O.C.-in Chief' five days later.

During research for this compilation over one thousand different poems and songs were discovered, scattered across nearly three hundred sources. The original idea was to publish everything, but the unexpected extent of the material made that impractical. The poems and songs left out would fill a second volume the size of this one. The ones included in this collection have been chosen to reveal something of the ferment of literary creativity sparked by the events of our period. They have been grouped into sections representing various themes, such as 'The War', 'The Rising' and so on. Many of the items would fit comfortably into more than one section, such as the songs written in Knutsford internment camp, but written about events in World War I, which are here allocated to the latter section. The choices had to be made, and they were.

Of the known authors, the most heavily represented here are Maeve Cavanagh, James Connolly, Peadar Kearney, Sean O'Casey and Brian O'Higgins, all of whom require some comment.

Maeve Cavanagh was a personal friend and confidante of James Connolly, who referred to her as 'the poetess of the revolution.' Her brother was the political cartoonist Ernest Kavanagh, who was shot dead in front of Liberty Hall during the 1916 Rising, and her husband was the musician Cathal MacDubhghaill, who published many 'rebel songs' at the time, both arrangements and original compositions. Cavanagh published a play and several collections of poems. Most of her poetry is political in nature, and usually appeared first in the radical press of the time. For some years before the Rising a week could seldom pass without one of her inflammatory squibs appearing, urging the necessity of armed action. It would not be too much of an exaggeration to say that she nagged the IRB into rebellion. Despite her role in the Rising, she seems not to feature in any of the recently published books about the women of the period.

James Connolly's songs can be recognized as conforming to the conventions of 'socialist verse' of which there was a respectably long tradition by his time. What is of equal interest is the fact that the names of the tunes to which he set his verses reveal him to have been familiar with the version of Irish traditional music then available to Ireland's working and middle classes. This consisted of the old airs to which Thomas Moore had set his songs a century earlier. Most of Connolly's prescribed airs are the titles of different Moore songs, but not the original titles of the airs that Moore had used. Interestingly, Connolly also used for one song the air of the Transvaal National Anthem. Perhaps he learned the tune from Griffith or MacBride, both of whom had spent time in South Africa.

Peadar Kearney is celebrated as the author of the Irish national anthem, although it is another writer's translation of his text into Irish that is the anthem rather than his English-language original. More than other writers, he was able to employ the language register of the folk song, and consequently many of his songs have slipped seamlessly into tradition and will probably remain in use for many years.

Sean O'Casey was involved in different cultural and political activities, including trade-unionism, socialist politics, the Citizen Army, and the St Laurence O'Toole Pipe Band, among others. At the time these would have all been seen as complementary parts of an ethical, nationalist outlook on life as, indeed, for many Irish people, they still are. His songs are not as singable as Kearney's. The combination of contemporary references and wordiness would deter many singers. His clearly intense early interest in song foreshadows its inclusion in his plays, especially his later ones. The airs to which he set his songs are a mixture of music-hall songs and Irish folk songs. His choices from the latter store tend to show him as being less indebted to Moore and more in touch with traditional song than was Connolly.

Brian O'Higgins wrote hundreds of songs and poems that he published at great length himself, mostly in his *Wolfe Tone Annual*, which ran for three decades. His verse is written with great skill and humour, but most of his songs consist of attacks on those he deemed to be insufficiently nationalistic. He was seemingly able to turn them out on demand. He records on several occasions how he prepared poems and songs at short notice for various events, such as a visit to Tone's grave at Bodenstown, or a demonstration against some manifestation of the British crown or empire. He was one of the seven abstentionist TDs who took part in the farcical 'transfer of authority' from Dáil Éireann to the IRA Army Council in December 1938.

More generally, the fact that so many of the leaders and participants in the Rising were poets or songwriters is significant. These men and women were not thugs, although that is how they were treated by the British state. In executing the leaders the authorities scored two own-goals. The killings did more than the Rising itself to turn Irish public opinion. They also removed from the scene the most competent figures with whom Britain could have negotiated an ethical settlement, years earlier than when such negotiations eventually became inescapable, and possibly without the bloodshed and destruction of the following seven years.

The illustrations scattered throughout the collection are contemporary and are included to add to the entertainment and instruction value of the book. They have been carefully chosen to illustrate the texts that they accompany, in the hope that they will enlarge and enhance the experience of reading those texts.

Most of the songs for which appropriate airs are known are accompanied by those airs. It was once customary to provide an indication to a prescribed melody: 'Air: The Wearing of the Green' or suchlike, the writer taking it for granted that readers would know the named airs. However, my experience is that such familiarity with the national music has become a thing of the past, hence the decision to include the music. This publication is the first location in which many of the songs have appeared with their prescribed airs. The two items by James Joyce are cases in point. In those instances, and probably many others, the author named an air to which the text was set, but probably never envisaged the piece actually being sung. The air would have been simply the rhythmic scaffolding on which the poem was constructed. Nevertheless, even if it is never sung, a knowledge of the air enables the reader to apprehend the poem in the way the author conceived it.

There is one final curiosity connected with the songs here. The creation of 'rebel songs' was quite continuous – there are thousands – but upon the split in the republican movement caused by the division over the Treaty, only one side continued to produce them, the anti-Treaty faction. I have found no songs or poems produced by the pro-Treaty side, unless one counts the laments for the death of Michael Collins. The late, great Frank Harte was fond of repeating the formula 'those in power write the history, those who suffer write the songs'. However true that may be, it certainly seems to be the case that those in power don't write the songs. If it were desired to conduct an experiment to test the thesis, no better test bed could be found than the transition during the Civil War of one faction from revolutionary guerillas to defenders of the State and the status quo. Perhaps those writers who supported the Treaty, having achieved an acceptable settlement, no longer felt the urge to vent their grievances in verse, or no longer felt aggrieved. Or perhaps it is the case that those given to songwriting were always going to be the ones who would reject any compromise. If that's the case, then monitoring the production of dissenting verse could well be a useful tool for governments around the world. Harte was also known to remark 'If you want to know the facts, read the histories; if you want to know how it felt, read the songs'. That's as accurate a description of this project as I could wish for.

I cannot finish without drawing the readers' attention to another musical aspect of this collection. While searching for the illustrations, pictures were found of several dozen musicians who had been involved in the events of the time. All the pictures of actual musicians turned out to be of pipers. The melodeon player on page 19 and the concertina player on page 27 (both illustrating events in the Boer War) may have been real people, but there is no way of knowing. The players of the bones, tambourine, violins and banjos on page 125 are a mixture of known personalities and cartoon characters. The known ones did not play the instruments associated with them in the picture. In contrast, there are photographs of thirty actual pipers, most of them players of the warpipes. Ten warpipers may be seen in the picture of the Gaelic League gathering on page 45, including Jimmy Ennis and Éamonn Ceannt, both of whom also played the uilleann pipes; Ceannt is shown playing those on page 345. The other uilleann piper shown is Denis Delaney, on page 480. Two other groups of warpipers are to be seen – Harry Hough and his comrades accompanying the funeral of Terence MacSwiney on page 571, and the unnamed members of the Black Raven Pipe Band at the funeral of Thomas Ashe on page 505. Thomas Ashe was himself a member of that band and can be seen in the garb of the band on page 258. The remaining figures are Flor Begley, who famously played Tom Barry's troops to victory at the battle of Crossbarry (page 590) and Sean O'Casey (page 235) who was a member of the St Laurence O'Toole Pipe Band. Players of other instruments surely took part in the events we are covering, but no pictures of them surfaced in the research. No doubt the foregoing account will serve to confirm for many readers their impression of pipers as turbulent, intractable characters.

A more considered study of the songs and poems of this era remains to be done, for which I hope this work will provide both the stimulus and the gateway.

Terry Moylan

Acknowledgments

This book would not exist without the support and encouragement of my partner Pascale Gaudry.

I am indebted to Liam McNulty, who provided detailed historical notes to many of the songs, particularly those of the later period, from the O'Casey songs on, but who firmly refused to allow his name to be included on the title page as a contributor. Liam also provided the historical bibliography. His notes are identified by the initials 'LM'.

Cormac O'Malley assisted me with access to the collection of songs assembled by his father Ernie O'Malley, which are now in New York University.

Francy Devine shared with me his researches into the Dublin radical press of the pre-1916 period, in which I found several songs to include in the collection, and Fergus Russell shared with me songs that he had researched, and his own tunes to accompany them.

The Mansfield Library at the University of Montana assisted me with access to the collection of songs in their Archives & Special Collections Department, and Chelsea Shriver of the University of British Columbia provided information, available nowhere else, about the authorship of the anonymous poems in *Aftermath of Easter Week*.

Nicholas Carolan and the staff of the Irish Traditional Music Archive were, as ever, unfailingly courteous and helpful during my visits, and Nicholas Carolan provided much-appreciated advice as well as help in proofreading Irish language texts.

The poems and songs of Sean O'Casey are included by kind permission of the Estate of Sean O'Casey. Dermot O'Byrne's poems are carried with the permission of the estate of Sir Arnold Bax, the poems of Patrick Macgill with the permission of Knight Features, London, and those of Leo Maguire with the permission of Walton's, Dublin.

For the use of illustrations included in this book I am grateful to Thomas Ryan, RHA, and to the Sweeney, O'Rahilly and Curran families, as well as to Trinity College, Dublin; the National Library of Ireland; the Royal Irish Academy; the Crawford Gallery; the South Dublin Libraries; An Chartlann Mhíleata/The Military Archives, Irish Defence Forces; Na Píobairí Uilleann; and the website comeheretome.com.

Antony Farrell of the Lilliput Press made many helpful suggestions during the compilation of the work, and provided very welcome encouragement throughout the process, while his daughter Bridget proved a meticulous proof-reader.

Luke Cheevers, Sally Corr, Tim Dennehy, Sean Garland, Des Geraghty, Barry Gleeson, Tony McGaley, Pat Mitchell, Shivaun O'Casey, Antaine Ó Faracháin, Michael O'Rahilly, Jerry O'Reilly, Manus O'Riordan, Noel Pocock, Sandie Purcell, Ruth Sweeney and Aoife Whelan assisted me in various ways for which I am very grateful.

Every effort has been made to identify and acknowledge the copyright holders of the poems, songs and illustrations used in this collection. If a copyright holder advises the publisher of the inclusion of unacknowledged material here, an appropriate acknowledgment will be carried in any subsequent edition.

NOTE ON THE TEXT

The observant reader will notice variant spellings of 'Shan Van Vocht', 'Cuchullain', etc, denoting the progression from oral to printed sources, and the standardization that the latter imposed across time.

The Indignant Muse

J.F. O'Hea, 'Rejoice, Oh! Greatly. Erin having deposited her decoration at the shrine of "Loyalty"
retires (on invitation) to an Imperial Institute to celebrate the Queen's Jubilee.'
Supplement with *The Weekly Freeman*, 4 June 1887.

A Jubilee Ode, 1887
Modified by Irish Circumstances
Thomas O'Hagan (1855–1939)

Dear gracious Queen, we're loyal too,
    And full of love and kindly part;
Our tears have trickled to the ground
    When famine reigned in Erin's heart;
We know the age and watch its plans,
    Its deeds of fame, its brilliant glory –
And love you true – as England's Queen;
    But not in Erin's tear-clad story.

On every field where valor led
    Our swords have leapt, our hearts have panted,
To smite the foe with deadly blow,
    To rout the foe with hearts undaunted;
On Afric's coast, through burning sands,
    The Arab flew in wild commotion,
Nor dared to meet the waves so wild
    That heaved 'round Ireland's brave devotion.

Dear gracious Queen, we're loyal too –
    And faithful to the land that bore us –
Thro' weal and woe, thro' smiles and tears
    Our hearts have sung an Irish chorus:
Across the years that bind your reign
    We catch a glimpse of England's glory,
And love you true – as England's Queen
    But not thro' Erin's tear-clad story.

The arts have flourished in your reign –
    What are so dear as Irish freedom?
Than wealth of Ind a little love
    Will better cheer our hearts and lead them;
In every land we built a cairn
    With pebbles stained with heart-bled sorrow,
That you, our Queen, we hail today –
    And hail not Ireland's peace tomorrow!

Dear gracious Queen, we're loyal too –
    But not to power that strikes our kinsmen;
For justice loves a kindly deed
    And through the heart she always wins men:
Look to the land of ivied tower –
    Of ruined castle old and hoary,

Queen Victoria's reign had included the years of the Famine and its aftermath, when millions of Irish died and millions more left Ireland in hopes of a better life overseas; and also the colossal expansion of Britain's empire, in which Irish soldiers played a significant part.

Her jubilee year provided an occasion for taking stock and questioning the status quo.

Text: *The Collected Poems of Thomas O'Hagan*, McClelland & Stewart, Toronto, 1922.

And say, great Queen of Britain's realm,
    Have you a pride in Ireland's story?

O, mighty voices of the past,
    Long hushed in death in Ireland's pleading –
O'Connell, Davis, Mitchell, Butt,
    Join hearts with those who now are leading!
And tell us what have fifty years
    Brought to a land 'neath cruel oppression?
From every mound and patriot grave
    Come forth one great heav'n-swept procession.

Dear gracious Queen, we're loyal too –
    In cabin, cot and stately mansion,
And love you true – as England's Queen –
    Your wealth of power and cash expansion;
But blame us not if in our cot
    We mourn because the crowbar stings us,
And crying for bread you reach a stone –
    The gift each tyrant landlord brings us.

Dear gracious Queen, we're loyal too –
    And faithful to the land that bore us;
Though darkest hour beset our way
    Our hearts will sing an Irish chorus;
For tenfold fifty years have we
    Knelt at the shrine of Ireland's glory –
We love you true – as England's Queen
    But not thro' Erin's tear-clad story!

A Jubilee Song
(1897)
Jim Connell (1852–1929)

Text: Jim Connell, *Red Flag Rhymes*, The Agitator's Press, Huddersfield, c. 1900.

Withered waste of the molten steel,
Lungless wreck of the grinder's wheel,
Palsied drudge of the pois'nous mine,
Paupered ghost of a manhood fine:
    Come lift your glasses with three times three,
    And toast Victoria's Jubilee.

Scottish crofter of visage gaunt,
Victim ever of toil and want;
Irish peasant of ragged coat,
Whom landlord swindled and ruler smote:
    Come lift your glasses with three times three,
    And toast Victoria's Jubilee.

Maimed survivor of glory's host,
Legless, foodless, and fortune-tossed;
Shrivelled drift of the chilling sea,
Mate of pains and poverty:
    Come lift your glasses with three times three,
    And toast Victoria's Jubilee.

Famished ryot of Hindustan,
Plundered Burmese and wronged Afghan,
Hunted Zulu and threatened Boer,
Swell the music and foot the floor:
    Come lift your glasses with three times three,
    And toast Victoria's Jubilee.

The Royal Irish Regiment storming Egyptian entrenchments at the Battle of Tel El Kebir in September 1882. The campaign left traces in Dublin in the form of the Tel el Kebir Dairy in Dún Laoghaire, which was founded by an Irish veteran of the battle, and Wolseley Street, named after the British commander. Dufferin Avenue, which crosses Wolesley Street, is named after another Irish imperialist involved in the affair.

Served Him Right

Arthur M. Forrester (1850–1895)

[An Irish girl, hearing that her brother Pat had been killed in the Royal Irish, fighting against the Mahdi, said: 'It served Pat right. He had no business going out there to fight those poor creatures (the Arabs). May God strengthen the Mahdi.' *London Graphic*]

The fifth line of this poem is echoed by Yeats's line, 'Those that I fight I do not hate' in his 'An Irish Airman Foresees his Death', see p. 184.

Text: Arthur M. Forrester, *An Irish Crazy-Quilt*, Alfred Mudge & Son, Boston, 1891.

I have no tears for brother Pat,
    Though stark he lies, and stiff and gory,
On the Egyptian desert, that
    He might assist in England's glory.
The foes he fought were not his own,
    Nor his the tyrant's cause he aided;
Then why should I his fate bemoan?
    O brother, faithless and degraded!

He saw how Saxon laws at home
    Had crushed his sires and banned his brothers,
Why should he cross the ocean's foam
    To place that hated yoke on others?
The Arabs slew him in a fight
    For all by brave and free men cherished –
Ay, for the cause of truth and right,
    For which his kith and kin had perished.

No Arab chief in ninety-eight
    Placed foot on Erin's shore as foeman;
They lent no spears to swell the hate
    Of Hessian hound and Orange yeoman.
But those who wrapt our homes in flame
    And trod us down like dumb-brute cattle –
It was for them – oh, burning shame!
    My brother gave his life in battle.

Sure, every memory of late
    Must from his wretched heart have vanished;
Our hills and valleys desolate,
    Our ruined homes, our people banished.
And yet, God knows, he learned in youth
    The gloomy story of his sireland –
Drank in at mother's knees the truth
    That England is the scourge of Ireland.

I cannot weep for brother Pat –
    I hate the hellish cause he died for;
False traitor to the the freedom that
    His brothers strove, his sisters sighed for,

E'en when in tearful dreams I see
    The parching sands drift blood-stained o'er him,
My grief is changed to anger. He
    Was treacherous to the land that bore him!

Richard Simkin, 'The Royal Irish in Egypt'.

Latest Version of the Shan Van Vocht
or
Queen Victoria's Recruiting Trip to Ireland
Edward Fitzwilliam (1833–1912)

You have heard of old Queen Vic, says the Shan Van Vocht.

Her late ca-pers make me sick, says the Shan Van Vocht.

In her war a-gainst the Boer, Ir-ish fools had suf-fered sore,

Then she came to get some more, says the Shan Van Vocht.

'If Queen Victoria was the great queen she is represented to be, in the silly slobber over her remains since her death, she could have prevented the Boer War, she could have prevented the periodical (English-made) famines in Ireland and India. One fourth of what it has cost to rob the Boers would have saved the millions that have starved to death in India, not to mention the tremendous loss of life. Well may she be called the famine queen of history.

In this ballad, Ireland is represented as a poor but proud old woman who although robbed of everything, including her children, still holds up her head and gives her reasons for refusing to aid and assist *her* robbers in killing and robbing the Boers.' Note on song in source.

See p. 278 for a note on the reference in verse 6 to the 'filthy *London Times*'.

The wearing of green, the Irish national colour, had once been proscribed as a marker of disloyalty. Verse 9 refers to the fact that Victoria, faced with mounting losses in the Boer War, created a new unit, the Irish Guards. She granted them the privilege of wearing shamrock in their caps to celebrate St Patrick's Day.

Text: Edward Fitzwilliam, *Songs and Poems, American and Irish, National and International, Patriotic, Political, Economic and Miscellaneous*, The J.K. Waters Co., Boston, 1906.

Air: 'The Shan Van Vocht'.

You have heard of old Queen Vic,
   Says the Shan Van Vocht,
Her late capers make her sick,
   Says the Shan Van Vocht,
In her war against the Boer,
Irish fools had suffered sore,
Then she came to get some more,
   Says the Shan Van Vocht.

'Twas a shameful sight to see,
   Says the Shan Van Vocht,
After all she's done to me,
   Says the Shan Van Vocht,
In no land beneath the sun,
Has such heartless things been done,
Since her cruel reign begun,
   Says the Shan Van Vocht.

Away back in forty-five,
   Says the Shan Van Vocht,
(It's a woundher I'm alive)
   Says the Shan Van Vocht,
I had most two million sons,
Fit to march and shoulder guns,
But from home they had to run,
   Says the Shan Van Vocht.

In forty-seven and forty-eight,
   Says the Shan Van Vocht,
England made a famine great,
   Says the Shan Van Vocht;
She took off her oats and whate,
Our sweet butter, eggs and mate
And left little we could ate,
   Says the Shan Van Vocht.

Vic did not come then nor send,
   Says the Shan Van Vocht,
As a ruler or a friend,
   Says the Shan Van Vocht;
Hunger, sickness and despair,
You could feel them in the air,
But one rap she didn't care,
   Says the Shan Van Vocht.

When the filthy *London Times*,
   Says the Shan Van Vocht,
Adding to its other crimes,
   Says the Shan Van Vocht;

Bragged how the Irish ran away,
'With a vengeance' day by day,
And prayed that they long might stay,
    Says the Shan Van Vocht.

This same heartless British Queen,
    Says the Shan Van Vocht,
Though then young, was just as mean,
    Says the Shan Van Vocht;
She once never raised a hand,
But to send an armed band,
To evict them from their land,
    Says the Shan Van Vocht.

So, for over fifty years,
    Says the Shan Van Vocht,
I have scarcely dried my tears,
    Says the Shan Van Vocht;
All those years they dhrove away,
My brave sons across the say,
But they want them bad to-day,
    Says the Shan Van Vocht.

When the grand heroic Boer,
    Says the Shan Van Vocht,
Frightened England to the core,
    Says the Shan Van Vocht;
They all, with their famine queen
Wore the outlawed Irish Green,
'Twas the quarest sight I've seen,
    Says the Shan Van Vocht.

'Twas chape blarney nothing more,
    Says the Shan Van Vocht,
To get men to fight the Boer,
    Says the Shan Van Vocht;
But although she lost her shame
My young men saw through her game,
And she went back as she came,
    Says the Shan Van Vocht.

There is freedom in the air,
    Says the Shan Van Vocht,
England wallows in despair,
    Says the Shan Van Vocht;
Though my sons are much reduced
Irish chicks come home to roost,
They'll give freedom yet a boost,
    Says the Shan Van Vocht.

A demonstration in December 1899 against the presence of Joseph Chamberlain in Trinity College, Dublin. Chamberlain was the Colonial Secretary, responsible for the conduct of the Boer War, and his visit occurred shortly after the British army had suffered reverses at Colenso and elsewhere. The flag is that of the Transvaal Republic.

The Queen's After-Dinner Speech

(As Overheard and Cut into Lengths of Poetry
by Jamesy Murphy, Deputy-Assistant-Waiter at
the Viceregal Lodge)

Percy French (1854–1920)

'Me loving subjects,' sez she,
'Here's me best respects,' sez she,
'An' I'm proud this day,' sez she,
'Of the illigant way,' sez she,
'Ye gave me the hand,' sez she,
'Whin I came to land,' sez she.
'There was some people said,' sez she,
'They were greatly in dread,' sez she,
'I'd be murthered or shot,' sez she,
'As like as not,' sez she,
'But 'tis mighty clear,' sez she,
''Tis not over here,' sez she,
'I have cause to fear,' sez she.
''Tis them Belgiums,' sez she,
'That's throwin' bombs,' sez she,
'And scarin' the life,' sez she,
'Out o' me son and the wife,' sez she.
'But in these parts,' sez she,
'They have warrum hearts,' sez she,
'Barrin' Anna Parnell,' sez she.
'I dunno, Earl,' sez she,
'What's come to the girl,' sez she,
'And that other wan,' sez she,
'That Maud Gonne,' sez she,
'Dhressin' in black,' sez she,
'To welcome me back,' sez she;
'Though I don't care,' sez she,
'What they wear,' sez she,
'An' all that gammon,' sez she,
'About me bringin' famine,' sez she.
'Now Maud Gonne 'ill write,' sez she,
'That I brought the blight,' sez she,
'Or altered the saysons,' sez she,
'For some private raysins,' sez she,
'An' I think there's a slate,' sez she,
'Off Willie Yeats,' sez she.
'He should be at home,' sez she,
'French polishin' a pome,' sez she,
'An' not writin' letters,' sez she,
'About his betters,' sez she,
'Paradin' me crimes,' sez she,

W.B. Yeats and Maud Gonne had been involved
together in organizing events to oppose Queen
Victoria's Jubilee in 1897, and to mark the
centenary of the United Irishmen's rebellion
the following year. They followed this up with
opposition to the Boer War (see picture on
p. 10), and to the Queen's visit to Dublin in
April 1900, with Yeats writing letters of protest
to *The Irish Times*.

The cartoon below is from the Irish-American
periodical *The Gael* of June 1903, and shows
Maude Gonne plucking the strings of a harp
labelled 'Factionalism', 'Intolerance', and 'Love
of notoriety'. It accompanies a report in the
magazine on the activities of a 'small irreconcil-
able faction who call themselves "The People's
Protection Society" ' – a 'notoriety-seeking
association recently formed for the purpose
of exciting a feeling of hostility towards any
proposal for presenting an address to the King
on the occasion of his approaching visit to
Dublin.'

Text: Mrs De Burgh Daly, *Percy French, Prose,
Poems and Parodies*, Talbot Press, Dublin, 1929.

11

'In the 'Irish Times',' sez she.
'But what does it matther,' sez she,
'This magpie chatther,' sez she,
'When that welcomin' roar,' sez she,
'Come up from the shore,' sez she,
'Right over the foam?' sez she,
''Twas like comin' home,' sez she,
'An' me heart fairly glowed,' sez she,
'Along the Rock Road,' sez she,
'An' by Merrion roun',' sez she,
'To Buttherstown,' sez she,
'Till I came to the ridge,' sez she
'Of the Leeson Street Bridge,' sez she,
'An' was welcomed in style,' sez she,
'By the beautiful smile,' sez she,
'Of me Lord Mayor Pile,' sez she.
'(Faith, if I done right,' sez she,
'I'd make him a knight,' sez she).
'Well, I needn't repeat,' sez she,
'How they cheered in each street,' sez she,
'Till I came to them lads,' sez she,
'Them 'undergrads',' sez she.
'Indeed, an' indeed,' sez she,
'I've had many a God-speed,' sez she,
'But none to compare,' sez she,
'Wid what I got there,' sez she.
'Now pass the jug,' sez she,

'And fill up each mug,' sez she,
'Till I give ye a toast,' sez she,
'At which you may boast,' sez she.
'I've a power o' sons,' sez she,
'All sorts of ones,' sez she:
'Some quiet as cows,' sez she,
'Some always in rows,' sez she,
'An' the one gives most trouble,' sez she,
'The mother loves double,' sez she,
'So drink to the min,' sez she,
'That have gone in to win,' sez she,
'And are clearin' the way,' sez she,
'To Pretoria to-day,' sez she.
'In the 'Gap o' Danger',' sez she,
'There's a Connaught Ranger,' sez she,
'An' somewhere near,' sez she,
'Is a Fusilier,' sez she,
'An' the Inniskillings not far,' sez she,
'From the Heart o' the War,' sez she;
'An' I'll tell you what,' sez she,
'They may talk a lot,' sez she,
'And them Foreign Baboons,' sez she,
'May draw their cartoons,' sez she.
'But what they can't draw,' sez she,
'Is the Lion's claw,' sez she,
'And before our flag's furled,' sez she,
'We'll own the wurruld,' sez she.

They Gave Him a Doublet of Scarlet
Russell Gray

These verses appeared in an Australian newspaper in 1900, contributed by a correspondent signing himself W.J.D. His letter introduced the poem as follows:

Sir— The magnificent attack of the Dublin and Enniskilling Fusiliers in the face of a veritable hail of lead at Pieter's Hill brings into splendid relief the unique bravery of the Celtic race.

Nothing more gallant or dauntless has been done throughout the whole campaign, and the message from the Queen to General Buller expressing her deepest concern at the heavy losses sustained by the brave troops will

They gave him a doublet of scarlet,
    And a rifle to hold in his hand,
And they bade him strike for his Sovereign,
    And fight for his native land.
They came and they 'listed' my darling
    And the Mother of Sorrows above
Can feel for the heart of a mother,
    For she knew how the Irish can love.

The challenge of England has summoned
    Her sister, the Emerald Isle.
And brothers-in-arms are their children,
    Now mustering, file upon file.

They gave me the paper that told it,
    And I read with my tear-dimming sight,
While it spoke of the glory of battle,
    And told how the Irish can fight.

But the voice of the bugle that called him,
    And the song of the slumbering deep,
Have killed the young heart in his bosom,
    And hushed my poor darling to sleep.
He is there – in the list of the slaughtered;
    But they tell me that I mustn't cry,
For he fell where the battle was thickest,
    To prove how the Irish can die.

awaken a re-echoing note throughout the length and breadth of Australia. The Irish race are ready to shed their life's blood on the field of battle, but there will be many a tear-stained eye and a sorrow-stricken heart in the Green Isle when the news of the brilliant, but expensive, victory is sent through. The feelings of the bereaved relatives have been so beautifully expressed in the following pathetic verses written by an officer's wife, an Irish lady, who writes under the *nom de plume* of 'Russell Gray' that perhaps you may find room for them.

Text: *The Advertiser,* Adelaide, 15 March 1900.

A Mother's Lament for Her Son

One evening late, when friends did meet, I heard a mother
    say,
'My child, my son, my chief support, alas, is gone away;
Hard I had to rear him since the day his father died,
Happy, happy would I be if he were by my side.'

'He joined the Munster Fusileers, a brave and active corps,
I little thought they'd send him out to tamper with the
    Boer;
From the day that he enlisted he sent me half his pay –
I'd give up what the Queen is worth to see my son to-day.'

'I gave him my blessing leaving Queenstown Quay,
With many more young Irish boys to cross the raging sea;
Many a mother now in Cork is in grief as well as me,
To think the son she cared and reared, his face she'll never
    see.'

'When the battle rages fiercely our boys are in the van;
How I do wish the blows they struck were for dear Ireland;
But duty calls, they must obey and fight against the Boer,
And many a cheerful Irish lad will fall to rise no more.'

'I wish my boy was home again, oh, how I'd welcome him;
With sorrow I'm heartbroken, my eyes are growing dim.
The War is dark and cruel, but whoever wins the fight,
I pray to save my noble lad and God defend the right!'

Text: Lady Gregory, *The Kiltartan History Book*, T. Fisher Unwin, London, 1926.

'Mothers, wives and sweethearts, cheer up and do not
    fret,
The men who are out in Africa we hope to see them yet.
Money plenty will be sent to help each family
From those who are in the battlefield before the enemy.'

'Sisters, wives and mothers should offer up a prayer
For those who are in South Africa, the friends we loved
    so dear;
God be their protection, shield them from the foe,
Many of them alive to-day I fear will be laid low.'

Royal Munster Fusiliers fighting from behind the redoubt at Honey Nest Kloof, South Africa (16 February, 1900).

The Poor Old Man

God bless and save all here, says the poor old man,
If allowed to take a chair, says the poor old man,
  Some few words I'd like to say on the topic of the day,
It will pass an hour away, says the poor old man.

Aren't the Boers a noble race, says the poor old man,
Such an army for to face, says the poor old man,
  Such men don't fear to die, Independence is their cry,
It's enough to make me sigh, says the poor old man.

Now De Wet is all the rage, says the poor old man,
They can't get him in the cage, says the poor old man,
  We're told they're on his heel, yet he slips through like
    an eel,
And the lead he makes them feel, says the poor old man.

Now the only child I reared, says the poor old man,
Great Britain has not spared, says the poor old man,
  But if my only child in freedom's cause had died,
I could think of him with pride, says the poor old man.

What has England sent to me? says the poor old man,
A few lines of sympathy, says the poor old man,
  To say it's with regret they inform me of his death,
That's the way they pay their debt, says the poor old man.

What's poor Ireland to gain, says the poor old man,
For her children who were slain, says the poor old man,
  Some millions she must pay a noble foe to slay,
But there'll come a time some day, says the poor old man.

The mills of God grind slow, says the poor old man,
And the seed the tyrants sow, says the poor old man,
  They will have to reap some day, with Russia in the
    fray,
Who an old debt longs to pay, says the poor old man.

Now I'll say farewell to all, says the poor old man,
And the next time that I'll call, says the poor old man,
  I'll have something to unfold that'll make your blood
    run cold,
It's a pity that I'm old, says the poor old man.

Christiaan De Wet (verse 3) was a
guerilla commander during the
Second Boer War, whose repeated
attacks on British forces brought him
to the attention of the Irish public.

His name would be known to
people nowadays through the reference in George Hodnett's song 'The
Monto':

You're seen the Dublin Fusiliers
The dirty ould bamboozeleers,
De Wet will get the childer,
One, two three.

Text: Lady Gregory, *The Kiltartan
History Book*, T. Fisher Unwin,
London, 1926.
  The air to which this song was
intended to be sung is clearly
'The Shan Van Vocht' (see p. 7).

The Song of the British 'Ero

Arthur Griffith (1872–1922)

Written in response to British imperialist adventures in Africa. The first (1893) and second (1896) Matabele [*sic*] wars resulted in the creation of the state of Rhodesia, comprising the territories now occupied by the states of Zambia and Zimbabwe.

Griffith was in South Africa during the Second Matabele War. In this song he is deliberately parodying the style and 'cockney diction' of Rudyard Kipling. See p. 48 for another piece from an Irish poet critical of Kipling's work.

Text: Piaras Béaslaí (ed.), *Songs, Ballads and Recitations by Famous Irishmen – Arthur Griffith,* Waltons, Dublin, n.d.

Air: No air is indicated but the text would fit very well to the tune and metre of the Irish song 'An Crúiscín Lán'.

I'm Trooper Robin Rape, a sojer from the Cape,
　　A supporter of hold Hengland's glorious cause
And I've taken one man's share in that little 'ere affair
　　When we taught the Matabili British laws:
　　　　Bless their eyes!
　　When we taught the Matabili British laws.

You should have seen the fun when we worked the
　　Maxim gun
And the niggers fell like locusts all around;
How our leaders' faces glowed when they saw the blood
　　that flowed
　　And we stabbed the dying devils on the ground:
　　　　Save their souls!
　　We stabbed the wriggling beggars on the ground.

We captured in the kraals all the blessed nigger gals;
　　'Twas funny, boys, to listen to them sue
For mercy and release, but we made them hold their
　　peace,
　　And we treated them as British sojers do –
　　　　Don't you know?
　　We treated them as British 'eroes do.

Royal Dublin Fusiliers and their Maxim gun, forming part of Hart's Irish Brigade (*With the Flag to Pretoria,* 1901).

I guess the Gawd-saved black will respect the Union
 Jack
  For the future, boys, where'er it may be seen,
And we'll put a lump of lead through the blessed
 nigger's head
  Who doesn't learn to sing 'Gawd save the Queen'.
    Dear old Queen!
  We'll teach the dogs to sing 'Gawd save the Queen'.

Come Along, Paddy
Arthur Griffith

Paddy, dear, there's wealth before you;
  Come and take a gun or lance;
Come and help us kill the Boer, you
  Ne'er again may have the chance –
    Kill the Boer!
    Wealth galore!
  Watches, trinkets, clothes and gold!
    Help us shoot –
    Help us loot –
  Help us as you did of old!

Paddy, darling, let us 'list you;
  Come along and don't be shy!
Take the shilling in your fist, you
  Needn't stay to say good-bye.
    Soon you'll come
    With rolling drum
  Like a hero marching back,
    When we've raised –
    The Lord be praised! –
  Above the Rand the Union Jack.

Paddy, come, we'll quickly teach you
  Murder, Theft – don't be afraid!
Human law can never reach you
  Once you join the Black Brigade.
    Come, be willing:
    Take the shilling
  In your fist and all is well;
    Cross the water,
    Rob and slaughter,
  Please old Hecate, Queen of Hell.

Text: Piaras Béaslaí (ed.), *Songs, Ballads and Recitations by Famous Irishmen – Arthur Griffith*, Waltons, Dublin, n.d.

17

Hand Me Down Me Petticoat

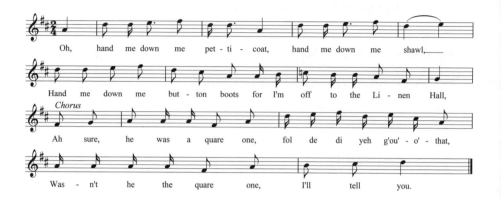

Oh, hand me down me pet-ti-coat, hand me down me shawl,___
Hand me down me but-ton boots for I'm off to the Li-nen Hall,

Chorus

Ah sure, he was a quare one, fol de di yeh g'ou' o' that,
Was-n't he the quare one, I'll tell you.

The Linen Hall was a market house for the linen trade, which was established in 1728 on a site south of, and adjacent to, the site now occupied by the King's Inns. The site is now occupied by Coleraine House, the DIT School of Trades, and a couple of residential roads.

By the 1870s it had passed into the control of the army and the Army Pay Corps was based there. The wives of soldiers on service abroad went there to draw their allowance.

In 1916 the complex was destroyed by fire by the rebels to prevent its use by the army.

Text and air: From memory.

Oh hand me down me petticoat,
  Hand me down me shawl,
Hand me down me button boots,
  For I'm off to the Linen Hall.

Chorus
Ah sure, he was a quare one,
Fal de di yeh g' ou' o' that
Wasn't he the quare one, I'll tell you.

If you go down to the Curragh Camp
  Just ask for number nine,
You'll find three squaddies standing there
  And the best-looking one is mine.

Well if he's joined the army
  All under another name,
For to do me out of my pension
  It's his ould wan is to blame.

When they go out to Africa
  To fight the savage Boers,
For God's sake hold the Dublins back
  Let the bogmen go before.

My love has gone across the sea,
  My love is far away,
My love has gone to America
  And left me in the family way.

The Song of the Dublin Fusilier

(Left behind, wounded, to die, by the British in their
retreat from Dundee, South Africa in October 1899)

Arthur Griffith

'If ye wear the coat of England,' sez me mother wance to
  me,
  'The curse of God will fall upon your head;
A thraitor to your country and your father you will be.'
  But I little heeded what the mother said.

Me father – Heaven rest him! died twelve years ago in jail,
  A Fenian – and they used him like a hound.
Still, I took the English shilling, though I knew me
  mother'd wail –
God curse him! – when the sergeant kem around.

'I'll larn to be a sojer, and some day I'll have a chance
  To fight for Ireland's freedom like a man,
When help is coming over here from Russia or from
  France
An' I'll be thrained,' sez I, 'then. That's the plan.'

The Battle of Dundee, also known as
the Battle of Glencoe and as the Battle
of Talana (see pp. 20, 25, 28, 30),
took place on 20 October 1899, and
was the first engagement of the
Second Boer War.

  Piet Joubert (verse 6) was
prominently involved, politically and
militarily, in the First Boer War and to
a lesser extent in the Second Boer War.

Text: Piaras Béaslaí (ed.), *Songs,
Ballads and Recitations by Famous
Irishmen – Arthur Griffith*, Waltons,
Dublin, n.d.

Sketched by Ernest Prater for *The Sphere*, 28 April 1900, the picture above is titled *'How the Irish soldiers in
Ladysmith celebrated St Patrick's Day'*. A legend to the picture relates how 'The Patron Saint's Day was
celebrated with great enthusiasm in the Irish camp at Ladysmith. In the evening a huge bonfire was lit, and a
platform erected on the top of an ox waggon. Many an Irish song was sung, and Drummer Kelly and Private
O'Leary of the Dublins crowned the evening with a typical Irish step dance.'

19

Yes, I thought that I was clever to join the English foe,
    And make them larn me how to shoot and dhrill,
Oh! little did I think then – oh! little did I know
    I'd be sent out here old Ireland's friends to kill.

'Charge up, boys,' sez the Colonel, and I charged straight
    up the hill
    To strike down freemen battling for their right –
To make meself a murdherer – for England's sake to kill,
    The pathriots standing out agin her might.

An' a freeman's bullet struck me, and I fell upon the ground
    An' they brought me to the camp back here to die,
An' now the dogs have left me – for Joubert is coming round,
    An' without a dhrink of water here I lie.

Yes, the curse of God is on me, an' I broke me mother's heart,
    An' me father's curse is on me, too, as well,
But wan thing cheers me still – when me life tonight I part,
    I'll meet the man that listed me in hell.

The Battle of Dundee;
Or, How President Kruger's Irish
Took In Her Majesty's Hibernians.
Rev. I. Dempsey

(With apologies to the Ancient Order of Hibernians, the
Knights of St Patrick, the Clan-na-Gael, the Fenians and
other fighters.)

The English and the Dutch of this
poem turn out to be the Irish units of
the British army, such as the Dublin
Fusiliers, and the Irish volunteers,
fighting on the side of the Boer
settlers, the original colonizers of
South Africa.
    The A.O.H. (verse 3) is the fraternal
organization, the Ancient Order of
Hibernians. See also note p. 19.

Text: *San Francisco Call*, Volume 87,
Number 108, 18 March 1900.

On the mountain's side the battle raged, there was no stop
    nor stay;
Mackin captured Private Burke and Ensign Michael Shea.
Fitzgerald got Fitzpatrick, Brannigan found O'Rourke;
Finnigan took a man named Lynch and a couple of lads
    from Cork.
Sudden they heard Martin cry, 'Hands up or I'll run you
    through!'
He thought he had a Yorkshire boy– 'twas Corporal
    Donoghue.
McGarry took O'Leary, O'Connell took McNamee –
That's how the 'English fought the Dutch' at the battle of
    Dundee.

Then someone brought in Casey; O'Connor took O'Neill;
Riley captured Cavanaugh while trying to make a steal.
Hogan caught McFadden, Corrigan found McBride.
And Brennan made a handsome touch when Kelly tried to
    slide.
Dacey took a lad named Walsh; Dooley got McGuirk;
Gilllgan turned in Fahey's boy – for his father he used to work.
They had marched to fight the English – but Irish were all they
    could see –
That's how the 'English fought the Dutch' at the battle of
    Dundee.

Spillane then took O'Madigan; Shanahan took Magee;
While chasing Jerry Donovan, Clancy got shot in the knee.
He cursed the Queen's whole army, he cursed the English race,
Then found the man who fired the shot – 'twas a cousin,
    Martin Grace.
Then Maginnis caught an A.O.H. who came from Limerick
    town,
But Sullivan got an Orangeman from somewhere in County
    Down.
Hennessy took O'Hara; Hennigan took McFee –
That's how the 'English fought the Dutch' at the battle of
    Dundee.

The sun was sinking slowly, the battle rolled along;
The man that Murphy 'handed in' was a cousin of Maud
    Gonne.
Then Flannigan dropped his rifle, shook hands with Bill
    McGuire,
For both had carried a piece of turf to light the schoolroom
    fire.
Then Rafferty took in Flaherty; O'Connell got Major McGue;
O'Keeffe got hold of Sergeant Joyce and a Belfast lad or two.
Some swore that 'Old Man Kruger' had come down to see the
    fun;
But the man they thought was 'Uncle Paul', was a Galway man
    named Dunn.
Though war may have worse horrors, 'twas a frightful sight to
    see;
The way the 'English fought the Dutch' at the battle of Dundee.

Just when the sound of firing in the distance fainter grew,
Ryan caught McCloskey, and Orderly Donegan, too.
O'Toole he found McCarthy; O'Mahony got Malone,
Duffy got a pair of lads from Connaught near Athlone.
Then Dineen took O'Hagan; Phelan got Kehoe.

Dempsey captured Callahan, but Gallagher let him go.
You'd have thought the 'Belfast Chicken' had tackled the 'Dublin
    Flea',
The way the 'English fought the Dutch' at the battle of Dundee.

Then Powers began to intervene – the Waterford Powers I mean –
And took a lad named Keenan and a captain named Mulqueen;
Then Brady captured Noonan; Maher got McIldoo;
McGovern got O'Hanlon and Colonel McLaughlin, too.
'Twas now the hour of sunset, the battle was nearly o'er
When McCormick came in with Hoolan and Lieutenant Roger
    Moore.
But 'twas a great day for Ireland, as you can easily see;
That's how the 'English fought the Dutch' at the battle of Dundee.

They marched them all to Kruger's town for supper and a bed.
O'Halloran was the rear guard; the way McNulty led.
When they got them to the race course the Boers were full of glee,
While Kruger never expected 'so many English to see'.
They told him they were Irish; it puzzled the old man's head,
For the Irish he'd seen were dressed in green, while these were togged
    in red.
But 'tis a passing story; on history's page you'll see,
That "twas the English fought the Dutch' at the battle of Dundee.

'Arrival in Pretoria of the Royal Irish Fusiliers captured near Ladysmith, c. 1900', by Thure de Thulstrup (1848–1930).

Cogadh na mBórach

Mícheál Ruiséal (d. 1928)

Éistigh go fóill go 'neosfad eachtra
    Do dhóigh sliocht Chailbhin is do chráidh a gcroidhe,
Cogadh na mBórs le Tóraibh Shasana
    Ar chóstaíbh Aifrice dá dtnáthadh síos;
Tá gunnaí breágh' nódha le fórsa 'cnagarnaigh,
    'Gus púdar go leor 'na smólaibh dearga,
Tá fearaibh breágh' óg' sa ghleo 'á dtreascairt,
    Is brón dá ndeascaibh ar a gcáirdibh gaoil.

Tá aicme chlann Lútair dá gcrústach eatartha
    Agus dúil dá ghlacadh gach lá 'na ndia'
'Ge *President* Crúger 'sa thrúpaí chalma,
    'Gus súil 'ge 'faireadh ar gach stráile dhíobh,
Tá *Orangemen* Gallda 'na gcamthaí leagaithe,
    Sasanaigh ramhra dá lamhach ar chapallaibh,
Tá pléascáin ann mar splannca lasarach.
    Ag pleanncadh an aicme úd, sliocht gránna 'Lís.

This song and the next one are two of the few pieces in the Irish language about events covered in this collection. The author, Mícheál Ruiséal, was a fisherman and small farmer living in West Kerry. Although he could not read nor write, he made many songs, and carried many more.

Texts: Seán Ó Dubhda (eag.), *Duanaire Duibhneach*, Oifig Dhíolta Foilseachán Rialtais, Baile Átha Cliath, 1933.
    Air: 'Táimse im Chodhladh'.

Tá 'n gasra tréan de laochfhir chalma,
　D'réir mar mheasaim, i gcáil 's i ngníomh,
Chun ailpeanna 'n Bhéarla féin úd Shasana,
　Go léir do leagadh, do chráidh riamh Gaoidhil.
Tá loingeas ó Éirinn ag tréall go hAifric,
　Le gasra tréan de laochaibh calma,
Tá galar ón spéir 's an t-éag dá nglacadh,
　Ceal éadach leabtha ná faghálthas bídh.

Cogadh na mBórach

Mícheál Ruiséal

Tháinig scéal ó Shasana ar *wire* san *October*
Go raibh na búirthí piléar san Aifrice ag pléascadh mar bheadh
　　tóirnigh,
Go raibh na Bórs go calma is gunnaí gléasta nódh' 'ca,
Is iad ag déanamh marbhuithe ar gach n-aon dá dtéigheadh
　'na gcómhgar.

Is tá camthaí 'n Bhéarla úd Shasana mar mheasaim-se go
　　brónach,
Cé gurbh iad na hailpeanna do chleachtuigh puins is rósta,
Tá Crúger thall ag faireadh ortha is scata de sna Bóraibh,
Is púdar ann dá lasadh 'ca 'sna *cannons* fé n-a gcómhair siúd.

Is tá Clanna Gaedheal bocht eatartha 'na ngasra breágh
　　óigfhear,
Is lámhach na bpiléar dá leagadh is gan aon tais' 'á dhéanamh
　　dóibh siúd;
Tá an *Major* féin ag faireadh ortha agus *flag* aige mar
　　chómhartha,
'Á rádh gan aenne 'casadh anois ón lasair úd sa ghleo 'ca.

Tá Clanna Gaedheal chómh hacfuinneach, is an lasair ag
　　g'bháilt thórsta,
Go dtéighid siad ar na bagnaití ceangailte ins na Bóraibh,
Le lúth a ngéag is acfuinne na bhfear úd chun cómhraic
Go n-éaluigheann fé sna leacachaibh le heagal uatha an Bór
　　bocht.

An té bheadh i *South Africa* ag amharc uaidh tráthnóna,
Ar na laochaibh úd ann treascartha, idir Shasanaigh is Bóraibh,
Is Clanna Gaedheal fós eatartha 's a dteanga 'paidir-eoireacht,
Chun trócaire Dé dá n-anam súd, go dtugadh Dia na Glóire.

John MacBride's Brigade

From land to land throughout the world the news is going round
That Ireland's flag triumphant waves on high o'er English ground.
In far-off Africa to-day the English fly dismayed
Before the flag of green and gold borne by MacBride's Brigade.
Three thousand sons of Erin's Isle, with bayonets flashing bright,
For Ireland's cause and Kruger's land right gallantly they fight;
And Erin watches from afar, with joy, and hope, and pride,
Her sons who strike for liberty, led on by John MacBride.

Three thousand Transvaal Irishmen, with spirits brave and free,
They struck the Saxon foeman down at Glencoe and Dundee.
From Ladysmith to Spion Kop their flag victorious waved,
And well they wreaked revenge on those who Erin's Isle enslaved.
With guns and bayonets in their hands, their Irish flag on high,
As down they swept on English ranks out rang their battle cry –
'Revenge! Remember '98, and how our fathers died.'
'We'll pay the English back today,' cried fearless John MacBride.

And soon, my boys, we all shall see on Ireland's soil again
Our dashing, dauntless John MacBride with all his fighting men.
They'll raise the flag of Emmet, Tone, and Mitchel up once more,
And lead us in the fight to drive the tyrant from our shore,
From Cork right up to Derry's Walls – from Dublin to Mayo.
Once more we'll meet and this time beat the cursed English foe,
And he who'll lead us in the cause for which our heroes died,
Is brave old Mayo's peerless son – our glorious John MacBride.

Text: Georges-Denis Zimmermann, *Songs of Irish Rebellion*, Figgis, Dublin, 1967. Originally published in *The United Irishman* on 24 February 1900.

The picture to the left shows Major John MacBride, Transvaal Irish Brigade, holding the sight of a British cannon captured at Colenso.

Song of the Transvaal Irish Brigade
(At Ladysmith)

A brigade of Irishmen, commanded by Major John MacBride, who fought for the Boers against the British in the South African war, 1899–1902.
Arthur Griffith

The Cross swings low,— the morn is near, now com-rades fill— up high;

The can-non's voice— will ring out clear when mor-ning lights— the sky.

A toast we'll drink to-ge-ther, boys, ere dawns the bat-tles's grey,

A toast to Ire— land, dear old Ire— land, Ire-land far— a-way!

Ire-land far a-way! Ire-land far a-way!

Health to Ire— land, strength to Ire— land, Ire-land, boys,— hur-rah!

The 'Cross' of the first line is the constellation Crux Australis or The Southern Cross, which is visible only in the southern hemisphere, and which is featured on the modern flag of Australia.

Text: Piaras Béaslaí (ed.), *Songs, Ballads and Recitations by Famous Irishmen – Arthur Griffith*, Waltons, Dublin, n.d.

The intended air is clearly that of T.D. Sullivan's 'Song from the Back-woods'.

The Cross swings low, the morn is near –
  Now comrades fill up high;
The cannon's voice will ring out clear
  When morning lights the sky.
A toast we'll drink together, boys,
  Ere dawns the battle's grey,
A toast to Ireland – dear old Ireland –
  Ireland far away!
    Ireland far away! Ireland far away!
      Health to Ireland! – strength to Ireland!
    Ireland, boys, hurrah!

Who told us that her cause was dead?
  Who bade us bend the knee?
The slaves! Again she lifts her head –
  Again she dares be free!
With gun in hand, we take our stand
  For Ireland in the fray –
We fight for Ireland – dear old Ireland!
  Ireland far away!
    Ireland far away! Ireland far away!
      We fight for Ireland – die for Ireland!
    Ireland, boys, hurrah!

O Mother of the Wounded Breast!
   O Mother of the Tears!
The sons you loved and trusted best
   Have grasped their battle-spears.
From Shannon, Lagan, Liffey, Lee,
   On Afric's soil to-day –
We strike for Ireland – brave old Ireland!
   Ireland far away!
      Ireland far away! Ireland far away!
         We smite for Ireland – brave old Ireland!
      Ireland, boys, hurrah!

The morning breaks – the bugle calls!
   Now, comrades, for the fight!
A hero's grave be his who falls
   Ere comes again the night.
For Freedom's flag – for Ireland's cause –
   Strike stout and swift to-day!
Hurrah for Ireland – brave old Ireland!
   Ireland far away!
      Ireland far away! Ireland far away!
         God guard old Ireland – dear old Ireland!
      Ireland, boys, hurrah!

The Irish Brigade, which fought on the side of the Boers.

27

Bravo! Dublin Fusiliers
or Ireland's Reply
G.D. Wheeler

Some dare to say that Ir-ish-men should re-fuse to fight for Bri-tain's crown;

Some dare sug-gest that they should pre-pare to turn and strike the Eng-lish down.

What co-ward-ly trai-tors to try and in-cite our sol-diers to be-come mu-ti-neers!

Those a-gi-ta-tors have had their re-ply from the gal-lant Dub-lin Fu-si-liers.

Chorus

Bra-vo! Dub-lin Fu-si-liers! You're no cra-ven mu-ti-neers,

You brave-ly storm'd and won the Glen-coe height; Put four thou-sand craf-ty Boers to flight,

Twas a grand and glo-rious sight, Bra-vo! Dub-lin Fu-si-liers!

Text and air: Sheet music published in 1899 by Francis, Day & Hunter, London.

Some dare to say that Irishmen should refuse to fight for
    Britain's crown,
Some dare suggest that they should prepare to turn and
    strike the English down.
What cowardly traitors, to try and incite our soldiers to
    become mutineers! –
Those agitators have had their reply from the gallant
    Dublin Fusiliers.

Chorus
Bravo! Dublin Fusiliers! You're no craven mutineers,
    You bravely stormed and won the Glencoe height;
    Put four thousand crafty Boers to flight,
'Twas a grand and glorious sight, Bravo! Irish Fusiliers!

Boers have derided men of our race, insulted Britain's
    dear old flag;
Boasted Majuba – said we were curs, called our flag 'The
    old white rag'.
Sanguine of victory and anxious to fight they came to
    Glencoe Hill to attack;
They'll cease to boast of Majuba – they've seen the
    colour of the Union Jack.

'Rushing the Boers at Spion Kop,'
How the Dublin Fusiliers and Border Regiment rushed the Boer Trenches on 23 January 1900.
(Sketch by Ernest Prater, drawn by J. Finnemore, R.I.) *The Sphere*, 24 February 1900.

Brave General Symons led our attack amidst the deadly
    shot and shell;
Foremost and first were brave Irish boys, and many
    gallant soldiers fell.
Dear was the price – for that victory we paid with many,
    many British lives;
'Tis but our duty if help we provide for those heroes'
    children and their wives.

What Do You Think of the Irish now?

Albert Hall (1864–1907) and Harry Castling

The Sham-rock has lost, and the Sham-rock has won, as she of-ten has won for the Rose,

For whilst the boat "Sham-rock" was beat by your friends, the Sham-rock was thra-shing you foes!

On far-off Glen-coe, when the morn-ing sun broke, the can-non were si-lenced 'mid cheers,

And then, like the wind, up that red hill of Death rush'd the boys who have ne-ver known fear,

The Dub-lin and I-rish Fu-si-liers!

Chorus

What do you think of the I-rish now? What do you think of the boys?____

You said we were trai-tors, but u-pon my soul, you read the names on Glen-coe's death-roll!

What do you think of the Fu-si-liers, who dashed o'er the fire-swept brow?____

You used to call us trai-tors, be-cause of a-gi-ta-tors, but you can't call us trai-tors now!____

Written for the music-hall performer Pat Rafferty, this song was published in sheet music in 1900 by Francis, Day & Hunter, London.

The Shamrock has lost, and the Shamrock has won,
    As she often has won for the Rose,
For whilst the boat 'Shamrock' was beat by your friends,
    The Shamrock was thrashing your foes!
On far-off Glencoe, when the morning sun broke,
    The cannon were silenced 'mid cheers,
And then, like the wind, up that red hill of Death
    Rush'd the boys who have never known fear –
    The Dublin and Irish Fusiliers!

Chorus
What do you think of the Irish now?
    What do you think of the boys?
You said we were traitors, but upon my soul,
You read the names on Glencoe's death-roll!

What do you think of the Fusiliers,
    Who dashed o'er the fire-swept brow?
You used to call us traitors, because of agitators,
    But you can't call us traitors now!

We've heard a few Irish speak out for the Boers,
    And the methods of England condemn,
If they thought they were speaking the thoughts of our
    race,
    What a lesson Glencoe was to them.
Their names may be Irish, their births Irish too –
    Black sheep may be found anywheres –
In the Fusiliers' wounded and glorious dead
    All the names are as Irish as theirs!
    The sort of Irishman who does and dares.

For you the Irish have oft fought before,
    And pulled you safe out of a row,
But people have said 'They to traitors have turned –
    The Irish won't fight for you now!'
If those people wondered what Ireland would do
    When she stood up to face England's foe,
Let them gaze on the lines of our glorious dead
    On those blood-reddened heights of Glencoe,
    And then like the foeman well they'll know!

In years that have passed, when the country had need
    'Twas the Irish who oft bore the brunt;
Lord Beresford now, and Lord Kitchener too
    Stern duty has called to the front.
And one whom the whole nation loves and reveres,
    Though stricken with grief cruel and keen,
Like his son, he's prepared – aye, to lay down his life,
    For the sake of his country and Queen.
    Lord Roberts is the General I mean.

Caoineadh na gCuradh

Tomás Ó Flannghaile (1846–1916)

Mo bhrón go deo, mo chreach, mo chrádh!
Na leómhain fé dheoidh faoi neart a námhad –
An tsaoirse thíos, 's laoich á gclaoidheadh,
A dtír fé chíos 's a ndaoine ag caoidh!
    Caoin, caoin, a chinneamhain ghéar,
    Is bí go faoidheach ag sileadh déar,

Another poem in the Irish language in support of the Boer cause.

Text: *Irish Political Review*, Vol. 21, issue 2, Dublin, 2006.

31

'Na luighe tá mílte groidhe-fhear tréan
'S a sliocht gan bhrígh, mo loma léin!

'S bhuaidhir mo chroidhe im' chlí thar meodhan,
Gan truagh an tsaoighil do shíol na mBóer,
An domhan go dúr, gan rún, gan báidh,
Gan cabhair, gan súil, le congnamh d'fhagháil;
    Caoin, caoin, an tsaoirse ar lár,
    An comhthrom thíos, an claon ar bhárr,
    Neamh-shuim 'sa cheart, 'san neart go géar,
    Na gaiscidhigh theas gan reacht, gan réim!

Acht bíodh gur buaileadh líon a bhfear,
Is gidh gur chuaidh sé díobh le seal,
D'fhág siad a rian go dian go trom,
I lár na ndiabhal do chiap tré feall;
    Cian, cian, bheidheas cumha na nGall
    I ndiaidh an ghéar-chrádha fuair siad thall,
    Minic do theicheadar le n-a sluagh
    Cois abhann is sléibh' ó fhaobhar na mBuar.

Tá dóchas fós don laochraidh i ndán –
Ní neart i gcómhnaidhe bhéarfas bárr –
Fulaing fear groidhe don tsaoirse is síol;
Agus muinighin chroidhe 'seadh is treise brígh;
    Éistigh le ciall, ní buan droich-riaghail,
    Má's tréan an diabhal, is tréine Dia,
    Iad féin, leo féin, le congnamh Dé,
    Beidh Bóeir fós saor 'na ndúthaigh féin.

Ode of Welcome
Oliver St John Gogarty (1878–1957)

Upon the return of the Irish regiments from South Africa in June of 1900, Gogarty sent in this poem (anony-mously) to the conservative Anglo-Irish journal, *Irish Society*.
  Its hidden message was not noticed by the publisher but was quickly dis-covered by the public, and it became the talk of Dublin city.

Text: A. Norman Jeffares (ed.), *The Poems & Plays of Oliver St John Gogarty*, Colin Smythe Ltd, 2001.

The gallant Irish yeoman
Home from the war has come
Each victory gained o'er foeman
Why should our bards be dumb.

How shall we sing their praises
Or glory in their deeds
Renowned their worth amazes
Empire their prowess needs.

So to Old Ireland's hearts and homes
We welcome now our own brave boys
In cot and Hall; 'neath lordly domes
Love's heroes share once more our joys.

Love is the Lord of all just now
Be he the husband, lover, son,
Each dauntless soul recalls the vow
By which not fame, but love was won.

United now in fond embrace
Salute with joy each well-loved face
Yeoman: in women's hearts you hold the place.

Kruger's Army

The Boers they were marching
　　And the British went to fight,
The Boers took out their rifles
　　And they blew them out of sight.

Chorus
Sound the bugle, beat the drum.
And give three cheers for Kruger!
To hell with the Queen and her oul' tambourine
And hurrah for Kruger's army!

This song was sung in Dublin at least up to the early 1960s.

Air: 'The British Grenadiers'.

33

The Man Who Came Home from Pretoria

George Curtin (Mícheál Ó Tuama, 1877–1927)

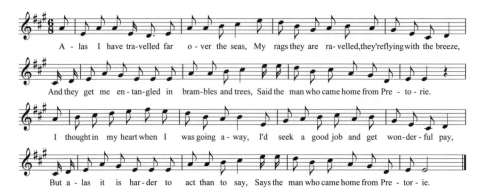

George Curtin, the author of this and several other witty songs, is said to have composed this piece to explain away an unfortunate trip to Scotland, from which he returned somewhat the worse for wear. See p. 15 for a note on Christiaan De Wet (verse 2).

The world of Irish traditional music and song offers an infinite number of treats to those who take the trouble to explore its byways. Very near the top of the pile is the experience of hearing this song performed, preferably at 'the Top of Coom', by one of the many superb singers that abound in the Cork district of Cúil Aodha.

Text: Dick Hogan, *The Hogan Collection,* Dublin, 2013.
Air: From memory.

Alas I have travelled far over the seas,
My rags they are ravelled, they're flying with the breeze,
And they get me entangled in brambles and trees,
 Said the man who came home from Pretoria.
I thought in my heart when I was going away,
I'd seek a good job and get wonderful pay,
But, alas! it is harder to act than to say,
 Said the man who came home from Pretoria.

Ah me, but De Wet gave us something to do.
I remember him well and I think so should you.
At the sight of him Kitchener turned quite blue,
 Said the man who came home from Pretoria.
Our long hours in ambush whilst dodging the Boers,
In anguish we languished while patching our sores,
Three of those men were a match for three score,
 Said the man who came home from Pretoria.

I slaved like a begger to come back again,
On board an oul lugger midst torrents of rain,
Sure the roar of the surges nigh put me insane,
 Said the man who came home from Pretoria.
After fourteen days sailing we came to Dundalk,
My limbs they were failing, I scarcely could walk,
And the peelers they stared with the eyes of a hawk,
 At the man coming home from Pretoria.

There was one with a squint, that insisted to know,
My name and my ways of existence also,

And says he 'you've the gimp and identical go,
    Of a man coming home from Pretoria.
Besides you've no visible means of support.
Your movements are strange since you came into port.
I will have you detained to explain it in court,
    Why you're tramping it home from Pretoria.'

Yes, I haven't a rap, that's a fact I allow,
But I broke in no shop, or I started no row,
I stole not a clock, a gold watch or a plough,
    Though I'm tramping it home from Pretoria.
I prayed and protested with the tears in my eyes,
For the sake of his dear ones who had fled from this life,
Not to have me arrested, me but let me pass by,
    On my way coming home from Pretoria.

He then marched me off like a horse going to pound,
With another poor straggler, strapped and well bound,
How I wish I was swallowed red hot through the
    ground,
    Or shot by the Boers in Pretoria.
Now I'll tell you the truth where they lodged us that
    night,
'Twas a dreary cold cell shut off from the light,
Where the fleas in battalions were having a fight,
    For the man coming home from Pretoria.

It was early next morning a raw boned J.P.
Subjected the law to a sharp scrutiny,
Says he 'there's no harm at all that I see,
    In that man coming home from Pretoria.'
And now I am back in Strickeen in the fall,
And candidly dream it's the grandest of all,
And those places I've seen from Benlee to Bengal
    Where I'll stick till my whiskers are hoary.

King Edward in Erin

Percy French

'Twas late in the evening as home I did go
To sweet Crossmolina in County Mayo,
I met an old harper who play'd on wan string,
And the tune he was playin' was 'God save the King'.

Edward VII visited Ireland in 1903. The sentiments in the final verse are also expressed in French's more famous song 'The Mountains of Mourne'. The Redmond of verse 3 is probably Willie Redmond, MP for East Clare. Saunderson is the MP for North Armagh who once challenged Redmond to a duel.

Text: James N. Healy, *Percy French and His Songs*, Mercier Press, Cork, 1966.

Chorus
'God save the King!'
He made the rocks ring
Wid de way he was weltin' out
'God save the King!'

Says I, 'Where's the tunes that wor' once in your pate?
Give us 'Erin Remember' or try 'Ninety-eight'.'
Says he, 'It is strange how they've all taken wing
Not a wan I remember but "God save the King!" '

Chorus
'God save the King!'
Not a taste of a thing,
Could the ould man remember
But 'God save the King!'

Says he, 'There's a change comin' over the land
That an old man like me cannot well understand
Wid Redmond and Saunderson all in wan ring
And footin' it nately to "God save the King!" '

Chorus
'God save the King!'
Together we'll cling,
All crackin' their voices wid
'God save the King!'

I mind well the day when the League of the Gael,
Would have scowled at the sight of a Sassenach sail
But now the King's yacht at her moorings may swing
Wid the Britain St band playing 'God save the King!'

Chorus
'God save the King!'
It's a wonderful thing
To see Capel Street marchin' to
'God save the King!'

For the King that's come over to see us at last,
Has nothin' to do wid the days that are past
And though there are some that to sorrows will cling,
For a while we'll forget them and welcome the King.

Chorus
'God save the King!'
For his reign seems to bring
A respite to Erin, so
'God save the King!'

The Fenian Girl's Song

'A Fenian Sister'

Oh, yes I am an Ir-ish girl, and glo-ry in the name___
And boast it with far great-er pride than glitt'-ring wealth or Fame.___
We en-vy not the Sax-on lass nor robes of beau-ties rare,___
Tho' dia-monds grace her snow-y brow and pearls be-deck her hair.___
Hur-rah!___ Hur-rah!___ for Ir-ish Rights so dear,___
Three cheers, for the Lin-sey dress, our Ir-ish girls can wear.___

Oh, yes I am an Irish girl, and glory in the name,
And boast it with far greater pride than glitt'ring wealth
    or Fame.
We envy not the Saxon lass nor robes of beauties rare,
Tho' diamonds grace her snowy brow and pearls bedeck
    her hair.
Hurrah! Hurrah! for Irish Rights so dear,
Three cheers for the Linsey dress, our Irish girls can
    wear.

My Linsey dress is plain I know, my hat is humble too,
But then it shows what Irish girls for Irish rights can do;
We'll send the bravest of our race, to fight the Saxon foe,
And we will give a helping hand, the English to
    o'erthrow.
Hurrah! Hurrah! for Irish Rights so dear,
Three cheers for the Green and Gold, our Fenian boys
    will wear.

Then English goods we won't receive, Victoria will
    blockade,
But Fenian girls will be content with goods that's Irish
    made;
We'll send our Fenians to the war, but girls never mind,

This song is a parody of 'The Home-spun Dress', a song popular in the southern states at the time of the American Civil War, also sung to the air here, 'The Irish Jaunting Car'.

Text and air: Sheet music published by J.J. Daly, New York, 1866.

Your Fenian love, can ne'er forget, the girl he left
  behind.
Hurrah! Hurrah! for Irish Rights so dear,
Three cheers for the Irish Flag, our Fenian boys will
  bear.

A Fenian is the lad for me. A brave heart I adore,
And when my Irish home is free, and fighting is no
  more,
I'll choose me then a lover brave, from out that gallant
  band,
The Fenian lad, I love the best, shall have my heart and
  hand.
Hurrah! Hurrah! for Irish Rights so dear,
Three cheers for the Fenian braves that will our colours
  bear.

And now young men, a word to you, if you would win
  the fair,
Go to the field where duty calls, and win your fair one
  there;
Remember that our brightest smiles, are for the true and
  brave,
And that our tears are all for those, who fill a Fenian's
  grave.
Hurrah! Hurrah! for Irish Rights so dear,
Ten thousand cheers for Fenian men who dare the Green
  to bear.

The Old Fenian's Address to His New Repeating Rifle

Edward Fitzwilliam

See p. 7 for another poem by Edward
Fitzwilliam.

Text: Edward Fitzwilliam, *Songs and
Poems*, The J.K. Waters Co., Boston,
1906.

Be-dad you are a dandy piece
    Your likes I never saw,
Right soon would Erin's trouble cease
    Well rid of England's law,
If every whole-souled Irishman;
    (But not the crawling few)
Were bound to work the one true plan,
    Each armed with such as you,
            My pet,
    Each armed with such as you!

When first I learned to hit the mark
    'Twas with an old Queen Anne,
With big flint-lock that struck a spark
    To powder in the pan;
But, human skill has been at work,
    John Bull might well feel blue
If all, from Donegal to Cork,
    Once owned a beaut like you,
          My pet,
    Once owned a beaut like you.

I have been listening all my life
    To eloquence most grand,
'Bout ways and means to end the strife
    In my loved native land;
And now drawing near my closing days
    I take a backward view;
I see that tyrants mock old ways
    But dread a crack from you,
          My pet,
    But dread a crack from you!

The times are changing very fast
    Invention's rising tide,
Makes what was best a few years past
    Now, rubbish cast aside:
Electric shocks may yet, perhaps,
    Displace the rifle too,
But 'till that day we Irish chaps,
    Must learn to shoot with you,
          My pet,
    Must learn to shoot with you!

In blood, the Boers have writ a page
    Of glorious human history,
That points, in this inventive age,
    The path to human liberty;
They talk not much, but just enough
    To make men dare and do;
The bravest soldiers give least 'guff',
    They talk through such as you,
          My pet,
    They talk through such as you!

You may, perchance, be rusty yet,
    'Though now so bright and clean,
But while I live, my trusty pet,
    No man shall use you mean:
Through your small bore there goes a pill,

Projected straight and true,
That bends the sternest tyrant's will,
Who'd bend alone to you,
My pet,
Who'd bend alone to you!

I know your voice is hard and sharp
And dreaded by mankind;
But musical as Erin's harp
On duty, well defined:
When rulers in this wondrous age,
Act bad as fiends can do;
The common people must engage
Strong pleaders such as you,
My pet,
Strong pleaders such as you!

I don't advise to kill a fly
Through malice or through spite;
But, wholesale robbers when they try,
Like burglars in the night,
The people's hard-earned wealth to loot
And tax them for it too;
Then, every man should learn to shoot,
And own a piece like you,
My pet,
And own a piece like you!

Peaceful agitation has
Been tried time-out-of-mind,
But every gain effected was
By means of another kind;
England likes peace measures well,
Talk tells her what to do,
But dreads, the world now can tell,
To face the likes of you,
My pet,
To face the likes of you.

Then, Irishmen each other trust,
Drop all dissension now,
A man to raise a crop, at first
Must dig, or hold the plow:
So, if you'd reap fair Freedom's fruit,
The proper thing to do,
Is: get a rifle, learn to shoot,
As I am doing with you,
My pet,
As I am doing with you!

'Constant Dropping Wears the Stone'

John Fitz-Gerald (1825–1910)

Little things have mighty power –
  Insects form the coral reef,
Stone on stone builds up the tower,
  Seedlings come to bough and leaf.
Grains of sand hem in the ocean,
  Where its wild waves high are thrown,
Trifles keep the earth in motion –
  'Constant dropping wears the stone.'

'Cast thy bread upon the waters,'
  'Twill return in many days,
If you help God's sons and daughters,
  Wandering in life's weary ways.
Little deeds when good, are splendid,
  Leaving you by God's bright throne,
When your life on earth has ended –
  'Constant dropping wears the stone.'

Leaf on leaf in autumn breaking,
  Leaves the forest brown and sere;
Wave on wave, 'mid sea-birds shrieking,
  Hews the sea-caves dark and drear.
Little clouds give timely warning,
  Ere the tempest blast has blown;
Little trifles bear not scorning –
  'Constant dropping wears the stone.'

Little pens, if tipped with fire,
  Cause the Revolution's shock,
Little blows that never tire,
  Fell the oak, and blast the rock.
Little steps ascend the mountain,
  Little wings long leagues have flown,
Little drops fill up the fountain –
  'Constant dropping wears the stone.'

Little leaks cause ships to founder,
  Little sparks explode the mine;
Little men, if they surround her,
  Make their land in honour shine.
Little streamlets swell the river,
  Little notes on trumpets blown,
Sound the charge where squadrons quiver –
  'Constant dropping wears the stone.'

Text: John Fitz-Gerald, *Legends, Ballads & Songs of the Lee*, Henry & Coghlan, Cork, 1862.

41

Little wrongs seem mean and trifling,
    Yet they all mount up in time;
Though a land its wrath be stifling,
    Some day it bursts, sublime.
Step by step, you goad a people,
    Till yourself like grass are mown,
And the tocsin shakes the steeple –
    'Constant dropping wears the stone.'

There's a small chain girds the world,
    Where the sun gets up or sinks –
Bent and strained, and downward hurled,
    Tiny shamrocks form its links.
Yet it keeps our sons united,
    Till a nation they have grown;
Wrong shall some day be requited –
    'Constant dropping wears the stone.'

Bide Your Time

M.J. Barry

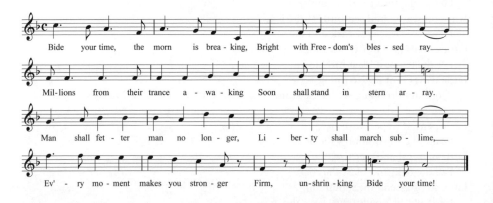

Bide your time, the morn is brea - king, Bright with Free - dom's bles - sed ray___

Mil - lions from their trance a - wa - king Soon shall stand in stern ar - ray.

Man shall fet - ter man no lon - ger, Li - ber - ty shall march sub - lime,___

Ev' - ry mo - ment makes you stron - ger Firm, un-shrin - king Bide your time!

This song was a favourite of James Connolly's. In *The Worker's Republic* in August 1915 he referred to the author: 'M.J. Barry, the gifted author of that splendid revolutionary song, all too seldom sung nowadays, Bide Your Time.' It was first published in *The Spirit of The Nation* in 1843, and was included in *Songs of Freedom by Irish Authors*, edited by Connolly and published in New York in 1906.

Text and air: *Spirit of The Nation*,
J. Duffy, Dublin, 1845.

Bide your time, the morn is breaking,
    Bright with Freedom's blessed ray –
Millions, from their trance awaking,
    Soon shall stand in firm array.
Man shall fetter man no longer,
    Liberty shall march sublime;
Every moment makes you stronger,
    Firm, unshrinking, Bide Your Time.

Bide Your Time – one false step taken
    Perils all you yet have done;

Undismayed, erect, unshaken –
　　Watch and wait, and all is won.
'Tis not by a rash endeavour
　　Men or states to greatness climb –
Would you win your rights forever
　　Calm and thoughtful, Bide Your Time.

Bide Your Time – your worst transgression
　　Were to strike, and strike in vain;
He, whose arm would smite oppression,
　　Must not need to smite again!
Danger makes the brave man steady –
　　Rashness is the coward's crime –
Be for Freedom's battle ready,
　　When it comes – but, Bide Your Time.

Ourselves Alone

John O'Hagan (1822–1890)

The work that should to - day be wrought De - fer not till___ to - mor - row;

The help that should with - in be sought Scorn from with - out to bor - row.

Old max - ims these, yet stout and true, They speak in trum - pet tone,

To do at once what is to do, And___ trust Our - selves___ a - lone.

The work that should to-day be wrought
　　Defer not till to-morrow;
The help that should within be sought,
　　Scorns from without to borrow.
Old maxims these – yet stout and true –
　　They speak in trumpet tone,
To do at once what is to do,
　　And trust ourselves alone.

Too long our Irish hearts were schooled
　　In patient hope to bide:
By dreams of English justice fooled,
　　And English tongues that lied.

Also first published in *The Spirit of The Nation*, under the pen-name 'Sliabh Cuilinn', the title of this song is probably the origin of the name of the Sinn Féin party.

Text and air: *Spirit of The Nation*, J. Duffy, Dublin, 1845.

That hour of weak delusion's past,
  The empty dream has flown;
Our hope and strength, we find at last,
  Is in ourselves alone.

Ay! bitter hate or cold neglect,
  Or lukewarm love at best,
Is all we've found or can expect,
  We aliens of the west.
No friend beyond her own green shore,
  Can Erin truly own;
Yet strongest is her trust, therefore,
  In her brave sons alone.

Remember when our lot was worse –
  Sunk, trampled to that dust –
'Twas long our weakness and our curse,
  In stranger aid to trust.
And if at length we proudly trod
  On bigot laws o'erthrown,
Who won that struggle? Under God
  Ourselves – ourselves alone!

The Rebel Heart

Francis A. Fahy (1854–1935)

Francis Fahy is best known for his
sentimental songs such as 'Galway
Bay' or 'The Ould Plaid Shawl',
but there was an undercurrent of
nationalism throughout his work,
best revealed in this song.

Text: Francis A. Fahy, *The Ould
Plaid Shawl and Other Songs*,
Three Candles, Dublin, 1949.
  The song was originally published
in *The Watchword of Labour*, Vol. 1,
No. 27, 3 April 1920.

From Rebel veins my life I draw,
  In Rebel arms I lay;
From Rebel lips my lessons knew,
  That led me day by day;
And rocked to rest on Rebel breast,
  And nursed on Rebel knee,
There woke and grew for weal or woe,
  A Rebel heart in me.

Chorus
A Rebel heart! A Rebel heart!
  From taint of thraldom free,
God strengthen still, through good and ill,
  A Rebel heart in me.

My home was where the Moher heights
  Rise rugged o'er the wave,
And nature's scenes and nature's sights
  Forbad me live a slave;

The billows on the crag that crashed
   Still thundered 'Liberty'!
And at the cry throbbed fast and high
   The Rebel heart in me.

I read my country's chequered page,
   I sang her deathless songs;
I wept her woes from age to age.
   And burned to right her wrongs;
And when I saw to alien law
   She never bent the knee,
O prouder yet for Ireland beat
   The Rebel heart in me.

I found my brothers scattered wide
   Still faithful to their own;
I found the tyrant in his pride
   A knave upon a throne.
'God ne'er designed a soulless hind
   Should lord of Ireland be'
And strove in vain to break her chain
   The Rebel heart in me.

I've wandered East, I've wandered West,
   'Mid scenes and faces strange,
And passing years have in my breast
   Wrought many a wondrous change;
One hope of old still firm I hold,
   And cold in earth I'll be,
Ere breaks or falls, or sinks or quails
   The Rebel heart in me.

The energy of the nationalist movement could not be more clearly demonstrated than by this photograph of a meeting of the Gaelic League in Galway in 1913, which includes three future presidents of Ireland, and many of the personalities mentioned in this book. They include Douglas Hyde, Eoin McNeill, James Ennis, Thomas Ashe, Éamonn Ceannt, Piaras Béaslaí, Seán Mac Diarmada, George Russell, Éamon de Valera, The O'Rahilly, Peadar Kearney, Cathal Brugha, Risteard Mulcahy, Willie Pearse, Seán Moylan, Pádraic Pearse and Constance Markievicz. (Courtesy: the Curran Family)

Where Is the Flag of England?

Henry Labouchère (1831–1912)

The author of this song, Henry Du Pré Labouchère, was an English publisher and Liberal MP of markedly conservative positions on social matters.

It was a piece of legislation which he had initiated in 1885 that was used to convict both Oscar Wilde and Alan Turing of the crime of gross indecency.

He was also a committed anti-imperialist, and a supporter of Gladstone in the matter of Home Rule for Ireland. He composed other poems on the same theme as this one, which has been re-worked by the ballad group The Wolfe Tones into the song 'The Butcher's Apron'. It has been reprinted several times in Irish nationalist songsters, as well as in Indian newspapers.

The original is reported to have been published during the Boer War, but it appeared in print at least as early as April 1896, in *The Evening Post* of Wellington, New Zealand, reprinted from Labouchère's own publication *London Truth*.

It may have been the stimulus for Rudyard Kipling's poem 'The English Flag', published in 1891 and included in *Barrack Room Ballads*.

Text: *Old 'Come-all-Ye's', The Derry Journal*, Derry, 1920s. See ITMA.ie.

And the winds of the world made answer,
    North, South, East and West –
'Wherever there's wealth to covet,
    Or land that can be possess'd;
Wherever there are savage races,
    To cozen, coerce and scare,
Ye shall find the vaunted ensign;
    For the English flag is there!'

'Ay, it waves o'er the blazing hovels
    Whence African victims fly
To be shot by explosive bullets
    Or to wretchedly starve and die!
And where the beachcomber harries
    Isles of the Southern seas,
At the peak of his hellish vessel
    The English flag flies free.'

'The Maori often has cursed it
    With his bitterest dying breath,
And the Arab has hissed his hatred
    As he spat at its folds in death.
The hapless Fellah has feared it
    On Tel-el-Kebir's plain
And the Zulu's blood has stained it
    With a deep indelible stain.'

'It has floated o'er scenes of pillage,
    It has flaunted o'er deeds of shame,
It has waved o'er the fell marauder
    As he ravished with sword and flame.
It has looked upon ruthless slaughter,
    And massacre dire and grim;
It has heard the shrieks of the victims
    Drown even the Jingo hymn.'

'Where is the flag of England?
    Seek the land where the natives rot;
Where decay and assured extinction
    Must soon be the people's lot.
Go! search for the once glad islands
    Where disease and death are rife,
And the greed of a callous commerce
    Now batten on human life!'

'Where is the flag of England?
    Go, sail where rich galleons come
With shoddy and loaded cottons
    With Beer and Bibles and Rum!
Go where brute force has triumphed
    And hypocrisy makes its lair.
And your question will find its answer,
    For the English flag is there.'

The Secret of England's Greatness.

BUCCANEER BULL.—"I have taken their country, I have taken the swag, I have taken their
bloomin' lives, and still they ain't satisfied."

This cartoon, from *The Lepracaun*, April 1906, may be meant to lampoon a famous painting,
Thomas Jones Barker's 'The Secret of England's Greatness', in which Queen Victoria is depicted
presenting a Bible to an African envoy, an entirely mythical event, but one which James Joyce has
'The Citizen' ridicule in the pages of *Ulysses*. The painting had been exhibited in Dublin in 1864.

47

Tim Healy
Jim Connell

There was a little office boy, conceited, sharp and mean,
Whose brazen face was seldom washed, whose shirt was
　　never clean;
The 'devil's luck', as one might guess, upon this urchin fell,
And he was gathered from the mud by Erin's chief, Parnell.

He did his master's menial work with quite congenial mind,
And ever chose as jobs of love the blackest he could find.
The whole immense establishment successfully he bled,
And fed and fattened on the fare his benefactor spread.

At length the day of trouble came, the chieftain had a fall.
With lion heart he faced his foes, his back against the wall.
The faithless rabble stoned him there, and fractured every
　　limb,
And foremost of the yelping pack was dirty little Tim.

Soon after that, with showman haste, the imp became a saint.
The bishops now his praises sing, the priests his merits paint.
He publishes a weekly sheet, of morals high and pure.
Oh, can there be a God above who lets such things endure?

Ulster
(A Reply to Rudyard Kipling)
Tom Kettle (1880–1916)

The red, redeeming dawn
　　Kindled in Eastern skies,
Falls like God's judgment on
　　Lawyers, and lords, and lies.
What care these evil things,
　　Though menaced and perplexed,
While Kipling's banjo strings
　　Blaspheme a sacred text.

Never did freemen stand,
　　Never were captains met,
From Dargai to the Rand,
　　From Parnell to De Wet,
Never, on native sod,
　　Weak justice fared the worst
But Kipling's Cockney 'Gawd'
　　Most impotently cursed.

So now, when Lenten years
    Burgeon, at last, to bless
This land of Faith and Tears
    With fruitful nobleness,
The poet, for a coin,
    Hands to the babbling rout
A bucketful of Boyne
    To put the sunrise out.

'Ulster' is ours, not yours,
    Is ours to have and hold,
Our hills and lakes and moors
    Have shaped her in our mould.
Derry to Limerick Walls
    Fused us in battle flame;
Limerick to Derry calls
    One strong-shared Irish name.

We keep the elder faith,
    Not slain by Cromwell's sword;
Nor bribed to subtler death
    By William's broken word.
Free from those chains, and free
    From hate for hate endured,
We share the liberty
    Our lavish blood assured.

One place, one dream, one doom,
    One task and toil assigned,
Union of plough and loom
    Have bound us and shall bind.
The wounds of labour healed,
    Life rescued and made fair –
There lies the battlefield
    Of Ulster's holy war.

A Call

Stephen O'Reilly (d. 1921)

Awake! for the dawn is breaking,
    And you lie sleeping on!
Comrades have buckled their armour –
    And forth to the fray are gone.
There's a gap in the ranks for you;
Come!
    Each one has a part to play,
And the wrongs of years may be righted
    By the fate that befalls to-day.

Stephen O'Reilly was killed, along
with his brother Paddy, during the
attack on the Custom House in 1921.

Text: Stephen O'Reilly, *Spirit Flowers*,
The Gael Co-op, Dublin, 1923.

The Limb of the Law

Brian O'Higgins (1882–1963)

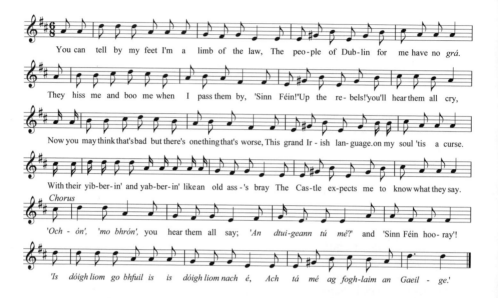

You can tell by my feet I'm a limb of the law, The peo-ple of Dub-lin for me have no *grá*.

They hiss me and boo me when I pass them by, 'Sinn Féin!'Up the re-bels!'you'll hear them all cry,

Now you may think that's bad but there's one thing that's worse, This grand Ir-ish lan-guage.on my soul 'tis a curse.

With their yib-ber-in' and yab-ber-in' like an old ass-'s bray The Cas-tle ex-pects me to know what they say.

Chorus

'Och-ón', 'mo bhrón', you hear them all say; 'An dtui-geann tú mé?' and 'Sinn Féin hoo-ray'!

'Is dóigh liom go bhfuil is is dóigh liom nach é, Ach tá mé ag fogh-laim an Gaeil-ge.'

This song satirizes the RIC (Royal Irish Constabulary) and/or DMP (Dublin Metropolitan Police). The DMP covered the city of Dublin while the RIC operated outside the capital city. While the RIC was an armed paramilitary force, the DMP was unarmed, except for its G Division, the political detectives who were prime targets for the IRA's active service unit and intelligence section in Dublin.

The DMP did earn a bad reputation during the 1913 Lockout, when it brutally attacked workers and raided and wrought destruction on their tenement homes. The G Division was active in picking out leaders from among the captured after the 1916 Rising. During the Anglo-Irish War the DMP avoided political involvement (with the notable exception of the G Division) and some were sympathetic to the freedom struggle, passing on information.

The song notes the unhappy lot of a policeman trying to do a job amidst a hostile public.

In the third verse the Irish phrases do not mean what the text says that they do, an added comic element designed to appeal to Irish speakers. [LM]

You can tell by my feet I'm a limb of the law,
The people of Dublin for me have no grá.
They hiss me and boo me when I pass them by,
'Sinn Féin!', 'Up the rebels!', you'll hear them all cry.
Now you may think that's bad but there's one thing
    that's worse,
This grand Irish language, on my soul 'tis a curse,
With their yibberin' and yabberin' like an old ass's bray
The Castle expects me to know what they say, with

Chorus
'Ochón', 'mo bhrón', you hear them all say;
'An dtuigeann tú mé?' and 'Sinn Féin hooray!'
'Is dóigh liom go bhfuil is is dóigh liom nach é,
Ach tá mé ag foghlaim an Gaeilge.'

I've a friend in the force and he's courting a cook,
And what do you know but she bought him a book,
With Irish on this side and English on that,
So small I could carry it round in my hat.
First learn the letters and then the whole phrase,
I'll have it all off in a couple of days.
Then their yibberin' and yabberin' I'll soon understand,
Such larnification will stagger the land.

This book I procured and to learn I must try.
'*An bhfuil mé?*' means 'Are you?', '*An bhfuil tú?*'
   means 'Am I?'
'*Is dóigh liom*', I think that I do understand.
'*Mo lámh*' is my foot and '*Mo chluas*' is my hand.
'*Tá mé ag foghlaim*', I'm learning you see.
If I keep on like this an inspector I'll be.
I'm getting so big that I don't know the cat.
My head is two sizes too large for my hat.

With larnification I'm bloody near dead,
I lie on the floor 'cause I can't lie in bed.
I am walking and talking when I'm fast asleep.
When I hear 'Up the rebels!' my flesh starts to creep.
My friends have all left me, I've now just a few,
I'm walking around like a wandering Jew.

Text and air: Frank Harte, *Songs of Dublin*, Ossian, Cork, 1993.

Comic postcard depicting Dublin Metropolitan Police constables carrying poles (and a banner) away from the scene of a protest in June 1911. A banner had been erected on Grafton Street, Dublin by the Independent United National Societies Committee in protest at the forthcoming visit of George V and Queen Mary to Ireland. The protest may have been lively, but was ultimately ineffectual, as thousands of people welcomed the king and queen as they proceeded down Grafton Street led by the Eighth Royal Hussars. The text printed on the back of the postcard reads:

The poles that once in Grafton Street
   Their tale of treason told,
Now lie confined in close retreat
   In Dublin Castle's hold.

Victorious are the brave blue coats;
   The rebel's reign is o'er.
The Union Jack serenely floats;
   The Empire's safe once more.

Send Us, O, God! the Revolution

Peter Golden (1877–1926)

Peter Golden was born in Cork in 1877 and emigrated to the United States in 1901, where he became an actor. He was a cousin of Terence MacSwiney and shared his republican sympathies, touring America and organizing, propagandizing and speaking in support of the nationalist movement in Ireland.

Text: Peter Golden, *Ballads of Rebellion*, 1914.

Perish the thought, and perish those
　　Who such a feeling now would foster,
Our country will not sink so low
　　Whatever treasure it may cost her.
We did not unto England yield
　　When on her noon the sun was shining,
And oh! we shall not do so now
　　When all her glory is declining.

What to that Empire do we owe
　　That we to save it now should gather?
Go ask of all our countless dead
　　Why we should not destroy it rather.
God shield us from contributing
　　To the foul thing's continuation,
But may He send us soon instead
　　The crash of its annihilation.

'No compromise' must be our cry,
　　No sign of wavering must we show them,
Until we have paid back the debt,
　　The awful, awful debt we owe them.
The conflict must be carried on
　　Though into dust each sword were shivered,
Until our Race stands forth alone,
　　Redeemed, enfranchised and delivered.

Small difference it makes to us
　　Which British Party robs our nation,
We're fighting for a holier cause
　　We're fighting for our liberation.
There's just one way and only one
　　To free us from the whole pollution
And to regain our Nationhood,
　　And that one way is Revolution.

You may decry it all you will
　　And any way you wish taboo it,
But if you'd with the strife be done
　　There is no other way to do it.
Humanity since Time began
　　Has had its every right resented,
Till its demands were made by men
　　And on a rifle's point presented.

'Divide and conquer' was the cry,
    Since first their hordes appeared upon us,
'Divide and conquer' is the cry
    That has today almost undone us.
And now again by fraud and guile
    Our lines they're seeking to dissever,
Oh! men, they must be stricken down
    Nor let them rule our land for ever.

Brothers, the spirits of the brave
    Intent to-day are bending o'er us,
And, oh! our Motherland to save
    With what appealing they implore us.
Let not our ranks, united now,
    By Party voicings be invaded,
And if we fighting have to fall,
    Let us fall gloriously as they did.

They who so long by Aileach's halls
    In readiness have been remaining,
Have sensed the struggle from afar,
    And at their leash their steeds are straining,
Give us, O, God! in this our day
    Of all our centuried strife the fruition,
The march, the muster, the array,
    Send us, O, God! the Revolution.

A Request

Peter Golden

For all the sorrows we withstood
Against the Saxon blackguard brood,
I raise my voice, O, God on high,
And crave of you to hear my cry!

When Britain is securely bound
And 'round her fast Fate's web is wound,
Lord, God in Heaven, I ask one prayer –
Grant me the glory to be there!

Give me the great boon to be nigh
When 'round her neck the noose they tie,
And send her shrieking in the air –
Grant, grant, O God, that I be there!

Text: Peter Golden, *The Voice of Ireland*,
Press of M.A. O'Connor, New York, n.d.

What Are You Going to Do About It?
Peter Golden

This poem expresses the attitude of
militant Irish-America in support of
the separatist movement at home.

Text: Peter Golden, *The Voice of
Ireland*, Press of M.A. O'Connor,
New York, n.d.

Yes, we're 'conspiring' as you claim,
    To save our kin across the water,
From being led forth in England's van,
    And sent into the shambles' slaughter;
We're putting rifles in their hands
    To use whatever time they'll need 'em –
Since when has it become a crime,
    America, to arm for Freedom?

Time was within your own domain
    When in the balance Freedom trembled,
The exiled children of the Gael
    Around you to a man assembled.
Nor was there found in that long roll
    One who disloyal was or traitor,
Nor have I heard that they were then
    Assigned the name of 'agitator'.

Our people's safety is at stake,
    The British desperately need 'em,
Out on the battlefields of France,
    There to the cannon's mouth to feed 'em.
By every means within their power
    The men of Ireland will oppose it,
And we'll uphold them to the end,
    Nor do we give a damn who knows it.

And may success be on their side,
    And may the God of battles speed 'em,
Who'll arm when, where, and how, they can,
    To fight again for Ireland's Freedom.
So let us send the *fiat* forth,
    Let no man for a moment doubt it,
We're with our people to the end,
    What are you going to do about it?

The Living Dead
(Bodenstown 1914)
Brian O'Higgins

Text: Brian O'Higgins, *The Voice
of Banba*, Dublin, 1931.

Hail to the brave and noble dead,
Who toiled and planned and fought and bled

In years forever flown;
That Eire's heart might know no pain,
That she once more might rule and reign –
   A queen upon her throne:
Hail to the hero, free from fear,
Who lies in sleep beside us here –
   Hail to the name of Tone!

When rang his country's battle call
He turned from kin and home and all,
   To walk the toilsome way
That led to pain and loss and grief,
And brought no joy or sweet relief
   To her he loved alway:
But O, his memory shall not die,
And here, beneath the Irish sky,
   We bless his name today.

We bless his name, and pledge our word
To cut our way – with fire and sword
   If need for them there be –
To where the bright and blessed Goal
That caught the ardour of his soul
   Shines out from sea to sea,
And bids us ne'er from toil retreat
Till on its crest we set our feet
   And find our Mother free!

The ones who fall in Freedom's fight,
Though round them close the shades of night,
   And lying foes defame;
Live on through ever-brightening years,
To kindle hopes, to banish fears,
   To fan into a flame
The fire of faith in Freedom's cause,
The fire of hate for alien laws –
   The fire no foe can tame!

O men of Ireland, lift your heads!
The Power on high that surely treads
   On tyrants in their pride,
That smites them for their greed and lust,
And lifts the down-trod from the dust,
   To be of joy the bride,
Is raising up your land and you,
Is making bright and clear and true
   The dreams of Tone who died!

We're Building for Ireland Now

Felix McGlennon (1856–1943)

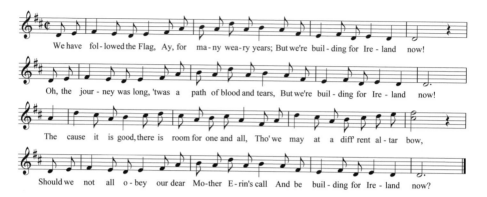

We have fol-lowed the Flag, Ay, for ma-ny wea-ry years; But we're buil-ding for Ire-land now!

Oh, the jour-ney was long, 'twas a path of blood and tears, But we're buil-ding for Ire-land now!

The cause it is good, there is room for one and all, Tho' we may at a diff'rent al-tar bow,

Should we not all o-bey our dear Mo-ther E-rin's call And be buil-ding for Ire-land now?

During the period when it appeared that Home Rule might be granted to Ireland, and with the foundation of the Volunteer movement in support of it, several writers made songs in support of that political end and in support of its promoters, the Volunteers and the Irish Parliamentary Party.

Three of these follow, from Felix McGlennon's *The Marching Songs of the Irish Volunteers*, London, c. 1914.

We have followed the Flag, Ay, for many weary years;
　　But we're building for Ireland now!
Oh, the journey was long, 'twas a path of blood and tears,
　　But we're building for Ireland now!
The cause it is good, there is room for one and all,
　　Tho' we may at a diff'rent altar bow,
Should we not all obey our dear Mother Erin's call
　　And be builders for Ireland now?

We were down in the dust but we've risen once again,
　　And we're building for Ireland now;
Let our daughters and sons in the old land still remain
　　And be builders for Ireland now.
We'll foster home trade and our commerce o'er the sea,
　　At the desk, or the workshop, or the plough;
So that all Erin's children enjoy prosperity,
　　We are building for Ireland now.

All the clouds will disperse 'neath the fire of Freedom's sun;
　　We are building for Ireland now.
All dissensions will cease, ev'ry heart will beat as one,
　　We are building for Ireland now.
We'll make our foundations of Hope and Love and Peace;
　　Then Erin, with calm, unruffled brow,
Will look to the future when factions all will cease;
　　We're all builders for Ireland now.

While Irish Blood Flows in the Veins of Irish Volunteers

Felix McGlennon

Oh Paddy dear, and did you hear the news that's going
    round?
Old Ireland's sons are drilling ev'rywhere on Irish ground;
Then stick the shamrock in your hat, be proud that there
    'tis seen,
For now at last triumphant is our own immortal Green.

I met with brave Joe Devlin and he took me by the hand,
And said he: 'All's well with Ireland, her future will be
    grand;
Home Rule is ours, and will remain, in spite of jibes and
    jeers,
While Irish blood flows in the veins of Irish Volunteers.'

There was a time when Irishmen let crafty foes divide;
But now, please God, all Irishmen in Ireland will take pride.
We crave for no Ascendancy, but laws made for us all,
By Irishmen for Irishmen, in Our Historic Hall.

We have our matchless leaders and we have our gallant
    men;
And, thank God, the tortures of the past will never come
    again,
Our glorious Nationality will outlive all their sneers,
While Irish blood flows in the veins of Irish Volunteers.

Text: Felix McGlennon, *The Marching Songs of the Irish Volunteers*, London, *c.* 1914.
    Air: 'The Wearin' of the Green', see 'The Demi-Semi Home Rull Bill', p. 246.

Joe Devlin (1871–1934), Parliamentary Party MP and supporter of Redmond's call for the Volunteers to support the British war effort.

The Irish Volunteers

Arise, you gallant young Irishmen, and ring the land with
    cheers;
Hurrah! Hurrah! at last we've formed the Irish Volunteers;
And every man who loves his land with rifle forth will go
For Erin's laws and Home Rule cause against the Orange foe.

O Carson thought his Ulster bluff would Irishmen dismay,
But now we have a brighter and better day;
For Munster men, Leinster men and Connaught men are here,
Already fit for action in the Irish Volunteers.

Text: Lady Gregory, *The Kiltartan History Book*, T. Fisher Unwin, London, 1926.

Too long we were trampled under foes, insulted and belied,
But an Irishman can soon stop that with a rifle by his side;
And if it is fighting they want, begob, from Bombay to Cape Clear,
They will find the hardest nuts to crack are the Irish Volunteers.

Success to brave John Redmond, who still pulls at the oar;
He will steer the ship to College Green and never leave it more,
And when we have our Parliament you will see the guns and spears
Defiant in the sunlight by Irish Volunteers.

So hearty lads of Erin join the National Brigade;
Take every drill and out the bill and never be afraid;
For you never know what other foe you will meet in future years,
But keep the foe subdued at home, brave Irish Volunteers.

Down with Carson and his brawling crowd, the day of power is o'er;
Although it took some hundred years, it's broken for evermore.
Bad luck go with Ascendancy, it died without a tear;
Emmet shed his blood for Ireland, boys, success to the Volunteers.

Hurray again for the National Cause, the cause that cannot die,
For coffins, ships, gibbets, starvation they did try.
But we'll tell to England straight, let her lend her mind to hear
Our National spirit she can't break while there is an Irish Volunteer.

So Irishmen and Irish boys join the ranks and join them soon,
And, please God, you will see us marching to the Rising of the Moon;
We will have Home Rule for Ireland, in spite of Carson's gang of Peers,
And our liberty we will maintain by the Irish Volunteers.

Cartoon by 'Spex' (John Fergus O'Hea) from *The Lepracaun*, showing Edward Carson and John Redmond.

Come All You Gallant Irish Boys

Felix McGlennon

Come all you gal - lant Ir - ish boys, Who love your Na - tive Land;___

The or - der has gone forth to join Our Isle's De - fen - sive Band,___

Our Ir - ish girls are watch - ing you, you'll hear their rou - sing cheers,___

But on - ly if___ you're in the ranks of the Ir - ish Vo - lun - teers.___

Our Ir - ish girls are watch - ing you, You'll hear their rou - sing cheers,___

But on - ly if___ you'll join the ranks of the Ir - ish Vo - lun - teers.___

Come all you gallant Irish boys,
　　Who love your Native Land;
The order has gone forth to join
　　Our Isle's Defensive Band.
Our Irish girls are watching you,
　　You'll hear their rousing cheers,
But only if you're in the ranks
　　Of the Irish Volunteers.

Our Irish girls are beautiful –
　　As all the world will own;
An Irish smile and Irish eyes
　　Would charm a heart of stone.
But all their smiles, and all their love
　　Will quickly turn to sneers,
If you won't work for Ireland now,
　　In the Irish Volunteers.

When, in the past, brave Irishmen
　　For Ireland took the field,
Our Irish maidens spurred them on
　　And bade them never yield.
And now, throughout our Own Dear Isle,
　　Our Irishwomen's cheers

Another of Felix McGlennon's songs
in praise of the Volunteers. Promising
that enlistment will win the hearts of
women is a not-uncommon basis for
appealing for recruits to the ranks.

Text: *The Marching Songs of the Irish
Volunteers*, London, *c.* 1914.
　　Air : 'Irish Molly O'.

59

Will light the eyes, and thrill the hearts
    Of our Irish Volunteers.

Then all you gallant Irish boys,
    Make haste, and don't delay,
Or, you may find our Irish girls
    Will bravely show the way.
They helped old Ireland in the past,
    For them no craven fears;
Don't hesitate, or they'll fill the ranks
    Of the Irish Volunteers.

The Irish Volunteers

Eleanor Rogers Cox (1865–1931?)

Text: *Volunteer Verses, Some Stirring Lines collected by R.J.K.*, James Duffy, Dublin, 1914.

And is it true that Spring is here,
    The Spring of all our dreaming –
And is it true that once again
Above the heads of armed men
    The old green flag is gleaming?

And is it true that from her eyes
    The long years' slumber shaking,
Her soul awake, from sea to sea,
Again among the peoples free
    Our land her place is taking?

The radiant spirit soars again,
    Again through hill and valley;
The bugle-notes of Freedom tall
And swift-responding to that call,
    Her sons united rally.

The hopes, the dreams that would not die,
    Oh! bright to-day they're burning,
As from her limbs for evermore
The chain that England forged of yore,
    Our Motherland is spurning.

And if the flag be Orange or Green,
    What matter if beneath it,
Beat hearts to God and Freedom true,
Oh! brothers, with a meaning new,
    Divine and fair we'll wreath it.

Not Orange, not Green, but IRELAND
    A free and chainless nation –
From Enniskillen of the North,
Lo! Freedom sends the world-word forth
    That heralds hate's cessation.

And blest are guns in freeman's hands,
    And blest of God for ever
Shall shine the year, shall rise the day
When the last link of slavery
    Our blended might shall sever.

The hour is here, the day begins,
    The fires of God are lighted,
Up, Ulster to your ancient place,
And flash it in the whole world's face,
    The Orange and Green's united!

Recruiting Song of the Irish Volunteers

Maeve Cavanagh (b. 1878*)*

Neath Ireland's flag they took their stand,
For her alone they wrought and planned,
When fools and knaves in panic fled,
To saneness back her forces led.
When War's red signs bewildered all,
No ears had they for England's call.

For what to them her whine of fear,
Whose path of duty shone so clear,
Where Emmet, Russell, Tone had led,
That sacred path they chose instead.
Not theirs the hireling's coat of shame,
They answered none – save Ireland's claim.

Long Ireland shall remember those,
Who in her day of trial rose,
Who kept the one great issue clear,
Who braved the worst, and had no fear,
Their Nation's soul they typify –
The men whom England could not buy!

See Introduction, p. xv for a note
on the writer Maeve Cavanagh.

Text: Maeve Cavanagh, *A Voice
of Insurgency*, Dublin, 1916.
    First published in *The Hibernian*,
17 July 1915.

Then join them as they marching go
The seeds of Ireland's faith to sow,
Nor longer carelessly delay,
Since Ireland calls you night and day.
Must braver men prise wide the gate,
Of Freedom whilst you shirk and wait?

The flames of War still higher soar,
Their tongues are scorching England's shore.
Her seas are strewn with dead and wreck,
The Teuton's heel is on her neck –
Then nerve the arm and train the eye,
For Ireland's sun flames in the sky.

Awaiting the Signal

Maeve Cavanagh

Text: Maeve Cavanagh, *A Voice of Insurgency*, Dublin, 1916.

Morrow by morrow brighter grows
    And hope that baffled Time and Death,
And hourly now the harvest grows
    Whiter, winnowed by Freedom's breath.
Close by my faithful reapers stand
Eager for signal and command.

In the red gateways of the West,
    In War's bright vestiture arrayed,
My hated foe again I breast,
    I, whom the Nations deemed decayed.
But fiercer flame is mine to-day,
Than ever lit my pilgrim way.

I know my time is near – I know
    That round me shrieks the battle gale,
That once again brave blood must flow,
    This too I know – I shall not fail.
Tho' God willed other – even so,
My soul, at bay, should thunder NO!

The Pass of Freedom

Maeve Cavanagh

The time is near – be watchful then my comrades and my
   brothers,
     We enter now the narrow gorge where courage shall be
      tried,
The Pass that leads to Freedom – henceforth Danger steps
   beside us,
     Then let the flippant and the weak be warned and
      stand aside.

The time is near – the place is by – search well your hearts
   my comrades,
     Come not adventure-seeking here – nor merely Fame
      to woo.
One noble motive guide you – the love of Ireland only,
     Thus worthily you'll take your place in Freedom's retinue.

The tyrant's arm is palsied – his own forsake and fail him,
     O'er sea and bloody battlefield his death-cry echoes wide;
His sun in shame is setting – while dawn our skies is
   flushing,
     Strike not too soon, nor bide too long, but wait the
      flowing tide.

The time is near – then falter not, tho' in the Pass Death
   waiteth,
     Far out beyond its shadow rise the heights that we
      must scale,
The goal of all our striving, thrice purchased – Freedom's
   haven,
     What matters then if in the gorge some few lie still and
      pale.

Text: Maeve Cavanagh, *A Voice of Insurgency*, Dublin, 1916. First published in *The Workers' Republic*, 11 September 1915.

Opportunity

Maeve Cavanagh

She stands outside our prison gates –
   Who nevermore may come our way;
She points the road where Freedom waits,
   And bids us haste ere wanes the day –
The wretched gates with rust are brown,
Yet none essay to break them down.

Text: Maeve Cavanagh, *A Voice of Insurgency*, Dublin, 1916. First published in *The Workers' Republic*, January 1916.

Wide arms she opes to daring souls,
    Adventure beckons from her eyes
How shall she tempt such prudent moles
    To trust the promise in their skies?
Tho' absent they had sung her charms,
Her coming fills them with alarms.

She says – 'On sea and plain your foe
    Has gone to meet a tyrant's fate,
Do you not then your new strength know
    That dazed, irresolute you wait –
Of what avail are gun and sword
If there be none dare give the word?

'On foreign fields your brothers fight
    Your tyrant's shamed cause to save,
Will you not risk as much for Right:
    Can only traitors then be brave?
E'en now the sun to West doth face,
And Ireland runs not in the race.'

Straining at the Leash

Maeve Cavanagh

Text: Maeve Cavanagh, *A Voice of Insurgency*, Dublin, 1916. First published in *The Workers' Republic*, 22 January 1916.

Unloose the leash; restraining hand,
    View! view! our harried enemy!
We wait in vain for your command.
    In fierce pursuit we fain would be.
We pray you loose us – bid us go,
Dost hear the thrilling 'Tally-Ho'?

The Day is fair – why vacillate?
    Soon fickle chance shall spread her wing,
And once again 'twill be 'Too Late',
    Back in Fate's lap her gift we'll fling.
Shame deep as ours shall never be,
Who trifled thus with Liberty.

The robber prey is sorely pressed,
    The Hounds of Justice on him gain,
Our place is there amongst the rest,
    Or merit we all men's disdain –
He wronged us most, – shall we delay
Whilst they our debt of Vengeance pay?

Nay, loose us or the leash we break,
   And join the Great Pursuit unbid,
No part in that last shame we'll take
   When Fear behind mean Caution hid –
Soon courage, too, would seem a vice,
And Freedom dear at any price.

We strain and pant, hark, hark away,
   Scant cover can the quarry find,
Yet chained and muzzled here we stay,
   Tho' clear for us the call doth wind,
And we who loudest bayed of all,
May not be there to see his fall.

Outward Bound (?)

Maeve Cavanagh

Moored in the river still we lie
Tho' fair the wind and still the sky
We wait the syren's last, shrill sound
The good ship 'Ireland' outward bound
O'er that wild sway, Insurgency,
To seek the port of Liberty.

The tide is full – why wait we here
Is there no fearless one to steer?
The restive crew their orders wait
To put to sea and challenge Fate.
Of little use their seaman's lore
If they must only hug the shore.

Ah! sweep the frightened ones aside,
Or we shall miss this glorious tide,
Put them ashore to plot and play
For the men who will act – Gangway!
Or else the gallant ship will stay
To rot in port till black Doomsday.

Text: Maeve Cavanagh, *A Voice of Insurgency*, Dublin, 1916. First published in *The Workers' Republic*, 29 January 1916.

Spring, 1916

Maeve Cavanagh

Quiet the prelude to the storm,
   Deep, ominous around me reigns,
In skies behind me cruciform,
   My Past's dread shadow slowly wanes.
The sword once more is in my hand,
An army moves at my command.

Text: Maeve Cavanagh, *A Voice of Insurgency*, Dublin, 1916. First published in *The Workers' Republic*, 19 February 1916.

And War's shrill bugle soon shall drown
    The miserere of the past,
When forth from valley, field and town,
    My soldiers gather at its blast,
The living heroes of my dream
Steeled for the sacrifice supreme.

Amongst my hills each mountain stream
    Still speaks with Winter's noisy voice,
Yet I can see the crocus gleam,
    Can hear Spring birds in woods rejoice;
Oh, would I knew what flower shall reign,
When I my throne and crown regain.

England's Difficulty – Ireland's Opportunity

Maeve Cavanagh

Text: Maeve Cavanagh, *Sheaves of Revolt*, Dublin, 1914.

I've hived the thought within my soul,
    Thro' centuries of blood and tears,
And worn it as Hope's Aureole,
    Above my crown of thorns for years.
Fierce war her lurid torch has lit,
    She stalks upon her fiery way,
And phantom-like, her shadows flit
    O'er England's craven heart to-day.

Do I to England service owe?
    Ask of my loved and murdered dead,
Methinks I hear their thundered 'No'!
    From out each martyr's crimsoned bed.
Let not the slave's advice prevail,
    Nor craven council bar my way,
They who for love of gold shall fail,
    And for its sake my cause betray.

The foe whose flag above me waves,
    Whose ruthless hand has maimed me oft,
A whining supplicant now craves
    My aid to keep that flag aloft.
I scorn the craven overture,
    And write this message on my brow –
No longer must my chains endure,
    Who'd serve me *true* must serve me *now*.

England's Downfall

Composed by Patrick 'Rocky Mountain' O'Brien
(1851–1919) and dedicated to the Traitors, Recruiting
Agents, Lickspittles and Bedwetters of Bantry Bay.
(San Francisco, California, USA)

O'Donovan is a boob, says the Shan Van Vocht,
And pro-British nincompoop, says the Shan Van Vocht,
And he lately got a tail, says the Shan Van Vocht
But he got it through the mail, says the Shan Van Vocht.
Nano Ryan and Tim Taboo, says the Shan Van Vocht,
Says Cullinane will never do, says the Shan Van Vocht.
He's not fit for the campaign, says the Shan Van Vocht,
Now he wags his tail in vain, says the Shan Van Vocht.

Desmond with his stick, says the Shan Van Vocht,
Says the Germans he could lick, says the Shan Van Vocht,
Little Hurley with his feet, says the Shan Van Vocht,
Says O'Leary he could beat, says the Shan Van Vocht.
When he comes back to Macroom, says the Shan Van
    Vocht,
In the Poorhouse is his doom, says the Shan Van Vocht.
Patrick Sheehan of the Glen, says the Shan Van Vocht,
Told the truth to Irishmen, says the Shan Van Vocht.

What about the Light Brigade, says the Shan Van Vocht,
When the English were afraid, says the Shan Van Vocht,
The men who fought and bled, says the Shan Van Vocht,
Had a workhouse for their bed, says the Shan Van Vocht.
Jail or workhouse was their doom, says the Shan Van
    Vocht,
Ere the guns had ceased to boom, says the Shan Van Vocht;
Sure, the Kaiser is our friend, says the Shan Van Vocht,
And our slavery he'll end, says the Shan Van Vocht.

Though Moll Dundon with his mouth, says the Shan Van
    Vocht,
Said the Germans he'd wipe out, says the Shan Van Vocht,
But that lying 'loop the loop', says the Shan Van Vocht,
Could not take a chicken coop, says the Shan Van Vocht.
No, nor Murphy's big tomcat, says the Shan Van Vocht,
The pro-British Redmond brat, says the Shan Van Vocht;
He's a bedwetter, they say, says the Shan Van Vocht,
And a shame to Bantry Bay, says the Shan Van Vocht.

Paddy Barry, the galoot, says the Shan Van Vocht,
That little he Bawd brute, says the Shan Van Vocht,

This *tour-de-force* of invective would
merit a place in any compilation of
comic verse. The author's chief target
could be Tim Healy, a native of
Bantry, who was regarded by many
as the architect of Charles Stewart
Parnell's political demise. See also
Jim Connell's poem on Healy, p. 48.

'Patrick Sheehan of the Glen' (verse
2) is a reference to Charles Kickham's
famous song 'The Glen of Aherlow'
in which a crippled army veteran
describes how he acquired his disabili-
ties fighting for the British army, and
how, now that he is no longer of any
use to them, he has to beg for a living.
The song became enormously popular
and was believed to have cost the
army thousands of recruits.

The author of the present piece
was born in Co. Cork in 1847. At the
age of seventeen he saw the local
bailiffs confiscating a cow from a
poor family, it being their only means
of livelihood. With others, he inter-
vened to recover it and restore it to
its owners, after which he became a
wanted man. He left Ireland soon
afterwards and settled in New York.

His entire subsequent life was
devoted to support for Irish separation
from Britain, and not just by words:
he led one of the companies that took
part in the Fenian invasion of Canada
in 1870.

His 1904 collection *Birth and
Adoption* (which does not include the
present piece) is one long tirade, in
verse and prose, against Britain.

Text: Ballad sheet in the Samuels
Collection, TCD.

If you saw this lump of muck, says the Shan Van Vocht,
For a year you'd curse your luck, says the Shan Van
    Vocht.
His nose is like a carrot, says the Shan Van Vocht,
And he prattles like a parrot, says the Shan Van Vocht,
A recruit he could not find, says the Shan Van Vocht,
For his brains are all behind, says the Shan Van Vocht.

And O'Driscoll, how he'd run, says the Shan Van Vocht,
If he saw a German gun, says the Shan Van Vocht;
Faith, he could not shoot a whale, says the Shan Van
    Vocht,
For his aim is in his tail, says the Shan Van Vocht.
There's another Canon Ryan, says the Shan Van Vocht,
Always loaded up with wine, says the Shan Van Vocht.
He's a lying, lazy lout, says the Shan Van Vocht,
And is shooting with his mouth, says the Shan Van Vocht.

The Canon up at Beare, says the Shan Van Vocht,
At mouth-fighting does his share, says the Shan Van Vocht,
When he should be with us all, says the Shan Van Vocht,
And make English tyrants fall, says the Shan Van Vocht,
But he is a Castle hack, says the Shan Van Vocht,
With John Redmond and his pack, says the Shan Van
    Vocht.
But the day is near at hand, says the Shan Van Vocht,
When we'll free our native land, says the Shan Van Vocht.

What did the Frenchmen do, says the Shan Van Vocht,
But rob Priests and Sisters, too, says the Shan Van Vocht,
They robbed the convents all, says the Shan Van Vocht,
Pulled the Virgin from the wall, says the Shan Van Vocht,
And they threw it in the street, says the Shan Van Vocht,
Where they kicked it with their feet, says the Shan Van
    Vocht,
And they robb'd the orphans' home, says the Shan Van
    Vocht,
Sent them friendless for to roam, says the Shan Van Vocht.

When they went to Germany, says the Shan Van Vocht,
That land of liberty, says the Shan Van Vocht,
What did Kaiser William say, says the Shan Van Vocht,
Every one of you can stay, says the Shan Van Vocht.
Tho' I'm of the Luther breed, says the Shan Van Vocht,
I care not what your creed, says the Shan Van Vocht,
And you'll not be in my way, says the Shan Van Vocht,
I'll protect you night and day, says the Shan Van Vocht.

Now let England fight her own, says the Shan Van
    Vocht,
And let Ireland fight at home, says the Shan Van Vocht.
Tell John Bull he'll look in vain, says the Shan Van
    Vocht,
Now he's got a German pain, says the Shan Van Vocht.
Let us learn the soldier's trade, says the Shan Van Vocht,
With Casement's new brigade, says the Shan Van Vocht,
With Sir Roger in the van, says the Shan Van Vocht,
That undaunted Irishman, says the Shan Van Vocht.

Now what will the traitors do, says the Shan Van Vocht,
They are looking black and blue, says the Shan Van
    Vocht.
We'll send them to Japan, says the Shan Van Vocht,
With John Redmond in the van, says the Shan Van
    Vocht.
For the Kaiser we adore, says the Shan Van Vocht,
For he'll free our Irish shore, says the Shan Van Vocht,
Then we'll have Old Ireland free, says the Shan Van
    Vocht,
From Kinsale to Tandragee, says the Shan Van Vocht.

Limerick's Bishop leads the van, says the Shan Van
    Vocht,
He's done more than any man, says the Shan Van Vocht,
For no traitor priest is he, says the Shan Van Vocht,
And his words came o'er the sea, says the Shan Van
    Vocht.
He dealt England a hard blow, says the Shan Van Vocht,
Which will send her down below, says the Shan Van
    Vocht,
And Redmond, that vile knave, says the Shan Van Vocht,
May he fill a traitor's grave, says the Shan Van Vocht.

The Canon of our town, says the Shan Van Vocht,
Is a priest of high renown, says the Shan Van Vocht,
For he's of the brave and true, says the Shan Van Vocht,
Loves his God and country, too, says the Shan Van
    Vocht.
Like His Grace, brave John McHale, says the Shan Van
    Vocht,
He is a credit to the Gael, says the Shan Van Vocht,
God bless him night and day, says the Shan Van Vocht,
He's the pride of Bantry Bay, says the Shan Van Vocht.

New Words to an Old Tune

Jim Connell

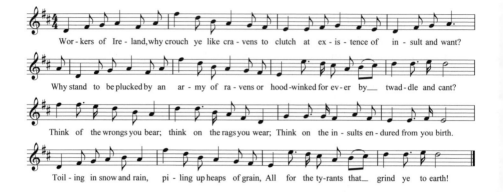

Modelled on the nationalist ballad 'O'Donnell Abú' by Michael McCann, Connell's poem is set to the same air here. It has been published in different versions, with the version in Connell's own collection *Red Flag Rhymes* commencing 'Workers of England . . .'.

Text: Leslie H. Daiken, *Goodbye Twilight*, Lawrence & Wishart, London, 1936.

Workers of Ireland, why crouch ye like cravens
    To clutch at existence of insult and want?
Why stand to be plucked by an army of ravens
    Or hoodwinked for ever by twaddle and cant?
    Think of the wrongs you bear;
    Think on the rags you wear;
        Think on the insults endured from your birth;
    Toiling in snow and rain,
    Piling up heaps of gain,
        All for the tyrants that grind ye to earth.

Your brains are as keen as the brains of your masters,
    In swiftness and strength you surpass them, by far.
Your brave hearts have taught you to laugh at disasters,
    You vastly outnumber your tyrants in war.
    Why, then, like cowards stand,
    Using not brain nor hand,
        Thankful like dogs when they throw you a bone?
    What right have they to take
    Things that we toil to make?
        Know ye not, comrades, that all is our own?

Despise all the talk of these fat agitators
    Who rave about *Ireland* or *Freedom* or worse,
Expect not your rights from political praters,
    But manfully trust in your courage and force.
    Waste not your ready blows,
    Seek not for foreign foes,
        Your bitterest enemy treads your own soil.

The sweaters that grind you,
The ranters that blind you,
   The gluttons that revel while you are at toil.

Arise in our might, brothers, bear it no longer,
   Assemble our masses throughout all the land,
We'll show these bloodsuckers who are the stronger
   When workers and robbers confronted shall stand.
   Through castle, court and hall,
   Over their acres all,
      Onwards we'll sweep like the waves of the sea,
   Claiming the wealth we've made,
   Ending the tyrants trade,
      Till Labour has triumphed and Ireland is Free!

The Cause Moves On
Jim Connell

Let us make a celebration
And proclaim to all creation
That our hearts are in elation
   O'er the dark days gone.
Deep-sown seed at last is springing,
Well-won triumph to us bringing,
And we here are gaily singing
   As the Cause moves on.

Hard our task when first beginning,
Hailed were we as sinners sinning,
But the thought that we were winning
   Made us deem all won.
Faced we calumny and slander,
Scorned we all to trim or pander,
Grew our efforts greater, grander,
   And the Cause moved on.

Now the baffled foe is quaking,
And his castle walls are shaking,
For the wide world is awaking,
   Since our sun has shone.
We can hear our friends advancing,
We can see their banners dancing,
And we find the scene entrancing,
   As the Cause moves on.

Text: Jim Connell, *Red Flag Rhymes*, The Agitators' Press, Huddersfield, *c.* 1900.

71

The Class War

Jim Connell

Text: Jim Connell, *Red Flag Rhymes*,
The Agitators' Press, Huddersfield,
c. 1900.

A ploughman, a landlord, a farmer,
    Were kneeling together in church;
The landlord was nearest the pulpit,
    The peasant was nearest the porch;
Each longed for a better condition,
    For temporal benefits prayed,
And fervently begged the Almighty
    To grant the request that he made.
        But then it unluckily happened
            In wishing, no two could agree,
        Cross purposes spoiled the petition,
            And yet they were honest, all three.

First Hodge, in a forcible fashion,
    Depicted his terrible lot,
And prayed for a raising of wages
    To fatten the family pot.
The farmer laid bare all his sorrows,
    Showed clearly his profits were small,
And hoped that his workmen should labour
    For just upon nothing at all.
        Omnipotence, puzzled extremely,
            Though kindly disposed to the two,
        Could not see his way to help either,
            Or think what the devil to do.

But further to add to his trouble,
    The farmer on business intent,
Sent skyward his prayers at the double
    And begged a reduction of rent.
The landlord, with acres embarrassed,
    From banker and Jew begged release,
And feeling financially harassed,
    Implored that his rents should increase.
        Jehovah at length comprehended
            The cause of their pitiful plight,
        And saw that a second Redeemer
            Was needed to guide them aright.

The parson, with eyes on promotion,
    Was fearful of possible frowns;
He talked about mansions hereafter,
    And angels and trumpets and crowns.
And when to the earth he descended,

He steered clear of points that were sore,
With eight or ten elderly daughters
    How could the poor fellow do more?
        The sorely perplexed congregation
            Filed outward discussing his worth,
            Where stuck on a stump by the roadside
                A Socialist preacher held forth.

He showed how this warring of classes
    Kept selfishness all to the front,
And how the result to the masses
    Was penury, misery, want.
He showed how collective possession
    Of capital, credit and land,
Would alter the foemen to brothers,
    And cause them to work hand in hand.
        He pleaded for knowledge and leisure,
            For living and raiment secure,
        To change to comparative pleasure
            The horrible lives of the poor.

The ploughman was held and delighted,
    The farmer was glad he had prayed,
The landlord began to grow hateful
    Of hollow and senseless parade.
The kindly old parson was softened,
    And cried, as he smother'd his greed,
'There pulses the heart of my Master,
    Though under a jacket of tweed.'
        The spring-time of hope is upon us,
            Its buds on the hedges are seen,
        Hurra! for the Red Revolution,
            'Twill come when the bushes are green.

Jim Connell.

73

A Song of Swords

G.K. Chesterton (1874–1936)

'A drove of cattle came into a village called Swords;
and was stopped by the rioters.' – Daily paper.

Chesterton may have been attracted
to this theme by the name of the place
where the incident he writes of took
place, a pitched battle between
striking farm labourers and blackleg
labour, with police protection, herding
cattle through the north Dublin
village in October 1913.

Text: G.K. Chesterton, *Utopia of
Usurers and other Essays*, Boni
& Liveright, New York, 1917.

In the place called Swords on the Irish road
    It is told for a new renown
How we held the horns of the cattle, and how
We will hold the horns of the devils now
Ere the lord of hell with the horn on his brow
    Is crowned in Dublin town.

Light in the East and light in the West,
    And light on the cruel lords,
On the souls that suddenly all men knew,
And the green flag flew and the red flag flew,
And many a wheel of the world stopped, too,
    When the cattle were stopped at Swords.

Be they sinners or less than saints
    That smite in the street for rage,
We know where the shame shines bright; we know
You that they smite at, you their foe,
Lords of the lawless wage and low,
    This is your lawful wage.

You pinched a child to a torture price
    That you dared not name in words;
So black a jest was the silver bit
That your own speech shook for the shame of it,
And the coward was plain as a cow they hit
    When the cattle have strayed at Swords.

The wheel of the torrent of wives went round
    To break men's brotherhood;
You gave the good Irish blood to grease
The clubs of your country's enemies;
You saw the brave man beat to the knees:
    And you saw that it was good.

The rope of the rich is long and long –
    The longest of hangmen's cords;
But the kings and crowds are holding their breath,
In a giant shadow o'er all beneath
Where God stands holding the scales of Death
    Between the cattle and Swords.

Haply the lords that hire and lend
   The lowest of all men's lords,
Who sell their kind like kine at a fair,
Will find no head of their cattle there;
But faces of men where cattle were:
   Faces of men – and Swords.

The Land to the Landlord
Eva Gore-Booth (1870–1926)

You hug to your soul a handful of dust
And you think the round world your sacred trust
But the sun shines and the wind blows
And nobody cares and nobody knows.
O the bracken waves and the foxgloves flame
And none of them has heard your name,
Near and dear is the curlew's cry
You are merely a stranger walking by.

Sheer up through the shadows the mountain towers
And dreams wander free in this world of ours –
Though you may turn the grass to gold
The twilight has left you out in the cold.
Though you are king of the rose and the wheat
Not for you, not for you is the bog-myrtle sweet,
Though you are lord of the long grass
The hemlock bows not her head as you pass.

The poppies would flutter amongst the corn
Even if you had never been born
With your will or without your will
The ragweed can wander over the hill.
Down there in the bog where the plovers call
You are but an outcast after all,
Over your head the sky gleams blue
Not a cloud or a star belongs to you.

Text: Eva Gore Booth, *The Perilous Light*, Erskine Macdonald, London, 1915.

A Village of the Heart of Stone
Réilthín Siúbhalach

A jewel in the harvest lands,
   That village hangs on a rocky stair,
Full in the sun; the reaping bands
   From field to field are spreading there.

Text: Réilthín Siúbhalach, *Rebel Songs*, Provinces Publishing Co., *c.* 1920. The copy of this collection in the National Library of Ireland has 'by Daniel Corkery' inscribed on the front cover.

Barn to barn the farmers build,
　　A shed for this, a shed for that,
Each thing is bought as soon as willed
　　For the hillside loam is deep and fat.

No dwelling lacks its orchard croft.
　　The gates are firm, the hedges clipped.
The cattle sink in pastures soft,
　　Week in, week out, the butter's shipped.

The men speak slow, their flesh is full.
　　Their eyelids thick with too much sun,
A pipe between their teeth they pull
　　Until the bargaining is done.

Who'd mind it if their sons were brave,
　　If courage lit the youthful eyes,
But never a boy that village gave
　　To any glorious enterprise.

Freedom's fight may wax or wane,
　　Their sons still saunter on the road,
Or help at night to count the gain
　　When they have sold another load.

If you whose soul has kept its fire
　　Strike on that place at height of day,
Your heart is drained of its desire,
　　Your limbs are cold as churchyard clay.

September 1913

Thomas MacDonagh (1878–1916)

Text: Thomas MacDonagh, *Lyrical Poems*, *The Irish Review*, Dublin, 1913.

I, Adam, saw this life begin
And lived in Eden without sin,
Until the fruit of knowledge I ate
And lost my gracious primal state.

I, Nero, fiddled while Rome burned:
I saw my empire overturned,
And proudly to my murderers cried –
An artist dies in me! – and died.

And though sometimes in swoon of sense
I now regain my innocence,

I pay still for my knowledge, and still
Remain the fool of good and ill.

And though my tyrant days are o'er
I earn my tyrant's fate the more
If now secure within my walls
I fiddle while my country falls.

September 1913
W.B. Yeats (1865–1939)

What need you, being come to sense,
But fumble in a greasy till
And add the halfpence to the pence
And prayer to shivering prayer, until
You have dried the marrow from the bone;
For men were born to pray and save:
Romantic Ireland's dead and gone,
It's with O'Leary in the grave.

Yet they were of a different kind,
The names that stilled your childish play,
They have gone about the world like wind,
But little time had they to pray
For whom the hangman's rope was spun,
And what, God help us, could they save?
Romantic Ireland's dead and gone,
It's with O'Leary in the grave.

Was it for this the wild geese spread
The grey wing upon every tide;
For this that all that blood was shed,
For this Edward Fitzgerald died,
And Robert Emmet and Wolfe Tone,
All that delirium of the brave?
Romantic Ireland's dead and gone,
It's with O'Leary in the grave.

Yet could we turn the years again,
And call those exiles as they were
In all their loneliness and pain
You'd cry, 'Some woman's yellow hair
Has maddened every mother's son':
They weighed so lightly what they gave.
But let them be, they're dead and gone,
They're with O'Leary in the grave.

Reacting both to the Lockout and to
the rejection by the Dublin bourgeoisie
of Hugh Lane's offer to donate his art
collection to their city, Yeats's criticism
of the philistinism of the Dublin business class contains an eternal message.

John O'Leary was born in Tipperary
town in 1830, and took part in the
abortive Young Ireland rebellion in the
year of revolutions, 1848. In 1865 he
was convicted of treason felony and
given a twenty-year sentence, five of
which he served before being exiled.

He lived in Paris during his exile,
while also visiting the United States,
and remained active in the IRB. He
returned to Ireland in 1885 and mixed
in political and cultural circles with
figures such as W.B. Yeats and Maude
Gonne. He led the Irish support for the
Boer republics during the Boer Wars.

Text: W.B. Yeats, *The Poems*,
Everyman, London, 1992.

The Fenian leader John O'Leary
(1830–1907).

Dublin City

Donagh MacDonagh (1912–1968)

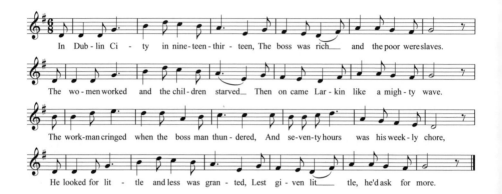

In Dub-lin Ci - ty in nine-teen-thir - teen, The boss was rich___ and the poor were slaves.

The wo - men worked and the chil - dren starved__ Then on came Lar - kin like a migh - ty wave.

The work-man cringed when the boss man thun - dered, And se-ven-ty hours was his week - ly chore,

He looked for lit - tle and less was gran - ted, Lest gi - ven lit___ tle, he'd ask for more.

The background and events of the great Lockout and the workers' struggle in Dublin in 1913 are outlined in this song (see also notes to 'The Citizen Army', p. 397). The reference to 'When Larkin left us …' is to the fact that James (Big Jim) Larkin went to the USA in 1914. While there he was active in union affairs and left-wing politics, was imprisoned for 'criminal anarchy' in 1920, and was deported in 1923. To this day the name of Jim Larkin is held in high esteem in working-class Dublin.

The song continues with some detail of the 1916 Easter Rising and of the executions in its aftermath, and ends with a tribute to James Connolly. [LM]

Text: John McDonnell, *Songs of Struggle and Protest*, Irish Labour History Society, 2008.
Air: 'Preab san Ól'.

In Dublin city in nineteen-thirteen,
  The boss was rich and the poor were slaves.
The woman worked and the children starved
  Then on came Larkin like a mighty wave.
The workman cringed when the bossman thundered
  And seventy hours was his weekly chore.
He asked for little, and less was granted,
  Lest, given little, he'd ask for more.

Then on came Larkin, in nineteen-thirteen,
  A mighty man with a mighty tongue.
The voice of Labour, the voice of Justice
  And he was gifted and he was young.
God sent us Larkin in nineteen-thirteen,
  A Labour man with a Union tongue,
He raised the worker, and gave him courage,
  He was their hero, the worker's son.

In the month of August the bossman told us
  No union man for him would work.
We stood by Larkin, we told the bossman
  We'd fight or die, but we would not shirk.
Eight months we fought and eight months we starved,
  We stood by Larkin through thick and thin,
But foodless homes and crying children,
  They broke our hearts and we could not win.

When Larkin left us we seemed defeated.
  The sky seemed black for our workless men.

But on came Connolly with new hope and counsel.
    His motto was that 'We'll rise again.'
In nineteen-sixteen in Dublin city,
    The English soldiers, they burned our town.
They shelled the buildings and shot our leaders,
    The harp was buried beneath the crown.

They shot MacDermott and Pearse and Plunkett.
    They shot MacDonagh and Clarke the brave.
From bleak Kilmainham they took their bodies
    To Arbour Hill to a quicklime grave.
But last of all of the seven leaders,
    I'll sing the praise of James Connolly,
The voice of Labour, the voice of freedom,
    Who gave his life that men might be free.

Jim Larkin addresses a meeting in Dublin after his return from the United States of America in 1924.

Lines to the Brotherhood of Cain

Maeve Cavanagh

Written during the Dublin Lockout, 1913.

Text: Maeve Cavanagh, *Sheaves of Revolt*, Dublin, 1914.

Drive them back to their wretched dens
    With brutal baton and sword,
And raise to a patient God your thanks
    That evil and power have scored.

Suffer them not to know of aught
    But squalor and toilsome days;
Live on their little one's sweated toil
    Whilst your own child thrives and plays.

Fetter their minds with ignorance –
    With puerile fears and with lies;
Preach glibly 'The poor must always be,'
    Lest they dare to think and rise.

Divide their ranks with bigotry
    Whilst you rob the wealth they made;
Then go to your vaulted church and pray
    Still shameless and unafraid.

Whilst you list to the organ's notes
    A fierce gale shrieks and raves;
Where far from your tranquil church
    Your ships are fighting the waves.

O'er freighted and ill-equipped,
    Death traps for their doomed crew,
With cargo high o'er the load line piled –
    But what is their plight to you?

If they ride the seas 'tis well –
    Should they sink – 'tis better still;
The widows' and orphans' curse
    Is powerless to work you ill.

When the writhing and mangled forms
    Are snatched from your burning mine,
Do you think of the desolate homes
    Whilst you languidly dine and wine?

Yet spite of your fiendish wiles –
    And canting, blasphemous prayer –
Right shall prevail, on your gilded walls
    The writing is surely there.

More Lines to the Brotherhood of Cain

Maeve Cavanagh

Do you dream that we are vanquished,
    That our great and holy cause
Can be killed by want or bludgeons
    Or a thousand rich men's laws?
Do you think you still can plunder,
    Cheat and sweat us to the end,
Because the Churches sanction, and
    The State its bayonets lend?

In the reeking lanes and alleys,
    Where diseases lurking lie,
You have herded us like cattle,
    There you thrust us back to die;
When our weary hearts and sinews
    To your spur respond no more,
Where Want and gaunt-eyed Hunger wait
    Loud clamouring at our door.

You have thrown the dust of hoary
    Superstitions in our eyes,
And have told us Christian teaching,
    Greed and plunder justifies.
But your Citadel is crumbling –
    Lo! it rocks with every gust,
And the hands that builded cities
    Shall yet raze it to the dust.

Written during the Dublin Lockout, 1913.

Text: Maeve Cavanagh, *Sheaves of Revolt*, Dublin, 1914.

Maeve Cavanagh.

Join the Union, Boys!

This poem appears to be an appeal
for trade union organization in the
armed forces.
   The Hetherton mentioned in verse
3 was one of the leaders of an attempt
to organize the members of the DMP.

   Text: Samuels Collection, TCD.

We appeal to all our comrades,
   From Cork to Donegal,
To join the Union, join at once –
   We're brothers one and all.

Disorganized and scattered
   For many years we've been;
Our wedding day has come at last,
   Let nothing stand between.

Heed not old 'crocks', nor spineless men,
   There's danger in delay,
Send off your names to Hetherton,
   Don't wait another day.

There are forty men in our dug-out,
   Thirty-five have joined,
So you can see the strength we have,
   There are only five behind.

These five poor moths will rue the day
   They failed at duty's call;
This very hour some of them see
   The writing on the wall.

Our comrades o'er the water, boys,
   They loudly call on you –
They are watching and waiting
   To see what we may do.

They want our strength and friendship,
   With them we stand or fall,
They are fighting for a living wage
   And standard pay for all.

Remember, men, the Union
   Has already fought for you,
Repay your debt, join up at once –
   'Tis all you're asked to do.

Heed not the weak-kneed creatures
   Who shiver in their clothes
At every scare that goes the rounds
   And every wind that blows.

An Irish branch, established
   Just two short months ago,
Boasts of five thousand members
   From Bantry to Dungloe.

To those who have not yet joined up
   In God's name we appeal
To go over the top with their comrades
   And join them in the field.

But, of course, you all have learned
   The news that's going round –
They want to separate us
   From the boys in London town.

We fought with them, and bled with them,
   In a land that's far away.
But we cannot be permitted
   To join with them to-day.

The Kaiser, with his shining sword,
   Was hurled from his throne;
He trampled on the rights of men –
   He's whining now alone.

His downfall was a blessing
   To all liberty-loving men;
But the job is yet unfinished,
   Although he's 'on the run'.

Oh! men, I say, be men,
   Fight for your rights to-day –
Enrol your names with Hetherton,
   Be sure, make no delay.

Show your manhood and your courage,
   And your fighting spirit too,
Be not like dumb-driven cattle –
   Don't let others fight for you.

These are days of swift upbuilding,
   Reconstruction and reforms,
Let not 'Robert' sit in silence
   With his pipe and folded arms.

Take your stand beside your comrades,
   Look not lightly on the past,
We have waited long and patiently,
   The day has dawned at last.

I will now conclude and finish
   With a fervent prayer for all
The members of the Union
   From Cork to Donegal!

A Song for the Times (Dublin)

Text: Ballad sheet.
  Air: The verses were united with this air by singer and researcher Fergus Russell.

We slave and starve together
  Beneath the rich man's thrall,
In warm and wintry weather
  While the bosses rob us all,
And as we're being exploited
  Our priests tell us to 'pray
For all those in high station'
  Who fleece us every day.
A toiling, a moiling,
  Oh! What a life of bliss!
They preach reward in the next life
  While they plunder us in this.

The bosses, the courts and the clergy
  And the forces of the Crown,
They all combined together
  To crush us workers down,
And if we seek more wages
  Or 'gainst their greed rebel,
We're the enemies of religion
  And deserve reward in hell.
A toiling, a moiling,
  Oh! What a life of bliss,
They'll promise you heaven in the next life
  While they're robbing you in this!

Despise all worldly comfort
　　As through this vale of tears you plod,
To be poor and cold and hungry
　　Is the Holy Will of God.
Heed not the vile sedition
　　That you hear from the Labour crew,
If you do, there's but perdition
　　After death awaiting you.
A toiling, a moiling,
　　Oh! What a life of bliss!
You may live in hope for the next life
　　While you die of want in this.

The limbs of law and order
　　Whom the foes of Labour bless,
Defenceless workers murder
　　Our meetings to suppress.
Before a smug shareholder
　　On the Bench with brazen jaw
And the aid of police perjurers
　　They will teach you love the law.
A toiling, a moiling,
　　Oh! What a life of bliss!
Trials may be just in the next life
　　But they're seldom just in this.

The politicians fool us,
　　For with lies their mouths are full,
The thugs in blue that baton us,
　　Won't fail to smash our skull.
And when the bosses' luck is out
　　Your leisure to employ,

They'll treat us to the pleasures
　　And the comforts of Mountjoy.
A toiling, a moiling,
　　Oh! What a life of bliss!
They love their foes in the next life,
　　But they'll cripple us in this.

We're counselled to be patient
　　By those who live at ease,
While we exist in hovels
　　Mid squalor and disease.
It's time all pious humbug
　　And cant came to an end,
We've learnt to know the worker
　　Alone is Labour's friend.
A toiling, a moiling,
　　Oh! What a life of bliss!
You're welcome rebel in the next life
　　But be patient here in this.

Oh! Workers held in bondage
　　By a cruel, crafty foe
If patience purchased freedom,
　　'Twas purchased long ago.
Let us arise, from off our knees,
　　And be no longer fooled
By those who aid the system
　　Whereby we're robbed and ruled.
A toiling, a moiling,
　　Oh! What a life of bliss,
To hell with them in the next life
　　We must help ourselves in this.

Cartoon by Ernest Kavanagh, *The Irish Worker*, 1914.

Advice to the Lawless

'Oscar'

Oh, this is a most sus - pi - cious age, and dan - ger - ous to boot,

And those who feel dis - posed to talk had bet - ter far be mute.

Oh, speak not a - bove a whis - per, don't let your feel - ings throb,

For to wink your eye, as like as not, might cost you for - ty bob.

For__ to wink your eye, as like as not, might cost you for - ty bob.

Text: *The Irish Worker,* 24 October 1913.
  Air: Composed for this song by Fergus Russell.

Oh, this is a most suspicious age
  And dangerous to boot,
And those who feel disposed to talk
  Had better far be mute.
Oh, speak not above a whisper,
  Don't let your feelings throb,
For to wink your eye as like as not
  Might cost you forty bob!

Don't gape at Sergeant Eastwood
  When strolling down the street,
You might as well stand by and sing
  An ode about his feet.
Oh, for heaven's sake don't look as though
  You envy him the job!
I've known a chap for less than that
  To fork out forty bob!

Don't pause upon the footpath
  If your pipe you want to light,
But wait until the boys in blue
  Are safely out of sight.
For with swords and batons hanging round
  It is no easy job.
A broken skull in half a tick
  Might end in forty bob!

Oh, perchance you take an evening stroll
    Away from strife and care,
And amble at a gentle pace,
    To breathe the country air,
Don't linger by the tempting hedge
    The blackberries to rob –
For if the local nark is nigh –
    Well, bang goes forty bob!

Mayhap whilst wandering about
    When you are stoney broke,
You see a G-man lounging by
    Exuding clouds of smoke,
Oh, don't stop to sniff that fragrant weed
    Or watch his grinning gob,
For down you'll go for loitering
    And forfeit forty bob!

Now last of all – take heed of this –
    And let me not be scorned!
Don't stare too hard at Murphy's trams,
    Remember, now, you're warned.
Oh, just pass upon your peaceful way,
    Sweet-tempered or begob!
You'll find yourself in duress
    Or minus forty bob!

A Dublin Metropolitan policeman guards one of the United Tramways Company's trams during the 1913 Lockout.

Who Fears to Wear the Blood-Red Badge?

Andrew Patrick Wilson (1886–1950)

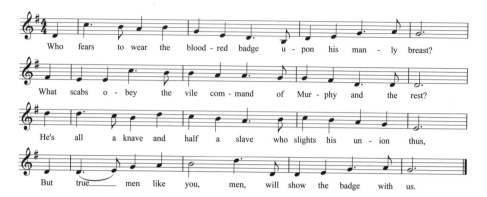

Who fears to wear the blood-red badge u-pon his man-ly breast?
What scabs o-bey the vile com-mand of Mur-phy and the rest?
He's all a knave and half a slave who slights his un-ion thus,
But true men like you, men, will show the badge with us.

'Harvey Duff' (verse 2), was originally a character in Dion Boucicault's play *The Shaughraun*. The character, an informer in the play, was based on a real person, Thomas Talbot, a former head constable of the RIC and a scourge of the Fenians.

The name came to be a slogan used to insult the police. See Georges-Denis Zimmermann, *Songs of Irish Rebellion*, Allen Figgis, Dublin, 1967, p. 273.

Text: *The Irish Worker*, 11 October 1913

Air: The song was clearly intended to be sung to the air of John Kells Ingram's 'The Memory of the Dead'.

Who fears to wear the blood-red badge?
  Upon his manly breast,
What scab obeys the vile command
  Of Murphy and the rest;
He's all a knave and half a slave
  Who slights his union thus,
But true men, like you men,
  Will show the badge with us.

They dared to fling the manly brick
  They wrecked a blackleg tram,
They dared give Harvey Duff a kick,
  They didn't care a damn.
They lie in gaol, they can't get bail
  Who fought their corner thus,
But you men, with sticks men,
  Must make the Peelers 'cuss'.

We rose in sad and weary days
  To fight the workers' cause,
We found in Jim, a heart ablaze,
  To break down unjust laws.
But 'tis a sin to follow him,
  Says Murphy and his crew,
Though true men, like you men,
  Will stick to him like glue.

Good luck be with him, he is here
  To win for us the fight;
To suffer for us without fear,
  To champion the right.

So stick to Jim, let nothing dim
   Our ardour in the fray,
And true Jim, our own Jim,
   Will win our fight today.

Jem Larkin Is a fighting man

When first he came to man's estate,
   Jem Larkin is a fighting man,
He then decided to emigrate,
   Jem Larkin is a fighting man.

He stowed away on a Liverpool ship,
   Jem Larkin is a fighting man,
And to New York he made a trip,
   Jem Larkin is a fighting man.

So out of Liverpool he set sail,
   Jem Larkin is a fighting man,
And in New York he arrived in gaol,
   Jem Larkin is a fighting man.

In gaol he heard the workers' call,
   Jem Larkin is a fighting man,
'If one is injured it hurts us all,'
   Jem Larkin is a fighting man.

In Liverpool he fought that fight,
   Jem Larkin is a fighting man,
And in Belfast he lit that light,
   Jem Larkin is a fighting man.

The Green and Orange, he said, are one,
   Jem Larkin is a fighting man,
They marched together in Belfast town,
   Jem Larkin is a fighting man.

So, we are with him, he'll fight our fight,
   Jem Larkin is a fighting man,
We'll prove together that right is might.
   Jem Larkin is a fighting man.

Text: The Donagh MacDonagh Song Collection. See http://songbook1.tripod.com/ (accessed 3 April 2015).
Air: MacDonagh specified the air 'Caleno Custure Me' for this song.

Sunday 31 August 1913, hundreds of people were injured when the DMP and RIC baton-charged the crowd in Dublin.

It's a Wrong Thing to Crush the Workers

The Red Hand (chorus, line 4) was the symbol of the Transport Workers' Union.

Text: Ballad sheet.
Air: 'It's A Long Way To Tipperary', see p. 201.

Grouped in dear old Dublin town the 'Polis' stand each day
Thirsting for their schoolmates' blood with whom they used to play,
Irishmen, remember, never let the Police be
Forgiven for their fierce assault and brutal cruelty.

Chorus
It's the wrong thing to crush the workers, it's the wrong thing to do,
It's the right thing to wipe out Murphy, Eason and his crew,
Fight on, Transport Workers, prove that you are true,
To the Cause of Labour and Big Jim Larkin and the Red Hand Abú!

A lockout was caused by Murphy, who did his best to try
To force all men in his employment their Union to deny,
But, comrades, stand together, and let this tyrant see
That we mean to fight for Justice and life-long Liberty.

Inequality

Desmond Crean

I often wonder, brother of the poor,
    How with your lot in this world you're content
When reason must inform you so that God
    Created not the world with the intent
That few should roll in luxuries of wealth,
    And, holding fast the reins of life's control,
Enslave and persecute their brother man
    As if he were a brute devoid of soul.

Our great financial system, 'tis a curse –
    The hideous evil root of all our woe
Which moulds the man to be so vilely mean,
    So selfish, so deceitful, and so low.
For are not all the men who tread the earth
    Daily warring with each other to obtain
Security from poverty and want,
    Which only gold and gold alone can gain.

Behold the poorer brother but a slave
    Who toils with body or the feeble brain,
To multiply the wealth of the élite,
    The perfect-mannered, cultured, and the vain,
A victim of the most unequal laws,
    By low environment demoralized,
Existing in his poverty and want,
    Uncouth, unlearned, uncultured and despised.

The daily wealth production of this world
    Is e'er produced by man from day to day,
And should this vast production ever cease,
    Then all the wealth we cherish would decay.
For lo! the very homes in which we live,
    The gold for livelihood to which we trust,
Our wearables, our ornaments, our all,
    Indeed in passing time become but dust.

Then if the daily labour of all men
    Produces all our never-ending wealth
On which the rich and poor alike depend,
    The daily worldly needs for human health,
Why should the few so covet all the gain?
    By legalized forms of robbery so defraud,
Denying brother man his daily bread
    Whilst calling loud 'Our Father' to their God!

Text: Desmond Crean, *Songs of an Old IRA Man*, Frederick Press, Dublin, 1939.

The Bold Labour Men

'To my life-long friend, Mick Halpin, and all the old hands who stood shoulder to shoulder in 1913.'

Joe O'Grady (1891–1960)

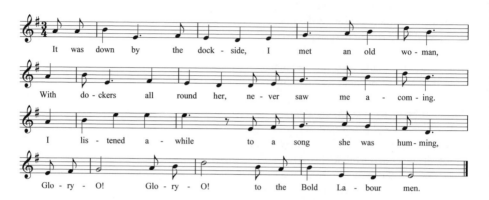

It was down by the dock-side, I met an old wo-man,
With do-ckers all round her, ne-ver saw me a-com-ing.
I lis-tened a-while to a song she was hum-ming,
Glo-ry - O! Glo-ry - O! to the Bold La-bour men.

The 'place that's named after Saint Kevin' (verse 10) refers to the South Dublin Union, where Éamonn Ceannt commanded a company of Volunteers during the 1916 Rising. It was developed into a hospital in later years and after the Treaty it was renamed Saint Kevin's Hospital. In 1971 it was renamed Saint James's Hospital. Among Dubliners of an older generation it never lost the stigma of its origins and was commonly referred to, up to the 1960s, as 'The Workhouse'.

Text: http://eastwallforall.ie/?p=1551 (accessed 3 April 2015).
    Air: The song is clearly modelled on Peadar Kearney's 'Down by the Glenside'.

It was down by the dockside, I met an old woman,
With dockers all round her, never saw me a-coming.
I listened awhile to a song she was humming,
    Glory O, glory O to the Bold Labour Men.

When I was a young maid the workers were sweating,
And struggling to live on the pay they were getting.
At many a fireside their families sat fretting,
    Glory O, glory O to the Bold Labour Men.

Then our leader appeared with a voice that was gifted,
Slave-drivers and yes-men he very soon shifted.
He championed our cause and our hearts were up-
        lifted,
    Glory O, glory O to the Bold Labour Men.

But the Bosses resented his vigorous manner,
When he upset their plans sympathetic, the spanner,
The dockers and coalies all flocked to his banner,
    Glory O, glory O to the Bold Labour Men.

Now Murphy, he swore, with the aid of his papers,
To break up our Union and stop Larkin's capers,
But the workers just smiled and said 'Never, be Japers!'
    Glory O, glory O to the Bold Labour Men.

One bright August day, when we went for our money,
They gave us a Form, sure the reading was funny,

Saying 'Sign on the line, or leave your job, Sonny.'
    Glory O, glory O to the Bold Labour Men.

For six weary months we had bloodshed and friction,
Hunger and want, baton charge and eviction,
But stuck to our guns, I defy contradiction,
    Glory O, glory O to the Bold Labour Men.

They filled up our jobs with free labour and squealers,
From all over Ireland they brought up the Peelers.
If you wore the Red Hand, sure, down came their
    feelers,
    Glory O, glory O to the Bold Labour Men.

The Judge or the Jury were not in our favour,
For saying the word 'scab' you got six months' Hard
    Labour,
And up in Mountjoy, you met many a neighbour.
    Glory O, glory O to the Bold Labour Men.

Some died in the place that's called after Saint Kevin,
While Nolan and Byrne we laid in Glasnevin.
They were killed by the Dockside, their souls now in
    Heaven.
    Glory O, glory O to the Bold Labour Men.

God rest you, Jim Larkin, James Connolly, and Foran,
Our two delegates, jailer Redmond and Nolan,
No more from Butt Bridge to the Point you're
    patrollin',
    Glory O, glory O to the Bold Labour Men.

The Bosses they granted a nice little pension,
To the 'scabs' and the 'squealers' who stood to
    attention.
You meet them each day, but their names I won't
    mention.
    Glory O, glory O to the Bold Labour Men.

I passed on my way with a heart that was aching,
When I think of those Old Hands now poor and
    forsaken,
While the Union now boasts of the thousands they're
    making.
    Glory O, glory O to the Bold Labour Men.

The Irish Citizen Army

Jo Connolly

The I-rish Ci-ti-zen Ar-my is the name of our wee band.

With our mar-chin' and our dril-lin', I'm sure you'll call it grand.

And when we start our figh-tin' it will be for Ire_____ land,

And we'll still keep mar-ching on!

Chorus

Glo-ry, glo-ry to old Ire_____ land! Glo_____ ry, glo-ry to our sire_____ land!

Glo-ry to the me-mo-ry of those who fought and fell, And we'll still keep mar-ching on!

'The Irish Citizen Army song was written by Jo Connolly, a young working-man, whose brother, Sean Connolly, was killed while leading the attack on Dublin Castle Easter Monday. Jo was the boy who cut loopholes in the roof of the College of Surgeons. He was deported to Wandsworth Prison, but after a few months was released.' Note in source.

Text: Margaret Skinnider, *Doing My Bit for Ireland*, The Century Co., New York, 1917.
Air: 'The Battle Hymn of the Republic'.

The Irish Citizen Army is the name of our wee band,
With our marchin' and our drillin', I'm sure you'll call it grand;
And when we start our fightin' it will be for Ireland,
　　And we'll still keep marching on!

Chorus
Glory, glory to old Ireland!
Glory, glory to our sireland!
Glory to the memory of those who fought and fell,
　　And we'll still keep marching on!

We've got guns and ammunition, we know how to use them well,
And when we meet the Saxon, we will drive them all to Hell;
We've got to free our country and avenge all those who fell,
　　So we still keep marching on!

King George he is a coward, that no one can deny,
When the Germans come to England, from there he'll have to fly;
And if he comes to Ireland then, by God, he'll have to die,
　　And we'll still go marching on!

When the Germans come to free us, we will lend a helping hand,
For we believe they're just as good as any in the land,
They're bound to win our rights for us, let England go be damned!
　　And we'll still keep marching on!

The Blackleg

Jim Connell

There's a cuc-koo in our house-hold and he ter-ri-fies our young,

For the ha-bits of the trai-tor have been of-ten told and sung.

Though his fea-thers flut-ter soft-ly, there is mur-der in his heart,

And all down the toi-ling a-ges he has played the vil-vain's part.

Chorus

Oh we hate the cru-el ti-ger and hy-e-na and jac-kal,

But the false and dir-ty black-leg is the vi-lest beast of all.

There's a cuckoo in our household
  And he terrifies our young,
For the habits of the traitor
  Have been often told and sung.
Though his feathers flutter softly,
  There is murder in his heart,
And all down the toiling ages
  He has played the villain's part.

Chorus
Oh, we hate the cruel tiger
  And hyena and jackal;
But the false and dirty blackleg
  Is the vilest beast of all.

When we dress our brave battalions
  And confront the lords of loot,
We behold the scab desert us
  Ere the guns begin to shoot;
Just to gorge his greedy stomach
  And to save his coward's skin,
With salvation in the balance
  He betrays his kith and kin.

Jim Connell put a note to this song:
'The appearance of a blackleg in
public constitutes a very apposite
occasion for practising the cuckoo's
call.
  "Blackleg" was derived from the
fact that scab miners who worked
during a strike could be identified by
their blackened legs. Another, early,
nineteenth century name for a scab
was "dunghill"; stalwart unionists
were called "flints".'
  To 'cut' someone (final verse) is an
old expression meaning to ignore
them or refuse to acknowledge them
when meeting them in public.

Text: *The James Connolly Songbook*,
Cork Workers' Club, 1972.
  The air is the one associated with
the song 'Do Me Justice', sometimes
known as 'Paddy's Lamentation'.

You can tell him midst a thousand
   By his cringe and by his crawl,
For of dignity and courage
   He possesses none at all.
In the aleshop he's a sponger,
   In the workshop he's a spy,
He's a liar and deceiver
   With low cunning in his eye.

Let us flout him in the market,
   Let us cut him in the street,
Let us jeer him from all places
   Where the honest workers meet;
When to his brazen features
   Every decent door is slammed,
We will leave him burst and broken
   To go down among the damned.

A Limerick Ballad

Air: *Shan Van Voch*

Text: Samuels Collection, TCD.

Oh! Limerick is on strike,
   Sez the Shan Van Voch,
Did you ever hear the like?
   Sez the Shan Van Voch,
For the city is 'Proclaimed',
And the people all are blamed
For being criminals untamed,
   Sez the Shan Van Voch.

Oh! to work they cannot go,
   Sez the Shan Van Voch,
If a permit they don't show,
   Sez the Shan Van Voch,
So a strike they did declare
'Gainst the British laws unfair,
And they'll ask no permits there
   Sez the Shan Van Voch.

John Bull has all his guns,
   Sez the Shan Van Voch,
It reminds me of the Huns,
   Sez the Shan Van Voch,
There're tanks in every street,
And peelers with big feet,

Sure 'tis really quite a treat,
    Sez the Shan Van Voch.

Then the people all went out,
    Sez the Shan Van Voch,
To enjoy themselves no doubt,
    Sez the Shan Van Voch,
But they all came back again,
On a very early train,
And no permits did obtain,
    Sez the Shan Van Voch.

Can Limerick win the day?
    Sez the Shan Van Voch,
That is what the people say,
    Sez the Shan Van Voch,
Yes! Limerick will win,
For Ireland's standing in,
And collecting all the tin,
    Sez the Shan Van Voch.

They have fought the fight before,
    Sez the Shan Van Voch,
In the far off days of yore,
    Sez the Shan Van Voch,
So all stand side by side,
No matter what betide,
An' we'll humble British pride,
    Sez the Shan Van Voch.

The Internationale
Teresa Brayton (1868–1943)

I heard the Song of the Red Flag yesterday
Sung in a hive beside my garden way,
Where maddened bees, to hold and guard their own,
Flung from their honey cells drone after drone.

Text: Teresa Brayton, *The Flame of Ireland,* New York, 1926.

97

26th July, 1914

Lily M. O'Brennan (1878–1948)

The song commemorates the Howth (Co. Dublin) gun-running episode, when 900 German single-shot Mauser rifles and 29,000 rounds of ammunition were landed from the yacht *Asgard*, crewed by Conor O'Brien, Erskine Childers, Molly Childers, Mary Spring Rice and two Gola islanders, Patrick McGinley and Charles Dugen. The Irish Citizen Army, Fianna Éireann and the Irish Volunteers took delivery of the cargo.

The gun-running was emulating that of the Ulster Volunteers, who had successfully landed much larger quantities of arms at Larne in April 1914. There are a number of accounts of the efforts to avoid surrendering the guns to the police and British military who attempted to seize the guns nearer Dublin. Only three rifles were seized.

A detachment of the King's Own Scottish Borderers, on being jeered by bystanders at Bachelor's Walk for their failure to seize the arms, opened fire on the crowd, killing three people. This atrocity outraged public opinion.

The rifles landed at Howth were used in the 1916 Rising. After the surrender prisoners were frequently told to remove their shirts, to see if

Oh, the guns are on the say,
 Says the Sean Van Vocht;
They're landed at Howth Bay,
 Says the Sean Van Vocht;
Oh, what a mighty cheer
Went ringing down the pier
From each Irish Volunteer!
 Says the Sean Van Vocht;

Now what will the Ulsters do?
 Says the Sean Van Vocht;
Sure they've broke my heart in two,
 Says the Sean Van Vocht.
But wouldn't it be great,
If they'd share their country's fate,
And join each fellow mate,
 For the Sean Van Vocht.

Oh! 'twould be the glorious sight,
 Says the Sean Van Vocht;
The day that they'd unite,
 Says the Sean Van Vocht.
From Bantry to Lough Neagh,

Picture from the *Illustrated London News* of 1 August 1914, showing the Volunteers returning to Dublin on 26 July, carrying the rifles that had just been been landed at Howth.

Sure who would say us nay!
For 'tis ours would be the sway
   Says the Sean Van Vocht.

And so I'm dreaming long,
   Says the Sean Van Vocht;
To hear their marching song,
   Says the Sean Van Vocht.
Oh! the orange and the green
Are fit colours for a queen
And they'll wave once more I ween
   O'er the Sean Van Vocht.

Oh! it was the famous day,
   Says the Sean Van Vocht,
When they doubled on the quay,
   Says the Sean Van Vocht.
And how they marched along
In bold battalion strong
Sure they'll right my every wrong
   Says the Sean Van Vocht.

their shoulder was bruised from using
a Howth rifle, which had a heavy
'kick'. Those with bruised shoulders
were not very popular, as the round
fired was a short round-nosed one,
which inflicted a nasty wound. [LM]

Text: Un-dated newspaper cutting in
the Ceannt Papers, Brother Allen
Library, Dublin.
   Air: 'An Seanbhean Bhocht', see p. 6.

Bachelor's Walk

Mournful Lines on the Military Outrage in Dublin

You true-born sons of Erin's Isle, come listen to my
   song.
My tale is one of sorrow but I won't detain you long,
Concerning the murderous outrage that took place in
   Dublin town
When a cowardly regiment was let loose to shoot our
   people down.

Text and air: Colm O Lochlainn, *Irish Street Ballads*, Three Candles, Dublin, 1939.

On the 26th day of July, the truth I'll tell to you,
The Irish Volunteers all swore their enemies to subdue,
They marched straight out to Howth and soon the people
    were alarmed,
When they heard the glorious news: 'Our Irish Volunteers
    are armed.'

The crowds they all kept cheering on as our brave
    defenders passed,
But their cheers were stopped by an outrage which for
    some time did last.
Our gallant men, the Volunteers, were met in front and
    rear,
By the King's Own Scottish cowards who are doomed for
    everywhere.

God save our gallant Captain Judge, the hero of the band,
Who nearly gave his precious life for the just cause of his
    land,
In spite of terrible injuries and weak from loss of blood,
He fondly hugged his rifle grand the prize of this
    brotherhood.

'Scene of the slaughter of Dublin citizens by military.'

Picture published in a contemporary newspaper showing the scene of the Bachelor's Walk killings. It was captioned as follows: 'A view of the scene of the shooting outrage yesterday in Bachelor's Walk. At the spot indicated by "A" a couple of soldiers were jostled by a crowd, and one of the men lost his cap. The officer in command went back to pick it up, and rejoined his Company at "B". Having marched to point "C" he ordered a squad of his men to fire. The bullets swept in the direction of O'Connell Bridge, mowing down about 20 people. A young cyclist crossing O'Connell Bridge fell a victim at point "D".' (Picture from the Ceannt Papers, Brother Allen Library, Dublin.)

Next in the list of heroes is the scout so well renowned,
With the butt end of his rifle felled a Borderer to the
    ground.
He disarmed him of his weapons and soon made his
    escape,
By climbing a wall in Fairview, for his young life was at
    stake.

The Dublin Police were ordered the Volunteers for to
    subdue,
But O'Neill and Gleeson boldly replied: 'Such a thing we
    decline to do,
For to fight against our countrymen would on us put a
    stain,
For we wish to see our native land a Nation Once
    Again.'

On Bachelor's Walk a scene took place, which I'm sure
    had just been planned,
For cowardly Scottish Borderers turned and fired with-
    out command.
With bayonets fixed they charged the crowd and left
    them in their gore,
But their deeds will be remembered in Irish hearts for
    evermore.

God rest the souls of those who sleep apart from earthly
    sin,
Including Mrs Duffy, James Brennan and Patrick Quinn.
But we will yet avenge them and the time will surely
    come
That we'll make the Scottish Borderers pay for the
    cowardly deeds they done.

Requiem

Maeve Cavanagh

Furl the flag and roll the muffled drum,
Add three lives more to the countless sum
    Who for Ireland died;
Number them with the wanton slain
Whose blood cries out from each reeking plain,
    Unavenged, undried.

Written in memory of the victims of
the King's Own Scottish Borderers,
26 July 1914, and published in *The
Irish Worker*, 1 August 1914.

Whence Ireland forges with bruisèd feet,
Thro' tenebrous years the dawn to greet,
    To her crown and throne;
Nor gallows, nor sword her way could bar,
Ever she worshipped the one fair star,
    From fields death strown.

Unfurl her flag, her dead are at rest,
Like mourning pearls on her throbbing breast,
    She will wear for aye;
No longer muted her Clarion cry,
Her armèd columns go marching by
    To the opening day.

The scene of the shootings at Bachelor's Walk, *Illustrated London News*, 1 August 1914.

My Old Howth Gun

Séamus McGallogly (James Doherty)

There is sorrow in my heart,
  O, my old Howth Gun!
Since we lately had to part,
  O, my old Howth Gun!
For in Ireland's day of need
Well you proved a friend indeed,
When you made the bullets speed,
  O, my old Howth Gun!

I was glad when you were near,
  O, my old Howth Gun!
And no foeman did I fear,
  O, my old Howth Gun!
For your bark and bitter bite
Put the Saxon curs to flight,
And they wouldn't dare to fight
  With my old Howth Gun!

How glorious was your feel,
  O, my old Howth Gun!
When you made the Saxons reel,
  O, my old Howth Gun!
When the Lancers, trim and neat,
Charging down O'Connell Street,
Had to beat a quick retreat
  From my old Howth Gun!

The parting it was sore,
  O, my old Howth Gun!
Sure I ne'er may see you more,
  O, my old Howth Gun!
There was glorious hope that we
Could have set old Ireland free,
Now you're parted far from me,
  O, my old Howth Gun!

But a day will come again,
  O, my old Howth Gun!
When I'll join the fighting men,
  O, my old Howth Gun!
With some brave, determined band,
Proudly there I'll take my stand
For the freedom of our land,
  O, my old Howth Gun!

A ballad slip version of this song
carries the information: 'Written
by an Irish Rebel in Knutsford Jail.'

Text: *The 1916 Song Book*, Irish Book
Bureau, Dublin, 1930.
  Air: 'The Shan Van Vocht', see p. 7.

Ireland to England

Patrick Sarsfield Gilmore (1829–92)

A Simple Peasant Ballad on the Question of the Day
– 'Home Rule for Ireland' –
Respectfully Dedicated to the Great Leaders:
William E. Gladstone and Charles S. Parnell,
As also to the Rank and File of the Irish and
English People the Whole World Over.

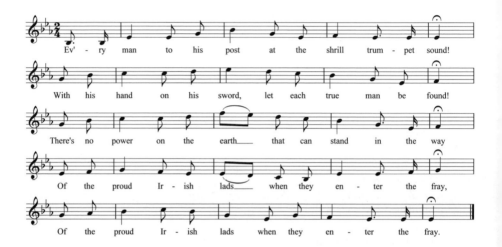

Ev' - ry man to his post at the shrill trum - pet sound!

With his hand on his sword, let each true man be found!

There's no power on the earth___ that can stand in the way

Of the proud Ir - ish lads___ when they en - ter the fray,

Of the proud Ir - ish lads when they en - ter the fray.

Patrick Sarsfield Gilmore, celebrated as 'the father of the American band', was born near Dublin and emigrated to the United States as a nineteen-year-old.

Text and music: Sheet music published by Hitchcock's Music Stores, New York, n.d.

Ev'ry man to his post at the shrill trumpet sound!
With his hand on his sword let each true man be found!
There's no power on the earth that can stand in the way
Of the proud Irish lads when they enter the fray,
Of the proud Irish lads when they enter the fray.

With a cause that is just and a heart that is brave,
Is there one son of Erin who would be a slave?
If there is, let him die – he's a stain on the land!
For we'll have none but freemen with strong heart and
        hand,
For we'll have none but freemen with strong heart and
        hand.

See the rivers of blood that for England we've shed,
Fighting battles for her in the coat that is red!
If she'll not do us justice let none stand between
And we'll march to our graves in the coat that is green,
And we'll march to our graves in the coat that is green.

But if England will come with her heart in her hand,
And will say, 'My brave boys, you shall have your own
    land
If you swear that our union you'll never oppose
We will drink to the shamrock that clings to the rose,
We will drink to the shamrock that clings to the rose.'

'We will give you 'Home Rule' with its pleasures and
    cares;
Go and make your own laws for your local affairs;
But the Crown of Great Britain shall reign over all –
You must stand by forever in its rise or its fall,
You must stand by forever in its rise or its fall'.

'Then what more do you ask, will you answer us now?
And for ever more banish that frown from your brow?
'Tis the voice of all England your rights to restore
And from Ireland's old heart to remove ev'ry sore,
And from Ireland's old heart to remove ev'ry sore.'

Patrick Sarsfield Gilmore.

Let these words once be heard in the isle ever green,
And a million of healths will be drank to the Queen.
If our rights we can have without striking a blow
Then we'll stand by Britannia – our breasts to her foe,
Then we'll stand by Britannia – our breasts to her foe.

May the Lord in His mercy these tidings soon send,
Then the whole heart of Erin with England's will blend,
We will bury our sword – there'll be joy in the land –
And for ever and ever united we'll stand,
And for ever and ever united we'll stand.

Says Mr John E. Redmond, O!

Phil O'Neill

Now list to what I've got to say,
    Says Mr John E. Redmond, O!
About the no far distant day,
    Says Mr John E. Redmond, O!
Home Rule is coming now at last,
The critical stage is almost passed,
And I've nailed my colours to the mast,
    Says Mr John E. Redmond, O!

John Redmond's assurance to the Irish people, that Home Rule would be delivered at 'no far distant date', was used afterwards as a stick with which to beat him. This song has also been printed and circulated under the title 'Says the Parliamentary Party, O!'

The B.O.E. (verse 5) was the Board of Erin, one of the two factions that emerged from a split in the Ancient Order of Hibernians in the early 1900s. It supported John Redmond and his party, and was controlled by Joe Devlin.

'John Redmond moves his resolution to give Home Rule to Ireland'
The Graphic, 4 April 1908.

Home Rule is cheap at any price, says Mr John E. Redmond, O!
If we only get a little slice, says Mr John E. Redmond, O!
So I told the boys to play the game,
Enlist and win a glorious name,
Sure my son is after doing that same, says Mr John E. Redmond, O!

Text: Samuels Collection, TCD.
  Air: 'Leather away the wattle O', see 'The Grand Oul' Dame Britannia', p. 235.

For this is Ireland's war, you know, says Mr John E. Redmond, O!
'Tis up to us to make a show, says Mr John E. Redmond, O!
So Irishmen tell all your sons,
Their duty is to fight the Huns,
And I'll change the old Italian guns, says Mr John E. Redmond, O!

Home Rule is on the Statute Book, says Mr John E. Redmond, O!
The other day I had a look, says Mr John E. Redmond, O!
And there 'twas down in black and white,
So boys enlist and join the fight,
When the war is o'er you'll find I'm right, says Mr John E. Redmond, O!

And when we're back in College Green, says Mr John E. Redmond, O!
What a grand assembly will be seen, says Mr John E. Redmond, O!
The bosses of the B.O.E.,
Little wee Joe and brave John D.,
Dillon and myself and of course T.P., says Mr John E. Redmond, O!

And every man that takes the bob, says Mr John E. Redmond, O!
I'll put his name down for a job, says Mr John E. Redmond, O!
For when I'm spouting on the floor,
I'll want a hundred men or more,
To keep Sinn Féiners from the door, says Mr John E. Redmond, O!

And when the opening day will come, says Mr John E. Redmond, O!
My speech will make the 'Old House' hum, says Mr John E. Redmond, O!
And when the doors I'll open fling,
The party songsters all will sing,
'God save Ireland and the King,' says Mr John E. Redmond, O!

So boys enlist, don't act the fool, says Mr John E. Redmond, O!
And take my word we've got Home Rule, says Mr John E. Redmond, O!
'Tis coming across in a ship I've seen,
If it doesn't meet a Submarine,
'Twill be landed safe at College Green, says Mr John E. Redmond, O!

Sinn Féin, I fear, is gaining ground, says Mr John E. Redmond, O!
But wait till I my plans expound, says Mr John E. Redmond, O!
I'll show 'tis but a rainbow chase,
But my Home Rule will change the case,
For I'm still the leader of the Irish Race, says Mr John E. Redmond, O!

107

To J.E.R.

J.E.R. is John E. Redmond. Francis Higgins and Leonard McNally were informers who betrayed the leaders of The United Irishmen in 1798, and Lord Castlereagh (Robert Stewart) was the Chief Secretary of Ireland at the time, who put down the rebellion with great brutality.

Text: *Poems and Songs of Easter Week,* undated ballad sheet.

You sought, of old, an honoured place
As Leader of the Irish race.
Know that we hold your peers to-day,
Higgins, McNally, Castlereagh;
Yet in this company alone,
A strange distinction you have won!
These for the price of soul disgrace,
Gained wealth or title, land or place;
But what is yours, O pitiful
Apostate Leader, England's Tool?
Your country sold, the price unpaid.
Hide thee! Betrayer – and Betrayed.

Commotion in Hades
Peter Golden

'Arnold' is Benedict Arnold, a general in the American army during the War of Independence who defected to the British.

This verse, and the next, are from Peter Golden, *The Voice of Ireland*, Press of M.A. O'Connor, New York, n.d.

Judas, Arnold and Castlereagh
    Spoke loudly through the gloom:
'Redmond, our master, comes to-day,
    Make room there, boys, make room.'

Rats!
Peter Golden

The fetid corpse of cut-throat Castlereagh
With rats was pelted on its burial day,
But now so many Castlereaghs abound
Where will the rats to pelt them with be found?

John Redmond presenting the flag to the Volunteers, August 1914.

Oul' Lloyd George's Bill

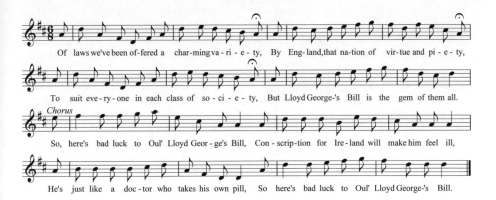

Of Laws we've been offered a charming variety
By England, that nation of virtue and piety,
To suit everyone in each class of society,
    But Lloyd George's Bill is the gem of them all.

Chorus
So here's bad luck to oul' Lloyd George's Bill
Conscription for Ireland will make him feel ill,
He'll be just like a doctor who takes his own pill
So here's bad luck to oul' Lloyd George's Bill.

The Priests and the Bishops are villains atrocious
At least England says so, in terms quite ferocious,
For out to strafe Germans, she likes for to coax us,
    But our nation and clergy won't have it at all.

The Kaiser, the divil, he can't be kept under,
He's knocking the lines of the Allies asunder,
While our Great British Statesmen have made a big
        blunder
    With Conscription for Ireland they'll have a big fall.

Refrain
So here's be damned to oul' Lloyd George's Bill
For bow to the Tyrants, our sons never will,
For Erin will fight it, and beat it until
You will then hear the last of oul' Lloyd George's Bill.

Text: *The Granuaile Song Book*, The
Irish Supply Depot, Dublin, 1922.
    Air: 'Father O'Flynn'.

109

Give Us Something To Be Loyal To

Felix McGlennon

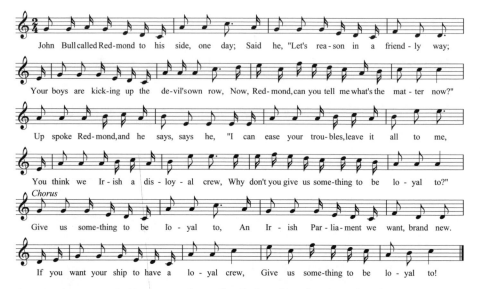

John Bull called Redmond to his side, one day; Said he, "Let's rea-son in a friend-ly way;

Your boys are kick-ing up the de-vil's own row, Now, Red-mond, can you tell me what's the mat-ter now?"

Up spoke Red-mond, and he says, says he, "I can ease your trou-bles, leave it all to me,

You think we Ir-ish a dis-loy-al crew, Why don't you give us some-thing to be lo-yal to?"

Chorus

Give us some-thing to be lo-yal to, An Ir-ish Par-lia-ment we want, brand new.

If you want your ship to have a lo-yal crew, Give us some-thing to be lo-yal to!

There was always a considerable proportion of the Irish population willing to follow the lead of the Irish Parliamentary Party. Their need for some gesture is expressed in this song.

Text and music: *The Marching Songs of the Irish Volunteers*, Felix McGlennon, London, n.d.

John Bull called Redmond to his side, one day;
Said he, 'Let's reason, in a friendly way;
Your boys are kicking up the devil's own row,
Now, Redmond, can you tell me, what's the matter now?'
Up spoke Redmond, and he says, says he,
'I can ease your troubles, leave it all to me,
You think we Irish a disloyal crew,
Why don't you give us something to be loyal to?'

Chorus
Give us something to be loyal to,
An Irish Parliament we want, brand new,
If you want your ship to have a loyal crew,
Give us something to be loyal to.

John Bull says, 'I have given you new laws,
And still you sing and speak about the Cause.
You make more trouble, and you worry me,
Far worse than all the others of my familee.'
Up spoke Redmond, and he says, 'Well, John,
With Irish sentiment you can't get on,
We won't be satisfied until you say:
"Let Irishmen rule Ireland in their Irish way".'

John Bull says, 'Aren't your laws the same as ours?
Than all my children do you want more pow'rs?'

Says Redmond, 'Most of them have failure shown,
We know they'd be much better if we made our own.'
John Bulls says, 'To chase your discontent,
You can try your Irish Parliament.'
Let Irishmen forget their bigotry,
For Ireland's sake all work for her prosperity.

Chorus
Now we've something to be loyal to,
An Irish Parliament at home, brand new,
The Ship of State will have a loyal crew,
Now we've something to be loyal to.

The Coming of the Irish Judas and his Paymaster.

The cartoonist Ernest Kavanagh (Maeve Cavanagh's brother) used the tag 'Empire John' to denigrate Redmond in a sketch lampooning Asquith's rally (see below) in *The Irish Worker* on 3 October 1914.

The Coming of the Irish Judas and his Paymaster

Maeve Cavanagh

Men of the martyred Emmet's race
   The arch betrayer comes,
With his English master Asquith,
   With beat of English drums.
Men of the race of peerless Tone
   These knaves greet as you ought –
Show to the world that Irishmen
   Can not be duped or bought.

The subjects of this poem are John Redmond, leader of the Irish Parliamentary Party, and Prime Minister Herbert Asquith, who visited Dublin in the autumn of 1914 to attend a recruitment rally.

Text: Maeve Cavanagh, *Sheaves of Revolt*, Dublin, 1914.

111

The English trickster and his tool
Come seeking Ireland's aid,
And 'Empire John' has vowed to form
An 'Irish Slaves' Brigade.
So, English poltroons, sit ye tight,
Give Redmond your command,
To find you Irish dupes enough
To save your craven land.

Where are the careless shepherds now?
The wolves are on the fold!
Is there a man in all the land
Not gagged by English gold?
If justice lives a day must come
Of reck'ning and revenge
When all that's true in Ireland, will
This day of shame avenge.

Then England send your ghouls to lure
A gallant nation's soul
To trade in Irish flesh and blood
And win us from our goal.
Your whippers-in, will bring to heel
But worthless curs – not men
So haste and take your wastrel pack
Nor bring them back again.

And beat your English drums, ye knaves
And ply your shameful trade
The while, with tongue in cheek you fake
An Irish Slaves' Brigade.
True Irishmen, close up your ranks,
The prowling wolves disperse –
Where'er the traitor pack may go
Shall follow Ireland's curse.

Johnnie I Hardly Knew You

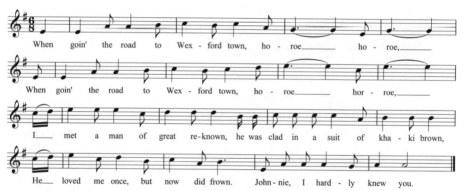

This song is a parody of Joseph B. Geoghegan's song of the same name, published in London in 1867, which begins 'While going the road to sweet Athy'. That song, in turn, was set to the air of the American Civil War song 'When Johnny Comes Marching Home Again' by Patrick Gilmore, published in Boston in 1863.

Text: Michael Mulcahy and Marie Fitzgibbon, *The Voice of the People*, The O'Brien Press, Dublin, 1982.
Air: The American Civil War song, 'When Johnny Comes Marching Home Again'.

When goin' the road to Wexford town, horoe, horoe,
When goin' the road to Wexford town, horoe, horoe,
I met a man of great renown,
He was clad in a suit of khaki brown.
He loved me once but now did frown,
Johnnie I hardly knew you.

With drums and guns and guns and drums, horoe, horoe,
With drums and guns and guns and drums, horoe, horoe,
With drums and guns and guns and drums,
The English lords did woo you.
Och darling dear you look so queer,
Johnnie I hardly knew you!

Where is the Bill that looked so fair, horoe, horoe,
Where is the promised Bill so fair, horoe, horoe,
In which my dead sons were to share,
You drove them forth and did not care,
Since you their anguish would not share,
Och Johnnie I hardly knew you.

You drove them forth to slay the Hun, horoe, horoe,
You drove them forth to slay the Hun, horoe, horoe,
Yes every single mother's son,
Though a million English slackers run,
And all for this precious Bill you've won,
Och Johnnie I hardly knew you.

You're worse than famine in the land, horoe, horoe,
You're worse than famine in the land, horoe, horoe,
With lords and ladies so fine and grand,
To finish the Gaels you well have planned,
And leave for the Saxons your native land,
Och Johnnie I hardly knew you.

To Ireland's Betrayers
Maeve Cavanagh

A curse on the helots and renegades
    Who are selling our land to-day,
On the craven and knavish 'leaders'
    Who are showing the shameful way.
Mean breed of lackey and sychophant –
    They are serving their masters well –
The faithless brood have one sole regret
    That they have but one land to sell.

Alas for the hapless land that bore
    Such a soulless, carrion horde,
They who for office and English gold
    Our centuried flag have low'red.
Who lured their dupes in the sacred names
    Of our rebel and martyred dead
And ruined the fruit of their noble creed
    Whilst they taught the cravens instead.

Then tear the mask from each traitor's face,
    Let their names ever numbered be
With all who have struck at our country's heart
    As she struggled towards Liberty,

Text: Maeve Cavanagh, *Sheaves of Revolt*, Dublin, 1914.

And you who would serve our loved land best,
    Who are guarding her honour still,
Strike first at the knaves who are selling that land –
    Then on to the fight with a will.

Sir Edward, My Boy
T. McGrattan

Addressed to Sir Edward Carson,
leader in Ulster of the opposition to
Home Rule, this is one of a relatively
small number of contemporary loyalist pieces on the politics of the time.

Text: Samuels Collection, TCD.
  Air: 'Father O'Flynn', see 'Oul'
Lloyd George's Bill', p. 109.

Sir Edward, my boy, you've a wonderful way wid ye,
All loyal Ulster has fallen in love wid ye,
Joe Devlin and Redmond are shaking for fear of ye;
    In spite of the traitors, ye'll best them all.
There's Craig – yes, and Wallace, Smiley and others –
Unionists together and good loyal brothers;
Lonsdale and Thompson, M'Mordie and t'others –
    All working like Turks for the good of our cause.

Chorus
Here's a health to ye, Sir Edward, my boy;
We bless you, and bless you, and bless you again;
So stand by the Union, and down wid the Fenians,
For gallant Sir Edward's the best of them all!

On the Twelfth of July, on the field of Craigavon,
The Orangemen assembled to hear you unburden
Your heart to them all concerning the trouble
    That Home Rule would bring to our own dear land.
Right nobly you stood by your Covenant that day,
And have shown all traitors ye mean what ye say;
Now Sir Edward, my boy, we're yours in this struggle,
    And we'll stand by the Union – yes, sir, to a man!

Here let us say, when our freedom is threatened,
That Rome we'll not trust no more we would Satan,
For history has told us, and by the same token,
    In spite of all promise she'd make slaves of us all.
Asquith and Churchill, Lloyd-George and the rest,
Hibernians and traitors may give up their jest;
For learning and bravery, Sir Edward's our darling,
    And in spite of the Pope he'll make fools of them all.

Cartoon by 'Spex' (John Fergus O'Hea) from *The Lepracaun, c.* 1912.
John Redmond drives Ireland (the queen) towards Home Rule, while Edward Carson, Bonar Law and
Lord Londonderry howl with rage over their bones of hatred and bigotry.

Ulster's Watch

Thomas Canning

Dedicated to our Brave Leaders – Sir Edward
Carson and Mr Bonar Law, and our Grand
Old Orange Institution. (Belfast, July 1913)

This poem was possibly inspired by
the German song 'The Watch on the
Rhine'.

Text: Samuels Collection, TCD.

Ulster? What of the night?
   The call resounds afar;
Your watchtowers guarded keep,
   For any evil hour;
Like campfires by their light,
   On fields of battle known;
Our sentries guard their posts
   Until the night has flown.

And at the break of day,
   Prepared are we for all,
Nor like a garrison besieged,
   But ready at the call.

Leaders strong, brave-hearted,
   Men we have not less
Resolute, unshaken in
   The cause of righteousness.

115

To Britain now we say,
  If from her flag we go,
Remember we shall hold our own,
  Nor fear to tell her so;
For Ulster is her shield
  And buckler in this hour,
When inward breach imperils
  And tampers with her power.

Our fixed resolve is scorned,
  But wait; O England, hear!
You deal with fearless loyal men,
  And you have such to fear;
A people strong of will,
  Courageous; of a race
That never can be budged one inch
  From our firm Empire place.

England! never shall your flag,
  By Ulstermen be furled,
For we are of her Empire strong,
  And dare to tell the world,
If ministers in power,
  For votes of 'eighty-four',
Will barter liberty for chains,
  A million souls and more;

Our red right-hand will glow,
  And with our leaders stand
For England, home and glory,
  For faith and Fatherland.

The Orange Cat & Rebel Rat
September 1913

Sir Ed - ward Car — son— has— a— cat, that— cat he— is— a— dan—— dy,

But Red-mond keeps a— re— bel— rat that— thrives on— cakes and— bran—— dy.

This mus - ty rat he goes a - bout and dir - ty's Ul - ster's pan—— try,

But Car - son's cat soon spots him— out and— cha - ses— him to— Ban—— try.

Text: Samuels Collection, TCD.
Air: 'The Boyne Water'.

Sir Edward Carson has a cat
  That cat he is a dandy,
But Redmond keeps a rebel rat
  That thrives on cakes and brandy.

This musty rat he goes about
  And dirtys Ulster's pantry
But Carson's cat soon spots him out
  And chases him to Bantry.

Sometimes John's rat goes out to sniff
    The place that pussy watches,
But in an instant smells the cat
    And off he goes like matches.

So Carson's cat keeps on the go
    As he is very handy
At dealing with a rat or so
    When out upon the randy.

For pussy now and then starts out
    To see a bit around him,
And if that rat is on the spot
    Squeeks out, the duce confound him.

If Carson's cat and Johnny's rat
    Should meet too close together,
Well, it would be a bit of hell
    That rat won't like – no rather.

When next you hear about the rat
    Twill be a new creation,
For Carson's cat will get him yet
    E'er Ireland is a nation.

They Can't Bell Carson's Cat

J.P.G., Belfast

Said Redmond to Joe Devlin:
    'Ten thousand pounds you'll get,
If you will undertake to bell
    Carson's big Orange cat.

Its offspring is over Ulster.
    In Halls and Clubs they dwell,
So you must try, upon the sly,
    Carson's Orange cat to bell.'

Said Joe Devlin, then, to Redmond:
    'I'd like to shed its blood,
Since I've been Member for the West
    At it I have thrown mud.

It always stands and humps its back,
    And spits when I am near;
I'd rather not take on the job,
    I hold my life too dear.

'Begone,' said Redmond, 'do your work,
    If not, why you'll regret;
March forth your mighty Ribbonmen,
    And bell that Orange cat.'

'No, no,' said Joe, 'I will not go
    Into the mouth of hell,

Text: Samuels Collection, TCD.

117

I'd rather throw up my M.P.,
    Than try that cat to bell.'

Then, ring loud the bells in Ulster,
    Lest that we should forget,
That they have not got the courage,
    To bell that Orange cat.

Men, Keep Your Rifles Free from Rust
J.P.G., Belfast

Text: Samuels Collection, TCD.

Let Ulstermen determined stand
Against Home Rule with heart and hand,
Or Rome her rule will on us thrust –
Men, keep your Rifles free from rust!

Rouse, Ulstermen, in vale and hill,
Be up and active – Drill, drill, drill!
Our Leaders tell us that we must –
Men, keep your Rifles free from rust!

That dear old Flag, the Union Jack,
Fight for its honour back to back;
Dare Rebel tramp it in the dust –
Men, keep your Rifles free from rust!

The Jesuits, through Redmond's mouth,
Speak to their dupes in West and South:
'There's gold up North, no more dry crust' –
Men, keep your Rifles free from rust!

We know what Rome did in the past,
When Spain her great Armada massed:
It came to glut her bloody lust –
Men, keep your Rifles free from rust!

King William at the glorious Boyne,
Our Fathers did his forces join,
And through King James's army burst –
Men, keep your Rifles free from rust!

The Freedom that our Fathers won
On bloody field midst crash of gun:
God did them help, their cause was just –
Men, keep your Rifles free from rust!

Jerry Connor's Forge

Teresa Brayton

By the crossroads of Knockallen where the bog and upland
   meet,
There's a tidy row of houses that the neighbours call 'the
   street';
It is free and independent, though it pays its tax to George,
For it runs its own Home Parliament in Jerry Connor's
   forge.

In the quiet dusk of evening, when the iron hammer rings,
That mighty song of labour that has raised and routed kings,
The members take their places, with their backs against the
   wall,
And who but Jerry Connor should be leader of them all.

For the tangles of Westminster there's little patience here,
Where State affairs are settled in the shoeing of a mare;
And bills that Whig and Tory view with sinking of the heart
Are fixed while Jerry rims the wheel of Kelly's donkey cart.

'Tis there the Kaiser's law is scorned, the Czar is roundly
   cursed,
And every ruling head declared no better than the worst,
When the world around, from China to the Rockies'
   farthest gorge,
Is tried before the Parliament in Jerry Connor's forge.

Pat Murphy is Conservative, and likes to hold his views,
Apart from other people's, like the bluest of the 'blues';
So when 'you're right there, Jerry, lad,' arises from the
   throng,
He'll croak: 'Bedad ye may be right – but then ye may be
   wrong.'

Mat Reilly is a Socialist, Jim Byrne stands for peace,
But little Billy Hennessy has little time for these,
With five foot two drawn up to look like six he'll fiercely
   cry –
'Thank God, I'm still a Fenian, boys, and not afraid to die.'

So though Westminster debates Home Rule for Erin still,
It long has passed the Parliament beside Knockallen hill;
Where destinies of nations, from the Caesars down to
   George,
Are settled while a mare is shod in Jerry Connor's forge.

Text: Teresa Brayton, *Songs of the Dawn and Irish Ditties*, P.J. Kennedy & Son, New York, 1913.

'Imperial Measure' by Thomas Fitzzpatrick, *The Lepracaun*, October 1906.

Paddy

Tom Kettle
(After Mr Kipling)

I went into the talkin' shop to see about the Bill;
The Premier 'e ups and says: 'We're waitin' . . . waitin' still!'
The Tories grinned, and Balfour strung our gamble Harman-high,
I outs into the street again, and to meself sez I:
O, it's Paddy this, and Paddy that, an' 'A cattle-driven crew!'
But 'twas 'Murphy o' the Munsters!' when the trump of battle
    blew.
When the wind of battle blew, my boys, when the blast of battle
    blew,
It was Burke, and Shea and Kelly when we marched to Waterloo.

I looked into a newspaper to see about the land
That bred the man who broke the sin that Bonaparte planned;
They'd room for cricket scores, and tips, and trash of every kind,
But when I asked of Ireland's cause, it seemed to be behind.
For it's Paddy this, and Paddy that, and 'Don't annoy us please!'
But it's 'Irish Rifles forward – Fast!' when the bullets talk like bees,
When the bullets yawn like bees, my boys, when the bullets yawn like
    bees,
It's 'Connaught blood is good enough' when they're chanting
    RIPs.

Yes! Sneerin' round at Irishmen, and Irish speech and ways
Is cheaper – much – than snatchin' guns from battle's red amaze:
And when the damned Death's-Head-Dragoons roll up the ruddy
    tide
The *Times* won't spare a Smith to tell how Dan O'Connell died.
For it's Paddy this, and Paddy that, and 'The Fifth'll prate and prance!'
But it's 'Corks and Inniskillings – Front!' when Hell is loose in France,
When Clare and Kerry take the call that crowns the shrapnel dance,
O, it's 'Find the Dublin Fusiliers!' when Hell is loose in France.

We ain't no saints or scholars much, but fightin' men and clean,
We've paid the price, and three times thrice for Wearin' o' the
    Green.
We held our hand out frank and fair, and half forgot Parnell,
For Ireland's hope and England's too – and it's yours to save or sell.
For it's Paddy this, and Paddy that, 'Who'll stop the Uhlan blade?'
But Tommy Fitz from Malahide, and Monaghan's McGlade,
When the ranks are set for judgment, lads, and the roses droop and
    fade,
It's 'Ireland in the fightin' line!' when the price of God is paid.

This is a parody of Rudyard Kipling's poem 'Tommy' which starts, 'I went into a public-'ouse to get a pint o' beer'.

Text: Tom Kettle, *Poems & Parodies*, The Talbot Press, Dublin, 1916.

121

Prepare Again, Brave Irishmen

Text: Samuels Collection, TCD.

Prepare again, brave Irishmen,
    Be ready for the Call,
Your motherland is waiting
    And watching for you all
To free her from the bondage
    Of British slavery,
And to strike again another blow
    For Erin's liberty.

We're proud that we are Irish,
    And Irish Volunteers,
Who dread no Saxon tyranny,
    Or heed their cruel sneers.
Our leaders have proved true to us,
    For us they nobly died;
But vengeance shall be with us
    Ere the widows' tears are dried.

Thanks to Judas Redmond
    For our hard and bitter case,
And all the cruel misfortunes
    That befell our Irish race.
He was the only lapdog
    That our British Tyrant had,
To them he sold his country
    As Judas sold his God.

With 'Home Rule' on the statute book,
    Recruiting he did go,
In hopes to gain more British gold
    For himself and honest Joe.
He thought to dupe our Irish boys
    To fight the honest Hun,
To the shambles out in Flanders
    He would send them one by one.

No wonder that our country
    In mourning deep should be,
Since they shot down Clarke and Plunkett,
    And Pearse and Connolly,
McDermott, Daly, Eamonn Kent,
    And Colbert from Athea,
They are numbered with the martyred ones
    Who rose to set us free.

May God be with those heroes,
    Their troubles are all o'er;
They are looking down from Heaven
    For the freedom of our shore –
The freedom which they strove for;
    But the fight was not in vain,
They raised our land and made her
    The 'one bright Spot' again.

123

When the Pigs Begin to Fly
A Song of the Irish Parliamentary Party, 1914

Brian O'Higgins

The songs and poems of Brian
O'Higgins (aka 'Brian na Banban')
would fill a book on their own. He
was incredibly prolific, and several
of his pieces have entered the Irish
tradition and become 'folk-songs'.

Text: Brian O'Higgins, *The Voice
of Banba*, Dublin, 1931.

Don't fret about Ireland's freedom,
   'Twill come when we see Home Rule,
'Tis as sure as there's wool on a nanny-goat,
   Or twenty tails on a mule;
Don't fret about Ireland's freedom,
   Fight on, and never say 'why?'
We'll win it yet on the Floor of the House
   (When the pigs begin to fly).

This talk about over-taxation
   Is only a blooming hoax,
And making us pay for the dish he eats
   Is one of John Bull's wee jokes;
His Liberal boys are with us,
   Telling us how to die,
And we'll bluff him yet on the Floor of the House
   (When the pigs begin to fly).

Our noble and gallant Party
   Are true to the inmost core,
And are willing to make more speeches
   Than ever they made before;
They'll tell us that hens wear feathers,
   That the stars are up in the sky,
And they'll tell the truth about Ireland's needs
   (When the pigs begin to fly).

So, gallop along to the colours,
   The 'no-far-distant day'
Is nearer than ever it was before
   (No matter how far away);
We must help the Belgians first, you know,
   And the Serbians by-and-by,
And we'll think about Ireland later on
   (When the pigs begin to fly).

The United Irish Parliamentary Minstrels

'Way down beside the old Thames river –
  Over the way –
Now won't we make old John Bull shiver
  If he tries any more delay;

All up and down the 'Old Saint Stephen's' –
  Sadly we roam –
Still hollering the old, old grievance,
  The loss of the Old House at Home.

Chorus
Now behold us all united
  'Neath Westminster's dome;
Soon will we have our wrongs all righted
  Safe in the Old House at Home.

Saint Stephen's Hall is a part of the Palace of Westminster, and 'The Old House' is the former Irish parliament house in Dublin's College Green, since the Act of Union a branch of the Bank of Ireland.

A parody of Stephen Foster's minstrel song 'The Old Folks at Home', this song, and the accompanying cartoon by Thomas Fitzpatrick, were published in *The Lepracaun* in February 1908.

The United Irish Parliamentary Minstrels.

The figures depicted in the cartoon above are (l–r):
Tim Healy, John Dillon, John Redmond, T.P. O'Connor and William O'Brien.

125

The Wreck of the Party

This poem is a parody of Longfellow's 'The Wreck of the Hesperus'.

Tay Pay (verse 2) was T.P. O'Connor MP, and 'melancholy John' was John Dillon MP.

Major General Friend, mentioned in this song (verse 5) and in the next (verse 2), was the British army commander-in-chief in Ireland from 1914 to 1916.

The Spark was a nationalist newspaper, published by Joseph Stanley's Gaelic Press.

The cartoon below is of 'Melancholy John' Dillon MP, by G.R. Halkett, from Charles L. Graves, *The Blarney Ballads*, Swan Sonnenschein & Co., London, 1893.

Text: Ballad sheet in The National Library of Ireland.

It was the Irish Party
   That sailed the Political Sea,
And the Leader had taken little Home Rule Bill
   As a cu-ri-os-i-ty.

Poor Bill had an accident at his birth,
   Tho' his godfather was Tay Pay,
'We'll land him in Ireland,' the Leader said,
   'At no far distant day.'

'Full steam ahead,' the Leader cried,
   'Let each man search his soul,
And, Joe, you re-organize the "Lague",
   Tell 'em we're in sight of goal.'

Then up and spoke 'Melancholy John',
   Who had tried to lead in vain,
'I pray thee, of the "sharp curve" beware,
   For I hear on the breeze "Sinn Féin".'

Last night the moon was a German gold,
   And to-day 'The Spark' is out,
But the Leader, he said, 'Friend and myself
   Know well what we're about.'

Bolder and bolder grew 'The Gael',
   It spread from town to town,
The Fossils in Kildare Street Club
   Said 'The Gael' must be put down.

Down came 'The Castle' in the night
   With all its bag of tricks;
They stole a blue lead pencil and
   A Postal Order for two-and-six.

Come hither! come hither! my little Charter,
   And do not trouble so,
For I can weather the toughest Gael
   That e'er Sinn Féin did blow.

He wrapped him in his Union Jack,
   'Oh, Bill, how pale you look?'
Then with a vote of confidence
   Bound Bill to the Statute Book.

'Oh, Leader, I hear the people's voice
   And 'tis not the voice of a mouse';
''Tis but the whine of Factionists,'
   And he steered for the 'Floor of the House'.

'Oh, Leader, I hear the sound of a gun,
    May I its meaning learn?';
''Tis the Sinn Féin mob in Tullamore,
    But they've only shot Ahern.'

'Oh, Leader, I see no ray of light;
    Oh, now unloose my cords';
But the Leader answered: 'The game is up,
    I'm off to the House of Lords.'

A Peer of the Realm, God save the King,
    With his jaw turned towards the Queen,
And the people said as they turned away,
    Good Lord what mugs we've been.

The One Bright Spot

Oh! we've changed the name of Erin
    To 'The One Bright Spot',
And an Empire now we're sharing
    In the One Bright Spot.
For we've got Home Rule, they say,
Or, at least, it's on the way,
Yes, and so is Judgment Day,
    To the One Bright Spot,
And till Tib's Eve, wait we may,
    In the One Bright Spot.

Oh, we send all cranks to jail,
    In the One Bright Spot,
If they dare use *Teanga na nGaedheal*,
    Or such beastly rot.
For the Realm we'll defend,
And to jail the lot we'll send,
If they don't obey our 'friend'
    In the One Bright Spot,
Oh, the prison is their end,
    In the One Bright Spot.

We've got a guard of G-men,
    In the One Bright Spot,
Just to let us know we're free-men,
    In the One Bright Spot.
You will find them in the street –
You will know them by their feet –
They're the boys that can retreat,
    If they hear a shot,
And they're always on the beat,
    In the One Bright Spot.

On the eve of the war, 3 August 1914, the Foreign Secretary Sir Edward Grey made a speech in the House of Commons that led Parliament to declare war on Germany. In the course of it he reflected on the situation in Ireland. Giving his assessment that the House need not regard Irish affairs as a factor that might deter the United Kingdom from going to war, he said: 'One thing I would say. The one bright spot in the whole of this terrible situation is Ireland.'

The text is taken from *Songs & Poems, The Rebels Who Fought and Died for Ireland in Easter Week, 1916*, copies of which may be found in the National Library of Ireland and in the Samuels Collection in TCD.
    Again, 'The Shan Van Vocht' is clearly the model on which the song was made.

And we've taxes now *go leor*,
   In the One Bright Spot,
Only just eight millions more,
   In the One Bright Spot.
For we've got to help the 'boss',
Johnny Bull, who lives across,
Oh, he runs us 'at a loss',
   In the One Bright Spot,
Mrs Britannia might be cross
   With the One Bright Spot.

But I'm told there are soldiers too,
   In the One Bright Spot,
Who are pledged to Ireland true,
   In the One Bright Spot.
For old Eire still has sons
Who are fit to 'man the guns',
And to drive all British Huns
   From the One Bright Spot,
And to keep them on the run,
   From the One Bright Spot.

Cartoon by Ernest Kavanagh, *The Irish Worker*, 7 November 1914.

All by the Baltic Say

Percy French

Once there was a Kyser
Whose head was of great size, sir,
And lived by telling lies, sir,
    All by the Baltic Say.

He'd wire to Pretoria
'Dear Kruger I implore ye
Knock spots off Queen Victoria
    All by the Baltic Say.'

And when the Queen resinted
Such conduct, he repinted
An' said he never mint it
    All by the Baltic Say.

He'd an army of five millions
Who treated all civilians
As low and vulgar villyans
    All by the Baltic Say.

Sez he, 'Me proper station
And natural vocation
Is King of all creation
    All by the Baltic Say.'

'I'll mobilize me Prooshans
And send them dirty Rooshans
To finish their ablutions
    All by the Baltic Say.'

'All treaties I'm evadin'
An' with high Heaven aidin'
In blood I'll soon be wadin'
    All by the Baltic Say.'

But Belgium said 'I bar you'
And Britain said 'I dar you'
And France said, 'Vell vare are you?'
    All by the Baltic Say.

So while his army waited
Till Liège was occupied
His plans they were frustrated
    All by the Baltic Say.

'Yunkers', properly 'Junkers' (verse
13) is a reference to the landed gentry
and aristocracy of Germany.

Text: James N. Healy, *Percy French &
His Songs*, Mercier Press, Cork, 1966.

The great siege guns they thunder'd,
The Germans killed and plunder'd,
But soon they found they'd blunder'd
    All by the Baltic Say.

For men who go to battle
Like droves of driven cattle
Feel bad when bullets rattle
    All by the Baltic Say.

An' now that they've retreated,
Dishearten'd and defeated,
They'll not be so conceited
    All by the Baltic Say.

The officers called 'Yunkers'
May not be quite such funkers
But they are well named 'Young Curs'
    All by the Baltic Say.

And hymns of peace will rise, sir,
From Europe to the sky, sir
When there shall be no Kyser
    All by the Baltic Say.

'Am Tag'
(To the Day)
Percy French

The 'double-faced fowl' of the second refrain is the double-headed eagle, the heraldic emblem of the Hapsburg Dynasty.

Text: James N. Healy, *Percy French & His Songs*, Mercier Press, Cork, 1966.

For years I have heard a curious word,
    'Tis German, I'm told, for the Day;
'Am Tag' it is spelt, and to Saxon or Kelt
    A thread it is meant to convey.
It means the dread hour when Germany's power
    Shall pull down Britannia's Flag,
And Kings will Kow-tow to old Billy Bow-wow,
    That's what Germany means by 'Am Tag'.

Refrain
Oh Bill, with the bluster and brag,
You may rage at that 'little red rag';
    I'll bet you a crown
    that you don't pull it down,
For all your tall talk and 'Am Tag'.

'You are arming for war,' cried Bill to the Czar,
    'An' what if I am' said old Nick;
'Oh, nothing,' said Bill, 'If you will, sure you will,
    But I call it a scoundrelly trick.'
'I could flatten out France, and then there's a chance
    Of adding John Bull to my bag;
But the Belgians and you 'leppen' out at me too,
    Is playing the puck with 'Der Tag'.'

Refrain
'But,' says he, with his bounce and his brag,
As he flourished his freak of a flag,
    'I'll sit cheek by jowl
      on Windsor, yer sowl,
With this double-faced fowl on 'Der Tag!"

So he trained every one to handle a gun,
    And kept them three years at their drill;
But they never could hit a haystack if it
    Didn't keep most uncommonly still.
'Keep charging en masse,' said the Kaiser; 'alas,
    If they shoot you, die for the flag;
There are millions behind, so I don't really mind
    How many they shoot on 'Der Tag'.'

Refrain
Oh Bill, with your bounce and your brag,
There are ghosts at your carriage wheels drag,
    And the victims that call
      from Louvain's blackened wall
Will hasten your fall on 'Der Tag!'

You may train up your sons to be latter-day Huns,
    But we'll catch you and cage you at last;
For you've proved such a pest that no nation can rest
    Till Prussia's a thing of the past.
The God that you prized was the devil disguised,
    And while you sail under his flag,
There is rapine and loot for each beer-sodden brute,
    But we'll send in the bill on 'Der Tag'.

Refrain
But it's no time to boast or to brag,
While the pendulum's still on the wag;
    The peril's not passed,
      to the Standard fly fast,
Or we'll ne'er hear the last of 'Am Tag!'

At the Cross Roads
Maeve Cavanagh

Maeve Cavanagh saw the outbreak of war as an opportunity for Ireland to stage a rebellion, and expressed this view forcefully in several poems.

Text: Maeve Cavanagh, *Sheaves of Revolt*, Dublin, 1914.

Whilst a craven England struggles for life,
    And continents lock in the throes of war,
The roar of the tumult to Ireland comes
    As the voice of Freedom's ambassador.

And many a boundary line shall fade,
    And ancient standards be lowered for aye –
Will Ireland alone stand effortless, bound,
    When the war dust, at last, has cleared away?

Nay – hark to the call of Ireland ringing,
    Over her cities and yellowing plains;
You who would free her, strike now and quickly,
    Ere forever the one great moment wanes.

The call and the moment have come at last –
    As we prayed and hoped – did we mean that prayer?
Would you traitors prove to the creed of Tone –
    Who dally and halt at the cross-roads there?

Ireland your answer impatiently waits –
    Beware of the traitorous council now,
History shall tell of the choice you made
    Of the perjured oath, or the rebel's vow.

The Wreck of the S.S. 'Britannia'
Maeve Cavanagh

Text: Maeve Cavanagh, *A Voice of Insurgency*, Dublin, 1916.

In War's fierce hurricane she sinks,
    Her flag droops lower day by day,
And every nation from her shrinks,
    The know the End – and go their way.
An evil ship that founders fast,
The pirate's sign still at her mast.

Her decks defeats' dark waters sweep,
    The rats in panic leave her sides,
Towed by the battered, sinking heap,
    A captive ship beside her rides.
Must she, too, in Death's course be set
Because some weakling cries 'Not Yet'?

Has fear or sleep her crew o'erborne
 That ne'er from scabbard flashes sword
To cut the tow-rope, thin and worn;
 Is there no man to give the word.
Must Ireland ever captained be
By landsmen scared of storm and sea?

Ireland to Germany

Maeve Cavanagh

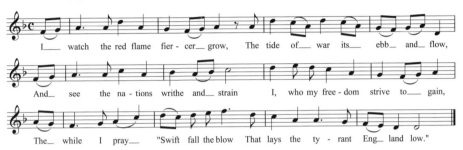

I watch the red flame fiercer grow,
The tide of war, its ebb and flow,
And see the nations writhe and strain.
I, who my freedom strive to gain,
The while I pray 'Swift falls the blow
That lays the tyrant England low.'

On her whose fetters seared my soul,
Whose rule is cursed from pole to pole,
Whose track across my hist'ry lies
One reeking path of infamies.
Whose brutal hoofs scarce left a trace
Of my past beauty in my face.

Thy stroke be sure, O Germany,
This wish I send thee o'er the sea,
From Shannon fair to lordly Rhine;
The foe who fronts thee, too, is mine;
I would my hosts with thine could be,
And my revenge thy victory.

My sons, as thine, are true and brave
To aid thee in thy task they crave,
To bring the pride of England low,
And vengeance wreak for all my woe;
God grant 'tis thine to overthrow,
And crush to earth our common foe.

This piece was first published as a
poem in *Irish World* in August 1915,
and subsequently issued as sheet music
with an air by Cavanagh's husband
Cathal Mac Dubhghaill. There are
slight differences in the text of the two
versions. The text here is the one that
was published in sheet-music form..

In *The Worker's Republic* of 11
December 1915, James Connolly
referred to it in these terms: 'A piece of
verse calculated to make the red blood
hot in the veins of every true lover of
freedom in Ireland. We had it in type
for publication when the Competent
Military Authority swooped down
upon us, and suppressed us.'

133

The Last Hill

Maeve Cavanagh

Text: Maeve Cavanagh, *Sheaves of Revolt*, Dublin, 1914.

Bayonets are clashing and trumpets blare
    O'er the red plains of a continent vast,
And England our foe, is struggling there
    For a prestige and power now waning fast.

And the gates of the City of Freedom ope
    To her who long watched by her western sea,
Who Destiny challenged with quenchless hope,
    Born of a vision of greatness to be.

You who for Ireland that hope would fulfil,
    Sink creed and party and severing line,
Linked in brave brotherhood storm the last hill,
    Thus from war's chaos will rise Ireland's sign.

Ireland's Overture to Germany

Maeve Cavanagh

Text: Maeve Cavanagh, *A Voice of Insurgency*, Dublin, 1916.

Before the conquering Teutons' might
My ancient foe reels in affright,
Soon History shall breathless write
    A tyrant's doom.

No puling pity, basely born
For her that day shall stem my scorn,
When from its pinnacle is torn
    Her crime-smirched flag.

For centuries I've lived for this
E'en in the depths of woe's abyss,
No phase of England's shame to miss,
    When came her hour.

Proud Germany, if thou had'st been
The fiercest nation earth had seen,
With no one thing to choose between
    Your sins and hers.

I'd still to thee my hand extend,
Thy hate and mine for her should blend
For e'er her foe shall be my friend
    Her friend my foe.

No helot I who'd masters change,
Nor wanton fain for lovers strange,
But one who Freedom's heights shall range
　　　In Fate's despite.

Then lend me of your power to-day
To wrest my land from England's sway,
Nor cost, nor recompense I'll weigh
　　　That honor knows.

Another Chant of Hate

Rosalie M. Moynahan

French and Russian, they matter not,
Some wrong remembered, some good forgot.
England stands at the Bar alone,
Nemesis rises to claim her own.
Ireland or Belgium – dare you say
Whose wrongs cry loudest this Judgment Day,
　　ENGLAND?

For not in a sudden, swift campaign,
The World as Mourner, was Ireland slain;
No soldier's steel plunged straight to her heart –
The sword you wield has a finer art.
Deep in the darkness of your hold
You forged it with hate, you weighed it with gold;
You drew it with lust, you swung it with sin,
Sure and stealthy you thrust it in,
And never have plucked it out again,
　　ENGLAND!

You cry aloud through the printed page
'For Liberty, Honor, the fight I wage!'
Australia, Canada, governed well'
Aye! They are distant, might rebel.
Ireland, helpless under your heel,
Proof of the value those words conceal!
You have wrenched their Celtic tongue away,
But their hate cries out in your tongue today,
And casts your treacherous past in the way,
　　ENGLAND!

Yet why the past do we judge you by?
Stricken Belgium must deny,
But we aloud to the world can cry:

Shortly after the outbreak of the war a poem by Ernst Lissauer was published in the Munich illustrated paper *Jugend*. Translated by Barbara Henderson, it was published in the *New York Times* on 15 October 1914 under the title 'A Chant of Hate', and inspired several imitations, including this one, published two days later, which preserves Henderson's first line. On 14 November the same year it was published in *The Irish Volunteer*, Vol. 1, No. 41.

Text: This poem was anthologized in *Contemporary War Poems*, New York, 1914.

'You pledged your power to be her shield,
You pledged her the millions your conquests yield;
What help can now the wrong atone?
You pledged your honor – She fought alone,
  ENGLAND!'

They have stood at the Judgment-Place,
The Saints, the Heroes of our race.
Through the long Night of the Tyrant's sin
Ireland has trusted her Cause to Him.
'Vengeance is Mine, I will repay,'
And God fulfills His Word today
  Through GERMANY!

Ireland to the British Empire

This piece has also been published as 'Ireland's Hymn of Hate' in *Songs & Poems, The Rebels Who Fought and Died for Ireland in Easter Week, 1916.*

Text: *The 1916 Song Book*, Irish Book Bureau, Dublin, n.d.

A withering curse upon thee –
  A curse from the vaults on high –
That shall wither your callous heartstrings
  Till the world shall hear you sigh!
Till the souls of the nations plundered
  To fill up your maw of greed
Shall laugh while your limbs are sundered
  And take a hand in the deed.

A curse from the God of Justice,
  A curse from the God of Might,
And thrice from a God of Nations,
  And again from a God of Right.
Across your path is a shadow,
  In your ears the eternal din
Of an Army that's ever marching
  To wipe out your heinous sin.

Then cursed be with gun and sabre,
  And cursed be with sword and pen;
On the sides of the lonely mountains
  'Midst the bustle and throng of men.
Accursed be with lead and burning,
  With boiling lead and brands
Snatched from the fires of nations
  By the bravest of many lands.

We have waited this hour of reckoning,
    We have longed for this day of strife,
As, back in the hours of anguish,
    Did the fathers who gave us life.
It has come with unmeasured slaughter,
    But there, 'midst the ruin and death,
The hosts of the Lord are waiting
    To stifle your poisonous breath.

C.E.B. Bernard, 'The Hole in the Wall', *The Literary Digest*, London, 2 April 1921.

The Shan Van Vocht

Text: Recruiting poster for the Munster Fusiliers.

Sound the bugles to advance!
    Says the Shan Van Vocht.
For the Germans are in France,
    Says the Shan Van Vocht.
On their track there lies a stain
From their frontier to the Aisne,
And their brand is on Louvain,
    Says the Shan Van Vocht.
And their brand is that of Cain,
    Says the Shan Van Vocht.

Oh! we're always for a fight,
    Says the Shan Van Vocht.
Whether wrong or whether right,
    Says the Shan Van Vocht.
But the sons of Erin know –
For they learned it long ago
How to strike their hardest blow,
    Says the Shan Van Vocht.
When their foe is Freedom's foe,
    Says the Shan Van Vocht.

Oh! from Cork to Donegal,
    Says the Shan Van Vocht.
We have answered to the call,
    Says the Shan Van Vocht.
We are off to take our chance,
Sound the bugles to advance!
For the Germans are in France,
    Says the Shan Van Vocht.
And we'll drive them out of France,
    Says the Shan Van Vocht.

Trade As Usual

Text: *The Workers' Republic* Vol 1, No. 19, 2 October 1915.

We fight 'gainst Might for Truth and Right, we stand for civilization.
We're known thro' all the ages as a Justice-loving Nation.
We never blew with dynamite, the Zulus from their caves.
We never paid for massacres of Yanks by Indian braves.
Our Cousins 'neath the Stars and Stripes revere and love us greatly,
For whenever we got half a chance we cozened them completely.
In 1812 our sympathy for them was quite amazing,
Ere we could tear ourselves away their Capitol was blazing,

And after when their fields were red with brother's life-blood flowing,
'Twas we supplied the weaker side to keep the struggle going.
The Fellaheens of Egypt our conduct will forgive,
For though we took their surplus wealth, we showed them how to live.
By shelling Alexandria we simply taught those slaves
That then as now the British fleet was built to rule the waves.
In Freedom's Cause at Omdurman our mercy was made plain,
When we killed the wounded Arabs, just to put them out of pain.
We saved the Danes some trouble once, just outside Copenhagen,
Before they knew we were at war their blooming fleet was taken.
And when the sands of India drank the blood of India's sons
We taught them rapid transit by blowing Sepoys from our guns.
We kept the Turk upon our side as long as he was wanted
Till Cyprus Island we secured, then from his cause Levanted.
The Boers once thought we were their foes, we cured them of their blindness
By catering for their wives and kids, and killing them with kindness.
The Treaty Stone of Limerick remains a faithful token
Beside the Lordly Shannon of our plighted word unbroken.
At Drogheda and Wexford town, with gun and pike and rapier,
We proved the sanctity we had for little scraps of paper.
The Wild Geese Ireland once produced are now domestic ganders,
They're highly prized and utilised upon the fields of Flanders.
When victory crowns our banners and we take the Dardanelles
High over all the warring notes, will ring with brave Irish yells.
But when they claim the price – Home Rule – we'll give them a refusal
Perhaps, Coercion we'll apply – Our Motto: Trade as Usual.

Preparing to blow Sepoys from the cannon's mouth, during the 'Indian Mutiny' of 1857.

We're Fighting Now for Christianity

Sliabh Ruadh (Phil O'Neill)

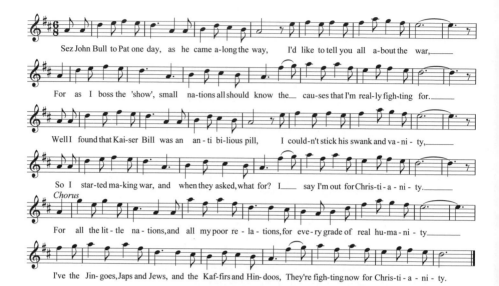

Sez John Bull to Pat one day, as he came a-long the way, I'd like to tell you all a-bout the war,

For as I boss the 'show', small na-tions all should know the cau-ses that I'm real-ly figh-ting for.

Well I found that Kai-ser Bill was an an-ti bi-lious pill, I could-n't stick his swank and va-ni - ty,

So I star-ted ma-king war, and when they asked, what for? I say I'm out for Chris-ti-a - ni - ty.

Chorus
For all the lit - tle na-tions, and all my poor re - la - tions, for eve - ry grade of real hu-ma-ni - ty

I've the Jin- goes, Japs and Jews, and the Kaf-firs and Hin-doos, They're figh-ting now for Chris-ti - a - ni - ty.

'Sliabh Ruadh' was the *nom-de-plume*, if not *nom-de-guerre*, of Irish Volunteer Phil O'Neill.

The fact that colonial troops, from both the British and French overseas empires, fought on the Western Front for the allies in World War 1 was not very well publicized in later years, although it seems to have been well known to the writer of this song.

The epithets used to signify the various races would be considered offensive nowadays, but were unremarkable at the time.

René Viviani, a freemason (verse 4), had been Prime Minister of France before the war.

Text: Samuels Collection, TCD.
Air: The tune 'Killaloe', which has been used as a regimental march in the British army since the late nineteenth century.

Sez John Bull to Pat one day, as he came along the way,
   I'd like to tell you all about the war,
For as I boss the 'show', small nations all should know
   The causes that I'm really fighting for;
Well I found that Kaiser Bill was an anti-bilious pill,
   I couldn't stick his 'swank' and vanity,
So I started making war, and when they asked 'What for'?
   I say I'm out for Christianity!

Chorus
For all the little Nations,
And all my poor relations,
   For every grade of real humanity!
I've the Jingoes, Japs and Jews,
And the Kaffirs and Hindoos,
   They're fighting now for Christianity!

I've got every class and clan, I've got every race of man,
   From Esquimaux to foolish Irishmen,
There's Arabs, Jews and Japs, and some flat-nosed nigger
   chaps
   Who'll prove to all that I'll be boss again;
Mike O'Leary from Macroom, and Sheik Haffi from
   Khartoum,
   Have enlisted in the cause of sanity,

There's the Gurkhas and the Sikhs, and the Mongos and
    the Mikes,
      All fighting now for Christianity!

There's Dagoes and Fijies, and now I've got Chinese,
    There's Cannibals and Hottentots galore,
There's men from God knows where, with feathers in their hair,
    To stop the Hun from landing on our shore;
So Pat my cordial friend, I'd like the war to end,
    Or else 'twill drive me to insanity,
'Tis for 'Faith and Fatherland', that all the Allies stand,
    For we're fighting now for Christianity!

I've Freemasons on my side, who you know are true and tried,
    You've heard of Viviani on the sly,
Who tried to stop the sun, if he couldn't stop the Hun,
    And put the stars from shining in the sky;
'Tis a just and blessed war, tho' slaughter I abhor,
    For I couldn't 'stick' the Kaiser's vanity,
So, Pat my gallant son, now's the time to get your gun,
    For we're fighting now for Christianity!

Indian soldiers at the Western Front in World War I.

The Huns

Text: Ballad slip, National Library of Ireland.

While your King and your country
    Are giving the call,
The factor and landlord
    Are making a haul.

At home quite contented
    Increasing the rent,
While Tommy poor devil
    Must go where he's sent.

To lighten their burdens
    The rents they increase.
It's poor Tommy's friends
    They're intending to fleece.

For such reasons as these
    We're entitled to grunt,
Till the factors and landlords
    Are sent to the front.

Screens
(in a hospital)
Winifred Mary Letts (1882–1972)

Text: Winifred Mary Letts, *Hallow-e'en and Poems of the War*, E.P. Dutton, New York, 1916.

They put the screens around his bed;
    A crumpled heap I saw him lie,
White counterpane and rough dark head,
    Those screens – they showed that he would die.

They put the screens about his bed;
    We might not play the gramophone,
And so we played at cards instead
    And left him dying there alone.

The covers on the screens are red,
    The counterpanes are white and clean; –
He might have lived and loved and wed
    But now he's done for at nineteen.

An ounce or more of Turkish lead,
    He got his wounds at Suvla Bay;
They've brought the Union Jack to spread
    Upon him when he goes away.

He'll want those three red screens no more,
  Another man will get his bed,
We'll make the row we did before
  But – Jove! – I'm sorry that he's dead.

The Call to Arms in Our Street

Winifred Mary Letts

There's a woman sobs her heart out,
  With her head against the door,
For the man that's called to leave her,
  God have pity on the poor!
    But it's beat, drums, beat,
    While the lads march down the street,
    And it's blow, trumpets, blow,
    Keep your tears until they go.

There's a crowd of little children
  Who march along and shout,
For it's fine to play at soldiers
  Now their fathers are called out.
    So it's beat, drums, beat;
    But who'll find them food to eat?
    And it's blow, trumpets, blow,
    Ah! the children little know.

There's a mother who stands watching
  For the last look of her son,
A worn poor widow woman
  And he her only one.
    But it's beat, drums, beat,
    Though God knows when we shall meet;
    And it's blow, trumpets, blow,
    We must smile and cheer them so.

There's a young girl who stands laughing,
  For she thinks a war is grand,
And it's fine to see the lads pass,
  And it's fine to hear the band.
    So it's beat, drums, beat,
    To the fall of many feet;
    And it's blow, trumpets, blow,
    God go with you where you go
    To the war.

Text: Winifred Mary Letts, *Hallow-e'en and Poems of the War,* E.P. Dutton, New York, 1916.

The Deserter

Winifred Mary Letts

Text: Winifred Mary Letts, *Hallow-e'en and Poems of the War,* E.P. Dutton, New York, 1916.

There was a man – don't mind his name,
    Whom Fear had dogged by night and day.
He could not face the German guns
    And so he turned and ran away.

Just that – he turned and ran away,
    But who can judge him, you or I?
God makes a man of flesh and blood
    Who yearns to live and not to die.

And this man when he feared to die
    Was scared as any frightened child,
His knees were shaking under him,
    His breath came fast, his eyes were wild.

I've seen a hare with eyes as wild,
    With throbbing heart and sobbing breath.
But oh! it shames one's soul to see
    A man in abject fear of death,

But fear had gripped him, so had death;
    His number had gone up that day,
They might not heed his frightened eyes,
    They shot him when the dawn was grey.

Blindfolded, when the dawn was grey,
    He stood there in a place apart,
The shots rang out and down he fell,
    An English bullet in his heart.

An English bullet in his heart!
    But here's the irony of life, –
His mother thinks he fought and fell
    A hero, foremost in the strife.

So she goes proudly; to the strife
    Her best, her hero son she gave.
O well for her she does not know
    He lies in a deserter's grave.

'The Deserter', Octav Bancila, 1906.

The Connaught Rangers
Winifred Mary Letts

I saw the Connaught Rangers when they were passing by,
On a spring day, a good day, with gold rifts in the sky.
Themselves were marching steadily along the Liffey quay
An' I see the young proud look of them as if it were to-day!
The bright lads, the right lads, I have them in my mind,
With the green flags on their bayonets all fluttering in the wind.

A last look at old Ireland, a last good-bye maybe,
Then the grey sea, the wide sea, my grief upon the sea!
And when will they come home, says I, when will they see once more
The dear blue hills of Wicklow and Wexford's dim grey shore?
The brave lads of Ireland, no better lads you'll find,
With the green flags on their bayonets all fluttering in the wind!

Three years have passed since that spring day, sad years for them and me.
Green graves there are in Serbia and in Gallipoli.
And many who went by that day along the muddy street
Will never hear the roadway ring to their triumphant feet.
But when they march before Him, God's welcome will be kind,
And the green flags on their bayonets will flutter in the wind.

Text: George Herbert Clarke (ed.), *A Treasury of War Poems 1914–1918*, Hodder & Stoughton, London, 1917 [sic].

Epiphany 1916
Winifred Mary Letts

The Kings still come to Bethlehem
    Though nineteen centuries have fled;
The Kings still come to Bethlehem
    To worship at a baby's bed.
And still a star shines in the East,
For sage and soldier, king and priest.

They come not as they came of old
    On lordly camels richly dight;
They come not bearing myrrh and gold
    And jewels for a king's delight.
All battle-stained and grim are they
Who seek the Prince of Peace to-day.

Text: Winifred Mary Letts, *Hallow-e'en and Poems of the War*, E.P. Dutton, New York, 1916.

They bring not pearls nor frankincense
　　To offer Him for His content.
Weary and worn with long suspense
　　With kingdoms ravished, fortunes spent,
They have no gifts to bring but these –
Men's blood and women's agonies.

What toys have they to please a child?
　　Cannon and gun and bayonet.
What gold? Their honour undefiled.
　　What myrrh? Sad hearts and long regret.
For they have found through bitter loss
That Kings are throned upon the cross.

The Kings still come to Bethlehem
　　With broken hearts and souls sore-vexed.
And still the star is guiding them
　　Through weary nights and days perplexed.
God greet you, Kings, that you may be
New-crowned at His Epiphany.

An Irish Mother's Lament

Text: Samuels Collection, TCD.

On Saturday night, when friends met, a mother did say:
'My son, my child and chief support, he is gone away.'
Hard I had to rear him since the day his father died,
And happy would I be today if he were by my side.
He joined the 18th Royal Irish, a smart and active corps,
And now he is at the Front where German cannons roar.

He left his good employment – many as well as he,
And went out to the battlefield to fight England's enemy.
I wish my boy was home again, how I'd welcome him,
My heart is bursting with grief, my eyes are growing dim.
Many a mother in Erin's Isle is grieved as well as me,
Thinking of the child she reared his face no more she'd see.

After every battle it is a dismal sight to see
Heaps of dead upon the field and more in agony.
Numbers of Irish boys, may the Lord receive their souls,
Without a shroud or coffin are buried in one hole.
Some of them died from hunger and more from plague,
To tell the truth, some from thirst, hardship and fatigue.

146

The shot and shell are roaring, as hundreds deplore
And many a cheerful Irish lad has fallen to rise no more.
Widows, wives and orphans, cheer up and do not fret,
For the boys who are at the front we will see them yet.
Plenty of money will be spent to support each family
Whilst Irishmen are fighting against England's enemy.

Mothers, wives and orphans, I hope you'll breathe a prayer
For poor sons on the battlefield, and do not shed a tear,
For God is their protection and will save them from the foe,
But many a mother's hard-reared son is in a trench laid low.

Gods of War
1914
George Russell (1867–1935)

Fate wafts us from the pygmies' shore:
   We swim beneath the epic skies:
A Rome and Carthage war once more,
   And wider empires are the prize;
Where the beaked galleys clashed; lo, these
Our iron dragons of the seas!

High o'er the cloudy battle sweep
   The winged chariots in their flight:
The steely creatures of the deep
   Cleave the dark waters' ancient night:
Below, above, in wave, in air,
New worlds for conquest everywhere.

More terrible than spear or sword
   Those stars that burst with fiery breath:
More loud the battle cries are poured
   Along a hundred leagues of death.
So do they fight. How have ye warred,
Defeated Armies of the Lord?

This is the Dark Immortal's hour,
   His victory, whoever fail;
His prophets have not lost their power:
   Caesar and Attila prevail.
These are your legions still, proud ghosts,
These myriad embattled hosts.

Text: George Russell, *Collected Poems*, Macmillan, London, 1919.

How wanes Thine empire, Prince of Peace!
   With the fleet circling of the suns
The ancient gods their power increase;
   Lo, how Thine own appointed ones
Make holy all Thy soul abhorred,
The hate on which Thy love had warred.

Who dreamed a dream mid outcasts born
   Could overbrow the pride of kings?
They pour on Christ the ancient scorn.
   His Dove its gold and silver wings
Has spread. Perhaps it nests in flame
In outcasts who abjure His name.

Choose ye your rightful gods, nor pay
   Lip reverence that the heart denies.
O Nations, is not Zeus to-day,
   The thunderer from the epic skies,
More than the Prince of Peace? Is Thor
Not nobler for world at war?

They fit the dreams of power we hold,
   Those gods whose names are with us still,
Men in their image made of old
   The high companions of their will.
Who build in air an empire's pride –
Would they pray to the Crucified?

O outcast Christ, it was too soon
   For flags of battle to be furled
While life was yet at the hot noon.
   Come in the twilight of the world:
Its kings may greet Thee without scorn
And crown Thee then without a thorn.

Apocalyptic
1915

George Russell

Text: George Russell, *Collected Poems*, Macmillan, London, 1919.

Our world beyond a year of dread
   Has paled like Babylon or Rome.
Never for all the blood was shed
   Shall life return to it as home.
No peace shall e'er that dream recall;
The avalanche is yet to fall.

Laugh, you whose dreams were outlawed things.
   The sceptre from the tyrant slips.
Earth's kings are met by those wild kings
   Who swept through the Apocalypse.
Ere the first awful hand be stayed,
The second shall have clutched the blade.

On the white horse is one who rides
   Until earth's empires are o'erthrown,
And a red rider yet abides
   Whose trumpet call is still unblown,
Whose battlefield shall be the grave
Either for master or for slave.

Once in a zodiac of years
   Earth stirs beneath her heaving crust,
And high and low, unheeding tears,
   Are equal levelled with the dust.
Laugh, slave, the coming terror brings
Thee to that brotherhood with kings.

Laugh too, you warriors of God,
   The tyrants of the spirit fail.
The mitred head shall no more nod
   And multitudes of men be pale.
When empires topple here below
The heavens which are their shadows go.

If the black horse's rider reign,
   Or the pale horse's rider fire
His burning arrows, with disdain
   Laugh. You have come to your desire,
To the last test which yields the right
To walk amid the halls of light.

You, who have made of earth your star,
   Cry out, indeed, for hopes made vain:
For only those can laugh who are
   The strong Initiates of Pain,
Who knows that mighty god to be
Sculptor of immortality.

Statesmen

George Russell

They tell us that they war on war. Why do they treat our wit with scorn?
The dragon from the dragon seed, the breed was true since life was born.
When has the lioness conceived the lamb beneath her tawny side?
When has the timid dove been born the offspring of the eagle's pride?
When Cherubim smite at their Light, oh! yes, we may believe this thing.
When Eblis risen in revolt casts from its shades their awful king.
We know how from the deeds men do a sudden blackness blinds the soul,
How kindled by their sacrifice lights up the instant aureole.
The thought, the deed, breed always true. Shall nations not the law obey?
Has not the Mighty Father store within His Treasure House to pay?
The noble and the base beget their kin, and empires ere they pass
See their own mirrored majesty arise within Time's looking-glass.
The pride that builded Babylon of Egypt was the mighty child:
The beauty of the Attic soul in many a lovely city smiled.
The empire that is built in pride shall call imperial pride to birth,
And with that shadow of itself must fight for empire of the earth.
Fight where ye will on earth or sea, beneath the wave, above the hills,
The foe ye meet is still yourselves, the blade ye forged the sword that kills.

Text: George Russell, *Collected Poems*, Macmillan, London, 1919.

P. Madeline, 'The Burning of Louvain' (*La Guerre documentée, 1914–1915*, No. 8).

Eight Millions of Englishmen

Brian O'Higgins

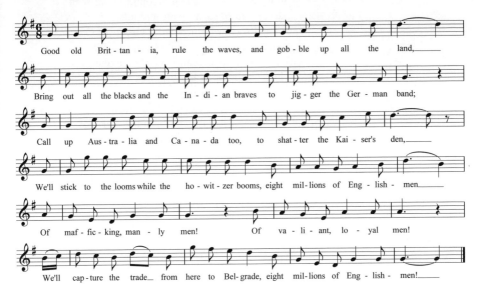

Good old Brit-tan-ia, rule the waves, and gob-ble up all the land,

Bring out all the blacks and the In-di-an braves to jig-ger the Ger-man band;

Call up Aus-tra-lia and Ca-na-da too, to shat-ter the Kai-ser's den,

We'll stick to the looms while the ho-wit-zer booms, eight mil-lions of Eng-lish-men

Of maf-fic-king, man-ly men! Of va-li-ant, lo-yal men!

We'll cap-ture the trade from here to Bel-grade, eight mil-lions of Eng-lish-men!

Good old Britannia! Rule the waves,
     And gobble up all the land.
Bring out the blacks and the Indian braves,
     To jigger the German band:
Call up Australia and Canada, too,
     To shatter the Kaiser's den,
We'll stick to the looms while the howitzer booms,
     Eight millions of Englishmen;
               Of mafficking, manly men!
               Of valiant, loyal men!
We'll capture the trade from here to Belgrade –
     Eight millions of Englishmen.

There are plenty of fools in Ireland still;
     Just promise them something soon –
A Union Jack or a Home Rule Bill,
     Or a slice of the next new moon –
And they'll rush to the colours with wild hurroos,
     What price the War Lord then?
They'll settle his hash, and we'll collar his cash,
     Eight millions of Englishmen;
               Of undersized, able men!
               Of home-loving, handy men!
We're shy of the guns, but we'll beggar the Huns,
     Eight millions of Englishmen.

Text: Brian O'Higgins, *The Voice of Banba*, Dublin, 1931.
Air: 'The Low-backed Car'.

151

So lug them along! It's a glorious thing
    To answer the Empire's call!
And it needn't cost you a bloomin' wing
    To get rid of them – one and all.
For we'll stay at home – stout Hearts of Oak –
    And with hammer, and plane, and pen,
We'll grab what we can from the furriner man,
    Eight millions of Englishmen;
        Of subborn, sturdy men!
        Of beef-eating, bulldog men!
We'll wave little flags and brandish our fags,
    Eight millions of Englishmen.

From the Trenches

Brian O'Higgins

Text: Brian O'Higgins, *The Voice of Banba*, Dublin, 1931.

We were out picking blackberries
    Along the River Aisne,
When up came seven thousand Huns
    Without a bally sign.
They shelled us hard from where they lay
    Upon a bally hill,
But we were British Tommies
    And we meant to have our fill.
We gathered all the blackberries
    (About a bally ton),
And then we charged the savages
    And set them on the run.
We slaughtered near a thousand –
    Shot the beggars as they ran –
And never lost a blackberry,
    Not to speak about a man!

'Gassed' by John Singer Sargent.

The Dreadnought Press

Brian O'Higgins

Ten little German armies, fresh from the Rhine,
The Freeman's Journal shattered one, then there were nine.
Nine little German armies, out one night too late,
Met *The Evening Telegraph*, then there were eight.
Eight little German armies – heedless all of heaven –
Crossed *The Irish Catholic*, then there were seven.
Seven little German armies, feeling in a fix,
Up came *The Independent*, then there were six.
Six little German armies, glad to be alive,
Down swooped the *Evening Herald*, then there were five.
Five little German armies, very sick and sore,
Faced the haughty *Irish Times*, then there were four.
Four little German armies, trying hard to flee,
Bumped against the Early Buff, then there were three.
Three little German armies, beaten black and blue,
Met *The Cork Examiner*, now there are two.
Two little German armies, always on the run;
Soon they'll meet *The Irish News*, then there'll be none.
No little German armies – hip, hip, hooray!
Home Rule in College Green at no far distant day!

Text: Brian O'Higgins, *The Voice of Banba*, Dublin, 1931.

Hearts of Oak

Brian O'Higgins

We don't want to work; but by Jingo if we do,
We'll capture all the German trade from Paisley to Peru;
We'll sweep it from the sea, and we'll wipe it from the
    land,
If only in the factories our boys united stand.
The Irish and the Scotch, they were born to be killed,
The Belgians and the Frenchy chaps for the same bright
    fate are billed;
But the gallant Hearts of Oak, for whose Ma the earth
    was made,
Are to dodge the fight in war-time and to capture
    German trade!

This poem is a parody of 'MacDermott's War Song' by George William Hunt, which was first performed in 1878.

That song caused the expression 'by jingo' (which used to be a minced oath, a euphemism for 'by Jesus') to assume its modern meaning. The word 'jingoism' is now a codeword for imperial bravado. An early example of this usage can be found in the poem 'Where is the flag of England?' on p. 46 (verse 4).

Text: Brian O'Higgins, *The Voice of Banba*, Dublin, 1931.

The Peelers and the German Spies

Brian O'Higgins

O, Pee-ler, 'tis pain-ful to hear, that your trou-bles are twice what they were, man,

And you'll soon be com-man-ded, I fear,___ to take up the stu-dy of Ger-man.

For the spies that come o - ver the seas to look at our bays and our har-bours,

Are be - co-ming as bu-sy as bees, and as plen-ty as ba-kers or bar-bers.

Chorus

Ri fol the dol ol the dol ay,___ ri fol the dol ol the dol a - mi-ty,___

Ri fol the dol ol the dol ay,___ yer - ra, man, it's an aw-ful ca - la-mi-ty!___

Text: Brian O'Higgins, *The Voice of Banba*, Dublin, 1931.
Air: 'In Glendalough Lived a Young Saint'.

O Peeler, 'tis painful to hear
    That your troubles are twice what they were, man,
And you'll soon be commanded, I fear,
    To take up the study of German:
For the spies that come over the seas
    To look at our bays and our harbours,
Are becoming as busy as bees,
    And as plenty as bakers or barbers.

Chorus
Ri fol the dol ol the dol ay,
    Ri fol the dol ol the dol amity,
Ri fol the dol ol the dol ay,
    Yerra, man, it's an awful calamity!

O Peeler, 'tis surely a sin
    What I hear has been ordered by Birrell –
That you'll have to get terrible thin,
    And as quick on the feet as a squirrel.
That you'll have to be up at the dawn,
    Patrolling the heath and the clover,
And listening for every yawn
    That comes on the breezes from Dover.

154

O Peeler, 'twas pleasure and peace
    To stop the unlawful trespasses
Of hens and of ducks and of geese,
    Of dogs and of goats and of asses;
To play with your curls in the court,
    And wink at your legal adviser;
But, my boy, it's a new kind of sport
    To be watching the spies of the Kaiser.

And to think, when you're going to bed,
    That as soon as your dreams are in motion,
A spy may be there at your head,
    To give you immediate promotion!
And a score of them out in the street,
    And a dozen in every passage,
To stab all the Peelers they meet,
    And chop them as fine as a sausage!

O Peeler, clear out with your life,
    And look for a new occupation,
Or seek for the right sort of wife
    That will save you from Germanization.
For 'the Force' is no longer a prize,
    Not a banquet of porter and chicken;
Between hunting for microbes and spies
    The profession has gone to the dickens.

When Tommy Comes Marching Home

Brian O'Higgins (1915)

When Tommy comes marching home again,
    Hurrah! Hurrah!
When Tommy comes marching home again,
    Hurrah! Hurrah!
We'll open the House in College Green,
And sweep the streets of Dublin clean,
And shout 'God Save the King!' –
    When Tommy comes marching home.

When Tommy comes limping home again,
    Hurrah! Hurrah!
When Tommy comes limping home again,
    Hurrah! Hurrah!

Text: Brian O'Higgins, *The Voice of Banba*, Dublin, 1931.
    Air: 'When Johnny Comes Marching Home Again', see p. 112.

155

With half a leg and a pair of toes,
A twisted head and a broken nose,
We'll wash every workhouse ward,
    When Tommy comes limping home.

When Tommy comes hopping home again,
    Hurrah! Hurrah!
When Tommy comes hopping home again,
    Hurrah! Hurrah!
We'll give him a penn'orth of English fags,
A bundle of disinfected rags,
And say 'Good-bye, Tom' –
    When Tommy comes hopping home.

When Tommy comes tumbling home again,
    Hurrah! Hurrah!
When Tommy comes tumbling home again,
    Hurrah! Hurrah!
We'll vaccinate the mice and rats,
And isolate the dogs and cats,
And sail for Timbuctoo –
    When Tommy comes tumbling home.

A War-Time Serenade

Brian O'Higgins (1915)

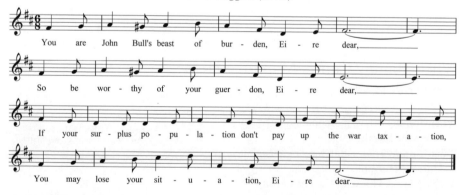

Text: Brian O'Higgins, *The Voice of Banba*, Dublin, 1931.
   Air: 'Sweet Marie' by Percy French.

You are John Bull's beast of burden,
        Eire dear,
So be worthy of your guerdon,
        Eire dear,
If your surplus population
Don't pay up the war taxation,
You may lose your situation,
        Eire dear.

Sure your Master owes you millions,
   Eire dear,
And he means to make it billions,
   Eire dear;
But he'll pay it all when Blarney
Changes places with Killarney,
And Fermoy flies up to Farney,
   Eire dear.

Weigh your words and don't offend him,
   Eire dear,
While his cousin tries to end him,
   Eire dear;
Pay the piper for his prancing,
But be sure to call it dancing,
And to say it's quite entrancing,
   Eire dear.

When the holy war is over,
   Eire dear,
That's the time you'll be in clover,
   Eire dear;
You'll have piles of presentations
From your Master's Little Nations –
But they'll all be new taxations,
   Eire dear.

The Tale of the Tinker Man

Sigerson Clifford (1913–1985)

Here's a health to you, Bard,
 And there's *sláinte* to me,
And may we both have thirsty throats
 Till Ireland will be free.
And the bed we'll get in heaven
 Let it be 'longside a pub;
Once eternity has liquor,
 Hell the use we'll have for grub.

I was never a chap for trouble,
 You might class me a man of peace,
If I ever saw fighting in the west
 I went whistling to the east.
For a broken skull's no ornament
 And bones are hard to mend,

A 'gom' (verse 4) is a foolish or innocent fellow.

Text: Sigerson Clifford, *Ballads of a Bogman*, Mercier Press, Cork, 1986.

157

And the big ashplant I carry,
    Sure it only flogs the wind.

In Dingle town I met Kitchener
    On a day I was five parts full,
And he gave me the silver shilling
    To win the war for Bull.
I swapped my ashplant for a rifle,
    Wrapped the puttees about my shins,
And clipped three years off Purgat'ry
    In France for my liquid sins.

'Twas a queer hotel in the trenches,
    Death paged us by day and dark,
For those wicked German snipers
    Could shoot the eye from a lark.
But a lifetime of dodging peelers
    Is training enough for a *gom*,
And devil the hole they drilled in me
    With bullet, bayonet or bomb.

One day there came a regiment,
    To beat a drum in the show,
And an English boy walked towards me
    And smiled, and said hello.
Shining gold he was, and handsome
    With his bandolier and gun;
Maybe he knew Greek and Latin
    But he didn't know the Hun.

So I sat me down to teach him,
    Praying he would not forget,
'Boy, don't you show an inch of hair
    Above that parapet.'
The laughter crinkled up his lips
    And wiped away the rule;
He like every beardless scholar
    Thought his schoolmaster a fool.

I tiptoed towards the dugout,
    At the door I turned around
As the boy fell like a broken branch
    From the parapet to the ground.
He lay there silent on his back,
    Staring at the skies,
And he never saw the round red hole
    Between his blind blue eyes.

Well, here's a health to you, Bard,
    And there's *sláinte* to me,
And may we both have throats to cool
    Till Ireland will be free.
And when we own four seas again
    We'll right our country's wrongs;
Till then I'll drink your stout, Bard,
    And you can sing my songs.

A Song for Cork

Dearest Nancy de Kaiser surrendered
    But don't be the least bit surprised
All his daring ambitions got hindered,
    When Redmond's bold troops mobilized.
All de Mollies from Morrison's Island,
    Dose brave hayroes that gained de Home Rule,
Were delighted at being united
    With O'Brien's Brigade from Blackpool.

Brudder Crosbie, whose writin's are famous,
    He refers to the Germans as Huns,
Said he'd order the Aicho shame us,
    If we didn't get Eyetalun guns.
All our men were in splendid condition,
    Fatty Higgins was leading the van,
Whilst the Lord Mayor with stately precision
    Kep de step close beside Squire M'Garm.

On de right Colonel Jameson Byrne,
    So-called since de night of de raid,

This song is a parody of Richard Milliken's 'De Groves of de Pool'.
    In verse 3 'Colonel Jameson Byrne' probably got his honorary rank as a result of his name, the satirical reference being to the provocative 'Jameson Raid' carried out against the Transvaal Republic in December 1895 by the British colonial official, Leander Starr Jameson.

Text: The *Workers' Republic*, Vol 1, No. 17, 18 September 1915.
    Air: 'The Groves of the Pool'.

159

Was explaining de right about turn,
    Dat's de goose-step to Redmond's Brigade.
On de left was that modern giant,
    He was formed by nature to rule,
Captain Donegan bould and defiant,
    Was de pictur of famed Finn Mc Cool.

When de Regiment marched past de Grand Stand, boys,
    With loud cheering de welkin did ring;
And de remnant of Barrack Street Band, boys,
    Made an effort at 'God Save the King'.
All de troops gave three cheers for de 'Ladder',
    For Great Britain, and Belgium and France,
For Ould Ireland, although they betrayed her,
    And den back to de pubs they advanced.

The Last Crusade
A Song of the Irish Armies
Tom Kettle

This song supports the 'fighting for England in WWI' stance. Tom Kettle served as an officer in the Royal Dublin Fusiliers, a British army regiment, and was killed on 9 September 1916 during the Battle of the Somme. Kettle, a Nationalist, had been influenced greatly to fight against Germany by the treatment of the Belgian civilian population by the German troops, when he was a newspaper correspondent in Belgium. The Mike O'Leary mentioned in 'The Old Soldiers Sing', is Sergeant Mike O'Leary VC, about whom there is a song entitled 'Sgt Michael O'Leary VC' in this collection. See p. 164. [LM]

Text: Stephen Gwynn and T.M. Kettle, *Battle Songs for the Irish Brigades*, Maunsel and Company, Dublin, 1915.

A wind blew out of the Prussian plain;
It scourged Liège, and it broke Louvain,
And Belgium shook with the trump of Cain,
    That a Kaiser must be mad.
'Iron is God!' – and they served him well –
'Honour a mark for shot and shell.'
So they loosed the devils out of Hell
    From Birr to Allahabad.

THE OLD SOLDIERS SING:
But we took them from Mons to the banks of the Marne,
And helped them back on their red return;
We can swim the Rhine if the bridges burn,
    And Mike O'Leary's the lad!

Not for this did our fathers fall;
That truth, and pity, and love, and all
Should break in dust at a trumpet call,
    Yea! all things clean and old.
Not to this had we sacrificed;
To sit at the last where the slayers diced,
With blood-hot hands, for the robes of Christ,
    And snatch at the Devil's Gold.

THE NEW SOLDIERS SING:
To Odin's challenge we cried Amen!
We stayed the plough, and laid by the pen,
And we shouldered our guns like gentlemen,
  That the wiser weak should hold.

Blood on the land, and blood on the sea?
So it stands, as ordained to be,
Stamp, and signet, and guarantee
  Of the better ways we knew.
Time for the plough when the sword has won;
The loom will wait on the crashing gun,
And the hands of peace drop benison
  When the task of death is through.

OLD AND NEW SOLDIERS SING:
Then lift the flag of the last Crusade!
And fill the ranks of the Last Brigade!
March on to the fields where the world's remade
  And the ancient dreams come true!

A Nation's Freedom

Tom Kettle

Word of the Tsar! and the drowse malign is broken;
  The stone is rolled from the tomb, and Poland free.
This is the strong evangel. The guns have spoken;
  And the scribble of flame of the guns is: Liberty.

Have you not met her, my lords, a-walk in the garden,
  Ranging the dawn, even she, the three times dead?
Nay! But in bondage, sundered from light and pardon –
  But now the water is wine, and the marriage read.

Word of the Tsar! My lords, I think of another
  Crowned with dolour, forbidden the sun, abased,
Bloodied, unbroken, abiding – Ah! Queen, my Mother,
  I have prayed the feet of the Judgment of God to
  haste.

Count me the price in blood that we have not
  squandered,
  Spendthrifts of blood from our cradle, wastefully true

This song draws a comparison between Poland and Ireland, and both countries' struggle for freedom. Verse 4 refers to the Irish who found a place in foreign armies, the Wild Geese who departed Ireland following the defeat of the Irish cause in the Williamite Wars in the late seventeenth century. [LM]

Text: Stephen Gwynn and T.M. Kettle, *Battle Songs for the Irish Brigades*, Maunsel and Company, Dublin, 1915.

161

Name me the sinister fields where the Wild Geese wandered!
  Lille and Cremona, and Landen, and Waterloo.

When the white steel-foam swept up on the tidal onset,
  When the last wave lapsed, and the tide turned back to
    the deep,
We were there in the waste and the wreckage, Queen of the
    Sunset!
  Paying the price of the dreams that cannot sleep.

The altar is set; uplifted again the chalice;
  The priest is in purple; the bell booms to the sacrifice,
The trumpets summon to death, and Ireland rallies –
  Fool or free? We have paid, and overpaid, the price.

Word of the Tsar! And Russia rises to vision,
  Poland and Ireland – that, my lords, was an augured fate.
The days draw in, and ways narrow down to decision –
  Will they chaffer, and cheapen, and ruin, or yield to be
    great?

WORKING ON CREDIT.

POLAND—" What are you getting for this job?"
ERIN—" A promise of Home Rule. And you?"
POLAND—" The same. I hope they won't both turn out to be 'Scraps of Paper.' "

Cartoon by 'Spex' (John Fergus O'Hea) in *The Lepracaun*, October 1914.

To My Daughter Betty, The Gift of God

Tom Kettle

The field, before Guillemont, Somme, 4 September 1916.

Text: Tom Kettle, *Poems & Parodies*, Talbot Press, Dublin, 1916.

In wiser days, my darling rosebud, blown
To beauty proud as was your mother's prime,
In that desired, delayed, incredible time,
You'll ask why I abandoned you, my own,
And the dear heart that was your baby throne,
To dice with death. And oh! they'll give you rhyme
And reason: some will call the thing sublime,
And some decry it in a knowing tone.
So here, while the mad guns curse overhead,
And tired men sigh with mud for couch and floor,
Know that we fools, now with the foolish dead,
Died not for flag, nor King, nor Emperor,
But for a dream, born in a herdsman's shed,
And for the secret Scripture of the poor.

Sergeant Mike O'Leary

Tom Kettle

It was Sergeant Mike O'Leary who broke the barricade,
Who took the chance, and won the Cross that crowns
　　the bayonet trade;
'Twas 'M'anam do Dhia,' and 'How's your heart', and
　　'How could we forget?'
But Michael from Inchigeela will fill a ballad yet.

Text: Tom Kettle, *Poems & Parodies*, Talbot Press, Dublin, 1916.

Oh! a fair and pleasant land is Cork for wit and
　　courtesy,
Ballyvourney East and Baile Dubh and Kilworth to the
　　sea:
And when they light the turf to-night, spit, stamp, swear
　　as of yore,
It's the Sergeant Mike O'Leary's ghosts that ward the
　　southern shore.

Sergeant Michael O'Leary, V.C.

Samuel S. McCurry

This song recounts and lauds the exploits of Sgt Mike O'Leary (1890–1961) of the Irish Guards Regiment of the British army. He was awarded the highest British military honour, the Victoria Cross, for his feat on the Western Front during WWI.

O'Leary hailed from Inchigeela, near Macroom, in West Cork. Macroom and Newtownards (verse 1), are towns in Cork and Down respectively, while Ballingeary, last verse, is another West Cork town, close to Macroom. [LM]

Text: Samuel S. McCurry, *The Ballads of Ballytumulty*, R. Carswell & Sons, Belfast, n.d.

Have you read of Mike O'Leary,
    Of the gallant Irish Guards?
Sure his raid upon the Germans
    Stirs the blood of Irish bards;
Through the world his fame is ringin'
And his feat of arms they're singin'
Where the shamrock green is springin'
    From Macroom to Newtownards.

Cried the Colonel one fine mornin',
    'We must take yon barricade,
Let the Huns have little warnin',
    Is there e'er a man afraid?'
'Not a man,' they answered cheery,
Then in front leapt Mike O'Leary,
And he fought till he was weary,
    He was perfect at his trade.

Five he felled with little trouble,
    Smashed them like a house of cards,
On he darted at the double
    For another sixty yards;
There he found three Germans standin',
Slew them while he had his hand in,
Och! he needed no commandin' –
    Mike O'Leary of the Guards.

But his heart withal was tender,
    And the final two he spared,
They thought better to surrender
    Seein' how the others fared;
Back he marched them single-handed,
On each arm a German bandit,
Not a man could understand it,
    While the Colonel laughed and stared.

When the thing got in the papers
    Sure at Windsor there was fun,
And the King himself danced capers
    When he found what Mike had done;
'Why,' he cried, 'this surely glosses
All our noble Army's losses,
Send him two Victoria Crosses,
    'Twere a shame to send him one.'

Then hurrah for Mike O'Leary,
    He's the boy of Irish vim,
From New York to Ballingeary
    May his glory never dim;
Sure the war would soon be over,
And the troops get back to Dover,
And the King would be in clover
    If he had some more like him.

'How Sergeant O'Leary of the Irish Guards won the VC', *The Sphere*, 13 March 1915.

165

Government

Eva Gore-Booth

Text: Eva Gore-Booth, *Poems of Eva Gore-Booth*, Longmans, Green & Co., London, 1929.

The rulers of the earth, savage and blind,
Have dug Gethsemane for all mankind.
For their honour and their glory and their pride,
In every age the heroes of all nations died.
Thus Joan of Arc and Socrates were slain
By the world's bane,
Jesus Christ a thousand years ago,
They servèd so,
And Roger Casement, just the other day,
Went the same way.
Now is their hour of power and life's despair
From blasted earth and desecrated air
The universal death that is their dream
Flows o'er the earth in a great lava stream,
Whelming men's thoughts in floods of liquid fire,
To light the old world's funeral pyre.
Shall then our hearts in hell-fire burn
To serve their turn?
God's splendid rebels, and men's stupid slaves
Earn the same graves.
Oh! rather let us scorn life's baser gains,
The joyless spoils of death-strewn battle plains,
Where for our rulers' glory and their lust
Some million human brains are bloodstained dust.
Far better labour for that purpose known
Unto the gods alone,
That hides behind the darkness and the storm
In every human form,
If but to die on God's dear battle plain,
Where daisies mount to life through sun and rain,
Whilst the wild winds their rapturous tumults rouse,
And the trees fight for beauty in green boughs.
Peace be to those who rule and hate and kill –
The world's true will
Has brought, in this dark hour of pain and strife,
A violet to life.

166

The Everyday of War
Patrick Macgill (1889–1963)

Text: Patrick Macgill, *Soldier Songs*,
E.P. Dutton & Co., New York, 1917.

A hand is crippled, a leg is gone,
    And fighting's past for me,
The empty hours crawl slowly on;
    How they flew where I used to be!
Empty hours in empty days,
    And empty months crawl by,
The brown battalions go their way,
    And here at the Base I lie!

I dream of the grasses the dew-drops drench,
    And the earth with the soft rain wet,
I dream of the curve of a winding trench,
    And a loop-holed parapet;
The sister wraps my bandage again,
    Oh, gentle the sister's hand,
But the smart of a restless longing, vain,
    She cannot understand.

At night I can see the trench once more,
    And the dug-out candle lit,
The shadows it throws on wall and floor
    Form and flutter and flit.
Over the trenches the night-shades fall
    And the questing bullet pings,
And a brazier glows by the dug-out wall,
    Where the bubbling mess-tin sings.

I dream of the long, white, sleepy night
    Where the fir-lined roadway runs
Up to the shell-scarred fields of fight
    And the loud-voiced earnest guns;
The rolling limber and jolting cart,
    The khaki-clad platoon,
The eager eye and the stout young heart,
    And the silver-sandalled moon.

But here I'm kept to the narrow bed,
    A maimed and broken thing –
Never a long day's march ahead
    Where brown battalions swing.
But though time drags by like a wounded snake
    Where the young life's lure's denied,
A good stiff lip for the old pal's sake,
    And the old battalion's pride!

The ward-fire burns in a cheery way,
    A vision in every flame,
There are books to read and games to play
    But oh! for an old, old game,
With glancing bay-net and trusty gun
    And wild blood, bursting free! –
But an arm is crippled, a leg is gone,
    And the game's no more for me.

Sir William Orpen, 'Soldiers Resting at the Front'.

The Dug-Out

Patrick Macgill

Deeper than the daisies in the rubble and the loam,
Wayward as a river the winding trenches roam,
Past bowed, decrepit dug-outs leaning on their props,
Beyond the shattered village where the lightest limber stops;

Through fields untilled and barren, and ripped by shot and shell –
The bloodstained braes of Souchez, the meadows of Vermelles,
And poppies crown the parapet that rises from the mud –
Where the soldiers' homes – the dug-outs – are built of clay and
blood.

Our comrades on the level roofs, the dead men, waste away
Upon the soldiers' frontier homes, the crannies in the clay;
For on the meadows of Vermelles, and all the country round,
The stiff and still stare at the skies, the quick are underground.

Text: Patrick Macgill, *Soldier Songs*, E.P. Dutton & Co., New York, 1917.

Dug-Out Proverbs

Patrick Macgill

Here are the Old Sweats' sayings. He tells the tale of his trade –
Gleanings from trench and dug-out, battle, fatigue, parade.

'Tis said the Boche has pluck enough. Of this I have no doubt,
But see him in the darkest light until you've knocked him out.

Your dug-out took you hours to build. Got broken in a minute!
A rotten shame! Be thankful, son, your carcass isn't in it.

And if one shelters you a night tend it roof and rafter,
And make it better than it was – for those who follow after.

'The trench is calm,' you say, my son. The Boche is keeping quiet.
Then keep your rifle close at hand. We soon shall have a riot.

A soldier's life is risky; it may end damn quick. Well, let it!
Since we get five francs every week we'll burst it when we get it.

You may cough and sneeze in your dug-out, but you can't go
anywhere.
There's little health around the house – the dead are lying there.

The word 'dirt' (verse 9) was the trench term for shells.

Text: Patrick Macgill, *Soldier Songs*, E.P. Dutton & Co., New York, 1917.

169

You may dig as deep as a spade can dig, but the Boche's eye can tell
Where the khaki moles have plied their trade, and the beggars burrow well.

Pray to God when the dirt flies over and the country flops about,
But stick to your dug-out all the same until you're ordered out.

When guns are going large a bit and sending gifts from Krupp,
You've got to keep your napper low, but keep your spirits up.

These are the dug-out maxims which the 'Old Sweats' fling about,
For the better education of the 'rooky' newly out.

The Guns

(Shivery-shake Dug-out, Maroc.)

Patrick Macgill

Text: Patrick Macgill, *Soldier Songs*, E.P. Dutton & Co., New York, 1917.

There's a battery snug in the spinney,
    A French seventy-five in the mine,
A big nine-point-two in the village
    Three miles to the rear of the line.
The gunners will clean them at dawning
    And slumber beside them all day,
But the guns chant a chorus at sunset,
    And then you should hear what they say.

Chorus
Whizz bang! pip squeak! ss-ss-st!
Big guns, little guns waken up to it.
We're in for heaps of trouble, dug-outs at the double,
And stretcher-bearers ready to tend the boys who're hit.

And then there's the little machine-gun –
    A beggar for blood going large.
Go, fill up his belly with iron,
    And he'll spit in the face of a charge.
The foe fixed his ladders at daybreak,
    He's over the top with the sun;
He's waiting; for ever he's waiting,
    The pert little vigilant gun.

Chorus
It's tit-tit! tit-tit! tit! tit! tit!
Hark the little terror bristling up to it!
See his victims lying, wounded sore and dying –
Red the field and volume on which his name is writ.

The howitzer lurks in an alley
   (The howitzer isn't a fool)
With a bearing of snub-nosed detachment
   He squats like a toad on a stool.
He's a close-lipped and masterly beggar,
   A fellow with little to say,
But the little he says he can say in
   A most irrepressible way.

Chorus
OO-plonk! OO-plonk! plonk! plonk! plonk!
The bomb that bears the message riots through the air.
The dug-outs topple over on the foeman under cover,
They'll slumber through revelly who get the message there!

The battery barks in the spinney,
   The howitzer plonks like the deuce,
The big nine-point-two speaks like thunder
   And shatters the houses in Loos,
Sharp chatters the little machine-gun,
   Oh! when will its chattering stop? –
At dawn, when we swarm up the ladders;
   At dawn we go over the top!

Chorus
Whizz bang! pip squeak! OO-plonk! sst!
Up the ladders! Over! And carry on with it!
The guns all chant their chorus, the shells go whizzing
   o'er us: –
Forward hearties! Forward to do your little bit.

A Lament
(The Ritz-Loos Salient)
Patrick Macgill

I wish the sea were not so wide
   That parts me from my love;
I wish the things men do below
   Were known to God above.

Text: Patrick Macgill, *Soldier Songs*,
E.P. Dutton & Co., New York, 1917.

171

I wish that I were back again
   In the glens of Donegal,
They'd call me coward if I return,
   But a hero if I fall.

'Is it better to be a living coward,
   Or thrice a hero dead?'
'It's better to go to sleep, my lad,'
   The Colour Sergeant said.

In the Morning
(Loos, 1915)
Patrick Macgill

Café Pierre le Blanc, Nouex les Mines, Michaelmas Eve, 1915.

Text: Patrick Macgill, *Soldier Songs*, E.P. Dutton & Co., New York, 1917.

The firefly haunts were lighted yet,
As we scaled the top of the parapet;
But the East grew pale to another fire,
As our bayonets gleamed by the foeman's wire;
And the sky was tinged with gold and grey,
And under our feet the dead men lay,
Stiff by the loop-holed barricade;
Food of the bomb and the hand-grenade;
Still in the slushy pool and mud –
Ah! the path we came was a path of blood
   When we went to Loos in the morning.

A little grey church at the foot of a hill,
With powdered glass on the window-sill.
The shell-scarred stone and the broken tile,
Littered the chancel, nave and aisle –
Broken the altar and smashed the pyx,
And the rubble covered the crucifix;
This we saw when the charge was done,
And the gas-clouds paled in the rising sun,
   As we entered Loos in the morning.

The dead men lay on the shell-scarred plain,
Where Death and the Autumn held their reign –
Like banded ghosts in the heavens grey
The smoke of the powder paled away;
Where riven and rent the spinney trees
Shivered and shook in the sullen breeze,
And there, where the trench through the graveyard
     wound,

The dead men's bones stuck over the ground
   By the road to Loos in the morning.

The turret towers that stood in the air,
Sheltered a foeman sniper there –
They found, who fell to the sniper's aim,
A field of death on the field of fame;
And stiff in khaki the boys were laid
To the sniper's toll at the barricade,
But the quick went clattering through the town,
Shot at the sniper and brought him down,
   As we entered Loos in the morning.

The dead men lay on the cellar stair,
Toll of the bomb that found them there,
In the street men fell as a bullock drops,
Sniped from the fringe of Hulluch copse.
And the choking fumes of the deadly shell
Curtained the place where our comrades fell,
This we saw when the charge was done
And the East blushed red to the rising sun
   In the town of Loos in the morning.

After Loos

Patrick Macgill

Was it only yesterday
Lusty comrades marched away?
Now they're covered up with clay.

Text: Patrick Macgill, *Soldier Songs*,
E.P. Dutton & Co., New York, 1917.

Seven glasses used to be
Called for six good mates and me –
Now we only call for three.

Little crosses neat and white,
Looking lonely every night,
Tell of comrades killed in fight.

Hearty fellows they have been,
And no more will they be seen
Drinking wine in Nouex les Mines.

Lithe and supple lads were they,
Marching merrily away –
Was it only yesterday?

A.D. 1916
Patrick Macgill

Text: Patrick Macgill, *Soldier Songs*,
E.P. Dutton & Co., New York, 1917.

The sky shows cold where the roof has been,
    But the stars of night are none the dimmer,
Where the home once stood are the ruins seen,
    But the brazier glows with a cheery glimmer.
And the old life goes and the new life fills
    The scenes of many a pleasant story,
And the bursting shells on the sentried hills
    Whisper of death but shout of glory!

Gutted and ripped the stricken earth,
    Where the bones of the restless dead are showing;
But the great earth breathes of life and birth,
    And ruin shrinks from the blossoms blowing.
The old life fails, but the new life comes
    Over the ruins scarred and hoary,
Though the thunder of guns and the roll of drums
    But make for death while they shout of glory.

The Night Before and the Night After the Charge
Patrick Macgill

Text: Patrick Macgill, *Soldier Songs*,
E.P. Dutton & Co., New York, 1917.

On sword and gun the shadows reel and riot,
    A lone breeze whispers at the dug-out door,
The trench is silent and the night is quiet,
    And boys in khaki slumber on the floor.
        A sentinel on guard, my watch I keep
        And guard the dug-out where my comrades sleep.

The moon looks down upon a ghost-like figure,
    Delving a furrow in the cold, damp sod.
The grave is ready and the lonely digger
    Leaves the departed to their rest and God.
        I shape the little cross and plant it deep
        To mark the dug-out where my comrades sleep.

The Listening Patrol

Patrick Macgill

With my bosom friend, Bill, armed ready to kill,
   I go over the top as a listening-patrol.
Good watch we will keep if we don't fall asleep,
   As we huddle for warmth in a shell-shovelled hole.

In the battle-lit night all the plain is alight,
   Where the grasshoppers chirp to the frogs in the pond,
And the star-shells are seen bursting red, blue, and green,
   O'er the enemy's trench just a stone's-throw beyond.

The grasses hang damp o'er each wee glow-worm lamp
   That is placed on the ground for a fairy camp-fire,
And the night-breezes wheel where the mice squeak and
   squeal,
   Making sounds like the enemy cutting our wire.

Here are thousands of toads in their ancient abodes,
   Each toad on its stool and each stool in its place,
And a robin sits by with a vigilant eye
   On a grim garden-spider's wife washing her face.

Now Bill never sees any marvels like these,
   When I speak of the sights he looks up with amaze,
And he smothers a yawn, saying, 'Wake me at dawn,'
   While the Dustman from Nod sprinkles dust in his eyes.

But these things you'll see if you come out with me,
   And sit by my side in a shell-shovelled hole,
Where the fairy-bells croon to the ivory moon
   When the soldier is out on a listening-patrol.

Text: Patrick Macgill, *Soldier Songs*,
E.P. Dutton & Co., New York, 1917.

A Soldier's Prayer

Patrick Macgill

Givenchy village lies a wreck, Givenchy Church is bare,
No more the peasant maidens come to say their vespers there.
The altar rails are wrenched apart, with rubble littered o'er,
The sacred, broken sanctuary-lamp lies smashed upon the floor;
And mute upon the crucifix He looks upon it all –
The great white Christ, the shrapnel-scourged, upon the
   eastern wall.

Text: Patrick Macgill, *Soldier Songs*,
E.P. Dutton & Co., New York, 1917.

He sees the churchyard delved by shells, the tombstones
   flung about,
And dead men's skulls, and white, white bones the shells
   have shovelled out;
The trenches running line by line through meadow fields
   of green,
The bayonets on the parapets, the wasting flesh between;
Around Givenchy's ruined church the levels, poppy-red,
Are set apart for silent hosts, the legions of the dead.

And when at night on sentry-go, with danger keeping
   tryst,
I see upon the crucifix the blood-stained form of Christ
Defiled and maimed, the merciful on vigil all the time,
Pitying his children's wrath, their passion and their
   crime.
Mute, mute He hangs upon His Cross, the symbol of His
   pain,
And as men scourged Him long ago, they scourge Him
   once again –
There in the lonely war-lit night to Christ the Lord I call,
'Forgive the ones who work Thee harm. O Lord, forgive
   us all.'

The Simple Soldier Man
William Orpen (1878–1931)

Text: *The Hobart Mercury*,
6 January 1933.

I hate the modern, simp'ring girls,
Their foolish walk, their stupid curls.
I hate all over-dressed young 'earls'
And ladies' bodies coiled with pearls –
To flaunt in earth's poor hungry face.

I hate society's worst disgrace,
Old women, who do keep their place
By mothering young men of talent
Until they spoil them,
Sicken and soil them
With all their useless nutriment.

Sir William Orpen, 'South Irish Horse, a Dubliner resting on his way to Arras Front'.
This image was used as the cover of the magazine *The Irish Soldier,* published by Easons of Dublin during WWI.
(Courtesy of Anne S.K. Brown Military Collection, Brown University Library.)

177

I hate myself
I hate them all,
All,
Except one man
Alone.
He I can admire
Truly
And with all my soul
Entire.

I mean the simple soldier man
Who when the Great War first began
Just died stone dead
From lumps of lead
In mire.
Or lived through hell
Words cannot tell
For four long years
And more
Of misery,
Until the war
Was ended.

No man did more
Before.
No love has been
By this world seen
Like his, since Christ
Ascended.

I am a coward –
And I hate
Myself
As much, or more
Than others of my breed.
Likewise
I hate the bully,
I hate the 'swank'
I hate the braggart.
I hate the 'crank'.

I hate all men who talk too loud,
Like those who glory when a crowd
Doth cheer them
On, to make long-winded words
About themselves.
And how the nations all do need them,
They, and their cursed breed, to lead them.

The South Down Militia

Oh___ boys, it was fine, when in bat - tle we did join
A___ long with good King Bil - ly at the bat - tle of the Boyne,
Says James "I'll take the first train home it's more than I can stand,
For the South Down Mi - li - tia is the ter - ror of the land."

O Boys, it was fine, when in battle we did join
Along with good King Billy at the Battle of the Boyne
Says James: 'I'll take the first train home; it's more than I
   can stand,
For the South Down Militia is the terror of the land!'

Chorus
You may talk about your Queen's Guards, Scots Greys and all,
You may rave about your Kilties and your gallant Forty-twa,
Or any other regiment under the King's command,
But the South Down Militia is the terror of the land!

When we went up to London, in September, '62,
The King and Queen and Dukes were there, parading for review,
'Oh, blood an' thunder!' says the Queen, as she waved her
   lily-white hand,
'Sure, the South Down Militia is the terror of the land!'

When Kruger heard the regiment was landed at Cape Town,
'De Wet,' says he, 'we're bet,' says he, 'they've sent out the
   South Down;
And De Wet, my boyo, that is true, we'll have to leave the Rand,
For the South Down Militia is the terror of the land!'

When we went out to Flanders to fight the awful Hun,
The Kaiser said to old Von Kluck: 'The war is nearly done!
I never thought the Orange Drum would beat the German Band –
Oh! the South Down Militia is the terror of the land!'

When the Sultan heard the regiment was at the Dardanelles,
He rushed out of his harem and gave three awful yells –
'Allah! Allah save us, save us or be damned!
For the South Down Militia is the terror of the land!'

See p. 13 for note on De Wet (verse 3).
   Another version may be found in the *Donagh Mac Donagh Songbook*, online at http://songbook1.tripod.com/So uthDownMilitia.html (accessed 12 April 2015).
   Peadar Kearney also wrote a version of this song which can be found below at p. 382.

Text: *The National Comic Song Book*, Irish Book Bureau, Dublin, n.d.

179

Neuve Chappelle

For— when we lan-ded in Bel— gium the girls— all danced with joy.—

Says one un-to the o - ther, "Here comes— an I - rish boy."—

Then it's fare thee well dear mo - ther, we'll do— the best we can,—

For you all— know well— that Neuve Cha-pelle was won by an I - rish - man.—

A note in the source states that this song was heard from a street-singer who was an ex-private in the Royal Inniskilling Fusiliers, and that it had been written by a Sergeant in the 27th Division. We are also told that 'it was the favourite song of the Inniskillings or the Irish Rifles, and was commonly sung when leaving the trenches or in the estaminets.'

Text: Gale Huntington and Lani Herrmann, *Sam Henry's Songs of the People*, The University of Georgia Press, Athens (GA) and London, 1990. It was originally published in Sam Henry's *Northern Constitution* newspaper column in December 1933.
Air: 'The Rambling Irishman', from *Songs of the People* and edited to fit the first verse.

For when we landed in Belgium the girls all danced with joy;
Says one unto the other, 'Here comes an Irish Boy.'
Then it's fare thee well, dear mother, we'll do the best we can,
For you all know that Neuve Chappelle was won by an Irishman.

Chorus
Then here's good luck to the Rifles, the Inniskillings, too;
The Royal Irish Fusiliers and the Royal Artillery, too;
For side by side they fought and died as noble heroes can,
And you all know well that Neuve Chappelle was won by
    an Irishman.

Said von Kluck unto the Kaiser, 'What are we going to do?
We're going to meet those Irishmen – the men we never
    knew.'
Says the Kaiser unto old von Kluck, 'We'll do the best we can,
But I'm telling you true that Waterloo was won by an Irishman.'

Paddy Atkins

This is another parody on Kipling's 'Tommy'. See p. 121. For a note on 'The Celt is going fast' (verse 3), see p. 278.
Note: the final verse is incomplete. No other version of the poem is known.

Text: E.G.B., *Songs & Poems, The Rebels Who Fought and Died for Ireland in Easter Week, 1916* (Samuels Collection, TCD).
Air: 'The Wearing of the Green'.

Oh, we slaughtered and we hunted them
    To Connaught or to hell,
Their babes we spiked, their boys and girls,
    To planters we did sell.
We hanged their priests, we banned their schools,
    We ground their very face,
We did our bit to wipe from earth
    The hated Irish Race.
'Twas Paddy here and Paddy there!
    And Papish dogs away!

But it's Paddy come and join us
    When the band begins to play.
And when the band begins to play, my boys,
When the band begins to play,
Oh, Paddy comes in useful when the band begins to play.

In later days we did not change,
    The self-same game we played;
We sent them off in coffin ships,
    Brought famine to our aid.
We killed their industries, we did,
    We made them starve or fly,
And if they asked for work, we said,
    No Irish need apply.
'Twas Paddy here and Paddy there!
    And dirty Irish swine;
But it's Paddy come, you're wanted,
    When we form the firing line.
When we form the firing line, my boys,
When we form the firing line,
You'll do to stop the bullets when we form the firing line.

We chuckled and we cried with glee,
    The Celt is going fast,
But times are changed, and we have found
    A use for him at last.
We've bitten off a bit too much,
    Our boys don't like the game;
So Pat can do the fighting while
    Old England gets the fame.
It's Paddy here and Paddy there,
    And Paddy form and dress,
But it's gallant English soldiers
    When the papers go to press.
When the papers go to press, my boys,
When the papers go to press,
We never mention Paddy when the papers go to press.

We've closed the ocean now to Pat,
    There's one place he must go –
Right across the way to Flanders,
    To fight our German foe;
And we put him in the fore front,
    To draw the Turkish shells –
We got rid of a lot of Paddies
    At the bloody Dardanelles.
It's Paddy here and Paddy there!

And skulking coward, we cry!
We won't even ask you nicely,
    But will make you come and die,
For our lads are very shy,
    And the Empire's going dicky,
    So you'll have to come and die.
It's Paddy here and Paddy there!
    And anything you please;
If Paddy's not a blinded fool,
    I fancy Paddy sees.

With the Dublin Fusiliers
Alfred Perceval Graves (1846–1931)

Text: A.P. Graves.
  Music: Irish air arranged by Charles
Villiers Stanford, published as sheet
music in 1924 by J.B. Cramer, London.

With lip contemptuous curling, she cried 'Is our flag
    above
Fold on fold unfurling, and Patrick pleading love?
When Irishmen together band in arms to aid a Sister
    Land,
And free her from a tyrant's hand, what true man wooes
    a woman?'
But when upon the morrow we marched to Death or
    Fame,
Full of sweet sorrow, my proud one weeping came.

Ah! have you seen Atlantic advance his green, relentless
    line
Against the cliffs gigantic and bury them in brine?
Thus on our stubborn foe we fell, while all around
    became one hell
Of bursting horror, wailing shell, dull glare and dreadful
    shadow.
Yet still with forward faces went down our dauntless men,
Still to their places as gallant hearts stepped in.

Until our onset glorious the foe's fastness thundered
    through,
And from our van victorious his sullen rank withdrew.
Then Peace returned and from the war by land and sea we
    homeward bore
Till all along old Dublin's shore rang out a shout of
    welcome.
Then when my Colleen found me, what joy through her
    dear eyes passed,
Tight her two arms bound me, and we were one at last.

The Rocky Road to Berlin

Cathal Mac Dubhghaill (d. 1926)

In nineteen-and-fourteen says Asquith to me
I'm going away Kaiser Wilhelm to see,
He's not the nice monarch I took him to be,
    For he's after committing a sin!
The crime of invasion is hard to believe,
Yet he waltzed into Belgium without any leave,
And he's laughing at all of us up in his sleeve,
    So I'll talk to him down in Berlin.

Chorus
'Twas a rough road
    A tough road
A terrible journey we had to begin,
    But only for Huns
    And their dirty old guns
We'd be dining this day in Berlin.

The road it was lovely, the scenery was grand,
With trenches and pill-boxes over the land,
But the worst of it was, they were all of them manned
    By some gentlemen down from Berlin.

The musician Cathal Mac Dubhghaill
was the husband of Maeve Cavanagh.

Text: Samuels Collection, TCD.

183

They caused us a great deal of trouble and woe.
Nothing we said would persuade them to go.
So it wasn't our fault if we found the road slow,
    To the beautiful town of Berlin.

In nineteen-and-sixteen we got some hard blows,
The dirty Sinn Féiners in Dublin they rose,
And they shot the poor soldiers like you would shoot
    crows,
    Oh it made my old blood boil within!
But we got forty-thousand tried soldiers and true,
Soon made the rotten old 'shinners' look blue
(They're a hard lot of roots, though, between me and
    you,
    And they spoiled half the trip to Berlin.)

Though the journey is tedious, we're sticking it still.
Sir Douglas is feeling decidedly ill,
He won't try a pill box in search of a pill,
    He's afraid it might damage his skin.
Our case it is dreadful, alas and alack!
We sometimes go forward, but more often back;
Sincerely I hope we won't all get the sack,
    But I know we can't get to Berlin.

An Irish Airman Foresees his Death

W.B. Yeats

The Irish airman of the title was Lady
Gregory's only son Robert, who was
killed fighting in Italy in January
1918.

Text: W.B. Yeats, *The Poems,*
Everyman, London, 1992.

I know that I shall meet my fate,
    Somewhere among the clouds above;
Those that I fight I do not hate,
    Those that I guard I do not love;
My country is Kiltartan Cross,
    My countrymen Kiltartan's poor,
No likely end could bring them loss
    Or leave them happier than before.
Nor law, nor duty bade me fight,
    Nor public men, nor cheering crowds,
A lonely impulse of delight
    Drove to this tumult in the clouds;
I balanced all, brought all to mind,
    The years to come seemed waste of breath,
A waste of breath the years behind
    In balance with this life, this death.

Aviators' Hymn

Arthur Campbell Ainger (1841–1919) / Charles Villiers Stanford (1852–1924)

Thy mes-sen-gers are winds, O God, Thy clouds___ the char-iot of Thy path.

The tem-pest ra-ges at Thy nod, The light-nings tes-ti-fy Thy wrath;

And if to scale Thy heav'ns a-bove On earth-born wings Thy crea___ tures dare,

Shield___ them with Thy pro-tec-ting love,___ Who ride___ u-pon the view-less air.___

Thy messengers are winds, O God
   Thy clouds the chariot of Thy path.
The tempest rages at Thy nod,
   The lightnings testify Thy wrath;
And if to scale Thy heav'ns above
   On earth-born wings Thy creatures dare,
Shield them with Thy protecting love,
   Who ride upon the viewless air.

Aloft they cleave the misty shroud,
   They scorn the danger, scorn the foe;
Athwart the blinding thundercloud,
   They go, where duty bids them go.
Yet while, amid the heav'ns above,
   The instant face of death they dare,
Shield them with Thy protecting love,
   Who ride upon the viewless air.

Thro' crash of war, thro' storm and fire,
   With stiff'ning limbs and vision strain'd,
Still on, still upward high and higher,
   They work untired the work ordained;
While, risking life in heav'ns above,
   To friends and comrades life they bear,
Shield them with Thy protecting love,
   Who ride upon the viewless air.

Text: A.C. Ainger
Music: Charles Villiers Stanford, published in sheet music by Stainer & Bell, London.

Dooleysprudence
1916–18

James Joyce (1882–1941)

Who is the man when all the gal-lant na-tions run to war

Goes home to have his din-ner by the ve-ry first ca-ble-car

And as he eats his can-ta-loups con-torts him-self in mirth

To read the bla-tant bul-le-tins of the ru-lers of the earth?

It's Mis-ter Doo-ley, Mis-ter Doo-ley

The coo-lest chap our coun-try ev-er knew

They're out to col-lar the dime and dol-lar

Says Mis-ter Doo-ley-oo-ley-oo-ley-oo.

This poem is inspired by the character created by Chicago-born newspaper writer Finley Peter Dunne (1867–1936). Mr Martin J. Dooley was his satirical mouthpiece, a saloon-keeper given to sharp, humorous pronouncements on current events, both local and international, delivered in an 'Irish' accent.

Text: James Joyce, *Poems and Shorter Writings*, Faber and Faber, London, 1991.

Air: 'Mr Dooley' indicated by Joyce. Composed by Jean Schwartz and published in sheet music by Shapiro, Bernstein & Von Tilzer, New York, 1903.

See link to recording on Library of Congress website (accessed 7 April 2015): www.loc.gov/jukebox/recordings/detail/id/7988/

Who is the man when all the gallant nations run to war
Goes home to have his dinner by the very first cablecar
And as he eats his cantaloups contorts himself in mirth
To read the blatant bulletins of the rulers of the earth?
   It's Mr Dooley,
   Mr Dooley,
   The coolest chap our country ever knew
   'They are out to collar
   The dime and dollar'
   Says Mr Dooley-ooley-ooley-oo.

Who is the funny fellow who declines to go to church
Since pope and priest and parson left the poor man in the lurch
And taught their flocks the only way to save all human souls
Was piercing human bodies through with dumdum bulletholes?

It's Mr Dooley,
Mr Dooley,
The mildest man our country ever knew
'Who will release us
From Jingo Jesus?'
Prays Mr Dooley-ooley-ooley-oo.

Who is the meek philosopher who doesn't care a damn
About the yellow peril or problem of Siam
And disbelieves that British Tar is water from life's fount
And will not gulp the gospel of the German on the Mount?
   It's Mr Dooley,
   Mr Dooley,
   The broadest brain our country ever knew
   'The curse of Moses
   On both your houses'
   Cries Mr Dooley-ooley-ooley-oo.

Who is the cheerful imbecile who lights his long chibouk
With pages of the pandect, penal code and Doomsday Book
And wonders why bald justices are bound by law to wear
A toga and a wig made out of someone else's hair?
   It's Mr Dooley,
   Mr Dooley,
   The finest fool our country ever knew
   'They took that toilette
   From Pontius Pilate'
   Thinks Mr Dooley-ooley-ooley-oo.

Who is the man who says he'll go the whole and perfect hog
Before he pays an income tax or licence for a dog
And when he licks a postage stamp regards with smiling scorn
The face of king or emperor on snout of unicorn?
   It's Mr Dooley,
   Mr Dooley,
   The wildest wag our country ever knew
   'O my poor tummy
   His backside gummy!'
   Moans Mr Dooley-ooley-ooley-oo.

Who is the tranquil gentleman who won't salute the State
Or serve Nabuchodonosor or proletariat
But thinks that every son of man has quite enough to do
To paddle down the stream of life his personal canoe?
   It's Mr Dooley
   Mr Dooley,
   The wisest lad our country ever knew

'Poor Europe ambles
Like sheep to shambles!'
Sighs Mr Dooley-ooley-ooley-oo.

Who is the sunny sceptic who fights shy of Noah's arks
When they are made in Germany by Engels and by Marx
But when the social deluge comes and rain begins to pour
Takes off his coat and trousers and prepares to swim ashore?
    It's Mr Dooley,
    Mr Dooley,
    The bravest boy our country ever knew
    With arms akimbo
    'I'll find that rainbow!'
    Shouts Mr Dooley-ooley-ooley-oo.

On Rudolf Goldschmidt
1917

James Joyce

Text: James Joyce, *Poems and Exiles*,
Penguin, London, 1992.
   Air: 'The Amorous Goldfish', indi-
cated by Joyce, is from the musical *The*

A Goldschmidt swam in a Kriegsverein
As wise little Goldschmidts do,
And he loved every scion of the Hapsburg line,

Each Archduke proud, the whole jimbang crowd,
And he felt that they loved him, too.
Herr Rosenbaum and Rosenfeld
And every other Feld except Schlachtfeld
All worked like niggers, totting rows of crazy figures,
To save Kaiser Karl and Goldschmidt, too.

Chorus
For he said it is bet – bet – better
To stick stamps on some God-damned letter
Than be shot in a trench
Amid shells and stench,
Jesus Gott, Donnerwet – wet – wetter.

Geisha, composed by Sidney Jones,
and published in sheet music by
Hopwood & Crew, London, 1896.

The Munster Fusiliers

Come pass the call 'round Munster.
　　Let the notes ring loud and clear.
We want the merchant and the squire,
　　The peasant and the Peer.
For we mean to whip those Germans,
　　So away with your paltry affairs
And come join that grand Battalion
　　Called the Munster Fusiliers

The Kaiser knows each Munster
　　By the shamrock on his cap
And the famous Bengal tiger
　　Ever ready for a scrap.
With all his big battalions,
　　Prussian Guards and Grenadiers,
He feared to face the bayonets
　　Of the Munster Fusiliers

When marching up through Belgium
　　Sure we thought of days of old.
The cruel sights that meet your eyes
　　Would make your blood run cold
To see the ruined convents
　　And the Holy nuns in tears.
'By God on high, avenge or die'
　　Cried the Munster Fusiliers.

God rest our fallen comrades,
　　May they take their long last sleep

Text: Ballad sheet, quoted in *History Ireland*, Spring 1998.

Royal Munster Fusiliers cap badge
with 'the famous Bengal tiger'.

189

On the fields of France and Flanders.
Sure, we have no cause to weep,
For their deeds will live in history
And the youth of future years
Will read with pride of the men who died,
The Munster Fusiliers.

The Munster Fusiliers

N.H. Gubbins / Arthur Foote (1853–1937)

Text and music: N.H. Gubbins and Arthur Foote, published as sheet music by The Arthur P. Schmidt Co., Boston & New York, 1918.

What's the happy hearted shouting?
    Shouting on the hilltop over there?
Shure, it cannot be a two-step
    At a Ballylongford Fair?
Though the battle's never fiercer,
    They're the gayest, maddest cheers.
'Tis the boys from County Kerry
    In the Munster Fusiliers.

What's the noise of happy shouting?
    Shure, there is no noise at all,
Save the music of the fiddlers
    Who play at Satan's ball.
Dark figures dot the hillside,
    Now the sky is full of tears
For the men who died for England,
    In the Munster Fusiliers.

190

'The Last General Absolution of the Munsters at Rue du Bois', by Fortunio Matania, depicts an incident on 8 May 1915. The chaplain, Fr Francis Gleeson of Templemore, is shown blessing the 2nd Battalion of the Royal Munster Fusiliers the day before they suffered very heavily at the Battle of Aubers Ridge. Of the 800 who went into that battle, only 200 survived. The picture was reproduced in *The Sphere* in November 1916, and the following year in the *Weekly Freeman's*.

The Irish Guards

Rudyard Kipling (1865–1936)

We're not so old in the Army list,
    But we're not so young at our trade,
For we had the honour at Fontenoy,
    Of meeting the Guards' Brigade.
'Twas Lally, Dillon, Buckley, Clare,
    And Lee that led us then,
And after a hundred and seventy years,
    We're fighting for France again.

Old Days! The wild geese are flighting
    Head to the storm as they faced it before!
For where there are Irish there's bound to be fighting,
    And when there's no fighting, it's Ireland no more
    Ireland no more!

The fashion's all for khaki now,
    But once through France we went
Full-dressed in scarlet Army cloth,
    The English left at Ghent.

Text: *Rudyard Kipling's Verse*, Doubleday, Page & Co., Garden City, 1922.

They're fighting on our side to-day
  But, before they changed their clothes,
The half of Europe knew our fame,
  As all of Ireland knows!

Old Days! The wild geese are flying
  Head to the storm as they faced it before!
For where there are Irish there's memory undying,
  And when we forget, it is Ireland no more
  Ireland no more!

From Barry Wood to Gouzeaucourt,
  From Boyne to Pilkem Ridge,
The ancient days come back no more
  Than water under the bridge.
But the bridge it stands and the water runs
  As red as yesterday,
And the Irish move to the sound of the guns
  Like salmon to the sea.

Old Days! The wild geese are ranging,
  Head to the storm as they faced it before!
For where there are Irish their hearts are unchanging,
  And when they are changed, it is Ireland no more!
  Ireland no more!

We're not so old in the Army list,
  But we're not so new in the ring.
For we carried our packs with Marshal Saxe
  When Louis was our King.
But Douglas Haig's our marshal now,
  And we're King George's men
After one hundred and seventy years
  We're fighting for France again.

Ah, France! And did we stand by you
  Then life was made splendid with gifts, and rewards?
Ah, France! And will we deny you
  In the hour of your agony, Mother of Swords?

Old Days! The wild geese are flighting,
  Head to the storm as they faced it before,
For where there are Irish, there's loving and fighting,
  And when we stop either, It's Ireland no more!
  Ireland no more!

Clare's Brigade
A Marching Song for the Irish Division
Stephen Gwynn (1864–1950)

When the gentlemen of Ireland went to France, so long ago,
They learnt about the soldier's trade just all there was to know.
Glory danced upon each blade when the sun of battle shone;
And the cry was – 'Clare's Brigade – Who's afraid? – Carry
    on!'

The simple way in Clare's Brigade at sea or on the shore,
Was to do what other men could do, and do a little more:
In the fiercest fusillade, by ten thousand set upon,
Still their word was – 'Clare's Brigade – Who's afraid? –
    Carry on!'

Now the old Brigade is ended, and the new one is begun,
And there's big work for Irishmen a-waiting to be done.
If before the last parade many a gallant lad is gone,
What is left, boys? – The Brigade – Who's afraid? –
    Carry on!

In the late seventeenth century Irish soldiers went to France in exchange for French soldiers augmenting the Jacobite ranks in Ireland to campaign in the Williamite Wars. Following the defeat of the Jacobites further Irishman went to France as 'The Wild Geese'.

The first two verses refer to these seventeenth-century soldiers, and in the third verse the author attempts to link the past with the British recruiting effort to enlist Irishmen to serve in WWI. The author, a Home Ruler, did himself serve as a British officer, with the Connaught Rangers. [LM]

Text: Stephen Gwynn and T.M. Kettle, *Battle Songs for the Irish Brigades*, Maunsel and Company, Dublin, 1915.

The Irish Brigade, 1914
Stephen Gwynn

From Fontenoy, from Landen, the message runs again,
Once more the fields of Flanders are strewn with Irish slain,
And once again, oh! once again, the herald thrills to tell
How gloriously an Irish charge avenged the brave who fell.

And we who sit at home and read – the tale rings in our ears,
We know our part, we claim our right, in those victorious cheers,
We boast our splendid heritage in the old fighting race;
Yet, have we marked the cry that comes from each dead
    soldier's place?

Half-overwhelmed, they rallied fierce: they bled, yet held
    their ground,
Though three to one the German hordes outflanked and
    hemmed them round;
But, oh! exultant hearts who praise their valour, must it be
That Ireland leaves her sons to fight for ever one to three?

This song invokes the name of the Irish Brigade, mainly used to describe the Irish forces who fought in continental armies, principally in the French army, after the collapse of the Jacobite cause in Ireland in 1691. Gwynn took the Redmondite (National Volunteer) stance in WWI, and believed that Irishmen should fight for the British crown and empire, in the belief that Home Rule would be given to Ireland after British success in the war.

Others (the Irish Volunteers) differed from this view and believed that Irishmen owed allegiance to Ireland alone, should not fight for the British empire and should remain in Ireland so that if fighting was to be done it would be done in Ireland and for Ireland.

Advanced nationalist opinion differed greatly from Gwynn's view that

Irishmen should fight for England, as noted above, and would take great issue with equating the 1798 Rising, when an attempt was made to overthrow English rule in Ireland, with Irishmen enlisting to fight for England.

Many would see this as a total distortion of history and a denial of reality, although many of those who followed Redmond quite genuinely held these beliefs. This issue can still be most contentious. In 1798 the population of Ireland was rising towards eight million, while in 1914 it was declining towards four million.

The Battles of Fontenoy (1745) and Landen (1693), verse 1, were battles in which Irish troops figured prominently.

Rangers (Connaught Rangers), Munsters (Munster Fusiliers), Inniskillings (Royal Inniskilling Fusiliers), Irish Guards, verse 4, were all Irish regiments of the British army.

Wild Geese, last line, verse 6, is the name by which those exile Irish soldiers of the late seventeenth and early eighteenth century were known.

Louis and James, verse 8, refer to the French and English monarchs for whom the Wild Geese fought.

Sarsfield, Patrick Sarsfield (1660–1693), verse 9, was an Irish cavalry officer of renown, killed at Landen in 1693, and Clare's Brigade, verse 10, was an Irish Wild Geese unit that fought for France.

Verses 9 and 10 have many Irish placenames, and the 'Ninety-eight' reference at the end of verse 10 recalls the Rising of 1798.

Verse 11 – Tara is the Hill of Tara, in Co. Meath; the cairn of Maeve is on Knocknaree in Co. Sligo; the birthplace of (Saint) Columba is Gartan, Co. Donegal; (Saint) Patrick's grave is in Downpatrick, Co. Down; Slieve Donard, Croagh-patrick, the Galtees, the (Mag-illicuddy) Reeks, are mountains or mountain ranges in counties Down, Mayo, Tipperary and Kerry respectively. [LM]

Text: Stephen Gwynn and T.M. Kettle, *Battle Songs for the Irish Brigades*, Maunsel and Company, Dublin, 1915.

Must English fill the Rangers' ranks? Welsh pad the
    Munsters' line?
Where stood the Dublin Fusiliers, Scots give the
    counter-sign?
Or when the Inniskillings faint, shall Sikhs the trench
    re-man?
Pathan and Gurkha finish what the Irish Guards began?

No shame for comrades' help to seek; but when the Irish
    fall,
To Ireland for more Irishmen first comes the clarion call.
Who says she cannot spare her sons to pay her honour's
    debt?
Poor Ireland is poor Ireland still – but abject, never yet.

One vast adventure shakes the pulse of Europe far and
    near,
Young gallant hearts leap up in pride the battle-cry to hear,
Yet now, when Fontenoy's Brigade unfurls the flag anew,
What wakes on shores where the Wild Geese soared up
    and wheeled and flew?

They fought for Louis, fought for James, for every despot's
    throne;
Shall we not fight who may defend a freedom like our
    own?
To choke the spoiler from his grip on ravaged homes and
    land –
God, to what nobler enterprise could chivalry set hand?

Or must we seek a counsel from the poisoned hiss of hate?
Our neighbor burns – we laugh, and, lo! the fire is at our
    gate.
Ah, tardy then the penitence, bitter the reckoning then,
But now, but now, the day is ours to take our part like
    men.

A Sarsfield lies there, fallen – an O'Brien – an O'Neill.
Wake the trump in Tipperary! down the Shannon let it
    peal!
Raise the slogan in Tyrconnell, send the call across Tyrone,
Over Munster, Leinster, Connaught, be the battle-music
    blown.

Clare's Brigade! what ghosts are stirring on the stony hills
    of Clare?
Let the cry go out through Galway, in Mayo let bugles blare:

Shall the Decies, or shall Desmond, to the muster-roll come
    late?
From Kildare to dauntless Wexford rouse the heirs of
    Ninety-eight.

Set the standard up on Tara; plant it on the cairn of Maeve;
From the birthplace of Columba speed the cross to
    Patrick's grave!
On Slieve Donard, on Croaghpatrick, on the Galtees, on
    the Reeks,
Waken memory, waken vision, by the beaconed mountain
    peaks.

Not for ourselves, but for our sons, and for the blessed sake
Of Ireland and of Freedom, be the high resolve we take;
The work begun cannot be done, our warfare may not cease,
Till on the hearth of Liberty we have established – Peace.

The Somme
1st July, 1916
Ruddick Millar (1907–1952)

'Tis zero hour!
A word of swift command,
A shower of shrapnel,
And the valiant band
Begin the forward rush,
While, near at hand –
The stilled note of a thrush.

They stumble on,
These gallant boys in brown,
From Antrim and from Down,
On and yet on!

Then clash of steel,
Blood like the river's foam;
While women kneel
In some far Ulster home.

And so they die,
With 'No surrender' on their lips,
These weavers of linen,
These builders of ships.

Text: Leslie H. Daiken, *Good-bye,
Twilight – Songs of the Struggle in
Ireland*, Lawrence & Wishart,
London, 1936.

Ulster on the Somme
In Memoriam E.G.B., Killed in Action, 1 July 1916
Frederick S. Boas

The 'Red Branch' (verse 4) is a
reference to the 'Red Branch Cycle'
of Gaelic legends, located in Ulster,
and dealing with the exploits of
Cuchullain and the Red Branch
Knights. [LM]

Text: Frederick S. Boas, *Songs of Ulster
& Balliol*, Constable and Company,
London, 1917.

'Twas two short years ago – they seem
    Fate-laden aeons now –
Faith saw the destined glory gleam
    O'er Ulster's helmèd brow.

Yet Faith itself might not foretell
    Such transcendental dower,
When yawned the gates of Death and Hell,
    And broke the awful hour.

From Antrim glens and hills of Down,
    And moaning Northern Sea,
From mill and mart and thronging town,
    Strode Ulster's chivalry.

Heroes re-born of the Red Branch,
    They leapt into the fray,
Whelmed by the steely avalanche,
    That long Midsummer day.

Life? – 'twas a little thing to give:
    Death? – 'twas a toy to try.
They knew that Ulster dared not live,
    Did they not dare to die.

There, blithely venturing in the van,
    A kinsman of mine own,
In years a boy, in heart a man,
    Was radiantly o'erthrown.

'Gay as a lark' – the tribute this
    By chief and comrade penned –
He sang his way to the Abyss,
    And smiled on Death as friend.

For him no somber requiem,
    No threnody of tears,
Who bartered for Youth's diadem
    The dross of After-Years.

The Charge of the Ulster Division at Thiepval, 1 July 1916

Samuel Kennedy Cowan (1850–1918) / W. Hamilton Burns (1858–1928)

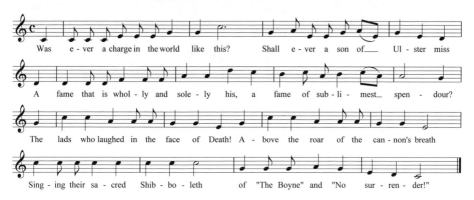

Was ever a charge in the world like this? Shall ever a son of—— Ul - ster miss
A fame that is whol - ly and sole - ly his, a fame of sub - li - mest— spen - dour?
The lads who laughed in the face of Death! A - bove the roar of the can - non's breath
Sing - ing their sa - cred Shib - bo - leth of "The Boyne" and "No sur - ren - der!"

Was ever a charge in the world like this?
Shall ever a son of Ulster miss
A fame that is wholly and solely his –
   A fame of sublimest splendour?
The lads who laughed in the face of Death!
Above the roar of the cannon's breath
Singing their sacred shibboleth
   Of 'The Boyne' and 'No Surrender!'

Giant-strong, with the strength of Right –
Fired, by the soul of their sires, to fight –
What cared they for the foeman's might,
   Or how many cannons thundered?
Face to face with a hundred Huns,
Half-a-score of Ulster's sons
Silenced the thunder of the guns –
   Ten – a match for a hundred!

Nought could stay them: nought them stop:
A thirst for blood to the last red drop,
Charging along on the topmost top
   Of the waves of Fire that bore them!
On, with a thirst that nought could quell,
Thro' a hurricane-shower of shot and shell,
To fight – or fall, as their Fathers fell,
   In the doughty days before them!

Merrily – every mother's son –
Laughing, as tho' they fought for fun,

This poem by S.K. Cowan was published in *The Belfast Newsletter* on 19 July 1916. It was later set to music by W.H. Burns and published in sheet music form by his music company in Belfast.

It celebrates the effort made at the Battle of the Somme when the Ulster Division was the only one in its Corps to achieve its objectives, at a cost of over 5500 casualties.

The image below is from a greeting card published at Christmas 1916.

Text and music: Sheet music published by Walter Burns & Son, Belfast, 1916.

At Thiepval, 1st July, 1916.

With a song and a cheer they charged the Hun,
    Marring his Maker's image!
Chaffing, as tho' each shell might be
The whistle-call of a Referee!
And the bloodiest tussle in History
    Only – a Football scrimmage!

Into the Hell of 'No Man's Land',
Thro' poisoned air, at their souls' command,
And a shrapnel-storm that none could stand,
    Charging, in wild derision.
Past Sentry Death, who, wondering, kept
His vigil there – on, on they swept,
Where never a man could live – except
    Ulster's Divine Division!

Flinging his fun in the face of Death –
Above the roar of the cannon's breath
Singing his sacred shibboleth
    Of 'The Boyne' and 'No Surrender!'
Wherever a son of Ulster is,
Honour and Glory shall aye be his!
Was ever a fight in the world like this,
    Or a charge of sublimer splendour?

James Prinsep Beadle, 'Battle of the Somme: Attack of the Ulster Division, 1 July 1916'.

Marching to Berlin

Jimmy Mulkerns 'The Rajah of Frongoch' (d. 1956)

1914

Loudly sound the trumpet, boys – by jingo, we will fight
For France and plucky Belgium in the sacred cause of right.
'Tipperary' we will whistle as the Germans feel our might,
      As we go marching to Berlin.

Chorus
Hurrah! Hurrah! in three weeks we'll be back,
And from the Kaiser's Palace we'll fly the Union Jack;
A hundred thousand million quids we'll take from Billy's sack
      As we come marching from Berlin.

1915

We hadn't got enough of shells when first we fought the Hun.
You'll want to send us thousands more to get him on the run.
Let 'More Shells' be England's cry, then all that's to be done
      Is to proudly go marching to Berlin.

Although it appears to chart the whole course of the war, the final verse reveals that this song was written before the outcome was known.

See the note on the expression 'by jingo' on p. 153.

Text: Samuels Collection, TCD.
    Air: The song is modelled on the American Civil War song 'Marching through Georgia' by Henry Clay Work.

Chorus
Hurrah! Hurrah! We're only here a year,
And if we were set back a bit of that you have no fear.
More Shells! More Shells! More Shells! We want to
    make Old England cheer,
        As we go marching to Berlin.

1916
We had the Germans beaten till the Irish they did rise.
The 'dogs' they stabbed us in the back and caused a big
    surprise.
But now we've shot their leaders, plainer still the road it
    lies
        On to our goal – that is Berlin.

Chorus
Hurrah! Hurrah! We've got the shot and shell.
Lloyd George he swears we're going to give 'em Hell.
The bells of old Cologne will ring the Kaiser's death-
    knell,
        As we come marching from Berlin.

1917
You must conscript the Irish crowd if we are going to
    win.
Nine hundred miles it must be tramped before we strike
    Berlin,
The Hun will not be beaten if the Irish won't come in –
        There's no use talking of Berlin.

Chorus
Hurrah! Hurrah! was what we used to cheer,
But now the sound grows fainter every year.
Oh, back to dear old Blighty I wish we all could steer,
        There's no use talking of Berlin.

1918
Final Chorus
Hurrah! Hurrah! Old Ireland she is free,
John Bull at last no longer rules the sea,
The world in arms had no effect on good old Germany.
        The joy-bells are ringing in Berlin.

It's a Long Way to Tipperary

Jack Judge (1872–1938)

Up to mighty London came an Irishman one day,
As the streets are paved with gold, sure, everyone was
    gay.
Singing songs of Picadilly, Strand and Leicester Square,
Till Paddy got excited, then he shouted to them there.

Chorus
It's a long way to Tipperary, it's a long way to go.
It's a long way to Tipperary, to the sweetest girl I know!
Goodbye Picadilly, farewell Leicester Square!
It's a long, long way to Tipperary, but my heart's right
    there.

Paddy wrote a letter to his Irish Molly-O,
Saying, 'should you not receive it, write and let me
    know!'
'If I make mistakes in spelling, Molly, dear,' said he
'Remember, it's the pen that's bad, don't lay the blame
    on me!'

This 'comic Irish' song was written,
supposedly for a bet, in 1912. Its first
sighting in a military context is said
to have been when a detachment of
the Connaught Rangers was heard
singing it as they arrived in France in
August 1914, after which it spread to
other units of the British army.

It is not unique in the canon of
Irish song in portraying the hero as
'not quite the full shilling'. Another
example, quite relevant in this
context, would be 'My Irish Molly O',
which was a popular success for
Maura O'Connell and De Danann
in the 1980s.

The troops produced their own
version of this song, beginning 'It's the
wrong way to tickle Mary'.

Text and music: Sheet music published
by B. Feldman & Co., London, 1912.

'Tipperary' by John Charles Dollman (1851–1934).

Molly wrote a neat reply to Irish Paddy-O,
Saying 'Mike Maloney wants to marry me and so,
Leave The Strand and Picadilly or you'll be to blame,
For love has nearly drove me silly: Hoping you're the same.'

Old Gallipoli's a Wonderful Place

Text: Max Arthur, *When This Bloody War Is Over*, Judy Piatkus Publishers, London, 2001.
Air: 'The Mountains of Mourne' or 'Bendemeer's Stream'. See 'The Mountjoy Hotel', p. 527.

Oh, old Gallipoli's a wonderful place,
Where the boys in the trenches the foe have to face,
But they never grumble, they smile through it all,
Very soon they expect Achi Baba to fall.
At least when I asked them, that's what they told me
In Constantinople quite soon we would be,
But if war lasts till Doomsday I think we'll still be
Where old Gallipoli sweeps down to the sea.

We don't grow potatoes or barley or wheat,
So we're aye on the lookout for something to eat.
We're fed up with biscuits and bully and ham
And we're sick of the sight of yon parapet jam.
Send out steak and onions and nice ham and eggs
And a fine big fat chicken with five or six legs,
And a drink of the stuff that begins with a 'B'
Where the old Gallipoli sweeps down to the sea.

The Dublin Fusiliers

Harry O'Donovan (1896–1973)

You may talk about the Injuns with their tommyhawks
and spears,
Of Balfour's royal peelers, the heroes of recent years,
And also, I might mention, the British Grenadiers,
Sure, none of them were in it with the Dublin Fusiliers.
You've heard about the Light Brigade and of the deeds
they've done,
And of the other regiments that many victories won,

This music-hall piece was written for
the comedian Jimmy O'Dea.

In the 1960s it was recycled by The
Dubliners, with changes to the lyrics.
The original version is presented here.

Text and air: Transcribed from recording of Jimmy O'Dea.

203

But the pride of all the armies, dragoons and carabineers
Is that noble band of warriors, the Dublin Fusiliers.

So, then, left turn, right about face, this is the way we go,
Charging with fixed bayonets, the terror of every foe.
The glory of ould Ireland, as proud as bucaneers,
And a terror to creation are the Dublin Fusiliers.

Now you've heard about the war between the Russians and the Brits,
The Czar, one day, was reading an ould copy of '*Tit-bits*',
When a general came to him and threw himself down in tears,
Said he 'We'll be defeated, here's the Dublin Fusiliers.'
The Czar commenced to tremble and bit his under-lip,
'Begorrah, boys,' says he, 'I think we'd better take the tip.
Them divils come from Dublin and to judge from what I hears,
They're demons of militia men, them Dublin Fusiliers.'

The Czar he said 'Get ready, lads, lay down each sword and gun,
Take off your shoes and stockings and, when I tell yiz, run.'
Well they didn't stop but started, and midst the ringing cheers
Came showers of bricks and bullets from the Dublin Fusiliers.
Now the time that Julius Caesar tried to land down at Ringsend,
The Coastguards couldn't stop them so the Dublins they did send,
And just as they were landing there they heard three ringing cheers,
'Go back to Rome like blazes, here's the Dublin Fusiliers.'

A company of the Dublin Fusiliers leaving the Royal Barracks, Dublin (now the National Museum of Ireland)
in April 1915 on their way to Gallipoli.

The Army's Full of Irish

Bert Hanlon (1890–1972) / Walter Donaldson (1893–1947)

It's always taken an Irishman to prove that might was right,
For there never was an Irishman who did not love to fight.
There never was a battle that the Irish didn't win.
There never was a battle that the Irish weren't in.
There's thousands in every regiment. The Irish always go.
They've heard there's fighting somewhere and that's all
    they want to know.

Chorus
The Army's full of Irish, they're Irish to a man;
A bugle call is music sweet to Casey or McCann.
They're all a bunch of noble sons
A fighting lot of sons o' guns,
A man from Erin never runs, he's Irish.

The figure of the 'fighting Irishman' was a constant theme of Irish-American vaudeville song. This was exploited for recruiting purposes in the USA when America entered the war.

Text and music: Sheet music published in 1917 by M. Witmark & Sons, New York.

It's always taken an Irishman to win the slightest brawl,
You'll always find him up on his feet, he don't know
how to fall.
An Irishman is never wrong, he's always in the right.
It matters not what he might weigh, it matters not his
height,
Whenever he sees a quarrel any hour of the night,
You'll find him in the middle if it's not a private fight.

Songs from an Evil Wood

Edward Plunkett (Lord Dunsany) (1878–1957)

Lord Dunsany was the patron and
publisher of the poet Francis Ledwidge, and a poet in his own right.
'Plugstreet' (verse 8) was the
British soldier's rendering of the
Belgian placename Ploegsteert,
between Messines and Armentières.

Text: George Herbert Clarke, *A
Treasury of War Poetry, British and
American Poems of the World War,
1914–1919*, Hodder and Stoughton,
London, 1917.

I

There is no wrath in the stars,
    They do not rage in the sky;
I look from the evil wood
    And find myself wondering why.

Why do they not scream out
    And grapple star against star,
Seeking for blood in the wood,
    As all things round me are?

They do not glare like the sky
    Or flash like the deeps of the wood;
But they shine softly on
    In their sacred solitude.

To their happy haunts
    Silence from us has flown,
She whom we loved of old
    And know it now she is gone.

When will she come again
    Though for one second only?
She whom we loved is gone
    And the whole world is lonely.

And the elder giants come
    Sometimes, tramping from far,
Through the weird and flickering light
    Made by an earthly star.

And the giant with his club,
    And the dwarf with rage in his breath,
And the elder giants from far,
    They are the children of Death.

They are all abroad to-night
    And are breaking the hills with their brood,
And the birds are all asleep,
    Even in Plug Street Wood.

II

Somewhere lost in the haze
    The sun goes down in the cold,
And birds in this evil wood
    Chirrup home as of old;

Chirrup, stir and are still,
    On the high twigs frozen and thin.
There is no more noise from them now,
    And the long night sets in.

Of all the wonderful things
    That I have seen in the wood,
I marvel most at the birds,
    At their chirp and their quietude.

For a giant smites with his club
    All day the tops of the hill,
Sometimes he rests at night,
    Oftener he beats them still.

And a dwarf with a grim black mane
    Raps with repeated rage
All night in the valley below
    On the wooden walls of his cage.

III

The great guns of England, they listen mile on mile
To the boasts of a broken War-Lord; they lift their
    throats and smile;
      But the old woods are fallen
        For a while.

The old woods are fallen; yet will they come again,
They will come back some springtime with the warm
    winds and the rain,
      For Nature guardeth her children
        Never in vain.

THE HARVESTER.

"HOW THAT RED RAIN HAS MADE THE HARVEST GROW."—Byron.

Mary FitzPatrick, 'The Harvester' (*The Lepracaun*, November 1914).

They will come back some season; it may be a
    hundred years;
It is all one to Nature with the centuries that are
    hers;
    She shall bring back her children
        And dry all their tears.

But the tears of a would-be War-Lord shall never
    cease to flow,
He shall weep for the poisoned armies whenever the
    gas-winds blow,
    He shall always weep for the widows,
        And all Hell shall know.

The tears of a pitiless Kaiser shallow they'll flow and
    wide,
Wide as the desolation made by his silly pride
    When he slaughtered a little people
        To stab France in her side.

Over the ragged cinders they shall flow and on and
    on
With the listless falling of streams that find not
    Oblivion,
    For ages and ages of years
        Till the last star is gone.

IV

I met with Death in his country,
    With his scythe and his hollow eye
Walking the roads of Belgium.
    I looked and he passed me by.

Since he passed me by in Plug Street,
    In the wood of the evil name,
I shall not now lie with the heroes,
    I shall not share their fame.

I shall never be as they are,
    A name in the land of the Free,
Since I looked on Death in Flanders
    And he did not look at me.

To the Fallen Irish Soldiers

Edward Plunkett (Lord Dunsany)

Merrion Square, in the centre of
Dublin, was the first site proposed, in
1927, for the Memorial to the nearly
50,000 Irish who died in WWI.

Due to opposition to this scheme,
the Memorial was eventually built on
the south bank of the River Liffey,
near Kilmainham.

In 2008 a memorial was built in
Merrion Square, dedicated to members
of the Defence Forces who died in the
service of the State.

Text: Lord Dunsany, *Fifty Poems*,
G.P. Putnam, London, 1929.

Since they have grudged you space in Merrion Square,
    And any monument of stone or brass,
    And you yourselves are powerless, alas,
And your own countrymen seem not to care;
Then let these words of mine drift down the air,
    Lest the world think that it has come to pass
    That all in Ireland treat as common grass
The soil that wraps her heroes slumbering there.

Sleep on, forgot a few more years, and then
    The ages, that I prophesy, shall see
Due honours paid to you by juster men,
    You standing foremost in our history,
Your story filling all our land with wonder,
Your names, and regiments' names, like distant thunder.

The Irish in Gallipoli

Francis Ledwidge (1887–1917)

Text: Alice Curtayne (ed.), *The
Complete Poems of Francis Ledwidge*,
Martin Brian & O'Keeffe, London,
1974.

Where Aegean cliffs with bristling menace front
The threatening splendour of that isley sea
Lighted by Troy's last shadow, where the first
Hero kept watch and the last Mystery
Shook with dark thunder, hark the battle brunt!
A nation speaks, old Silences are burst.

Neither for lust of glory nor new throne
This thunder and this lightening of our wrath
Waken these frantic echoes, not for these
Our Cross with England's mingle, to be blown
On Mammon's threshold; we but war when war
Serves Liberty and Justice, Love and Peace.
Who said that such an emprise could be vain?
Were they not one with Christ Who strove and died?
Let Ireland weep but not for sorrow. Weep
That by her sons a land is sanctified
For Christ Arisen, and angels once again
Come back like exile birds to guard their sleep.

The Landing
From *The Watchers of Gallipoli*, A Poem
George Chester Duggan (1887–1969)

V.

Text: G.C. Duggan, *The Watchers on Gallipoli*, Hodges Figgis, Dublin, 1921.

Hushed are men's lips, only one hears
Lap of the waves like the falling of tears.
Shadowy hulls bear an army. They see
A loom of far coast-line. Like souls just set free
'Twixt two worlds they stand,
And only the dark
Is around: a new land
Is ahead, and the stark
Stretch of sea is below.
Launched on the void
To no haven they go:
Uncharted, unbuoyed
Is the space, and they know
No gate wide-unbarred,
No strong-clasping hands
Await them. Storm-scarred
Cliffs are there, and the sands
Are barb-strewn where death
Is at watch, and men's breath
Comes quick, so quickly that men pant to hear
The screaming of shells chant aloud in their ear,
The cry of men fighting that makes the earth reel,
The cheer of their comrades, the clash of bright steel.

VI.

There is silence on the beaches, there is stir upon the sea,
Where the lighters and the horse boats fill in darkness on the lee
Of the warships, and the long tows leave to span the
    narrow way
Before the dawn comes and the mists have opened to the day.

What of that crash of cheering they heard by Mudros town
But yesterday, when all the ships out of the bay sailed down
To Tenedos, and all the sky was splashed with red and gold?
It echoes still, though making dim their eyes as men grown old.

The ripples of the water below the boat-keels sing
With memories of primrose banks and the fierce blossoming

A Royal Irish Fusilier in Gallipoli in 1915, trying to draw the fire of a Turkish sniper.

Of gorse in June. It lit their eyes with a wild wistfulness,
And made a homeland of the dark Ægean wilderness.

The eastern sky looms shadowy, save where in silver fringed
Great Sari Bair athwart the dawn is with the daylight tinged.
Swifter the tows move, nearer the sandy bluffs grow: still
As the turning tide are all things. Then a sound comes shivering, shrill;

Sweeping the quiet waters, and flinging high the spray,
Rending the timber transoms, it takes its onward way;
And in that quiet morning, outside a ruthless door,
Men's souls went up to God like chaff from off death's threshing-floor.

Out went the stars, and life went out, but clearer burned the flame
Of courage in men's hearts. Through choke of blood-stained sea they came,
Up mine-strewn beaches, over webs of steel, and on the sand
Men's bodies lay like bundled wheat dropped from the reaper's hand.

Lancashire Landing, Sedd-el-Bahr, beaches and bluffs that ring
With a fierce undying one day's spell and an agelong glorying,
Where life was naught and death was life and men gave all to win
A hand's breadth on a barren coast to take their slumber in!

Through daylight into evening they fought: the wailing night
Was seared with flashes as in storm the sea-troughs glimmer white:
Here from a battered hulk men steal across the dead who ne'er
Will see again Cork's rising hills or hear the winds of Clare.

And this is theirs – a little space upon the southern spit,
A cove whence hills rise steeply up, and in that space is writ
A song that sweeps tumultuous upon the harp of years,
A tale that sets the blood aflame and fills the eyes with tears:

An unrecorded tale of deeds known only to the dead,
Where friend for friend gave up his life and went unheralded
Beyond the dark, that stole about with grey-spun sandals shod,
Where man's enduring patience brought his stature nearest God.

Our Dead at Suvla Bay

George Chester Duggan

For three short weeks they fought and died; they crept
   O'er bent-strewn plain, up stony hills, those men
     Fresh from the homeland, from the English fen,
Welsh valleys, Ireland's hills. At times they slept,
Their eyes weary with dust and vigils kept
     In blazing day and stifling night; each glen
      A hell of living death, and where were ten
Now one man stood. From furze and trench there swept
The slaying fire. On the sea's edge they fell

Text: G.C. Duggan, *The Watchers on Gallipoli*, Hodges Figgis, Dublin, 1921. It was published first in *The Irish Times*, 16 August 1916.

Or on far uplands, captains with their troops,
Who strove on until death; and in the grey
Dawn the waves sang for them a soft farewell.
The sleeping lily of a good death droops
Upon their eyes who died at Suvla Bay.

Say not in vain they died, though they will see
No more the green hills, not the blue peat-haze,
Nor gorse aflame in spring – aye, tho' our days
Are robbed of song and youth's gay witchery.
Who knows but thereby in far Picardy
Some village sleeps in peace; some maiden prays
Safe in her Russian border home? The rays
Of victory broaden: justice and chivalry
See the light coming. In their long, last sleep
Dimly our dead hear the great bugle-notes
Of armies closing in. Have you not caught
Their whispering voices? On shell-splintered steep,
On Suvla's hills a far-off vision floats –
Our dead Crusaders watching where they fought.

The Healer

Padric Gregory (1886–1962)
(In memory of my friend, Francis Wisely, M.D., who died
of wounds received at Gallipoli, 14 September 1915).

Text: Padric Gregory, *Ireland: A Song of Hope and Other Poems*, Talbot Press, Dublin, 1917.

Not yours to heed the battle-trumpet's call,
And order slaughter with your latest breath,
Not yours locked in your comrades' ranks to fall,
But yours to clutch their bleeding forms from death.

And yours to wash their wounds, to soothe their cries,
And whisper them: 'Though troubled of your scars –
Bear ye, for Justice' sake, and lift your eyes,
And set your foreheads to the flaming stars.'

Friend of the healing hands! rest now, and know
The fruits of your sweet ministering they reap;
That Time shall not your memory overthrow,
And your long sleep shall be no barren sleep.

Salonika

Me hus - band's in Sa - lo - ni - ka, I won - der if he's dead,_____

I won - der if he knows he has a kid with a fox - y head,

Chorus
So right a - way,_____ so right a way_____

So right a - way Sa - lo - ni - ka, right a - way my sol - dier boy.

Me husband's in Salonika
 I wonder if he's dead,
I wonder if he knows he has
 A kid with a foxy head.

Chorus
So right away,
So right away
So right away, Salonika
Right away, my soldier boy

Now when the war is over
 What will the slackers do?
They'll be all around the soldiers
 For the loan of a bob or two.

But when the war is over
 What will the soldiers do?
They'll be walking around with a leg-and-a-half
 And the slackers will have two.

And they tax the pound o' butter
 They tax the halfpenny bun,
But still with all their taxes
 They can't beat the bloody Hun.

And they tax th' old Coliseum
 They tax Saint Mary's Hall.
Why don't they tax the bobbies
 Wi' their backs ag'in' the wall?

This Cork street-song is closely
associated with the singer Jimmy
Crowley.

Text: *Jimmy Crowley's Irish Song
Book*, Mercier Press, Cork, 1986.
Air: from memory.

215

But when the war is over
    What will the slackers do?
For every kid in Americay
    In Cork there will be two.

For they takes us out to Blarney
    They lays us on the grass.
They puts us in the family way
    And leaves us on our arse,

There's lino in the parlour
    And in the kitchen too.
A glass-backed chevonier
    That we got from Dicky Glue,

And before that I got married
    Sure I used to wear a shawl
But now the war is over
    'Tis hanging in Jones' pawn.

And never marry a soldier,
    A sailor or a Marine,
But keep your eye on the Sinn Féin boy
    With his yellow, white and green.

A Turkish fort on the Asian side of the entrance to the Dardanelles. *The Childrens' Story of the War, Vol. 4.*

War News

Jimmy Mulkerns 'The Rajah of Frongoch'

Ten million Germans are now dead,
   Killed – by the *'Daily Mail'*.
The *'Freeman'* shouts because of this
   'Our' next push will not fail.
Three years of war, *'The Sketch'* cries out,
   Have shown these Hunnish knaves
That British bands they yet can play
   'Britannia Rules the Waves'.
'We'll win this war,' says Davenport,
   If you all eat less bread.
Half of the people in 'Hunland'
   With hunger are now dead.
Keep up the fight, you Britons brave,
   Yourselves with food don't gorge,
One hope remains – that is the plough,
   I know it – says Lloyd George.
Conscript the Irish slacker,
   Exclaims the *'Morning Post'*.
No Home Rule for my loyal band
   Is Carson's latest boast.
The Russian army is intact,
   With valour they're afire.
'Official' reads this stunning fact
   In Martin Murphy's Liar.
The fake Convention meets again
   Within Mahaffy's Hall.
The Sinn Féin crowd they are not missed,
   The *'Telegraph'* does bawl.
Joe Devlin writes to Colonel Moore
   That Ireland wants no guns.
Dear England must not be disturbed
   While trying to smash the Huns.
T.P., the movie man, came back
   Across the raging foam;
New Ireland didn't want him there,
   So told him to clear home.
'Stop Press!' the cry is loudly heard,
   About the war in France.
I buy it – Heavens! what a scare –
   The Allies still advance.
What's happened this while back out East?
   The *'Globe'* asks, rather sad.
Why don't you tell us what is up
   With the troops around Baghdad?

This is a rhymed version of the 'Official War News' since the European War started in August 1914. My advice to the man in the street is never to purchase the morning, evening or weekly papers – go home and read the wall-paper, the information is just the same and it works out far cheaper. – 'The Rajah of Frongoch'.

For a similar piece see 'The Dreadnought Press', p. 153.

'Martin Murphy's Liar' was the *Independent* newspaper, owned at the time by William Martin Murphy. For information on the events mentioned in Roscommon, etc., see 'The Wreck of the "No Far Distant Date",' p. 538.

Text: Samuels Collection, TCD.

We haven't very long to wait
    To see how things do work.
Next morning comes the old, old yarn –
    Complete rout of the Turk.
And on and on the Paper Clique
    The same old game does play,
And fights the battle with their Press
    On all the fronts each day.
But at last their armies in the field
    White men they've got to face,
Not coloured tribes in far Soudan,
    Or harmless savage race.
But men trained in the art of war,
    And men whose hearts are brave,
With scorn they meet the Saxon Band,
    Their Fatherland to save.
And, blind with fury, East and West
    The British lion does grope,
And a loyal packed Convention
    Is now Ireland's only hope.
But the cry went from Roscommon,
    And it rang through Longford Town,
And brave East Clare swore by that flag
    That never shall fall down.
God bless you, old Kilkenny,
    You have joined the onward tide
That rushes on to Freedom
    With Cosgrave by your side.
And England now to us she pleads,
    But her pleading is in vain;
We swear to be her slaves no more –
    We'll have our own again!

The Day of the Scagger Wreck
(Knutsford, June 19, 1916)

The title of this poem is a pun on the Skagerrak, the strait between Denmark and Sweden, near which the Battle of Jutland took place on 31 May 1916.

Oh where will the gathering be, says the Sean Bhean Bhocht;
At the Skagger Rock 'twill be, says the Sean Bhean Bhocht;
    Where we'll give John Bull a shock,
    That will make his empire rock,
Till they hear him in L Block, says the Sean Bhean Bhocht.

Oh, the Allies at Verdun, says the Sean Bhean Bhocht;
They are nearly on the run, says the Sean Bhean Bhocht;
    But the navy of the Hun,
    Sure, it fairly takes the bun,
And Britannia's fleet is done, says the Sean Bhean Bhocht.

Oh, Trafalgar's out of date, says the Sean Bhean Bhocht;
German gold and hymns of hate, says the Sean Bhean Bhocht;
    Have the Bulldog's bottom bate,
    And their knocked out all concate,
From the empire, quite complete, says the Sean Bhean Bhocht.

And what will the rebels say, says the Sean Bhean Bhocht;
When they hear about the day, says the Sean Bhean Bhocht;
    Why, they'll get right down and pray,
    That the Huns may shoot away,
Every scrap of England's sway, says the Sean Bhean Bhocht.

This poem, and others, were written in Knutsford Internment Camp by a Volunteer who had been arrested after the Easter Rising.

Text: E.G.B., *Songs & Poems, The Rebels Who Fought and Died for Ireland in Easter Week, 1916* (Samuels Collection, TCD).

The Rats
(Knutsford, 1916)

Last night we heard the rats were out,
    And punctured John Bull's navy,
To-day we heard the news is true,
    Poor Bull is in the gravy.
At Skagger Rock, a mighty shock –
    The Huns were out of righting,
Then John Bull knew the rats had teeth,
    For Jack Tar felt them biting.
The Bull-dog's breed has gone to feed
    The fishes in the ocean –
And how the divil they'll ever survive,
    I haven't the faintest notion.

The British press described the German fleet's exit from their home bases as 'like rats leaving their holes', taking their cue from Winston Churchill's remark about 'digging them out like rats'. The British claimed victory in the battle, although they lost more ships and men than their opponents.

Text: E.G.B., *Songs & Poems, The Rebels Who Fought and Died for Ireland in Easter Week, 1916* (Samuels Collection, TCD).

When the Rats Came Out

'Britannia rules the waves! Britons never shall be slaves!'
    We've been told that tale so often, that we've scarcely room
        for doubt,
Irish rebels in their graves, done to death by cowardly knaves,
    Would sleep peacefully, I'm certain, if they knew the rats
        came out.

The reference in verse 4 to the Battle of Jutland being 'different from the Liffey' is a recollection of the fact that the British naval vessel *Helga* sailed up the Liffey and shelled rebel-held targets in

219

Dublin, including Liberty Hall, during the Easter Rising.

Text: Ballad sheet entitled *Poems & Songs of Easter Week.*

'Twas on the 31st of May, for ever blessed be the day,
  The British fleet off Denmark's coast, were cruising round
      about;
They felt safety in numbers, and no fear disturbed their slumbers,
  Never dreaming for an instant that the rats were coming out.

Those tars renowned for bravery, those sworn foes of slavery,
  Were out upon a pic-nic; German merchant ships to rout.
They thought they had an easy thing, their bands were playing
  'God save the king',
      But soon they changed their tune – they found the rats were
      out!

'Queen Mary' had a thousand men, their like we'll never see again,
  Because they're food for fishes now, and cods dislike
      'Sauer-Kraut',
They got bowled out in a jiffy, 'twas different from the Liffey,
  And not at all like Liberty Hall, the time the rats came out.

Because they knew these German Huns are well supplied with
  shells and guns,
      Besides they've gelignite in tons – they're quick to hand it out.
Behaving reprehensible, they sank the great 'Invincible',
  And our Bulldogs got insensible – just when the rats came out.

That gallant ship, the bold 'Defence', she cost a good few English
  pence,
      Displayed a proper lack of sense by going down, no doubt.
She found she couldn't get away – the course she wasn't fit to stay,
  And though 'twas night she said 'Day-day' – the time the rats
      came out.

The beggars then they gave 'what-for' to the 'Black Prince' and the
  'Warrior',
      And now our claim to rule the waves, those barbarous Germans
      flout.
Between ourselves, I'm free to say, 'twas better far we stayed away
  From Jutland shores that awful day the German rats came out.

Moral
The blood of murdered Irishmen appeals to Heaven once again;
  The fleet that shelled old Dublin Town has got a clean
      knock-out.
True Irish hearts will ever pray, that God may speed the coming
  day,
      And Britain's fleet get swept away, when next the rats come out.

Erin and John Bull
(At the Peace Conference)
Air: Tooraloo

The Great Big War was over, and all the nations came,
      Tooral, ooral, ooral, ooral, ooo!
To settle peace for Europe, and each one knew the game,
      Tooral, ooral, ooral, ooral, ooo!
They all sat down to table, to show that they were able,
  And competent to see the matter through;
To give self-determination, and stop warlike animation,
  For the future good of mankind, Tooral oo.

Sez Russia now I want to say a word or two in here,
      Tooral, ooral, ooral, ooral, ooo!
For I've been through the mill myself, I pray you give me ear,
      Tooral, ooral, ooral, ooral, ooo!
There's a nation old called Erin, whose gallant sons non-
  fearin'
  Who have fought and died for her the ages through,
So I think this ancient nation must get first consideration,
  In this hall of free oration, Tooral oo.

Just then a Lady entered and quickly took her seat,
      Tooral, ooral, ooral, ooral, ooo!
On her all eyes were centred, she looked so smart and
  neat,
      Tooral, ooral, ooral, ooral, ooo!
Sez John Bull to France, I'm fearin', this Lady's name is
  Erin
  An' I think she's out for business now don't you?
I'm afraid it's no use bluffin' tho' I'm fond of Home
  Rule Stuffin'
  But I'll try and camouflage 'em – Tooral oo.

Sez Erin to the Big Powers then, full freedom I demand,
      Tooral, ooral, ooral, ooral, ooo!
With Sovereign Independence for the children of my
  land,
      Tooral, ooral, ooral, ooral, ooo!
Sez the Powers we all are willing (since no more blood
  we're spilling)
  To guarantee full liberty to you,
For your Isle of saints and scholars there dawns a bright
  tomorrow
  What has Johnny Bull to say, now? Tooral oo.

Text: Samuels Collection, TCD.
  Air: 'Sergeant William Baily',
see p. 382.

FIFTH CONTORTION

Sez Johnny Bull this turn of things it grieves my poor
    heart sore,
        Tooral, ooral, ooral, ooral, ooo!
Sure I offered all her members full Home Rule the day
    before,
        Tooral, ooral, ooral, ooral, ooo!
What about my Naval Bases, when Erin cuts the traces?
    Oh Gentlemen! Oh! what am I to do?
Sez the court your warlike crazes, an' yerself may go to
    blazes
    For Erin's now a nation, Tooral oo.

To a Crippled Soldier

Ben O'Hickey

Text: Ben O'Hickey, *From Prison
Cells*, The Elo Press, Dublin, 1935.

You have done your best for England,
    But you are useless now,
So, she's cast you off to beg or starve,
    Or live no matter how;
That empty sleeve once 'cased an arm,
    You lost in England's war,
That face that once was handsome,
    Now is marred by many a scar;
And this is your reward, poor wretch,
    For all that bloody strife,
This little bit of ribbon,
    And ten pence a day for life.

Oh! those who fight for England,
    And forget their own dear land,
Must take what they are offered,
    From their betrayer's hand;
And England always casts away,
    What she no longer needs;
E'en though you in her service may,
    Have done some doughty deeds,
'Twere better far you stayed at home,
    And after all the strife,
What have you gained? – An empty sleeve
    And tenpence a day for life.

Ireland and World Freedom

Padric Gregory

Ireland! this is my song of you –
  This is the song I give your sons
(Patriots all, and staunch and true),
  To sing in despite of the brattling guns.

Text: Padric Gregory, *Ireland: A Song of Hope and Other Poems*, Talbot Press, Dublin, 1917.

The drums of doom, at Islam's gate,
  Shall beat full soon, nor be denied!
The virgin torn, the grey-beard spate,
  Whose ghosts to God for vengeance cried

Shall be avenged; and spectral hosts
  Of slain from Greece and Macedon,
From Crete to the Dalmation coasts,
  Shall rise to see the vengeance done.

The worms shall glut and feast their fill
  Upon the bones of throneless Czars,
The Muscov speak his sons his will
  About this age's freeing wars.

The Pole, the Magyar, held in thrall,
  And all who knew the bondsman's shame
Shall crash aside the cup of gall
  And break the bonds that sear and maim.

The races tyranny long smote
  Shall beat their swords to ploughing-shares,
Armenian, Albanian, Croat,
  Shall hymn High-God in lauding prayers.

And as the peoples rose and broke
  The power of eldern Aryan kings:
In distant Cathay burst the yoke,
  Thro' Babylon's walls clove openings.

And left the Pantheon a place
  Where now but green-backed lizards bide,
Exterminated Philip's race,
  And crushed the haughty Bourbons' pride.

So shall the peoples bring to dust
  The Teuton's breed: his power shall wane,
And battle-fields shall gape and lust
  For sacrificial blood in vain.

223

And men shall rally, as of yore,
   Whatever nurtures in them still
The faith that thrills the brave heart's core,
   And 'courages the constant will.

And they who suffered and stood fast
   That justice might the weak uphold
Shall come into their own at last:
   Their blessings shall be manifold.

And in its death-throes Tyranny
   Shall see the dusk of ruin stain
Its capitals, and, blightingly,
   Fire mosque, and minaret, and fane.

And when the Maori takes his stand
   On London Bridge's crumbling walls,
To limm – perchance with trembling hand –
   'The broken ruin of St Paul's.'

Then, then, O Ireland! thou who brought
   Forth men of wisdom and of worth,
Ere Pharaohs ruled, or Caesars fought,
   Or Christ came down to save this earth –

Then, then, O Motherland! shalt thou
   Still stand resplendent, fair, and free,
Victor and vanquished to endow
   With thine own love of liberty.

Ireland! this is my song of you –
   This is the song I give your sons
(Patriots all, and staunch and true),
   To sing in despite of the brattling guns.

Lament on the Death of Lord Kitchener

In 1914 Lord Kitchener was created Secretary of State for War, and placed Britain on a war-footing in terms of manpower and material. While on a diplomatic mission to Russia in June 1916, Lord Kitchener's ship HMS

Oh Lord Kitchener is dead, says the Sean Van Vocht.
Without tombstone at his head, says the Sean Van Vocht
He has gone to his reward, he'll be welcomed by the Lord.
I don't think a bad record, says the Sean Van Vocht.

Have you heard of Omdurman? says the Sean Van
  Vocht.
Try and spell if it you can, says the Sean Van Vocht
Where the river Nile ran red, with the blood of Arab
  dead,
Butcher Kitchener had shed, says the Sean Van Vocht.

Oh Lord Kitchener the proud, says the Sean Van Vocht
Has gone to join the crowd, says the Sean Van Vocht
The crowd that's gone to – well – where they're learning
  how to spell,
That old England isn't well, says the Sean Van Vocht

And is Maxwell still alive? says the Sean Van Vocht.
Will the Great God let him thrive? says the Sean Van
  Vocht.
He is riding for a fall, o'er his course now draw the pall,
For forth has gone the call, says the Sean Van Vocht.

Hampshire struck a mine and was lost with all on board. He had been one of Britain's foremost figures in the nineteenth-century colonial 'scramble for Africa'.

'Omdurman' (verse 2) refers to the battle in the Sudan in 1898 where General Kitchener's army, armed with artillery and Maxim guns, killed and wounded 34,000 of the Mahdist forces, armed with swords, spears and muskets, while suffering a few hundred casualties themselves.

General Maxwell (verse 4) served with Kitchener in the war in Sudan, and in 1916 ordered the execution of the leaders of the Easter Rising.

Text: The Ernie O'Malley Papers, New York University.
  Air: 'Love's Young Dream' is specified in the source. This is the title of the song written by Thomas Moore to the air of 'The Shan Van Vocht', see p. 6.

The Second Coming

W.B. Yeats

Turning and turning in the widening gyre
The falcon cannot hear the falconer;
Things fall apart; the centre cannot hold;
Mere anarchy is loosed upon the world,
The blood-dimmed tide is loosed, and everywhere
The ceremony of innocence is drowned;
The best lack all conviction, while the worst
Are full of passionate intensity.

Surely some revelation is at hand;
Surely the Second Coming is at hand.
The Second Coming! Hardly are those words out
When a vast image out of *Spiritus Mundi*
Troubles my sight: somewhere in sands of the desert
A shape with lion body and the head of a man,
A gaze blank and pitiless as the sun,
Is moving its slow thighs, while all about it
Reel shadows of the indignant desert birds.
The darkness drops again; but now I know
That twenty centuries of stony sleep
Were vexed to nightmare by a rocking cradle,
And what rough beast, its hour come round at last,
Slouches towards Bethlehem to be born?

The poem was written in 1919, and expresses Yeats's horror at the carnage that Europe had just experienced in the war.

Text: W.B. Yeats, *The Poems*, Everyman, London, 1992.

What Will the Next Move Be?

James McLaughlin

Text: Leslie H. Daiken, *Good-bye, Twilight – Songs of the Struggle in Ireland*, Lawrence & Wishart, London, 1936.

What will the next move be, O, wise old wizard of Time?
Will the world engage in another great war, and our youth
    be cut down in their prime?
With all the love ties severed, and in anguish and grief of
    soul
Be forced to pass through the shell and gas, to dig down
    and die in a hole?

What are the wise Gods planning, say, O Wizard, say!
Will the moneybags once more open, will they do it the
    same old way?
Will they lend it to save the Nation on bonds that are
    more than secure
And when all is done, and the danger's gone, collect it
    again off the poor?

Must the toiler do the fighting, and when he has the
    victory won
Must he then pay through the noddle for the good work
    he has done?
Must he fight for the gold that he dare not touch and
    comfort he shall not share
For a land – ah, where has he a land? O Wizard, come tell
    me, where?

I stand on the brink of the river and I'm tired enough of
    life
When I look at my half-clad children, my drudged and
    care-worn wife
And I note the cost of living rising day by day
Ever upon the upward grade to a price that I cannot pay.
And, Wizard, I wish you could answer a question that runs
    through my head –
Will the man at the top of the ladder still fix the price of
    bread?

Where is the good Samaritan, when will they play the
    game?
When will we meet together a little bit more the same?
Who will preach the Gospel to teach the grabbing elves
The good and holy maxim, 'Our neighbours as ourselves'?
I feel the pinch of the present, the future, I cannot see –
O Wizard. I'd like you to tell me, what will the next move
    be!

The Fighting 69th

Jerome J. McCuen and Everett J. Evans

There's a band of I-rish sol-diers on the fi-ring line in France,___ And when the Ger-mans see them,___ they'll all go in a trance,___ Their fame has spread be-fore them,___ for va-lour there is none to com-pare with the six-ty-ninth boys. In Eu-rope or at home

Chorus

They are I-rish,___ yes, they're I-rish.___ Old E___ rin gave them birth.___ They've ne-ver yet been con-quered___ on this___ or Eu-rope's earth,___ When France_ sent out her S. O. S. to the U. S. A. for help,___ The six___ ty-ninth were first in line,___ to get___ the Kai-ser's scalp.___

There's a band of Irish soldiers on the firing line in France,
And when the Germans see them, they'll all go in a trance.
Their fame has spread before them, for valour there is none
To compare with the sixty-ninth boys, in Europe or at home.

Chorus
They are Irish. Yes, they're Irish. Old Erin gave them birth.
They've never yet been conquered on this or Europe's earth.
When France sent out her SOS to the USA for help
The sixty-ninth were first in line to get the Kaiser's scalp.

They are first in all engagements. They are noted for their grit.
And like all true-born Irishmen, they were never known to
     quit.
When the band plays 'Garryowen' 'tis then the Germans
     holler,
But the yell that starts them all on the run, shure is old
     'Faugh-a-bollaugh!'

The commercial music industry in the USA did not neglect the war as a source of inspiration and profit. The next five songs were products of that commercial machine.

'The Fighting 69th' is the nickname of the 69th Infantry Regiment of the US army, based in Manhattan.

'Faugh-a-bollaugh!' (properly Ir. *'fág an bealach'*, 'clear the way') was originally the war-cry of the 87th Regiment of the British army, the Royal Irish Fusiliers.

Text & music: Sheet music published by Arbor Music Co., Albany, 1918.

Faugh – a – Ballah

Edward Rose and Abe Olman (1888–1984)

Text & music: Sheet music published in 1917 by Forster Music, Chicago.

There's a new word used today, in the trenches, so they say,
It makes them fight with all their might, and it means to clear the way.
It's Irish as can be and it scares the enemy,
For when they hear this battle cheer it's goodbye Germany.

Chorus
Faugh-a-ballah! the Dublin boys are here, Faugh-a-ballah! just listen to them cheer.
We'll carry on till the last one is gone, And even then we will come again
Just to help the boys along by singing Faugh-a-ballah!
There's something troubling Dublin and, begob, we know just who,
For we'll march right thru like the Irish always do,
When we sing Faugh-a-ballah! in the morning.

Next day the regiment across the top was sent.
They fought and fought and never stopped till every man was spent.
The captain cried, 'Now men, we'll have to rescue them,'
Then came a cheer and we could hear the battle cry again.

The Irish Laddies to the War Have Gone

Dedicated to the 208th Battalion Canadian Irish

Frank O. Madden

Now— Pad-dy dear and did you hear the talk that's go-ing round,
That ould Ire-land's sons aren't lo-yal to the core,
And they're mur-mur-ing that still there are some I-rish to be found,
Who have not yet en-lis-ted for the war.
Sure and Pad-dy dear it's us that knows the fol-ly of such talk,
And how all her sons have gone to meet the foe.
Faith there's no-one left but chil-der and gos-soons too young to walk,
But e-ven they are dril-ling for to go.
Chorus
Faith and who— can be de-ny-ing— that our I-rish lads are there.

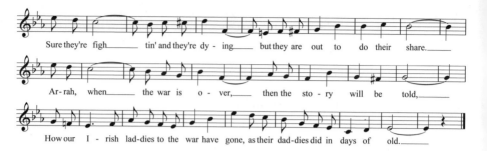

Sure they're figh_____ tin' and they're dy - ing_____ but they are out to do their share._____

Ar- rah, when_____ the war is o - ver,_____ then the sto - ry will be told,_____

How our I - rish lad-dies to the war have gone, as their dad-dies did in days of old._____

Text & music: Sheet music published in 1918 by Anglo Canadian Music, Toronto.
The air cleverly incorporates musical phrases from 'The Wearing of the Green' and 'The Minstrel Boy'.

Now Paddy dear and did you hear the talk that's
  going round,
That auld Ireland's sons aren't loyal to the core?
And they're murmuring that still there are some Irish
  to be found,
Who have not yet enlisted for the war.
Sure and Paddy dear it's us that know the folly of such
  talk,
And how all her sons have gone to meet the foe,
Faith there's no one left but childer' and gossoons too
  young to walk,
But even they are drilling for to go.

Chorus
Faith and who can be denying that our Irish lads are
  there,
Sure they're fightin' and they're dying but they are out
  to do their share,
Arrah! When the war is over, then the story will be
  told,
How our Irish laddies to the war have gone, as their
  daddies did in days of old.

Do you know of any decent fight in all of history,
Where the Irish were not foremost in the fray?
Have you heard of any battles on the land or on the
  sea,
Where the Irish did not fight and win the day?
Sure you'll find our Irish fighting men in every fighting
  force,
Where they know they fight for liberty and right.
Faith, they'd rather fight than eat, although they some-
  times eat of course,
But it's only to fit them for the fight.

My Barney Lies Over the Ocean
(Just the way he lied to me)

Sam M. Lewis (1885–1959), Joe Young (1889–1939) and Bert Grant (1878–1951)

Barney Carney promised he'd be true to Molly-O
The day he went away to war about a year ago.
In every note that Barney wrote he called her 'Ma Cherie,'
She read the name and said with shame, 'this isn't meant
    for me.'
All the neighbours noticed there were teardrops in her eye;
And when they asked her how was Barney, she'd begin to cry:

Text & music: Sheet music published
in 1919 by Waterson, Berlin & Snyder,
Canada.

231

Chorus
My Barney lies over the ocean,
My Barney lies over the sea;
Sure he said he went to war to help the women,
And I think he's helped himself to two or three;
Now he's got a little girl in Belgium and one in Paree,
And I know the little things he tells 'em, when they're on his knee,
Sure my Barney lies over the ocean,
Just the way he lied to me.

Barney wrote a letter home the day the war was through,
He started off with 'Molly, dear, I'm coming home to you.'
He didn't say what week or day, nor did he say what year,
And Molly O said 'Wurra-woe, it's all a joke I fear.'
People said he'd have to wait until the ships come back;
And Molly said 'Why wait for them, why don't he take a hack?'

When Germany Licks England
Old Ireland Will Be Free

Charles A. Meyers

When Ger - ma - ny licks Eng - land old Ire - land will be free
And migh - ty proud we'll be of dear old Ger - ma - ny.
The jinx is on the Bel - gians, the French and Rus - sians, too,
And Eng - land's best like all the rest, they don't know what to do,___
De - fea - ted soon they'll be, they're all up in a tree,
For Ger - ma - ny spells vic - to - ry on a - ny land or sea;
Chorus
Oh, Ger - ma - ny, oh, Ger - ma - ny, Fight on to vic - to - ry,___

When Germany licks England, old Ireland will be free
And mighty proud we'll be of dear old Germany.
The jinx is on the Belgians, the French and Russians too,
And England's best, like all the rest, they don't know
    what to do.
Defeated soon they'll be, they're all up in a tree,
For Germany spells victory on any land or sea.

Chorus
Oh, Germany, oh, Germany, fight on to victory,
Tho' you may be on land or sea, old Ireland's by your
    side.
So strain each gun and make them run, pull down their
    haughty pride,
Then dear old Ireland will be free, so fight on to victory.

We're proud that there's a country like dear old Ger-
    many
That conquers when it fights like Ireland for its rights.
The 'Johnny Bulls', the Belgians, the French and Russians
    too,
They all may fight, but Germany has told us what she'll
    do,
She'll set old Ireland free, so take this tip from me,
With just one gun the Kaiser is the man that makes them
    run.

Text & music: Sheet music published in
1915 by Independent Music Publishers,
Kenosha, Wisconsin.

Faithful Forever

Sean O'Casey (1880–1964)

Text: This poem was originally published in *The Irish Worker* on 26 April 1913, and re-published in Robert Hogan (ed.), *Feathers from the Green Crow – Sean O'Casey 1905–1925*, University of Missouri Press, Columbia, 1962.

Dost hear the tale the traitors tell,
  Ireland, dear Ireland?
In whisper low or joyous yell,
   Of thee, of thee, dear Ireland?
That thou dost eat the Saxon bread;
That all the hopes thy soul hath wed.
Now prostrate lie with all thy dead,
  Ireland, dear Ireland!

They lie, they lie – the cowards – they lie,
  Ireland, dear Ireland.
Nor blazing guns, nor measures sly,
   Can conquer thee, dear Ireland.
Our blood may tinge our rivers' tide,
Our bodies lie our home beside –
We stand where stood all those who died,
   For Ireland, for Ireland.

Ay, till this earth has ceased to roll,
  Ireland, dear Ireland.
Till death has snatched off every soul
   That pants for thee, dear Ireland.
We'll kindle freedom's magic blaze,
And stand defiant 'neath its rays,
Till, armed and strong, the Gaodheal repays
   His bloody debts, dear Ireland.

Mark that man's face – worn and pale,
  Ireland, dear Ireland.
'Twas fashioned so in England's gaol –
   He fought for thee, dear Ireland.
Her bloody mark is on his brow,
But, as of old, he hates her now,
Her fall is still his prayer and vow,
   His love is thine, dear Ireland.

Beneath thy flag fresh hopes we feel,
  Ireland, dear Ireland.
We'll gild its folds with glint of steel,
   And rifles' flame, dear Ireland.
In garish day, 'neath night's damp dew,
Its green and white and orange hue
Shall signal death to England's crew,
   And hope to thee, dear Ireland.

God of the Gael! our banner bless,
    And Ireland, dear Ireland.
And in the battle's tedious stress
    Oh! nerve our arm for Ireland!
Now Fenian proud, lift high your head,
'Twas vows, but now 'tis blows instead,
For vengeance, for our Martyred Dead,
    For Freedom and for Ireland!

Sean O'Casey as a young man.

The Grand Oul' Dame Britannia

Sean O'Casey

Och, Ireland, sure I'm proud of you –
    Ses the Grand Oul' Dame Britannia,
To poor little Belgium tried and true
    Ses the Grand Oul' Dame Britannia.
Ye've closed your ear to the Sinn Féin lies,
For you know each Gael that for England dies
Will enjoy Home Rule in the clear blue skies,
    Ses the Grand Oul' Dame Britannia.

Ah, Casement! Damn that Irish pig,
    Ses the Grand Oul' Dame Britannia,
We'll make him dance an English jig
    Ses the Grand Oul' Dame Britannia.
But Redmond's here – the good and great,
A pillar of the English State.
Who fears to speak of 'Ninety-eight'–
    Ses the Grand Oul' Dame Britannia,

The 'Grand Oul' (Old) Dame Britannia' is of course England, and the word 'Ses' is colloquial Dublinese for 'says'.

Verse 1 recounts the propaganda of WWI – 'poor little Belgium' and the 'freedom of small nations', while Ireland was being held in subjection by England. The Home Rule reference is to the prospect of Home Rule being granted to Ireland following a British victory in WWI, but in this instance the reference is sarcastic as the Irish who would die for England would not be around to enjoy anything.

In verse 2 the English jig for Casement is the dance at the end of the hangman's rope, which was the fate of Casement. The references to Redmond, here and throughout the poem (John Redmond, (1856–1918), the leader of the Irish Parliamentary

235

Party), depict England being grateful to their supporter, Redmond. A moderate Nationalist, he had urged the Irish Volunteers, in his famous Woodenbridge speech of 20 September 1914, to join the British army for service in WWI. This split the Volunteers, the majority of whom did in fact follow Redmond's advice.

In verse 4 O'Casey alludes to the fact that there are still, despite the subservience of Redmond and his followers, unreconstructed separatists roaming about the country spreading sedition.

'The Castle' (verse 3) is Dublin Castle, the centre of British power in Ireland. See the reference to 'Shane the Proud' on p. 254.

''67' refers to the Fenian Rising of 1867, and 'Bachelor's Walk' recalls the incident in 1914, when the King's Own Scottish Borderers, a British army regiment, on returning empty-handed from an exercise to seize the guns being landed at Howth, Co. Dublin, were jeered by a crowd, and opened fire on unarmed civilians, killing three (see the song '26th July 1914', page 98).

The Hibernian Academy of verse 5 is the Royal Hibernian Academy, an organization of and for artists, founded in 1823 and still extant. Britain is here saying that she needs every penny for weaponry, and thus cannot give anything to artists; an O'Casey sideswipe at artistic servility. In verse 6 England calls on all Irishmen to enlist in the Irish Guards, a regiment of the British army, and their reward will be a tombstone and a shroud ('winding sheet').

Verse 7 returns to the theme of treating Redmond with sarcasm. In November 1915 he made a well-publicized visit to the front lines in France and while there was allowed to fire a round from a cannon, an event that excited ridicule rather than admiration at home. In the final verse the 'Inspector' Quinn referred to is Superintendent Fergus Quinn (DMP), who was in charge of the police during the 1913 street violence. O'Casey would have seen Quinn, a Nationalist, as a class-enemy and a tool of the capitalists. In 1920 Quinn was summarily dismissed, despite his long years of loyal service, as his loyalties were suspect.

The poem ends on a panic note, the news that the British have had to retreat from the Dardenelles.

The Castle's now an altered place,
    Ses the Grand Oul' Dame Britannia,
It's the Drawing Room of the Irish race
    Ses the Grand Oul' Dame Britannia.
John Redmond to the throne is bowed
'Mid a frantic cheerin' Irish crowd.
Sure it's like the days of Shane the Proud,
    Ses the Grand Oul' Dame Britannia.

For Redmond now Home Rule has won,
    Ses the Grand Oul' Dame Britannia,
And he's finished what Wolfe Tone begun
    Ses the Grand Oul' Dame Britannia
Yet rebels through the country stalk,
Shouting ''67' and 'Bachelor's Walk'–
Did ye ever hear such foolish talk?
    Ses the Grand Oul' Dame Britannia.

Ye want a pound or two from me!
    Ses the Grand Oul' Dame Britannia,
For your oul' Hibernian Academy!
    Ses the Grand Oul' Dame Britannia.
Don't ye know we've got the Huns to quell,
And we want the cash for shot and shell.
Your artists! – Let them go to hell,
    Ses the Grand Oul' Dame Britannia.

Ah Scholars, Hurlers, Saints and Bards!
    Ses the Grand Oul' Dame Britannia,
Come along an' list in the Irish Guards,
    Ses the Grand Oul' Dame Britannia.
Each man that treads on a German's feet
'ill be given a parcel – tied up neat –
Of a Tombstone Cross an' a winding sheet,
    Ses the Grand Oul' Dame Britannia.

Be jabers, Redmond, you're the Bhoy!
    Ses the Grand Oul' Dame Britannia,
Sure you're Ireland's pride and England's joy,
    Ses the Grand Oul' Dame Britannia.
Like a true-born Gael he faced the Hun,
Then he jumped around an' fired a gun.
Faix, you should have seen the Germans run!
    Ses the Grand Oul' Dame Britannia.

Sure I spoke today with Inspector Quinn,
    Ses the Grand Oul' Dame Britannia,

An' he told me straight we were bound to win!
    Ses the Grand Oul' Dame Britannia.
What mean these deafening newsboys' yells?
What tale is this the Paper tells –
A British retreat from the Dardanelles!
    Ses the Grand Oul' Dame Britannia.

O! these Irish that our interests vex,
    Ses the Grand Oul' Dame Britannia.
We'll put the rope around their necks,
    Ses the Grand Oul' Dame Britannia.
Look! See those march with rousing cheers;
Who dare to talk of Saxon fears –
Hurrah for the Dublin Fusiliers,
    Ses the Grand Oul' Dame Britannia.

Oh! Fearless, Fulsome, Firey Gael,
    Ses the Grand Oul' Dame Britannia.
Strike now for Right and Inishfail,
    Ses the Grand Oul' Dame Britannia.
We've cut the curls from 'The Dear Dark Head',
We've pulled the green below the red,
Mitchell, Tone! ah! sure they're dead;
    Ses the Grand Oul' Dame Britannia.

God strengthen you, my Irish son,
    Ses the Grand Oul' Dame Britannia.
In your fight against the bloody Hun,
    Ses the Grand Oul' Dame Britannia.
What! a half-brained, stupid, sinful Gael
Hopes the British arms will fail?
God! clasp the scoundrel into gaol;
    Ses the Grand Oul' Dame Britannia.

For La Belle France and Belgium's love,
    Ses the Grand Oul' Dame Britannia.
For England and for God above,
    Ses the Grand Oul' Dame Britannia.
The land of Hypocrites and whines,
Where sin is not, and virtue shines –
The land of truth and Wild Woodbines!
    Ses the Grand Oul' Dame Britannia.

The 'Wild Woodbines' of the last verse were a brand of cigarette, the cheapest on the market. [LM]

Text: Four different versions of this song have been found. The first eight verses here are from the version published in *The Workers' Republic* in January 1916, and reproduced in *Feathers from the Green Crow*. O'Casey's *Windfalls* (1934) contains a seven-verse version, lacking the final verse here, and having a different version of the second verse. The final four verses here are from a ballad sheet.
    Air: 'Leather Away the Wattle O!'.

The Lepracaun, February 1915.

If the Germans Came to Ireland in the Mornin'

Sean O'Casey

There are men in this 'ere Nation without any
  education –
  An asylum ward they ought to be adornin' –
For they tell us – holy Moses – life 'ud be a bed o' roses
  If the Germans came to Ireland in the mornin'.

To capture, sure, they're eager, each United Irish
  Leaguer,
  In Home Rule Sauce to give them all a cornin';
An' the men that serve King Billy, they'd be fed on
  Popish skilly
  If the Germans came to Ireland in the mornin'.

Now, the noble men that lade yez, they'd imprison in
  bird cages,
  An' make them whistle God Save Ireland, out o'
    scornin' –
Oh! the Germans are such damn rogues, they'd destroy
  our harps an' shamrogues,
  If they came and landed here now in the mornin'.

Billy Brien an' Johnny Dillon one another 'ud be killin';
  The Nation inside out, sure, they'd be turnin';
Foul faction would be loosed, sir, an' the Home Rule
  Bill be goosed, sir,
  If the Germans came to Ireland in the mornin'.

In our noble secret service the peelers now are nervous,
  For they'd kill these gentle creatures without warnin'

Sean O'Casey's comic/satirical song
makes fun of those who forecast dire
consequences of the Germans coming to
Ireland. The song is of WWI vintage,
when anti-German propaganda and
horror-stories were part and parcel of
the English war effort and recruitment
campaign.
  United Irish League (second verse)
– the political party, founded in 1898
with its slogan 'The Land for the
People' – championed land reform.
  Home Rule (second verse) – this was
a measure of limited independence, the
struggle for which commenced in the
1860s. The first two Home Rule Bills,
1886 and 1893, were defeated. The
Third Home Rule Bill was passed by the
British parliament in 1914, but was set
aside for the duration of WWI. Events
overcame it and, after the 1916 Rising,
Home Rule was no longer seen to be
enough, full independence being then
demanded.
  The men that serve King Billy (second verse) – the Unionists, who opposed Home Rule and wished to remain
an integral part of the United Kingdom.
  Billy Brien and Johnny Dillon (third
verse) – William O'Brien, a social
reformer and agrarian agitator, founder
of the United Irish league (UIL); John
Dillon was another leader of the UIL.
  Peelers (verse 4) were the Royal Irish
Constabulary (RIC), the para-military
police force, drawn mainly from the
Irish, nationalist, rural population,
which policed Ireland in England's
interest and vigorously suppressed

239

sedition and rebellion – hence the later violence against the RIC by the IRA.

The reference in the last verse to 'the Sinn Féin rainbow chaser' is an indication of O'Casey's distrust of 'nationalism'. O'Casey, a member of the Irish Citizen Army, the workers' protection corps, was himself socialist and suspicious of 'green tories'. [LM]

This song, and the seven that follow, are from O'Casey's three *Songs of the Wren* songsters, published in 1918.

Air: 'I'm Off to Philadelphia in the Mornin' '.

Every peeler on his beat, sir, they'd cut off his little feet, sir,
   An' make submarines of his boots, then, in the
     mornin'.

Sure as God made little apples, they'd demolish all our chapels,
   An' our grand homes in the slums that we were
     born in –
With their big guns firing' shrapnel, well – God help
   poor Charlie Chaplin –
   If the Germans came to Ireland in the mornin'!

Now take heed to what I'm sayin', they'd destroy potato
   sprayin' –
   Sure with indignation sore my hear is burnin' –
And what would happen, pray, sir, to the Sinn Féin
   rainbow chaser
   If the Germans came to Ireland in the mornin'!

We've Captured the Cave of Machpelah

Sean O'Casey

'The British ams have scored a great victory by the capture of Hebron, which contains the Cave of Machpelah, the tomb of Abraham.' *The Daily Mail.*

This mock-heroic song is typical of O'Casey's output. He wrote many of these in the WWI period. The tone of this song is seemingly boastful at the wonderful military achievements of the British, but in reality the song is

In the fight for Poor Freedom against the Huns,
We've lost thousands and thousands and thousands of
   guns;
But still in the struggle we're givin' them tons,
   An' we've captured the Cave of Machpelah!

Chorus:

Hurrah! for John Bull and for Uncle Sam –
We're losin' the War, but we don't care a damn,
For we've taken the tomb of poor Abraham,
    An' we're captured the cave of Machpelah!

To triumph they'll carry the Union Jack –
Our warriors bold, brown, red and black
The Germans hit us, but we're hittin' them back –
    An' we're captured the cave of Machpelah!

With joy an' with Pride, now, our bosoms thrill!
Tho' we're losin' each dale an' we're losin' each hill,
But we're givin' the bloodthirsty Germans their fill,
    For we're captured the cave of Machpelah!

Wirrastrue, Wirrastrue, we have lost Trieste,
An' the Germans are reignin' in Bucharest –
But these losses are now but a mighty jest,
    Since we're captured the cave of Machpelah!

We're proud, aye, we're proud of our British pluck,
That fought against Hope and the hardest of luck,
We've won all we want an' we've settled Von Kluck,
    For we're captured the cave of Machpelah!

Mackensen may brag and the Kaiser may blow
About Russia's and Italy's overthrow,
But they'll soon change their tune when they get to know
    That we're captured the cave of Machpelah!

mocking and sarcastic, as the Cave of Machpelah and Abraham's tomb were of no military significance and indeed worthless.

In the fourth verse – 'wirrastrue' is 'A Mhuire, is truagh' (Mary, it is sad'), an exclamation.

Von Kluck, fifth verse, was General Alexander Heinrich Rudolph von Kluck (1846–1934) a German general of WWI.

Mackensen, sixth verse, refers to General August von Mackensen (1849–1945) a German WWI general, and readers may wish to read of the MacDonald/Mackensen myth, a somewhat fantastical conspiracy tale of two generals, on the one hand Major-General Hector Archibald MacDonald (*c.* 1852–1903), a British general of Scots origin, and the above General von Mackensen. [LM]

Air: The air specified by O'Casey was 'Under the Willow Tree'. It is assumed that this is the air used here: Stephen Foster's 'Under the Willow She's Sleeping'.

The Divil's Recruitin' Campaign

Sean O'Casey

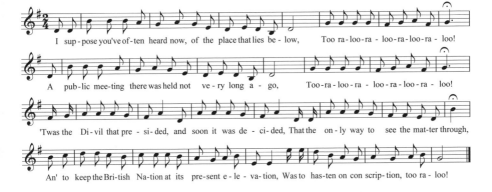

I suppose you've often heard now, of the place that lies below, Too ra-loo-ra - loo-ra-loo-ra - loo!

A public meeting there was held not very long ago, Too-ra-loo-ra - loo-ra-loo-ra - loo!

'Twas the Divil that presided, and soon it was decided, That the only way to see the matter through,

An' to keep the British Nation at its present elevation, Was to hasten on conscription, too ra - loo!

A different, six-verse version of this song, credited to Brian O'Higgins, was published in *The Workers' Republic* Vol 1, No. 33, 8 January 1916. Only verses 1 and 4 here are shared with the other version, which can be found on p. 269.

Air: 'Sergeant Willy Baily'.

I suppose you've often heard, now, of the place that lies
 below –
 Tooral ooral, ooral, ooral, ooo!
A public meeting there was held not very long ago,
 Tooral ooral, ooral, ooral, ooo!
'Twas the Divil that presided, and soon it was decided
 That the only way to see the matter through,
An' to keep the British Nation at its present elevation,
 Was to hasten on Conscription, tooral ooo!

Ses the Divil, 'Things in Ireland, now, they will not do at
 all' –
 An' he spoke in tones of thunder, tooral ooo!
'All the men that's left in Ireland, now, will have to hear
 the call
 To get out and to get under, tooral ooo!'
Ses his Secretary, 'Look, sir, Home Rule's on the Statute
 Book, sir;
 And we've only just another thing to do:
The Duke of Connaught swear in as the great High King
 of Eireann,
 And we'll get recruits in thousands, tooral ooo!'

Ses the Divil, 'In our Empire things have reached a pretty
 pass,
 Tooral ooral, ooral, ooral, ooo!
With their air raids, submarines an' all their latest
 poisoned gas,
 Tooral ooral, ooral, ooral, ooo!
But I wouldn't still be carin' if it wasn't now for Erin,
 And the doings of the silly Sinn Féin crew;
I'm beginnin' to feel queer, oh! with this cursed De
 Valera –
 Tooral ooral, ooral, ooral, ooo!'

An' the Divil sent his agents out to gather in recruits,
 Tooral ooral, ooral, ooral, ooo!
To preserve the Saints in England an' destroy the
 German Brutes,
 Tooral ooral, ooral, ooral, ooo!
You'll get a welcome hearty from the gallant Irish
 Party –
 Tell them to spread an' preach what isn't true –
'Twas written by St Kevin that no Gael could enter
 Heaven,
 Unless he dyed the green, red, white and blue.

After years an' years an' years of work his agents all
   came back,
   Tooral ooral, ooral, ooral, ooo!
They carried an old man just nicely tied up in a sack,
   Tooral ooral, ooral, ooral, ooo!
We could only just get one sir, to put the khaki on, sir –
   Tho' we searched an' searched the country through
   an' through;
He'll join the British Awmy, but the doctors say he's
   bawmy –
   Tooral ooral, ooral, ooral, ooo!

The Man from the 'Daily Mail'

Sean O'Casey

Ireland is a very curious place, sir –
   Far stranger than Japan –
Where the boys are a very curious race, sir,
   An' each girl's becomin' a man!

This sarcastic song mocks the English
newspaper correspondents and their
prejudiced views of Ireland, its affairs
and its people.
   The *Daily Mail* was an English
newspaper, which still exists.

THE NEW "OLD MAN OF THE SEA."

"I am convinced that Parliamentary agitation, as now conducted, has spent its force,
and that nothing more can be gained by it on its present lines." . . . . . "I do not
believe that the English-speaking people will ever grant Home Rule or anything like it."

Letter from SIR THOMAS ESMONDE, M.P.—*Daily Papers*, July 22nd, 1907.

Thomas Fitzpatrick, 'The Old Man of the Sea', *The Lepracaun*, August 1907. In the tale from *The Arabian Nights* the Old Man of the Sea tricks travellers into carrying him across a stream, and then refuses to release them.

No matter where you travel to discover,
    How are all in Inisfail –
You'll find that, begorra, things will change by tomorrow
    Says the man from the *Daily Mail!*

Every night, in the pale moonlight,
    They're all drillin' oh! it's thrillin'
Every lad is gone ravin' mad,
    Over here, now; oh! it's queer now.
Armed with skeens and sharp dudeens,
    That would make your stout heart quail –
Oh! I'm shakin' in my shoes as I'm sendin' on the news–
    Says the man from the *Daily Mail!*

The country's now a fire of ragin' passions,
    And it's Sinn Féin, through and through;
And the Polis, now are joinin' the Dalcassians,
    While their pass-word's 'dhiginn thu'.
Every doggie has a tri-coloured banner
    Tied firmly to his tail –
Ah! I'll have to quit the service, for bedad, I'm getting nervous
    Says the man from the *Daily Mail.*

Every time the church bells chime,
    The crowd comes out, sir, an' run about, sir;
Every boy, with a shout of joy,
    Eats a spud, then, steep'd in blood, then;
The drums then beat in a fierce retreat,
    An' the war-pipes wildly wail –
Oh! all the country's shaken, or I'm very much mistaken–
    Says the man from the *Daily Mail!*

The other day I travelled down to Clare, boys,
    An' I saw in the old boreen,
A squad of brave and busy ganders there boys,
    Dress'd in orange, white an' green;
They marched with the German goose-step
    As they warbl'd Granuaile –
Oh! it won't be surprisin,' if there be another risin' –
    Says the man from the *Daily Mail.*

Every bird, upon my solemn word,
    Is singing treble, I'm a rebel,
The hens – the jades – are layin' hand grenades,
    By the score, now, ay, an' more, now;

Inisfail, verse 1, (Inis Fáil, the Island of Destiny) is another name for Ireland.

Skeens and dudeens, verse 2, are knives and clay pipes; obviously a mock reference.

Verse 3 – Polis are the RIC (Royal Irish Constabulary), Dalcassians are in this context the Irish, but strictly speaking the people of Dal gCais, an area approximating the present County Clare. 'dhiginn thu' is 'an dtuigeann tú? (do you understand?). Tri-coloured banner is a reference to the then-revolutionary flag of green, white and orange.

Verse 5 – boreen, a small, very often unpaved road, from 'bóthairín' little road. Granuaile, from Gráinne Ní Mháille, Grace O'Malley (*c.* 1530 – *c.* 1603), Connaught sea queen and pirate who was a most formidable foe of English (Elizabeth I) rule in Ireland. The name Granuaile has been some-times used to personify Ireland, and can be taken so in this song.

Verse 7 makes the point that nei-ther inducement nor repression will succeed in weaning the Irish from their devilish ways and in the last verse the Man from the *Daily Mail* says that if the Irish were outright foes then the English could kill them, and the word Hottentot, now re-garded as derogatory, refers to the in-digenous Khoi people of South Africa. The term 'Irish Hottentot' is another way of saying 'Irish savage'. [LM]

Although O'Casey attacks the newspaper for its supposed attitude to Ireland, in fact, according to John Simpson, it was *Daily Mail* reports that revealed to the British public the nature and extent of Black and Tan outrages in Ireland.

Air: Percy French's 'The Girl from the County Clare'.

Every cock in the farmer's stock
  Crows the triumph of the Gael.
Oh, our power may be pretended, but I fear our day
  is ended
  Says the man from the *Daily Mail.*

It's useless to be trying for to coax them
  With Conventions in the air,
For they're thinkin' that we're tryin' hard to hoax them,
  An' they're laughin' everywhere,
An' we only make them worse an' worse than ever,
  If we clap them into jail.
I'm afraid we'll never win them, for, bedad, the divil's
  in them,
  Says the man from the *Daily Mail.*

Heaven knows, we wish they weren't foes,
  For then we'd send them where war 'ud end them;
Happy lot for an Irish Hottentot
  A grave to find, sir, to save mankind, sir,
But faith I'll pack my luggage on my back
  An' for England now I'll sail –
There's no further use o' spakin', for my counsel won't
  be taken –
  Says the man from the *Daily Mail.*

The Demi-Semi Home Rule Bill

Sean O'Casey

The__ strug - gle now is o - ver, oul' Ire - land, sure, is free,
An' if you don't be - lieve__ it, well just you wait and see.
For the fruits of th'Ir - ish Par - ty, tho' Sinn Féi - ners say they're nil,
Is a de - mi, se - mi, se - mi, de - mi, de - mi Home Rule Bill.
With__ knives and forks stuck in them the__ pigs will run a - bout

And___ when they see a green flag, "Who'll___ eat me?" they will shout!

An' each fish 'll come to the land and use his tail as a wri - tin' pen,

An' they'll write on all the rocks an' trees "A Na - tion once a - gain"

The struggle now is over, oul' Ireland, sure, is free,
An' if you don't believe it – well, just you wait an' see!
For the fruits of th' Irish Party – tho' Sinn Féiners say
    they're nil –
Is a demi-semi, semi-demi, demi-i-i-i-i-i-i-i-i-i-i Home
    Rule Bill!

With knives an' forks stuck in them the pigs will run
    about,
And when they see a green flag 'who'll eat me' they
    will shout;
An' each fish 'ill come to the land and use his tail as a
    writin' pen,
An' they'll write on all the rocks an' trees 'A Nation
    Once Again!'

The peelers then will meet us with faces mild and bland –
Instead of batons each'll wave green shamrocks in his
    hand.
'Twill be a thing of joy to meet them as they march
    along the street,
For they'll all look like fairies – if it wasn't for their feet!

To make us saints an' sages will only take a week,
An' we'll all be speakin' Latin, Esperanto, ay, an' Greek;
Every hungry man an' woman will then eat an' drink
    their fill,
When in the Statute Book they'll send along the demi-
    semi Home Rule Bill!

Oh! the Force of Evolution may be workin' in the land;
An' Dunraven's Devolution, yet, may get the upper
    hand;
Or a Sinn Féin Revolution may be brewin' here – but,
    still,
We'll know no peace in Ireland till we get the Home
    Rule Bill!

O'Casey makes fun of the Home Rule movement, and this would be consistent with his socialist political view – he seeing Home Rule as a bourgeois settlement, with it having little or no positive effect upon the worker's lot.

The Irish Party of verse 1 is the Irish Parliamentary Party, which sat in Westminster and the Sinn Féiners are the nationalists of Arthur Griffith's pre-1916 Sinn Féin.

'A Nation Once Again', verse 2, is the popular nationalist song, written by Thomas Davis (1814–45).

The peelers, verse three, were the police, the members of the RIC (Royal Irish Constabulary), the paramilitary police force composed mainly of Irishmen, and which was the main agent in maintaining English rule in Ireland.

Dunraven's Devolution, verse four, refers to the movement of Irish gentry and landlords, which met in Dublin in 1904. The Irish Reform Association, in which the Earl of Dunraven was a leading figure, arose from this meeting, and the aim of this body was to achieve, by moderate means, a form of Home Rule. [LM]

Air: 'The Wearin' o' the Green'.

I Don't Believe It, Do You?

Sean O'Casey

'Twould sic-ken a sen-si-ble man, now, to hear The way some peo-ple talk of the war,

For they say, sure, in spite of all that we've gained, That we sim-ply don't know where we are;

They should view the per-spec-tive and then they would see All the things that we know are-n't there,

For though lo-sin' an' lo-sin' an' lo-sin' in fights We're win-nin' now eve-ry-where.

Chorus

But I don't be-lieve it, do you It's real-ly too good to be true;

We're ma-kin' a won-der-ful change in the maps Through the pluck of our sai-lors an' khar-ki-clad chaps

And we'll be in Ber-lin in a twelve month, per-haps! But I hard-ly be-lieve it, do you?

This song lampoons the propaganda of the British in WWI.

The Zeppelins, verse 3, were the airships used for military purposes, and also for transport of people up to the late 1930s, when their use fell into rapid decline following the 'Hindenburg' disaster of 1937.

General Friend, verse 4, is a reference to Major-General Friend, commander of British troops in Ireland, who was on leave in England when the 1916 Rising broke out. He returned immediately to Dublin and took part in the suppression of the Rising.

'By the Police joinin' the Hibs' – a mocking suggestion of the RIC (Royal Irish Constabulary), the paramilitary police force that held Ireland for England, joining the Ancient Order of Hibernians, a nationalist organization. [LM]

Air: 'I've Never Been Courting Before'.

'Twould sicken a sensible man, now, to hear
    The way some people talk of the war,
For they say, sure, in spite of all that we've gained,
    That we simply don't know where we are;
They should view the perspective and then they would see
    All the things that we know aren't there –
For tho' losin' an' losin' an' losin' in fights
    We're winnin' now everwhere.

Chorus
But I don't believe it, do you, oo oo?
It's really too good to be true;
We're makin' a wonderful change in the maps
Through the pluck of our sailors an' kharki-clad chaps
An' we'll be in Berlin in a twelvemonth – perhaps!
But I hardly believe it, do you?

Don't believe all you hear about Zeppelin raids –
    That we're all frightened out of our wits.
And every night that they come over here

That they always blow London to bits.
Sure, we laugh as we see them up high in the skies,
    For a Zeppelin nobody hurts,
An' we sing Rule Britannia an' God Save the King,
    An' we dance in the streets in our shirts!

Chorus
But I don't believe it, do you?
It's really too good to be true!
The other night one came across in the dark,
And dropped a big bomb right on top of Hyde Park –
And knocked the wing off a linnet, a thrush and a lark –
    Oh! I hardly believe it, do you?

Some say, now, Sinn Féin our dear Country will save,
    From the top, sure, right down to the end;
Some say our one hope is a Government firm,
    Exercised now by General Friend.
A new Party proclaim that these methods are crude,
    And they're only political squibs,
And Ireland, they say, will be saved from her foes
    By the Police now joinin' the Hibs!

Chorus
Now, I don't believe it, do you,
It's really too good to be true!
Fancy these men as they go to and fro,
Shouting out 'I'm a rebel,' be japers, an' so –
Well, that's just the absolute limit you know,
    So I don't believe it, do you?

The Bonnie Bunch of Roses, O!

Sean O'Casey

Dear England, now we'll take a walk,
    Says the Bonnie Bunch of Roses O,
An' we'll have a quiet little talk,
    Says the Bonnie Bunch of Roses O,
An' I'll show you places in the land
Where the stroke of your soft, gentle hand
Ruled – for our good – you understand?
    Says the Bonnie Bunch of Roses O.

This song recounts the historic wrongs done to Ireland by England. The phrase 'the Bonnie Bunch of Roses' originally referred to the British army, because of their red uniforms, but in this song it would seem to refer to Ireland.
    Verse 2 brings 'England' to Saint Catherine's Church, Thomas Street, Dublin, outside of which Robert Emmet (1778–1803) was executed, for organizing an insurrection in Dublin in 1803.

249

Mullaghmast, verse 3, is a place in Co. Kildare, where, about 1578, over one hundred Irish Chieftains and their followers were entrapped and slaughtered, some slain and some burned, by the English. The Irish had been lured to the fortress on a pretext, for the purpose of annihilation.

Newgate, verse 3, was the Dublin prison in which Lord Edward Fitzgerald (1763–98), the revolutionary and United Irishman leader, died from wounds received during his arrest. Wolfe Tone actually died in the Provost's Prison in the Royal Barracks, now the NMI. Regarded as the father of Irish Republicanism, Tone died from a throat wound, generally believed to have been self-inflicted to cheat the hangman, but here O'Casey claims that Tone was murdered by the English – a possibility that cannot be discounted.

The Quays and the North Wall in verse 4 refers to the transportation through Dublin, where these places are located, of John Mitchel (1815–75), to Van Diemen's Land (Tasmania) in 1848, following the failed Young Ireland Rising of that year. Mitchel, like Tone, believed that the freedom struggle should be based on the 'men of no property'. Mitchel escaped in 1853 and went to America.

Verse 5 refers to Limerick, Sarsfield and the Treaty Stone. The Siege of Limerick took place in 1691; Patrick Sarsfield (c. 1660–93) was an Irish cavalry commander who fought in the Williamite War (1689–91), which ended with the Siege of Limerick. Of the Treaty of Limerick, it was said "Twas broken ere the ink wherewith 'twas writ could dry' – an allusion to the treachery of the English. The Treaty Stone is allegedly the stone on which the treaty paper was signed. The stone features as a monument on the banks of the River Shannon in Limerick City.

In verse 6, O'Casey's own strong Labour feelings can be detected. He refers to James Connolly (1868–1916), the Labour leader and Marxist revolutionary, executed after the 1916 Rising.

In the final verse, O'Casey refers to a topic of the day in 1918, and the threat of conscription in Ireland (to supply troops for the British army in WWI). There was massive Irish opposition to the conscription threat, hence the statement that though Ireland be crammed with soldiers (English) and guns, conscription and England 'be damned'. [LM]

The Church that stands here in this place,
   Says the Bonnie Bunch of Roses O,
Looked down on Emmet's noble face,
   Says the Bonnie Bunch of Roses O,
Just here his sacred blood was shed –
I hear now what the hangman said:
'Behold the shameless traitor's head' –
   Says the Bonnie Bunch of Roses O.

Now, isn't this a lovely scene?
   Says the Bonnie Bunch of Roses O,
With its trees an' grass an' rath serene,
   Says the Bonnie Bunch of Roses O,
This place links up our country's past –
No wonder, now, you stand aghast –
For there's blood on the slopes of Mullaghmast,
   Says the Bonnie Bunch of Roses O.

The jail of Newgate once stood here,
   Says the Bonnie Bunch of Roses O,
Why do you shake like that with fear?
   Says the Bonnie Bunch of Roses O,
Before me visions sadly float;
'Twas here poor Eire's heart you smote,
When you cut poor helpless Wolfe Tone's throat,
   Says the Bonnie Bunch of Roses O.

We're walkin', now, along the Quays,
   Says the Bonnie Bunch of Roses O,
I hope, dear friend, my words will please –
   Says the Bonnie Bunch of Roses O,
When Mitchel answered Ireland's call
He passed in chains down this North Wall –
We've forgot all this? Oh, not at all –
   Says the Bonnie Bunch of Roses O.

This place we're in is Limerick Town,
   Says the Bonnie Bunch of Roses O,
Ah, England, dear, why do you frown?
   Says the Bonnie Bunch of Roses O,
For here your word was overthrown,
When Sarsfield left the land alone –
Ah, a teacher great is the Treaty Stone!
   Says the Bonnie Bunch of Roses O.

Strong Labour here his vigil keeps,
   Says the Bonnie Bunch of Roses O,
O'er the place where Connolly calmly sleeps,

Says the Bonnie Bunch of Roses O,
His teachings true in Ireland soon
Shall flourish like the flowers in June –
I'm afraid they'll hasten on your ruin –
Says the Bonnie Bunch of Roses O.

Conscript the Gael is now your cry,
Says the Bonnie Bunch of Roses O,
Ah, listen to our calm reply,
Says the Bonnie Bunch of Roses O,
Tho' the country be with soldiers crammed,
Tho' every street with guns be jammed –
Conscription, ay! an' you be damned!
Says the Bonnie Bunch of Roses O.

Air: 'The Grand Oul' Dame Britannia',
see p. 235.

We Welcome the Aid of Japan

Sean O'Casey

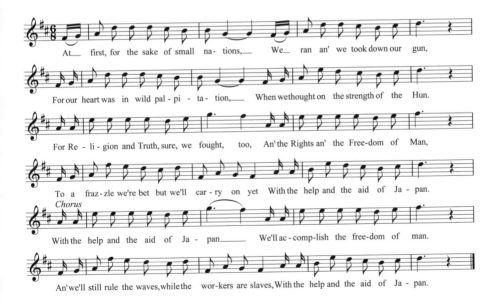

At first, for the sake of small nations,
We ran an' we took down our gun,
For our heart was in wild palpitation
When we thought on the strength of the Hun.

This is another typical O'Casey song, in a humorous, mocking vein, and with a social message, though relatively little in this case. As if written by an Englishman, the song recounts

251

the events of WWI, and mentions countries involved in the conflict. The chorus has the social message, in 'while the workers are slaves' – a reference to the fact that no matter what the nationality of the ruling class, the workers will remain in their condition of slavery.

The fifth verse notes the rise of Sinn Féin, the Irish nationalist movement, and the 'For she didn't act fair' phrase in the penultimate line of that verse probably refers to the 1916 Rising, which England and its Irish supporters saw as a stab in the back.

Nelson and Drake, in the sixth verse, refers to the two English naval heroes, and the word 'haythen' in the last verse is 'heathen'. [LM]

In October 1914 the United Kingdom enlisted Japan's assistance to besiege and take the Chinese port of Tsingtao, which was the home base of the German Navy's East Asia Squadron.

Air: 'Twenty-Four Strings to My Bow' by James J. Wills and Joseph Gabriele.

For Religion and Truth, sure, we fought, too,
   An' the Rights an' the Freedom of Man –
To a frazzle we're bet – but we'll carry on yet
   With the help and the aid of Japan!

Chorus:
With the help and the aid of Japan,
   We'll accomplish the freedom of man:
An' we'll still rule the waves, while the workers are
   slaves,
   With the help and the aid of Japan!

Poor Belgium, like a little goose, sir,
   Answered quickly fair Honour's loud call,
But Germany's strength was let loose, sir,
   And, faith, she soon ended them all;
And now our poor Belgium is numbered
   With horses that then also ran –
Sure, that's just as well – let her now go to hell,
   For we've captured the aid of Japan!

On Russia for years we depended,
   But their tidy and trim apple car
The merciless Hun soon upended,
   And, now, we've no use for the Czar!
And the Bolshevicks fierce have destroyed, too,
   Our nicely developing plan –
But now we don't care for the great Russian bear,
   For we've collared the aid of Japan!

Roumania, all caution and cunning,
   Came out on the side of the Right,
Bur, faith, sure, I hear they are running –
   They never had stomachs for fight.
And these gilded chocolate soldiers
   Finished up well before they began;
But we've got to, now, keep our hands to the plough,
   So we welcome the aid of Japan!

Now, Ireland is blighted with Sinn Féin –
   Tho' we thought that she'd give us her aid –
For they're all thinkin' now of their own gain
   By diggin' up plots with a spade.
But if ever we get a good chance, boys,
   Her obstinate hide we will tan,
For she didn't act fair – ah! but still we'll get there,
   With the much welcome aid of Japan!

Tho' Providence helped us before, boys,
    In the great days of Nelson and Drake,
I'm afraid that she'll help us no more, boys,
    For she thinks that we're out on the make!
But now we can well do without her,
    And we laugh at her pitiful ban –
For we don't care a damn, now, for Bible or psalm,
    For we've captured the aid of Japan!

The Japanese may be a haythen –
    A bloody and villainous tyke –
But when we're at war we're not playin',
    And that's just the thing that we like!
For Civilization needs, now, boys,
    The help, sure, of every man,
And the Savage, we find, is a help to Mankind –
    So we welcome the aid of Japan!

'The Anglo-Japanese Alliance – 'Will you come into my parlour' said the Spider to the Fly.'
This cartoon by Thomas Fitzpatrick was published in *The Lepracaun* in October 1905.

England's Conscription Appeal to Ireland's Dead

Sean O'Casey

Saint Pa - trick, save the na - tion kind, That la - boured hard your flock to teach,

A ful - ler des - ti - ny to find Like co - ckles on a san - dy beach.

Now we want them all to help us, Though it seems they'd ra - ther skelp us.

Hear us and your praise we'll hymn it. Says Saint Pa - trick: that's the li - mit.

Ha, ha, ha, Ha, ha, ha, Says Saint Pa - trick: That's the li - mit. Ha, ha, ha.

This song is dated about 1918, when 'the conscription threat' emerged. England wished to impose conscription in Ireland to augment its armies on the Western Front, where the Germans had made advances in early 1918, and this move was very strongly resisted by all shades of nationalist opinion in Ireland. While large numbers of Irishmen had volunteered to fight in the British army from 1914 onwards, conscription was another matter entirely, especially after the shelving of the Home Rule Bill in 1914, and the events of 1916 in Dublin. By 1918 opinion had swung firmly behind Irish nationalism and so conscription was bound to be virulently resisted, with people believing that if there was fighting to be done it would be in Ireland, for Ireland's freedom, and not against Germany, which was not seen as Ireland's enemy.

St Patrick, Wolfe Tone, Shane O'Neill, John Mitchell, the Sinn Féiners of the day and the 'Shades of those in Easter Week', the executed leaders of the 1916 Rising, are all invoked at the beginning of the verses, to support the English conscription effort and defeat the Germans. In the latter part of each verse those invoked delight in the opportunity to once again oppose England. [LM]

Air: 'Harp and Lion' / 'Tow Row Row'. Another song to this air, entitled 'Harp or Lion', may be found in Margaret Skinnider's book *Doing my Bit for Ireland*, The Century Co., New York, 1917.

Saint Patrick, save the nation kind,
    That laboured hard your flock to teach,
A fuller Destiny to find –
    Like cockles on a sandy beach –
Now we want them all to help us –
Though it seems they'd rather skelp us –
Hear us, and your praise we'll hymn it!
Says Saint Patrick: That's the limit!

Chorus
Ha, Ha, Ha, Ha, Ha, Ha,
Says Saint Patrick: That's the limit – Ha! Ha! Ha!

Shade of Tone! Remind the Gael
    For Freedom once you bravely died;
Hear, oh, hear, our heart-wrung wail,
    And range yourself on England's side!
Ah, we know – we're sure you'll do it –
If you don't, you know you'll rue it –
Bring the Irish now to reason –
Says Tone: Ah, yes, I'll teach High Treason!
Ha, Ha, Ha, Ha, Ha, Ha,
Says Tone: Ah, yes, I'll teach High Treason! Ha! Ha! Ha!

Ghastly head of Shane the Proud,
    Blood-stained upon the Castle gate,
Save us now, we cry aloud,
    From Germany's malignant hate.

By your body that we sundered,
Save us now from being plundered;
We can't withstand our foes much longer –
Says Shane the Proud: God make them stronger.
Ha, Ha, Ha, Ha, Ha, Ha,
Says Shane the Proud: God make them stronger. Ha! Ha! Ha!

John Mitchel, now, we turn to thee,
    Though once we wrapped your limbs in chains,
Help us to strive for Liberty,
    While yet one manly Gael remains!
Turn the sore-head, mad Sinn Féiners
Into England's best campaigners,
Save us from our peril appalling –
Says Mitchel: Hurrah! the Empire's falling!
Ha, Ha, Ha, Ha, Ha, Ha,
Says Mitchel: Hurrah! the Empire's falling! Ha! Ha! Ha!

With confidence we beg to speak
    In words of friendship, smooth and fair,
To Shades of those in Easter Week,
    We shot within the Barrack Square;
Brave, noble Spirits, whisper, hark ye,
Make the Irish don the khaki,
And we promise that we'll grant ye
Home Rule so full, 'twill sure enchant ye!
Ha, Ha, Ha, Ha, Ha, Ha,
The Spirits only said: We taunt ye! Ha! Ha! Ha!

The Constitutional Movement Goes On and On

Sean O'Casey

We're leaders of this mighty Irish Nation
Though some folk say our leading days are done.
But don't forget what e'er may be our station
The Constitutional movement must go on.

Chorus:
And on and on and on for ever more.

Gather the Party round, Sinn Féin a-scorning
And let your speeches roll across the floor.
For the Constitutional Movement, now take warning,
Must go on and on for evermore ... Amen.

Variously attributed to Sean O'Casey and Fergal O'Connor and, in one work, to both jointly. Two quite different versions are to be found. This one was included, without attribution, in Ernie O'Malley's *On Another Man's Wound*. The other version may be found on p. 519.

The *Sean O'Casey Review*, Vol 5, No. 2, Spring, 1979, reveals that Fergus O'Connor wrote the first two verses and O'Casey wrote the remainder

Four hundred pounds was the annual salary of an MP at the time. The final verse refers to the moderately nationalist *Freeman's Journal*, which supported the Anglo-Irish Treaty.

255

We've Home Rule now the Statute Book adorning
It's there to be seen by every mother's son.
We brush the cobwebs off it every morning
For the Constitutional Movement must go on.

Four hundred pounds a year is very handy
It helps the Party now to carry on.
In London, boys, we all can act the dandy
For the jobbery and corruption must go on.

Now Ireland can no longer be excluded
Lloyd George he flung his speech across the floor.
No matter what you think about conscription
But the Constitutional Movement must go on.

When Lloyd George will threaten Ireland with
    conscription
We'll stop him with our gas, lead on by John.
And the *Freeman* will write a grand description
For the Constitutional Movement must go on.

The Sweet Little Town of Killwirra

Sean O'Casey

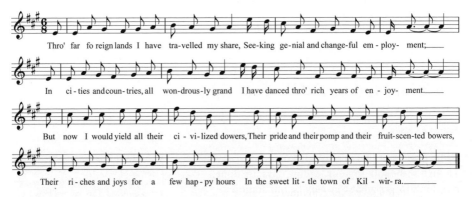

Thro' far fo reign lands I have tra-velled my share, See-king ge-nial and change-ful em - ploy- ment;____

In ci - ties and coun-tries, all won-drous-ly grand I have danced thro' rich years of en - joy- ment.____

But now I would yield all their ci - vi-lized dowers, Their pride and their pomp and their fruit-scen-ted bowers,

Their ri-ches and joys for a few hap-py hours In the sweet lit-tle town of Kil - wir-ra._____

Text: David Krause (ed.), *The Letters of Sean O'Casey 1959–64, Vol. IV*, Catholic University of America Press, Washington, D.C., 1992.

Air: Traditional, 'Cnocáinín Aerach Chill Mhuire'. O'Casey also used this air for his love-song 'As I Wait in the Boreen for Maggie'. There are dozens of places in Ireland named Cill Mhuire, which is usually anglicized as 'Kilmurry'.

Thro' far foreign lands I have travelled my share,
    Seeking genial and cheerful employment;
In cities and countries all wondrously grand
    I have danced thro' rich years of enjoyment.
But now I would yield all their civilized dowers,
Their pride and their pomp and their fruit-scented
    bowers,
Their riches and joys for a few happy hours
    In the sweet little town of Killwirra!

There the rich-throated lark in the frame of the sky,
    A mantle of music is weaving;
And the seagull, with strong discontent in his cry,
    A way through the still air is cleaving.
And when, in a garment of orange and red,
The day-weary sun is enfolding his head,
Boys and girls dance together till twilight has fled
    From the sweet little town of Killwirra!

As the morn's opening eyes see the fruit-laden trees,
    And the dew-spangled flowers gaily glistening,
The huntsman's loud horn often shatters the breeze –
    While the fox in his covert is listening:
Then the birds from their nests in the trees swiftly fly,
As the fox, panting hard, with the hounds in full cry,
And the gay-coated huntsmen come galloping by,
    Through the sweet little town of Killwirra!

To those that oppression's wild, withering laws,
    In thought and in action are spurning, –
Remaining still faithfull to Eire's dear Cause –
    With hope in my heart, I'm returning.
And now fill a full, flowing bumper with me,
Till we drink a deep health to the day that shall see
A chance for a blow that shall make Ireland free,
    And one more to the town of Killwirra!

Lament for Thomas Ashe

Sean O'Casey

The breasts of the mountains with anger are heaving,
    Swift rivers of tears down their rugged cheeks flow;
Their mantle of heather the wild wind is reaving,
    And their proud heads are capp'd with a storm cloud
    of woe,
Why gathers the gloom in a manner appalling –
    What causes the sunshine in terror to flee?
The mountains of Erin are plaintively calling –
    Thomas Ashe, Thomas Ashe, we are mourning for thee!

The wild mountain glens are now silent and lonely,
    And Grief on their bosom has laid her poor head,
Here thoughts of new life have no place, for now only
    The green woods are wrapped in dear thoughts of the
    dead!

Sean O'Casey here mourns the death of Thomas Ashe, who died (as a result of force-feeding while on hunger strike) in Dublin's Mountjoy Jail on 25 September 1917. Further details concerning Ashe are to be found in 'Let Me Carry Your Cross for Ireland, Lord', in this collection. The poem laments the death of Ashe, who hailed from Kinard, Lispole, near Dingle (Daingean Uí Chúis) in Co. Kerry.

Text: This poem was published in 1917 as part of a pamphlet about Thomas Ashe, and re-published in Robert Hogan (ed.), *Feathers from the Green Crow – Sean O'Casey 1905–1925*, University of Missouri Press, Columbia, 1962.

257

'Thomas Ashe' by Leo Whelan.

The leaves from the trees, sadly sighing, are falling
    And form a bronze pall for the once flower'd lea,
The winds rustling thro' them, are plaintively calling –
    Thomas Ashe, Thomas Ashe, we are mourning for thee!

In the ears of the coast Erin's grey waves are beating
    A curse on the Power that his life would not spare,
And mingle a prayer in their gloomy retreating,
    With a caoine for the soul that had courage to dare!
The grey restless waves are all rising and falling –
    Oh! a sorrowful breast is the breast of the sea –
And her waters, uneasy, are plaintively calling –
    Thomas Ashe, Thomas Ashe, we are mourning for thee!

Shall we then to Nature's sad, heart-broken grieving
    Our own Gaelic Nature in apathy close?
Ah! No! To our hearts this dear sorrow receiving
    We'll send in a shout to our circle of foes!
Your thoughts, Thomas Ashe, now, shall shortly be ours–
    As you fought the good fight so we'll fight to be free.
'Gainst all the vain pomp of their princes and powers,
    Made strong by the thought of dear vengeance for thee.

Thomas Ashe

Sean O'Casey

Text: Courtesy of UCD Archives.

The Children of Eireann are listening again
    To Death's sullen, sad, sombre beat of the drum;
Oppression has seized on a man amongst men,
    And an eloquent life's stricken senseless and dumb,
      While we, left behind, wait the life from your death
        that shall come!

In your fight to unfetter Humanity's soul,
    Your body was blazoned with scars,
To oppression you fearlessly tendered the toll,
    Removing for progress the Bolts and the Bars.
    With your hand to the Plough and your eyes on the
      stars.

On the cold seat of Death now your body's enthroned,
    And your warm heart is silent and still,
For our life that is Death, your great life has atoned,
    And we feel in our hearts a swift answering thrill,
    To take up your work, all hard fallow nature to till.

Here hope and Endeavour with energy braid
    Leaves of honour to garland the Dead,
Here Liberty rests with calm Courage arrayed,
    By the side of the Kingly but now passive head,
    Anointed with blood that this Hero has shed.

Huge Labour looks down on your battle-scarred face,
    Ignoble and noble with sweat on his brow,
Unable to fathom this soul of his race,
    Half conscious that soon, when he springs from the Slough,
    He shall understand then, if he can't do it now!

To your soul, for awhile, we all murmur, Farewell!
    And we take the Dear Gift that you gave,
For your great Life stamped out in the cold prison cell
    Shall be potent our own slavish nature to save,
    Tho' your body we leave in the drear hidden gloom of the grave.

Private Cassidy, V.C.

Sean O'Casey

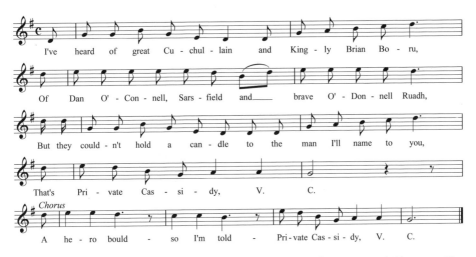

I've heard of great Cuchullain & Kingly Brian Boru,
Of Dan O'Connell, Sarsfield, and brave O'Donnell Ruadh!
But they couldn't hold a candle to the man I'll name to you –
    That's Private Cassidy, V.C.

Chorus
A hero bould – so I'm tould – Private Cassidy, V.C.

This song was probably prompted by one Private Cassidy, a winner of the Victoria Cross, whose exploits were used in a British army recruiting poster.

A 'pinkeen' (verse 2) is the Dublin slang term for the small fish properly called the stickleback.

Kut (verse 6) is a town south of

Baghdad, in which a British force was besieged by the Turkish army from December 1915 until the following April, when the garrison surrendered.

Text: New York University Library. The item bears the following note:
'Copied 27/4/1963 from original manuscript of Sean O'Casey, Irish Dramatist. Written about 1917; the property of Fergus O'Connor, Publisher, dec'd 1952, late of Lowell House, 23 Herbert Avenue, Merrion, Dublin.'
Air: 'The Lowlands Low'.

When fishing in the Liffey on a balmy summer e'en –
His bait a wee electrified and dynamoed Pinkeen,
Who with his line and hook brought up a German
    Submarine?
    Private Cassidy, V.C.

When a Zeppelin come over camp and caused a frightful fuss,
Who was it that jumped out of bed and ran out with a cuss,
And downed it with an antiquated Irish blunderbuss?
    Private Cassidy, V.C.

When we lost a forty-ton gun and had to do a stump,
Who was it came runnin' up with a hop, step and a jump,
An' brought the gun back safe to camp upon his bally hump?
    Private Cassidy, V.C.

When a German shell burst over us on a mornin's calm and still,
And we felt that we were passin' thro' a movin' mortar mill,
Who was well again when he just took an anti-bilious pill?
    Private Cassidy, V.C.

All our affairs in Asia, now, are in a frightful rut,
Townshend and all his army have surrendered out in Kut –
Victorious in Baghdad he'd be, if he had had the nut,
    of Private Cassidy, V.C.

They may decimate our army and destroy our navy great,
They may give us Standard Bread and raise the Health
    Insurance Rate,
But we've still a great man left, my boys, to guard and save
    the State –
    That's Private Cassidy, V.C.

Chant in Prerumble
Sean O'Casey

Text: these two verses are from O'Casey's play *The Drums of Father Ned*.
Air: Printed at the back of the published text of O'Casey's play is a version of 'The Star of the County Down'.

The Black and Tans are blasting now
Ireland's living into the dead;
Her homes and shops in flames fall down
In red ashes on her bonny head.

May God leave none of th' Tans alive,
May His big fist destroy them all!
Each curse of the Holy Book of th' Psalms
An' the Prophets upon them all!

The United Irish Volunteers

C.B. Armstrong

Island of dreams, thy dawn is breaking,
    Breaking with storm and sword and flame.
Spirits of battle attend your waking,
    You of the Irish name!
All that is fair and true and holy
    Springs to birth from the fire of strife;
Erin the dreamer, sad and lowly,
    Wakes to a nobler life.

Now, when Britain's might and glory
    Rise in anger to guard the right,
Rise to write in her ancient story
    One more legend bright.
You, the guard of a land united,
    Heal a wound at the Empire's heart,
Pledge of a thousand errors righted,
    Playing a nation's part.

Emerald field and purple heather
    Pour to the fight their armed hosts,
North and South forever together
    Guard our island coasts.
One in love of the land that bore you,
    One the King and the Flag you claim,
God of Battles keep watch before you,
    Men of the Irish name.

This poem embodies Redmond's appeal to the Volunteers to join the British army and fight in the war.

Text: R.J. Kelly, *Volunteer Verses*, James Duffy & Co. Ltd, Dublin, 1914.

England's Recruiting Jackals

Maeve Cavanagh

Like a swarm of jackals hunting their prey
    The minions of England prowling go,
The manhood and youth of Ireland to snare
    By every dastardly wile they know.

For a Ruin stands knocking at England's gates,
    And Panic and Fear flit thro' her halls;
For help in her dire extremity now
    To the land she wronged she wildly calls.

Text: Maeve Cavanagh, *Sheaves of Revolt*, Dublin, 1914.

CONSCRIPTION.

John Bull:— "I am on the Rocks, my dear, but let us DIE TOGETHER!"

Samuels Collection, TCD. Reproduced courtesy of Trinity College Dublin.

See starkly before her shuddering soul
    The legions of Retribution stand –
Whilst with dripping scythe and with swerveless stroke
    Death waits the doomed armies of her land.

Manhood of Ireland, be deaf to her call,
    Stand passive and let her flag go down –
Let the Judas among you take her bribe
    And brand himself with a vile renown.

Whilst the Eagle grips with the Vulture foe
    Who wrought our country's woe and decay,
Wrest NOW from her talons your own fair land
    And grudge not Liberty's price to pay.

The Song of Lloyd George

Maeve Cavanagh

I hatched a plot – a crafty plan –
    With Long and Short in London, O
Against the rebel Sinn Féin clan –
    A master stroke – a knock-out blow.
I told the world a good George lie,
    Of how I caught collogueing O
The Kaiser dread, and Sinn Féin's 'Head',
    And, Pigott-like, forged proofs to show.

This scornful Ireland must be crushed,
    She blocks our path by every way;
Conscription swiftly must be rushed –
    Though French may find 'tis not child's play.

The first verse here refers to the trumped-up 'German Plot' of 1918.

Viscount Walter Long (1854–1924) was the chief drafter of the 1920 Government of Ireland Act, and Edward Shortt (1862–1935) was the Irish Chief Secretary.

Richard Pigott (1835–89) was the fabricator of the forged letters that purported to tie Charles Stewart Parnell to the Phoenix Park murders. Parnell sued *The Times* for publishing the forgeries and won the case. Pigott later shot himself in a Madrid hotel.

John French was the Lord Lieutenant of Ireland at the time.

Text: Samuels Collection, TCD.
Air: 'The Peeler and the Goat'.

But we must risk it – big the game,
    The odds are good that we shall win,
I swear those Irish (H)'uns to tame –
    Who said 'Small Nations', Justice, Sin?

The leaders are all safe in jail,
    I trust I've got the right ones, though
Sometimes I feel a trifle pale,
    These Irish (H)'uns can cod us so.
I hope old French won't get cold feet
    (He wasn't much missed at the Front);
But there – 'tis good to be discreet,
    And Christian Charity's my stunt.

So I must hurry on the fight,
    The Hun is at our very gate,
And soon he'll serenade, some night,
    Old England with his 'Hymn of Hate';
Then we would see on Ireland's face
    A grin as broad as Dublin Bay –
To 'down' ere then this taunting race
    Conscription is the only way.

Col. Downing's 7th 'Pals' Battalion

Maeve Cavanagh

Lieutenant Colonel Geoffrey Downing, a former rugby player, was involved with the Irish Rugby Football Union in recruiting the 7th Battalion of the Royal Dublin Fusiliers, of which D Company was to be reserved for volunteers from the IRFU.

The 'Borderers' (verse 3) refers to the shooting of civilians by the King's Own Scottish Borderes the previous July. See notes on pages 98–100.

Lord Aberdeen (verse 4) was Lord Lieutenant of Ireland at the time.

Text: Maeve Cavanagh, *Sheaves of Revolt*, Dublin, 1914.

Now Dublin men make haste and join
    'Pal' Downing's 'Pals" Brigade,
He'll let you bring your mother, too,
    In case you feel afraid;
Grand-aunts or old-age pensioners
    He'll welcome each and all –
No end of kind concessions
    If you answer England's call.

He'll let you drill beside your 'pals'
    (And starve beside them, too),
So quit your rebel sneering
    And join the Colours, do.
Upon the field of battle,
    Sure the 'Huns' will run for life
From the 'Pals' and 'Johnnie Ghoorka'
    With his disembowelling knife.

You'll fight in goodly company,
    You men from Dublin town.
With the jail-bird and the 'Borderers'
    You'll surely save the Crown.
If you'll only sell your country
    You'll get 1s. 9d. a day –
You can save it or invest it –
    But don't squander it away.

So hurry up, the next 'platoon',
    Ye men of Dublin town;
Sure you couldn't have the heart to see
    Old England's flag go down.
Is it live without her 'Peelers',
    Her Workhouse and her Jail,
Her Aberdeens and Garrison?
    The thought would turn you pale.

So hurry up and take the 'bob',
    The 'Butcher' cannot wait;
The German guns are talking
    At a most terrific rate.
And if you should crawl back
    Minus arm or minus leg,
You'll get leave to roam your city
    To sell matches – or to beg.

The Dublin 'Pals' marching along Nassau Street in September 1914, on their way to
Kingsbridge railway station, the Curragh Camp, and Gallipoli.

Conscription
The Prayer of Ireland
Maeve Cavanagh

Lord, that this cross may pass a - way, yet not my__ will but Thine be done,

I ne'er have shunned the__ fie - ry way, nor craved the crown be__ for 'twas won,

With__ con - science clear__ Thy will I wait, while round me surge__ fierce waves of hate!

A - lone a__ mong the Na - tions all, I wit - ness__ for true Li - ber - ty.

Yet none__ I__ know will heed my call, when kneel I in Geth__ se - ma - ne,__

Though they, too, in a lit - tle while, will un der - stand, who__ now re - vile,

When spent they__ sheath the sword, and wake, fresh fet - ters__ on their limbs to see,

More gal - ling than they__ sought to break, then chas - ten'd they__ may__ think of me,

For__ though my flag__ be spread or furled, my__ sa - cra - fice__ will save the world.

In - to my hand the sword is thrust, be - hold, Lord,__ not on me the blame,

For right I war,__ if__ war I must, let them be - ware__ who__ light the flame,

For__ all who now__ shriek "Cru - ci - fy" will__ rue its kin - dling ere it die!

Text: Samuels Collection, TCD.
  Air: From a manuscript copy in the hand of Maeve Cavanagh's husband Cathal MacDubhghaill, in the National Library of Ireland.

Lord, that this cross may pass away,
  Yet not my will, but Thine be done,
I ne'er have shunned the fiery way,
  Nor craved the crown before 'twas won;

With conscience clear Thy will I wait,
Though round me surge fierce waves of hate.

Alone, among the nations all
    I witness for true Liberty –
Yet none I know will heed my call
    When I kneel in Gethsemani –
But they, too, in a later while
Will understand, who now revile.

When spent they sheathe the sword, and wake
    Fresh fetters on their limbs to see,
More galling than they sought to break,
    Then, chastened, they may think of me;
For tho' my flag be spread or furled
My sacrifice will save the world.

Into my hand the sword is thrust;
    Behold, Lord, not on me the blame,
For Right I war, if war I must –
    Let them beware who light the flame,
For all who now shriek 'Crucify'
Shall rue its kindling ere it die.

'The first Irish conscript' (postcard).

Come Listen Friends

Text: Ernie O'Malley Papers,
New York University.
   Air: see p. 252, 'England's
Conscription Appeal'.

Come listen friends good news I bring, conscription into law
   has passed
We're loyal now to George our King, and we must forget old
   Ireland's past.
We'll double to the English now, to fight we'll show the
   Germans how
And we will not shield a sword or blade till we've captured
   all the German trade.

Ha ha ha
Till we've captured all the German trade.

Surely friends you will agree our doubting was a sour disgrace
For England, Masters of the Sea, a nation small she'll never face
She brought the Boers and Indians peace, she guarded well
   poor little Greece
And were it not for German gold, she'd still have Russia in her fold.

Ha ha ha, She'd still have Russia in her fold.

Faith I'd fight and fight right willin' if I only had the killin'
Of every British Saxon in the morning.

'Mobilising an Irish conscript' (The second Irish Conscript, postcard).

The Irish M.P.'s Advice

Brian O'Higgins

Fly to France and Belgium,
     That's where Ireland needs you;
Fight for Russia's gentle Czar,
     Who with his flour feeds you;
Help the yellow Jap to be
     Your future lord and master;
Rush to aid your foreign friends,
     Faster, boys, and faster!
And in case there's no one left
     To give you half a cheer,
When your heads and legs come home –
     I'll stay here.

Text: Brian O'Higgins, *The Voice of Banba*, Dublin, 1931.

Recruiting!

Brian O'Higgins

You have all heard before today of the place that lies
     below,
     Tooral, ooral, ooral, ooral, oo!
A public meeting there was held a day or two ago,
     Tooral, ooral, ooral, ooral, oo!
'Twas the Divil that presided, and then it was decided –
     That the only way to see the matter through,
An' to keep the British Nation at its present elevation,
     Was to hasten on Conscription, tooral oo!

Then the Divil sent his agents out to gather in recruits – Tooral etc,
To preserve our glorious Empire and destroy the German brutes, Tooral etc,
You'll get a welcome hearty from the gallant Irish Party;
     Tell them to preach and spread what isn't true –
That no Gael can enter Heaven, as 'twas written by Saint Kevin,
     Unless they dyed the Green Red, White and Blue.

The first man that they brought in, sure they found in lands afar,
     Of his name indeed they couldn't get a clue.
In a jungle wild in Asia, on the map called 'Verdon Bar' –
     When they found him he was shoutin' 'tried and thrue'.
Ses the Divil, 'Sure he's dotin'; he asked me was I votin' –
     Just then the prisoner shouted 'Pillaloo!'
The Divil's got a turn – but 'twas only Alfie Byrne,
     Tooral, ooral, ooral, ooral, oo!

Alfie Byrne (verse 3) was the Lord Mayor of Dublin.

Text: *The Workers' Republic*, Vol 1, No. 33, 8 January 1916.
     Air: See p. 241 for 'The Divil's Recruiting Campaign', Sean O'Casey's version of this song, and the air.

The next they brought 'twas Nugent, poked the Divil in the ribs,
  And he asked him in a whisper for a chew.
Have you ever tried for bold recruits in the Branches of the 'Hibs',
  The members there are very loyal to you!
These vile pro-German swabs are all bailiffs mixed with scabs;
  To let them enter here now wouldn't do.
So if you've any jobs for storemen, or for uniformed doormen,
  The Hibernians are the very men for you.

The next the agents brought along had said he'd fight the Huns,
  Tooral, ooral, ooral, ooral, oo!
For the sake of Erin's virtue and the holy priests and nuns –
  An' he wanted nothing for it – Tooral oo!
Ses the Divil – 'Fetch a barrow, now Mr Kelly Sparrow,
  I'm not bad enough to work along with you.'
They caught hold of poor Saturnus and they dumped him in the furnace,
  Then they ran for respirators, Tooral oo!

Then the next man that they brought in looked a fierce and dreadful Tyke –
  The Divil's heart with terror quickly fills.
He was dressed all out in Khaki and was mounted on a bike,
  In his hand he waved a box of Beecham's Pills.
Ses the Divil – 'Morrow' mildly; but he shouted at him wildly,
  'I'll kill the German Kaiser and his crew!'
Now dear England needn't falter, for she's got J.C. M'Walter –
  Tooral, ooral, ooral, ooral, oo!

'The third Irish conscript' (postcard).

A Tale of Tails

Brian O'Higgins

I met a man in Belfast
    That met a man in Larne,
That knew a man that saw a man
    That heard an awful yarn
Of how the German soldiers,
    One day in holy France,
Cut off the tails of twenty cats
    And fried them on a lance;
Then with the gravy stuck them on
    The poor, wee things again –
Now, shouldn't tales like that recruit
    All Ireland's able men?

Text: Brian O'Higgins, *1916 Before and After, Wolfe Tone Annual 1950*, Dublin, 1950.

A Recruiting Come-All-Ye

Brian O'Higgins

Come all ye true-hearted Irish youths
    And listen to my lay;
I've enlisted for fame as a warrior bold
    At ten bright pence a day;
And I've sworn by every virtuous king
    That England ever knew,
To defend her cause and uphold her laws
    From Tara to Timbuctoo.

Chorus
From Tara to Timbuctoo,
From Tara to Timbuctoo,
To defend her cause and uphold her laws
From Tara to Timbuctoo.

My drill and my training are all complete,
    I can curse like a Colonel now;
I can show you the way to retreat in time
    When anyone starts a row.
I can sport a fag, I can boast and brag,
    I can drink till I'm bold and brave;
I can swagger and swear, I can whistle the air
    Of 'Britannia Rules the Wave'.

Text: Samuels Collection, TCD.
    Air: 'Ireland, Boys, Hurrah!' or 'Song from the Backwoods', see 'Song of the Transvaal Irish Brigade', p. 26.

Chorus
Britannia rules the waves, etc.

I'm loyal and true to the English King,
    And I cheer for the English Crown,
And dressed in a cast-off khaki coat,
    I dazzle the bloomin' town.
I'm one of the Empire's warrior sons,
    But I hope there'll never be war,
For my liver gets white when I think of a fight,
    And my legs wouldn't carry me far.

Chorus
And my legs wouldn't carry me far, etc.

Come all ye true-hearted Irish youths
    And throng to the Empire's aid;
Who cares a rap about Ireland's wrongs
    When he's clothed and grubbed and paid?
You're sure of a share in the orphan's prayer
    While Britannia rules the wave,
An Imperial kick when your day is done
    And an Irish pauper's grave.

Chorus
And an Irish pauper's grave, etc.

To Any Unbought Irishman
Brian O'Higgins

Text: Brian O'Higgins, *The Voice of Banba*, Dublin, 1931.

Don't be downhearted! there's nothing to dread,
    Though taxes may gather and grow,
You never need go without champagne to bed
    Or ride on shanks' mare in the snow;
Though jobs may be few and the pay may be small,
    And your spirits may droop for a spell,
There's one solid blessing that's left after all –
    You still have a country to sell!

Ballad of Sinn Féiners

Our God is self; though nations die
　　And countless thousands writhe in pain,
We shut our ears to moan and cry
　　And close our eyes to all the slain.
We frown not on the foulest deed
　　The reason for our stand is plain:
'Ourselves Alone'; that is our creed.

An outraged maiden's dying sigh
　　Fills us with nought but cold disdain;
And when the Prussians crucify
　　Our friends we never wax insane
And curse the beasts who so bestain
　　This world of ours. Oh no, indeed.
By doing so what would we gain?
　　'Ourselves Alone'; that is our creed.

The first verse of this piece has only
seven lines in the original.

Text: Recruiting poster with text of
poem originally published in the New
York magazine *Life*.

What Have You Done for Ireland?

What have you done for Ireland?
　　How have you answered the call?
Are you pleased with the part you're playing
　　In the job that demands us all?
Have you changed the tweed for the khaki
　　To serve with the rank and file
As your comrades are gladly serving,
　　Or isn't it worth your while?

Can you meet the eyes of soldiers?
　　Or have you to turn away?
When they talk of the stay-at-home slacker,
　　Have you never a word to say?
When you read the roll of honour
　　Of living and dead – what then?
Does the voice within approve you
　　As one to be ranked with men?

For if in Ireland's glory
　　Each soldier may claim his share,
So he who would shirk his duty,
　　His burden of shame must bear.

Text: Recruiting poster published
in Dublin in March 1915.

273

You who are strong and active,
You who are fit for the fray,
What have you done for Ireland?
Ask of your heart to-day!

Michael Dignam, 'The Recruiting Post at Grattan's Statue, Dublin, on the Royal Dublin Fusiliers Flag Day'.
The Lady of the House, Christmas 1915. (Courtesy of Dublin City Library and Archive)

God Save Ireland from Conscription

Sliabh Ruadh (Phil O'Neill)

Hear the cry that wakes the land
    Swelling forth from each strong band,
That musters in one common cause today;
    To Lloyd George's 'Man-Power Bill',
    We oppose a Nation's will,
And with earnest hearts together here we say –

Chorus
'God Save Ireland – from Conscription',
    God Save Ireland, say we all,
And United now we stand,
For our Faith and Fatherland,
    Pledged in Freedom's fight to conquer or to fall!

    Green and Orange side by side,
    Now to face the battle's tide,
A common country now alone we know!
    And no more shall class or creed
    Faction foul among us breed,
For a common front in Ireland's cause we show!

Text: Samuels Collection, TCD.
    Air: 'Tramp, Tramp, Tramp' or
'God Save Ireland'.

275

North and South are gathered here
From the Causeway to Cape Clear!
From Dublin's Town across to Galway Bay;
'Conscription we defy,'
Let that chorus reach the sky
And let England hear united Ireland say –

Where our martyred heroes lie
We shall raise our banners high,
'Neath its folds we'll marshal every creed and clan
And emblazoned there will be
Marked in letters bold and free,
'No Conscription whilst there lives one Irishman.'

John Bull's Appeal
Sliabh Ruadh (Phil O'Neill)

Text: S.S. Breathnach, *The Barricade
Song Sheet*, Dublin, n.d.
  Air: 'Moses Ri-toorli-Toorli-i-ay'
or 'The Ould Orange Flute'.

John Bull, as you know, is a clever old man,
He gives little away but he grabs all he can,
But when he went looking for spoils to Berlin,
He found his mistake for the Kaiser was 'in!'

Then John says to Frenchy: 'Come on – twiggez-vous?
We'll forget Fontenoy and of course Waterloo
For my heart bleeds for Belgium so stout and so brave
Sure only for them I'd be now in my grave.'

'The Russians,' he says, 'too, will join before long,
'Twill be nothing like war – 'twill be merely ping pong!
If you like, you can fight for I'll give you the 'tin,'
But I must be Boss when we get to Berlin!'

'The Dagos,' he says, 'with their mandoline band,
Are out for a deal so they'll give me a hand,
If I give them the cash and I tell them what for,
You may swear on your oath, they'll be stuck in
    the war!'

'My Navy, of course, is queen of the waves!
And Britons, remember, will never be slaves,
But a canny old German, they call him Tirpitz,
Brought out submarines and he's giving them fits.'

Says John Bull to Paddy, 'My true-hearted son,
I hope now you'll help me to smash up the Hun,
Forget Ninety-Eight and the black Famine years,
When the war is all over I'll pay me arrears.'

Says Paddy to John, 'Well you've said that before,
And now you are coming again to my door,
Well here is my answer, I'll state it quite plain,
I'll now stay at home organizing Sinn Féin.'

'It pays not,' says Paddy, 'to send my best sons
Away out to Flanders, as food for your guns,
If the boys want a fight – well we'll fight for our own,
And leave Bull and his Allies severely alone.'

Well, John Bull went off and he took to his bed,
And he told all his friends he was sorely misled,
'Without Paddy,' says he, 'sure I couldn't well win,
So 'tis off for the present – my trip to Berlin!'

Join the British Army

When I was young I used to be
As fine a man as you could see.
The Prince of Wales he said to me
    'Come, join the British army.'

Chorus
Too-ra-loo-ra-loo-ra-loo
They're looking for monkeys up in the Zoo
And if I had a face like you
    I'd join the British army.

Text: Dominic Behan, *Ireland Sings*,
Music Sales, London, 1973.
Air: Traditional.

277

Corporal Daly's gone away.
His wife is in the family way
And the only thing that she can say is
  'Blame the British army.'

Sergeant Doyle, he has the drought.
Give him a load of Guinness stout.
He'll beat the enemy with his mouth
  And save the British army.

Kilted soldiers wear no drawers,
Won't you kindly lend them yours?
The poor should always help the poor,
  God help the British army.

They'll beat the Germans without fuss
And lay their bones out in the dust;
I know, for they quite near beat us –
  The gallant British army.

An Anti-Conscription Ballad
'Rory of the Hill'

The imperial ambitions that Germany had nurtured, in the decades before the outbreak of war, were expressed in the speech made by the German Foreign Secretary, Bernhard von Bülow, in the Reichstag in 1897, in which he stated that Germany demanded its own place in the sun.

During the Irish Famine of the 1840s *The Times* newspaper is said to have welcomed the prospect of some ethnic cleansing, and to have expressed the hope that 'Soon a Celt will be as rare on the banks of the Liffey as a red man on the banks of the Hudson' (see lines 55/6).

Text: The Workers' Republic, Vol 1, No. 32, 1 January 1916.
The air of this song is that of 'The Irish Jaunting Car' by Val Vousden, which was also used for 'The Fenian Girl' (see p. 37).

The Lion's teeth were getting frayed
  The Lion's day was done
He heard the Eagle screaming for
  'A place beneath the Sun'.
The noble Eagle soared aloft
  On steady, silent wing,
The Lion, roaring, left his food
  And to his slaves did sing.

'That Eagle's getting out of hand,
  He wants to make us slaves;
And if we don't soon clip his wings
  We'll cease to Rule the Waves.'

The Lion then asked in to tea
  His olden Gallic foe,
The Russian bear he'd slandered once,
  The Yellow Jap also,
And many an Irish slave as well,
  Like Redmond and Tay Pay –
Whom he had kept to clean his sewers
  And make his house look gay.

Said he – 'My friends, this Eagle is
    Your foe as well as mine,
So just surround him ere I go
    To cross the bloomin' Rhine.'
And when the Lion thought he had
    The Eagle netted well
He turned his face to those he'd sent
    To Connaught or to Hell.

'Ye gallant boys, I've loved ye long
    (My lads must stop at home),
And though I've lads *go leor* to fight
    For me from o'er the foam.

'You wouldn't see your dear old dad,
    The German Eagle's prey,
You wouldn't see your dear green Isle
    Beneath the German's sway!'

Some fools in Ireland heeded him
    And started off to kill
Brave men who never did them wrong,
    More stayed in Ireland still.
The Eagle bold put up a fight
    That made the Lion pale,
'If somebody don't stop him soon,
    It's over here he'll sail.'

His Zeppelins already fly
    Across with every breeze,
The while his submarines – O my,
    Does Britain rule the seas?

Meantime the men of Ireland stood
    Well armed for Ireland's weal,
''Tis not for my behest,' he snarled,
    'They mean that lead and steel.'
'Ho, ho, you cowards, come and fight
    And help me beat the Hun,
In former days I laughed, 'The Celts
    Are with a vengeance gone'.'

'But now you are not to emigrate
    To far off Amerikee,
For Flanders and the Dardanelles
    Is just the place to be.'

Up spake the men of Ireland,
  'For Ireland's sake alone –
We'll fight to place Dark Rosaleen
  Again upon her throne.
Not Flanders or the Dardanelles
  Nor yet Columbia's shore,
Will be our home while England's rag
  Flies hopeless Ireland o'er.'

'We'll stand or fall with Ireland
  Despite of foes and slaves.
We'll stand redeemed on Irish soil
  Or lie in Irish graves.'

Ernest Kavanagh, 'The Coming of the Hun', *The Irish Worker*, 21 November 1914.

Anti-Recruiting Song

Constance Markievicz

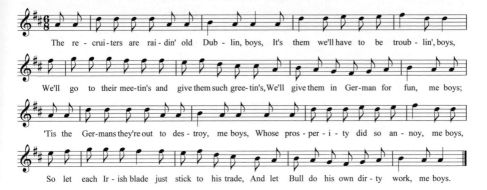

The recruiters are raidin' old Dublin, boys,
It's them we'll have to be troublin', boys,
We'll go to their meetin's and give them such greetin's,
We'll give them in German for fun, me boys;
'Tis the Germans they're out to destroy, me boys,
Whose prosperity did so annoy, me boys,
So let each Irish blade just stick to his trade
And let Bull do his own dirty work, me boys.

Text: Margaret Skinnider, *Doing My Bit For Ireland*, The Century Co., New York, 1917, where it is attributed to Constance Markievicz.
   Air: 'The Gallant Tipperary Boys' or 'The Young May Moon'.

Chorus
For the Germans are winning the war, me boys,
And England is feeling so sore, me boys,
They're passing conscription, the only prescription
To make Englishmen go the the front, me boys.

Your boss, he won't go to the war, me boys,
Hun bullets do him so annoy, me boys,
So kindly he frees you, he does it to squeeze you
To fight for his money and him, me boys;
They've hunger conscription in Ireland, boys,
You'll starve till you're thin as a wire, me boys,
You'll get very thin, but you won't care a pin
For you'll know it's for Ireland's sake, my boys.

Chorus
For the English are losing the war, me boys,
And they want us all killed before, me boys,
The great German nation has sworn their damnation,
And we'll echo the curse with a will, me boys.

Then hurrah for the gallant old Dublin, boys,
And if you wouldn't be muddlin', boys,

Join a Volunteer corps, or, if that is a bore,
The Citizen Army's as good, me boys.
Then hurrah for the Volunteers, me boys,
Ireland in arms has no fears, me boys,
And surely if we would see Ireland free,
We'll arm and we'll drill for the Day, my boys.

Chorus
For the Germans are going to win, me boys,
And Ireland will have to butt in, me boys,
From a Gael with a gun the Briton will run,
And we'll dance at the wake of the Empire, boys!

The Dublin Recruiting Song

Another version of the preceding song.

Text: Samuels Collection, TCD.

The recruiters are raiding Dublin, boys,
And its them that we'll have to be troublin', boys;
We will go to their meetings and give them such
    greetings,
We'll greet them in German for fun, me boys.

'Tis the Germans they're out to destroy, me boys,
Their prosperity did them annoy, me boys;
But let each Irish blade just stick to its trade,
And let Bull do his own dirty work, me boys.

Our men are dead in the Dardanelles, me boys,
At Mons and at other hells, me boys;
But they needn't have died, they'd be here at our side,
If they'd only been true to their country, boys.

The Germans are winning the war, me boys,
And the English are feeling quite sore, me boys;
For they brought in Conscription, the only prescription,
To make Englishmen go to the front, me boys.

The fools who forget '98, me boys,
Will meet with a very sad fate, me boys;
They'll be put in the front, and made bear all the brunt,
And cover the Brit-huns' retreat, me boys.

Then hurrah for dear old Dublin, boys,
And sure if you wouldn't be muddlin', boys,
Join a Volunteer Corps, and if that is a bore,
The Citizen Army's as good, me boys.

Then hurrah for the Volunteers, me boys,
Ireland in arms has no fears, me boys;
So just join them today, and drill right away,
And be ready to fight on the day, me boys.

The Germans are going to win, me boys,
The Irish will have to butt in, me boys;
For the great German nation has sworn England's
    damnation
And we'll echo that curse with a will, me boys.

The Recruiting Sergeant
Seamus O'Farrell (1886–1973)

As I was strolling down the street,
    I was feeling nice and larky, O,
A recruiting sergeant says to me:
    'Faith, you'd look fine in khaki, O.
The King he is in need of men,
    Just read this proclamation, O,
And the life in Flanders for you then
    Will be a fine vacation, O.'

'That may be true,' I said to him
    'But tell me sergeant, dearie, O,
If I had a pack upon me back,
    Would I look bright and cheery, O?
You'd make me train and drill until
    You had me one of French's, O,
It may be warm in Flanders, but
    It's draughty in the trenches, O.'

The sergeant swung his little cane,
    And his smile was most provoking, O,
As he twirled and twirled his wee moustache
    Says he: 'I hope you're joking, O.
The sandbags are so nice and high,
    The wind you won't feel blowing, O.'
But I winked at a cailín passing by,
    And I said: 'It might be snowing, O.'

Seamus O'Farrell, a journalist, was
a Dublin man. He assisted with the
formation of the Irish Transport &
General Workers' Union. He was very
involved with nationalist movements
and wrote for the 'mosquito press'; as
one might say, 'He wrote when it was
dangerous to write!'

He worked on the staff of the *Irish
Independent* and then *The Irish Press*.
Later he edited the *Longford Leader*
and the *Leinster Leader*. He contributed a column ('Speaking for Myself') to the *Nationalist* and *Leinster
Times* during the sixties.

He was a founder member of
Muintir na Tíre and an active member
(and one-time President) of the
National Agricultural and Industrial
Development Association. He was a
member of Seanad Éireann during the
first Coalition Government.

'The Recruiting Sergeant' was published in some subversive paper; it
was intended to be sung to the tune of
'The Peeler and the Goat' (see 'The
Song of Lloyd George', p. 263). [LM]

Text: *The National Comic Song Book*,
Irish Book Bureau, Dublin, n.d.

283

'But hail or rain or hail or frost or snow,
We're not going out to Flanders, O,
While there's fighting to be done at home,
Let your Privates and Commanders go.
Let Englishmen for England fight;
It's nearly time they started, O.'
Then I bade the Sergeant a nice good night,
And there and then we parted, O.

Come Along and Join the British Army

Jimmy Mulkerns 'The Rajah of Frongoch'

Last week I met Joe Dev - lin, and he took me by the hand.

Said he your king and coun - try need you, A - gainst the foe you ought to make a stand.

But, said I, I do not mind the Kai - ser, For that, said Joe, I'll make it ve - ry hot,

Be - cause ac - cor - ding to law that is high trea - son, So at dawn to-mor-row morn I'll have you shot.

But just then a big crowd passed us by, Through a me - ga-phone Jo - ey Dev - lin did cry:

Chorus

Come a-long and join the Bri - tish Ar - my, Show that you're not a - fraid,

Put your name up-on the roll of hon - our In the Dub - lin Pals Bri - gade.

We'll send you out to die in France or Bel - gium, 'Twill show that you are True Blue.

When the war is o'er if we want you a - ny more. We'll find you in the S. D. U.

Last week I met Joe Devlin
    And he took me by the hand.
Said he, your King and country need you
    Against the foe you ought to make a stand.
But said I, I do not mind the Kaiser,
    For that, said Joe, I'll make it very hot
Because according to law that is high treason
    So at dawn tomorrow I'll have you shot.
But just then a big crowd passed us by.
Thro' a megaphone Joe Devlin did cry:

Chorus
Come along and join the British army,
    Show that you're not afraid.
Put your name upon the roll of honour
    In the Dublin Pals Brigade.
We'll send you out to die in France or Belgium,
    'Twill show that you are True Blue.
When the war is o'er, if we want you any more
    We'll find you in the S.D.U.

Said I to Joe, you're very young and healthy,
    So o'er to Grafton Street you run.
I've nothing for to fear from an invasion,
    It's men like you should chase the Hun.
Then Josie started singing 'Rule Britannia',
    From his eye there fell a tear.
We have to find the mugs to do the fighting,
    For it we get 400 quid a year.
John Dillon then he roared out loud,
King George of the Irish now is proud.

Repeat chorus

When the scrap broke out on Easter Monday,
    And loudly rang the old Howth gun,
When the khaki sons of Mother England
    Were trying to get the rebels on the run,
The Irish Party held a special meeting,
    Because they knew their little game was o'er,
And visions of their past fame – they were fleeting –
    'Twas their heads this time (not ours) were feeling
    sore.
Stephen Gwynn, in a voice so sad, did sigh:
The rebels win the game, so no more we can cry:

Repeat chorus

For the 'Dublin Pals' (chorus) see the note on p. 264. The S.D.U. (chorus) was the South Dublin Union, the Workhouse, which was garrisoned by the Volunteers during the Rising, under the command of Éamonn Ceannt.

Text and music: Samuels Collection, TCD. In her book *Doing my Bit for Ireland*, Margaret Skinnider attributes this song to Thomas McDonagh's brother Jack.

'Tis the Wrong Way to Tipperary

'Irish Americans consider the so-called song entitled 'It's a Long Way to Tipperary' as a vile, vulgar caricature of their race, a product of the cheap London Music Hall, which manufactures filthy red-light literature.

The subjoined verses have been written by a member of the Irish Literary Society of Chicago for the millions of American homes that exclude silly doggerel.' (Note accompanying this text in the source.)

Text: *Songs & Poems, The Rebels Who Fought and Died for Ireland in Easter Week, 1916* (Samuels Collection).
Air: 'It's a Long Way to Tipperary', see p. 201.

Up to Tipperary came an Englishman one day,
Ribbons flying from his cap and mudguards half the
  way;
With three V's upon his sleeve and shillings in his
  hand,
He wanted Irish boys to go and fight for Saxon Land.

Chorus
'Tis the wrong way to Tipperary – 'tis the wrong way
  you know;
'Tis the wrong way to Tipperary, when recruiting you
  must go.
Good-bye English army, farewell friend and foe;
'Tis the wrong way to Tipperary, for our boys won't go.

Tommy wrote a letter unto Kitchener next day,
Saying, 'h'Irish won't h'enlist, no matter what h'I say;
Answer not by telegraph, nor lay the blame on me;
They'll recognize your writing on the telegram, you
  see.'

Kitchener wrote to Tommy, and what do you think he
  said:
'You can't fool the Irish now, nor are they easily led;
They will fight in front of us, and cover our retreat –
Just promise them Home Rule again, and safety by
  our Fleet.'

Ireland needs her boys at home to battle for her rights;
They fought too long, alas, and won, the other fellow's
  fights;
Curragh's Kicks and King's Own Troops, they'll not
  forget for years,
My soul, we never doubted you, brave Irish
  Volunteers.

If you want a fighter, who was looking for a fight,
Call on Mr Carson, for you know it's his delight;
Bluff and bluster he put forth, and to him you did
  cling,
Now Irish boys will stay at home, and this is what
  they'll sing:

'Tis the wrong way ... etc.

T.P. O'Connor's Trip to New York

Be Japers, Balfour, we are bet,
    Says the grand old dame Britannia,
For I see no Yankees coming yet,
    Says the grand old dame Britannia;
Small Nation stunts don't work out there,
They say we don't treat Ireland fair,
And they give three cheers for De Valera
    Says the grand old dame Britannia.

We must get one of Redmond's crew,
    Says the grand old dame Britannia;
For to tell them Ireland loves us, too,
    Says the grand old dame Britannia;
He must tell them Ireland hates the Hun,
That her boys to join in our troops still run,
And that Easter Week was only fun,
    Says the grand old dame Britannia.

T.P. O'Connor is the boy,
    Says the grand old dame Britannia;
And a trip on the ocean he'll enjoy,
    Says the grand old dame Britannia;
We'll take him away from his cinema screen,
And send him across in a submarine,
And be sure he wears a tie of green,
    Says the grand old dame Britannia.

Let Charley Chaplin 'peg away',
    Says the grand old dame Britannia;
We must move his picture o'er the Bay,
    Says the grand old dame Britannia;
And I'll make him a knight, in a coat of mail,
If he succeeds – But if he should fail
He can look for a job on the *'Daily Mail'*,
    Says the grand old dame Britannia.

Be Japers, Balfour, we are burst,
    Says the grand old dame Britannia;
For Doc. MacCartan got there first,
    Says the grand old dame Britannia:
O'Connor's tour is all in vain –
For the Yanks are shouting 'Up Sinn Féin.'
Oh, bring Tay Pay back in a aeroplane,
    Says the grand old dame Britannia.

Text: *Marching Songs of Ireland, No. 2,*
Fergus O'Connor, Dublin, n.d. (Samuels
Collection, TCD).
    Air: 'The Grand Oul' Dame Britannia',
see p. 235.

T.P. O'Connor in 1917.

287

Under Which Flag

The day has dawned for Ir-ish-men to show once more by deed

That E-rin on-ly holds their love, for her a-lone they'll bleed.

That not one drop of pa-triot's blood in Eng-land's cause we'll shed.

We swear that now in Hea-ven's sight, we pledge it to our dead.

Text: Ballad sheet in the National
Library of Ireland. Originally printed
in *The Shan Van Vocht*.
  Air: 'Paddies Evermore'.

The day has dawned for Irishmen
  To show once more by deed
That Erin only holds their love,
  For her alone they'll bleed.
That not one drop of patriot's blood
  In England's cause we'll shed.
We swear that now in Heaven's sight,
  We pledge it to our dead.

The Dead who died for Ireland, boys
  On scaffolds England reared.
The Dead whose blood makes every glen
  And mountain side revered.
The thousands that the Saxon slew
  By famine, fire and blade.
Hark! how their memory calls on you,
  'Will you their murderers aid?'

Britannia's Pirate flag has waved
  O'er blackened hearths and spread
Its hated folds like vultures' wings
  Where lay our martyred dead.
It's stood for all that wrecked our hopes,
  Our nation overthrown.
It blessed the assassins' poisoned cup,
  The knife that slaughtered Tone.

And will you fight beneath that rag
  Of Famine, crime and greed
Or rally round your own green flag,
  And serve your Country's need.

If you be men of Irish race
  Then answer with this cry,
For Eire only and her flag
  We'll arm and fight and die.

What Do You Think of the 'Covenant' Now?

The English papers told us, just a few short months ago,
That a hundred thousand Orangemen would make the red
  blood flow.
The Empire is in danger now, what will those heroes do?
Perhaps the German blood, like theirs, is just a trifle blue,
Or maybe what is keeping them from going across the seas,
Is that the German Army will not give them guarantees.

For there must be some strong reason –
Either German gold or treason –
  That keeps those troops from crossing o'er the say, Sir.
Maybe 'tis the square and compass,
That withholds them from the rumpus,
  Or that Carson signed a treaty with the Kaiser.

Those grim Ulster Volunteers have been drilling hard for
  years,
  Whilst the Tory papers daily sing their praises.
Then what keeps them from the fighting, they should know
  it is the right thing.
  Are they waiting till the Empire goes to blazes?
They just keep their powder dry, saying they'll want it bye
  and bye.
  They're not fools to go to fight where General French is
And, begor, be the same token, since the weather became
  broken,
  'Tis unhealthy to be dying in the trenches.

'Tis a valid Orange reason –
Neither German gold nor Treason –
  That keeps those troops from crossing o'er the say, Sir.
Their war system isn't thorough,
It won't work beyond the Curragh,
  And Ould Carson wouldn't dare to kill the Kaiser.

The 'square and compass' (line 10)
form the symbol of the Freemasons.
The reference to 'the Curragh' (line
25) is to the Curragh Mutiny in
March 1914, when a group of army
officers resigned rather than obey
an anticipated government order to
suppress an expected UVF revolt.

Text: *The Workers' Republic,* Vol 1,
No. 21, 16 October 1915.
  Air: possibly 'Sergeant William
Baily', see p. 384.

The 'square and compass' –
the emblem of the Freemasons.

289

England – Our Enemy Always

Edward F. McKenna
'But grief shall come to our heartless foe,
and her throne in the dust be seen!'

For a note on the last two lines on the facing page, see p. 278.

Text: *Marching Songs of Ireland, Number Three*, Fergus O'Connor, Dublin, n.d. (Samuels Collection, TCD).

When from my shores I swept the Dane,
And peace was in my home again;
When Art and Learning made of me
A shrine to which, by land and sea,
Came worshippers from every clime,
Partaking of my fruits sublime;
When forth my children went to spread
The Gospel of the Crucified,
And on my name a lustre shed
That filled my heart with hopeful pride –
Who took to heart my recreant son,
Condon'd the deed that he had done,
Heark'd to the tale he had to tell,
And taught him 'gainst me to rebel?
Who, posing in Religion's garb,
Sunk in my breast the poisoned barb?
                              England!

Who laid the most ingenious plans
To bring dissension 'mong my clans?
Who planted in my soil the seeds
That fructified in traitorous deeds?
Who on my children dared to thrust
A new religion, born in lust?
And with a fierce, malignant hate –
To Justice's cry paid little heed –
Endeavoured to exterminate
My name, my race, my ancient creed?
Who murdered Shane and banished Hugh
Because they fought, as men should do?
Who poisoned Owen, my valiant son,
Because he did what Hugh had done?
Who slew and robbed and slew again
Till on the rack I writh'd with pain?
                              England!

Who gloried in the crimson tide
That flowed behind the Regicide?
Who broke a Treaty, clause by clause,
And passed instead the Penal Laws,
When winged my 'Wild Geese' o'er the sea
And none were left to fight for me?

Who banished bishop, monk and friar,
Or set a price upon their head?
Who stifled learning's keen desire
Or foul'd the fount where it fed?
Who crushed my industries and trade
And tried to brutalize, degrade,
And trample me in the dust –
A beggar fawning for a crust?
And laughed in triumph at the thought
My hope was gone, my last fight fought?
                              England!

When full the chalice of my woes,
Who goaded me until I rose,
Frenzied and frail, to strike again
The tyrant who had forged my chain?
Who wrought the pitch-cap – instrument –
Of torture that from hell was lent?
Who vaunted of the deeds of shame
That bring the blush to manhood's face?
On whom the everlasting blame
For horror's time can ne'er efface?
Who slew the Geraldine, my pride?
A soldier's death to Tone denied?
And from the heart of Emmet drew
The young life's tide, so pure and true?
Who drenched my valleys fair with blood
And robbed me of my nationhood?
                              England!

When Famine's pestilential breath,
Consumed me like a blast of death,
Who took my cattle and my grain –
The food that would my life sustain –
Told me I was a beggar knave,
And sold the bread that others gave?
Who broke Mitchel down with chains,
And broke O'Connell's generous heart?
Who drained the life blood from my veins,
As day by day were forced to part
From me my children young and old,
Like sheep compelled to flee the fold?
Who triumph'd in the hellish deed
That scattered o'er the earth my seed,
And boasted that at last was dealt
The blow to extirpate the Celt?
                              England!

Who tortured in the prison cell
The Fenian men who loved me well?
And traitors called the Martyred Three
Because they proved their love for me?
Who fostered the unholy trade
Of spy, informer, renegade?
Who left in ruins the peasant's cot
(A home it was, though poor and bare)
Nor pity showed, nor heeded not
The cries of anguish and despair?
Who promise breaks as soon as 'tis made
And ne'er a debt of honour paid?
Who bullies every puny foe
And often strikes the coward's blow?
Who has a history dark with stains
Of blood and lust and ill-got gains?
                    England!

And now at last, in terror dire,
With conscience wrought and brain on fire,
She comes to me to seek my aid
Because, forsooth, the German blade
Is drawn, and plunged unto the hilt
To penetrate her heart of guilt.
May God forbid true son of mine
Should e'er forget his heritage –
The deeds illustrious that shine
Upon my checkered history's page;
Should e'er forget my scroll of woe
Was written by the Saxon foe,
And that e'en now he does not try
The wrongs of years to rectify.
Though Justice long has stayed her hand,
Now Retribution makes demand
                    On England!

The Old Grey Mare

Pádraic Pearse (1879–1916)

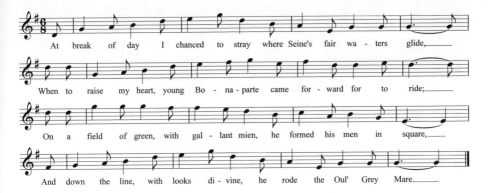

At break of day I chanced to stray where Seine's fair waters glide,
When to raise my heart, young Bonaparte, came forward for to ride;
On a field of green, with gallant mien, he formed his men in square,
And down the line, with looks divine, he rode the Oul' Grey Mare.

My sporting boys that's tall and straight, take counsel and be wise;
Attention pay to what I say, my lecture don't despise;
Let patience guide *yous* everywhere, and from traitors now beware,
For none but *min* that's sound within can ride my Oul' Grey Mare.

Now Bonaparte on her did start, he rode too fast, *is truagh!*
She lost a shoe at Moscow fair, and got lamed at Waterloo;
But wait till she comes back again where she'll have farrier's care,
And the very next *hate*, she'll win the plate, my sporting Oul' Grey Mare.

'Can't you hear some blind ballad-singer trolling out these lines at an Irish country fair? And if you found them in a collection of anonymous Irish street-songs, would you not pronounce them authentic? But the lines were written by Pádraic Pearse to embody a fragment of a genuine traditional song.

In a characteristic Irish way, using the figure of a grey mare as other Irish ballads use the figures of a bunch of roses or a green linnet, the original seems to have lamented the eclipse of the Napoleonic cause and prophesied its triumph.

Pádraic Pearse's re-construction was typical of the illiterate ballad-maker's productions ... The last stanza was the genuine relique.

Pádraic Pearse was devoted to the memory of the Corsican and one of his cherished possessions was a lock of hair said to be Napoleon's.

He used to say – 'Hold your breath now while I'm showing you this.' I remember being with him in the Abbey Theatre and seeing him read during the intervals a book called *The Corsican* that was made up of extracts from the diaries, proclamations and despatches of Napoleon. He reminded me that in the beginning Napoleon was the ardent lover of a poor and unhappy motherland. 'He took the bribe and went over to the big country,' I said.

"Yes," said Pearse, "Napoleon the patriot let himself be bribed with glory."'

– Padraic Colum, *The Irish Rebellion of 1916 and Its Martyrs*, The Devin-Adair Company, New York, 1916.

Text: Padraic Colum, *The Irish Rebellion of 1916 and Its Martyrs*.
Air: Colm O Lochlainn, *Irish Street Ballads*, At the Sign of the Three Candles, Dublin, 1939.

Amhrán na nÓglach

Pádraic Pearse

'Sé do bhea - tha, a bhean ba léan - mhar,

Dob' é ár gcreach do bheith in ngéi - bheann,

Do dhú - thaigh bhreá i____ seil - bh méir - leach____

'Stú____ díol - ta leis na Gal - laibh.

This very popular song (always sung in its Irish-language version) addresses Ireland as a woman, a common theme in song and poetry.

Granuaile, in verses 2 and 3, is the sixteenth-century Connacht pirate queen, Grace O'Malley, referred to in other items in this collection. The reference to the French and Spaniards is to the historic aid efforts by those people to help the Irish in their struggle against the English. Pearse's vision is that it will be Irishmen who will defeat the English – referred to in verses 3 and 4 as 'the stranger'. [LM]

This seems to be the original version of this piece. It was printed in the first issue of *The Irish Volunteer*, 7 February 1914, with the note: 'After the Galway meeting Sir Roger Casement suggested that 'Searlus Óg' would make a splendid march tune for the Volunteers. The foregoing is an adaptation of the old Jacobite words to the modern situation by P.H. Pearse.'

It is more often known nowadays under the title 'An Dord Féinne', but it was first printed under the title used here.

Text: *The Irish Volunteer*, Vol. 1, No. 1, 7 February 1914. The translation is from P. Browne (ed.), *The Collected Works of Pádraic H. Pearse*, Maunsell and Company, Dublin, 1917.
Air: 'Searlus Óg'.

'Sé do bheatha, a bhean ba léanmhar:
Dob' é ar gcreach do bheith i ngéibheann,
Do dhúthaigh bhreagh i seilbh méirleach,
  'S tú díolta leis na Gallaibh.

Óró, 'sé do bheatha a bhaile,
Óró, 'sé do bheatha a bhaile,
Óró, 'sé do bheatha a bhaile,
  Anois ag theacht an tSamhraidh!

A buidhe le Dia na bhfeart go bhfeiceam,
Muna mbímíd beo 'na dhiaidh acht seachtmhain
Gráinne Mhaol is míle gaisgídheach
  Ag fógairt fáin ar Ghallaibh!

Tá Gráinne Mhaol ag teacht tar sáile,
Óglaigh armtha léi mar ghárda,
Gaedhil féin 's ní Franncaigh ná Spáinnigh,
  Agus ruagairt ar Ghallaibh!

'Sé do bheatha, O woman that wast sorrowful.
What grieved us was thy being in chains,
Thy beautiful country in the possession of rogues,
And thou sold to the Galls,

Chorus
Óró 'sé do bheatha abhaile,
Óró 'sé do bheatha abhaile,
Óró 'sé do bheatha abhaile,
Now at summer's coming!

Thanks to the God of miracles that we see,
Altho' we live not a week thereafter,
Gráinne Mhaol and a thousand heroes
Proclaiming the scattering of the Galls!

Gráinne Mhaol is coming from over the sea,
The Fenians of Fál as a guard about her,
Gaels they, and neither French nor Spaniard,
And a rout upon the Galls!

The Fool

Pádraic Pearse

Since the wise men have not spoken, I speak that am only a fool;
A fool that has loved his folly,
Yea, more than the wise men their books or their counting houses, or
    their quiet homes,
Or their fame in men's mouths;
A fool that in all his days hath done never a prudent thing,
Never hath counted the cost, nor reckoned if another reaped
The fruit of his mighty sowing, content to scatter the seed;
A fool that is unrepentant, and that soon at the end of all
Shall laugh in his lonely heart as the ripe ears fall to the reaping-hooks
And the poor are filled that were empty,
Tho' he go hungry.

I have squandered the splendid years that the Lord God gave to my
    youth
In attempting impossible things, deeming them alone worth the toil.
Was it folly or grace? Not men shall judge me, but God.

I have squandered the splendid years:
Lord, if I had the years I would squander them over again,
Aye, fling them from me!
For this I have heard in my heart, that a man shall scatter, not hoard,
Shall do the deed of today, nor take thought of tomorrow's teen,
Shall not bargain or huxter with God; or was it a jest of Christ's
And is this my sin before men, to have taken Him at His word?

The lawyers have sat in council, the men with the keen, long faces,
And said, 'This man is a fool,' and others have said, 'He blasphemeth';

Text: P. Browne (ed.),
*Collected Works of
Pádraic H. Pearse*,
Maunsel and Company,
Dublin, 1917.

Pádraic Pearse.

And the wise have pitied the fool that hath striven to give a life
In the world of time and space among the bulks of actual things,
To a dream that was dreamed in the heart, and that only the heart
    could hold.

O wise men, riddle me this: what if the dream come true?
What if the dream come true? and if millions unborn shall dwell
In the house that I shaped in my heart, the noble house of my
    thoughts?
Lord, I have staked my soul, I have staked the lives of my kin
On the truth of Thy dreadful word. Do not remember my failures,
But remember this my faith.

And so I speak.
Yea, ere my hot youth pass, I speak to my people and say:
Ye shall be foolish as I; ye shall scatter, not save;
Ye shall venture your all, lest ye lose what is more than all;
Ye shall call for a miracle, taking Christ at His word.
And for this I will answer, O people, answer here and hereafter,
O people that I have loved shall we not answer together.

The Rebel

Pádraic Pearse

I am come of the seed of the people, the people that sorrow,
That have no treasure but hope,
No riches laid up but a memory
Of an Ancient glory.
My mother bore me in bondage, in bondage my mother
    was born,
I am of the blood of serfs;
The children with whom I have played, the men and
    women with whom I have eaten,
Have had masters over them, have been under the lash of
    masters,
And, though gentle, have served churls;
The hands that have touched mine, the dear hands whose
    touch is familiar to me,
Have worn shameful manacles, have been bitten at the
    wrist by manacles,
Have grown hard with the manacles and the task-work of
    strangers,
I am flesh of the flesh of these lowly, I am bone of their
    bone,
I that have never submitted;
I that have a soul greater than the souls of my people's mas-
    ters,
I that have vision and prophecy and the gift of fiery speech,
I that have spoken with God on the top of His holy hill.

And because I am of the people, I understand the people
I am sorrowful with their sorrow, I am hungry with their
    desire:
My heart has been heavy with the grief of mothers,
My eyes have been wet with the tears of children,
I have yearned with old wistful men,
And laughed or cursed with young men;
Their shame is my shame, and I have reddened for it,
Reddened for that they have served, they who should be
    free,
Reddened for that they have gone in want, while others
    have been full,
Reddened for that they have walked in fear of lawyers and
    of their jailors
With their writs of summons and their handcuffs,
Men mean and cruel!
I could have borne stripes on my body rather than this
    shame of my people.

Text: P. Browne (ed.), *Collected Works of Pádraic H. Pearse*, Maunsel And Company, Dublin, 1917.

297

And now I speak, being full of vision;
I speak to my people, and I speak in my people's name to
    the masters of my people.
I say to my people that they are holy, that they are august,
    despite their chains.
That they are greater than those that hold them, and stronger
    and purer,
That they have but need of courage, and to call on the name
    of their God,
God the unforgetting, the dear God that loves the peoples
For whom he died naked, suffering shame.
And I say to my people's masters: Beware,
Beware of the thing that is coming, beware of the risen peo-
    ple,
Who shall take what ye would not give. Did ye think to
    conquer the people,
Or that Law is stronger than life and than men's desire to be
    free?
We will try it out with you, ye that have harried and held,
Ye that have bullied and bribed, tyrants, hypocrites, liars!

A Mother Speaks

Pádraic Pearse

In Mr Pearse's last letter to his mother
he says: 'You asked me to write a little
poem which would seem to be said by
you about me. I have written it, and one
copy is in Arbour Hill Barracks, with the
papers, and Father Aloysius is taking
charge of another copy of it.' (The above
is the little poem referred to.)
Note in source.

Text: *Songs & Poems, The Rebels Who
Fought and Died for Ireland in Easter
Week, 1916* (Samuels Collection, TCD).

Dear Mary, that didst see Thy First-born Son
    Go forth to die amid the scorn of men,
        For whom He died,
Receive my first-born son unto Thy arms,
    Who also hath gone forth to die for men,
And keep him by Thee, till I come to him.
    Dear Mary, I have shared Thy sorrow,
And soon shall share Thy joy.

Ireland, 1905

Thomas MacDonagh

Text: Thomas MacDonagh, *The Golden
Joy*, O'Donoghue & Co., Dublin, 1906.

Thomas Davis loved his land,
    Dreamt a dream, and dared to trust –
Sixty years ago his hand
    Fell to useless dust.

Sixty dismal years, alas!
    Fraught with death and wrong and scorn –
Memory from him doth pass
    As he ne'er were born.

All the brave are o'er the sea,
    All that were the fair and good! –
All the strong that would be free
    Shun our Nationhood.

Huddle here the weakling few,
    Murmur that 'twere good to die –
Let this race die, and a new
    Erin glorify.

Sure our fathers chose the wrong,
    Ne'er content with foe to treat –
Down the losing ages long
    Keens their shrill defeat.

Let the flag at last be furled
    And the bootless quarrel cease,
With the Empire of the World
    Let us stand in peace! –

Davis – ah! he loved this land,
    And he dared in her to trust –
Sixty years his tongue and hand
    Have been nerveless dust!

But the voice – it dies not yet,
    And the spirit lives for aye,
And his race shall not forget,
    May not pass away!

Down the ages of defeat
    Sire to son a duty gives,
While a patriot heart doth beat
    Still the Nation lives!

We were we ere England rose,
    England falls and still we are –
Saxon foes as Danish foes
    Meteors to our star!

Easy 'twere in peace to dwell,
    To give o'er the ancient fight, –
Easy the descent of Hell,
    High are Heaven and Right!

England prays you now to take
    At her feet an easy place –
Take it, slaves, – but nought can make
    Saxons of your race.

You are Irish to the end!
    Ease for this your sires withstood:
Down the glorious years they send
    Life-long Nationhood.

Far the end and Life is long;
    For the spirit wakes anew,
And again are born the strong
    Where the strong were few –

Strong and brave and many and young
    Dwelling within Irish seas,
Speaking their proud Gaelic tongue,
    Craving no new ease.

Keeper of their fathers' hest,
    Lovers of their fathers' ways,
Guarding the sublime bequest
    'Gainst the coming days –

Days of glory, days of peace,
    Days that Davis yearned to see,
Hail! With you the wars shall cease,
    Crowned with victory!

No defeat doth mar the past,
    Not in vain our fathers fought,
If the strife goes well at last
    For the Right they sought.

Thomas Davis in his grave
    Sleeps, for all his dreams of trust –
But his soul is with the brave
    Though his heart is dust!

Thomas MacDonagh.

Marching Song of the Irish Volunteers

Thomas MacDonagh

Greater than word in any age
    The care of God for Ireland still;
Under His guidance we engage
    For Ireland now to work His will.
We have no hate for Irishman,
    Our land we love from sea to sea;
And heed no mark of creed or clan –
    But Ireland claim and Ireland free.

When in the morn of time the Gael
    Saw Ireland rising o'er the foam,
He left his labouring oars to hail
    This lovely land, his destined home;
He loved this island's ancient grace,
    And here in glory long he throve;
His children's Gaelic pride of race
    Hallows the island of their love.

Text: Ballad slip in the Samuels
Collection, TCD. Originally published
in *The Irish Review* (Dublin), Vol. 3,
No. 34, December 1913.

A thousand years ago the Dane
    With raven banner swept the seas,
To win this land he sought in vain,
    Then left the ways of war for peace;
Tired of wayfaring here he found
    The welcome due to valiant foe;
The Viking stock on Irish ground
    Has grown and strongly still shall grow.

The Norman came in evil hour,
    When Ireland's passion had begun
And matched against an Empire's power
    The clans were broken one by one;
But yielded not and to this day
    Unconquered stand and wait the word;
The Normans took the Danish way
    And Ireland's is the Norman sword.

The clans were broken but to weld
    Into one mighty Irish strength;
The Dane and Norman force were held
    To build the Irish race at length,
We Gael, we Dane, we Norman now
    Have heard the word we waited long;
In arms we come and take this vow
    To make our country free and strong.

The Irish race, united, new,
    The youngest nation of the earth,
Shall to the elder race be true,
    And guard the glory of our birth;
Never for gain of praise or gold
    Our race has sold the sacred gift,
Unsullied still our right we hold
    And freedom's flag unstained we lift.

Our fathers, who foresaw the noon,
    Unfurled this flag before the dawn;
Its fringes caught the light but soon
    Back to the darkness it was drawn;
The dawn is come, the night is o'er,
    With joy we face the future years;
And now in freedom's cause once more
    Arise the Irish Volunteers.

Oh! sacred light of Liberty,
    Oh! Nation hallowed by thy cause,

We hail the glorious destiny
    That comes with right of native laws.
Oh! God, our comfort in the night,
    Be still our guardian in the day
And lead Thy people in Thy sight
    To follow still Thine ancient way.

Chorus
For Ireland, for Ireland, for Ireland all,
    Our ranks we band in might,
From her four seas, we at Ireland's call,
    In Ireland's cause unite
And march to the hosting of Gael and Gall,
    To claim our freedom's right.

The Rose Tree
Thomas MacDonagh

The Rose and the Thorn –
    Life's ancient story,
Ever reborn,
    Of Sorrow and Glory.

And the after-lot
    That Time discloses,
The thorns forgot
    In dreams of the roses.

Text: Thomas MacDonagh, *The Golden Joy*, O'Donoghue & Co., Dublin, 1906.

Let Erin Remember
Thomas MacDonagh

Let Erin remember the heroes brave,
    And gild their names in her story,
Who nobly fought their land to save,
    When knaves forgot her glory.
Ah! bold and leal in the Bearna Baoghail,
    Like brothers at last uniting;
Stout heart and hand they took their stand,
    And died for Ireland fighting.

Text: not found in any of the published collections of MacDonagh's poetry, this poem is attributed to him in *Songs of Freedom*, an anonymous, undated songster included in the Samuels Collection in TCD. A note after the poem reads 'Composed by An Ceann Catha, T. Mac Donnchadha, RIP'.
    The poem is modeled on Thomas Moore's 'Let Erin Remember the Days of Old'.

Some speak of vict'ries of battles fought,
    With never a gun's loud pealing;
Of Freedom won and the rights long sought,
    With never a life-blood's sealing.
Ah! with ring of steel the Bearna Baoghail
    Ever echoes the nation's calling,
And he loves her best who with dauntless breast
    Dies there for Ireland falling.

For Victory

Thomas MacDonagh

Text: Thomas MacDonagh, *The Golden Joy*, O'Donoghue & Co., Dublin, 1906.

We thank Thee, God,
For the love Thou hast given us,
Though late, for the country of our fathers!–
Late, not over late,
We thank Thee through Patrick
That we serve the country of our fathers.

We toil by day,
And we dream in the sleep-time,
And our toil and our dreams are for Erin:
We hold the flag
That our sires held always,
And we make new dreams for Erin.

O Victory
How fair thou comest,
Young, though the ages are thy garments!
Of Gaelic mouth
How sweet thou singest –
How splendid in the beauty of thy garments!

All radiant thou
In grandeur of the Fenians,
Or crowned with the memory of Tara!
In the fame of kings,
In the might of chieftains,
Bound in the memory of Tara!

Sweet as May dream,
Sweet is our Gaelic –
How Erin shall teem with its glory!
Brave in the North
And melodious in Munster
And impetuous in Connacht its glory!

An old man weeps
And a young man sorrows,
While a child is busy with his gladness!
The old shall cheer
And the young shall battle –
The child shall tremble for their gladness.

Sweet little child
To thee the victory –
Thou shalt be now as the Fenians!
For thee the feast,
For thee the lime-white mansions,
And the hounds on the hills of the Fenians!

Song from the Irish

Thomas MacDonagh

(Táid na réalta 'na seasamh ar an aer)

The stars stand up in the air,
   The sun and the moon are gone,
The strand of its waters is bare,
   And her sway is swept from the swan.

The cuckoo was calling all day,
   Hid in the branches above,
How my *stóirín* is fled far away –
   'Tis my grief that I give her my love!

Three things through love I see,
   Sorrow and sin and death –
And my mind reminding me
   That this doom I breathe with my breath.

But sweeter than violin or lute
   Is my love, and she left me behind –
I wish that all music were mute,
   And I to all beauty were blind.

She's more shapely than swan by the strand,
   She's more radiant than grass after dew,
She's more fair than the stars where they stand –
   'Tis my grief that her ever I knew!

Text: Thomas MacDonagh, *Songs of Myself*, Hodges Figgis, Dublin, 1910.

305

The Poet Captain

Thomas MacDonagh

Text: Thomas MacDonagh, *The Golden Joy*, O'Donoghue & Co., Dublin, 1906.

They called him their king, their leader of men, and
    he led them well
For one bright year, and he vanquished their foe,
Breaking more battles than bards may tell,
Warring victoriously – till the heart spake low,
And said – Is it thus? Do not these things pass? What
    things abide?
They are but the birds from the ocean, the waves of the
    tide;
And thou art naught beside – grass and a form of clay,
And said – The Ligurian fought in his day –
In vain, in vain! Rome triumphs. He left his friends to
    the fight,
And their victory passed away,
And he like a star that flames and falls in the night.

But after another year they came to him again,
And said – Lead us forth again. Come with us again.
But still he answered them – You strive against fate, in
    vain.
They said – Our race is old. We would not have it pass.
Ere Rome began we are, a gentle people of old,
Unsavage when all were wild.
And he – How Egypt was old in the days that were old,
Yet is passed, and we pass.
They said – We shall have striven, unreconciled.
And he went with them again, and they conquered
    again.
Till the same bare season closed his unquiet heart
To all but sorrow of life – This is in vain! Of yore
Lo, Egypt was, and all things do depart,
This is in vain! And he fought no more.

He conned the poems that poets had made in other days,
And he loved the past that he could pity and praise.
And he fought no more, living in solitude,
Till they came and called him back to the multitude,
Saying – Our olden speech and our old manners die.
He went again, and they raised his banner on high:
Came Victory, eagle-formed, with wings wide flung,
As with them awhile he fought, with never a weary
    thought, and with never a sigh,
That their children might have again their manners and
    ancient tongue.

But again the sorrow of life whispered to his soul
And said – O little soul, striving to little goal!
Here is a finite world where all things change and change!
And said – In Mexico a people strange
Loved their manners and speech long ago when the
    world was young!
Their speech is silent long – What of it now? Silent and
    dead,
Their manners forgotten, and all but their memory sped!
And said – What matter? Heart will die and tongue;
Or if they live again they live in a place that is naught,
With other language, other custom, different thought.
He left them again to their fight, and no more for him
    they sought.

But they chose for leader a stern sure man
That looked not back on the waste of story:
For his country he fought in the battle's van,
And he won her peace and he won her glory.

Wishes for My Son
Born on St Cecilia's Day, 1912
Thomas MacDonagh

Now, my son is life for you,
And I wish you joy of it –
Joy of power in all you do,
Deeper passion, better wit
Than I had who had enough,
Quicker life and length thereof,
More of every gift but love.

Love I have beyond all men,
Love that now you share with me –
What have I to wish you then
But that you be good and free,
And that God to you may give
Grace in stronger days to live?

For I wish you more than I
Ever knew of glorious deed,
Though no rapture passed me by
That an eager heart could heed,
Though I followed heights and sought
Things the sequel never brought.

Text: Thomas MacDonagh, *Lyrical Poems*,
The Irish Review, Dublin, 1913.

Wild and perilous holy things
Flaming with a martyr's blood,
And the joy that laughs and sings
Where a foe must be withstood,
Joy of headlong happy chance
Leading on the battle dance.

But I found no enemy,
No man in a world of wrong,
That Christ's word of charity
Did not render clean and strong –
Who was I to judge my kind,
Blindest groper of the blind?

God to you may give the sight
And the clear undoubting strength
Wars to knit for single right,
Freedom's war to knit at length,
And to win, through wrath and strife,
To the sequel of my life.

But for you, so small and young,
Born on St Cecilia's Day,
I in more harmonious song
Now for nearer joys should pray –
Simpler joys: the natural growth
Of your childhood and your youth,
Courage, innocence, and truth:

These for you, so small and young,
In your hand and heart and tongue.

The Singer's Grave

Thomas MacDonagh

Text: Thomas MacDonagh, *Through
the Ivory Gate,* Sealy, Bryers and
Walker, Dublin, 1902, re-printed as
'The Easter Rose Tree' in Brendan
Mary Mac Thormaid, *Deathless Glory,*
Dublin, 1966.

If in my life I shall have sung or done
  Some thing
For which mankind may praise me when I'm gone
  Then bring
A rose-tree to my grave, and plant it in the Spring.

'Tis not alone because I love the rose
  That I
Would crave a living rose-tree fair from those
  Who sigh
And weep my passing, for my poor grave when I die.

The War Legacy
Thomas MacDonagh

Be it War like the War that we waged, like the wind that withers
 the wold
All the howling night (and the people in horror holy within the
 house)
Uprooting the stark strong trees and riving the ruins of old,
Making tremble the animal – brute and man – the king of men
 and the mouse.

For better War's battering breeze than the Peace that barters the
 Past,
Better far the fear of our fathers' Father than friendship false
 with their foe,
And better anointed Death than the Nation's damnation at last,
And the crawling of craven limbs in life and the curse of the
 coward below.

Let the forest be felled and the roof-tree riven by wind of War,
Let mortals tremble and totter to death and the fight fare on
 anew,
With a soul for prize, and the trust of the sword of a Son for star,
And Victory and Heaven of Heroes for end, and revenge for the
 lives of the true.

Text: Thomas MacDonagh,
The Golden Joy, O'Donoghue
& Co., Dublin, 1906.

I See His Blood Upon the Rose
Joseph Mary Plunkett (1887–1916)

I see His blood upon the rose
And in the stars the glory of His eyes,
His body gleams amid eternal snows,
His tears fall from the skies.

I see His face in every flower;
The thunder and the singing of the birds
Are but His voice – and carven by His power
Rocks are His written words.

All pathways by His feet are worn,
His strong heart stirs the everbeating sea,
His crown of thorns is twined with every thorn,
His cross is every tree.

Text: Geraldine Plunkett (ed.),
The Poems of Joseph Mary Plunkett,
The Talbot Press, Dublin, 1916.

1867

Joseph Mary Plunkett

Text: Geraldine Plunkett (ed.),
The Poems of Joseph Mary Plunkett,
The Talbot Press, Dublin, 1916.

All our best ye have branded
When the people were choosing them,
When 'twas Death they demanded
Ye laughed! Ye were losing them.
But the blood that ye spilt in the night
Crieth loudly to God,
And their name hath the strength and the might
Of a sword for the sod.

In the days of our doom and our dread
Ye were cruel and callous,
Grim Death with our fighters ye fed
Through the jaws of the gallows;
But a blasting and blight was the fee
For which ye had bartered them,
And we smite with the sword that from ye
We had gained when ye martyred them!

The Dark Way

Joseph Mary Plunkett

Text: Geraldine Plunkett (ed.),
The Poems of Joseph Mary Plunkett,
The Talbot Press, Dublin, 1916.

Rougher than death the road I choose
Yet shall my feet not walk astray,
Though dark, my way I shall not lose
For this way is the darkest way.

Set but a limit to the loss
And something shall at last abide,
The blood-stained beams that formed the cross,
The thorns that crowned the crucified;

But who shall lose all things in One,
Shut out from Heaven and the Pit
Shall lose the darkness and the sun,
The finite and the infinite;

And who shall see in one small flower
The chariots and the thrones of might
Shall be in peril from that hour
Of blindness and the endless night;

And who shall hear in one short name
Apocalyptic thunders seven
His heart shall flicker like a flame
'Twixt Hell's gates and the gates of Heaven.

For I have seen your body's grace,
The miracle of the flowering rod,
And in the beauty of your face
The glory of the face of God,

And I have heard the thunderous roll
Clamoured from heights of prophecy,
Your splendid name, and from my soul
Uprose the clouds of minstrelsy.

Now I have chosen in the dark
The desolate way to walk alone
Yet strive to keep alive one spark
Of your known grace and grace unknown.

And when I leave you lest my love
Should seal your spirit's ark with clay
Spread your bright wings, O shining Dove –
But my way is the darkest way.

To Caitlín Ní hUallacháin
Joseph Mary Plunkett

The Little Black Rose shall be Red at Last

Because we share our sorrows and our joys
And all your dear and intimate thoughts are mine,
We shall not fear the trumpets and the noise
Of battle, for we know our dreams divine,
And when my heart is pillowed on your heart
And ebb and flowing of their passionate flood
Shall beat in concord love through every part
Of brain and body – when at last the blood
O'erleaps the final barrier to find
Only one source wherein to spend its strength
And we two lovers, long but one in mind
And soul, are made one only flesh at length;
Praise God if this my blood fulfils the doom
When you, dark rose, shall redden into bloom.

Text: Geraldine Plunkett (ed.),
The Poems of Joseph Mary Plunkett,
The Talbot Press, Dublin, 1916.

Frontispiece from *The Poems of Joseph Mary Plunkett*, captioned 'from a memory drawing by Mrs Joseph Plunkett'. Grace Plunkett (1888–1955), née Gifford, was one of the six Gifford sisters (Grace, Kate, Ada, Muriel, Nellie and Sydney), from a Dublin Unionist background. All went on to take part in the Irish independence struggle from the 1913 Lockout onwards, some more actively than others. Grace studied art, under William Orpen. Shortly before his execution on 4 May 1916, Grace married Joseph Mary Plunkett. Grace's sister Muriel was married to Thomas MacDonagh, another of the executed leaders. Muriel died in a drowning accident in 1917 and Grace was imprisoned in Kilmainham Jail during the Civil War.
See *Unlikely Rebels – The Gifford Girls and the Fight for Irish Freedom*, Anne Clarke, Mercier Press, 2011, for the story of these remarkable activist women. [LM]

The Glories of the World Sink Down in Gloom

Joseph Mary Plunkett

The glories of the world sink down in gloom,
And Babylon and Nineveh and all
Of Hell's high strongholds answer to the call,
The silent waving of a sable plume.
But there shall break a day when Death shall loom
For thee, and thine own panoply appal
Thee, like a stallion in a blazing stall,
While blood-red stars blaze out in skies of doom.
Lord of sarcophagus and catacomb,
Blood-drunken Death! With the columned hall
Of time, thou diest when its pillars fall.
Death of all deaths! Thou diggest thine own tomb,
Makest thy mound of Earth's soon-shattered dome,
And pullest the heavens upon thee for a pall.

Text: Padraic Colum and Edward J. O'Brien (eds.), *Poems of the Irish Revolutionary Brotherhood*, Small, Maynard & Co., Boston, 1916.

The Stars Sang in God's Garden

Joseph Mary Plunkett

The stars sang in God's garden;
The stars are the birds of God;
The night-time is God's harvest,
Its fruits are the words of God.

God ploughed His fields at morning,
God sowed His seed at noon,
God reaped and gathered in His corn
With the rising of the moon.

The sun rose up at midnight,
The sun rose red as blood,
It showed the Reaper, the dead Christ,
Upon His cross of wood.

For many live that one may die,
And one must die that many live –
The stars are silent in the sky
Lest my poor songs be fugitive.

Text: Geraldine Plunkett (ed.), *The Poems of Joseph Mary Plunkett*, The Talbot Press, Dublin, 1916.

This Heritage to the Race of Kings

Joseph Mary Plunkett

Text: Geraldine Plunkett (ed.),
The Poems of Joseph Mary Plunkett,
The Talbot Press, Dublin, 1916.

This heritage to the race of kings –
  Their children and their children's seed
  Have wrought their prophecies in deed
Of terrible and splendid things.

The hands that fought, the hearts that broke
  In old immortal tragedies,
  These have not failed beneath the skies,
Their children's heads refuse the yoke.

And still their hands shall guard the sod
  That holds their father's funeral urn,
  Still shall their hearts volcanic burn
With anger of the sons of God.

No alien sword shall earn as wage
  The entail of their blood and tears,
  No shameful price for peaceful years
Shall ever part this heritage.

The Ballad of the Foot and Mouth

Joseph Mary Plunkett

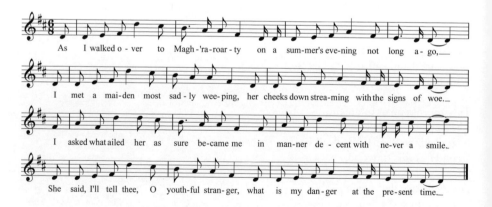

As I walked o - ver to Magh -'ra-roar - ty on a sum-mer's eve-ning not long a - go,—

I met a mai-den most sad - ly wee-ping, her cheeks down strea-ming with the signs of woe.—

I asked what ailed her as sure be-came me in man-ner de - cent with ne-ver a smile.—

She said, I'll tell thee, O youth-ful stran-ger, what is my dan-ger at the pre-sent time.—

Plunkett used a different register of
language for this song than he em-
ployed in his formal poetry. It is included in the collection edited after
his death by his sister Geraldine with

As I walked over to Magheraroarty
  On a summer's evening not long ago,
I met a maiden most sadly weeping,
  Her cheeks down streaming with the signs of woe;

314

I asked what ailed her, as sure became me
    In manner decent with never a smile,
She said I'll tell thee, O youthful stranger,
    What is my danger at the present time.

On my father's lands there are many mansions
    With sheep and cattle, and pigs *go leór*,
Until the Saxon came over the border
    With detention orders that raked him sore.
His herds they plundered and killed five hundred,
    And the rest they sundered north, east and south,
Saying, keep the hides and the woolly fleeces
    For the beasts have diseases of the foot and mouth!

With these words deceitful, sure he was cheated,
    Not a mouth was dropping, not a foot was sprung,
But the only disease came over from England
    The Cloven Hoof and the Dirty Tongue.
Now what can avail me, O youthful stranger,
    To save the beasts and my father's life
And my marriage portion that's my only fortune
    For the lad that's courting me to be his wife?

the comment, 'The ballad of the "Foot and Mouth" is an extremely good imitation of the old topical ballad, with all its beautiful badnesses. It is sung to "The Groves of Blarney".'

Text: Geraldine Plunkett (ed.), *The Poems of Joseph Mary Plunkett*, The Talbot Press, Dublin, 1916.
Air: 'The Groves of Blarney'.

The Legacy
(A Dying Socialist to His Son)
James Connolly (1868–1916)

Come here my son, and for a time put up your foolish play,
Draw nearer to your father's bed, and lay your games away.
No sick man's plaint is this of mine, ill-tempered at your noise,
Nor carping at your eagerness to romp with childish toys.
Thou'rt but a boy, and I, a man outworn with care and strife,
Would not deprive you of one joy thou canst extract from life;
But o'er my soul comes creeping on death's shadow, and my lips
Must give to you a message now ere life meets that eclipse.
Slow runs my blood, my nether limbs I feel not, and my eyes
Can scarce discern, here in this room, that childish form I prize.

Aye, death's grim hand is on my frame, and helpless it lies here,
But to my mental vision comes the power of the seer,
And time and space are now as naught as with majestic sweep,
I feel my mind traverse the land and encompass the deep;
Search backwards over history's course, or with prophetic view,
And sounding line of hope and fear, gauge man's great destiny too,
The chasm deep 'twixt life and death, I bridge at last tonight,

James Connolly, Union Leader, Marxist, Revolutionary and 1916 Rising leader, penned many songs and poems promoting the rights of the worker and economic freedom for the working class.

Connolly, being a Marxist, saw political freedom as a consequence of the economic freedom for the working class, as opposed to the non-Marxist view of achieving political freedom and then perhaps trying to improve the lot of working people. Connolly did have an input into the 1916 Proclamation of the Irish Republic, and his thinking, albeit in very broad terms, can be seen in the document.

315

It is erroneous to attribute Socialist or left-leaning motives to the main leaders of the 1916 Rising and the subsequent Anglo-Irish War. While some few were undoubtedly emotionally and perhaps philosophically of the Left, the predominant thinking of the time was conservative, as can be clearly seen in the result, the very conservative Irish Free State. [LM]

Text: James Connolly, *The Legacy and Songs of Freedom*, Socialist Party of Ireland, Dublin, 1918.

And with a foot on either side absorb their truth and light,
And thus, though reft of strength, my limbs slow turn to clay,
Fired by this light I call you here to hear my Legacy.

'My Legacy.' Ah, son of mine! Wert thou a rich man's pride,
He'd crown thee with his property, possessions far and wide,
And golden store to purchase slaves, whose aching brain and limb
Would toil to bring you luxury as such had toiled for him.
But thy father is a poor man, and glancing round you here,
Thou canst see all his property – our humble household gear.
No will we need by lawyers drawn, no witnesses attest,
To guard for you your legacy, your father's last bequest.

'Thy father is a poor man,' mark well what that may mean,
On the tablets of thy memory that truth write bright and clean.
Thy father's lot it was to toil from earliest boyhood on,
And know his latent energies for a master's profit drawn.
Or else, ill-starred, to wander round and huxter-like to vend
His precious store of brain and brawn for all whom fate may send
Across his path with gold enough to purchase Labour's power
To turn it into gold again, and fructify the hour
With sweat and blood of toiling slaves, like unto us my son;
Aye, through our veins since earliest days, 'tis poor man's blood
    has run.

Yes, son of mine, since History's dawn two classes stand revealed,
The Rich and Poor, in bitterest war, by deadliest hatred steeled.
The one, incarnate greed and crime, disdaining honest toil,
Has grasped man's common birthright and treasure house, the soil.
And standing 'twixt their fellow men and all that earth could give,
Had bade them render tribute if they would hope to live.
And, building crime on top of crime, had pushed their conquests on,
Till, arbiters of life and death, they stood with weapons drawn,
And blades athirst to drink the blood, on land and over sea,
Of him who dared for human rights to stem this tyranny.
They held our lands, our bodies ruled, and strove to rule the mind,
And Hell itself could not surpass their evil to mankind.
And all who strove for human rights to break their cursed yoke –
The noblest of our race, my child – went down beneath their stroke,
And over all earth's sweetest spots, in nature's lovliest haunt,
Each built his fort or castle grim the poor of earth to daunt.

And issuing forth from walls of stone, high over cliff and pass,
With sword in hand would gather in the tribute for his class,
And grimmest emblems of their rule flaunting to human ken,
The pit to drown our women, the gibbet for our men
Stood, aye, beside their fortresses; and underneath the moat

Tier under tier of noisome cells for those the tyrant smote.
Thumbscrew and rack and branding rod, and each device of Hell
Perverted genius could devise to torture men to sell
(For brief respite from anguish dire to end their wretched lives)
The secrets of their comradeship, the honour of their wives.
As fabled as the tree of old, by ancient poets sung,
Consumed with blight each living thing that 'neath its branches
    sprung.
The rich man's power o'er all the earth had spread its baleful
    blight,
Respecting neither age nor sex to sate its lust for might.
It stole the harvest from the field, the product from the loom,
Struck down the old man in his age, the young man in his bloom.
It robbed the carrier on the road, the sailor on the tide,
And from the bridegroom of an hour it took the new-made bride.
Such crimes it wrought – not Hell itself and its satanic school
Could fashion crimes to equal those wrought by the rich man's
    rule.
'The past?' Ah, boy, the method's past; the deed is still the same,
And robbery is robbery yet, though cloaked in gentler name.
Our means of life are still usurped, the rich man still is lord,
And prayers and cries for justice still meet one reply – the sword!
Though hypocrites for rich man's gold may tell us we are free,
And oft extol in speech and print our vaunted liberty.
But freedom lies not in a name, and he who lacks for bread
Must have that bread tho' he should give his soul for it instead.
And we, who live by Labour, know that while they rule we must
Sell Freedom, brain, and limb, to win for us and ours a crust.

The robbers made our fathers slaves, then chained them to the
    soil,
For a little longer chain – a wage – we must exchange our toil.
But open force give way to fraud, and force again behind
Prepares to strike if fraud should fail to keep man deaf and blind.
Our mothers see their children's limbs they fondled as they grew,
And doted on, caught up to make for rich men profits new.
Whilst strong men die for lack of work, and cries of misery swell,
And women's souls in cities' streets creep shuddering to Hell.
These things belong not to the past, but to the present day,
And they shall last till in our wrath we sweep them all away.

'We sweep them!' Ah, too well I know my work on earth is done,
Even as I speak my chilling blood tells me my race is run.
But you, my last born child, take the legacy I give,
And do as did your father whilst he yet was spared to live.
Treasure ye in your inmost heart this legacy of hate,
For those who on the poor man's back have climbed to high estate.

The lords of land and capital, the slave lords of our age,
Who of this smiling earth of ours have made for us a cage,
Where golden bars fetter men's souls, and noble thoughts do flame
To burn us with their vain desires, and virtue yields to shame.
Each is your foe, for to your class, of human rights, the foe.
Be it your thought by day and night to work their overthrow;
And howsoe'er you earn your wage, and wheresoe'er you go,
Be it beneath the tropic heat or mid the northern snow,
Or closely pent in factory walls or burrowing in the mine,
Or scorching in the furnace hell of steamers 'cross the brine,
Or on the railroad's shining track you guide the flying wheel,
Or clambering up on buildings high to weld their frames of steel,
Or use the needle or the type, the hammer, or the pen,
Have you one thought, one speech alone to all your fellow-men.
The men and women of your class, tell them their wrongs and yours,
Plant in their hearts that hatred deep that suffers and endures.
And treasuring up each deed of wrong, each scornful word and look,
Inscribe it in the memory, as others in a book.
And wait and watch through toiling years the ripening of time,
Yet deem to strike before that hour were worse than folly – crime.

This be your task, oh, son of mine, the rich man's hate to brave,
And consecrate your noblest part to rouse each fellow-slave,
To speed the day the world awaits when Labour, long oppressed,
Shall rise and strike for Freedom true, and from the tyrants wrest –
The power they have abused so long, Oh, ever glorious deed!
The crowning point of history, yet, child, of bitterest need.

Ah, woe is me, thy father's eyes shall not behold the day.
I faint and die; child, hold my hand –
Keep – thou – my – legacy!

A Father in Exile

James Connolly
(Written in the United States, Christmas 1903)

Text: James Connolly, *The Legacy and Songs of Freedom*, Socialist Party of Ireland, Dublin, 1918.

'Tis Christmas Day in Ireland, and I'm sitting here alone,
  Three thousand miles of ocean intervene,
And the faces of my loved ones in my little Irish home
  Come glancing in and out my thoughts between;
O, to catch the loving kisses from my little children flung,
  To feel the warm embrace when wife and husband meet,
To hear the boisterous greeting in the kindly Dublin tongue
  That makes brightness of the dullness of our murky Dublin
  street.

'Tis Christmas Day in Ireland, and I, my lot bewailing,
    Am fretting in this Western land, so cold,
Where the throbbings of the human heart are weak and unavailing,
    And human souls are reckoned less than gold;
O, the headache and the heartache and the ashes at the feast
    Attend us every hour of our sojourn in this land,
Till the heart-sick Irish exile turns his face towards the East,
    To that land where love and poverty can wander hand in hand.

'Tis Christmas Day in Ireland, and ringing over yonder
    Are Dublin streets with Irish love of life,
And I'm here in exile moping, in spirit yearning wander
    To that Irish land to meet my Irish wife;
O, the lovings and the strivings and the griefs we shared in common
    And the babes that came to bless us as sweet buds upon a tree,
O, curses on the cruel fate that sent a father roaming,
    And blessings still this Christmastide my Irish home on thee.

Lift the Flag

James Connolly

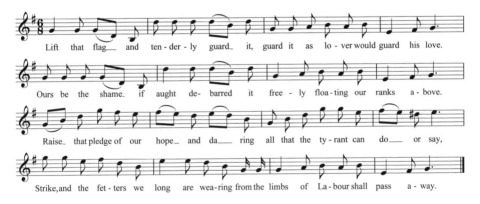

Lift that flag and tenderly guard it,
    Guard it as lover would guard his love,
Ours be the shame if ought debarred it
    Freely floating our ranks above.
Grasp that flag, and proudly daring
    All that the tyrant can do or essay,
Strike, and the fetters they long are wearing,
    From the limbs of Labour shall fall away.

The flag involved here is the red flag of the Socialist movement. [LM]

Text: James Connolly, *Songs of Freedom by Irish Authors*, J.E.C. Donnelly, New York, 1907. Slight differences in the text appear in subsequent publications – 1918 by the Socialist Party of Ireland, and 1972 by the Cork Workers' Club.
    Prescribed air: 'The Legacy'.

319

Hail that flag, my brothers, 'tis ours,
  Ours the life-blood that gave it its hue,
For us it waved thro' darkest hours,
  Waiting 'till Labour its destiny knew.
See that flag, now floating on high
  Free as the eagle flies to the sun,
Token and sign tho' men may die
  The cause persists whilst blood doth run.

Pledge that flag; my brothers, your glasses
  Never were drained to a holier toast;
Never shall Time reveal as it passes
  A grander mission than Labour can boast,
Fill up the glass! no stinted measure
  Shall serve to pledge this day with me,
The Cause we love, the Hope we treasure,
  The Flag that beckons to Liberty.

Freedom's Sun

James Connolly

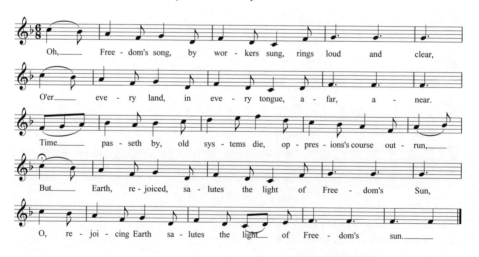

Oh,___ Free - dom's song, by wor - kers sung, rings loud and clear,

O'er___ eve - ry land, in eve - ry tongue, a - far, a - near.

Time___ pas - seth by, old sys - tems die, op - pres - ions's course out - run,___

But___ Earth, re - joiced, sa - lutes the light of Free - dom's Sun,

O, re - joi - cing Earth sa - lutes the light___ of Free - dom's sun.___

Text: James Connolly, *Songs of Freedom by Irish Authors*, J.E.C. Donnelly, New York, 1907.
  Air: 'Love's Young Dream', or 'The Shan Van Vocht'.

Yes, Freedom's song, by workers sung,
  Rings loud and clear,
O'er every land, in every tongue,
  Afar, anear;

Time passeth by,
Old systems die –
Oppression's course outrun,
But Earth, rejoiced, salutes the light
Of Freedom's sun;
O, rejoicing Earth salutes the light
Of Freedom's sun.

Yes, all men then their lives may live
From grim want free,
And all the joys that life can give,
Their lot shall be;
And care shall fly,
And sea and sky
Acclaim the work well done,
When Earth, rejoiced, salutes the light
Of Freedom's sun,
O, rejoicing Earth salutes the light
Of Freedom's sun.

No longer now revolt need hide
In holes and caves,
While those who brave Oppression's pride
But find their graves.
No tyrant's ban
Can now make man
The truths of knowledge shun;
All Earth, rejoiced, salutes the light
Of Freedom's sun,
O, rejoicing Earth salutes the light
Of Freedom's sun.

Our fathers saw the master's sword
His plunder glean,
But specious fraud and lying word
His thefts now screen;
Yet fraud shall fail
And Truth prevail,
And Justice shall be done,
When Earth, rejoiced, salutes the light
Of Freedom's sun,
O, rejoicing Earth salutes the light
Of Freedom's sun.

Be Moderate

James Connolly

Some men, faint hear-ted, e-ver seek our pro-gramme to re touch,
And will in sist, when e'er they speak, that we de-mand too much.
'Tis pas-sing strange, yet I de-clare, such state-ments cause me mirth,
For our de-mands most mo-dest are, we on-ly want the Earth.

This song pours scorn on the moder-ates and compromisers, and verse 3 is sarcastic. The whole tenor of the song is to resist any demands or sug-gestions that anything less than the ultimate goal of full freedom and full control over one's own destiny is ac-ceptable. 'We only want the earth' is a good slogan for Republicans and Socialists. [LM]

Text: James Connolly, *The James Connolly Songbook*, Cork Workers Club, n.d.
The first verse here is not found in the 1972 edition by the Cork Workers' Club, nor in the 1918 version published by the Socialist Party of Ireland.
Air: 'A Nation Once Again'.

Some men, faint-hearted ever seek
   Our programme to retouch.
And will insist, whene'er they speak
   That we demand too much.
'Tis passing strange, yet I declare
   Such statements cause me mirth,
For our demands most modest are,
   We only want THE EARTH.

'Be moderate,' the timerous cry,
   Who dread the tyrant's thunder,
'You ask too much, and people fly
   From you aghast, in wonder.'
'Tis passing strange, and I declare
   Such statements cause me mirth
For our demands most moderate are,
   We only want THE EARTH.

Our masters all – a godly crew,
   Whose hearts throb for the poor –
Their sympathies assure us, too,
   If our demands were fewer.
Most generous souls, but please observe
   What they enjoy from birth,
Is all we ever had the nerve
   To ask, that is, THE EARTH.

The Labour Fakir, full of guile,
   Such doctrine ever preaches,
And, whilst he bleeds the rank and file,
   Tame moderation teaches.
Yet, in his despite, we'll see the day
   When, with sword in its girth

Labour shall march in war array,
    To seize its own, THE EARTH.

For labour long with sighs and tears
    To its oppressors knelt,
But never yet to aught save fears
    Did heart of tyrant melt.
We need not kneel; our cause is high,
    Of true men there's no dearth,
And our victorious rallying cry
    Shall be, WE WANT THE EARTH.

Saoirse a Rúin

James Connolly

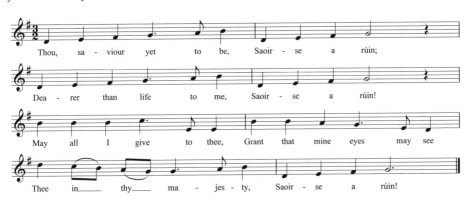

Thou, saviour yet to be,
    Saoirse a ruin!
Dearer than life to me,
    Saoirse a ruin!
May I give all to thee,
Grant that mine eyes may see
Thee in thy majesty,
    Saoirse a ruin!

Hard was our travail past
    Saoirse a ruin!
Long held in bondage fast,
    Saoirse a ruin!
Weary the road we've passed,
By error's clouds o'ercast,
Thy light breaks in at last,
    Saoirse a ruin!

The word 'Saoirse' is the Irish word for 'freedom'. The third verse is missing a line in all printed versions.

Text: James Connolly, *The Legacy and Songs of Freedom*, Socialist Party of Ireland, Dublin, 1918.
    Air: The air prescribed for this song in 1918 was Moore's 'Erin the tear and the smile in thine eye', which uses the traditional air 'Eibhlín a Rúin'.

323

Oft hath our master's tongue,
   Saoirse a ruin!
Glibly thy glories sung,
   Saoirse a ruin!
Loudly thy harp they've strung,
Wildly thy praises flung –
   Saoirse a ruin!

Long have we sought thy light,
   Saoirse a ruin!
Through Oppression's darkest night,
   Saoirse a ruin!
And ne'er shall cease the fight
'Gainst the tyrant's hateful might,
Till thou shalt bless our sight,
   Saoirse a ruin!

Forth, then, we march today,
   Freedom, our own!
Eager, panting for the fray,
   Freedom our own!
'Neath thy sun's enlight'ning ray
Naught shall our progress stay,
Soon thou shall reign alway,
   Freedom our own!

The National Executive of the Irish Trades Union Congress and Labour Party in 1914,
with James Connolly on the extreme left of the picture, and James Larkin, front row, second from the right.

Arouse

James Connolly

A—— rouse! The ral - ly - ing cry sends its cho - rus up on high,

Let—— cra - ven co - wards fly—— to the rear.——

While— we ral - ly to the fight, to do our com - bat for the Right,

And Op - pres - sion—— put to flight, we swear.——

For—— ty - rants we have fought,—— and our blood (their gold had bought),——

They have la - vished, ca - ring naught,—— in red streams,——

But— the fight we have be - gun, on this earth shall ne'er be done

Till the light of Free - dom's Sun—— on us gleams.——

Arouse! The rallying cry
Sends its chorus up on high,
Let craven cowards fly
   To the rear;
While we rally to the fight,
To do our combat for the Right,
And Oppression put to flight,
   We swear.

For tyrants we have fought,
And our blood (their gold had bought),
They have lavished, caring naught,
   In red streams,
But the fight we have begun,
On this earth shall ne'er be done
Till the light of Freedom's sun
   On us gleams.

At our lot might angels weep,
While we toil our masters sleep,

Text: James Connolly, *The Legacy and
Songs of Freedom*, Socialist Party of
Ireland, Dublin, 1918.
   Air: 'Pearla an Brollaig Bain', or
'The Snowy-Breasted Pearl'.

What we make our masters keep,
    And our gains,
Are the wage – to buy our food,
The poor shelter for our brood,
And the fever which our blood
    Ever drains.

By our toil they keep their state,
On our woes they rise, elate,
Yet wonder when our hate
    To them ascends;
Where we build they enter in,
What we earn these spoilers win,
But we swear our slav'ry's sin
    Soon shall end.

Then arouse! ye workers all,
Braving scaffold, sword and ball,
And at Labour's trumpet call
    Quick appear,
For the day we long have sought,
For which our fathers fought –
The day with Freedom fraught
    Now is here!

A Festive Song

James Connolly

Com-rades, clasp hands, the time de-mands this night we spend en-joy-ing
The jo-vial word round fes-tive board, grim, car__ king care__ de-stroy-ing.
Li-quor__ this night shall spar__ kle bright, with ho__ mage pay__ to Beau-ty,
And brave men__ who oft con__ flict knew, shall take__ a rest__ from du-ty.

Chorus

Then fill the cup with li-quor up, pledge eve-ry man__ his neigh-bour,
That in the light of truth he'll fight to win__ the world__ for La-bour.

Comrades, clasp hands,
The time demands
This night we spend enjoying
The jovial word
Round festive board,
Grim, carking care destroying.
Liquor this night
Shall sparkle bright,
With homage pay to Beauty,
And brave men who
Oft conflict knew,
Shall take a rest from duty.

Text: James Connolly, *The Legacy and Songs of Freedom*, Socialist Party of Ireland, Dublin, 1918.
Air: 'Wreathe the Bowl'.

Chorus

Then fill the cup
With liquor up,
Pledge ev'ry man his neighbour,
That in the light
Of Truth he'll fight
To win the world for Labour.

Comrades, the tears
Our Class thro' years
Hath shed the wide world over,
Have taken root,
And soon the fruit
Our tyrants shall discover;
And when at length
We show our strength
And send each despot flying,
With joy and mirth,
Like ours, the Earth
Shall hail Oppression dying.

For who with zest
Can laugh the best
But he who laughs the longest,
And in the fight
'Twixt wrong and right
The laugh is with the strongest;
Since Time began
Fate's mighty plan
The laugh gave to the proudest
But History
Shall tell that we
Did laugh the last and loudest.

327

Then, comrades, toast
Great Freedom's host,
And loudly sing her praises,
And honoured be,
O'er land and sea,
Whoe'er her banner raises;
So, ere we leave,
A wreath we'll weave
Of flow'rs of Earth's best gleaning,
With Maid and Wife,
With Hope of Life
Free from a Tyrant's scheming.

The Message

James Connolly

Our mes - sage send a - gain_____ pea - ling thro' hill and glen,_____

Free - dom for wor - king men_____ is_____ free - dom for all;_____

Free - dom from dread of want,_____ from hun - ger, lean and gaunt,_____

From all the ills that daunt_____ and keep us in thrall._____

Up on the moun - tain side_____ far o'er the o - cean wide,_____

Cir - cling the world wide,_____ that mes_____ sage is borne;_____

Bring-ing to those whose hearts_____ ache 'neath the stings and darts,_____

Bon - dage to men im - parts,_____ hope of_____ Free - dom's morn._____

Our message send again
Pealing thro' hill and glen,
Freedom for working men
    Is freedom for all;
Freedom from dread of want,
From hunger, lean and gaunt,
From all the ills that daunt
    And keep us in thrall.

Up on the mountain side,
Far o'er the ocean tide,
Circling the world wide,
    That message is borne;
Bringing to those whose hearts
Ache 'neath the stings and darts
Bondage to man imparts,
    Hope of Freedom's morn.

Morning when man shall rise
And face, with gladdened eyes,
The truth that Freedom lies
    In Labour's arms alone;
Labour, which makes to bloom
Mountain steppe and desert gloom,
Yet finds this life a tomb,
    And each hour a moan.

Moaning for manhood lost,
For noble purpose crossed,
For hopes and bright dreams tossed
    In that yawning grave,
Where wealth, the tyrant, stands,
Grasping with greedy hands,
And binding in iron bands,
    The life of its slave.

That message send again
Pealing thro' hill and glen,
Freedom for working men
    Is Freedom for all;
Freedom from dread of want,
From hunger, lean and gaunt,
From all the ills that daunt
    And keep us in thrall.

Text: James Connolly, *The Legacy and Songs of Freedom*, Socialist Party of Ireland, Dublin, 1918.
    Air: 'Seaghan O Duibir an Gleanna'.

329

The Call of Erin

James Connolly

With the en - gines 'neath us throb bing,_____ and the wind u - pon our stern,

Lit - tle reck we of the dis - tance_____ that di - vides us now from Erin,

For we hear her voi - ces cal - ling,_____ swee-ping past us on the west,

Cal - ling home to her the chil - dren_____ She once nou - rished on her breast.

Chorus

She is cal - ling, cal - ling, cal - ling,_____ in the wind and o'er the tide,

We, her chil - dren hear her voi - ces_____ call us e - ver to her side.

This song expresses Connolly's
thoughts as he returned to Ireland
from the USA. [LM]

Text: James Connolly, *The Legacy and
Songs of Freedom*, Socialist Party of
Ireland, Dublin, 1918.
   Air: 'Rolling Home to Bonnie
Scotland', which was later used for
the popular song 'Kevin Barry'.

With the engines 'neath us throbbing,
    And the wind upon our stern,
Little reck we of the distance
    That divides us now from Erin,
For we hear her voice a calling,
    Calling past us from the West,
Calling home to us her children
    She once nourished on her breast.

Chorus
She is calling, calling, calling,
    In the wind and on the tide,
We her children, hear her voice
    Call us ever to her side.

Oh! ye waters, bear us onward
    And ye winds your task fulfil,
Till our Irish eyes we feast on
    Irish vale and Irish hill;
Till we tread our Irish Cities,
    See their glory and their shame
And our eyes, like skies o'er Erin,
    Through their smiles shed tears of pain.

Glorious is the land we're leaving,
    And its pride shall grow through years;
And the land that calls us homewards
    Can but share with us her tears;
Yet our hearts her call obeying,
    Heedless of the wealth men crave,
Turneth home to share her sorrow
    Where she weeps beside the wave.

For Labour's Right

James Connolly

Up, brothers, up! The drums are beating,
    And see on high the banners wave,
Close up your ranks, let no retreating
    Be ours while earth contains a slave.
        'Till all alike our triumph won
        Shall know the splendor of the sun,
        And drink of wisdom's holiest spring,
        This is the prize our armies bring.

    Chorus
    A holy war for Labour's right,
    A holy war for Labour's right,
            For Labour's cause,
            For Labour's cause,
    Shall win the fight.

Text: James Connolly, *Songs of Freedom by Irish Authors*, J.E.C. Donnelly, New York, 1907.
    A note to the text reads 'Translation of the famous revolutionary song "Auf Socialisten" sung in chorus by the German Socialists at the close of the Stuttgart Congress.'
    Air: The air, by J.J. Hughes, was published in tonic sol-fa format in the *Connolly Souvenir*, a programme for a commemorative concert in The Mansion House on 5 June 1919, Connolly's birthday.

O, brothers we, whose hurts uncounted
    Must toil to earn a scanty wage,
Whose backs were bent that robbers mounted,
    Might ride thereon from age to age.
No longer now in thralldom grown
Your strong right hand must take your own;
And by that act to manhood spring
This is the prize our armies bring.

The tyrants hope a conquering sword
    Shall stem the onward march of right,
But Truth o'er all their barbarous horde
    Leads Freedom's host to Freedom's height.
To break the sword of War and Pain
That peace and joy o'er Earth may reign
And conquering hosts of Labour sing
This is the prize our armies bring.

A Rebel Song

James Connolly

Come, wor-kers, sing a re-bel song, a song of love and hate,
Of love un— to the low-ly and of ha— tred to the great,
The great who trod our fa— thers down, who steal our chil-dren's bread,
Whose hand of greed is stretched to rob the li-ving and the dead.

Chorus

Then sing our— re-bel song, as we proud ly sweep a-long,
To— end the age-long ty-ran-ny that makes for— hu-man tears;
Our march is nea-rer done with each set— ting of the sun,
And the ty-rant's might is pas-sing with the pas-sing of the years

Come workers, sing a rebel song,
    A song of love and hate
Of love unto the lowly
    And of hatred to the great;
The great who trod our fathers down,
    Who steal our children's bread,
Whose hands of greed are stretched to rob
    The living and the dead.

Chorus
Then sing our rebel song,
As we proudly sweep along,
To end the age-long tyranny
    That makes for human tears,
Our march is nearer done
With each setting of the sun,
And the tyrant's might is passing
    With the passing of the years.

We sing no more of wailing
    And no song of sighs or tears.
High are our hopes, and stout our hearts
    And banished all our fears.
Our flag is raised above us
    So that all the world may see
'Tis Labour's faith and Labour's arm
    Alone can Labour free.

Out from the depths of misery
    We march with hearts aflame,
With wrath against the rulers false
    Who wreck our manhood's name;
The serf who licks the tyrant's rod
    May bend forgiving knee,
The slave who breaks his slavery's chain
    A wrathful man must be.

Our army marches onward
    With its face towards the dawn,
In trust secure in that one thing
    The slave may lean upon;
The might within the arm of him
    Who, knowing Freedom's worth,
Strikes home to banish tyranny
    From off the face of earth.

Text: *The Connolly Souvenir*, Cumannacht na hÉireann, Dublin, 1919.
    The music, by G.W. Crawford, a Scottish socialist, was included in tonic sol-fa form in the publication.

A Love Song

James Connolly

I— love you, I   love you, tho' toil may ob - scure   and make dar - ker the light of my   eye,___

Tho' slow runs my blood, and my heart, if   as   pure,   beats cal-mer when wo - men are   nigh;

Yet   out from my heart comes a   pas-sio-nate wail,   with a   note   of sin - ce - ri - ty   true,___

The pro-test   of that heart, tho' its   vi-gor may fail, yet beats stron-ger its   love, dear, for   you.___

Named in later publications as 'Love of Freedom'.

Text: James Connolly, *Songs of Freedom by Irish Authors*, J.E.C. Donnelly, New York, 1907.
  Air: 'Believe me if all those endearing young charms'.

I love you, I love you, tho' toil may obscure
  And make darker the light of my eye,
Tho' slow runs my blood, and my heart, if as pure,
  Beats calmer when women are nigh.
Yet out from my heart comes a passionate wail,
  With a note of sincerity true,
The protest of that heart, though its vigor may fail,
  Yet beats stronger its love, dear, for you.

I love you, I love you, no swain to his dear,
  Nor mother to first fruit of her womb,
Nor thinker to truths he has garnered in tears,
  From the deserts which hid them in gloom,
Hath love more devoted, more unfailing than he
  Now laying this poor wreath at thy shrine,
In hope that accepted that offering will be
  And remembered when victory is thine.

Yes, Freedom, I love you, my soul thou hast fired
  With the flame that redeems from the clay,
Thou hast given to me, as to Moses inspired,
  A glimpse of that land bright as day,
Whither Labour must journey, tho' each foot of the road
  Sweated blood from the graves of its best,
Where built upon justice and truth, the abode
  Thou preparest awaits the opprest.

The Watchword

James Connolly

Oh! hear ye the Watchword of Labour!
    The slogan of they who'd be free,
That no more to any enslaver,
    Must labour bend suppliant knee.
That we on whose shoulders are borne,
    The pomp and the pride of the great;
Whose toil they repay with their scorn,
    Must challenge and master our fate.

Chorus
Then send it aloft on the breeze, boys!
    That watch-word, the grandest we've known
That Labour must rise from its knees, boys,
    And claim the broad earth as its own.

Aye! we who oft won by our valour,
    Empire for our Rulers and Lords,
Yet knelt in abasement and squalor,
    To the thing we had made by our swords.
Now valour with worth will be blending,
    When answering Labour's command,
We arise from our knees, and ascending
    To manhood for freedom take stand.

This song, more commonly known as 'The Watchword of Labour', is regarded by the Irish Labour Party as its own anthem.

Text: James Connolly, *Songs of Freedom by Irish Authors*, J.E.C. Donnelly, New York, 1907.
    Air: 'Take and Hold'. That air may be the one above, by J.J. Hughes, to which the text was set in tonic sol-fa format in the 1919 *Souvenir Programme*, and in the 1920s in the sheet music version published by the ITGWU.

Then out from the field and the city,
From workshop, from mill, and from mine,
Despising their wrath and their pity,
We workers are moving in line,
To answer the watchword and token,
That Labour gives forth as its own;
Nor pause till our fetters we've broken,
And conquered the spoiler and drone.

Freedom's Pioneers

James Connolly

Text: James Connolly, *Songs of Freedom by Irish Authors*, J.E.C. Donnelly, New York, 1907.
Air: 'The Boys of Wexford'.

Our feet upon the upward path
Are set, where none may tread
Save those who to the rich man's wrath
Dare turn rebellious head,
And heart as brave; no cringing slave
In all our ranks appears;
Our proudest boast, in Labour's host,
We're Freedom's Pioneers.

Chorus
Oh, slaves may beg, and cowards whine;
We scorn their foolish fears.
We dare and plan to lead the van,
With Freedom's Pioneers.

Too long upon our toil were built
    The palaces of power,
When at our word those forts of guilt
    Would crumble in an hour;
Now each day brings on swiftest wings
    To their unwilling ears,
The shouts that greet our marching feet
    ''Tis Freedom's Pioneers!'

The rich man's hate, the rich man's pride,
    Hath held us long in awe,
Our Right to Life is still denied,
    And wealth still rules the law.
But man shall bow no longer now,
    But welcome with his cheers
The ringing stroke to break his yoke
    Of Freedom's Pioneers.

Shake Out Your Banners

James Connolly

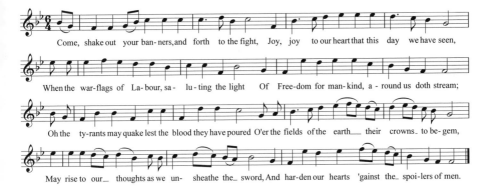

Come, shake out your banners, and forth to the fight,
    Joy, joy to our heart that this day we have seen,
When the war-flags of Labour, saluting the light
    Of Freedom for mankind, around us doth stream;
Oh the tyrants may quake lest the blood they have poured
    O'er the fields of the earth their crowns to be-gem,
May rise to our thoughts as we unsheathe the sword,
    And harden our hearts 'gainst the spoilers of men.

Text: James Connolly, *The Legacy and Songs of Freedom*, Socialist Party of Ireland, Dublin, 1918.
    Air: 'Come, Send Round the Wine', or 'Thugamar Féin an Samhradh Linn'.

337

Ay the sword glitters grandly, but not as of yore,
  When brother smote brother in murderous feud,
Or the nod of a tyrant rushed nations to war,
  And the hopes of our race were o'erwhelmed in blood.
Nay the fight that we fight is a fight for our own,
  And 'Freedom for Labour' our war's tocsin shall be,
Through the broad earth resounding, till Capital's throne
  Lies shattered for aye, and the toiler is free.

Hymn to Freedom

James Connolly

Text: James Connolly, *Songs of Freedom
by Irish Authors*, J.E.C. Donnelly, New
York, 1907.
  Air: 'The Holy City'.

Here at her altar kneeling,
  Sweet Freedom we adore,
And swear to hold her honour
  As sacred as of yore.
Did all her holy martyrs,
  When, recking life as naught,
They went to death to guard the faith
  Her love to man had brought.

Chorus
O Freedom! O Freedom!
  Thy worshippers are we;

Here kneeling, our allegiance
    We render unto thee.

And as our fathers prayed to see
    The glories of her face,
We kneeling at her altar
    Beseech her longed-for grace,
She needs no gory sacrifice
    Laid on her altar stones,
Our pilgrimage of poverty
    For all our faults atones.

She comes not clothed in majesty,
    No terrors in her tone,
Her priesthood is of Labour,
    Her service is our own.
To toil, and pain, and penury,
    Wherever manhood dwells,
She speaks and lo, responsive,
    The heart of Labour swells.
She builds her altar in our hearts,
    Her ritual on our lives,
And they who yield her service
    Need not the grace that shrives.

Human Freedom

James Connolly

Come, hear-ken all, the__ day draws nigh, when must-'ring hosts the cause shall__ try
Of__ La-bour's right to__ live and die en-joy-ing hu-man free____ dom;
Then La-bour's force shall take the field, the li-be-ra-ting sword to__ wield,
For La-bour's own right arm must shield the cause of hu-man free____ dom.

Chorus
Shout hur-ra for__ free-dom's host, for free-dom's ban-ner nob__ ly__ borne,
Shout hur-ra, though tem-pest tossed, Free-dom's barque shall ride the storm.

Text: James Connolly, *Songs of Freedom by Irish Authors*, J.E.C. Donnelly, New York, 1907.

Air: The prescribed air for this song is 'Happy We've Ben A' Thegither', which is the first line of the chorus of a song sometimes ascribed to Robert Burns, entitled 'Happy Friendship'. That song is found set to several tunes, including the Scots 'Willie Was a Wanton Wag' (better known in Ireland as 'Clare's Dragoons'), to which it is set here.

'Happy Friendship' is now sung to a different air (one that does not fit Connolly's song), which was collected from Willie Scott, 'the Border Shepherd', by the Scottish singer and collector Alison Mac Morland.

Come, hearken all, the day draws nigh,
When mustering hosts the cause shall try
Of Labour's right to live and die
    Enjoying human freedom;
Then Labour's force shall take the field,
The liberating sword to wield,
For Labour's own right arm must shield
    The cause of human freedom.

Shout hurra for freedom's host,
    For freedom's banner nobly borne,
Shout hurra, though tempest tossed,
    Freedom's barque shall ride the storm.

The rights our heroes' lives have bought,
The truths our martyrs, dying, taught,
The hearts of men with passion hot,
    Prepare for human freedom;
Its roots are in no barren soil,
But, watered by the tears of toil,
Are spreading fast, no storms can spoil
    The plant of human freedom.

Our Native Land! Alas, the name
Is but a sound to tell our shame,
What land have they whose spirits tame
    Brook loss of human freedom?
When lake and river, hill and dale,
Hear children's cry and women's wail
Of suffering rise on every gale,
    For lack of human freedom.

Our banner waves o'er many bands,
Thro' mount and ocean-severed lands,
With active brain and skilful hands
    Working for human freedom;
For ancient feuds no more divide,
And ancient hates we thrust aside,
Our class, we know, thro' battle's tide
    Must bear the flag of freedom.

For this, since ere the world began,
Their troubled course the ages ran,
And earth, in long travail for man,
    Bare seed of human freedom.
For us and ours that heritage
Was handed down from age to age,
That we might write on Hist'ry's page –
    The Birth of Human Freedom.

O Slaves of Toil!

James Connolly

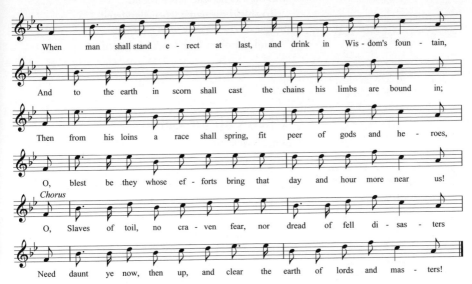

When man shall stand e-rect at last, and drink in Wis-dom's foun-tain,

And to the earth in scorn shall cast the chains his limbs are bound in;

Then from his loins a race shall spring, fit peer of gods and he-roes,

O, blest be they whose ef-forts bring that day and hour more near us!

Chorus

O, Slaves of toil, no cra-ven fear, nor dread of fell di-sas-ters

Need daunt ye now, then up, and clear the earth of lords and mas-ters!

When man shall stand erect at last,
   And drink at Wisdom's fountain,
And to the earth in scorn shall cast
   The chains his limbs are bound in;
Then from his loins a race shall spring,
   Fit peer of gods and heroes,
O, blest be they whose efforts bring
   That day and hour more near us!

Chorus
O, Slaves of toil, no craven fear,
   Nor dread of fell disasters
Need daunt ye now, then up, and clear
   The earth of lords and masters!

Like brazen serpents raised on high,
   In Israelite tradition,
Our cause in each believing eye
   Mean slavery's abolition;
We see the day when man shall rise,
   And, firm on science building,
From Theft's thick mask of fraud and lies
   Strip all the specious gilding.

O, blest are they whom wind and tide
   Are wafting fortune's graces,

A note in the source records that the fourth line of the second verse 'was indistinct in original MS; Maeve Cavanagh has substituted the above'.
   Cavanagh was a close friend of Connolly, who referred to her as 'the poetess of the revolution'.

Text: James Connolly, *The Legacy and Songs of Freedom*, Socialist Party of Ireland, Dublin, 1918.
   Air: 'O, For the Swords of Former Time!'.

341

And blest the man whose blushing bride
    Returns his rapt embraces,
And blest is he who has a friend
    To shield his name when slandered,
But blest o'er all they who contend
    And march in Freedom's vanguard.

When Labour Calls
James Connolly

When La-bour calls her chil-dren forth, a wai-ting world to win,

Earth's no-blest breed, true men of worth___ her___ ranks shall en-ter in.

Then, com-rades all, pre-pare that we___ may hear that call a-non,

And drive the hosts of ty-ran-ny___ like clouds be-fore the dawn.

And drive our foes, and drive our foes, our foes like clouds be-fore the dawn.

In the 1918 Socialist Party edition of Connolly's songs the second half of the second verse is as follows:

But Time rolled on, and Earth and Sky
    New Powers to man revealed,
And Science echoes Labour's cry,
    'King Capital must yield,'
      At last must yield,
      At last must yield,
King Capital at last must yield!

Text: James Connolly, *Songs of Freedom by Irish Authors*, J.E.C. Donnelly, New York, 1907.
    Air: 'Transvaal Volkslied or National Anthem'.

When Labour calls her children forth,
    A waiting world to win,
Earth's noblest breed, true man of worth,
    Her ranks shall enter in.
Then comrades all, prepare that we
    May hear that call anon,
And drive the hosts of tyranny
    Like clouds before the dawn.
        And drive our foes,
        And drive our foes,
Our foes like clouds before the dawn.

Thou knowest, long has Labor groaned,
    A robbed and beaten thrall,
Whilst Capital, on high enthroned
    Reigned, lording over all.
But knowledge came and to the slave
    His power at last revealed,

He stands erect, his heart is brave,
   The tyrant's doom is sealed.
      His doom is sealed,
      His doom is sealed,
   Thy tyrant's doom at last is sealed.

We work and wait till womb of Time
   Shall give fair Freedom birth,
To Labour's host that hope sublime
   Regenerates the earth.
And by that hope we toilers fired
   To nobler deeds shall be,
That we may guide, by it inspired,
   Our class to Liberty,
      To Liberty,
      To Liberty,
   To guide our class to Liberty!

My Jimmy, Dear

Thomas J. Clarke (1858–1916)

My Jimmy, dear,
   Another year
Has snail-like crept away
   Since you I wrote
   That 'P.P.' note
My gift last Christmas Day.

   And I again
   Unearth the pen
To try what I can do
   At stringing rhyme
   This Christmas time
For comrades staunch and true.

   Another year
   For Ireland, dear,
We've spent in these drear cells
   Where England strives
   To blast our lives
With torments fierce as hell's.

Tom Clarke wrote of his experiences in English prisons, where he spent fifteen years, from 1883 to 1898. To lighten their load he and his fellow prisoners would write and exchange verses. Of this piece he wrote

'I ... have by me a copy of one of my own effusions, and a few verses of it will serve as a sample of our prison rhymes and show the spirit in which we were facing the Chatham music.'

And he adds,

'On the previous Christmas I had written to Daly and Egan a skit on Pontius Pilate, *alias* Governor Harris.'

Text: Thomas J. Clarke, *Glimpses of an Irish Felon's Prison Life*, Maunsell & Roberts, Dublin, 1922.

Tom Clarke.

But their worst we scorn,
　For we're Fenians born,
And, by heaven, the same we'll die;
　No slaves are we,
　We bend the knee
To none but God on high.

Ah! no, old man,
　They never can
Our Fenian souls subdue,
　For our love is bound
　Too firmly round
Our cause to prove untrue.

Here's to our land,
　May she withstand
The might of England vile;
　May the future bring
　On swifter wing
True freedom to our Isle.

Image courtesy of the
National Library of Ireland.

Con Colbert (pictured above) was
based in Marrowbone Lane during
the Rising, and at the surrender
assumed command of his unit in
order to save the life of his superior
officer, a married man.

Text: Brendan Mary Mac Thormaid,
Deathless Glory, Dublin, 1966.

May Sharp Swords Fall on Ireland's Foe
Con Colbert (1888–1916)

May sharp swords fall on Ireland's foe
May all her hills be rifle lined,
May I be there to deal a blow,
For Ireland, Faith and womankind.

God's good mercy if I fall
And Ireland lives, strongly free.
If I live and Ireland lives
Oh! God is very good to me.

And may the song of battle soon
Be heard from every hill and vale,
May I be there with the marching men
Who fight to free our Gráinne Mhaol.

344

Ireland Over All

Éamonn Ceannt (1881–1916)

Ireland, Ireland, 'fore the wide world, Ireland, Ireland o - ver all!

When we fight we'll fight for Ireland, An - swer on - ly Ireland's call;

Plain and moun - tain, rock and val - ley, From the Shan - non to the sea,

Chorus

Ireland, Ireland, 'fore the wide world, Ireland one and Ireland free!

Ireland, Ireland, 'fore the wide world, Ireland one and Ireland free.

Ireland, Ireland, 'fore the wide world,
    Ireland, Ireland over all!
When we fight we'll fight for Ireland,
    Answer only Ireland's call;
Plain and mountain, rock and ocean,
    From the Shannon to the sea,
Ireland, Ireland 'fore the wide world,
    Ireland one and Ireland free!

Ireland's land and Ireland's Nation,
    Ireland's Faith and Hope and Song,
Irishmen will yet redeem them,
    From the Foreign Tyrant throng.
Ireland's homes and Ireland's hillsides,
    Shall be freed from slavery;
Ireland, Ireland 'fore the wide world,
    Ireland one and Ireland free!

Unity and Right and Freedom,
    For our Irish Fatherland,
Strive we all we may secure them,
    Strive we shall with heart and hand;
Be our aim, then, God defending,
    Right, Eternal Liberty,
Ireland, Ireland 'fore the wide world,
    Ireland one and Ireland free!

Text and music: Sheet music published by Whelan and Son, Dublin, accessed on the website of the Irish Traditional Music Archive.

The music, by Josef Hayden, is that usually associated with the German anthem 'Deutschland Über Alles'.

Éamonn Ceannt the piper.
Picture courtesy of Na Píobairí Uilleann.

345

Parnell

Roger Casement (1864–1916)
6th October, 1891

Text: Gertrude Parry (ed.), *Some Poems of Roger Casement,* The Talbot Press, Dublin, 1918.

Hush – let no whisper of this cruel strife,
Wherein he fell so bravely fighting, fall
Nigh these dead ears; fain would our hearts recall
Nought but proud memories of a noble life –
Of unmatched skill to lead by pathways rife
With danger and dark doubt, where slander's knife
Gleamed ever bare to wound, yet over all
He pressed triumphant on – lo, thus to fall.
Through and beyond the breach he living made
Shall Erin pass to freedom and to will,
And shape her fate: there where his limbs are laid
No harsh reproach dare penetrate the shade;
Death's angel guards the door, and o'er the sill
A mightier voice than Death's speaks 'Peace, be still!'

Roger Casement

Translation from Victor Hugo's 'Feuilles d'Automne'

Roger Casement

Casement's poem is a translation of 'Amis, un dernier mot', poem XL in Victor Hugo's *Feuilles d'Automne.*

Text: Gertrude Parry (ed.), *Some Poems of Roger Casement,* The Talbot Press, Dublin, 1918.

I hate oppression with a hate profound,
And wheresoever in the wide world round,
Beneath a traitor king, a cruel sky,
I hear appeal a strangled people's cry –
Where mother Greece, by Christian kings betrayed
To butcher Turks, hangs disembowelled, flayed,
Where Ireland, bleeding on her Cross expires,
And German truth in vain fronts royal liars.

Oh then, upon their heads my curse I launch,
These kings whose steeds pace bloody to the paunch:
I feel the poet speaks their judgment, and
The indignant Muse, with unrelenting hand,
Shall bind them pilloried to their thrones of shame,
And press their dastard crowns to shape a name
That on their brows the poet's hand shall trace –
So man may read their calling in their face.

Armed for the Battle

Constance Markievicz (1868–1927)

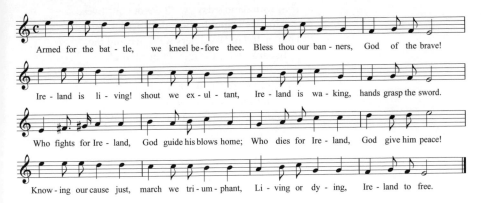

Armed for the bat - tle, we kneel be - fore thee. Bless thou our ban - ners, God of the brave!

Ire - land is li - ving! shout we ex - ul - tant, Ire - land is wa - king, hands grasp the sword.

Who fights for Ire - land, God guide his blows home; Who dies for Ire - land, God give him peace!

Know - ing our cause just, march we tri - um - phant, Li - ving or dy - ing, Ire - land to free.

Armed for the battle, we kneel before thee.
Bless thou our banners, God of the brave!
Ireland is living! shout we exultant,
Ireland is waking, hands grasp the sword.
Who fights of Ireland, God guide his blows home;
Who dies for Ireland, God give him peace!
Knowing our cause just, march we triumphant,
Living or dying, Ireland to free.

The spirit of freedom floats on the ether,
Souls of our heroes march by our side.
Tone is our battle cry; Emmet inspires us,
Those who for freedom fall never shall die.
England is breaking! shout we exultant;
England is beaten, Ireland is free!
Charge for the old cause: down with the old foe!
Giving our heart's blood Ireland to free.

Text: *Songs of Battle*, The Art Depot, Dublin, 1918.
    Music: C. Desmond Greaves, *The Easter Rising in Song & Ballad*, Kahn & Averill, for the Workers' Music Association, London, 1980, where it is described as the air of a Polish hymn.

Constance Markievicz.

Our Faith

Constance Markievicz

We are ready to fight for the land we love,
    Be the chances great or small,
We are willing to die for the flag above,
    Be the chances nothing at all.

We have sworn by prison, and torture, and death,
    By the faith of Emmet and Tone,

Text: Samuels Collection, TCD.

347

By the martyr men of our noble race,
  By the peaceful days that are gone.

That to Ireland's days we'll devote our lives,
  That we'll stand where our forbears stood;
That as Ireland's soldiers we'll live and die
  In ranks with the men of our blood.

An injury done to one of our band
  Is an injury done to all;
Shoulder to shoulder we take our stand,
  Together we fight or fall.

Our Leader we trust, for we know full well,
  Our honour is safe in his hands;
Each comrade would follow his pal to hell,
  Fulfilling friendship's demands.

So we're waiting till 'Somebody' gives the word,
  That sends us to freedom or death,
As freemen defiant we'd sooner fall
  Than be slaves to our dying breath.

The Call

Constance Markievicz

Text: Samuels Collection, TCD.

Do you hear the call of the whispering wind?
  The call to our race today,
The call for self-sacrifice, courage and faith,
  The call that brooks no delay.

The storm-beaten rose lifts a pale green shoot,
  To meet the rising sun;
Young grass-plants push up their sword-like blades,
  To tell us the day has come!

The call of Freedom rings loud and clear,
  It shouts on the rising gale:
'Buckle on your swords, with never a fear,
  Our foe is stricken and pale.'

For the dawn-light shines in the eastern sky,
  Faint glow from the rising sun,
Are you sleeping or watching, oh, men of the Gael?
  To Arms! for the day has come.

Freedom, with wild, tumultuous wings,
    Is beating the bars in vain;
Oh! men, are you men of Irish blood
    That you wait and watch and refrain?

Do you hear the call in the howling wind?
    It storms down the mountain side,
For Freedom! for Ireland! for Honour! for Right!
    Choose now – 'tis the time to decide.

We answer the call with a ringing cheer,
    With bayonets fixed we stand,
We are ready and steady, without a fear,
    To die for our native land.

Heroes and Martyrs

Constance Markievicz

You died for the Ireland of yesterday,
    With her broken hopes and tears,
You defied the foe with your dying breath,
    And your battle prayer rang in their ears.
      God save Ireland you prayed that day,
        Just fifty years ago,
      And that prayer will ring in the dying ears
      Of our brutal uncivilized foe.

They hung you in Manchester Jail that day,
    That the world might point with scorn;
But out of a shameful felon's death
    A wonderful hope was born.
      God save Ireland from England's chains
        Was the Manchester Martyr's prayer;
      God give us courage to follow their lead,
      God give us hearts to dare.

They hung you for daring to take up the fight
    Of a nation tortured and bound,
For a desperate rescue of leaders beloved,
    And a policeman dead on the ground.
      God save Ireland from England's yoke,
        Her soldiers, her police, her laws,
      God bless the men with arms in their hands,
      God prosper Ireland's cause.

Below the title in the source is the inscription 'Dedicated to Na Fianna Éireann (As recited by Commandant Garry Houlihan)', and below the text, 'Constance de Markievicz, IRA.' and 'November 23rd, 1917'.

Garry Houlihan (or Holohan) was the commander of the Dublin Brigade of Fianna Éireann, and had been involved in the raid on the Magazine Fort in the Phoenix Park, during the 1916 Rising.

Text: Samuels Collection, TCD.

The prayer you prayed with your dying breath
Was caught by a passing wind;
It snatched it back from the gates of death
For those you left behind.
God save Ireland with Ireland's guns
Was the prayer of the Volunteers,
When the sun rose bright on an Easter dawn,
Trembling 'twixt hopes and fears.

And we fought in the streets of Dublin Town
Till the gutters were heaped with dead,
And the same immortal cause was ours
For which the martyrs had bled.
God save Ireland we prayed that day,
When the tricolour floated on high,
God save Ireland we shouted with joy
As we watched the English fly.

And we hoisted the flag on the G.P.O.,
And it floated on Stephen's Green,
From Boland's mills down to far Clontarf
The Republican Flag was seen.
God save Ireland, a soldier's prayer,
The prayer of Ireland's sons,
As with Ireland's honour our only care
We faced the English guns.

And the battle raged on the Liffey's banks,
And the streets were piled with dead;
We shot them down at the barricades,
And cheered as the regiments fled.
God save Ireland we cried that day,
And death took up the cry,
As we saw them stagger on Mount-Street Bridge
And many a soldier die.

O'Connell Street flamed in a funeral pyre,
With shrapnel they battered it down,
And cannon boomed thro' the terrible night
In the streets of Dublin Town.
God save Ireland we prayed with hope,
Tho' we knew that the battle was lost;
What matter our lives in Ireland's fight
When England must count the cost.

Soldiers guarding the ruins of
Clanwilliam House, the command-
post of the insurgents during the
Battle of Mount Street Bridge.

But the flag that was burned on the G.P.O.
   Lit the sky with a marvellous light,
Triumphantly flaming o'er ruin and death,
   Prophetic, unconquered and bright.
      God save Ireland, flamed in the hearts
        Breaking for Ireland's sake,
      And the sunburst lighting the midnight sky
        Flamed out that the day must break.

They murdered our men in the grisly dawn,
   In unhallowed graves they lie,
And we proudly honour our martyred dead
   As we raise the triumphant cry:
      God save Ireland, so small and great,
        With her armies of martyred dead,
      Fighting and praying the great hosts march,
        We following in their tread.

And the Fianna martyrs have left a word
   To every boy in the land:
For Ireland's sake take up the gun
   That fell from our dying hand.
      God save Ireland and Ireland's boys,
        Was Colbert and Heuston's prayer.
      As, crowned with the martyr's holy crown,
        They mounted the golden stair.

Like the Martyr murdered in Mountjoy Jail,
   The last to fall in the fight.
Take up your cross for Ireland, boys,
   Nor fear to die for the right.
      God save Ireland through Ireland's men,
        Who steadfastly bear her cross,
      Triumphantly marching in serried ranks,
        Not counting death or loss.

And the prayer goes up from our martyred dead,
   And we echo it here to-day;
For the army, where dead and living unite,
   No English force can stay.
      God save Ireland, altho' we, too,
        Must fight and suffer and fall,
      The Republican Army is ready to-day
        To march at the battle call.

The O'Rahilly (Michael Joseph O'Rahilly).

Thou Art Not Conquered Yet, Dear Land

The O'Rahilly (1875–1916)

Thou art not conquered yet, dear land,
    Thy spirit still is free.
Though long the Saxon's ruthless hand
    Has triumphed over thee.
Though oft obscured by clouds of woe,
    Thy sun has never set,
'Twill blaze again, in golden glow,
    Thou art not conquered yet!

Chorus
Thou art not conquered yet, dear land,
    Thy sons must not forget.
The day will be, when all will see
    Thou art not conquered yet!

Though knaves may scheme and slaves may crawl
    To win their master's smile,
And though thy best and bravest fall,
    Undone by Saxon guile.
Yet some there be, still true to thee,
    Who never shall forget
That though in chains and slavery
    Thou art not conquered yet.

Through ages long of war and strife,
    Of rapine and of woe,
We fought the bitter fight of life
    Against the Saxon foe.
Our fairest hopes to burst thy chains
    Have died in vain regret,
But still the glorious truth remains
    Thou art not conquered yet!

The O'Rahilly (the definite article
'The' was used to indicate that the
person was the clan head; a Gaelic
custom) was Michael Joseph
O'Rahilly, a Republican and Irish language enthusiast. He was prominent
in the founding and in the continuing
activities of the Irish Volunteers.

When he discovered that the Easter
Rising was being secretly planned he
opposed it, as he believed it would
end in failure, and he travelled about
spreading the countermanding order
of Eoin MacNeill.

Despite being opposed to the
Rising he nonetheless took part and
fought in the GPO in Dublin. He was
seriously wounded on Friday 28 April
1916, while leading a body of men
trying to break out from the GPO.

He died in Sackville Lane, off
Moore Street, where an elegant
plaque has been erected to his
memory, the engraving on which
is a facsimile of the letter he wrote,
while lying wounded, to his wife.
[LM]

Text and air: C. Desmond Greaves,
The Easter Rising in Song & Ballad,
Kahn & Averill, for the Workers'
Music Association, London, 1980. In
1915 the air was taken from the Petrie
collection by Fr Pádruig Breathnach to
set a poem of the same title by John
Keegan Casey. O'Rahilly seems to have
modelled his song on the earlier one in
Breathnach's *Songs of the Gael*.

The chorus is sung to the second two
lines of the air.

353

Let Me Carry Your Cross for Ireland, Lord

Thomas Ashe (1885–1917)

Let me carry your cross for Ire-land, Lord, the hour of her trial draws near.

And the pangs and the pain of sa-cri-fice may be borne by com rades_ dear.

But, Lord, take me from the off-'ring throng, there are o-thers far less pre-pared.

Though anx-ious and all as they are to die that Ire__ land might be spared.

Written in Lewes Jail in 1916. Thomas Ashe had led the Volunteers in North Co. Dublin during Easter Week, and his was the only unit that met with military success, when it defeated a large force of Royal Irish Constabulary (RIC) at Ashbourne (the placename and Ashe's name are purely coinciden-tal). Jailed for making a seditious speech, Ashe went on hunger strike and died on 25 September 1917, from pneumonia, as a result of force-feeding in Dublin's Mountjoy Jail. A warpiper, Ashe founded the Black Raven pipe band in Skerries, Co. Dublin. He was exceptionally able and charismatic and would probably have been a major figure in the freedom struggle that later developed.

Róisín Dubh (Little Black Rose) in the song is an allegorical name for Ireland. [LM]

In her statement to the Bureau of Military History (ref. W.S. 330), Mrs Batt O'Connor related how Ashe had stayed at her home for a week shortly before his arrest, and that he had sung this song for them during his stay. This was the only occasion on which he sang it, as he told them he had never had any other opportunity to do so.

Text: *The 1916 Song Book*, The Irish Book Bureau, Dublin, *c.* 1930.
Air: 'The Felons of Our Land'.

Let me carry your cross for Ireland, Lord!
    The hour of her trial draws near.
And the pangs and the pains of the sacrifice
    May be borne by comrades dear.
But, Lord, take me from the offering throng,
    There are many far less prepared.
Though anxious and all as they are to die
    That Ireland may be spared.

Let me carry your cross for Ireland, Lord!
    My cares in this world are few.
And few are the tears will for me fall
    When I go on my way to You.
Spare, oh! spare to their loved ones dear
    The brother and son and sire,
That the cause we love may never die
    In the land of our heart's desire!

Let me carry your cross for Ireland, Lord!
    Let me suffer the pain and shame.
I bow my head to their rage and hate,
    And I take on myself the blame.
Let them do with my body whate'er they will,
    My spirit I offer to You.
That the faithful few who heard her call
    May be spared to Róisín Dubh.

Let me carry your cross for Ireland, Lord!
    For Ireland weak with tears,
For the aged man of the clouded brow,
    And the child of tender years;
For the empty homes of her golden plains;
    For the hopes of her future, too!
Let me carry your cross for Ireland, Lord!
    For the cause of Róisín Dubh.

Battle-Cry

Terence MacSwiney (1879–1920)

Glory to God, we shall not die without another blow.
Glory to God, the living flood is sweeping all below.

The flame has cleft the darkness, the old and fierce desire
Has even swept the slave into a white and mounting fire.

'Tis no mad dream: I hear the tread of countless marching men.
Old Ireland is ablaze, ablaze in city, field and glen.

'To arms!' the cry goes down the wind, and with a wild delight
We rush to arms, and pray 'God speed another gallant fight'.

And we had cursed our bitter time of black and freezing shame –
Christ, on our knees for this brave hour we bless Thy Sacred Name.

We shall not perish off the land in dastardly disgrace.
Glory to God, we'll do a deed worthy our royal race.

Old Shane the Proud, look up in Heaven, we send it to the stars:
We shall be proud, and you shall hear the clamour of our wars.

Old Brian, smiter of the Dane, and you shall hear as we
Shout your great name, and smite the foe and sweep them to the sea.

In this poem MacSwiney invokes the names of the following Gaelic heroes:
Shane the Proud – Shane O'Neill, a member of the O'Neill dynasty of Tyrone; after his murder in 1567 his head was brought to Dublin and spiked on the Castle Gate, an event to which Sean O'Casey also refers, see p. 254; Brian – Brian Boroimhe, whose victory over a mixed force of Norse and Leinster Irish at Clontarf in 1014 put an end to 'Danish' power in Ireland; Red Hugh – Hugh O'Neill, the leader of the Irish resistance to Elizabeth in the Nine Years' War; mighty Aodh – either the afore-mentioned Hugh (Aodh) O'Neill, or Red Hugh O'Donnell who fought with O'Neill at the Battle of the Yellow Ford in 1598; Owen Roe – Owen Roe O'Neill (c. 1585–1649), leader of the Confederate armies against the Cromwellians, and victor at the Battle of Benburb in 1646.

Text: Toirdhealbhach Mac Suibhne, *Battle Cries*, 1918.

What happy field in Heaven holds you, our brave Red
    Hugh?
But you must flash in spirit down the battle to renew.

And mighty Aodh shall soar above the well-known
    Yellow Ford,
And smile to see us bare again the freedom-winning
    sword.

Oh, shade of valiant Owen Roe, the old black treachery,
That struck you down, has burst upon the ancient
    enemy.

The evil game they tried again – set their own train afire!
Glory to God, we'll give them now more than their
    heart's desire.

Shout for the long-despaired-of fight. By Heaven, we
    shall not fail,
Led by the hosted spirits of the warriors of the Gael.

From out the shining East they come, up the undying
    West,
From Donegal to Desmond, with glory manifest.

But soft, and still awhile the exultation fierce and loud,
Oh, martyred spirit, see where stands our Emmet pale
    and proud.

One passionate prayer we breathe below our hushed,
    exulting laugh:
We swear it by the living God to write his epitaph.

Oh, by the Cross of Agony, where Christ our Saviour
    died,
Let not the kiss of death itself by one man be denied.

Oh, Thou who holdest in Thy Hands the issue of this
    strife,
We freely offer pain in death and every hope in life.

Only set on the battle swift, and make us fit and free.
Yea, reckon up the price for us, however great it be,
We'll pay it in our best of blood for Ireland's liberty.

A Call to Arms

Terence MacSwiney

Sons of the Gael, to your glory awaking,
  Fling ye to earth all the fears of the slave.
Hark, now our tyrants in battle are shaking;
  Now our old banner forever shall wave.
      Where slaves were wont to weep,
      Men to the struggle leap:
  Lo! in their thousands they form o'er the plain,
      What shall our war-cry be?
      Shout it from sea to sea:
'For God and our country to arms again.'

Long in the gloom was our motherland calling
  The sons of our once gallant race to the fray;
Long were our hopes like the autumn leaves falling –
  Now the pure breath of freedom arrests the decay.
      Perish the dark despair!
      Spirits sing in the air
A rally to battle our land to regain.
      Soldiers with gallant mien
      Grasp gun and sabre keen,
And strike for old Ireland in arms again.

Mark, as ye rise how the tyrant is trembling,
  Our day fair is dawning, and he in his might
Must yield to the strength of our thousands assembling
  In battle-array, and all hot for the fight.
      Where is the one who fears?
      Think of the glorious years
Full in the freedom long fought for in vain.
      Fling the old flag on high;
      Vow ye to win or die,
And strike for the old cause. To arms again.

Swift now above us the war-clouds are rolling,
  But the blaze of our banner is bright in the sky;
And the crash of our rifles the death-knell is tolling
  Of England's dark reign, now the last hour is nigh.
      Now make her armies reel
      Back from your gleaming steel,
While on their ear falls the old war refrain,
      Loudly from wood and glen,
      Shout it, my gallant men,
For God and for Ireland. To arms again.

Text: Toirdhealbhach Mac Suibhne,
Battle Cries, 1918.
  Air: 'O'Donnell Abú', see p. 70.

Terence MacSwiney.

Casement
(Executed 3rd August, 1916)
Terence MacSwiney

Text: Toirdhealbhach Mac
Suibhne, *Battle Cries*, 1918.

They have immortalized another day
Who struck you down. And oh, we burn with pride
Because of you, our peerless one, who died
In the old proud, unbending, Irish way.

Fearless and kingly, you; as base were they,
Smarting at your disdain, they vilified
The soul we loved. Who now its light can hide,
Where it soars liberated from the clay.

And you are victor. See their rabble rage
As the bolt falls, and shout their hellish glee,
Frenzied with hate and their impotency,
While you hand on to us our heritage
And make us sharers in your victory:
One with our conquering Dead you rule the age.

Parley
Terence MacSwiney

Text: Toirdhealbhach Mac
Suibhne, *Battle Cries*, 1918.

What! come you at the eleventh hour –
You! trembling for your shaking power –
You! wolf that would our land devour
    If you were strong?
But now God's wrath is out at last,
But now your day is slipping past,
And the dread thunder-bolt is cast –
    Oh, fierce sweet song!
And now comes retribution fast.
    'Twas prayed for long.

And now you offer terms of peace!
You see the clouds above increase;
You cannot make the thunders cease;
    Your sun has set.
But still you make a show of state,
To prove your condescension great –
But oh, remember, we can wait
    A little yet.

And why you condescend thus late
   We don't forget.

Remember in our bitter woe,
As we did feel it, lying low,
That all the world our shame did know:
   Our cup was full.
God, all that agony of shame,
It scorched us more than any flame,
For, oh, some souls were still untame,
   Not dead nor dull:
But you, you ever were the same,
   Unpitiful.

But now, but now the hour is changed;
Your foes against you all are ranged;
Your frown is for a smile exchanged;
   You speak of peace.
But we can read behind a part
You fain would hide, a trembling heart,
Oh, is it strange fierce joy should start?
   'Tis our release!
While all wild terrors through you dart
   Our hopes increase.

And now 'tis fitter we should write
The terms of peace: we dread no night,
You've spent your strength; you made the fight;
   You have not won.
Take hence your weak half-measures now;
When strong our hearts you could not cow;
Then to the inevitable bow:
   Your race is run.
Behold us! Read it on each brow:
   Your day is done.

So, take our terms: you'll profit well.
What we have suffered, you can tell;
And now our hearts can even quell
   What vengeance cries.
We will not reckon tears and blood –
God, could we count all, if we would?
But this, this must be understood:
   Our flag here flies;
Your power entire ends, ends for good.
   No compromise.

Oh My Dark Rosaleen

Terence MacSwiney

Text: *Treoir* 42.1, Comhaltas Ceoltóirí Éireann, Dublin, 2010.
Air: 'Down by the Glenside', see p. 92.

Oh my dark Rosaleen by the light of thine eyes
May thy daughters the stranger's allurements despise
By thy purity sweet that flows out from your heart
May they live but to love thee and be what thou art.

May thy name be their glory, thine honour their pride
May they cling to thee closely whatever betide
May they dream of thy greatness tho' dark are the skies
Be their life's sweetest harbour to banish thy sighs.

When the false have betrayed thee and the weaklings
    have fled
May they breathe to thee softly that hope is not dead
May they urge the still faithful to efforts more great
To raise thee my sweet Queen, to thy former state.

Then my dark Rosaleen will their song be most sweet
In the light of thine eyes when they stand at thy feet
When they sing thy grand triumph, the clouds passed
    away,
The glory of freedom at the Dawn of the Day.

Shall My Soul Pass Through Old Ireland

Terence MacSwiney

The Lord Mayor of Cork, Terence MacSwiney, died on hunger strike in Brixton Prison, England, on 25 October 1920, after 74 days' fasting, and attempts to force-feed him. MacSwiney had been involved with the Irish Volunteers since 1913, the year of their founding, and was to be second-in-command of the Easter 1916 Rising in Cork, where no action took place due to Eoin MacNeill's counter-manding order. Active in the freedom struggle, and Commandant of Cork No. 1 Brigade, MacSwiney was elected Lord Mayor of Cork following the murder by British forces of Lord Mayor Tomás MacCurtain. Arrested in August 1920 for possession of seditious documents and a police code

In a dreary Brixton prison
    Where an Irish rebel lay,
By his side a priest was standing
    Ere his soul should pass away;
And he faintly murmured 'Father,'
    As he clasped him by the hand,
'Tell me this before I die,
    Shall my soul pass through Ireland?'

Chorus
'Shall my soul pass through old Ireland,
    Pass through Cork's old city grand,
Shall I see the old cathedral
    Where Saint Patrick took his stand?

Shall I see the little chapel
 Where I pledged my heart and hand?
Tell me this before you leave me
 Shall my soul pass through Ireland?'

'Twas for loving dear old Ireland
 In this prison cell I lie.
'Twas for loving dear old Ireland
 In this foreign land I die;
Will you meet my little daughter,
 Will you make her understand?
Tell me, Father, ere you leave me,
 Shall my soul pass though Ireland?'

With his heart pure as a lily
 And his body sanctified,
In that dreary English prison
 Our brave Irish rebel died.
Prayed the priest that wish be granted
 As in blessing raised his hand:
'O Father, grant this brave man's wish,
 May his soul pass through Ireland.'

cipher, which, as Lord Mayor, he was entitled to have, he was sentenced to prison and went on hunger strike, dying 74 days later. To prevent a huge demonstration in Dublin, his body was forcibly taken to Cork by British military and he was buried, after a massive funeral, in the Republican Plot in St Finbarr's Cemetery, Cork. See picture, p. 571.

His hunger strike and death drew worldwide attention to, and sympathy for, Ireland's struggle for freedom. Among those influenced by him were Jawaharlal Nehru, Mahatma Gandhi and Ho Chi Minh. [LM]

Text: *Walton's 132 Best Irish Songs and Ballads*, Walton's Musical Instrument Galleries, Dublin, n.d.

Air: 'Rolling Home to Bonnie Scotland', see p. 330.

How They Brought the Good News to Heaven
(A Dream)
Terence MacSwiney

'Twas the first that fell in battle as they swept to glory free,
And they flashed to Heaven's shining plain in battle-ecstasy.

And they cried to the radiant Seraphim word of the great new wars,
And their spirits bathed in battle-light outshone the splendid stars.

'Speed us swift to the happy field where our old heroes dwell,
For the first to fall have the privilege the glorious news to tell.'

And the Seraphim clashed their shining wings and swept their souls with fire,
Till the first who fell, in battle-joy flashed into the golden choir.

And they sang in the height of the music and they burned with the joy divine,
And Heaven was filled with their glory who fell in the battle line.

Text: Toirdhealbhach Mac Suibhne, *Battle Cries*, 1918.

But their spirits in all Heaven's splendour were flushed with a noble
    pride
To bear the news to the hero-souls who in other years had died.

And they cried to the shining leader of the soaring Seraphim:
'Oh, speed us swift to their happy field to the sound of our battle-
    hymn.'

And they formed in their battle order, and the angels ringed them
    round,
And a hush fell over Heaven at their music's noble sound.

A shining leader led them, and, lo! at a heavenly sign
They swept in their glory forward, who fell in the battle line.

But the light of their dauntless spirits was flashed to a field afar
Where the dauntless spirits of other days beheld a splendid star.

And they rose in the gleam of its beauty, a dazzling company,
And they cried in a voice: ''Tis the promised star, the star of the brave
    and free.'

'Long have we bathed in the glory that God has poured on these
    heights,
But now he unrolls the destined dream, and sends us the light of
    lights,
The crowning star of His Beauty, His Vision, the light of lights.'

And up in a stately column like soldiers who need no word,
They form to wait with their spirits high for the glory long deferred.

And out of the shining distance, with the blaze of a million stars,
Flashed forth the exultant spirits new-come from the glorious wars.

And they came in a rush of music while the angels ringed them
    round,
White with the great sun's splendour, they swept to the sacred
    ground.

Where the older heroes waited – oh, God, for an angel hand
To write of the joy of the meeting there of the brave united band.

When the news is heard of the victory of the white and the green
    and the gold,
Quick with the sweeping music, the warriors proud of old
Fight all their battles over again as they hear the story told.

Old Cormac of soul-deep wisdom sings of the brave and wise,
And Conn, the Hundred-fighter, peals forth his battle-cries.

And Brian, the great Dane-queller, cries: 'They shall be ever free,
Who form them straight in the battle-line as one from sea to sea.'

See Shane in the light of Heaven toss his splendid head in pride:
'In the worst of days our gallant men Clan London hordes defied.'

And Owen Roe to the mighty Aodh cries out triumphantly:
'For the soldier-work we were always fit, by the soldier's sword
    we are free.'

Hear Red Hugh laugh to MacSwiney: 'Is there aught our Heaven
    lacks?'
That great chief shook with the olden joy as he swung in his
    shining tracks,
'Oh for an hour in Ireland now, and my brave battle-axe.'

And Fiach MacHugh and Rory Ogue, whom the joy of Heaven fills,
Shout for the fire of Leix of old, and the light of the Wicklow hills.

And Emmet and Tone and Davis, the proud and the gay and serene
Are swept in the glory prophetic: but soft in the light is seen.

Where Mitchel turns to his brothers, saying, ever as void of guile:
'Down comes old Carthage with a crash.' – Heaven is in his smile!

They are all in the flush of the morning, they are all in the light elate,
For they all have the older spirit still, who have passed from the
    olden hate.

And now they pause from exulting, and clear in one mighty voice,
They cry to the whole of Heaven: 'For the glorious earth rejoice:

'For the land that has justified us, for the mighty deed it has done,
For its splendid pride as it lifts its head to the white majestic sun.'

And that is the morning music we hear in the Dawn's white fire,
Where our souls are hushed in the glory and our foes with the
    night retire.

After the age-long years and wars, by the Infinite God, we, we
Are given the time and the deed to do, to strike old Ireland free,
Are given our foremost place in the sun and our splendid destiny.

As in his poem 'Battle-Cry', p. 355, MacSwiney here again includes the names of Irish heroes of recent and earlier times:

Cormac – Cormac Mac Airt, a legendary high king of Ireland whose reign was some time between the second and fourth centuries AD;

Conn – Conn of the Hundred Battles, grandfather of Cormac, and ancestor, through Niall of the Nine Hostages, of the Uí Néill dynasty;

Red Hugh – Red Hugh O'Donnell (1572–1602), King of Tír Chonail and ally of Hugh O'Neill in the Nine Years' War against Elizabeth;

MacSwiney – the head of an Irish clan, with Scottish origins, which served the O'Donnells of Donegal as gallowglasses; their weapon of choice was the battle-axe;

Fiach MacHugh – Fiach MacHugh O'Byrne (1534–97), head of the O'Byrnes, with territory in Co. Wicklow, who waged war against the Elizabethan armies;

Rory Ogue – Ruairí Óg Ó Mórdha (d. 1578), Lord of Laois, one of the few survivors of the massacre at Mullaghmast in 1577, which event is mentioned by O'Casey, see p. 250;

Emmet – Robert Emmet, leader of the second insurrection of the Society of United Irishmen in 1803;

Tone – Theobald Wolfe Tone, leader of the first (1798) insurrection;

Davis – Thomas Davis, poet and journalist and leader of the Young Ireland movement; died at the age of thirty in 1845;

Mitchel – John Mitchel (1815–75), Young Irelander and author of the classic Irish nationalist text, *Jail Journal*.

To the Dead at Eastertide

Terence MacSwiney

Text: Toirdhealbhach Mac Suibhne, *Battle Cries*, 1918.

But yesterday you stood with us against the crowd.
We were not then a host, oh Dead, dispraise was loud.
Ah, not as loud, as deep, as pure as now your praise,
Who died, and brought us back the dream of purer days.

Yet still the many pause – they do not understand.
Children, they, wondering, touch the pure mysterious brand
You lit, and nursed to flame, till grew and grew the fire,
And you went forth to death – death, ah but your desire.

Over all broken plans. They were material things,
And the step seemed so wild – wild, now reflection brings:
All our contrivings were vain. God put them away.
'Twas God broke the plan, letting the spirit have sway.

Ah, how the spirit rose on its wings, and its flight
Gleamed in the dark, and challenged, and put to affright
The power material, holding our land in its chains,
Till the voice of the many, who trembled, that power disdains.

Ah, but their praise is in wise that was not your wise;
They have seen the earth rock but not the light in the skies,
Turn, turn but once, and draw them to gaze on the stars,
They try to bend down your dream to their own petty wars.

Ah, and your war was great, divine, and moved to your dream;
And the earth you loved as it caught from your vision a gleam.
Show them the earth in its glory, its beauty, its pride,
Kissed by the spirit, and pure, at its breath beautified.

Ah, but we stand, whom you knew, in the clamour all mute;
Silent we've taken the banner, its glory salute.
Give us to guard and advance it, your pure, burning brand,
To blaze in our battle, and light your dream in the land.

Oh, our brothers, our comrades, our champions, you gave
To victory its meaning, to the hope of our tyrants a grave:
This earth shall be ours for the deed of your last Easter morn,
When it laboured in pain of your pain, and the spirit was born.

Song

Terence MacSwiney

Brothers! have hope, my Brothers! know
The fight has not been ended yet;
Our right we never will forego –
    'Twere folly to forget.

Look back! see what we have survived.
Say, then, should we in terror bow?
Thus has my courage been revived,
    And I am hopeful now.

Tho' Freedom's Cause went down in blood,
To crush our Land it naught availed;
So evils, too, that from this flowed –
    Famine and fever – failed.

Our Land did rise in new-born hope.
Where lives the unbeliever, then,
Who questions that the skies will ope
    And light the Land again?

Trust, then, in God, as brave men should –
Doing the while all man can do;
If by our sires God had not stood,
    Our sires had not been true.

Be we, then, true and never swerve
One inch aside – strike for the whole;
Show God our freedom we deserve,
    And we shall reach the goal.

Text: Terence MacSwiney, *The Music of Freedom*, The Risen Gaedheal Press, Cork, 1907.

Song of the Streamlet

Terence MacSwiney

Love never maketh only
    Love in spaces;
Love would leave no part lonely –
    The whole its place is.

On brothers' dark suspicions
    Love cries 'Unseemly!'
For it is Love's true mission
    To rule supremely.

Text: Terence MacSwiney, *The Music of Freedom*, The Risen Gaedheal Press, Cork, 1907.

Love will not let light beaming
    Bless selfish brothers,
Who would its rays redeeming
    Deny the others.

Love is not proud, nor coldly
    Turns from the lowly;
It ever speaks – not boldly –
    In sweetness holy.

To those who low are drooping
    It steals down near them,
And in the darkness stooping
    It breathes to cheer them.

When those who had lived, hating,
    Find Truth to raise them
And grieve – they find Love waiting
    To bless and praise them.

Love could not rule, dividing.
    Its sway is tender;
So may all hearts confiding,
    To Love surrender.

A Roving We Will Go
Peadar Kearney (1883–1942)

There was a man lived in the East,
    And this man's name was John;
He had a most enormous waist,
    A wonder to look on.
He grabbed our Fathers' bright green fields
    And laid their homesteads low,
And oh we want to meet with him
    When a roving we will go.

Chorus
A roving, a roving high hills and lowlands low,
And oh we want to meet with him when a roving
    we will go.

We have a wee short rifle,
    We have a bayonet, too,
We have a big Howth Mauser –
    And you know what that can do.
A ten-foot pike to buck him up
    When he is feeling low;
We have them all for our friend John
    When a roving we will go.

A wise man said long, long ago
    That too far East is West,
And our friend John he carried all
    His courage 'neath his vest.
We'll slit his big fat belly
    And let his courage flow,
And all the world shall praise us
    When a roving we will go.

So we'll take our wee short rifle,
    And we'll take our bayonet, too,
We'll take our big Howth Mauser,
    And see what we can do;
We'll give them all to our friend John
    Who laid our homesteads low,
With hate and vengeance in our hearts,
    When a roving we will go.

The 'man whose name was John' is, of
course, John Bull, or England.

Text: Peadar Ó Cearnaigh, *Camp-Fire
Songs*, Art Depot, Dublin, n.d.

A Row in a Town

Peadar Kearney

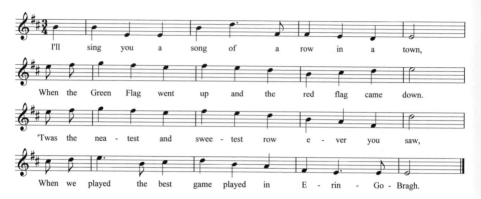

I'll sing you a song of a row in a town,
When the Green Flag went up and the red flag came down.
'Twas the nea-test and swee-test row e-ver you saw,
When we played the best game played in E-rin - Go - Bragh.

Text: Seamus de Burca, *The Soldier's Song*, P.J. Bourke, Dublin, 1957. This song has gone into the living tradition and has been changed in the mouths of singers over the years. A recent version may be found in Frank Harte, *Songs of Dublin*, Gilbert Dalton, Dublin, 1978.
  Air: 'Master McGrath'.

I'll sing you a song of a row in a town,
When the Green Flag went up and the Red Flag came
    down;
'Twas the neatest and sweetest row ever you saw,
When we played the best game played in Erin Go Bragh.

A thousand brave fellows of every degree,
With rifles and shotguns they swore to be free;
One fine Easter Monday they laughed at the 'Law',
And played the best game played in Erin Go Bragh.

A great English Captain was raging that day,
Saying: 'Give me one hour and I'll blow them away.'
But he never thought what he afterwards saw:
The dead khaki soldiers in Erin Go Bragh.

In thousands and thousands right on us they poured,
Their big guns and small guns they rattled and roared
But our Mauser bullets got stuck in their craw
And they died from lead-poisoning in Erin Go Bragh.

Our brave De Valera was down at Ringsend,
The honour of Ireland to hold and defend;
He had no veteran soldiers but volunteers raw,
Playing sweet Mauser music for Erin Go Bragh.

Bold Kent and his comrades, like lions at bay,
From the South Union windows poured death and
    dismay;
There was fear in their souls when the Saxon swine saw
How we played the best game played in Erin Go Bragh.

A health to Ned Daly and all his command,
From the Four Courts to King Street their fighting was grand;
For the might of the Empire they cared not a straw,
But played the best game played in Erin Go Bragh.

God rest gallant Pearse and his comrades who died:
Jim Connolly and Mallin, MacDonagh, MacBride,
And here's to young Heuston who gave one 'hurrah',
And faced the machine guns for Erin Go Bragh.

Forget not the men of the brave rank and file,
And the lion-hearted women of Erin's green isle;
Let true men salute them in wonder and awe,
The bravest and greatest in Erin Go Bragh.

Oh, Glory to Dublin! It's hers the renown,
Through long generations her fame shall go down,
And children shall tell how their forefathers saw
The red blaze of freedom o'er Erin Go Bragh.

'The GPO 1916' by Thomas Ryan RHA. This work was painted in 1966 and was exhibited to celebrate
the fiftieth anniversary of the Rising. (Courtesy of the artist.)

Arise
Ballykinlar March – 1921
Peadar Kearney

Ballykinlar internment camp, on the Co. Down coast, was opened in December 1920 and was used to intern men on suspicion of involvement with the IRA.

Text: Seamus de Burca, *The Soldier's Song*, P.J. Bourke, Dublin, 1957.
Music: Martin Walton.

In the screaming of the eagle
In the gentle murmur of the bees,
In the fury of the tempest,
In the whisper of the breeze,
'Tis freedom's voice pulsating
Thro' the nation's inmost core,
'Tis the song of hope vibrating
Through the land from shore to shore.

Chorus
Arise! ye slavelings, from your centuried thrall,
Arise redeemed in freedom's ray;
Arise! 'tis Ireland's myriad soldiers call,
As free men hail the coming day.
'Tis Ireland's voice, 'tis Ireland's soul,
That calls from sea to sea;
Our motherland, while ages roll,
Redeemed, erect and free.

List ye, nations of the world,
  To the message of the free,
Ireland stands with flag unfurled
  Sword in hand for liberty!
Ever shall her voice be heard
  In the councils of the free,
Ever shall her shining sword be bared
  For truth and liberty.

Down by the Liffeyside
Peadar Kearney

'Twas down by An-na Lif___ fey my___ love___ and___ I did stray,
Where in the good old slu-shy mud the sea-gulls sport and play.
We___ got the whiff of ray and chips, and Ma-ry soft-ly sighed,
"Yer-ra, John, come on, for a one-and-one, down by___ the___ Lif-fey - side".

'Twas down by Anna Liffey my love and I did stray,
Where in the good old slushy mud the seagulls sport and play.
We got the whiff of ray and chips and Mary softly sighed,
'Yerra, John, come along for a one-and-one down by the Liffeyside.'

And up to Rabiotti's together we did go,
And the rapture there that filled our hearts no poet e'er could know.
We started eating one-and-ones and Mary softly sighed,
'Oh! I'd live forever eating chips down by the Liffeyide.'

Then out along by George's Street, the loving pairs to view,
While Mary swanked it like a queen in a suit of royal blue.
Her coat was newly turned and her blouse was newly dyed
And you couldn't match her amber locks down by the Liffeyside.

And it's on her oul' melodeon so sweetly she did play
'Goodbye and don't sigh' and 'Rule Britann-i-ay'.
But when she turned Sinn Féiner sure me heart near burst with pride
For to hear her sing 'The Soldier's Song' down by the Liffeyside.

A 'one-and-one' is Dublin slang for a portion of fish and a portion of chips.

Text: Frank Harte, *Songs of Dublin*, Gilbert Dalton, Dublin, 1978, with additions from memory.
  Air: 'Down by the Tanyard Side'.

371

And on Sunday morning early to Meath Street we will go
And it's up to Father Murphy we both will make our vow.
He'll join our hands in wedlock bands and soon we'll be outside
For a whole afternoon for our honeymoon down by the Liffeyside.

And we'll have little children and raise them neat and clean
To shout 'Up the Republic' and to sing about Sinn Féin,
To emulate their auld fellas who England's laws defied
And send them off with guns to fight the Saxon Huns down by the Liffeyside.

DORA
A Love Ditty on True Blue West British Lines
Peadar Kearney

A sweet, lit-tle la-dy has lan-ded here late-ly be-low at the love-ly North Wall

She came here a-mong us to kiss us and hug us, and, oh! how she cud-dles us all!

Her blue eyes are bea-ming, like two bay'nets glea-ming, she brought a sup-ply of the same,

And if e-ver she'd leave us how sore-ly 'twould grieve us, and now I will tell you her name,

It's Do - ra, Do - ra, Oh, how we wor-ship our Do - ra.

She came here to teach our young men how to live, How to for-get, aye, and how to for-give,

And should we Do - ra e-ver dis-please or an-noy,

She'll treat us quite well in a first class ho-tel, With the beau-ti-ful name of Mount-joy.

DORA, the Defence of the Realm Act, which was passed by Parliament shortly after the start of the war in 1914, gave draconian special powers to the authorities.

Text and music: Sheet music published by The Art Depot, Dublin, n.d.

A sweet little lady has landed here lately
    Below at the lovely North Wall.
She came here among us, to kiss and to hug us,
    And oh! how she cuddles us all!
Her blue eyes are beaming like two bayonets gleaming,
    She brought a supply of the same.
And if ever she'd leave us, how sadly 'twould grieve us,
    And now I will tell you her name.

Chorus
It's Dora, Dora,
Oh, how we worship our Dora.
She came here to teach our young men how to live,
How to forget, aye, and how to forgive.
And should we Dora ever displease or annoy,
She'll treat us quite well in a first-class hotel,
With the beautiful name of Mountjoy.

Highest society, every variety,
    Welcomed this lady ashore.
From fear they were crazy, but now they'll be aisy,
    They'll quiver or shiver no more.
They know rebel cheering and all Volunteering
    In future must come to an end,
For Dora's a quare one, a fair one, a rare one,
    And she is the loyal man's friend.

Oh, Irish transgressors, give heed to your betters,
    And make up your minds to be good,
For ages and ages brave West-British sages
    Have taught all the lessons they could.
And now we have Dora, our own darling Dora,
    Who scatters her gifts with a smile,
And if she but wishes there'll be big loaves and fishes
    All over the Emerald Isle.

D O R A (Defence of the Realm Act), postcard.

373

Here's to Lloyd George
Peadar Kearney

To 'hoch him' (chorus) is, according to Wright's *English Dialect Dictionary,* to 'throw the leg over a person to express contempt at his small stature'. To 'bite a file' is to engage in some pointless activity.

Text: Samuels Collection, TCD.
Air: 'Master McGrath', see 'A Row in a Town', p. 368.

Lloyd George he was powerful, Lloyd George he was great,
But he left the poor Empire in a horrible state,
And he put on the kybosh in elegant style,
When he thought out conscription for Erin's Green Isle.

Chorus
So here's to Lloyd George, boys, and hoch him again,
He changed our old women into good fighting men;
What matter to us if he's biting a file,
Since he thought out conscription for Erin's Green Isle.

We fought with each other in the days that are gone,
While some died for Ireland the others looked on.
Now poor Mr George is disgorging his bile
Since he found he's uniting all Erin's Green Isle.

Now our Tricolour Flag is afloat in the sky,
For Ireland we're willing to live or to die.
Oh George dear, a miss is as good as a mile,
Since you thought out conscription for Erin's Green Isle.

O Loydy George
Peadar Kearney

Text: *Ná Bac Leis*, a prisoners' newspaper published in Ballykinlar camp.

My name is John FitzMulligan Smith,
    I come from Inchicore,
I was always brave and bold,
When down the Circular Road I strolled.
    But now alas! my rambling days are o'er,
For the bulldogs came one wintry night,
And dragged me off in a terrible fright
And landed me here an awful sight
    On Ballykinlar shore.

Chorus
I'm one of the Curfew birds,
    I'm an internee,
O! Loydy, Loydy, George,
    See what you've done for me.
You started out to buy a dog,
    And only got a pup,
O! Loydy, Loydy, George,
    See what you've rounded up.

You should see me cutting it fine,
    Along the Esplanade,
Whenever I had a bob to spare,
If you were in Bray you'd find me there,
    But now alas! I'm very much afraid
I'll spend the rest of my life instead
Gobbling spuds that feel like lead,
And spreading the Margo on my bread,
    Disguised with marmalade.

The Susans and the Mary Janes,
    May fade away and die.
They'll be all old maids I see,
If they sit on the bench to wait for me,
    For now alas! they'll never see me more.
I'll be here to the end of my days I know,
Carrying buckets to and fro,
And I'll go where martyrs go
    On Ballykinlar's shore.

Seán Treacy
Peadar Kearney

To you, O Flower of Ireland's Youth!
    Across the grave we send a Nation's praise
Hailing your name – the greatest name of all,
    Young Ireland's pioneers!
Chanting your courage cool;
    Your deathless love for her,
Your changeless hate for those
    Who sought her soul to rend –
Those you pursued and slew
    Without remorse –
Those you destroyed and conquered
    To the end.

To-day behold your Ireland!
    Eyes alight and hearts ablaze
No longer shivering slaves in
    Freedom's dawn.
Today each heath-clad hill,
    Each singing glen,
Re-echoes to the tramp of armed men,
    Whose guiding star thou art
Forever and for aye
    O Seán!

Text: Seamus de Burca, *The Soldier's Song*, P.J. Bourke, Dublin, 1957.

'The Birth of the Irish Republic – 1916', postcard published by The Art Depot, Dublin.

Gather Round the Flag

Peadar Kearney

Gather round the flag, my comrades, feast your eyes u-pon each fold,

See the sun of Free-dom shi-ning on the Green, White and Gold.

While we've hearts its fame to che-rish and we've hands its staff to hold,

It shall ne-ver bend to Ire___ land's___ foe!___

Chorus

By the flag that floats a-bove us, by our fa___ thers'___ graves,

By the dead who died for Ire-land long a-go,___

We shall ne-ver rest, my bro-thers, in this land of ours as slaves

While we've strength__ to__ face the Sa-xon foe.___

Gather round the flag, my comrades,
    Feast your eyes upon each fold,
See the sun of Freedom shining
    On the Green, White and Gold.
While we've hearts its fame to cherish,
    And we've hands its staff to hold,
It shall never bend to Ireland's foe!

Chorus
By the flag that floats above us,
    By our fathers' graves,
        By the dead who died for Ireland long ago,
We shall never rest, my brothers,
    In this land of ours as slaves,
        While we've strength to face the Saxon foe!

From Inishowen to Bearea
    We have raised that banner high,
Our lives are pledged to keep it there

Text: Samuels Collection, TCD.
Air: 'O'Neill's March'.

377

It foemen to defy;
And ere tyrant hands dare touch it,
    Round its staff we'll gladly die,
And in dying prove our words are true.

The deathless love of comrades true
    Shall cheer us on the way;
Hand in hand for Mother Ireland,
    We are brothers in the fray.
We shall never halt or waver
    Till the Dawning of the Day
Shines in glory on the conquering Gael.

Labour's Call
Peadar Kearney

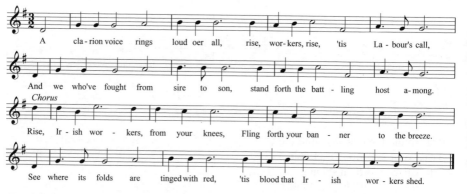

Text: ballad sheet.
    Air: 'The Red Flag' or 'O Tannen-
baum'.

A clarion voice rings loud o'er all,
Rise, workers, rise, 'tis Labour's call,
And we who've fought from sire to son,
Stand forth the battling host among.

Chorus
Rise, Irish workers, from your knees,
Fling forth your banner to the breeze,
See where its folds are tinged with red,
'Tis blood that Irish workers shed.

No worker shall forget the day
When Connolly stood 'mid war's array,
And sent aloft with volleys three
Our bright-hued flag of Liberty.

Our toiling millions claim their own,
From old Kinsale to Inishowen:
No hirelings' share shall they enjoy,
But all therein from sea to sky.

We send our hail to lands afar,
Where'er our struggling brothers are;
Each shattered crown, each crumbling throne,
Is Labour's call to claim its own.

Defeat ne'er gave us doubt or pain,
We've fought and failed and fought again.
But now the final die is cast,
We'll fight for Labour till the last.

The Three-Coloured Ribbon
(A Ballad of Easter Week)
Peadar Kearney

I had a true love, if ever a girl had one.
    I had a true love, a brave lad was he.
One fine Easter Monday, with his gallant comrades,
    He started away for to set Ireland free.

Chorus
All round my hat I wear a three-coloured ribbon O
    All round my hat until death comes to me.
And if anybody's asking why do I wear it,
    It's all for my true love I never more shall see.

His bandolier round him, his bright bayonet shining,
    His short service rifle, a beauty to see.

Peadar Kearney penned this still-popular song that narrates the tale of a young woman waiting for news and then lamenting the loss of her lover in the 1916 Rising. The Three-Coloured Ribbon is one of green, white and orange, the colours of Ireland's flag. This, however, was not the main flag that flew over Dublin's GPO (General Post Office), the headquarters of the insurrectionary forces in the then Sackville Street, now O'Connell Street, Dublin. The main flag was a green one, with the words Irish Republic in gold, in large print. The tricolour, which was also flown over the GPO, came more into prominence

379

post-1916 and the previously more popular flag of green with a gold harp fell into disuse. See picture, p. 435. [LM]

Text: *Songs of the Irish Republic*, Coiste Foillseacháin Náisiúnta, Cork, 1962.
    Air: 'All Round My Hat I Will Wear the Green Willow'.

There was joy in his eyes though he left me behind him
    And started away for to set Ireland free.

He whispered: 'Good-bye, love, old Ireland is calling.
    High over Dublin our tricolour flies.
In the streets of the city the foeman is falling,
    And wee birds are singing, 'Old Ireland, arise!"

In praying and watching, the dark days passed over,
    The roar of the guns brought no message to me.
I prayed for old Ireland, I prayed for my lover,
    That he might be saved, and old Ireland be free.

The struggle was ended, they brought me the story,
    The last whispered message he sent unto me:
'I was true to my land, love, I fought for her glory,
    And gave up my life for to make Ireland free!'

Up, De Valera!
Peadar Kearney

Text: Peadar Ó Cearnaigh, *Camp-Fire Songs*, Art Depot, Dublin, n.d.
    Prescribed air: 'That's What the People Say in Ireland'.

Oh, we've had many leaders,
    Both valiant, wise and true,
Who proved on many a battlefield
    What Irishmen can do.
Once more we're facing danger,
    And the man to see us through
Is Ireland's undaunted De Valera.

Chorus
Then up, De Valera! he's the man to lead us on,
We'll follow De Valera till English rule is gone.
We cannot lose the fight, boys, while God is looking on
    And we're led by undaunted De Valera.

We're marching on to Freedom,
    And we'll never halt again,
And should old Ireland need them,
    She'll have lots of fighting men.
They'll throng from every city,
    From every hill and glen,
To be led by undaunted De Valera.

They may brag about their millions
    And all their roaring guns,
But all their might shall not prevail
    'Gainst Ireland's fighting sons.
We'll beat the lot together –
    The English, French and Huns –
When we're led by undaunted De Valera.

The Bold Volunteer
Peadar Kearney

Oh, have you heard the call,
Ringing loud over all,
From Cork to Donegal,
    In this wonderful year

Text: Samuels Collection, TCD.
Air: 'The Bold Soldier Boy'.

There's the glory and renown,
Mother Ireland to crown,
Bayonet bright and rifle brown,
    For the Bold Volunteer.

Chorus
Then rally to the cause, boys,
'Tis Ireland over all, boys,
While she is held in thrall, boys,
    Shall we give heed to fear?
No! every drop our fathers bled,
And every tear our mothers shed,
Shall light the way to freedom
    For the Bold Volunteer.

Let dirty traitors whine,
Now's the time, into line!
Let your gleaming bayonets shine
    O'er each full bandolier.
Eyes front! shoulders squared!
Toe the line! Be prepared!
For there's danger to be dared
    By the Bold Volunteer.

Then think and work and plan,
Learn the trade every man,
For life is but a span,
    And the Great Day is near,
And if 'tis ours to fall
When we answer the Call,
'Tis the grandest fate of all
    For the Bold Volunteer.

The South Down Militia
Peadar Kearney

Text: *Walton's 132 Best Irish Songs and Ballads*, Walton's Musical Instrument Galleries, Dublin, n.d.
    Air: see p. 179.

You've heard of Julius Sayser
    And Alexander too,
And other famous haireos
    Who fought at Waterloo,
But if you read your history
    You'll quickly understand
That the South Down Militia
    Is the terrors of the land!

Chorus
You may talk about your King's Guard,
   Scots Guards an' a',
Your Black an' Tans, and Kilties
   An' the fighting Forty-twa,
Also our brave Auxiliaries –
   A most ferocious band –
But the South Down Militia
   Is the terrors of the land!

And when we marched thro' London
   In the year of brave '14,
Our gracious King reviewed us,
   With Her Majesty, the Queen,
'Och, bloody wars,' the Queen remarked
   And waved her lily hand,
'The South Down Militia
   Is the terrors of the land!'

When the Kaiser heard the regiment
   Had landed in France,
In wild despair he tore his hair,
   Then fell into a trance,
He never thought the Orange Drum
   Would bate the German Band,
But the South Down Militia
   Is the terrors of the land!

We'll tell the living world
   'Twas us that won the War,
We marched thro' France and Belgium
   An' never got a scar.
When the Germans saw us coming
   They wouldn't wait to stand,
For the South Down Militia
   Is the terrors of the land!

And now the War is over
   And peace is here again,
But peace or war, we'll do an' dar'
   Our rights for to maintain.
When the rebels cross the Border
   They'll never see the Bann –
For the South Down Militia
   Is the terrors of the land!

Sergeant William Bailey

Peadar Kearney

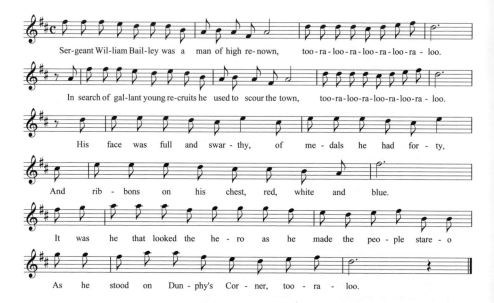

Although completely unconnected with this song, there actually was a Sergeant William Bailey in the British army during the First World War, an Australian soldier who was killed near Arras in 1917.

Text and air: Transcribed from the singing of Luke Cheevers, who added the second verse to the song.

Sergeant William Bailey was a man of high renown,
    Tooral looral looral looral loo,
In search of gallant young recruits he used to scour the town,
    Tooral looral looral looral loo.
His face was full and swarthy, of medals he had forty,
And ribbons on his chest red white and blue,
It was he that looked the hero as he made the people
    stare O,
    As he stood on Dunphy's Corner tooral loo.

Now, as Sergeant William Bailey at Dunphy's Corner
    stands,
    Tooral looral looral looral loo,
Enticing Dublin young lads for to die in foreign lands,
    Tooral looral looral looral loo.
For to improve their station, he shouts in high elation
To come and fight for King and country,
But for all the lies he's making, the bait they aren't taking
    From Sergeant William Bailey, tooral loo.

But alas for human greatness every dog he has his day,
    Tooral looral looral looral loo,
And Sergeant William Bailey he is getting old and grey,
    Tooral looral looral looral loo.

No longer youths are willing to take his dirty shilling,
And things for him are looking mighty blue,
In spite of fife and drumming no more recruits are coming,
    For Sergeant William Bailey tooral loo.

Sergeant William Bailey what a wretched sight to see,
    Tooral looral looral looral loo,
His back that once was firm and straight is almost bent
    in three,
    Tooral looral looral looral loo.
Some rebel youths with placards have called his army
    blackguards,
And told the Irish youth just what to do,
He has lost his occupation let's sing in jubilation,
    For Sergeant William Bailey tooral loo.

'The Recruiting Sergeant', *Punch*, 25 March 1914.

385

It's a Grand Old Country

Peadar Kearney

You've read of re-vo-lu-tions and you've read of the bloo-dy wars,

You've seen our land dis-fi-gured by the dir-ty Sax-on scars.

You know that ships went, sai-ling with our best from vale and hill,

But there's hearts and hands in Ire-land that will free old Ire-land still.

Chorus

For it's a grand old coun-try eve-ry time,

With its rocks and ri-vers, lakes and soil and clime!

We're God's own peo-ple and we'll shout from tower and stee-ple,

It's a grand old coun-try eve-ry time!

Dominic Behan recorded this song in 1959 on the Topic album *Easter Week and After,* and attributed it to his uncle Peadar Kearney.

Text and air: Transcribed from the singing of Dominic Behan.

You've read of revolution and you've read of the bloody
   wars,
You've seen our land disfigured by the dirty Saxon scars,
You know that ships went sailing with our best from
   vale and hill,
But there's hearts and hands in Ireland that will free old
   Ireland still.

Chorus
For it's a grand old country every time,
With its rocks and rivers, lakes and soil and clime!
We're God's own people and we'll shout from tower and
   steeple
It's a grand old country every time!

386

How often we've been flattened out, our history books
    will show.
When Mother England battened on our misery and woe.
She sacked us and she beat us and the snivellers cried
    'amen',
But the world knows how Ireland rose from out the dust
    again.

I'll pray for Mother England while I'm waiting on the
    day,
I'll pray for Mother England till I'm blind and bald and
    grey,
I'll pray that dying, she may die, and drowning, she may
    drown,
And if ever she tries to lift her head I'll be there to push
    it down.

ROBBED—FOR "ENGLAND, HOME, AND BEAUTY."

Cartoon by Thomas Fitzpatrick from *The Lepracaun*.

The Devil's Crew

Peadar Kearney

The expression 'unco guid' in the second verse is Scots, and Kearney is probably quoting from the title of Robbie Burns' poem 'Address to The Unco Guid, Or The Rigidly Righteous'.

Text: Broadsheet in the National Library of Ireland. The broadsheet includes MS corrections, some in Kearney's hand, which have been adopted here.
   Seamus de Burca included the first three verses in *The Soldier's Song*, P.J. Bourke, Dublin, 1957.

The poets have chanted their paeans of praise
   To the men who were pure of soul,
I'll tell of a bunch who in different ways
   Find a place on the muster roll.
'Tis very low down, still you'll all agree
   They have earned their places there,
Tho' their principal pastime seemed to be
   To drink and gamble and swear.
The chances are just a thousand to one
   This tale won't appeal to you,
Still, whether you like the yarn or not,
   Just give the devil his due
While I strive to outshine, minus trimmings or shine,
   My tale of the Devil's Crew.

Oh, a holy crush! not one of us
   But of devilment had our share.
We all had our jags on the backs of the books
   And most of us some to spare.
We sang our songs and courted the girls,
   And quaffed the eau-de-vie,
And seldom saw home till the rays of dawn
   Shot up from the Irish Sea.
We had no friends 'mong the 'unco guid',
   Tho' some of the brave and true
Would grin and say: 'That bunch, we guess,
   Are not God's chosen few.'
While the word-spinning hypocrites passing by
   Said: 'They are the Devil's Crew!'

There were none of us burdened with easy wealth
   When first we were planted here,
The wages we should have trebled by stealth
   We flung to the winds on beer.
And why should the worker worry himself,
   In the midst of a crazy slum,
'Bout the wherewithal or the where-with-which
   Or the day that might never come?
So we looked on the cheerier side of life
   As all good comrades do,
Recounting our various jamborees
   With Mary and Jane and Sue,
While the plaster invertebrates passing by
   Said: 'They are the Devil's Crew.'

Irish? Yes! As pure as ever was made,
    We drew our blood from the high green hill,
And up from the hazel glade:
The Barrow and Nore, the Suir and Boyne,
    To our sinew and bone paid toll.
But Dublin town, with its smoke and brown,
    Laid claim to our rebel soul.
And the love in our hearts for the motherland
    That stronger and stronger grew,
Was never discussed, tho' we often spoke
    Of the things that we hoped to do
If God in His own good time would give
    Once chance to the Devil's Crew!

One holiday morn when Ireland called
    And we joined in the great parade,
You never saw such an unsoldierly crush
    Since first the world was made,
But in spite of the canting cowards who preached
    From the depths of an easy chair,
One thing shall live when most things die:
    'By G—, boys, we were there!'
Tho' there wasn't one decent equipment,
    Either second-hand or new,
Save a water-flask here or a haversack there
    With maybe a puttee or two,
But a bandolier, bayonet and rifle were strapped
    On each man of the Devil's Crew!

From the crackle and crash of the first red night
    The sputtering bullets tore –
One fellow dropped like an empty sack
    And another in anger swore.
While a kid with rapidly glazing eyes
    Was crooning an Irish song,
And died as he watched the tiny stream
    Of his heart's blood creeping along –
We stemmed the rush of the khaki tide
    Whenever it came in view,
Spending red days and hideous nights
    In proving our worth tho' few
There were brave lads there, but the pick of the bunch
    Were known as 'The Devil's Crew!'

You know the rest – one short red week,
    A dream of a nation free –
An affair that gladdens an old man's heart

With a glorious memory.
Our leaders were wise and learned men
With a wisdom we never knew,
They gave their orders and we obeyed,
A thing we thought hard to do;
For had the orders been 'Carry on!'
I'm telling a thing that's true –
The last shot fired from Dublin's ruins
Would come from the Devil's Crew!

The Rainbow Chasers

Peadar Kearney

Text: Samuels Collection, TCD.
Air: The model for this song is clearly Dan Emmett's song 'I Wish I Was in Dixie'.

We've heard the traitors and the wasters
Tell us we are rainbow chasers,
So we are, we are, hurrah! hurrah!
We'll chase that rainbow till we find it,
And, what's more, we'll get behind it,
Then the Lord look on the poor Brithun.

Chorus
For we are rainbow chasers,
     We are! we are!
  Our arms are strong, our courage high,
  Our banner's planted in the sky,
Hurrah! hurrah! for we're the rainbow chasers.

Where brothers died in Freedom's furrow
Others, too, shall die to-morrow
  For the Flag that's planted in the sky.
Once more the Saxon boasts he'll break us;
Let the swine come here and take us,
  And they'll find how Irishmen can die.

So send us on more babes and sucklings.
By the Lord! for fight they're good things,
  But we've bogs right here to hold them all.
They'd rather fight a million Kaisers
Than face ten thousand rainbow chasers
  When we mobilize at Ireland's call.

To England
Peadar Kearney
September 25th, 1917

Hail! Mother of Civilization
  Hail! strength of the lowly and weak
(You sink of the earth's degradation),
  Give ear while we speak:
Once more you have bade us remember
  That your thrice-accursed flag is blood red,
And Ashe, in his glory and vigour,
  Is strangled and dead.

He is dead, but his spirit triumphant
  Soars high over thraldom and death
(And he scorned your friendship, O England,
  With his last dying breath).
You may smile in the filth of your brothels,
  You may sneer in your arrogant might,
But lo! Even now you are reeling
  'Neath a withering blight.

In this song Peadar Kearney laments
the death of Thomas Ashe. See also
pp. 257, 258, and 504.

Text: Samuels Collection, TCD.

391

And you stand in the market-place, England,
    With your leprous soul laid bare,
The scorn and contempt of the nations,
    Who spit on you there.
THEY know that your sentence is written,
    That Freedom and Right shall prevail,
But the Power that shall carve out that sentence
    Is the Power of the Gael.

And we call on the nations to witness,
    The sons of the Inde and the Gael,
Who have learned the truth of your teaching
    By gibbet and jail;
And their blood in one sacrifice column
    In Heaven shall justice demand,
And when Heaven shall mete out its justice,
    YOUR hour is at hand.

Then hail! to your mission, O England,
    To plunder and ravish and slay.
YOU gave us red milestones to Freedom,
    WE follow alway.
We'll follow that red road to Glory
    (The white-livered traitors assail),
And you'll hear with your death-rattle, England,
    The Curse of the Gael.

The Soldier's Song
Peadar Kearney

Text: Seamus de Burca, *The Soldier's Song*, P.J. Bourke, Dublin, 1957, where it is described as an 'Extra verse added to "The Soldier's Song" [see p. 429] in answer to a request that the Irish of the six north-eastern counties could register a protest against the British-planned partition of Ulster'.

And here where Eire's glories bide
    Clann London fair would flourish;
But Ulster-wide what e'er betide
    No pirate blood shall nourish;
While flames the faith of Con and Owen,
    While Cave Hill guards the fame of Tone,
From Gullion's Slopes to Inishowen
    We'll chant a Soldier's Song.

Whack Fol the Diddle!
Peadar Kearney

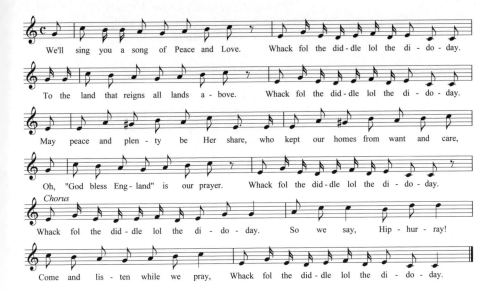

We'll sing you a song of Peace and Love, / Whack fol the did-dle lol the di-do-day. / To the land that reigns all lands a-bove. / Whack fol the did-dle lol the di-do-day. / May peace and plen-ty be Her share, who kept our homes from want and care, / Oh, "God bless Eng-land" is our prayer. / Whack fol the did-dle lol the di-do-day.

Chorus Whack fol the did-dle lol the di-do-day. So we say, Hip-hur-ray! Come and lis-ten while we pray, Whack fol the did-dle lol the di-do-day.

We'll sing you a song of Peace and Love,
    Whack fol the diddle lol the di-do-day.
To the land that reigns all lands above,
    Whack fol the diddle lol the di-do-day.
May peace and plenty be Her share,
Who kept our homes from want and care,
Oh 'God bless England' is our prayer,
    Whack fol the diddle lol the di-do-day.

Chorus
Whack fol the diddle lol the di-do-day.
So we say, hip-hur-ray!
Come and listen while we pray,
Whack fol the diddle lol the di-do-day.

When we were savage, fierce and wild,
    Whack fol the diddle lol the di-do-day.
She came as a mother to her child,
    Whack fol the diddle lol the di-do-day.
Gently raised us from the slime,
Kept our hands from hellish crime,
And sent us to Heaven in her own good time,
    Whack fol the diddle lol the di-do-day.

Béal 'n Áth Buidhe and Pieter's Hill (verse 3) are, respectively, the location of the Battle of the Yellow Ford, in 1598, when an English army was destroyed by O'Neill and O'Donnell, and the location of a battle between the British army and the Boers in 1900.

Text and music: Sheet music viewable on the website of the Irish Traditional Music Archive. The music is described as an 'Old Air, arranged by Cathal Mac Dubhghaill'.

393

Our fathers oft were naughty boys,
    Whack fol the diddle lol the di-do-day.
Pikes and guns are dangerous toys,
    Whack fol the diddle lol the di-do-day.
From Béal 'n Áth Buidhe to Pieter's Hill,
They made poor England weep her fill,
But old Britannia loves us still,
    Whack fol the diddle lol the di-do-day.

Oh, Irishmen forget the past,
    Whack fol the diddle lol the di-do-day.
And think on the day that is coming fast,
    Whack fol the diddle lol the di-do-day.
When we shall all be civilized,
Neat, and clean, and well advised,
Oh, won't Mother England be surprised,
    Whack fol the diddle lol the di-do-day.

Peadar Kearney.

Lonely Banna Strand

'Twas on Good Friday morning before the month of May,
A German ship was signalling beyond there in the bay.
"We've twenty thousand rifles, all ready for to land",
But no answering signal came from the lonely Banna Strand.

Twas on Good Friday morning before the month of May,
A German ship was signalling beyond there in the bay,
'We've twenty thousand rifles here, all ready for to land,'
But no answering signal came from the lonely Banna
Strand.

A motor-car was dashing through the early morning
gloom.
A sudden crash, and in the sea they went to meet their
doom.
Two Irish lads lay dying there just like their hopes so grand,
They could not give the signal now from lonely Banna
Strand.

'No signal answers from the shore,' Sir Roger sadly said.
'No comrades here to welcome me, alas! They must be dead;
But I must do my duty and at once I mean to land.'
So in a boat he pulled ashore on lonely Banna Strand.

The German ships were lying there with rifles in galore.
Up came a British ship and spoke, 'No Germans reach
the shore;
You are our Empire's enemy, and so we bid you stand,
No German foot shall e'er pollute the lonely Banna
Strand.'

They sailed for Queenstown Harbour. Said the Germans:
'We're undone.
The British are our masters man for man and gun for gun.
We've twenty thousand rifles here, but they never will
reach land.
We'll sink them all and bid farewell to lonely Banna Strand.'

The German ship, *The Aud*, under Captain Karl Spindler, had 20,000 rifles, machine guns, explosives and ammunition on board and was to land this weaponry in Kerry on Good Friday, 21 April 1916, to arm the Irish Volunteers. These weapons were badly needed for the imminent 1916 Rising. Due to a mishap, the on-shore signalling party, taking a wrong turn and driving into the sea and being drowned, no signal was received by *The Aud*, which was captured by the Royal Navy and then scuttled, with its cargo, near the entrance to Cork Harbour.

A German submarine, U19, with Sir Roger Casement on board, was to be part of the gun-running operation. As no communication had been established the submarine captain put Casement ashore, and he was captured by the Royal Irish Constabulary (RIC) the next morning. Casement was tried for high treason, as he had held office under the Crown, and hanged in Pentonville Prison, London on 3 August 1916. Some of his diaries, dubbed 'Black Diaries', outline explicit homosexual conduct, and were leaked in an effort to discredit him, homosexual acts being illegal in those times. There has been dispute as to whether they were forged or not, but modern research would suggest that they are authentic.

Casement is possibly better known internationally for his humanitarian work in exposing the atrocities committed against the indigenous people of the Congo, and the Putumayo Indians of Peru, by those extracting rubber from those regions. His work received widespread acclaim and was instrumental in stopping the barbaric treatment of the indigenous peoples concerned. He was knighted for his work, 'Sir' Roger Casement.

In 1965 Casement's remains were returned to Ireland and were interred in Glasnevin Cemetery, Dublin. [LM]

Text: *Songs of the Irish Republic*, Coiste Foillseacháin Náisiúnta, Cork, 1962.
Air: From memory.

The R.I.C. were hunting for Sir Roger high and low,
They found him at McKenna's Fort. Said they: 'You are
    our foe.'
Said he: 'I'm Roger Casement, I came to my native land.
I mean to free my countrymen on the lonely Banna
    Strand.'

They took Sir Roger prisoner and sailed for London
    Town,
And in the Tower they laid him as a traitor to the
    Crown.
Said he: 'I am no traitor,' but his trial he had to stand
For bringing German rifles to the lonely Banna Strand.

'Twas in an English prison that they led him to his
    death.
'I'm dying for my country,' he said with his last breath.
He's buried in a prison yard far from his native land.
The wild waves sing his requiem on the lonely Banna
    Strand.

The Breaking of Our Flag
To Commandant Connolly
Maeve Cavanagh

This poem was written about the unveiling of the Tricolour on Sunday, 16 April 1916.

Text: Maeve Cavanagh Papers, National Library of Ireland.

Thousands there 'neath the April sky
    The Liffey's banks beside,
They stand expectant, gazing high
    Eyes lit by hope and pride,
The young and old, the youth and maid,
    The grandsire and the child,
There too, the shame-faced renegade
    In England's garb reviled.

The sleuth-hounds of the foe are there
    Betrayers of their kin,
Who honour sell like merchantware
    And revel in their sin.
Yet not forever shall they go
    Unpunished and immune,
God's justice might be doubted so
    Nay – Vengeance cometh soon.

Thus side by side the brave and base
    For those few moments wait,
The martyr light on some young face
    A hero marked by fate,
For many too – the Fiery Cross
    Fierce trial, Death or Pain,
Who've spurned the world's appeal and dross
    To kneel at Freedom's fane.

See, to the brave west wind at last
    Leaps the immortal green,
To the clear sound of Trumpet blast
    Its floating folds are seen,
Whilst mounting to the fair spring skies
    The cheers of thousands go,
Fair omen, Ireland's standard flies
    A challenge to the foe.

Eastertide, 1916

Maeve Cavanagh

The warring nations mazèd heard
    The slogan cry of Eire ring,
And they who in her fain hope shared
    Exultant watched her gallant spring –
The wolf-dog stood at bay once more,
And heard unmoved the Lion's roar.

The hours were told – her time had come –
    At noontide on an April day,
She bore the Truth – the Lie struck dumb
    In all her glorious, deathless way.
Ere to his couch the Sun sank down
Her flag flew over Dublin town.

And Connaught o'er broad Shannon's tide,
    Her noble challenge swiftly sends,
True as of yore from Slaney's side
    Brave Wexford's thrilling answer wends –
And history stoops to write to-day
The fairest page she'll pen for aye.

What tho' our fairest, dearest fall?
    We shall not grudge the awful price,

'Written on the hoisting of the Irish Republican Flag over the GPO – Dublin, 24/4/1916.'

Text: Maeve Cavanagh, *A Voice of Insurgency*, Dublin, 1916.

To-day we stand in Freedom's hall,
    And freely make our sacrifice.
We've seen our Goddess face to face
All times cannot this hour efface.

The Call to Arms
On the recent mobilization of the Irish Citizen Army
Maeve Cavanagh

Text: Maeve Cavanagh, *A Voice of Insurgency*, Dublin, 1916. First published in *The Workers' Republic*, 8 April 1916.

Make way, oh gaping, careless crowds,
    Fall back, and let them by,
Fate even now may weave their shrouds,
    They go – to win or die.
Some moments since, at work they bent,
    In factory, mill, or street,
Till Eire her Reveille sent,
    Then thronged they to her feet.

Machines were stayed, tools thrown aside,
    'Twas Eire's hosting day,
Ne'er bridegroom to a regal bride,
    Went half so fleet as they.
With bandolier and trusty gun,
    Each busy street they tread,
Whilst England's craven garrison,
    Looks on in hate and dread.

They needed neither bribe not threat,
    'Twas love their service bought,
Had yielded life without regret,
    If but its gift had brought
The great, shy bird of Freedom near,
    To fold her wings at last,
And nest upon their land so dear,
    Till Time should wind his blast.

They kept their vigil, brave and true,
    No foe their fort assailed,
The British Bull-dog, loathe to woo
    New dangers, backed and quailed.
And slunk to kennel, baffled, sore,
    Too scared to bark or bite,
To weave his dastard plots once more,
    'Gainst men he dare not fight.

Citizen Soldier

Liam MacGabhann (1908–1979)

Citizen Soldier, whither bound?
In all the big city there's never a sound,
Bandolier and bayonet and big brown gun,
Out by the river at the rising o' the sun.
Whom have you been talking to,
Where are you walking to,
Is there something happening, something to be done?
The soldier laughed and pointed to the skies,
And a bright new banner was flashing on my eyes,
'There's a fight to be lost and won.'

Citizen Soldier, whither I,
I would be with you when the foe comes nigh?
Barricades are building by the bridges and the quays,
For battle with the British that are coming on the seas.
Connolly is planning them,
Someone will be manning them,
While the last man lives and the colours kiss the breeze.
And the soldier shouldered his big, brown gun,
And the banner flew at the setting of the sun,
And the night-wind sighed in the trees.

Citizen Soldier, whither thou?
In all the big city there's a silence now.
Never a flag or a muffling of the drum,
Or the pipers' playing, or the clarionaders' hum.
Where is your scheming now,
Planning and dreaming now,
Cold in the coffin there, motionless and dumb?
And the soldier lay with his gun-gashed breast,
And the wind was saying as he went to his rest,
'The fight has been lost and won.'

Text: Liam MacGabhann, *Rags, Robes and Rebels*, Republican Press, Dublin, 1933.

The Citizen Army

Liam MacGabhann

The Citizen Army is out today and if you wonder why,
Go ask the lords of the tram-lined way if their cash re-
    turns be high.
'Tisn't the bosses who bear the brunt, 'tisn't you and I,

The Citizen Army, full name 'Irish Citizen Army', was founded as a workers' protection force in the aftermath of the 1913 Dublin Lockout, when the employers, under the leadership of William Martin Murphy, locked out any worker who would not disassociate himself or herself from the Irish Transport and General Workers' Union (ITGWU).

The lockout was accompanied by Dublin Metropolitan Police (DMP) police brutality, on a wide scale, against the workers. Jim Larkin was the charismatic union organizer, prominent in the struggle.

The Plough and the Stars was the flag of the Citizen Army; a blue background with the Starry Plough on it. James Connolly, who left a number of works advocating socialism, and analyses of Irish history, was a trade union leader and Commandant General, Irish Citizen Army.

Prominent in the 1916 Rising and a signatory of the Proclamation of the Irish Republic, he was in overall command of the Dublin insurgents. He was wounded in the fighting in Dublin's GPO and was shot in Kilmainham Jail on 12 May 1916.

The execution of a wounded man, and after a lull in the executions, had a profound effect on public opinion and many believe that his shooting was in revenge for his socialist activities. A none-too-indirect editorial call for Connolly's execution, in a newspaper owned by William Martin Murphy helped support this theory.

The reference in verse 2 is to the unemployed being used as cannon fodder in what socialists regarded as a war of international capitalism. [LM]

Text: John McDonnell, *Songs of Struggle and Protest*, Irish Labour History Society, 2008.

The Starry Plough.

But the women and kids whose tears are hid as the
  strikers go stumbling by.
The docker loads two hundred tons to his master's ship
  per day.
At night the docker's daughter bends her weary limbs to
  pray.
From the old North Wall to Liberty Hall was a deadline
  of unskilled.
They heaved and hauled when the bosses called and
  stopped when the bosses willed.

The Citizen Army is out today and if you wonder why,
Go ask the troops in the masters' pay if the blood on
  their guns be dry.
Ah, well, they won and the baton and gun have swung
  where the dead men lie,
For the women and kids whose tears are hid as the
  wounded go stumbling by.
Jim Connolly watches ships go out through flags at
  Kingstown pier,
And starving Dublin sends its toll of guard and fusilier.
Food for the guns that over the world have thundered
  murder's peace
And Dublin's broken union men die first on Flanders'
  fields.

The Citizen Army is out today and if you wonder why,
Jim Larkin came this way to nail the bosses' lie.
That the iron gyves on their limbs and lives would crush
  them till they die!
Those women and kids whose tears are hid as the
  strikers go marching by.
The docker and carter and heaver of coal, were only the
  backwash then,
Till Larkin built the union up and the bosses feared again.
From the old North Wall to Liberty Hall came that
  deadline of unskilled,
In a new-born fight for the workers' rights that the
  bosses thought they had killed.

The Citizen Army is out today and if you wonder why,
Go ask the men in the grey and green why the Plough
  and Stars flag flies.
'Tisn't only the bosses we challenge now, 'tis Connolly
  has cast the die,
For the women and kids as the tears are hid as the
  soldiers go marching by.

Four hundred bosses planned to break that deadline of
    unskilled,
Four hundred bosses drink tonight for Connolly is
    killed.
But, dead or alive, there are those who strive a glorious
    thing to do,
For Connolly built that union up, for the likes of me and
    you.

The Citizen Army is out today and if you wonder why,
Go ask the lords of the banking house if their cash
    returns be high.
For they are there and we are here, and a fight to the
    knife again.
The Citizen Army is out today; come workers, are ye
    men?

The Irish Citizen Army

Leo Maguire (1903–1985)

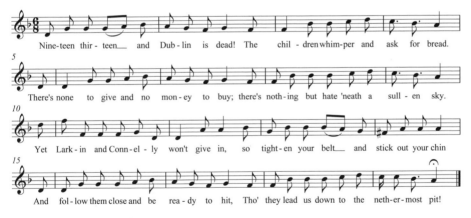

Nineteen-thirteen and Dublin is dead!
The children whimper and ask for bread.
There's none to give and no money to buy;
There's nothing but hate 'neath a sullen sky.
Yet Larkin and Connolly won't give in,
So, tighten your belt and stick out your chin
And follow them close and be ready to hit,
Tho' they lead us down to the nethermost pit!

Text: Leo Maguire, *The Faithful and the Few*, Walton's Musical Instrument Galleries, Dublin, 1959.
    Air: Written for the song by Sandie Purcell.

401

Aye, tighten your belt and grip your stick!
The batons are swinging, you'd better be quick!
If hunger has left any strength in your arm
You'll live thro' the day and you'll come to no harm.
The wife and the children sit 'round the black grate;
There's nothing to burn and nothing to eat.
There's nothing to pawn and nothing to sell,
So, face the Peelers and give them hell.

Nineteen-sixteen and the hour has come,
Without blast of bugle or tuck of drum.
It's 'Get to your post and do your best!'
With green jacket hiding a ragged vest.
What harm is in that if your bayonet's bright
And your face aglow with the battle-light?
So, it's 'shoulder your rifle and join the boys!'
Tho' the backside's out of your corduroys.

Into the Green, with the gates made fast.
Dig yourself in and look your last
On the Dublin you love and the Dublin you hate!
But, dig yourself in, for the hour is late!
Holy Mary! The end is near!
Speak to your Son for those we hold dear!
So, fire your last bullet and die with the boys
With the backside out of your corduroys.

The Irish Volunteer (1916)
(A. Coy.)

Ben O'Hickey

Text: Written in July 1916 and published in *From Prison Cells*, The Elo Press, Dublin, 1935.

With our bandoliers and rifles we are ready, one and all,
Every belt and buckle shining, we lined up before the Hall.
. . . Carry on by sections, numbers one and two keep still!
How our hearts all leaped from gladness,
. . . The boys who came to drill.

So we carried on in sections and carried on in squads,
We formed into companies . . . 'twas wonderful ye gods!
And at every twist and turn, how the hearts in us did
    thrill,
We were Ireland's steps to freedom,
. . . The boys who came to drill.

Now our ranks are thinned and broken, and our hearts are sick and sore;
We have fought and we've been beaten, just as others have before;
We've been beaten . . . but what matter, there are some remaining still,
Who will follow in the footsteps of
. . . The boys who came to drill.

The Dublin Brigade
Seosamh Mac Aonghusa (1875–1922)

It was on Eas - ter Mon - day the boys got the call

To___ join their bat - tal - ions · in park, glen and hall.

In less than an hour they were out on pa - rade;

There were true men, tho' few men, in the Dub - lin Bri - gade.

In___ less than an ho - ur they were out on par - ade,

There were true men, tho' few men, in the Dub - lin Bri - gade.

'Twas on Easter Monday the boys got the call
To join their battalions in park, square and hall,
And in less than an hour they were out on parade,
The faithful and true of the Dublin Brigade.
(Repeat last two lines of each verse for chorus)

And when they'd got orders they took up their posts,
And though few their numbers 'gainst England's proud
    hosts,
There was joy in their hearts, not a man was afraid,
For they're brave boys and true in the Dublin Brigade.

There was much work to do getting everything right,
But the old and the young they were anxious for fight.
Each worked hard to strengthen their own barricade,
And soon the rifles rang forth from the Dublin Brigade.

Dublin bore the brunt of the fighting in 1916, when about 1000 men, women and boys of the Irish Volunteers, Irish Citizen Army, Cumann na mBan and Fianna Éireann rose.

The song praises the Dublin Brigade for their fight and the last verse holds a promise for the future, that in spite of the leaders of the Rising having been shot and many others sent to jail, there will be a resurgence by the Dublin Brigade. This sentiment was prophetic, as Dublin was a hotbed of IRA activity during the Anglo-Irish War. [LM]

Text: The first five verses are from a contemporary ballad sheet, *The Irish Soldier's Song Book* (Fergus O'Connor, Dublin, n.d.), which also indicates that the song had been composed while the author was interned in Portland Prison, England.

403

The final verse and the air are from a slightly different version published in C. Desmond Greaves' *The Easter Rising in Song and Ballad,* Kahn & Averill, for the Workers' Music Association, London, 1980.
Air: 'Old Donegal'.

For a week without rest not a man showed a frown,
'Till the cowardly English set fire to the town;
Then to save it our leader had to be obeyed,
For he was the pride of the Dublin Brigade.

May God rest those brave men who gave up their lives
For Ireland, and Dublin's poor children and wives;
And their blood be on England till the last drop is paid
At the hands of the men of an Irish Brigade.

They have shot down our leaders and sent us to jail;
They have broken the spirit, they think, of the Gael.
But the day will come yet when they'll all be afraid
Of the true fighting men of the Dublin Brigade.

The Foggy Dew

Rev. Charles O'Neill

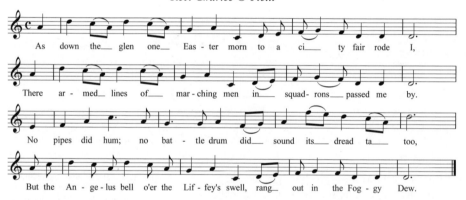

This is probably the most celebrated and most often performed song of the 1916 Rising.

Text and music: sheet music published by Whelan & Son, Dublin, *c.* 1919. The sheet music appeared in at least two different editions, which may be found on the website of the Irish Traditional Music Archive and in the Samuels Collection in TCD.
The author is identified in some publications as Rev. P. O'Neill , but most sources credit the song to Canon Charles O'Neill of Belfast.

As down by the glen one Easter morn to a city fair rode I,
There armed lines of marching men in squadrons passed me by;
No pipes did hum, no battle drum did sound its dread tattoo,
But the Angelus bell o'er the Liffey's swell rang out in the
   Foggy Dew.

Right proudly high over Dublin Town they hung out the
   Flag of War,
'Twas better to die 'neath an Irish sky than at Suvla or Sud
   El Bar;
And from the plains of Royal Meath strong men came
   hurrying through
While Britannia's Huns, with their great guns, sailed in by
   the Foggy Dew.

The night fell black, but the rifles' crack made perfidious
    Albion reel,
'Mid the leaden rain seven tongues of flame did burn o'er the
    lines of steel;
By each shining blade a prayer was said that to Ireland her
    sons might be true
And when morning broke still the War-Flag shook its folds in
    the Foggy Dew.

But the bravest fell, and the requiem bell rang mournfully and
    clear,
For those who died that Eastertide in the springing of the
    year;
And the world did gaze with deep amaze on those fearless
    men, but few,
Who bore the fight that Freedom's light might shine through
    the Foggy Dew.

'Twas England bade our 'Wild Geese' go that small nations
    might be free,
But their lonely graves are by Suvla's waves and the fringe of
    the grey North Sea.
Oh! had they died by Pearse's side or fought with Valera too,
Their place we'd keep where the Fenians sleep 'neath the
    shroud of the Foggy Dew.

Back to the glen I rode again, and my heart with grief was
    sore,
For I parted then with valiant men whom I never would see
    more;
But to and fro' in my dreams I go, and I kneel and pray for
    you,
For slavery fled, Oh! Rebel Dead, when you fell in the Foggy
    Dew.

The Foggy Dew

Leo Maguire

As I walked out on an Easter morn thro' Dublin city grand,
A maid I spied by the Liffey's side and weeping she did stand.
'O, wherefore weep, dear maid?' said I : she raised her eyes of blue
And sadly said 'I mourn the dead who must sleep beneath the
    Foggy Dew.'

Text: Leo Maguire, *The Faithful
and the Few*, Walton's Musical
Instrument Galleries, Dublin,
1959.

And as she spoke, thro' the pall of smoke that hung the city round
Came, fierce and high, the rallying cry and battle's dreadful sound.
She said 'They go to right my wrongs, the faithful and the few.'
Then the Angelus bell, like a funeral knell, tolled sadly thro' the Foggy Dew.

Then as I stood by Liffey's side I saw a glorious sight:
Brave men came marching, staunch and strong, to challenge England's might.
And high above O'Connell Street, for all the world to view,
No foreign rag, but our own dear flag, swung proudly o'er the Foggy Dew.

She said 'My sons face the tyrant's guns, 'tis a hopeless fight, but grand.
Their lives they give, but their dreams will live and bring hope to their
    martyred land.'
Then, as I gazed on her sad, sweet face, I said 'Dear Rosheen Dhu,
It is good to die under Ireland's sky and to sleep beneath the Foggy Dew.'

'Mavrone, mavrone,' she made sad moan, 'I am weary and sad this day.
The bravest and best are laid to rest in the cold unheeding clay.
Alas, my great strong sons are gone, who still had work to do:
My joy and pride, 'twas for me they died, and their shroud is the Foggy Dew.'

Then the blood-red sun sank slowly down in the brooding, angry West:
And we looked our last as the flames swept fast thro' a city that knew no rest.
I knelt and kissed her garment's hem, and said 'O, Rosheen Dhu,
May they sleep with God 'neath the Irish sod, who died in the Foggy Dew.'

Members of the Irish Volunteers and Irish Citizen Army inside the GPO during Easter Week.
(Courtesy of An Chartlann Mhíleata/The Military Archives, Irish Defence Forces.)

The ruins of Eden Quay after the Rising.

A Little Band of Rebels

A little band of rebels set out to fight one day,
To a spot in dear old Dublin not so very far away;
The seized upon the G.P.O., and made a gallant stand –
They fought a splendid battle to free old Ireland.

Text: Songs & Poems, The Rebels Who Fought and Died for Ireland in Easter Week, 1916 (Samuels Collection, TCD).

Chorus
So they started sniping day and night and never thought of rest,
Their hearts and souls were in their work, we know they did their best;
And ten to one the soldiers came and they began to sneer,
But they met a gallant fighter in each Irish Volunteer.
They kept the soldiers busy with their constant rifle shot –
The English had to admit they were a plucky lot.
The soldiers used artillery to make the rebels run,
And wrought such deeds of savagery, far worse than any Hun.

    The English said surrender, on conditions which we'll keep –
    The way they kept their promises will make the angels weep.
    The Volunteers to save us from the deadly British fire,
    They laid aside their rifles and their foes did then conspire.

Chorus
So they marched the leaders off to jail, with spirits still unbent –
Pearse, MacDonagh, Colbert, Heuston, Daly, also Ceannt,
MacDermott and O'Hanrahan, Plunkett, Clarke, MacBride,
And poor Connolly in a bath chair, who shortly would have died.
They allowed no plea of mercy on behalf of these brave men,
And the Treaty of Limerick was repeated once again;
They took them to Kilmainham Jail, and with cruel vengeance hot,
These noble Irish Volunteers in coldest blood were shot.

James Connolly's Grave
Tom Osborne

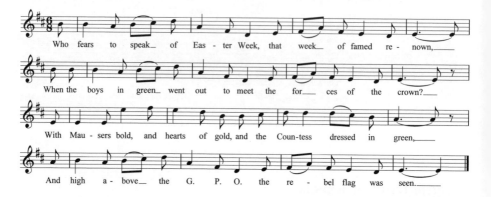

Who fears to speak of Eas-ter Week, that week of famed re-nown, When the boys in green went out to meet the for-ces of the crown? With Mau-sers bold, and hearts of gold, and the Coun-tess dressed in green, And high a-bove the G. P. O. the re-bel flag was seen.

This song was performed by Brendan Behan on the LP recording *Brendan Behan Sings Irish Folksongs and Ballads*, Spoken Arts SA760, 1960.

Louvain (verse 5), a university city, was destroyed by the German army in late August 1914, as part of a planned strategy of 'frightfulness' (*schrecklichkeit*), to intimidate civilians in occupied territories. The university library was singled out for attention and deliberately set on fire, leading to the loss of nearly a quarter of a million books. These actions caused outrage around the world. See picture p. 150.

Text: The only printed version is in *Songs and Recitations of Ireland, 3 – The Easter Lily,* published by Coiste Foillseacháin Náisiúnta, Cork in 1976.

Who fears to speak of Easter Week,
    That week of famed renown,
When the boys in green went out to face
    The forces of the Crown.
With Mausers bold, and hearts of gold
    And the Countess dressed in green,
And high above the G.P.O.
    The rebel flag was seen.

Then came ten thousand khaki coats
    Our rebel boys to kill,
But before they reached O'Connell Street
    Of fight, they'd had their fill.
They'd Maxim guns and cavalry
    And cannon in galore,
Bit it wasn't our fault that e'er a one
    Got back to England's shore.

They shot our leaders in a jail
    Without a trial, they say.
They murdered women and children
    Who in their cellars lay.
They dug their grave with gun and spade
    To hid them from our view,
Because they could not kill nor catch
    The rebels so bold and true.

May the Lord have mercy on three men
    Who faced the murderous foe.
There was Dixon, Sheehy-Skeffington
    And McIntyre also.

'Twas in a dismal barrack cell
    They met their fate so cruel.
Yes, they were shot, with no clergy got
    To prepare them for their doom.

For six long days we held them off
    At odds of ten-to-one.
And through our lines they could not pass
    For all of their heavy guns.
And deadly poison gas they used
    To try and crush Sinn Féin,
And they burned our Irish capital
    Like the Germans burned Louvain.

But we shall love old Ireland
    And shall while life remains.
And we shall say, 'God speed the day
    The rebels will rise again.'
Though Irish slaves and English knaves
    Will try you to deceive,
Remember those who died for you,
    And likewise James Connolly's grave.

The scene inside the GPO, just before its evacuation, as imagined by the British artist Walter Paget (1863–1935).
James Connolly, who had been wounded in the ankle, is lying on the stretcher.
(Courtesy of the National Library of Ireland.)

With the Irish Volunteers

Text: Samuels Collection, TCD.
Air: 'The Rising of the Moon' or
'The Wearin' of the Green', see p. 246.

Will you tell me Seamus Connor
   Why so quickly do you go?
With your men in double column
   Towards Old Dublin's G.P.O.
I will tell you then O'Donnell,
   Tho' it's only for your ears,
It's to strike a blow for freedom
   With the Irish Volunteers.

Chorus
With the Irish Volunteers,
   With the Irish Volunteers,
It's to strike a blow for freedom
   With the Irish Volunteers.

At noon our flag was floating,
   Over Dublin's ancient town,
And before the guns of Erin's sons,
   Full many a foe went down,
And the men who fought for freedom,
   Thro' that week of hopes and fears –
Saved Ireland's name and spread the fame
   Of the Irish Volunteers.

Of the Irish Volunteers
   Of the Irish Volunteers,
Saved Ireland's name and spread the fame
   Of the Irish Volunteers.

They saved our nation's honour
   And death but brought a smile,
For they knew they'd lit freedom's flame,
   Bright flashing through our Isle,
And we still have men like them again
   Who know not doubt or fears,
And we'll follow in the footsteps
   Of the Irish Volunteers.

Of the Irish Volunteers
   Of the Irish Volunteers,
And we'll follow in the footsteps
   Of the Irish Volunteers.

Up with the Barricades!

Phil O'Neill (Sliabh Ruadh)

Oh! flash the word from town and tower,
  Light beacons on each hill,
'Tis come at last the wished-for hour,
  With joy our bosoms thrill.
Send out the word to every man,
  To regiments and brigades,
Shout out the cry and raise it high –
  Up with the barricades!

Chorus
Then flash it forth from South to North
  To regiments and brigades,
The hour's at hand, our chiefs' command
  Up with the barricades.

The beacons blaze on Wicklow's peaks,
  To rouse the Wexford men,
The fire that blazed in Ninety-eight
  Is lighting once again.
The Enniscorthy boys are 'up',
  And ere the evening fades,
With rousing shout they rally out
  And raise the barricades.

Text: S.S. Breathnach, *Barricade Song
Sheet*, Dublin, n.d. (Samuels Collection,
TCD).
  Air: 'The Mountains of Pomeroy'.

411

The Galway men with eager hearts
　　Have heard the slogan cry,
Impatient for the coming fight
　　They march on Athenry.
A thousand more from Oranmore
　　The old cause nobly aids,
The West's Awake, let tyrants quake,
　　Up with the barricades!

The Louth men join across the Boyne,
　　To give a helping hand,
From old Fingal come one and all
　　To join our warlike band.
O'er Dublin's town the sun's gone down,
　　And as the evening fades,
Our stalwarts meet in every street
　　And raise the barricades.

From South and North they sally forth,
　　For Freedom calls again,
Our banners wave, our beacons blaze
　　O'er many thousand men.
Our boys are here from everywhere,
　　And many comely maids,
All thro' the land the sole command –
　　Up with the barricades!

Irish Rebellion ‒ May 1916.
Soldiers holding a Dublin Street..

For Erin Aboo!

Swiftly o'er Dublin the war cry is sounding,
　　Calling to Freedom the sons of the Gael,
And eager for battle each brave heart is bounding
　　To strike for the cause of the dear Innisfail.
Brave Pearse is in command of Erin's gallant band,
　　Pledged to the cause, steadfast, fearless and true.
Let every rifle well, death to the foeman spell –
　　And strike home for freedom and Erin aboo!

Proudly on high the Tricolour's waving,
　　The coward has fled and the tyrant dismayed,
And gone is the hireling, the slave and the craven –
　　And Dublin is held by the sons of the brave.
Up then, green, white and gold, out to the breeze unfold,
　　Symbol of freedom in every bright hue,
On courthouse, on mart, and mill, Hark! how their war cry thrill!
　　Strike home for freedom and Erin aboo!

God guard you now, Oh! brave sons of Erin,
　　The battle is raging and foes all surround,
Tho' ten times your number, the cost they've paid dear in
　　Their horse-men and foot-men lie dead on the ground.
Grasp every rifle tight, hail bullets at their might,
　　Wipe out the old score so long over due,
Brave Clarke and Plunkett well, bravely they've fought and fell–
　　For faith, home, and freedom, and Erin aboo!

Text: Samuels Collection, TCD.
Air: 'O'Donnell Abú', see p. 70.

In the Firing Line at Noon
Convict Reid

'Twas on Easter Monday morning Scout O'Kelly got the call,
To summon all his comrades to parade in their Drill Hall.
He'd got orders from his Captain get the boys out quick and
　　soon,
With their rifles on their shoulders in the Firing Line at Noon.

Chorus
In the Firing Line at Noon, in the Firing Line at Noon,
With their rifles on their shoulders, in the Firing Line at Noon,

Text: Samuels Collection, TCD.
Air: 'The Wearin' of the Green',
see p. 246.

When the boys had all assembled and each joined his company
'Twas a sight to be remembered in our country's history,
For they stood in marching order waiting for the word then soon,
To go forth and fight for freedom in the Firing Line at Noon.

Then the flag it was unfurl'd and around it were seen
The boys who stood for Ireland and the Orange, White and Green,
They were marched forth into action and the streets were quickly strewn
With the bodies of their foemen in the Firing Line at Noon.

They fought hard for Mother Erin 'gainst the ancient Saxon foe,
And they gloried in the fighting like their fathers long ago,
And if England thinks they're conquered she will quickly change her tune,
When the boys are again in action in the Firing Line at Noon.

The Heroes of Easter Week

Eileen O'Connor

Text: S.S. Breathnach, *The Victory Song Book*, J.J. Walsh, Dublin, 1920 (Samuels Collection, TCD).

O'er Eire's night of bitter woe,
  Full many a meteor flashed,
When patriots rose her wrongs to right,
  Her tyrant's power to blast.

Their blood was shed, the tyrant thought
  That Eire's soul was slain!
That blood was but as seed that's sown
  Whence heroes sprang again.

And now behold a glorious band,
  Defiant, – dauntless, brave,
Rise up against the ancient foe,
  Their native land to save.

They feared not 'mid the battle's roar,
  No thought of self they knew,
Outnumbered far by mighty hosts,
  More fierce their courage grew.

And on and on through shot and shell,
  They fought by day, by night,
Humane, Chivalric, high-souled, pure,
  Till Might had conquered Right!

Blood-thirsty tyrants then spring on
  Their hapless victims slay,

And loudly boast:– 'Sedition now
    Is dead and gone for aye.'

But hark! what are those mystic sounds
    That ring across the main?
Methinks I hear the marching men
    O'er hill and vale and plain.

Our gallant youths will join those bands
    Their battle-cry Sinn Féin,
This very year they'll make our land,
    A Nation once again.

The Dying Soldier

Rev. P. MacTomais

Mother Ireland! I have loved thee
    With a love that knew not fear.
I have drawn the sword to free thee
    At the flowering of the year.
But a hand was raised to smite me
    As I stooped to kiss thy brow,
And the arm that would have freed thee
    By my side hangs helpless now.

I have lived and loved and laboured
    With a patriot's heart and will,
That the dawning years might find thee
    Fearless and unfettered still.
I am vanquished, and my comrades
    In the glorious fight have bled,
And the dauntless hearts that loved thee
    Rest among the silent dead.

The reference in the first verse to 'the dawning of the year' can be taken to refer to the Easter Rising of 1916, of which The Dying Soldier is a casualty.

Text: *The 1916 Song Book*, Irish Book Bureau, Dublin, n.d.
    A note in the source states that the poem is 'Dedicated to Pádraig Pearse'.
    Air: A version of 'Boolavogue' to which the poem is set in C. Desmond Greaves' *The Easter Rising in Song & Ballad*, Kahn & Averill, for the Workers' Music Association, London, 1980.

415

But 'twere nobler thus to perish,
 Thus to wipe away their tears,
With the distant voice of Freedom
 Echoing in their dying ears,
Than to stand as fawning minions
 Of the sneering conqueror's race,
With the clanking chains of bondage
 Telling of our deep disgrace.

When the deathless glow of Freedom
 Flickering through the gloom of years,
Shall have flashed upon the hilltops,
 Conqueror of gloom and tears.
When a future age shall find thee,
 Freemen standing by thy side,
Mother Ireland, O, remember
 'Twas for Freedom's cause they died.

They are gone, and I must follow
 To the golden fields above,
Where the mighty God of Justice
 Shall reward a patriot's love.
Sweet it were to live and love thee,
 Sweeter far for thee to die,
With the flower-clad hills around me
 Echoing back my last good-bye.

The round-up of Irish Volunteers after the Easter Week Rising. The prisoners are seen being escorted by British soldiers with fixed bayonets, passing down Eden Quay en route to prisons in England.

The Dying Rebel

Seamus Kavanagh (d. 1969)

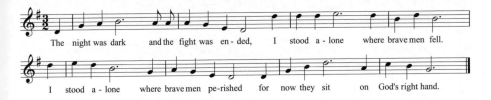

The night was dark and the fight was ended, I stood a-lone where brave men fell.
I stood a-lone where brave men pe-rished for now they sit on God's right hand.

The night was dark and the fight was ended
    I stood alone where brave men fell.
I stood alone where brave men perished
    For now they sit on God's right hand.

Chorus
My only son was shot in Dublin
    Fighting for his country bold.
He fought for Ireland, Ireland only
    The Harp and Shamrock, Green, White and Gold.

The first I met was a grey-haired Fenian
    Looking for his only son.
I said: 'Old man, there is no use searching,
    For straight to heaven your son has gone.'

'O God!' he cried, 'I am broken-hearted,'
    O God!' he cried, going on his knees.
'I knew my son was too kind hearted,
    I knew my son would never yield.'

The next I met was a fair young maiden
    Kneeling by her lover's side.
Praying to God, her Heavenly Father,
    Praying to God his soul to guide.

The last I met was a dying rebel.
    Kneeling low I heard him cry:
'God bless my home in dear Cork City,
    God bless the cause for which I die.'

This sentimental song could refer to either the 1916 Rising in Dublin, or to any of the street-fighting events of the Anglo-Irish War, 1919–21. It most likely refers to 1916, the only event of the period in which there was large-scale street-fighting and numbers of casualties. [LM]

Text: *Songs of the Irish Republic*, Coiste Foillseacháin Náisiúnta, Cork, 1962.
    Air: From memory.

417

The Bright Silvery Light of the Moon

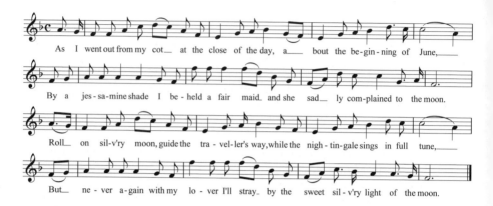

As I went out from my cot— at the close of the day, a— bout the be-gin-ning of June,—

By a jes-sa-mine shade I be-held a fair maid— and she sad— ly com-plained to the moon.

Roll— on sil-v'ry moon, guide the tra - vel-ler's way, while the nigh-tin-gale sings in full tune,—

But— ne - ver a-gain with my lo - ver I'll stray— by the sweet sil-v'ry light of the moon.

This is an example of a not-uncommon genre of republican ballad, in which an existing song is modified to refer to contemporary events. In this case the original song was the music-hall favourite 'Roll On, Silver Moon', by the British composer Charles Sloman, which was published in 1860 and became hugely popular in the United States of America.

Text: *Walton's 132 Best Irish Songs and Ballads*, Walton's Musical Instrument Galleries, Dublin, n.d.
Air: 'Roll On, Silver Moon' by J.W. Turner.

As I went out from my cot at the close of the day,
  About the beginning of June,
By a Jessamine shade I beheld a fair maid,
  And she sadly complained to the moon.
'Roll on, silvery moon, guide the traveller's way,
  While the nightingale sings in full tune;
But never again with my lover I'll stray
  By the sweet silvery light of the moon.'

As the hart on the mountain my lover is brave,
  And so handsome, so manly, and clean,
So kind, so sincere, and he loved me so dear,
  Oh Eamon, thy equal was never yet seen.
But now he is dead and gone to his lone bed,
  Cut down like a flower in full bloom,
He had fallen asleep, and poor Jane's left to weep
  By the bright silvery light of the moon.

For he died for his country, my sweetheart so true,
  For Ireland he gave his young life,
He fell with our heroes, when mourners were few,
  Mid the rifle-fire, cannon and strife.
And his brothers-in-arms, 'neath that bright Easter sun,
  Fought and prayed that the dawn would come soon –
'Gainst the fierce, foreign foe, till the Vict'ry was won
  By the sweet silvery light of the moon.

Bishop O'Dwyer and Maxwell

Come. join me in my dir - ty work, wrote Eng - land's bu - tcher bold;___

You're re - bel priests with - in your See that love us not, I'm told,___

Re - move these men where ne - ver - more they'll threa - ten Eng - land's sway,___

And__ Eng - land's love and gra - ti - tude shall be your own for aye.___

'Come join me in my dirty work,'
  Wrote England's butcher bold;
'You've rebel priests within your See,
  That love us not, I'm told,
Remove those men, where never more,
  They'll threaten England's sway,
And England's love and gratitude
  Shall be your own for aye.'

Then answer made the brave O'Dwyer:
  'My laws are not as thine,
For yours condemn in ruthless haste,
  It is not so with mine.
Ere I'll accuse, I'll know the charge,
  The witness, place, and time,
And ere I'll punish, I'll have proof
  That there has been a crime.'

And quickly came the bogus charge,
  In humbler accents framed:
'Methought it needed not to prove,
  The guilt of those I named.
They've hearkened to the rebels' word,
  They've blessed the rebels' cause –
By voice and pen they've taught their flocks
  To spurn the Empire's laws.'

Our Bishop true, no longer now
  His anger can restrain;
His words are cutting as the scythe
  That reaps the harvest's grain:

In the aftermath of the Rising, General Maxwell demanded of the Irish Hierarchy that they should dismiss or silence priests who were sympathetic to the rebels. Bishop O'Dwyer of Limerick rejected the demand, and condemned him for his brutality in the suppression of the Rising.

Text: *Songs & Poems, The Rebels Who Fought and Died for Ireland in Easter Week, 1916* (Samuels Collection).
  Air: C. Desmond Greaves, *The Easter Rising in Song & Ballad*, Kahn & Averill, for the Workers' Music Association, London, 1980.

Bishop Thomas O'Dwyer

419

'These men you name are godly men,
    In act and thought guilt free –
They serve their God, and love their Land,
    And that's no crime to me.'

'And were their guilt as black as night,
    Don't think at your behest,
I'd join with those whose hands are dyed
    In blood of Ireland's best.
Full many a ruthless English cur
    Has held our land in thrall,
But history sure will write you down
    The blackest of them all.'

'And do you think that I forget
    My Country's martyred dead:
The brave, the pure, the high-souled lads,
    Whose blood you foully shed?
Then here's your answer: I may share
    The fate of those who died,
But I'll not be the first O'Dwyer
    To take the Tyrant's side.'

Descendant of a noble clan,
    May you be left us long –
Fearless and true to uphold our cause
    'Gainst tyrants cruel and strong.
They thought that every voice was stilled,
    That hearts were cold with fear,
No coward threats your heart could chill,
    Nor make your voice less clear.

And, oh! thank God that there are men,
    To speak with love and pride
Of those who be in prison cells
    And those who nobly died.
And where the glorious tale is told
    Of Ireland's latest fight,
In letters golden shall be writ:
    O'DWYER UPHELD THE RIGHT!

We'll Remember

Our Leaders starved and thirsted as they waited there to
  die,
Bare was the bitter prison ground where they were forced
  to lie –
We'll remember, we'll remember! Thank the God that we
  adore,
Having drunk the Wine of Martydom, our heroes thirst no
  more;
No longer do they hunger, for Above the Feast is spread,
And the rest is sweet in Heaven of our holy martyred Dead,
No tyrant's hate can hurt them now, they're safe with God,
  and yet –
We'll keep their sufferings in our hearts, and we shall not
  forget!

Uplifted on the winds of heaven their souls are free at last,
And though their bodies scornfully in prison clay were cast!
We'll remember, we'll remember! Hate for hate we
  backward fling,
Building in our faithful hearts for each the cairn of a King.
We shall place them with the highest in the Annals of our
  Land,
Through the Thunder of the Centuries their memory shall
  stand,
And we know no scorn can touch them wheresoe'er they lie
  – and yet
We'll keep those graves within our hearts, and we shall not
  forget!

Weep not for them with useless tears, but think of them
  with pride,
For Ireland they fought the fight, for her, with joy, they
  died.
We'll remember, we'll remember! their wounds, their blood,
  their pain,
Though we know no pang was wasted, nor one drop was
  shed in vain.
For our Country has awakened; we have heard the trumpet
  blast,
The traitor's power is shattered, and the sleep of slaves is
  past.
Lo! the Dead arise triumphant, and the Living's task is set –
The cause is burning in our hearts, and we shall not forget!

Text: Ballad sheet, National Library
of Ireland.

The Irish Green
(A Romance of Easter, 1916)

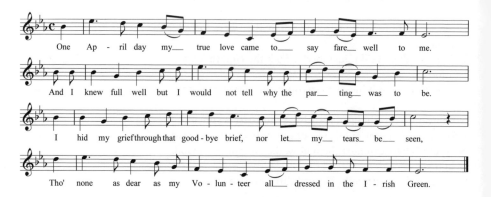

One   Ap - ril day   my__   true love came   to__   say   fare__ well   to   me.

And I   knew full well but I would   not tell why the par__ ting was to   be.

I   hid   my grief through that good - bye brief,   nor   let__   my__   tears__ be__   seen,

Tho' none   as dear   as my Vo - lun - teer   all__ dressed in the I - rish Green.

Text: Samuels Collection, TCD.
Air: 'The Jackets Green'.

One April day my true love came
    To say farewell to me.
And I knew full well but I would not tell
    Why the parting was to be.
I hid my grief through that good-bye brief,
    Nor let my tears be seen,
Tho' none as dear as my Volunteer –
    All dressed in the Irish Green.

The long hours passed, but no news came,
    From my own love brave and true.
That he'd gone to fight in Erin's name
    Was all I was told or knew.
And proud was I when his duty pressed,
    I did not go between,
But bid him go for freedom blest –
    'Neath the Orange, White and Green.

I heard the guns by the Liffey's side
    As they shrieked o'er Dublin's Town,
And I watched the flames rise to the skies,
    I did not feel cast down,
For my prayers were with my absent one
    That made my grief less keen.
I knew his duty had been done –
    As dressed in his Irish Green.

The waiting time is over now,
    They told me how he fell,
As he held the breach in a building, how
    That was stormed at by shot and shell,

But I do not weep but I think with pride
    Oh him who last I seen,
When he said good-bye and left my side –
    All dressed in his Irish Green.

The Mendicity Institute

Leo Maguire

Once in the twilight I walked beside a river,
The slow, dark Liffey that flows thro' Dublin Town;
And the wind from the sea made the waters quiver
As they flowed by an old house, all faded grey and brown.
Oh! This was once a proud house, all young and gay and sparkling
Where Lords and their Ladies lived and laughed and had no care;
To-night it's deserted and blank-faced and darkling,
With naught but ghostly whisperings within its chambers bare.

Lord Edward Fitzgerald and his young bride danced here,
And Ah! she was lovely! And Oh! he was gay!
And the wine flowed red and the music entranced here
And candles glittered by the score until the break of day.
Lord Moira stood here, where the ancient steps are crumbling,

The Mendicity Institute was established on the site of the home of Lord Moira, who had been a friend of Lord Edward Fitzgerald, the Commander-in-Chief of the armed forces of the United Irishmen in 1798, and of Fitzgerald's wife Pamela.

Text: Leo Maguire, *The Faithful and the Few*, Walton's Musical Instrument Galleries, Dublin, 1959.

The Mendicity Institute, facing the River Liffey on Usshers Island, before its demolition in the 1970s.

And wished them God-speed and watched them on their way;
And over the cobble stones the carriages went rumbling
And dawn came up and night-mists rolled out thro' Dublin Bay.

Aye! That was gay and that was grand, but not the crowning glory
Of this brave house; for once there came an Easter Monday morn
When the finest, proudest chapter in all its chequered story
Was writ in blood. Lord Edward's dying dream again was born
When Seán Heuston led his fighting men, and Oh! How few their numbers!
How poorly armed for battle as they tramped along the Quays!
But soon the crackling rifles roused the old house from its slumbers
While the green and white and orange flag swung proudly in the breeze.

Cuchulain at the Ford of Death faced never doom more surely
Than young Seán Heuston at his post on that clear April day;
But in his breast the ancient fire glowed steadily and purely,
And the spirit of Lord Edward was with him in the fray.
Night fell on the city and the bale-fires burned around them;
The roaring bomb-shells boomed a knell for many an Irish boy;
But dawn came struggling thro' the murk and dauntless still it found them,
The makers of a saga that nothing can destroy.

A few short days of glory and the gallant fight was ended;
The tattered flag was lowered and the barricades were down.
In all our country's story was never deed more splendid
Than Heuston's stand for freedom in storied Dublin town.
A mockery of a trial and the tale was well nigh finished;
They led him out to slaughter in all his youthful pride,
But Heuston faced the firing-squad with courage undiminished
And the spirit of Lord Edward was with him as he died.

Seán Heuston.

A Dublin Ballad – 1916

Dermot O'Byrne (1883–1953)

O write it up above your hearth
And troll it out to sun and moon,
To all true Irishmen on earth
Arrest and death come late or soon.

Some boy-o whistled *Ninety-eight*
One Sunday night in College Green,
And such a broth of love and hate
Was stirred ere Monday morn was late
As Dublin town had never seen.

And god-like forces shocked and shook
Through Irish hearts that lively day,
And hope it seemed no ill could brook.
Christ! for that liberty they took
There was the ancient deuce to pay!

The deuce in all his bravery,
His girth and gall grown no whit less,
He swarmed in from the fatal sea
With pomp of huge artillery
And brass and copper haughtiness.

He cracked up all the town with guns
That roared loud psalms to fire and death,
And houses hailed down granite tons
To smash our wounded underneath.

And when at last the golden bell
Of liberty was silenced, – then
He learned to shoot extremely well
At unarmed Irish gentlemen!

Ah! where were Michael and gold Moll
And Seumas and my drowsy self?
Why did fate blot us from the scroll?
Why were we left upon the shelf?

Fooling with trifles in the dark
When the light struck so wild and hard?
Sure our hearts were as good a mark
For Tommies up before the lark
At rifle practice in the yard!

Well, the last fire is trodden down,
Our dead are rotting fast in lime,
We all can sneak back into town,
Stravague about as in old time,

The tune that 'some boy-o' whistled was 'The Memory of the Dead', also known as 'Who Fears to Speak of '98?'. For the tune, see p. 88 and for a note on the consequences for performing it, see p. 481.

Text: Sir Arnold Bax, *A Dublin Ballad and Other Poems*, Candle Press, Dublin, 1918.

And stare at gaps of grey and blue
Where Lower Mount Street used to be,
And where flies hum round muck we knew
For Abbey Street and Eden Quay.

And when the devil's made us wise
Each in his own peculiar hell,
With desert hearts and drunken eyes
We're free to sentimentalize
By corners where the martyrs fell.

In Glencullen

Dermot O'Byrne

Mount Jerome (verse 1) is a cemetery
in the Harold's Cross district of
Dublin.

Text: Sir Arnold Bax, *A Dublin Ballad
and Other Poems*, Candle Press,
Dublin, 1918.

You can leave your slane to rust, old man,
  And stretch all day in bed;
No more I'll rinse out crock and pan,
  Or soak the flour for bread;
But think my fill of Mount Jerome
And a heap of nettles far from home
  Where Dan lies stiff and dead.

But first I'll burn the creepy-stool
  His little naked feet
Would dangle round and him from school
  (O! nice they were and neat!)
Yon creepy's pain that's fit to kill
Since Dan went whistling down the hill
  To die in Sackville Street.

The fluff may crawl about the floor
  And weeds whip in the thatch,
We'll twist no sods to stuff the door
  When big winds shake the latch,
The spuds may lie all in and out
For red fox-cubs to turn about
  And hares to paw and scratch.

No more he'll sing out through the fog
  To cheer a lambing sheep,
Nor drive the turf-cart from the bog,
  Nor rake the harvest heap,
Now earth is sick and sun gone mad
Ourselves may well lie down, old lad,
  And trust the saints for sleep.

426

After

Dermot O'Byrne

Last night I stumbled up and down
Through every quarter of the Town,
Hot hammers thumped inside my head
And soaring sparks of green and red
Stung at my eyes, and in my brain
Drink fought with memory in vain,
'Twas hell to think of going to bed!

And at the turn of Merrion Street
I found a man I used to meet
Among the poets of Rathgar,
And he was cursing sky and star,
And then he'ld stop awhile to damn
The place-names on a passing tram.

When he saw me his lips turned white
As moths on a midsummer night,
And then he laughed a bit and smote
His brow and muttered in his throat.

'My God,' he said, 'this is, I see,
Sure proof of immortality!
This man's as dead as anyone
That ever sinned beneath the sun,
And yet I hear his living feet
Knocking the stones of Merrion Street!

'My lively ghost, I have a tale
Will make your merry blood turn pale,
Each morning if you listen well
You'll feel a breeze blow up from hell
And bring from Richmond Yard the spit
Of shots that echo round and split
The sky as though 'twere suns that fell.

'Long strips of sky torn shed by shred
To bind the cerecloths of souls dead,
Mad souls that loved this tragic land
Better than God could understand.

'Now I've been drunk three nights and days
And swung out through a dizzy blaze
Of moons and suns as drunk as I
To the last corners of the sky.
But there's no place, I tell you plain,
Where you'll not hear that sound again,
The noise that makes a comrade die.'

Text: Sir Arnold Bax, *A Dublin Ballad and Other Poems*, Candle Press, Dublin, 1918.

He smiled a smile was all one side
And then he laughed and laughed and cried
'That day I wasn't there, my lad,
I'ld not the whimsy that some had
To barter all the estate of man,
The green world and life's lusty span
For Caitilin ni Hoolihan!'

Yet at that name his grey lips shook
Like the torn leaves of some old book
Left flapping on the window-sill,
And when his dry tongue clicked on still
Through rattling teeth 'I wasn't there,
I wasn't there, I wasn't there!'
His eyes were shrivelled up with fear.

I fled that babbling patriot,
His soul hitched to a rifle shot.
As through a funnel of red pain
The fumes were blown out from my brain,
And I went homeward to Clonskea
More sober than a man should be.

Muriel Brandt, 'The Breadline'. (Courtesy of The Crawford Gallery, Cork)

A Soldier's Song

Peadar Kearney

We'll sing a song, a soldier's song, with cheer-ing, rous-ing chor___ us,

As round our blaz-ing fires we throng, the star-ry heav-ens o'er us;

Im-pat-ient for the com-ing fight, and as we wait the morn-ing's light,

Here in the sil-ence of the night, we'll chant a sold-ier's song.

Chorus:

Sold_iers are we, whose lives are pledged to Ire-land; Some have come from a land be-yond the wave,

Sworn to be free, no more our anc-ient sire-land shall shel-ter the des-pot or the slave.

To-night we man the bear-na baoghail, in Er-in's cause, come woe or weal;

'Mid can-non's roar and rif le's peal, we'll chant a sold-ier's song.

We'll sing a song, a soldier's song,
With cheering, rousing chorus,
As round our blazing fires we throng,
The starry heavens o'er us;
Impatient for the coming fight,
And as we wait the morning's light,
Here in the silence of the night
We'll chant a soldier's song.

Chorus

Soldiers are we, whose lives are pledged to Ireland;
Some have come from a land beyond the wave,
Sworn to be free, no more our ancient sireland
Shall shelter the despot or the slave.
Tonight we man the *bearna baoghail*
In Erin's cause, come woe or weal;
'Mid cannon's roar and rifle's peal,
We'll chant a soldier's song.

Written in 1907 by Peadar Kearney, with music by Paddy Heeney, 'A Soldier's Song' was first published in 1912 in the newspaper *Irish Freedom*. It was first performed in public by the St James's Band at the graveside of Thomas Ashe in 1917.

Its use among the GPO garrison during the Rising led to its iconic status in Irish republican circles.

After the Rising it was frequently re-printed, sometimes with the sub-title 'Barricade Song of the Irish Volunteers, 1916'.

In her book *Doing my Bit for Ireland* (1917), Margaret Skinnider tells us:
'Here is the song of the Irish Volunteers, sung at all concerts held before the rising to get funds for rifles and ammunition. The Volunteers sang it whenever they marched, and I have been told the men in the rising of '67 also sang it. It was sung everywhere during

the last rising. When we first withdrew to the College of Surgeons, Frank Robins sang it, and we all joined in the chorus.

The air does not display any characteristically Irish features, and has been described recently as deriving more from mainstream European art music than from any native models.

Text and music: Sheet music published by Whelan & Son, Dublin. See p. 392 for an additional verse by Kearney, and p. 615 for a parody of the song.

In valley green, on towering crag,
　　Our fathers fought before us,
And conquered 'neath the same old flag
　　That's proudly floating o'er us.
　　　　We're children of a fighting race
　　　　That never yet has known disgrace,
　　　　And as we march the foe to face
　　　　　　We'll chant a soldier's song.

Sons of the Gael! Men of the Pale!
　　The long-watched day is breaking,
The serried ranks of Inisfail
　　Shall set the tyrant quaking.
　　　　Our camp fires now are burning low,
　　　　See, in the East a silv'ry glow,
　　　　Out yonder waits the Saxon foe,
　　　　　　So chant a soldier's song.

Amhrán na bhFiann
Translated : Liam Ó Rinn (1886–1943)

Peadar Kearney's song acquired such a celebrated status that in 1926, translated into Irish, it was adopted as the Irish national anthem.
　A shortened version of the air is used as the Presidential Salute.

Text: Website of the Department of the Taoiseach.

Seo díbh a chairde duan óglaigh,
Caithréimeach bríomhar ceolmhar,
Ár dtinte cnámh go buacach táid,
'S an spéir go mín réaltógach
Is fonnmhar faobhrach sinn chun gleo
'S go tiúnmhar glé roimh thíocht don ló
Faoi chiúnas chaomh na hoíche ar seol:
Seo libh canaigí Amhrán na bhFiann.

Curfá:
Sinne Fianna Fáil atá faoi gheall ag Éirinn,
Buíon dár slua thar toinn do ráinig chugainn.
Faoi mhóid bheith saor, seantír ár sinsir feasta
Ní fhágfar faoin tíorán ná faoin tráil
Anocht a théim sa bhearna baoil,
Le gean ar Ghaeil chun báis nó saoil
Le gunnascréach faoi lámhach na bpiléar
Seo libh canaigí Amhrán na bhFiann.

Cois bánta réidh, ar arda sléibhe,
Ba bhuach ár sinsir romhainn,
Ag lámhach go tréan faoin sárbhrat séin

Tá thuas sa ghaoth go seolta
Ba dhúchas riamh dár gcine cháidh
Gan iompáil siar ó imirt áir,
'S ag siúl mar iad i gcoinne namhad
Seo libh, canaigí Amhrán na bhFiann.

A bhuíon nach fann d'fhuil Ghaeil is Gall,
Sin breacadh lae na saoirse,
Ta sceimhle 's scanradh i gcroithe namhad,
Roimh ranna laochra ár dtíre.
Ár dtinte is tréith gan spréach anois,
Sin luisne ghlé san spéir anoir,
'S an bíobha i raon na bpiléar agaibh:
Seo libh, canaigí Amhrán na bhFiann.

Fonn na bhFiann

Árdóchaidh mé dhíbh, a cháirde croidhe
    Ámhrán na bhFiann, go spleódrach,
Annso dúinn cois na mbéilteach ngrinn,
    Fé dhíon na spéir-réalt n-órdha;
Go díoghraiseach toisc comhrac géar
    Bheith cinnte cughainn le breacadh an lae,
'S annso fé ciúneas mór na ré
    Árduighimís Dréacht na bhFiann!

Curfá
Sláinte geal na bhFiann, eochair-sgiath na Banban;
    Roinnt beag dínn ó chríoch thar lear i gcéin.
'Sé ár móid go fíor – gan Tír Chuinn d'fágaint feasta
    'Na fásgadh ag tíoráin' ná spréas.
Anocht féin seasfaimíd i mbearna 'n bhaoghail,
    Fé bhrat na nGaedheal le toil is mian;
Thar síon na cruaidhe, thar fuaim na bp'léar
    Árdóchaimíd fonn na bhFiann.

I ngleannta glas' 's ar árd-chraig duairc
    Do bhuaidh ár sinnsear romhainn
Fé'n sean-bhrat úd tá ár folumhain
    Go h-uaibhreach ós ár gcomhair
De threabhcas chalma chródha sinn
    Nár thaithigh riamh mío-chlú na ndaoi
'S ag tabhairt fé ár namhaid dúinn
    Árdóchaimíd fonn na bhFiann.

Liam Ó Rinn's was not the only
attempt at translating 'A Soldier's
Song' into Irish. This translation was
published anonymously in *The 1916
Song Book*, a small songster published
by the Irish Book Bureau, Dublin.

A chlanna Gaedheal! A ghasra an Pháil
   Tá fáinne 'n lae 'sna spéartha;
'S cuirfidh clanna Gaedheal fíor scáth
   Ar náimhdibh saoirse Éireann.
Ár dteinte táid 'nois éagtha fann;
   Béidh grian an lae ghil ann ar ball,
Ar aghaidh uainn thall thá slúagh na nGall,
   Árduighmís fonn na bhFiann!

The Cumann na mBan

Phil O'Neill (Sliabh Ruadh)

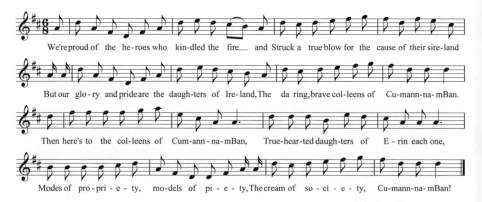

The Cumann na mBan (literally, 'Women's organization'), was an all-female paramilitary body formed in 1914 as an auxiliary to the recently established Irish Volunteers. During the Rising, as well as taking part in combat, they operated in intelligence, procurement, courier, despatch carrier and other roles. [LM]

Text: *New Songs, Ballads and Recitations*, Fergus O'Connor, n.d.
  Air: 'The Top of Cork Road'.

We're proud of the heroes who kindled the fire and
Struck a true blow for the cause of their sireland
But our glory and pride are the daughters of Ireland,
   The daring, brave Colleens of Cumann na mBan.
Then here's to the Colleens of Cumann na mBan,
True-hearted daughters of Erin each one,
   Modes of propriety,
   Models of piety,
   The cream of society, Cumann na mBan.

The khaki-clad maidens I oftentimes pity,
They seem out of place with the rest of our city;
No colleen more gracious, more graceful and witty
   Than those who the costume of Ireland put on.
Here's to the Colleens of Cumann na mBan
Who proved their devotion to them that are gone,
   Their services lending,
   On everyone tending,
   The flag, too, depending, brave Cumann na mBan.

They kept up our hearts when the stout ones were fading,
Bringing comfort to wounded with nursing and aiding
Through the grim gap of danger and death bravely wading,
    No truer colleens the sun ever shone on.
Here's to the colleens of Cumann na mBan,
Hearts true as gold and as pure as the swan,
    With time never missing,
    Expeditious at dressing,
    To Ireland a blessing, true Cumann na mBan.

Then here is a toast, and it gives me much pleasure
Their health to propose in a full flowing measure,
To those whom we all and our country treasure
    No matter what changes of time may come on.
Here's to the Colleens of Cumann na mBan,
May their Irish eyes soon see the long watched for dawn,
    Sweet modes of propriety,
    Models of piety,
    Cream of society, Cumann na mBan.

A party of Cumann na mBan on the march in Dublin.

'Tis Noble to Die for Ireland
Sliabh Ruadh (Phil O'Neill)

Text: *New Songs, Ballads and Recitations*, Fergus O'Connor, n.d.

'Tis noble to die for Ireland,
  To die for your native land,
And fearlessly fall by the foeman's ball,
  Marked by the martyr's brand;
What nobler death than life's last breath
  To give for the land you love?
And 'neath the folds while a shred still holds
  Of the flag that flies free above.

'Tis noble to die for Ireland,
  To die for the land of your birth,
For your blood is seed of a warrior breed
  That shall spring from Irish earth;
Tho' no trophies wave above your grave,
  Nor monument marks the mound
In days to be a nation free
  Shall guard it as sacred ground.

What nobler end than to yield one's life,
  Our mother to enthrone,
And by dying prove your lasting love
  To her and to her alone?
What nobler tomb – 'neath the heather bloom –
  The rugged mountain side?
Where often before in days of yore,
  Our forefathers fought and died.

What a glorious death to stand before
  The rifles at silvery dawn,
And an honoured name to give to fame
  For Caitlín Ní hUalacháin.
Oh, happy are those who thus repose
  Who Freedom's fire has fanned,
For though dead and gone their spirit lives on,
  Who died for their native land.

The Men of Easter Week
Phil O'Neill

Text: Samuels Collection, TCD.

As children of a suffering land, we always look with pride,
On those who for our country's cause have nobly fought and died,

The men who strove from age to age to set their country free
And perished on the battle-field or on the scaffold tree,
And now with those who thus repose, we'll reckon all who bled
Our chains to break, in Easter week, with Ireland's Martyred Dead.

For ne'er is Ireland's glorious list full writ or nigh complete,
Until it tells of fearless men who fell in Dublin's Street,
And raised once more with hopeful hearts our country's flag on high,
And showed that Ireland still has sons prepared to do or die,
And on our future history's page an epoch bright they'll mark,
To head that band for aye will stand McDonagh, Pearse and Clarke.

We'll tell of Heuston, Plunkett, Kent and Connolly we'll name
Whose names as heroes e'er will shine on Ireland's roll of fame,
McDermott, Mallin, Hannrachain, Daly, Colbert and McBride,
Are men who for our country's cause have nobly bled and died,
It shows to-day, that come what may our country always bred,
Hearts true and bold, like those of old, our country's martyred dead.

Then brothers all, be proud of those who fell in Easter week,
Be yours the task upon their foes a vengeance dire to wreak,
Resolve to-day within your hearts, some day your faith to show,
When Freedom's slogan calls again to deal a gallant blow,
For the blood of men must flow again though orphans tears are shed,
Till a nation free the shrine shall be of Ireland's Martyred dead.

At the Parnell monument at the north end of O'Connell Street, two British soldiers display the flag that had flown over the GPO. It is being deliberately held upside-down to dishonour it.

Rally Round the Banner, Boys!

Phil O'Neill

Text: *The 1916 Song Book*, Irish Book Bureau, Dublin, n.d.

Rally round the banner, boys,
    That now above us flies;
The die is cast, the night is past,
    The dawn is in the skies.
Come forth each one, each stalwart son,
    For Freedom calls again,
And see! her standard proudly flies
    O'er twice ten thousand men.

Chorus
Rally round the banner, boys,
    That now above us flies;
The die is cast, the night is past,
    The dawn is in the skies.

What care we for the tyrant's power!
    Our hearts are staunch and true.
Be ours the task to show once more
    What Irishmen can do.
Let coward and hireling stand aside,
    To linger still as slaves,
While we march on to Freedom's goal,
    Where Ireland's banner waves.

Then forward men! On, on again!
    Stout ships are on the sea,
And let us show the ancient foe
    That Ireland must be free!
And while our banner floats on high,
    Let every true man swear
To give his life in Freedom's strife
    To keep it floating there.

Come creed and clan, come every man;
    We stand for Ireland all;
If from her chains she'll soon be free,
    What matter if we fall?
Our flag unrolled – green, white and gold –
    Inspired with hope once more,
While we march on to greet the dawn,
    For slavery's night is o'er!

The King of Ireland
Dedicated to De Valera

When we were little children, Johnnie Redmond was a fool;   Text: Samuels Collection, TCD.
He told us to be satisfied with something called Home Rule;
But we have learned a thing or two since we attended school.
  And we want a republic now in Ireland.
But still, had we the proper man, a monarch we might crown,
For the Empire, with its army and its navy, will go down,
And I know a man who'd suit us and who fought in Dublin
  Town,
  The invincible and gallant De Valera.

Chorus
So, Up De Valera! He's the champion of the right:
We'll follow him to battle 'neath the orange, green and white.
When next we tackle England we will beat her in the fight,
  And we'll crown De Valera King of Ireland!

'Twas in Ringsend and Boland's De Valera took his stand;
A hundred of the boys at most were under his command,
Still, I fear the 'Tommies' thereabouts went slightly 'out of hand',
  But you wouldn't put the blame on De Valera.
On Wednesday, when the British fired their shells in British style,
Their lovely aim made De Valera's men begin to smile;
And, if that was the effect upon the common 'rank and file',
  Imagine, now, the grin on De Valera.

A great day for Ireland will be the crowning day,
The boys from every county will be there in great array –
From Donegal to Kerry, and from Clare to Dublin Bay,
  We will gather in the fighting men of Ireland.
There'll be gun-men and pike-men, with pipers on before,
We'll carry weapons openly, as in the days of yore:
The 'Defence of the Realm' won't be heard of any more,
  When we crown De Valera King of Ireland!

We think Sir Douglas Haig is trying to do his very best,
With his 'pushing' and his 'nibbling' on the front that's 'going
  West';
But nobody would blame him if he had a little rest,
  And came for a holiday to Ireland.
If De Valera took his place and tried to bate the Hun,
With Irish boys behind him, he could make the Germans run;
But John Bull's our only enemy, and when he's dead and gone
  We will still have De Valera here in Ireland.

437

Wrap the Green Flag Round Me Boys
Dedicated to Major John MacBride
J.K. O'Reilly

Oh,— wrap the Green Flag round me,— boys, to die were far more sweet

With— E - rin's no - ble em - blem,— boys, to be my win - ding sheet.

In life I longed to see it wave and fol— low— where it led,

But— now my eyes grow dim, my— hand would grasp its last bright shred.

Chorus
Oh, wrap the Green Flag round me, boys, to die— were— far more sweet

With— E - rin's no - ble em - blem,— boys, to be my win - ding sheet.

Text and air: Sheet music accessed at the website of the Irish Traditional Music Archive. www.itma.ie

Wrap the Green Flag round me boys,
    To die were far more sweet
With Erin's noble emblem, boys,
    To be my winding sheet.
In life I loved to see it wave,
    And follow where it led,
But now my eyes grow dim, my hand
    Would grasp its last bright shred.

Chorus
Oh, wrap the Green Flag round me, boys,
    To die were far more sweet
With Erin's noble emblem, boys,
    To be my winding sheet.

And I had hoped to meet you, boys
    On many a well-fought field,
When to our sacred banner, boys,
    The traitorous foe would yield.
But now, alas! I am denied
    My dearest earthly prayer,
You'll follow and you'll meet the foe,
    But I shall not be there.

But though my body moulders, boys
    My spirit will be free,
And every comrade's honour, boys,
    Will yet be dear to me.
And in the thick and bloody fight
    Let not your courage lag,
For I'll be there and hovering near
    Around the dear old flag.

The Flag on the G.P.O.
Easter 1917
J.J. Walsh (1880–1948)

Why gather the crowd in O'Connell Street?
    Why throng all the people there?
What eminent personage do they greet?
    With the shouts that fill the air?
Who comes this morning or what's to be seen
    That they hurry and push them so?
'Tis the rebel standard – white, orange and green
    That floats from the G. P. O.

With a message of hope it defiantly flies
    From the sullen and smoke-stained walls,
And moist are most of the watchers' eyes
    For a sacrifice brave it recalls;
But that soul-stirring cheer that rings out on the air
    Is a shout of revenge on the foe,
That tells him that men are still ready to dare
    For the flag on the G. P. O.

It brings back thoughts of another year
    When comrades marched side by side
And stood in that breach without falter or fear
    And gallantly fought and died,
And the flag seems to say 'Persevere to the end'
    Till the harvest again you mow,
When the manhood of Ireland again will defend
    The flag on the G. P. O.

Text: Samuels Collection, TCD.

A soldier guards the ruins of the GPO after the rebellion. (By permission of the Royal Irish Academy © RIA.)

The Old G.P.O.
M.J. MacManus (1888–1951)

Men lighted here a Paschal flame
To cleanse away a nation's shame.
It blazed a week, that Easter fire,
And then became their funeral pyre.

Text: M.J. MacManus, *Dublin Diversions*, Talbot Press, Dublin, 1928.

Éire – After the Storm
To Countess Markievicz
May, 1916
Maeve Cavanagh

Defiant still, though scarred by War's fierce passion
 In glorious unrepentance Ireland stands,
Her ruins stark repelling all compassion,
 Her broken sword still clasping in her hands.
Failure? Not so – no sigh her great heart troubles,
 No tears her brave eyes mar – Hope still reigns there;
This day and hence her lust for Freedom doubles
 E'en now she stoops to build up and prepare.
Though round her feet her martyred dead are lying,
 See from their blood her soul new life drinks in.
Stronger she'll rise from this last crucifying
 In Fate's despite she'll fight again and WIN.

Text: Maeve Cavanagh, *A Voice of Insurgency*, Dublin, 1916.

The Men of Dublin

They nailed their colours to the mast, the Orange, White
 and Green,
A nobler set of Irishmen the world has never seen;
They knew through sloth and idleness a nation's soul was
 lost,
They rose to save dear Ireland's soul and counted not the cost.

They knew well that two thousand men – they did not
 number more –
Could never break the tyrant's chain and drive him from
 our shore;

Text: *Songs & Poems, The Rebels Who Fought and Died for Ireland in Easter Week, 1916* (Samuels Collection, TCD).

441

But this they knew, and knew it well, they would not die in vain –
Their blood would save our Country's soul and give her life again.

Who was it led this noble band, and what has been their fate?
Was mercy shown to them at last? No, worse than Ninety-eight.
They fought 'gainst overwhelming odds and held them well at bay,
Till Britain swore that she would make the innocent to pay.

She swore that she would shell the town until its streets ran red,
And every inch was piled up high with dying and with dead.
Commandants Pearse and Connolly, Joe Plunkett and Tom
   Clarke,
To save the town, surrendered – it was unsafe at dark.

For woe betide the mortals who went abroad at night,
The soldiers lay in ambush hid and shot them down at sight;
They shot the women and the men, they shot the children too,
The 'DEFENDER OF SMALL NATIONS' showed herself in
   colours true.

For when all had surrendered there began a reign of blood
Unequalled in the history of the world since the flood;
The Brothers Pearse and Daly, young Colbert and Tom Clarke,
With Eamonn Ceannt and Connolly were shot down off the
   mark.

The same fate met young Heuston, MacDonagh and MacBride,
But 'twas outside the GPO the brave O'Rahilly died;
Mallon, Plunkett and McDermott fell before a firing squad,
Their blood with Miceal Hanrahan's, for vengeance cries to God.

Large numbers too were sentenced and treated as convicts,
Among them was a woman, the Countess Markievicz;
Gold could not buy those who fought for Ireland thro' that week,
And they to make their sacrifice no purer Cause could seek.

Enshrined are they for ever in every Irish heart,
God bless those men and women who played that noble part –
Who left their homes behind them, who left their kith and kin,
And rallied round their banner when the fighting did begin.

May their memory live forever; may our children bless the name
Of each one who fought for Ireland; may it ever be the same.
May our country still have heroes who are not afraid to die
On the battlefield or scaffold so our proud old flag may fly.

What Do You Think?

What do you think of the Irish now?
   (Who is it makes the noise?)
What do you think of the Knights of old?
What do you think of the heroes bold?
   What do you think of the boys?

What do you think of poor Emmet, too?
   (Never a word of Tone) –
What do you think of the life he gave?
What of the land he died to save?
   What of the uncarved stone?

What do you think of the glorious past?
   (Haven't we much to brag?)
What do you think of the Rope and Rack?
What do you think of the Union Jack?
   What do you think of the Flag?

What do you think of the dogs of war?
   (Britain shall rule the waves);
What do you think about England's foes?
What do you think of the land she rules?
   What do you think of her slaves?

What do you think of the German crew?
   (Do we not love the Gaul?)
What do you think? – It's a sorry job! –
How do you feel for the Irish mob?
   What do you think of them all?

What do we think of the Empire great?
   (See how we scrape and bow?)
What of 'our brothers across the foam'?
What of the Britisher's 'ruined home'?
   What do you think of them now?

What do you think of the olden days –
   Honoured in tale and verse?
What of the songs our fathers sung?
What do you think of the Irish Tongue?
   What do you think of the Erse?

What do you think of the Sean Bhean Bhocht?
   (How she will cease to wail!)
What of the desolate Irish coasts?

This song was probably inspired by the music-hall item at p. 30. The 'uncarved stone' (verse 2) refers to Robert Emmet's request at the end of his famous speech from the dock:

'I have but one request to ask at my departure from this world; it is—the charity of its silence. Let no man write my epitaph; for as no man who knows my motives dare now vindicate them, let not prejudice or ignorance asperse them. Let them and me rest in obscurity and peace, and my name remain uninscribed, until other times and other men can do justice to my character. When my country takes her place among the nations of the earth, then, and not till then, let my epitaph be written.'

Text: *Songs & Poems, The Rebels Who Fought and Died for Ireland in Easter Week, 1916* (Samuels Collection, TCD).

What do you think of the Rebel hosts?
What do you think of the Gael?

What do you think of the Irish now?
(Makers of all the noise),
What do you think of the Red Branch Knights?
What do you think of the Redmondites?
What do you think of the boys?

Resurrection

Pádraig de Brún (1889–1960)

Text: This poem exists in at least three quite different versions. The one here was included in Edna C. Fitzhenry's *Nineteen-Sixteen Anthology*, Browne & Nolan, Dublin, 1935.

The others, entitled 'Easter 1916' and 'Dublin 1916' can be found, respectively, on a ballad sheet in the Samuels Collection in TCD, and in *Songs & Poems, The Rebels Who Fought and Died for Ireland in Easter Week, 1916.*

Our day has seen the sacred fire again
Burst into flame, and from the new-born glow
We have re-lit the lamp within our souls,
Like the church tapers lighted row on row,
On Easter Saturday from the Paschal coals,
                And anxious throbs of pain
Are in the hearts that question their past mood
Of lethargy, remorseful that they slept,
While up the East another morn had crept
For watchers who had faith in nationhood.

But they, the faithful ones, are gone; they lie
In a strange bed, beneath a prison yard,
After the night of vigil, taking rest,
Outwearied sentries, now relieved from guard.
Quenched is the flame of passion in the breast
                And stilled the battle-cry,
That rang out clear at the red dawn of flame.
For darkness fell upon their day of strife,
And haughty courage and impetuous life
Were buried in a common pit of shame.

Their eyes were straining for the help to come
Over the sea, as in a far-off day
Men waited for the ships of Spain or France
Bearing on Bantry or Killala Bay;
And when none came, by force of evil chance,
                They dreaded that the sum
Of all their efforts would be as a wave
Broken to foam in one mad surging beat,
Like Emmet's handful in the Castle street,
And not a thrill would stir the passing slave.

All failed them but the strength of dauntless will
And mystic ardour that within them burned
To feel themselves the last-born chivalry
Of the Dark Rose, who had again returned
To band her knights in high-souled rivalry
       Her triumph to fulfil.
What though death's portal should before them loom,
And shadows hang around the path they trod,
They would press through to join the hosts of God
That shall be marshalled at the Day of Doom.

The burst of Spring has overswept the land
With irony of budding life, while they,
The life of Ireland's life, are lying cold
Under the Earth and mouldering to decay
With all who in that struggle centuries old
       Made the same fearless stand;
And we remain, in whom no hopes of Spring
Arise, and from whom all delight is fled
In life, which seems but shame since they are dead,
Careless what fate the morrow to us bring.

Yet from the dead speaks one with pale calm brow,
Most beautiful, who in a weakened frame
Possessed a heart of fire – I see his face,
And startled whisper Sean MacDermot's name –
As when I held him in a last embrace,
       His voice comes to me now,
Upbraiding me for toying with despair
And words compassionate, mere waste of breath
For one who never wavered unto death,
But passed to wait for me in God's clear air.

Seán Mac Diarmada.

And though this idle tribute of our tears
We pay to those who fell, we know 'tis vain;
For they have died with proud, unflinching gaze,
Glad that in death they wiped away the stain
Of servitude that marked us in the ways
       Of past disgraceful years,
And linked our time to ages long ago,
And chiefs who never to false altars bowed,
Whom gifts had never won nor threats had cowed,
Emmet and Tone, Sarsfield and Owen Roe.

Like Naoise when enmeshed by hunter's toils,
Or grim Cuchulainn battling with the sea,
They fought with souls that knew not of defeat,

445

That could in failure shout for victory,
Though for them came no years with memories sweet,
 Nor wealth of battle spoils.
A firing party and a bed of lime
Were all that fortune gave them in return,
And only with faith's ear could they discern
The songs of freedom in the coming time.

They have but died to strengthen our belief
That the Dark Rose can never die or fade;
Though failure and eclipse be now her lot,
The glory dimmed wherewith she was arrayed,
And she for her brave dead in some lone spot
 Lie folded up in grief,
The watchers of the coast shall yet behold
Her ship returning on a landward tide,
And send her word imperious far and wide,
Calling her Knights to battle as of old.

Resurrection of Ireland

J.J. Burke & J.J. Hughes

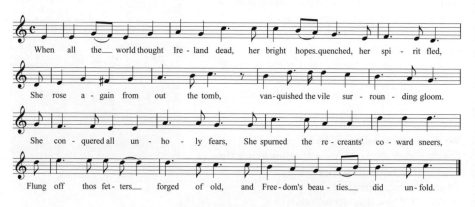

Text and air: Sheet music published by
Whelan & Son, Dublin, n.d.

When all the world thought Ireland dead,
Her bright hopes quenched, her spirit fled,
She rose again from out the tomb,
Vanquished the vile surrounding gloom.
She conquered all unholy fears,
She spurned the recreants' coward sneers,
Flung off those fetters forged of old,
And Freedom's beauties did unfold.

The men who were for Ireland slain,
They have not died for her in vain,
Though slaughtered in an Empire's wrath,
They've shown a nation Freedom's path.
Sold, kissed by Judas sadly shamed.
Deceived, degraded and defamed,
There was no other way to free,
Our Country but on Calvary.

Oh! Resurrected freedom fair,
Always may Ireland worship there.
Always with us be men to give,
Their lives that this our Country live.
To keep our land, our people true,
Like those who died for Her and You,
And guard for aye that flag whose rays,
Illumined those glorious Easter Days.

Easter Week
Eva Gore-Booth

Grief for the noble dead
Of one who did not share their strife,
And mourned that any blood was shed,
Yet felt the broken glory of their state,
Their strange heroic questioning of Fate
Ribbon with gold the rags of this our life.

Text: Eva Gore-Booth, *Poems of Eva Gore-Booth*, Longmans, Green & Co., London, 1929.

Heroic Death, 1916
Eva Gore-Booth

Na man shall deck their resting-place with flowers;
    Behind a prison wall they stood to die,
Yet in those flowerless tragic graves of ours
    Buried, the broken dreams of Ireland lie.

No cairn-heaped mound on a high windy hill
    With Irish earth the hero's heart enfolds,
But a burning grave at Pentonville,
    The broken heart of Ireland holds.

Ah! ye who slay the body, how man's soul
    Rises above your hatred and your scorns –
All flowers fade as the years onward roll,
    Theirs is the deathless wreath – a crown of thorns.

Text: Eva Gore-Booth, *Poems of Eva Gore-Booth*, Longmans, Green & Co., London, 1929.

447

Dublin

Text: *The 1916 Song Book*, Irish Book
Bureau, Dublin, n.d.

You poured your spies upon her streets,
    You ringed her round with steel;
For three most hideous centuries
    She lay beneath your heel.
You kept your forces round her gates,
    And built your barracks well,
And in your Castle's heart devised
    Foul deeds – too foul for hell.

And there you planned the Epitaph
    Of Ireland, day by day,
And watched our people fade and die,
    Our language pass away.
And undisturbed, and all secure,
    You sat the centuries,
And boasted of our loyalty,
    And fed the world with lies.

But Dublin tore from off her face
    The horrid mask she wore,
And all the nations saw again
    Her beauty as before.
She hurled you from your tyrant's seat,
    And clothed in flame and lead,
She stood, a captive unenslaved,
    And risen from the dead.

Sinn Fein Rebellion 1916.
D.B.C. Sackville Street, Dublin.

And though a few sad days will pass
   Till she is wholly free,
And though you claim her once again,
   God holds her destiny.
For He shall smite you to the earth,
   And raise her on a throne,
And for those ages of despair
   That triumph shall atone.

My Brief
Desmond Crean

I hold a brief for men who used the gun,
Who waged guerrilla war against the foe,
If blame must be assigned for war and hate,
The guilt rests with usurpers of the State.
They crushed the Gael, they confiscated lands,
They plundered ruthlessly with blood-stained hands,
Imprisoned, exiled, all who stood for right,
Illumed with burning homes the darkened night,
Did sanction, execute and thus fulfil
An alien rule against a Nation's will.
Till outraged justice bowed her sorrowed head,
And placed a shroud of mourning o'er the dead.
It is to those alone who wrought such wrongs,
I claim in justice that all blame belongs,
As right is right, in every age and clime,
So wrong is wrong, though law condones the crime.

I hold a brief for men who stood the test,
The pioneers of Irish Ireland thought,
Who laboured ceaselessly with racial pride,
Who faced the squads in Easter Week and died.
Died praying that their countrymen might see
The narrow suffering path that leads men free,
Who trod the scaffold, who in ambush fell,
Who hungered unto death in prison cell,
Till Erin in despair en masse arose
And waged guerrilla war against her foes.
Each man that fell, another took his place,
Unconquerable, symbolic of the race,
When despots found brute force of little use,
Then bitter foes with honour signed a truce.
Ye dead and living, who through years of grief
Fought to be free – with pride I hold your brief.

Text: Desmond Crean, *Songs of an Old IRA Man,* Frederick Press, Dublin, 1939.

A Litany, 1916

Teresa Brayton

Text: Teresa Brayton, *The Flame of Ireland*, New York, 1926.

Chant their names and tell their story,
They who died for Ireland's glory;
Breathe no sigh and shed no tear,
Hero souls are hovering near.

Chant their names as high priests might
Solemn canticle recite;
Tell their deeds as might be told
Michael's warrior deeds of old.

Speak their names until we see
The high-hearted company
Pass before our eyes tonight,
Ireland's claim in blood to write.

Ireland's claim, a ransomed nation,
Writ in deathless proclamation;
Ireland's name, a slogan hurled
Through the war camps of the world.

Chant them slowly, name by name,
Each a bead of living flame,
Each a bead of Victory,
Gemming Ireland's Rosary.

Patrick Pearse, for high deeds fashioned,
Dying for his dream empassioned;
Dauntless son of Liberty,
Lion-hearted Connolly;

Clarke, whose soul an English hell
Half a lifetime could not quell,
Fallen with his battle blade
Red on Ireland's barricade;

Colbert, Tom and Eamon Kent,
Heuston, broke but never bent;
Staunch to dare and swift to plan
John MacBride, O'Hanrahan;

Willie Pearse, his young days done;
Tom MacDonagh, Skeffington;
Mallon – patriot, husband, sire;
Plunkett with his song afire;

Sean McDermott, joyous, daring;
Daly, far from Munster faring;
The O'Rahilly, whose sword
Flashed the young Republic's word;

Casement, on a scaffold deck,
England's rope around his neck;
Ashe, by murderous hands down borne,
Dying in his cell forlorn.

Chant their glorious Litany,
Names that made and hold us free;
Chant them with uplifted head,
They are conquerors, Ireland's dead!

The executed leaders of the Rising.

Front (l-r): Pádraic Pearse, John MacBride, Tom Clarke, Éamonn Ceannt, James Connolly and Joseph Plunkett.
Rear (l-r): Willie Pearse, Thomas McDonagh, Sean Heuston, Michael Mallin, Seán Mac Diarmada, Michael O'Hanrahan, Edward Daly and Con Colbert.
On the wall behind can be seen pictures of Roger Casement and Thomas Kent.

Remembrance
M.J. MacManus

Text: M.J. MacManus, *Dublin Diversions*, Talbot Press, Dublin, 1928.

I fear there was something very wrong
   With that little war of ours,
Or we would laud its deeds with song
   And pretty flags and flowers.
It wasn't, I think, a respectable war,
   A really proper, civilized war,
It was, in fact, an amateur war,
   That little war of ours.

We had no uniforms at all
   (A thing that isn't done),
And we never hearkened to the call
   To go and fight the Hun.
But we fought at home a raggedy war,
   A most unpleasant, unmannerly war,
In fact, a most un-English war,
   That little war we won.

We honour Dublin's Fusiliers
   (Right gallantly they fell
When the cry went up for volunteers
   To storm the gates of hell).
But that was a really glorious war,
   A rescue-poor-little-Belgium war,
An altogether different war
   From the war in Dublin town.

If ever we shoulder guns again
   When the gage of war is thrown,
We'll find a nation smaller far
   (If possible) than our own.
And when it's attacked we'll wage a war,
   A world-safe-for-democracy war,
A high, religious, heavenly war,
   A war unlike our own.

And then the flowers will blossom red
   In the streets of Dublin town,
And our lame and crippled and blind and dead
   Will be men of high renown.
But it must be a really respectable war,
   An orderly, capitalistic war,
A God-damned, hypocritical war
   To be honoured in Dublin town.

For Ireland Alone

Not for the cause of faithless France,
　　Nor grasping Britain's greed;
Nor for the Russian Bear's advance
　　Was done this glorious deed.
Against grim foes at home they rose,
　　In manly patriot pride,
And though that birth was crushed to earth,
　　For Ireland's rights they died.

Not by the far-off Dardanelles,
　　Nor slimy Tigris' banks,
Nor mid the din of pagan yells
　　Went down their bleeding ranks.
O'er sainted ground, with glory crowned,
　　Rolled on the battle-tide,
And proudly, brave, their homes to save,
　　On Ireland's soil they died.

Text: *The 1916 Song Book*,
Irish Book Bureau, Dublin, n.d.

The Rose Tree
W.B. Yeats

'O words are lightly spoken,'
Said Pearse to Connolly,
'Maybe a breath of politic words
Has withered our Rose Tree;
Or maybe but a wind that blows
Across the bitter sea.'

'It needs to be but watered,'
James Connolly replied,
'To make the green come out again
And spread on every side,
And shake the blossom from the bud
To be the garden's pride.'

'But where can we draw water,'
Said Pearse to Connolly,
'When all the wells are parched away?
O plain as plain can be
There's nothing but our own red blood
Can make a right Rose Tree.'

Text: W.B. Yeats, *The Poems*,
Everyman, London, 1992.

Three Songs to the One Burden
W.B. Yeats

III

Text: W.B. Yeats, *The Poems*,
Everyman, London, 1992.

Come gather round me players all:
Come praise Nineteen-Sixteen,
Those from the pit and gallery
Or from the painted scene
That fought in the Post Office
Or round the City Hall,
Praise every man that came again,
Praise every man that fell.

From mountain to mountain ride the fierce horsemen.

Who was the first man shot that day?
The player Connolly,
Close to the City Hall he died;
Carriage and voice had he;
He lacked those years that go with skill
But later might have been
A famous, a brilliant figure
Before the painted scene.

From mountain to mountain ride the fierce horsemen.

Some had no thought of victory
But had gone out to die
That Ireland's mind be greater,
Her heart mount up on high;
And no one knows what's yet to come
For Patrick Pearse had said
That in every generation
Must Ireland's blood be shed.

From mountain to mountain ride the fierce horsemen.

Easter, 1916
W.B. Yeats

Text: W.B. Yeats, *The Poems*,
Everyman, London, 1992.

I have met them at close of day
Coming with vivid faces
From counter or desk among grey
Eighteenth-century houses.
I have passed with a nod of the head
Or polite meaningless words,
Or have lingered awhile and said

Polite meaningless words,
And thought before I had done
Of a mocking tale or a gibe
To please a companion
Around the fire at the club,
Being certain that they and I
But lived where motley is worn:
All changed, changed utterly:
A terrible beauty is born.

That woman's days were spent
In ignorant good-will,
Her nights in argument
Until her voice grew shrill.
What voice more sweet than hers
When, young and beautiful,
She rode to harriers?
This man had kept a school
And rode our wingèd horse;
This other his helper and friend
Was coming into his force;
He might have won fame in the end,
So sensitive his nature seemed,
So daring and sweet his thought.
This other man I had dreamed
A drunken, vainglorious lout.
He had done most bitter wrong
To some who are near my heart,
Yet I number him in the song;
He, too, has resigned his part
In the casual comedy;
He, too, has been changed in his turn,
Transformed utterly:
A terrible beauty is born.

Hearts with one purpose alone
Through summer and winter seem
Enchanted to a stone
To trouble the living stream.
The horse that comes from the road,
The rider, the birds that range
From cloud to tumbling cloud,
Minute by minute they change;
A shadow of cloud on the stream
Changes minute by minute;
A horse-hoof slides on the brim,
And a horse plashes within it;

The long-legged moor-hens dive,
And hens to moor-cocks call;
Minute by minute they live:
The stone's in the midst of all.

Too long a sacrifice
Can make a stone of the heart.
O when may it suffice?
That is Heaven's part, our part
To murmur name upon name,
As a mother names her child
When sleep at last has come
On limbs that had run wild.
What is it but nightfall?
No, no, not night but death;
Was it needless death after all?
For England may keep faith
For all that is done and said.
We know their dream; enough
To know they dreamed and are dead;
And what if excess of love
Bewildered them till they died?
I write it out in a verse –
MacDonagh and MacBride
And Connolly and Pearse
Now and in time to be,
Wherever green is worn,
Are changed, changed utterly:
A terrible beauty is born.

The Statues
W.B. Yeats

Text: W.B. Yeats, *The Poems*, Everyman, London, 1992.

Pythagoras planned it. Why did the people stare?
His numbers, though they moved or seemed to move
In marble or in bronze, lacked character.
But boys and girls pale from the imagined love
Of solitary beds knew what they were,
That passion could bring character enough;
And pressed at midnight in some public place
Live lips upon a plummet-measured face.

No; greater than Pythagoras, for the men
That with a mallet or a chisel modelled these
Calculations that look but casual flesh, put down
All Asiatic vague immensities,

And not the banks of oars that swam upon
The many-headed foam at Salamis.
Europe put off that foam when Phidias
Gave women dreams and dreams their looking-glass.

One image crossed the many-headed, sat
Under the tropic shade, grew round and slow,
No Hamlet thin from eating flies, a fat
Dreamer of the Middle Ages. Empty eyeballs knew
That knowledge increases unreality, that
Mirror on mirror mirrored is all the show.
When gong and conch declare the hour to bless
Grimalkin crawls to Buddha's emptiness.

When Pearse summoned Cuchulain to his side,
What stalked through the Post Office? What intellect,
What calculation, number, measurement, replied?
We Irish, born into that ancient sect
But thrown upon this filthy modern tide
And by its formless spawning fury wrecked,
Climb to our proper dark, that we may trace
The lineaments of a plummet-measured face.

Sixteen Dead Men
W.B. Yeats

O but we talked at large before
The sixteen men were shot,
But who can talk of give and take,
What should be and what not
While those dead men are loitering there
To stir the boiling pot?

You say that we should still the land
Till Germany's overcome;
But who is there to argue that
Now Pearse is deaf and dumb?
And is their logic to outweigh
MacDonagh's bony thumb?

How could you dream they'd listen
That have an ear alone
For those new comrades they have found,
Lord Edward and Wolfe Tone,
Or meddle with our give and take
That converse bone to bone?

Text: W.B. Yeats, *The Poems*,
Everyman, London, 1992.

Sixteen Dead Men
Dora Sigerson (1866–1918)

Text: Dora Sigerson, *Poems of the Irish Rebellion 1916*, Maunsel and Company, Dublin, 1916. The poem was re-printed in September the following year in *Aftermath of Easter Week*, published for the benefit of the Irish National Aid And Volunteers' Dependents Fund. See p. 474.

Hark! in the still night. Who goes there?
   'Fifteen dead men.' Why do they wait?
'Hasten, comrade, death is so fair.'
   Now comes their Captain through the main gate.

Sixteen dead men! What on their sword?
   'A Nation's honour proud do they bear.'
What on their bent heads? *'God's holy word:*
   All of their nation's heart blended in prayer.'

Sixteen dead men! What makes their shroud?
   'All of their nation's love wraps them around.'
Where do their bodies lie, brave and so proud?
   'Under the gallows-tree in prison ground.'

Sixteen dead men! Where do they go?
   'To join their regiment, where Sarsfield leads;
Wolfe Tone and Emmet, too, well do they know:
   There shall they bivouac, telling great deeds.'

Sixteen dead men! Shall they return?
   'Yea, they shall come again, breath of our breath.
They on our Nation's hearth made old fires burn,
   Guard her unconquered soul, strong in their death.'

The Sacred Fire
Dora Sigerson

Text: Dora Sigerson, *Poems of the Irish Rebellion 1916*, Maunsel and Company, Dublin, 1916.

They lit a fire within their land that long was ashes cold,
With splendid dreams they made it glow, threw in their hearts
   of gold.
They saw thy slowly paling cheek and knew thy failing breath,
They bade thee live once more, Kathleen, who was so nigh to
   death.

And who dare quench the sacred fire, and who dare give them
   blame,
Since he who draws too near the glow shall break into a flame?
They lit a beacon in their land, built of the souls of men,
To make thee warm once more, Kathleen, to bid thee live again.

The Story Without End
Dora Sigerson

Before my time my kindred were as felons in their land,
Because they claimed the liberty that freemen understand.

Ere I was born in Dublin town men's hearts were still aflame;
They spoke of Allen and O'Brien, and whispered Larkin's name.

When I slept on my mother's breast, a little babe, and frail,
Young Duffy's hearse went slowly by: he died in Milbank Jail.

When I could read, I spelt and knew the lives of patriot men;
When I could write, my pencil traced – 'A Nation Once Again'.

I learnt of those who often knew the baton and the cell,
Who asked for right by peaceful means – O'Connell to Parnell.

And once when thro' the cheering streets some 'felon' homeward
    came
I lit, amongst the gayer lights, my candle's tiny flame.

When I was but a tiny child I ran by Kickham's side;
I heard his bitter story told in reverence and pride.

And when with tears he passed away when life was young and fair,
I stood upon time's crowded path, and met O'Leary there.

I saw with pity and amaze a craven party go,
Obedient to a Scotsman's word, for Parnell's overthrow.

Before Kilmainham's bloodstained walls I stood all cold and still;
I lived through all the awful night that shadowed Pentonville.

If thus o'er one life's blotted page some neutral soul should bend,
He'll read to-day – as yesterday – the story without end.

William Allen, Michael Larkin and Michael O'Brien were known as the 'Manchester Martyrs'. They were members of a group of IRB men who attacked a prison van and rescued two of their comrades on 18 September 1867.
    A police officer was killed during the attack, and Allen, Larkin and O'Brien were hanged for murder.
    Edward Duffy, a comrade of the Fenian leader James Stephens, died, aged 28, in Millbank Prison in 1868.
    Charles Kickham (1828–1882) was a novelist, song-writer and member of the Irish Republican Brotherhood.

Text: Dan Barry (ed.), *The Tricolour*, Coiste Foillseacháin Náisiúnta, Cork, 1976.

To The Irish Dead
August 11th, 1917
Theodore Maynard (1890–1956)

You who have died as royally as kings,
    Have seen with eyes ablaze with beauty, eyes
        Nor gold nor ease nor comfort could make wise,
The glory of imperishable things.

Text: Theodore Maynard, *Poems by Theodore Maynard*, McClelland & Stewart, Toronto, 1919.

459

,Despite your shame and loneliness and loss –
 Your broken hopes, the hopes that shall not cease,
 Endure in dreams as terrible as peace;
Your naked folly nailed upon the cross

Has given us more than bread unto our dearth
 And more than water to our aching drouth;
 Though death has been as wormwood in your mouth
Your blood shall fructify the barren earth.

Easter Week
(Revised)
Ben O'Hickey (June 1916)

Text: Ben O'Hickey, *From Prison Cells,* The Elo Press, Dublin, 1935.

Who fears to speak of Easter Week,
 . . . Just words and nothing more . . .
But who would follow where they led,
 From Howth to Arranmore;
Aye, from Donegal to Cove of Cork,
 Let us raise our heads on high,
And follow where the heroes led,
 . . . Who taught us how to die.

MacDonagh, Pearse, and Plunkett,
 MacDermot and MacBride,
Clarke, Connolly and Daly,
 Like heroes all they died;
O'Hanrahan and Colbert
 . . . And one was but a boy!
All faced a grim death sentence,
 To teach us how to die.

And others too, who nobly fought,
 That their country might be free,
While grass grows green in Ireland,
 Remembered they shall be;
And in days to come, to beat of drum,
 We'll raise the flag on high,
And follow where the heroes led,
 Who taught us how to die.

Photograph from a contemporary newspaper, which has been annotated as follows: 'Lined up for Courtmartial Richmond Barracks 1916. (a) Major John MacBride, (b) W.T. Cosgrave, (c) Philip Cosgrave, (d) Commandant Eamonn Ceannt, (e) Michael Mallin, (f) Con Colbert.' (Ceannt Papers, Brother Allen Library.)

The Veterans
Donagh MacDonagh

Text: Roger McHugh, *Dublin 1916*, Hawthorn Books, New York, 1966.

Strict hairshirt of circumstance tears the flesh
    Off most delicate bones;
Years of counter and office, the warped mesh
    Of social living, dropping on stones,
Wear down all that was rough and worthy
    To a common denominator of dull tones.

So these, who in the sixteenth year of the century
    Saw their city, a Phoenix upturned,
Settle under her ashes and bury
    Hearts and brains that more frantically burned
Than the town they destroyed, have with the corrosion
    of time
    Spent more than they earned;

And with their youth has shrunk their singular mystery
    Which for one week set them in the pulse of the age,
Their spring adventure petrified in history,
    A line on a page,
Betrayed into the hands of students who question
    Oppressed and oppressor's rage.

461

Only the dead beneath their granite signatures
　　Are untroubled by the touch of day and day,
Only in them the first rich vision endures;
　　Those over clay
Retouch in memory, with sentiment relive,
　　April and May.

Easter Week

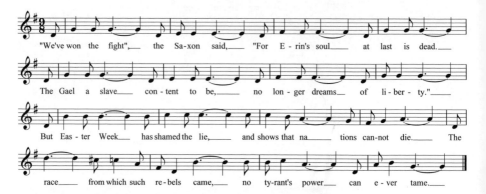

Text: *The De Valera Song Book,*
City Printing Co., Limerick, n.d.
(Samuels Collection, TCD).
　Air: 'The West's Asleep'.

'We've won the fight,' the Saxon said,
'For Erin's soul at last is dead.
The Gael a slave content to be,
No longer dreams of Liberty.'
But Easter Week has shamed the lie,
And shows that nations cannot die.
The race from which such rebels came,
No tyrant's power can ever tame.

'Tis true alas we were betrayed,
And while the patriots' part they played,
Their country's honour traitors sold
For England's smile and England's gold.
But now the nation starts to life,
To awake again the ancient strife.
No! shall truce or treaty be,
With England, till our land be free.

All honour to the men that kept
The watch-fires bright while others slept;
And sounding loud the morning call,
Did many a danger there forestall.
For it is true that Freedom's price
Should be for them life's sacrifice.

462

Heroes! their blood they gladly gave,
Their country's life and soul to save.

Say not that blood was shed in vain:
It fell in fertilizing rain.
And even now its fruit appears,
In Ireland's hopes and England's fears.
For now 'tis known the Gael retains
The will and power to burst his chains.
Oh! long shall Britain's warriors speak
With trembling voice of Easter Week.

Easter Week
In Memory of Joseph Mary Plunkett
Joyce Kilmer (1886–1918)

'Romantic Ireland's dead and gone,
It's with O'Leary in the grave.'
– W.B. Yeats

'Romantic Ireland's dead and gone,
    It's with O'Leary in the grave.'
Then, Yeats, what gave that Easter dawn
    A hue so radiantly brave?

There was a rain of blood that day,
    Red rain in gay blue April weather,
It blessed the earth till it gave birth
    To valour thick as blooms of heather.

Romantic Ireland never dies!
    O'Leary lies in fertile ground,
And songs and spears throughout the years
    Rise up where patriot graves are found.

Immortal patriots newly dead
    And ye that bled in bygone years,
What banners rise before your eyes?
    What is the tune that greets your ears?

The young Republic's banners smile
    For many a mile where troops convene,
O'Connell Street is loudly sweet
    With strains of Wearing of the Green.

Yeats's lines are from his poem 'September 1913', see p. 77.

Text: Edna C. Fitzhenry, *Nineteen-Sixteen Anthology*, Browne & Nolan Ltd, Dublin, 1935.

463

The soil of Ireland throbs and glows
    With life that knows the hour is here
To strike again like Irishmen,
    For that which Irishmen hold dear.

Lord Edward leaves his resting place
    And Sarsfield's face is glad and fierce.
See Emmet leap from troubled sleep
    To grasp the hand of Padraic Pearse!

There is no rope can strangle song
    And not for long death takes his toll.
No prison bars can dim the stars
    Nor quicklime eat the living soul.

Romantic Ireland is not old.
    For years untold her youth will shine,
Her heart is fed on Heavenly bread,
    The blood of martyrs is her wine.

Credo

Text: Manuscript copy book compiled at Mungret College, Limerick by a student named Eamon. (National Library of Ireland.)

I believe in Erin's glory
I believe in those who died
Passing on the deathless story
By the fate they met with pride.

I believe they live forever
In the bosom of their God.
I believe their blood has watered
Erin's green heroic sod.

I believe her women loved her
Grudged their best not for her sake.
Souls may give their tribute freely
Though the heart itself may break.

I believe that failure triumphs
When like theirs its fires are white.
Cast aside your rigid standard
For you know their will was right.

Erin Remember 1916

Lyrics: Peadar Mac Conna Midhe / Music: É. de Lásaigh

Strew wreaths before the hundred score
    Of Erin's daring sons,
Who triumphed o'er an army corps
    Of soldiery and guns.
Their action taught the foe that naught
    Our Nation can suppress;
The boys who fought, new spirit brought
    This dear old land to bless.

Chorus
For Pearse the brave would ne'er be slave,
    Mac Donagh nor Mac Bride;
And Plunkett's sons with loaded guns
    Went marching by their side.
Tom Clarke, made white with dungeon blight,
    One did not need to seek;
These heroes all faced shell and ball,
    For us in Easter Week.

Text and music: Sheet music published
by Quinn & Company, Dublin, 1919,
accessed on the website of the Irish
Traditional Music Archive.

Full seven days the cannon plays,
    The houses tumble down;
Amid the blaze the leader says
    'We yield to save the town,'
As rebels hot the brave were shot,
    In prison yard they lie;
That hallowed spot, forget it not,
    Its dead shall never die.

Their spirits bright in Freedom's light
    Shall hover o'er the Isle.
Let Ireland's might proclaim them right
    And ne'er those claims defile,
Who would repine shall now combine
    In accents bold shall speak;
'That Patriot line, their cause is mine,
    The men of Easter Week.'

Flood-Tide

To James Connolly

Maeve Cavanagh, 28 October 1916

Text: Maeve Cavanagh, *A Voice of Insurgency*, Dublin, 1916.

At last, at noon, flowed in the tide –
    Past was the waiting and the fear,
The dread that weakness might decide,
    And on the rocks the brave ship steer,
Or else in stagnant waters leave
Her, anchored, shamed beyond reprieve.

Past is the waiting, dead the fear,
    Ere ebbed the tide the ship sailed out,
She was not built for Fate so drear,
    Her place the sea's wild rush and rout,
Scant was she manned, but brave the crew
That from her mast her colours flew.

Out to the raging storm they rode,
    And dealt their blow at England's heart,
Whilst o'er their land the old Truth flowed,
    Blessed were their names in street and mart,
When, storm-tossed, proud, the ship came back,
Glory and Victory in her track.

But some that sailed came back no more,
    Yet were they envied who thus died,
And those who mourned beside the shore,
    Wept less for sorrow than for pride,
With each one's grief there too was blent,
Joy, Gratitude and Wonderment.

And you whose watch was on the bridge,
    Upon your soul a great joy shone,
That safely o'er the last Wave's ridge
    The ship you helped to steer had gone –
I know where'er you journey now,
Victory's smile is on your brow.

The Sinn Féin Dead

April 1916
W.N. Ewer (1885–1976)

When the dark world seems all too desperate,
    A hopeless, hideous struggle without cease,
    When hope is gone, what left but seek release
In one mad grapple with the thing you hate;
Flinging all counsel to the whirlwind, send
    Defiant challenge to the world, and so
    Recklessly facing your triumphant foe,
Pray that some welcome bullet bring the end?

Yours was the grim resolve that nerves the will
    When faith and hope are fled beyond recall,
As it was theirs who died at Bunker Hill,
    And those mad boys who held the Roman wall.
Your dreams, maybe, were madmen's dreams, but still
    You gave your lives for them – God rest you all!

The British journalist William
Norman Ewer was better known
as Trilby, and was said to have acted
as a spy for the Soviet Union during
the 1920s.

Text: W.N. Ewer, *Five Souls*,
The Herald, London, 1916.

Vengeance

In Dublin Town they murdered them,
    Like dogs they shot them down;
God's curse be on you England, now,
    God strike your London Town.
And cursed be every Irishman
    Alive, or yet to live,
Who'll dare forget the deaths they died,
    Who'll ever dare forgive.

Text: Samuels Collection, TCD.
(From *The Irish World*, America,
13 May 1916.)

467

In Kilmainham Jail they murdered them,
    Who fought for you and me.
Those men who dared to back with deeds
    Their dreams of liberty.
Whose strong hand clutching England's throat,
    Till all her veins ran chill,
Flung round the world a conquering note
    What time can never kill.

In Kilmainham Jail they murdered them,
    These men of Irish birth,
Kindly and tender, brave and warm
    As their own Irish earth.
Salt of the soil of Irish life,
    Bone of her bone were they,
Like carrion flung in a quick-lime grave
    In Dublin Town to-day.

Now eye for eye and tooth for tooth,
    Be this our Battle-cry,
Though ways run red, with hot blood shed,
    By men who dare to die;
Vengeance, that knows no rest or ruth,
    Vengeance, no power to stay,
This is the price of sacrifice,
    And we are here to-day.

From North to South, from East to West,
    Wherever England hurled
Her seed of old, we swear to-day
    To crush her round the world.
To stand as one, to plan as one,
    As one to fight or fall.
Till they who died in Dublin Town
    Are conquerors over all.

They murdered them in Dublin Town,
    Yes! and in Cork City, too.
These men who flung at Freedom's feet
    Their lives for me and you.
Then up with this for Battle-cry
    Thunder it up and down:
Revenge! Revenge! Revenge! for them
    Who died in Dublin Town.

General Sir John Maxwell
By an Irish Prisoner in Knutsford Prison

The divil sat by a lake of fire
On a pile of sulphur kegs.
His head was bowed upon his breast,
His tail between his legs.
A look of shame was on his face,
The sparks dropped from his eyes.
He had sent his resignation
To the throne beyond the skies.
'I'm down and out' the devil said,
He said it with a sob.
'There are others who outclass me
And I want to quit my job.'

'John Maxwell – Fenian hater
With his bloody shot and shell
Knows more about damnation
Than all the imps of Hell.
Give my job to General Friend
Or to Colthurst, the insane!
To Redmond or his followers,
'Tis all the blooming same.
I hate to leave the dear old home,
The spot I love so well,
But I feel that I'm not up to date
In the art of making hell!'
And the devil spat a squirt of fire
At a brimstone bumble bee,
And murmured 'I'm outclassed at last,
By Maxwell's devilry.'

General Maxwell, a veteran of colonial wars in The Sudan and South Africa, was sent to Ireland with absolute authority to deal as he saw fit with those who had taken part in the 1916 Rising. He organized the summary trial by secret court martial of nearly 200 rebels and secured ninety death sentences, of which fifteen were carried out.

General Lovick Bransby Friend was the Commander-in-Chief in Ireland from 1914 until he was replaced by Maxwell in the wake of the Rising.

Captain J.C. Bowen-Colthurst was the British officer who arrested the pacifist Francis Sheehy-Skeffington on the street, had him taken to Portobello Barracks, and murdered him there.

Text: Manuscript copy book compiled at Mungret College, Limerick by a student named Eamon. (National Library of Ireland)

To the Memory of Some I Knew Who Are Dead and Who Loved Ireland
George Russell (Æ)

Your dream had left me numb and cold
But yet my spirit rose in pride,
Re-fashioned in burnished gold
The images of those who died,
Or were shut in the penal cell –
Here's to you, Pearse, your dream, not mine,
But yet the thought – for this you fell –
Turns all life's water into wine.

This poem is usually entitled 'Salutation'. The text here is assembled from two versions. All but the second-last verse here is from George Russell, *Imaginations and Reveries,* Maunsel & Roberts Ltd, Dublin, 1921.

The second-last verse is included in the version in Roger McHugh, *Dublin 1916,* Hawthorn Books, New York, 1966. That version, however, does not include the verses which are in italics here, as they are in Russell's *Imaginations and Reveries*.

You who have died on Eastern hills
    Or fields of France as undismayed,
Who lit with interlinked wills
    The long heroic barricade,
You, too, in all the dreams you had,
    Thought of some thing for Ireland done.
Was it not so, Oh, shining lad,
    What lured you, Alan Anderson?

I listened to high talk from you,
    Thomas MacDonagh, and it seemed
The words were idle, but they grew
    To nobleness, but death redeemed.
Life cannot utter things more great
    Than life can meet with sacrifice,
High words were equalled by high fate,
    You paid the price. You paid the price.

You who have fought on fields afar,
    That other Ireland did you wrong
Who said you shadowed Ireland's star,
    Nor gave you laurel wreath nor song.
You proved by death as true as they,
    In mightier conflicts played your part,
Equal your sacrifice may weigh,
    Dear Kettle, of the generous heart.

The hope lives on, age after age,
    Earth with its beauty might be won
For labour as a heritage,
    For this has Ireland lost a son,
This hope unto a flame to fan
    Men have put life by with a smile,
Here's to you, Connolly, my man,
    Who cast the last torch on the pile.

You, too, had Ireland in your care,
    Who watched o'er pits of blood and mire,
From iron roots leap up in air
    Wild forests, magical, of fire;
Yet while the Nuts of Death were shed
    Your memory would ever stray
To your own isle, Oh, gallant dead –
    This wreath, Will Redmond, on your clay.

Here's to the women of our race
    Stood by them in the fiery hour,

Rapt, lest some weakness in their blood
    Rob manhood of a single power –
You, brave as such a hope forlorn,
    Who smiled through crack of shot and shell,
Though the world look on you with scorn,
    Here's to you, Constance, in your cell.

Here's to you, men I never met,
    Yet hope to meet behind the veil,
Thronged on some starry parapet
    That looks down upon Inisfail,
And see the confluence of dreams
    That clashed together in our night,
One river born from many streams,
    Roll in one blaze of blinding light.

On Behalf of Some Irishmen
Not Followers of Tradition

George Russell (Æ)

They call us aliens, we are told,
Because our wayward visions stray
From that dim banner they unfold,
The dreams of worn-out yesterday.
The sum of all the past is theirs,
The creeds, the deeds, the fame, the name,
Whose death-created glory flares
And dims the spark of living flame.
They weave the necromancer's spell,
And burst the graves where martyrs slept,
Their ancient story to retell,
Renewing tears the dead have wept.
And they would have us join their dirge,
This worship of an extinct fire
In which they drift beyond the verge
Where races all outworn expire.
The worship of the dead is not
A worship that our hearts allow,
Though every famous shade were wrought
With woven thorns above the brow.

Text: George Russell, *Collected Poems*, Macmillan, London, 1919.

471

We fling our answer back in scorn:
'We are less children of this clime
Than of some nation yet unborn
Or empire in the womb of time.
We hold the Ireland in the heart
More than the land our eyes have seen,
And love the goal for which we start
More than the tale of what has been.'
The generations as they rise
May live the life men lived before,
Still hold the thought once held as wise,
Go in by the same ancient door.
We leave the easy peace it brings:
The few we are shall still unite
In fealty to unseen kings
Or unimaginable light.
We would no Irish sign efface,
But yet our lips would gladlier hail
The firstborn of the Coming Race
Than the last splendour of the Gael.
No blazoned banner we unfold –
One charge alone we give to youth,
Against the sceptred myth to hold
The golden heresy of truth.

Sinn Fein Rebellion, 1916.
Hotel Metropole and
Post Office, Dublin.

Who Fears to Speak of Easter Week?

Who fears to speak of Easter Week?
  Who dares its fate deplore?
The red gold flame of Erin's name
  Confronts the world once more!
Oh! Irishmen, remember then,
  And raise your heads with pride,
For great men and straight men
  Have fought for you and died.

The spirit wave that came to save
  The peerless Celtic soul,
From earthly strain of greed to gain
  Had caught them in its roll;
Had swept them high to do or die,
  To sound a trumpet call:
For true men though few men
  To follow one and all.

Upon their shield a stainless field,
  With virtues blazoned bright;
With Temperance and Purity
  And Truth and Honour right.
So now they stand at God's Right Hand,
  Who framed their dauntless clay,
Who taught them and brought them
  The glory of today.

The storied page of this our age
  Will save our land from shame.
The ancient foe has boasted – ho!
  That Irishmen were tame.
They bought their souls for paltry doles,
  And told the world of slaves,
That lie, men! shall die, men!
  In Pearse and Plunkett's graves.

The brave who've gone to linger on
  Beneath the tyrant's heel –
We know they pray another day,
  With clash of clanging steel.
Now from their cell their voices swell,
  And loudly call on you.
Then ask men! the task, men!
  That yet remains to do.

This song is said to have been 'Written by a nun on 3 May 1916, when news of the first executions became known.'

Text: *The 1916 Song Book*, Irish Book Bureau, Dublin, n.d.
  Air: 'The Memory of the Dead', see p. 86.

Requiem
Seamus O'Sullivan (1879–1958)

The following fourteen pieces comprise all but one of the poems published anonymously in September 1917 in *Aftermath of Easter Week*, which was 'Published for the benefit of the Irish National Aid and Volunteers' Dependents Fund'. Dora Sigerson's 'Sixteen Dead Men' was also in that collection, but may be found here on p. 458, after W.B. Yeats's poem of the same name.

A copy of the collection in the Library of the University of British Columbia contains a typed note identifying the writers.

The collection's Foreword, by Rev. Patrick Browne, is as follows:

A year ago one might have said, 'Here is a garland for the graves of those who died'; now one must say, 'Here are flowers for the altars of those who live for ever.' Many thought then, like the Athenian statesman, that the spring was taken out of the year; at present they think rather of the grain of wheat which falls into the ground and dies, to bring forth much fruit.

The Nation's life has been purified and renewed; and, among other things, the national literature has experienced a new impetus and inspiration. A few friends of the Association which has been engaged in the noble work of assisting the families of those who suffered for their connection with the Easter Rising now wish, for the benefit of the Fund, to publish some of the poems that have been written. It is to be hoped that the public will respond generously, not so much for the sake of the poems themselves, as for the cause they are intended to help, and the illustrious dead whom they commemorate.

P.B.

18 September 1917.

Tears for the dead, but not for them
Spirits of wind and fire and flame,
For these a lordlier requiem.

Tears for the dead, who in the gloom
Of old despairs forlornly grope,
Forgetful that the dawn is come.

Tears for such living, but for them
Spirits of wind and flame and fire,
Raise we a loftier requiem,
Build we a lordlier funeral pyre.

Blow to us, wind of deathless hope,
And wake the swift avenging flame
Exultant, of their heart's desire.

The Seanachie Tells Another Story
Seamus O'Kelly (1881–1918)

Once upon a time in our townland
This vision came of a funeral band:
Coffins of gold and each silver hearse
Had a breast-plate with a shining verse,
While all the proud mourners on the march
Would reach from here to Saint Peter's Arch.

As sixteen coffins went by Kilgar,
A flaming spear leapt up to a star;
A sign that the men who lived in death
Were those who had drawn the hero breath;
England had bullets and burning lime,
And Ireland has names that march with time.

Quae est ista quae progreditur quasi aurora consurgens pulchra ut luna, electa ut sol

Rev. Patrick Browne (d. 1960)

Because they died and at the darksome door
Of death's house never quailed, nor o'er their eyes
Passed a faint hand to blot the shapes that rise
When blood runs cold and freezes at the core,
But kept her form before them to adore,
The passionate Dark Rose whose strange surprise
Of beauty nerved them to their enterprise
Till death nor life had moment any more,
They have passed to a galaxy of stars,
And throned her in an ether with no cloud,
A sun round which their circling orbits gleam,
While we through spaces of our prison bars
Watch in the firmament their courses proud
And feel life's light is darkness to their dream.

The Latin title of this poem is from *The Song of Solomon* (chapter 6, verse 10), and is translated in the King James version as 'Who is she that looketh forth as the morning, fair as the moon, clear as the sun'.

'The Rebels'

Oliver St John Gogarty

Not that they knew well, when they drew the blade,
That breaks for victory if gain were planned,
You never gave without a trembling hand;
But when they heard of sacred truth waylaid,
And meanness with grandiloquence gainsaid,
And Freedom, in the name of Freedom, banned;
And Friendship in this foulness, this, England –
This was the cause of that good fight they made.

They heard your mobsters mouthing at the hordes,
Who care not so the fight increase their store,
Hawking your honour on the sandwich boards;
But their's is safe, and to these things unlinked
They stood apart; and Death withholds them more,
Separate for ever and aloof – distinct.

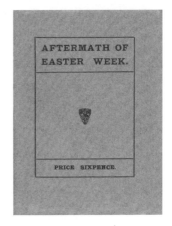

AFTERMATH OF EASTER WEEK.

PRICE SIXPENCE.

475

To Ireland, 1916
Michael Scot (Kathleen Goodfellow) (1891–1980)

These are your sons who bore your time of waiting
Smitten and mocked by brutal soldiery;
Each now has risen from the cross of hating
Winged with white flames of love and liberty.
Little Dark Rose, the rain is in their faces,
Mourn not the past of agony and drouth;
Proud-eyed and strong, they stride the starry spaces,
Laughter has flowered from every bleeding mouth.
Weep not their wounds who loved your eyes of sorrow,
Red wine of joy stains every pierced side,
Sons of young Angus, princes of the morrow,
Sunlight and wind acclaim the crucified!

Lacrymae Rerum
Rev. Patrick Browne

The title, a quotation from Virgil's
Aeneid, means 'the tears of things'.

Souls, your high fate with our sad thoughts allied
Has brought into the spring our Hallow-eve,
And lengthening days of life returning grieve
Holding the vigil of your passion tide.

Fresh flowers and leaves forget their wonted pride
And over all the fields conspire to weave
A wreath for hopes your lives could not achieve
A funeral tribute to your hearts that died.

So life at each recurring vernal bloom
Shall by your memory be overthrown;
No more a Victor on triumphal ways.

'Twill come, but in procession to your tomb,
While south-west winds that lead the spring intone
Your *Dies Irae* to the end of days.

The Boreen, 1916

Seamus O'Kelly

They whisper in the dark boreen,
Where all their mumbled words are mean,
Of who was wrong, and who was right,
(The hoots of blind bats in the Night!) –
From starry space we hear you sing,
O ye who grew the Eagle's wing.

They stumble on by crooked ways,
With empty clamour fill their days,
The nothingness of all they say
Is stamped upon an alien clay –
'Hearts to the golden sun,' you sing,
O ye who know the Eagle's wing.

'Be wise, be wise,' our old fools cry,
'You'll get your own wings by and by' –
And mumble on of insect things,
Of empire flights on pismire wings –
'Strain for the Golden sun,' you sing,
O ye who soar on Eagle's wing.

They shuffle down their dank boreen
By stagnant pools and on between
The lichened walls that map their sway
And mark them from freedom's highway –
'Eyes to the Golden sun,' you sing,
O ye who sweep on Eagle's wing.

Green meads and all the laughing seas,
The purple hills, the forest trees,
The glory of the sun's uprise,
Are not for folk with wintered eyes –
'Breasts to the Golden sun,' you sing,
O ye who rose on Eagle's wing.

To Thomas MacDonagh
Seamus O'Sullivan

You who had garnered all that old song could give you,
And rarer music in places where the bittern cries,
What new strange symphonies, what new music thrills you
Flashing in light-loud magic beneath wildering skies?

Singer of dawn songs, you who drink now at the fountains,
Cry out as your own poet of the bittern cried,
Flood that new song deep-drunken, rapturous about us,
So shall these parched sad hearts drink deep, satisfied.

To Sean MacDermot
Rev. Patrick Browne

Your pale dead face with sure insistent claim
Shall haunt my soul as long as thought endures,
Waking remembrance of your wasted frame
Afire with that all-conquering soul of yours –

As last I saw you, captive in the net,
And heard you in Kilmainham's prison cell
Review the patient years with no regret
And say in sight of death that all was well.

I know you walked (O sad, lame steps!) to die
With high disdain of all who hold life dear
And sacrifice their honour like a pawn;

No dimness born of agony and fear
Was in those spirit eyes when carelessly
They faced the rifles at the grey of dawn.

In Memoriam
Seán MacDermot
Seamus O'Sullivan

They have slain you, Seán MacDermot, never more these eyes will greet
The eyes beloved by women and the smile that true men loved.
Never more I'll hear the stick-tap and the gay and limping feet.
They have slain you, Seán the gentle, Seán the valiant, Seán the proved.

Have you scorn for us who linger here behind you, Seán the wise?
As you look about and greet your comrades in the strange new dawn.
So one says, but saying wrongs you, for doubt never dimmed your eyes,
And not death itself could make those lips of yours grow bitter, Seán.

As your stick goes tapping down the heavenly pavement, Seán, my friend,
That is not your way of thinking, generous, tender, wise and brave;
We who knew and loved and trusted you are trusted to the end,
Even now your hand grips mine as though there never were a grave.

Casement in Berlin

Rev. Patrick Browne
(Er lachte niemals – *Berliner Tageblatt*)

He never laughed – his soul within
Burned with a silent fire,
Wasted with thought that strove to spin
The web of his desire.

No giddy pleasures ever lured
His soul from her high road;
In a dumb vigil he endured
The spirit's secret goad.

He, wont to pale at Beauty's glance
That history half withheld,
Now on the later scrolls of chance
A sterner message spelled.

While guests their glasses raised to drain
In many a fervent toast,
He started like the thought-worn Dane
Before his father's ghost.

As though outside a window square
He heard a scaffold groan,
And saw fixed in an icy stare
The pallid face of Tone –

Assured that in Time's book the date
Was marked when he should seize
That chalice from the hands of fate
And drain it to the lees.

The expression in German under
the title means 'He never laughed'.

The vision passed and life again
Resumed its wonted ways;
Along his rugged path of pain
He went, nor turned his gaze.

Hourly he seemed to droop and fade
By fantasies possessed
Of some dim heaven, an exiled shade
Whose doom allowed no rest.

And when he vanished as he came
Like some migrating bird,
They who knew well the inward flame
Divined that he had heard

The voices calling from the graves,
Dead martyrs of his race,
And rising went out on the waves
To meet death face to face.

Denis Delaney (courtesy of Na Píobairí Uilleann).

Piper Denis Delany

Seamus O'Kelly

Play up the martial air
For all Mountbellew fair,
Enchantment is your trade
Your heart is unafraid;
You do your soul no wrong
To pipe a rebel song.

The message from your keys
Now loose upon the breeze,
Ah, soon the old desire
Will set men's hearts afire –
You do their souls no wrong
To pipe a rebel song.

Lift up that noble face!
Let all who care there trace
The passion that you woo
From olden days for new –
You do that face no wrong
To pipe a rebel song.

Warm now the magic flood
Of your piping Gaelic blood –
Wake mem'ries of our dead
And the tyrant's lure is fled!
You do his cause much wrong
To pipe a rebel song.

O man with blinded eyes
Piping under Irish skies,
The brightness of your art
Lights Eire's darkened heart –
You do her soul no wrong
To pipe a rebel song.

Play up the martial air
For all Mountbellew fair,
Enchantment is your trade,
Your heart is unafraid,
You do your soul no wrong,
To pipe a rebel song.

'Denis Delany, the famous Ballinasloe
piper, the winner of so many prizes
at Feiseanna, was arrested under the
Defense of the Realm Act for playing
'The Memory of the Dead' at Mountbellew Agricultural Show shortly after
the Insurrection of 1916. Delany is
blind and over eighty years of age.'
– daily papers.

481

The Leaders
Seamus O'Sullivan

Where loud-voiced leaders vaunt a claim
They have no place, they have no name,
The tenders of the Phoenix Flame;
Without a word, without a sign,
They move upon that old divine
High mission at the inmost shrine.

Yet have they more enduring place,
The men of Ireland's hero race,
And they have names that still can stir
The deep unconquered heart of her.

The Dead Who Live for Ireland
Blanaid Salkeld (1860–1959)

Because they were her best-loved sons –
In beauty, wisdom, valorous unrest,
She sent them forward on her ancient quest
With stainless courage and pure orisons.
In splendid youth and hope, her darling ones
Left friendship, praise, love, children – being's best,
Lest she of ultimate right be dispossessed . . .
It was her victory when callous guns
Made such dear dignity bow down to death;
Stamped on our hearts the gesture of their fall!
They are more dear to us than living friends,
Whose sacrifice re-fired our love and faith,
Lime has consumed their bodies; but the call
Of their inviolate souls all speech transcends.

To an Irish Patriot
Sir William Watson

Text: Sir William Watson, *Ireland Unfreed*, John Lane, London, 1921.

Your cause at its centre is pure : the wise plan
Is to keep it circumference pure – if you can.

Dark Rosaleen's Last Chaplet

Forty feet deep they dug his grave,   Samuels Collection, TCD.
   Toll the bells of Ireland, toll,
They buried the man who Ireland would save,
   But none could bury his soul.
Forty feet of Irish earth
   The true heart of Pearse they covered,
But over the city that gave him birth
   The wind of his spirit hovered.

His soul sailing under the morning star
   Heard the desecrate city sigh,
And bearing his brother's soul afar
   The red wind of death rushed by.
The winds of Ireland met up there,
   At dawn they met and at dark,
O'Hanrahan's soul on their wings they bore
   And the soul of Thomas Clarke.

The watchers down in the city heard
   MacDonagh's soul go by,
But hardly his sleeping children stirred
   So gently he passed them nigh.
The souls of Daly and John MacBride
   In the mist with Mallin's went,
And the Lord bade the soul of Thomas ride
   On His wind with Eamonn Kent.

And the Lord was for Joseph Plunkett grieved
   And said, 'I have a care for thee,
Since many a crown was for Ireland weaved,
   Like one that was wove for me.'
'Men knew that I broke not the braised reed,
   Yet they would not let me live,
My way was hard for my sons indeed,
   And My mind is to forgive.'

'I saw Colbert choose a felon's path,
   That a comrade might go free,
And much is pardoned to one that hath
   Loved another as much as he.'
The twelve winds of Erin went to find
   The scattered souls of the rest,
And Heuston was found by the grey-green winds
   The wind the wild birds love best.

The purple winds swept up the Liffey's tide
    For Connolly's soul unseen,
And Sean MacDermott's, the last that died,
    God counted in all fifteen.
The lights of Ireland gleamed below
    In the ring of her leaden sea,
And the voice of Ireland chanted slow
    Only my dead are free.

Dear Lord! Of a thorn-bush my wreath is made,
    So mourned my Dark Rosaleen,
My Chaplet to-night at Thy feet is laid,
    I give Thee my beads fifteen.
He heard who dwelt in the highest place,
    And His angels silent led
The waiting souls to His holy face,
    And He spoke unto the dead:

'There never yet dropped a feeble wing
    Too small for Mine eyes to see,
Nor ever was sought by a hunted thing
    A refuge in vain with Me.
I would the black story of England's way
    Were blasted from my sight,
I will show the dawning of Ireland's day,
    The passing of her night.'

Then God from the steps of His high throne
    Went down for many a mile,
And He saw great England hard as stone,
    And He bent in thought awhile.
'Too long hath Ireland the thorn path trod,
    I will turn my face away,
Vengeance is Mine!' said the mighty God
    'Is mine! I will repay.'

Immortal
In Memory of Padraic Pearse
Theodore Maynard

Text: Edna C. Fitzhenry, *Nineteen-Sixteen Anthology*, Browne & Nolan Ltd, Dublin, 1935.

In this grey morning wrapped in mist and rain,
    You stood erect beneath the sullen sky,
A heart which held its peace and noble pain,
    A brave and gentle eye.

The last of all your silver songs are sung,
    Your fledgling dreams on broken wings are dashed –
For suddenly a tragic sword was swung,
    And ten true rifles crashed.

By one who walks aloof in English ways
    Be this high word of praise and sorrow said:
He lived in honour all his lovely days,
    And is immortal, dead!

The Star
In Memory of Patrick Pearse
Dora Sigerson

I saw a dreamer, I saw a poet,
On the red battle-field fell my slow tear,
'Lover of birds and flowers, singer of gentle songs,
Dying with men of war, what do you here?'
Languid his closing eyes looked to the breaking dawn
Where the young day peeped out through prison bars,
'I on a high hill stood singing a dear old song,
I fell to earth,' he sighed, 'grasping at stars.'

He laid him softly down, cold was his paling cheek,
Silent and chill he grew as the dead are,
But from his folded hands on to the crimson earth
Glowing and shimmering fell a great star,
Out of the heavens there came a hand raising it,
Set in the green sky for all to see,
There it shone purely bright, faithful as planets shine,
There it sung loud and sweet, 'Come, follow me.'

Text: Edna C. Fitzhenry, *Nineteen-Sixteen Anthology*, Browne & Nolan Ltd, Dublin, 1935.

Patrick Pearse
Leo Maguire

I've sung many a song. I've told many a story
Of lovers so tender and battles so fierce.
Now, may God be my guide as I sing of the glory,
The goodness, the grandeur of bold Patrick Pearse.
All the virtues and graces that God ever granted
To mortal on Earth here in him were combined.
High honour and faith in his soul were implanted,
He was fearless in battle, yet gentle and kind.

Text: Leo Maguire, *The Faithful and the Few*, Walton's Musical Instrument Galleries, Dublin, 1959.

485

There are hills 'round Rosmuck, there are fields 'round Rathfarnham,
Where wild flowers grow brighter, the air is more clear,
And the grass seems to whisper, 'We'll always remember;
Tho' the whole world forget him, he used to walk here.'
When the westering sun sends the long shadows creeping
Thro' ancient Saint Enda's, the wind brings a sound
As a child hears its mother, 'twixt waking and sleeping,
'Walk softly, your feet are on sanctified ground.'

One glorious week when the red flame of battle
Wrapped Dublin around, and the staunch-hearted few
Stood with Pearse thro' the shell-bursts and the rifles' sharp rattle
While the bright torch of freedom was kindled anew.
Then the sad ending came, but still fearless it found them;
They lost, but, in losing, the battle was won;
They fought 'til old Dublin in ruins fell 'round them
Then to death with a smile walked our Land's bravest sons.

One short, whispered prayer, then the murderous thunder
Of rifles rang out in that bare prison yard;
While the grim fusillade tore his broad breast asunder
His pure soul ascended to Heaven, unmarred.
Not Ireland alone, but the whole world, should mourn him,
The selfless, the valiant, the friend of the meek.
Brave men, gather 'round me! Tho' hirelings may scorn him,
Remember brave Pearse and sublime Easter Week.

Connolly

Liam MacGabhann

Connolly, one of the leading Marxist theorists of his day, was shot in the Stonebreaker's Yard, Kilmainham Jail, Dublin, on 12 May 1916. Kilmainham Jail is now a fine museum with exhibits mainly relating to the 1913–24 period of Ireland's independence struggle. The Stonebreaker's Yard is open to visitors. [LM]

Text: Liam MacGabhann, *Rags, Robes and Rebels*, Republican Press, Dublin, n.d.

(The son of a Welsh miner, a member of the firing squad that shot James Connolly was so impressed by the bravery of the great leader that afterwards he paid a visit to Connolly's relatives to implore their forgiveness. The following poem is an impression of the soldier's story to his comrades.)

The man was all shot through that came today
Into the barrack square;
A soldier I – I am not proud to say
We killed him there;
They brought him from the prison hospital:
To see him in that chair
I thought his smile would far more quickly call
A man to prayer.

Maybe we cannot understand this thing
That makes these rebels die
And yet all things love freedom – and the spring
Clear in the sky.
I think I would not do this deed again
For all that I hold by;
Gaze down my rifle at his breast – but then
A soldier I.

They say that he was kindly
Apart from all the rest;
A lover of the poor; and all shot through,
His wounds ill drest.
He came before us, faced us like a man,
He knew a deeper pain
Than blows or bullets – Ere the world began;
Died he in vain?

Ready – present; And he just smiling – God
I felt my rifle shake.
His wounds were opened out and round that chair
Was one red lake.
I swear his lips said 'fire' when all was still
Before my rifle spat
That cursed lead; and I was picked to kill
A man like that.

To the Memory of James Connolly
John Hewitt (1907–1987)

A dozen years have passed since then,
    The memory has died away
Of Connolly and the martyred men
    Who rose on Easter Day.

When I was six years old I heard
    Connolly address a Labour crowd –
I cannot recollect a word
    Yet I am very proud –

As one who stood upon the edge
    Of Galilee to watch the ship
That waders pushed beyond the sedge
    While bright oars flash and dip;

Text: John Hewitt, *Collected Poems of John Hewitt*, Blackstaff Press, Belfast, 1991.

But not indeed as one who stood
Among the crowd on Calvary
To see Christ die for Brotherhood,
As Connolly died for me.

James Connolly

Patrick Galvin (1927–2011)

Where, O, where_____ is our James Con - nol - ly?_____

Where, O, where_____ is that gal_____ lant man?_____

He's_____ gone to or - ga - nise the Un_____ ion,_____

That wor - king men_____ might_____ yet be free._____

Text and music: Patrick Galvin, *Irish Songs of Resistance*, Workers' Music Association, London, 1955.

Where O where is our James Connolly?
Where O where is that gallant man?
He's gone to organize the union
That working men might yet be free.

Where O where is the Citizen Army?
Where O where are those fighting men?
They have gone to join the great rebellion
To smash the bonds of slavery.

And who'll be there to lead the van?
Oh who'll be there to lead the van?
Who should be there but our James Connolly
The hero of each working man.

Who carries high that burning flag?
Who carries high that burning flag?
'Tis our James Connolly all pale and wounded
Who carries high our burning flag.

They carried him up to the jail.
They carried him up to the jail,
And there they shot him one bright May morning
And quickly laid him in his grave.

Who mourns now for our James Connolly?
Who mourns for that fighting man?
O lay me down in yon green garden
And make my bearers union men.

We laid him down in yon green garden
With union men on every side
And swore we'd make one mighty union
And fill that gallant man with pride.

Now all you noble Irishmen
Come join with me for liberty
And we'll forge a mighty weapon
And smash the bonds of slavery.

Connolly
Thomas O'Brien (1914–1974)

We shall not gather like banshees around his grave
And wail a sentimental dirge,
As if his Death were all his life;
Far better leave him quiet in the shade
Than remember only that he died,
He lived, lest smothered in an earthy avalanche you forget.
He was the Man who stood with clenched fist
Under the workers Red;
He who like a miner went below
And brought forbidden objects to the light –
Slimy things that crawled across the earth
And looked with bulbous eyes at their creators.
He was a demolisher of capitalism,
He was the breath of the Revolution,
He was the Red Terror –
Connolly, lest you forget.

Text: Gustav Klaus, *Strong Words, Brave Deeds*, O'Brien Press, Dublin, 1994.

Eamonn Ceannt
Lily O'Brennan

He walked apart, God moulded his childhood
To understand His ways. Unobstrusive and quiet
Nature appealed to him, and the lark's lilt
Was ever in his heart and on his lips.

Eamonn Ceannt (1881–1916), Galway-born (Ballymoe) son of an RIC man, was very active in the language and revolutionary movements at the beginning of the twentieth century. He was also a piper, playing both the warpipes and the uilleann pipes, and he was active in the Dublin Pipers' Club.

A signatory of the 1916 Proclamation and a Commandant during the 1916 Rising, being in command at the South Dublin Union and Marrowbone lane Distillery, Ceannt was executed in Kilmainham Jail on 8 May 1916. The 'She' in verses 2, 3 and 4 is Ireland. [LM]

Text: Seán Reid Library, Na Píobairí Uilleann, Dublin.

And when he grew to Boyhood She called him
And brought him to her fount and there he drank
A Nation's purifying draught
In History, Language and Song.

And when he grew to man-hood's dreams
She placed a sword into his hands
And sent him forth to quell the foreigner
Who stole her mountain slopes and pasture fields.

And when he died She clasped him to her breast
And caoined and called him patriot.
But God who moulded him a child
And made him in his fuller years
Great and kindly and good,
Placed a crown upon his head
And called him Martyr.

They Did Not See Thy Face
In Memory of Thomas MacDonagh
Dora Sigerson

Text: Dan Barry (ed.), *The Tricolour,* Coiste Foillseacháin Náisiúnta, Cork, 1976.

Some on the pleasant hillside have thought they saw thee pass,
As flings a cloud before the sun a shadow on the grass,
They praised thy fairness and held dear thy meekness and thy grace;
They only saw thy shade, Kathleen, they did not see thy face.

Some on the purple mountains stood to see thee speeding by,
As glides a sudden golden shaft across a stormy sky;
And these were braggarts of their love within thy dwelling-place;
They saw thy beauty, Róisín Dubh, they did not see thy face.

But some in flames of battle strove their slender weight to throw
Against the bayonet and the gun that hid thy only foe;
They left for thee their earthly loves, these heroes of thy race,
And died, as all must die, Kathleen, who once have seen thy face.

So must thy grief be ever new who holds a love like this,
That thrusts away a dear one's heart, a little child's soft kiss,
That leaves behind an honoured home, a mother's fond embrace,
Till others seek again, Kathleen, to see thy hidden face.

The Poet Captain
Thomas MacDonagh
(1878–1916)
Padraic Colum (1881–1972)

How shall I show him? How his story plan?

Text: Padraic Colum, *Irish Elegies*,
The Dolmen Press, Dublin, 1961.

This you asked for him, the man in your first play,
And for another audience I ask this:
How shall I show you, how your story plan?

An excursion train
That's journey-bound for pilgrimage
Or tournament – I'll place you there.
The landscape changes, humours change,
And you who talked of thoughtful men
Of Villon, or of Horace, or
Of wild Catullus and his love,
Now raise for us a parish song
That brings to life the folk of those
Odd houses at the boro's end –
Local as jackdaws on the roofs
Of some small Tipperary town,
Lively as jackdaws on the slates,
And you, remarked for pompousness
Will be acclaimed for drollery.

How shall I show you? How your story plan?

In Saint Canice's: we walk down
An aisle and find ourselves beside
An effigy in black limestone
Of knight recumbent – here you speak
Of figure you have mind to form.
All we who carry banners dream,
And try to put our dream in text
Of play, or poem, or history.
This dream of yours you'd bring to life
Upon a stage. The hero? Who?
Someone in time that's yet to come –
The Poet-Captain who'll transmute
The word into the deed, the deed
Into the vibrating word.
The play I saw remembering
The chapel-aisle, the lonely knight

491

Whose word was in a language gone
As word on shield. I ask again –

How shall I show you? How your story plan?

You step into our company
In kilts and *brat* and with a brooch
As good as plume for gallant show,
And tell us poems will add to poems
Are in your scrip, and tell them well.
The Yellow Bittern, never out
In drinking bout is dead beside
The bog-drain that was all his booze:
He might have had a flightier life.

John-John is back to card-trick men
And Maggie-men at Nenagh Fair –
Not for the like of him a house
And household chores. Unseen, unheard
The dogs hunt over untracked field
At night, and have unkennelled life
Their sleepy owners cannot know.
Then from those earlier, I recall
An April verse –

The songs that I sing
Should have told you an Easter story
Of a long sweet spring
With its gold and its feasts and its glory.

How shall I show you? How your story plan?

Court-martial. Now you come before
The men with power of dealing death:
You speak to them of trialled man,
Of Savanarola, Florentine.
(And who but you would bring that name
Before a bench of medalled men?)
They judge you by their printed book.
Then in the barrack-yard you prove
That your own judgment's unrevoked –
The Poet-Captain; there you tear
From history the double word,
The envoi to your poems!

Thomas MacDonagh
Francis Ledwidge

He shall not hear the bittern cry
In the wild sky, where he is lain,
Nor voices of the sweeter birds
Above the wailing of the rain.

Nor shall he know when loud March blows
Thro' slanting snows her fanfare shrill,
Blowing to flame the golden cup
Of many an upset daffodil.

But when the Dark Cow leaves the moor,
And pastures poor with greedy weeds,
Perhaps he'll hear her low at morn
Lifting her horn in pleasant meads.

Text: Alice Curtayne (ed.), *Francis Ledwidge Complete Poems*, Martin Brian & O'Keeffe, London, 1974.

Joseph Mary Plunkett
Maeve Cavanagh

Tho' you be dead let no man mourn for you,
　　Whose brave life-song was ended,
E'en to the last full note
　　And with its music blended.
Love's song and War's, Glory's, Achievement's, too,
　　Its grand triumphant echo long shall float
Round you and glad your dream Death's twilight thro'.

Tho' you be dead, its fruits your life-dream bore,
　　Beyond all hope surpassing,
Your heart its wish had known,
　　Then let none mourn your passing.
You live in Ireland's heart for evermore,
　　In Life's flood-tide the death you craved you won,
Then fared with radiant face to Death's strange shore.

Text: Maeve Cavanagh, *A Voice of Insurgency*, Dublin, 1916.

A Song of Seán MacDermott

Teresa Brayton

When Sean Mc - Der - mott__ heard the call to__ shoul - der__ arms for Ire - land's sake,

The__ blood stream of__ his__ fa_____ thers all an-swered the__ sum-mons wide a - wake;

And__ out of Augh rim__ shrilled the__ cry: strike in our__ name a blow long due,

And__ we who dared do__ fight and die for__ E - rin__ will be there with you.

'Seán MacDermott was born in Kiltyclogher, Co. Leitrim, in 1886. While still in his teens he emigrated to Scotland where he worked as a gardener and tram-car conductor. Moving to Belfast, he joined the Irish Republican Brotherhood and became a full-time organizer in 1908. He was one of the seven signatories of the Proclamation of the Irish Republic and was executed in Kilmainham Jail on 12 May 1916.'

The note above accompanies this poem in Martin Shannon, *Ballads from the Jails and Streets of Ireland*, Red Hand Books, Dublin, 1966, where the prescribed air is named as 'Signal Fires'. No air by that name could be found.

Air: The air accompanying the text here comes from C. Desmond Greaves, *The Easter Rising in Song & Ballad*, Kahn & Averill, for the Workers' Music Association, London, 1980.

When Sean MacDermott heard the call
    To shoulder arms for Ireland's sake
The bloodstream of his fathers all
    Answered the summons wide awake;
And out of Aughrim shrilled the cry:
    Strike in our name a blow long due,
And we, who dared to fight and die
    For Erin, will be there with you.

For Connacht slumbered not, nor slept,
    Adown her years of scourge and thorn,
But silently a vigil kept,
    For some high resurrection morn;
And then it came; the very dust
    Of storied hill and valley stirred,
When shroud and tomb aside were thrust,
    And Easter flashed the gallant word.

Then Sean MacDermott fought his fight,
    And paid the price that heroes pay,
Who with their brothers scale the height
    Where men may face unfettered day;
Now Connacht bares her ancient head
    Before the shrine, with eyes love-lit,
When on the roll-call of her dead
    Brave Sean MacDermott's name is writ.

And not upon this shrine alone,
    That name, sealed with his blood is set;
'Twill flame where noble deeds are done
    In days unborn to history yet.
And men will feel their pulses thrill

To read of Erin's glorious scroll
Of those who broke a tyrant's will
    And saved from him their country's soul.

The O'Rahilly

W.B. Yeats

Sing of the O'Rahilly,
Do not deny his right;
Sing a 'the' before his name;
Allow that he, despite
All those learned historians,
Established it for good;
He wrote out that word himself,
He christened himself with blood.
        How goes the weather?

Sing of the O'Rahilly
That had such little sense
He told Pearse and Connolly
He'd gone to great expense
Keeping all the Kerry men
Out of that crazy fight;
That he might be there himself
Had travelled half the night.
        How goes the weather?

'Am I such a craven that
I should not get the word
But for what some travelling man
Had heard I had not heard?'
Then on Pearse and Connolly
He fixed a bitter look:
'Because I helped to wind the clock
I come to hear it strike.'
        How goes the weather?

What remains to sing about
But of the death he met
Stretched under a doorway
Somewhere off Henry Street;
They that found him found upon
The door above his head
'Here died the O'Rahilly
R.I.P.' writ in blood.
        How goes the weather?

Text: W.B. Yeats, *The Poems,*
Everyman, London, 1992.

F.T. Meloe, 'The O'Rahilly'.
(Courtesy of Ruth Sweeney and Michael O'Rahilly.)

495

Roger Casement and Daniel Bailey (of the Royal Irish Rifles) in the Dock at Bow Street Police Court.
The Children's Story of the War, Thomas Nelson & Sons, London, 1917.

The Ghost of Roger Casement

W.B. Yeats

O what has made that sudden noise?
What on the threshold stands?
It never crossed the sea because
John Bull and the sea are friends;
But this is not the old sea
Nor this the old seashore.
What gave that roar of mockery,
That roar in the sea's roar?

The ghost of Roger Casement
Is beating on the door.

John Bull has stood for Parliament,
A dog must have his day,
The country thinks no end of him
For he knows how to say
At a beanfeast or a banquet,
That all must hang their trust
Upon the British Empire,
Upon the Church of Christ.

The ghost of Roger Casement
Is beating on the door.

John Bull has gone to India
And all must pay him heed
For histories are there to prove
That none of another breed
Has had a like inheritance,
Or sucked such milk as he,
And there's no luck about a house
If it lack honesty.

The ghost of Roger Casement
Is beating on the door.

I poked about a village church
And found his family tomb
And copied out what I could read
In that religious gloom;
Found many a famous man there;
But fame and virtue rot.
Draw round, beloved and bitter men,
Draw round and raise a shout;

The ghost of Roger Casement
Is beating on the door.

Sir Roger Casement had been knighted by the British government for his investigations and exposure of dreadful human rights abuses in Peru and in the Belgian Congo. He tried, unsuccesfully, to organize an Irish Brigade among Irish prisoners-of-war in Germany during WWI, and also arranged a shipment of German weapons to arm the Volunteers. The arms landing failed, and he was captured, convicted of treason and sentenced to death.

His execution was arguably illegal, as his conviction turned upon how the sense of a passage in the original 1351 Anglo-French text of the Treason Act was affected by a single comma.

Widespread calls for clemency were silenced through the leaked publication of his diaries, which revealed that the writer had engaged in homosexual acts, a crime at the time. The diaries were condemned by nationalists as forgeries, but they are now generally accepted as being authentic.

His death inspired more praise poems than that of any other figure.

Text: W.B. Yeats, *The Poems,* Everyman, London, 1992.

Casement

Teresa Brayton

Text: Teresa Brayton, *The Flame of Ireland*, New York, 1926.

They took the title from his name,
    That paltry gift of Britain's hand,
Nor saw a laurel wreath aflame
    For him today in every land;
They stood him on a gallows tree
    With eyes blindfolded from the light,
Nor saw, down all the years to be,
    His soul a sword for truth and light.

They hanged him high in Pentonville;
    Uncoffined there his ashes lie,
A mound of dust that may not thrill
    To sun or shade, to sea or sky.
But somewhere, far beyond our ken,
    O'er awful vistas yet unrolled,
That dust shall spring to fighting men
    As sprang the dragon's teeth of old.

A Galahad of stainless name,
    A knight unstained midst wrong and strife,
Their lies could not besmirch his fame,
    Their rope could never end his life,
Their gallows was a pedestal
    Lifting him up for all to see
How Irishmen yet fight and fall
    And die for Ireland's liberty.

Fall as a wind-tossed billow falls
    To give new tides beyond it place,
When the uprisen ocean calls
    Its waters in a stormy race;
Fall as the martyrs of the world
    Shall fall forever, fearlessly,
Till the last wrong to hell is hurled
    And man, in God's high name, is free.

They murdered him in Pentonville
    While howling mobs profaned the air
Like wolves who only dare to kill
    When the full pack is gathered there;
But others, of his countrymen,
    Knelt in the dust for him who cried:
'I give my life for Ireland,' then –
    'God take my soul' – before he died.

God took his soul, God heard his cry,
   God gauged his reckoning, yea, and set
Above the farthest reach of sky,
   Casement's immortal coronet.
God ranged his coin of sacrifice –
   His life, 'twas all he had to give –
With theirs whose blood has paid our price,
   And died that Ireland's soul shall live.

Roger Casement in the custody of the English police in 1916.

Roger Casement
(After reading *The Forged Casement Diaries*
by Dr Maloney)
W.B. Yeats

Text: W.B. Yeats, *The Poems*,
Everyman, London, 1992.
    Air: This poem has been set to the air
of 'Skibbereen'.

I say that Roger Casement
Did what he had to do,
He died upon the gallows
But that is nothing new.

Afraid they might be beaten
Before the bench of Time
They turned a trick by forgery
And blackened his good name.

A perjurer stood ready
To prove their forgery true;
They gave it out to all the world
And that is something new;

For Spring-Rice had to whisper it
Being their Ambassador,
But then the speakers got it
And writers by the score.

Come Tom and Dick, come all the troop
That cried it far and wide,
Come from the forger and his desk,
Desert the perjurer's side;

Come speak your bit in public
That some amends be made
To this most gallant gentleman
That is in quick-lime laid.

The Choice
Dora Sigerson

Text: Dora Sigerson, *Poems of the
Irish Rebellion 1916*, Maunsel and
Company, Dublin, 1916.

This Consul Casement – he who heard the cry
Of stricken people – and who in his fight
To lift the torture load from broken men,
And shield sad women from eternal night,
Went through lone, hot, and fevered foreign lands.

For doomèd Casement, slaves that he raised up
Pray with strong voices, so a wide world hears.
Men saved from anguish, women saved from shame,
He dried your children's tears!
He gave you life – for him lift pleading hands.

Sir Roger Casement, honoured for his years
Of stress and struggle, of fatigue and work,
What is the claim of his frail human needs
For arduous hours he did not shun nor shirk,
A King's reward, a royal friendliness!

For honoured Casement titles and renown,
A future great with promise, all life's page
Writ in gold letters, and a path so soft
One could not hear the coming of old age
To point an honoured tomb that nations bless.

Ah! Irish Casement, in the roar of war
That stung his blood and whipped his manhood's fire,
What did he hear upon red shaken earth,
Where little nations struggle and expire?
Some banshee cry upon the hot wind thrills!

And Roger Casement – he who freed the slave,
Made sad babes smile and tortured women hope,
Flung all aside, King's honours and great years,
To take for *finis* here a hempen rope,
And banshee cries upon far Irish hills.

The Rebel
Roger Casement
Padraic Colum

They have hanged Roger Casement to the tolling of a bell,
    Ochone, och, ochone, ochone!
And their Smiths and their Murrays and their Cecils say
    it's well,
    Ochone, och, ochone, ochone!
But there are outcast peoples to lift that spirit high,
Flayed men and breastless women who laboured fearfully,
And they will lift him, lift him for the eyes of God to see,
And it's well, after all, Roger Casement!

Text: Padraic Colum, *Irish Elegies*,
The Dolmen Press, Dublin, 1961.

They've ta'en the strangled body and laid it in the pit,
　　Ochone, och, ochone, ochone!
And brought the stealthy fire to waste it bit by bit,
　　Ochone, och, ochone, ochone!
To waste that noble stature, that grave and brightening face
That set courtesy and kindliness in eminence of place,
But they – they'll die to dust that no poet e'er will trace,
While 'twas yours to die to fire, Roger Casement.

Roger Casement
Sigerson Clifford

Text: Sigerson Clifford, *Ballads of a Bogman*, The Mercier Press, Cork, 1986.

O let them rake their muck now and pile it Brandon-high,
And grind the bones to powder and spill it on the land;
Enough for us a tall man came with salt spray on his beard,
And smiled to see the ropes of weed on Lonely Banna Strand.

O let them fling their stones now nor heed the splintering glass;
I drained a dram with Monteith and he took me by the hand,
And he told me of the tall man with the green flag in his mind
Who rose from out the noose of sea on lonely Banna Strand.

The tall man in McKenna's Fort saw the dark upon the hills;
He touched his lantern to a star and lighted up the land.
Enough for us the blinds are drawn and crepe is on the door,
Enough we slept while Casement wept on lonely Banna Strand.

A Lament for Roger Casement
Leo Maguire

Text: Leo Maguire, *The Faithful and the Few*, Walton's Musical Instrument Galleries, Dublin, 1959.

A lonely wave is beating on the rocky Antrim shore
And a sighing wind is keening o'er the water's sullen roar;
The sea-birds sweep to haven with a loud and piercing wail;
'Tis the passing-knell for one who dies in a gloomy English
　　jail.

Along the swelt'ring Congo a ghastly silence falls;
The jungle trees hang lifeless, like a thousand funeral palls;
And dark-skinned men are heavy with a fear they cannot
　　name
While their gentle friend is led to death with mockery and
　　shame.

Ah! Lordly Roger Casement, you gave all a man could give
That justice be not mocked at and that liberty might live;
But, you hurt the high and mighty ones in pocket and in pride,
And that is why they hated you and that is why you died.

The greedy ones, the greasy ones, they clutched their money-bags
While the Irish peasant toiled and starved and his children froze in rags.
The dying screams of negroes 'neath the lash and on the rack
Were muffled in the stifling folds of the sacred Union Jack.

Aye, they stripped you of your honours and they hounded you to death;
And their blood-lust was not sated when you gasped your dying breath.
They've tried to foul your mem'ry as they burned your corpse with lime,
But God is not an Englishman and truth will tell with time.

Ah! Gentle Roger Casement, you have left us in your debt!
They've tried to blot you from our minds but we will not forget,
For God sits high in Heaven and your cause will yet prevail
Tho' your bones be trodden underfoot in a gloomy English jail.

Francis Sheehy-Skeffington
Dublin, April 26, 1916
Eva Gore-Booth

No green and poisonous laurel wreath shall shade
   His brow, who dealt no death in any strife,
Crown him with olive who was not afraid
   To join the desolate unarmed ranks of life.

Who did not fear to die, yet feared to slay,
   A leader in the war that shall end war,
Unarmed he stood in ruthless Empire's way,
   Unarmed he stands on Acheron's lost shore.

Yet not alone, nor all unrecognized,
   For at his side does that scorned Dreamer stand,
Who in the Olive Garden agonized,
   Whose kingdom yet shall come in every land,

When driven men, who fight and hate and kill
   To order, shall let all their weapons fall,
And know that kindly freedom of the will
   That holds no other human will in thrall.

Text: Edna C. Fitzhenry (ed.),
Nineteen-Sixteen Anthology,
Browne & Nolan Ltd, Dublin, 1935.

Marbhna Thomáis Aghais

Seo dán i n-omós do Thomás Ághas a fuair bás de bharr bídh a thabhairt dó i n-éadan a thoille, agus é ar stailc ocrais i bPriosún Mhuinseó, Baile Átha Cliath, ar an 25 Meán Fómhair 1917. Tá breis eolais faoi Thomás Ághas ar fail insna dánta/amhráin 'Let Me Carry Your Cross for Ireland, Lord' agus 'Lament for Thomas Aghas' sa chnuasach seo.

'Sé Cinn Áird, sa chéad agus sa tríú bhéarsa, baile fearainn dúchais Thomáis Ághais, i Lios Phóil, Co. Chiarraí.

Sa tarna bhearsa deintear tagairt do 'cath Ashbourne', an cath a tharla le linn Éirí Amach na Cásca 1916 – féach 'Let Me Carry your Cross for Ireland, Lord' chun tuile eolais a fháil faoi'n gcath sin. [LM]

Text: Ballad sheet.

I gCinn Áird fhéarghlais ar fhaobhar na taoide
Tá tinteán néata faoi dhubhnéal bróin
Faoin ngárlach rua cas ná fillfidh choíche
Ó d'fhág le haoibh é ar buí lá Fómhair.
Bhí Tomás Ághas geal glan, sé troigh ar airde,
Bánchnis shíodúil is croí mar leon,
Ba chaite snoite a chaolchorp sínte
Faoi bhrat na saoirse – ár laoch go deo.

I gcath Ashbourne ar theorann na Mí thuas
I mBearna an Bhaoil sheas an tÁghasach óg
'S gur le neart a ghéaga is cabhair a dhiorma
Do bhuaigh glan díreach ar bhuíon ní ba mhó
Ó bhuillí tréana ná feall dá ghéire,
Níor chúl ár laoch geal riamh aon ló
Ach ar fud na tíre ag adhaint na saoirse
Níor staon dá dhícheall gur gabhadh faoi dhó.

Ba thréan a mhóidigh aon bhia nach tógadh
I ngéibhinn fuar glas aon deoch níor ól
'S gur le fórsa pípe a baineadh díoltas
Ó Dhia 's a Shaoirse faraor go deo.
Ár gceannairí tréana ag Gaill dá sléachtadh
Ag dó san aol gheal taréis an áir
Is ar ghaoth an Gheimhridh cois faobhar na taoide
Tá monuar caointe ar thráig Chinn Áird.

Our Latest Hero Dead
(To the Memory of Thomas Ashe)
Lyrics: James Mulcahy Lyons (b. 1874) / *Music: A. Ryan*

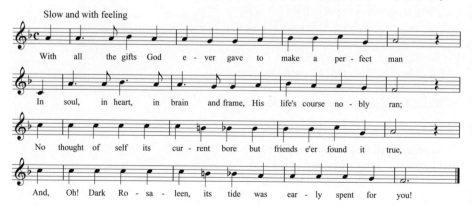

504

With all the gifts God ever gave
　　To make a perfect man
In soul, in heart, in brain and frame,
　　His life's course nobly ran;
No thought of self its current bore
　　But friends e'er found it true,
And Oh! Dark Rosaleen, its tide
　　Was early spent for you!

We miss the manly form we loved
　　Its splendour and its grace.
We miss the fearless heart, the soul
　　That held no essence base;
We miss the gifted tongue and pen,
　　The mind to music wed,
And dwell with mournful pride upon
　　Our latest hero, dead!

Text and music: Sheet music published by The Art Depot, Dublin, 1917.

The Black Raven Pipe Band at the funeral of Thomas Ashe, 30 September 1917.
The band, based in Lusk, Co. Dublin, had numbered Ashe among their members.

Rubaiyat of Knutsford

Knutsford Prison, near Manchester, was one of the English prisons to which Irish political prisoners and insurgents were sent, immediately after 1916, prior to their transfer to Frongoch internment camp in Wales.

The prison also housed Irish political prisoners during the following years, up to 1921.

A parody of Edward Fitzgerald's 'Rubaiyat of Omar Khayam', this extended piece cleverly parallels many of Fitzgerald's quatrains.

Text: *Songs & Poems, The Rebels Who Fought and Died for Ireland in Easter Week, 1916* (Samuels Collection, TCD).

Dreaming when dawn's bright face lit up my cell,
I woke to hear the chink of keys that tell
   The jailer's advent, and his summons brief –
'Up, sleeper, there!' which gave my sleep the knell.

'Tis 4 a.m., and Knutsford jail's alive;
Pardon, ye daylight savers, faith, 'tis five.
   Blinking my eyes – for sleep still veils their view –
But, howsomever, up, I must contrive.

Clanging of doors and keys and hurrying feet,
Washing of floors and warders' gentle bleat,
   Rush on my ears and rouse me to the fray;
I fix my plank and trim my cell complete.

Then, in a tin which flashes like a glass
(Result of bathbrick and my hands' compass),
   I wash my face, and feel the stubble there;
Razors, you know, are named seditious trash.

Then dawns event of morning's custom here:
To wit, our breakfast. Hark, it doth appear!
   Tea, in a vessel round, with slender waist;
Of bread one chunk, and margarine a smear.

Come, quaff with me this beverage of slops!
Drink! ere its heat to freezing point quite drops.
   Take, too, a bite of this delicious loaf,
Ere in my cell the watchful jailer pops.

Here, with a loaf of bread, aged twenty-three,
A cigarette, a jug of tea and thee
   Beside me weaving songs about the Knuts,
And Knutsford Jail is Paradise to me!

My cell, good friends, lacks ornament, say you?
Naught decorates it – whitewashed walls, 'tis true –
   But, see you now my washing on the line –
A shirt, a towel, and a sock or two?

My plank, behold it up against the wall,
Its sublime structure, three long boards and all;
   Observe its pose, and see my blankets, too,
When dusk appears, beneath them I shall crawl.

But hence! Such thoughts away! Let us arise,
And take the air beside my comrades five;
   For desperadoes, six in all, are we;
And you shall see them, if they still survive.

Here comes my guardian, Knight of jangling keys;
In khaki clad, a sergeant, if you please!
    He opes the door. Come, let us ramble forth,
Into the area fanned by gentle breeze.

And now, behold, with artist's eyes awhile,
The pride of Knutsford! See this red brick pile,
    Enobling grace in every feature teems;
Aesthetic triumph! Greco-Cheshire style!

These windows barred – observe them, line and line!
One for each cell – at least I've one in mine;
    And if your gaze some sweeter object seeks –
There is the gallows. Institution fine!

My five companions, yes, you see them there,
That's P----- M---------, for ladies' hearts a snare;
    Look how his pockets bulge with their tribute
His post it comes – well, just from anywhere!

But if M-------- breaks hearts and scruples not;
There's Doctor D-------- will cure them on the spot,
    And make his patients feel a sad regret
He's married – so his cures may go to pot!

Here stalks a man of mighty mien and jaw,
Well known to C--------, a Barrister-at-law;
    Puzzled is he to find himself in quod,
But that would puzzle even Bernard Shaw.

Then, sauntering slow, comes Rory of the Hill,
In search of parcels – or poetic thrill;
    In autographs, he earned an expert's fame
When Mitchell's sentence flowed from off his quill.

Such my companions, comrades in distress;
Two more were there, but now have no address;
    D-------- and B-------- off to Wales are fled;
But does it matter, one whit more or less?

Come, take a turn around this sun-rayed yard;
Forget awhile that egress here is barred;
    Survey the world, with Knutsford as Grand Stand,
With mind-lit eyes – we still hold one trump card.

Now fades before our gaze those lines of bricks;
Our khaki guardians follow in a tick;
    And standing here, exhaling gold-flake smoke.
We'll visualize all mankind pretty quick.

. . . .

What's that we view – a vista of decay?
A smouldering ruin, heaps of ashes grey;
    Is that Louvain, or Rheims, or famed Ypres,
Are the black debris marks of vile Huns' prey?

But no; methinks as strain my eyes thro' space,
Some signs familiar rise about the place;
    Those fire-scorched walls, this wreckage heaped
      grotesque,
It is old Dublin, wounded, war-scarred face.

These are the hall-marks of the gentle way
That petrol bombs preached 'Irish slaves, obey!'
    These conquest jewels gem 'the one bright spot',
I thank thee, War Lord, 'twas thy word, O Grey!

. . . .

But pass we on, not ended yet the sphere
Of our survey; methinks yon passing queer;
    A line of men with rifles stand erect,
Their target there – a green-clad Volunteer!

Rings now a volley – comrade, let us pray!
A living creature's form has passed to clay!
    A criminal, maybe, a trait'rous, odious rogue?
No – one we loved has winged his soul away.

But pause not here, to weep or mourn that deed;
For such, believe, are conquest's gory need;
    Buttressed with buildings, bulwarked by the dead,
'Tis Hades' offering to the Devil's creed.

In sooth, such are but Culture's talons spread
To clasp the erring sure by hair of head,
    And keep them, yoked to righteous Beelzebub,
So they the steps of Saint Bill Sykes may tread.

. . . .

But, Holy Moses. Here's a fine to do!
Are all the girls, from here to Timbuctoo,
    Besieging Knutsford with the wild design
Of freeing us? No – faith, I have a clue.

These serried ranks of damsels, blithe and gay,
Are merely seeking to find out a way
    To see M--------. Hark, how his name they call?
See how they jostle, in their grand array.

They shake his hands and seem inclined to tear 'em;
Some carry socks, and beg of him to wear 'em;
    Parcels, fruit, and odds and ends galore,
Beware, M--------, the law forbids a harem!

But, bless them all, each kindly Irish heart;
It makes me young to see how they impart,
    With eyes like sunbeams, gladness into jail;
But P----- M-------- is vanquished by their dart.

And now they're gone; and in we're marched to eat
A Knutsford meal – a gastronomic feat –
    Three spuds, a loaf, and something lacking name –
Some call it soup – the liars! – base deceit!

Once in my cell, with such repast set down,
Armed with a spoon, and on my face a frown;
    I fished amid its hazy depth to find
A substance spongy, tame and coloured brown.

Shades of Block L! My soul heaved with relief;
I called to mind my friend, Paudeen O'Keeffe,
    When we chummed there, and shared our frugal
      meal,
An iron biscuit and some bully beef.

For such it was now rushed upon my view –
An ancient relic of Chicago brew;
    Sturdy, tho' flabby, loud its voice exclaimed:
'I reckon, boss, that this is SOME stew.'

Too full for words I listened to the end
Of its discourse, but could not wholly bend
    My mind to task so meet for cannibal –
Like unto that of eating an old friend.

While gushed the tears from out my eyes in floods,
I gently laid Chicago near my duds;
    And, musing o'er our chequered fellowship,
I set to work to peel and eat my spuds.

The Spirit Invincible

A note in the source reads: 'The subject of this poem was suggested by a fellow-prisoner, namely, to express the motive and spirit of the rebel fighters, as contrasted with those of the mercenary, or even the soldiers who fight under the flag of a free country. (Knutsford, 22 June 1916).'

Text: *Songs & Poems, The Rebels Who Fought and Died for Ireland in Easter Week, 1916* (Samuels Collection, TCD).

Go forth in your mustered legions,
    Arrayed in your soldier gear,
To shake with your pent-up thunder
    The earth, till your enemies fear.
You are massed, you are girt for the tramping,
    Right down to the valley of fire;
And the heart of your people is thrilling,
    If in battle, you, fighting, expire.

Yes, ye of the freedom-won nations,
    You can lift up your eyes to the sun,
And hear on your ear-drums the plaudits
    Of a world, e'er the battle's begun.
'Tis spoken that foemen embattled
    Are nearing your land from afar,
And you rush with a gun to the standard
    That waves o'er the regions of war.

There are tears and sorrow at leaving,
    There are aching and sorrow of heart;
But there's pride and a glorious thrilling,
    'Mid the weepings and sighs when you part.

There's Honour and Duty to bid you
    Face Death, with a front undismayed.
There's none of the Homeland to chide you,
    Or scorn, then, the soldier's dread trade.
There's none then to tell you 'tis madness,
    There is none to acclaim you as great,
If you shun all the dangers of battle,
    And skulk till the foe's at the gate.

Yes, courage you show when you enter
    The lists of the war's bloody plain,
And face all its horrors undaunted,
    And die there, if fate so ordain.

You picture the valley of slaughter,
    The moans and the sobbings of woe;
The red-dripping bayonets that mangle,
    The shrieking as foemen meet foe.
The crackling of rifles, and thunder
    Of guns, that seem mouthpiece of hell,
The nerve-wracking waiting, half-frozen,
    Till it's time for advancing pell-mell.

You shudder and halt ere you face it,
    And you count up the loss and the gain,
E'en the bravest may wince at the prospect
    With its torture and carnage insane.
But the MAN in your heart calls for courage,
    And you conquer the pangs of dismay,
And you pray to your God for the spirit
    And strength for the mind-wracking fray;
And you go to the shambles, uplifted
    With the sense that God's finger is nigh,
And you strike for the Right in your contest,
    And, fighting thus, gloriously die.

But we, of the peoples imperilled,
    By the weight of a conqueror's heel,
We, sons of a nation in bondage,
    All such, and much more, do we feel.
When we face the grim ordeal of freedom,
    Of restoring the sway of the Right,
When we lift high the standard of Erin,
    To rally her sons to the fight.

'Tis not the mere woes of the conflict,
    And 'tis not the sharp, stabbing steel,
Nor is it the volleying thunder
    That rattles out, peal upon peal;
'Tis not only the charging entrenchments,
    'Mid the swift-winged, death-dealing lead,
'Tis not the hot anguish of dying,
    Unsuccoured, 'mid enemy's tread.

No, these be but part of the scourges,
    That fall on the patriot's soul;
Those but the least part of the ransom
    That he pays to reach liberty's goal.

There's the cold, jarring sneer of the cynic,
    There's the smile of the placeman's disdain,
There's the cloud o'er the vision-lost people,
    There's the tyrant, the spies in his train.
There's the slow stirring up of the embers
    Of hope, nearly quenched by despair,
There's the strain to inspire the awakening
    Of souls, till they plan and prepare.

There's the silent, subdued propaganda,
    To rouse and to cheer and to arm,
There's the danger from fools and from traitors,

The rash and the perilous calm;
There's the voice of the tempter seductive,
　　Oh! who shall portray the travail
Of the patriot, seeking life's substance,
　　When the tempter his soul shall assail.

There's the price on his head by the tyrant,
　　Urging vultures, alert, on his trail,
There's the soul-wracking fear of disaster,
　　A gibbet, or cell, if he fail.
No splendid array for his comrades,
　　As they gather for strife with the foe;
No trumpets or cheering, arousing
　　His land to its re-birth. Ah, no!
But waiting and counting their chances
　　In silence, these patriot hosts,
Till an hour which they deemed blest by Heaven
　　Cheers their souls, and they charge to their posts.

Perchance they shall win the encounter,
　　God willing, as victors to stand
With the ruins of serfdom beneath them,
　　And a crown on their loved Motherland;
Or the tyrant may trample them under,
　　Then woe, direst woe, be their fate;
His wrath shall surround them with dangers,
　　Their deaths be the gauge of his hate.

But the soul that hath visioned the splendour
　　For freedom, will glory to be
On the roll of the heroes, who, falling,
　　Made a nation, long struggling, free.

Knutsford Hotel

George Lashwood (1863–1942) was a popular British music-hall singer, and Sir Thomas Lipton (1848–1931) was the founder of the famous firm of tea merchants. He is referred to also in the poem 'The Irish Brigade' on p. 514.

Text: *Songs & Poems, The Rebels Who Fought and Died for Ireland in Easter Week, 1916* (Samuels Collection, TCD).

Oh, why do old misers their wealth grimly hoard,
And not live in peace like the Knuts at the Ford?
Or why does George Lashwood in town do the swell,
When there is such joy at old Knutsford Hotel?

Nice bacon for breakfast, and eggs newly laid,
Thin slices of bread, and some Scotch marmalade;
Fresh pots of tea, Tommy Lipton's best brew,
A can full to the brim of rich Irish stew.

MP's to talk to, and ices all hot;
Ladies when gazed on can ne'er be forgot;
Soft beds to lie on for quite a long spell,
Wakened at dawn by the ring of a bell.

Rich men and poor men, all on the mash,
No need for money and no use for cash;
Only polishing your tins, and scrubbing your cell,
So this is the way at the Knutsford Hotel.

The Captain, he calls, to your wants attending,
Looks to your boots in case they want mending;
Someone in poor clothes, all tattered and torn,
Seeming to say, sure my case is forlorn.

Felt hats that went thro' the thick of the fray,
Mascots to treasure when we've passed away;
Left to our grandsons, their tale to tell,
Of the owners who wore them at Knutsford Hotel.

We're facing the future, oh, what will it send?
Can it break the spirit that never will bend?
Can law or its arm make Irishmen fear?
Or hard labour's lot from us drag a tear?

Oh, no, Mother Erin, that never can be,
We're willing to suffer, my darling, for thee;
For Pearse and his heroes, our hearts all do swell,
Altho' we're locked up in the Knutsford Hotel.

A Jail Bird

Brian O'Higgins

What the dickens brought you to jail,
    You poor little timid grey thing?
Did you tread on some Constitutional tail,
    Or treat some Act as a gay thing?
Did you perch where tricolour flags were hung,
    Or heckle a platitude dealer?
Did you sing some song that shouldn't be sung
    Or go chirruping after a peeler?

Text: Brian O'Higgins, *1916 Before and After*, Wolfe Tone Annual 1950, Dublin, 1950.

513

Did you get mixed up in a German plot
    To shatter the glorious Realm? –
A collapsible boat in a lonely spot,
    With a mystery man at the helm;
Bombs from Berlin and guns from Kiel,
    And German Gold in billions –
A full-dress show for a cinema reel,
    And a thrill for the English millions!

Did you lay an egg in the Short Mare's Nest
    That is built of Long French flora?
Did you fail to obey the least behest
    Of the Dame we know as Dora?
Did you utter a counterfeit Treasury Note
    Or jeer a recruiting parson?
Did you rent a cage from a man who wrote
    The Exploits of Sir Edward Carson?

Whatever your 'crime', get far from here
    As fast as your wings can bear you,
And keep on singing your note of cheer
    As long as the Lord shall spare you.
Some suffering one shall make your song
    His memory's precious plaything –
God leave you freedom and keep you strong,
    You poor little timid grey thing!

The Irish Brigade

Like the poem on p. 506, this is another clever parody, this time of Thomas Davis's poem 'The Battle Eve of the Brigade'.

Text: *Songs & Poems, The Rebels Who Fought and Died for Ireland in Easter Week, 1916* (Samuels Collection, TCD).

They all watch their doors, each white face is set –
For supper is ready, though it isn't served yet;
The Staff-sergeant cries with an uplifted glance,
'Inside your rooms! With the supper advance!'
With shuffling and whispering they've done as he bade,
For they're all nearly starving, the Irish Brigade.

Now hear you that shuffling, and hear you that tramp –
As along come the Taymen, your mug just to damp.
Their two boys, with baskets of stuff they call bread –
It's usually half-baked and as heavy as lead.
Hurrah, for the glad hour of supper has come,
And soon we'll be bending o'er many a crumb.

As they sat at their tables, and the black tea they
   quaffed,
'Here's to bold Thomas Lipton!' – and fiercely they
   laughed!
And here's to the feeds, we ate long ago,
At ---------- in Dublin, where the Liffey doth flow.
God prosper the bakers, you'd think them afraid,
So pale grew the cheeks of the Irish Brigade.

So they feasted and revel'ed, fast, fiery, and true,
And of loaves, if they had them they'd eat just a few.
Like Lazarus, they picked up the crumbs off the floor,
And they begged of their people to send them some
   more
Meat, butter and bread and, oh, great cakes home-made,
To save from starvation the Irish Brigade.

Cowld Tay

Seán Etchingham (1870–1923) *13 December 1916*

We watched out if anyone knew us,
   But got no reward for our pains,
As we journeyed from Dartmoor to Lewes
   Secured in our handcuffs and chains.
But soon other thoughts we were thinking
   For 'ere we had reached the half way,
Like boys out of school we were drinking
   A glass of the cowldest of tay.

Chorus
So let us to England be grateful,
   And trust her by night and by day,
And swear that rebellion is hateful
   As long as she gives us cowld tay.

For she's out to save little nations,
   Isn't that what her leading men said?
To prove it she's now on half rations
   And fairly well stranded for bread.
So we rebels are resting contented,
   Our feelings light-hearted and gay,
For we see that 'John Bull' is demented
   And we toast his defeat in cowld tay.

Cowld tay (cold tea) is a satirical comment on the fare given to the Irish prisoners in their journeyings in England, following their imprisonment there (Dartmoor and Lewes jails being two of the places of detention) in the aftermath of the 1916 Rising.

Seán Etchingham was a leader of the Irish Volunteers in Enniscorthy, Co. Wexford, and he was among the Volunteers who took control of the town during Easter Week 1916. There was almost no fighting there, the orders being to disrupt the railway line to prevent British troops reaching Dublin, by rail, from the port of Rosslare.

Etchingham won a seat in the 1918 election and again in 1921. He opposed the Treaty of 1921 and was jailed during the Civil War. His health deteriorated while in jail and he died in April 1923. [LM]

Text: C. Desmond Greaves, *The Easter Rising in Song & Ballad*, Kahn & Averill, for the Workers' Music Association, London, 1980.

Frongoch was an internment camp in North Wales, close to the town of Bala and, before the arrival of the Irish in 1916, had been a German prisoner-of-war camp. Following the countrywide swoops in Ireland, after the 1916 Easter Rising, those arrested were interned in Frongoch. Some were not insurgents or activists, but were merely caught up in the large-scale arrests. It was in Frongoch that the plans were laid for a return to the independence struggle, the camp being referred to as the 'University of Revolution'. A very full account, including lists of those held in the camp, can be had in *Frongoch, University of Revolution*, by Seán O'Mahony, and published by FDR Teoranta. All the internees were released to return home by December 1916. [LM]

The Frongoch Roll-Call

Joseph Stanley (1889–1950) Hut 6 (352)

Fifteen forgetful rebels filed into the Frongoch 'clink',
  Shouting out the battle-cry of Freedom.
In a state of blank abstraction – of their names they
    couldn't think,
  So they shouted out the battle-cry of Freedom.

Chorus
Gott strafe the roll-call, hurrah for the 'Mikes',
Hurrah for the rebel boys that organized the strikes,
For everywhere the roll was called, their names they
    didn't know,
  So they shouted out the battle-cry of Freedom.

Now this caused a great commotion, but the rebels spent
    their time
  Shouting out the battle-cry of Freedom.
A court came down to 'sit on' them – the function was
    sublime –
  Shouting out the battle-cry of Freedom.

'While the IRA prisoners were
interned in Frongoch Camp, a general
roll-call was ordered by the British
military authorities, with a view of
identifying men for pressing them into
the army. The general body of the
men refused to answer the roll-call,
with the result that fifteen of the hut
leaders were arrested, courtmartialled,
and the majority were sentenced to a
month's imprisonment with hard
labour. Despite the hardships involved
for both leaders and men, the
"identity strike" was entirely successful, and the following lines commemorate the event.' Note in source.
  Joseph Stanley was a printer who
had published the underground, anti-
government newspaper *The Spark*. He
filled the role of Press Officer during
the Rising, and produced the rebels'
communiqué *Irish War News*.

Text: Samuels Collection, TCD.
  Air: 'The Battle-Cry of Freedom'.

517

With their speechifying and oratory the courthouse knew no rest,
 Shouting out the battle-cry of Freedom.
It was largely quite irrelevant, but they got things off their chest,
 Shouting out the battle-cry of Freedom.

And when the smoke of battle cleared, and th' air was free of dust,
 Shouting out the battle-cry of Freedom.
They got a month's hard labour, for their memories to adjust,
 And they shouted out the battle-cry of Freedom.

Now the moral of the story isn't very far to seek,
 Shouting out the battle-cry of Freedom.
In the fight against the Sassanach, don't turn the other cheek,
 Shouting out the battle-cry of Freedom.

A Mountjoy Ditty

I'll sing you a ditty___ of Dub - lin's fair ci - ty___
And a place called Mount - joy___ which all of you know.
'Twas there of all pla - ces,___ the boys cut the tra - ces,___
And got out___ of pri - son___ a - live, a - live, o.

Text: *The Granuaile Song Book*, The
Irish Supply Depot, Dublin, 1922.
 Air: 'Alive, Alive, O!' or 'Molly
Malone'.

I'll sing you a ditty of Dublin's fair city,
 And a place called Mountjoy which all of you know.
'Twas there of all places the boys cut the traces,
 And got out of prison alive, alive O.

The first was bold Barton, when he was departin',
 Left a note for the 'Boss' his politeness to show.
An' a 'dummy' in order to fool the poor warder,
 But Barton had 'hopped' it, alive, alive O.

J.J. Walsh and Pierce Beasley, the trick did quite easily,
 Some pro-German devil a ladder did throw.
Then 'some' twenty Sinn Féiners like acrobat trainers,
 Scaled the wall and got free all alive, alive O.

They're thinking to-morrow to call it 'Mount Sorrow',
    It's made of John Bull such a terrible show.
His prison no longer have bolts any stronger,
    To hold in Sinn Féiners alive, alive O.

I'll finish my rhyme now, and think it's near time now,
    The people are laughing wherever you go.
It caused great elation in this ancient nation,
    Sinn Féiners, Pro-Irish alive, alive O.

The Constitutional Movement Must Go On
Fergus O'Connor (b. 1876)

Through Britannia there is joy and exultation,
    And a statesman great proclaimed is brother John
Since at Waterford he made the declaration
    That the Constitutional Movement must go on.

Chorus
Then gather the Party round, Sinn Féiners scorning,
    And let your speeches roll across the Floor,
For the Constitutional Movement now, take warning,
    Must go on and on and on for ever more.

Great acts, with possibilities potential,
    And Home Rule upon the Statute Book we've won,
But connection with the Empire being essential,
    The Constitutional Movement must go on.

Until William Archer Redmond is made Colonel,
    Until every Irish goose becomes a swan,
While there's Castle Gold to keep the *Freeman's Journal*,
    The Constitutional Movement must go on.

While poor old Ireland with wild grief and lamentations
    Mourns o'er her heroes who are gone,
There's delight amongst the Party men's relations,
    For jobbery and corruptions must go on.

De Valera, in a burst of indignation,
    Says our methods, tried an' true, are nearly done,
But we'll soon convince him, thro' a deputation,
    That the Constitutional Movement must go on!

The following song was written in Dartmoor Prison on hearing that John Redmond had addressed a public meeting in Waterford, in which he declared that in spite of everything and no matter what happened 'the Constitutional Movement must go on.'
Note in source.
    See p. 255 for Sean O'Casey's version of this song.

Text: *The Irish Soldier's Song Book*, Fergus O'Connor, Dublin, n.d.
    Air: The prescribed air 'The Horse Shoe' could not be identified.

Tho' the land become a place of desolation,
 An' the wheat an' spuds an' all the crops are gone,
Our seats we'll hold with grim determination,
 For the Constitutional Movement must go on!

While the earth an' all the stars in space are blazin',
 An' Time, itself, his lengthy race has run,
In the next life the green banner we'll be raisin',
 For the Constitutional Movement must go on!

Manchester Ballad
On the Escape of the Sinn Féin Prisoners from Strangeways Gaol, 25 October 1919

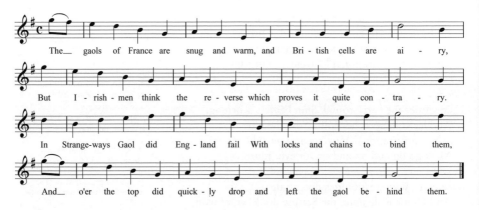

The__ gaols of France are snug and warm, and Bri - tish cells are ai - ry,
But I - rish - men think the re - verse which proves it quite con - tra - ry.
In Strange-ways Gaol did Eng - land fail With locks and chains to bind them,
And__ o'er the top did quick - ly drop and left the gaol be - hind them.

Text: Mansfield Library, University of Montana. Another version of this song with the title 'Escaping Men' may be found in the Donagh MacDonagh Song Collection (see p. 87).
 Air: 'The Girl I Left Behind Me'.

The Gaols of France are snug and warm,
 And British cells are airy,
But Irishmen think the reverse,
 Which proves it quite contrary.
In Strangeways Gaol did England fail
 With locks and chains to bind them,
And o'er the top did quickly drop
 And left the gaol behind them.

Pierce Beasley of Mountjoy fame,
 From bondage now has risen,
And won another victory
 In breaking out of prison.
And with his gallant comrades too,
 We pray they ne'er will find him,
He didn't stay to say good-day
 But left the gaol behind him.

Bold Austin Stack he knew the knack,
　　He watched the Bull Dog sleeping,
While friends outside their time did bide,
　　A watchful vigil keeping.
Hearts high with hope, a ladder rope,
　　Now let your warders find them,
Hurrah, they're out! and freedom's gained,
　　They've left the gaol behind them.

If England built a mighty fort,
　　A thousand feet or higher,
To keep our Irish prisoners –
　　To crush our hearts desire,
Some day they'd wake and find us gone,
　　Whilst ladder ropes remind them,
Of Austin Stack and his brave band,
　　Who left the gaol behind them.

THE REAL EXPLANATION.
(Not generally known, so keep it quiet).

Cartoon by 'Mícheál' from the comic periodical *Irish Fun*, suggesting that the Manchester prison guards were enjoying the periodical so much they never noticed the escape taking place.

Ná Bac Leis

J.S. Considine
Ballykinlar, September 1921

'Ná bac leis' means 'never mind'. This poem is modelled on a very old pattern, with many examples going back at least to the early nineteenth century, when one with the same metre and structure, entitled 'The Major', was published about Town Major Henry Sirr. The comedian Brendan Grace has a similar piece called 'The Mammy'.

The song on the following page is probably a parody of some spiritual or minstrel song, but no original could be identified.

Text: This poem and the one on the facing page are taken from *Ná Bac Leis*, a prisoners' newspaper published in Ballykinlar camp.

When life in Camp comes filled with care
And worries crowd you everwhere,
Be brave – give way not to despair,
    Nabacleis!

When laundry's done and hung to dry,
'Neath sunny morning's azure sky,
It rains in torrents bye and bye,
    Nabacleis!

When in a bout of football play,
You get a knock and bite the clay,
Keep cool – good temper wins the day,
    Nabacleis!

When named each day for Coal fatigue,
Through oversight or Hut intrigue,
You long to join the Looney League,
    Nabacleis!

When comes your turn for hot bath nice,
To banish dirt, disease and - - - other things,
You find the water cold as ice,
    Nabacleis!

When rowdy nights within your hut
Forbid your weary eyes to shut,
If boot or trestle finds your 'nut',
    Nabacleis!

When things move slowly with the Peace
Deferring hopes of quick release,
Take heart – your troubles soon shall cease,
    Nabacleis!

When racked with family cares outside,
Where loving wives and children bide,
Trust Him, who ever shall provide.
    Nabacleis!

Later On, Later On

J.S. Considine

The Prison Camps in Ireland are going to close down,
          Later on, later on.
When the brightest gem is won from the blood-stained British crown
          Later on, later on.
When De Valera forces George at last to sign the Peace,
And the joyful order issues for the Internees release,
Inspection, Coal and Hut fatigue for ever more shall cease.
          Later on, later on.

How lonely we shall all be when we have to leave the scene,
          Later on, later on.
Where we waxed so fat on mouldy bread, thin soup and margarine,
          Later on, later on.
No more the morning bugle note shall call us out of bed,
The crows and seagulls prancing in derision overhead,
But we'll ne'er forget the naughty things our comrades of them said,
          Later on, later on.

No more we'll hear the clatter of our Bedlam dining hall,
          Later on, later on.
When the thin veneer of Etiquette was rubbed off one and all,
          Later on, later on.
Then meals without Orchestra will to us seem very strange,
When spoons on bowls out-echoed all the rifles on the range,
And the lack of pounding hob-nails will be quite a pleasant change,
          Later on, later on.

We'll miss familiar faces of boot and clothes parade,
          Later on, later on.
Who, the role of human scare-crows in borrowed plumes essayed,
          Later on, later on.
No more they'll take their places quite fearful of detection,
As they turned up their ----- garments for the G.O.C.'s inspection,
And we'll miss the flow'ry metaphors of those that met rejection,
          Later on, later on.

In years to come when Peace is signed and all are once more free,
          Later on, later on.
Enshrin'd in happy mem'ry shall those times forever be,
          Later on, later on.
We'll long to clasp kind hands again, and o'er a friendly 'Jar',
Recall those cheery comrades from all Ireland near and far,
Who never let dull tedium our pleasant Camp Life mar,
          Later on, later on.

My Little Grey Home in Mountjoy

Text: *The Granuaile Song Book*, The
Irish Supply Depot, Dublin, 1922.
    Air: 'My Little Grey Home in the
West'.

I have roamed many lands o'er the sea,
    I have dwelt in an old French chateau,
And then once again in a castle in Spain,
    Some glad recollections I know.
But in Dublin's old city a place,
    I know with affection and joy,
In the world anywhere no place can compare
    To my little grey home in Mountjoy.

There were kind friends to welcome me in,
    And a prince he might envy my lot.
There was comfort all round, everything was all found,
    And a splendid reception I got.
My bedroom was on the first floor,
    And nothing my peace to destroy.
This was my first day, and my heart pined away
    For my little grey home in Mountjoy.

The grounds were all laid out in style,
    The avenues shady and cool.
A haven of rest, with attendants the best,
    With quiet and good order the rule.
The tea was all served on the lawn,
    'Twas a feast that the gods might enjoy.
Oh! where'er I may be, I will still think of thee,
    My little grey home in Mountjoy.

Of course you can quite understand,
    This grandeur was all forced on me,
And if I could choose, I could not refuse,
    So then I just let matters be.
Six months was not long going round,
    I had plenty my mind to employ.

At last came the day, I am speeding away
　　From my little grey home in Mountjoy.

They say there is no place like home.
　　I feel I've awoke from a dream.
Once more I am free and at sweet liberty,
　　And many old friends I must see.
They'll all ask me how I got on,
　　And I'll just make this answer, 'old boy –
Oh! from Land's End to Perth, there is no place on earth
　　Like my little grey home in Mountjoy.'

The Mountjoy Hotel

Sliabh Ruadh (Phil O'Neill)

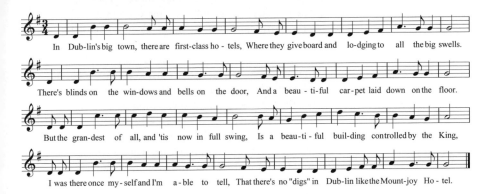

In Dublin's big town, there are first-class ho-tels, Where they give board and lo-dging to all the big swells.

There's blinds on the win-dows and bells on the door, And a beau-ti-ful car-pet laid down on the floor.

But the gran-dest of all, and 'tis now in full swing, Is a beau-ti-ful buil-ding controlled by the King,

I was there once my-self and I'm a-ble to tell, That there's no "digs" in Dub-lin like the Mount-joy Ho-tel.

In Dublin's big town, there are first-class hotels,
Where they give board and lodging to all those big
　　swells,
There's blinds on the windows and bells on the door,
And a beautiful carpet laid down on the floor.
But the grandest of all, and 'tis now in full swing,
Is a beautiful building controlled by the King.
I was there once myself, and I'm able to tell
That there's no 'digs' in Dublin like Mountjoy Hotel.

I was met at the train by the porter and 'bus,
And he took me along with a great deal of fuss.
We drove through the town like a Viceroy in state,
And we never drew rein till we stopped at the gate.

Text: *Songs and Recitations of Ireland, 2 – The Harp*, Coiste Foillseacháin Náisiúnta, Cork, n.d.
　Air: 'Bendemeer's Stream' or 'The Mountains of Mourne'.

525

I was brought to a room, where they took down my name,
They asked my address, and the reason I came,
When I answered those questions, the clerk rang the bell –
I was ordered a bath at the Mountjoy Hotel!

When I got in the bath, though my blood was nigh froze,
The attendant he brought me a new suit of clothes,
The finish was fine and the pattern grand,
And over them all was a beautiful brand.
Then dinner was served – 'twas a glorious feast,
It consisted of five or six courses at least,
But the brandies and liqueurs, they made my head swell
I got drunk as a lord at the Mountjoy Hotel.

The bedrooms were cosy, and carefully kept,
When I laid down to rest I immediately slept.
But early next morning, without 'By your leave',
'Get up' says the boots, 'here's hot water to shave.'
The breakfast consisted of fish, ham and eggs,
But I drained my old stirabout can to the dregs,
Then I asked for the bill; sure the waiter near fell,
''Tis all free, Sir,' said he, 'in the Mountjoy Hotel.'

I went for a walk every day round the grounds,
For the guests as you know, must keep within bounds.
When I asked for my pipe as I wanted a smoke,
Sez the boss, very stiff, 'Do you think it a joke?'
'I'm sorry,' I said, 'you've taken it so,
But please for a brandy and soda, now go.'
'Bread and water,' sez he, 'p'raps will do you as well.'
And I got it that week at the Mountjoy Hotel.

I stopped there some months, as I couldn't well go,
Where all were so kind, and they treated me so,
With light and attendance and everything free,
Not to mention the 'extras' and afternoon tea.
At last came the day when I had to depart –
I almost got sick with the joy in me heart –
For with all its grand comforts, the truth I must tell,
That I won't go again to the Mountjoy Hotel!

Ballykinlar, Co. Down

I've been in Der - by Bar - racks, I've been in Lich - field too.

I've sol - diered up at Walls - end Which was none too grand, 'tis true.

But the place I shall re - mem - ber, And re - mem - ber with a frown

Is that one - eyed, God - for - sa - ken Bal - ly - kin - lar, Coun - ty Down.

I've been in Derby Barracks,
  I've been in Lichfield too.
I've soldiered up at Wallsend
  (Which was none too grand, 'tis true).
But the place I shall remember,
  And remember with a frown
Is that one-eyed, God-forsaken
  Ballykinlar, Co. Down.

'Twas World's-End Camp they called it.
  That describes it to a 'T'.
Had it been a few yards further
  'Twould have been right in the sea.
And the man who first discovered
  This interesting spot
Should rank as an explorer
  With Shackleton and Scott.

We never saw a 'civvy'.
  We never saw a pub.
We never saw a paper.
  We didn't have much grub.
We were so isolated
  That we all agreed 'twas true
We might have been encamping
  In the wilds of Timbuctoo.

The wind was very 'icy'
  And all the fellows said
The only way of getting warm
  Was getting into bed.

Text: Mansfield Library, University
of Montana.
  Air: 'A Little Bit of Heaven'.

527

The cold was so intense there
    An unusual sight we saw,
A seagull from exposure
    Had snuffed it on the shore.

'A little bit of heaven'
    Old Ireland has been named.
The author's perhaps not seen 'World End',
    If so, he can't be blamed.
But I'll make a sweeping statement
    And all the world I'll tell,
If this is a bit of heaven,
    Then give me a bit of hell.

What Ireland Wants

In the course of a friendly chat, the prison
Chaplain asked me what Ireland really
wanted. Below is my reply.

Shepton Mallet Prison, '21

Ben O'Hickey

Text: Ben O'Hickey, *From Prison Cells*, The Elo Press, Dublin, 1935.

What Ireland wants, did you say, Sir? Do I think I could
    give it a name?
Well with all due respect to yourself, Sir, it's easy
    enough, is that same.
Sure Ireland is wanting her own, Sir, these seven long
    centuries past,
And if it takes as long more, Sir, her own she'll be having
    at last.

It isn't so much that she's sought for, a small nation's
    rights, and that's all,
The same England's boasted she's fought for, as well as
    my mind can recall;
She's wanting to cast off forever, the chains that have
    galled her full sore,
The ties of her bondage to sever, and reign as a nation
    once more.

She wants to be rid of coercion – God never made man
    for a slave!

Yet for centuries as serfs have been treated, her sons and
    her daughters so brave,
She wants just to frame her own laws, Sir, with no one
    to hinder or let,
To be brief, Sir, She's wanting her freedom, and freedom
    she's bound for to get.

After Lights Out

Ben O'Hickey
Shepton Mallet Prison, '21

The lights are extinguished, the guard has gone round,
And close to the floor on my pallet I lie,
All over the prison there isn't a sound,
Except an occasional moan or a sigh.

Thro' the iron-bound window that graces my cell,
I'm watching the beautiful star-lighted sky,
And I'm thinking of home, and the friends I love well,
As I gaze on the bright glowing planets on high.

I'm thinking of comrades who fought by my side,
And fell in the fight their loved country to free,
Some have fallen in battle, and bravely they died,
And others faced death on the grim gallows tree.

However they died, or wherever they sleep,
'Twas the one bond of love that united them all,
They fain would be sowers that others might reap,
They bravely made answer to liberty's call.

Peace, peace to their ashes, may God give them rest,
In memory they'll live while this world remains,
In the true Irish Hearts in the isle of the West,
The land which they sought to set free from her chains.

Thus night, after night, I think and I dream,
As steadily onwards the passing hours creep,
And the thoughts of the past drift along in a stream,
Until wearied with thinking I drop off to sleep.

Text: Ben O'Hickey, *From Prison Cells*, The Elo Press, Dublin, 1935.

The Home Coming
(Lewes to Dublin, 18 June 1917)
Alice Milligan (1865–1953)

Text: Samuels Collection, TCD

They have come, and after the prison walls
    Freedom is sweet;
And after the warder's churlish word
Oh, how some boyish hearts are stirred
    By the cheers in the street;
After bread that was broken in solitude
The feast that is shared this day is good
    When with friends is their seat.

Thousands on thousands since early day
    Have waited and thronged,
Wives who have suffered and wept are there,
Girls who have lifted their hearts in prayer,
    Who have hoped, who have longed.
And boys come by with uplifted head
Saying, see we live though the best are dead;
We shall muster and march and stand instead
    For our country wronged.

A shout goes up at the station gate
    Where the guard is set.
A shout goes up from the crowd in the street
    There they are – they are met.
A shout goes up at College Green,
A shout where the Easter flag was seen,
    Shout louder yet.
Shout loudly, loud was the cannonade
Which our noble city in ruins laid,
Yes loudly show we are not dismayed
    And shall not forget.

And not in Dublin streets alone,
    Though Dublin is great,
Oh, not in Dublin streets alone,
But all over Ireland be it known
    Does the welcome wait.
And some are here who must haste away
To Wexford hills or to Galway Bay,
    To Belfast, though late;
And some must travel from Liffey to Lee,
To Shannon shore and to true Tralee;
For not in Dublin streets alone

Should the shots have rung, when the flag was flown
   On the day of fate.
So not in Dublin streets alone
   Does the welcome wait.

Oh, hush the laughter and cease the song,
   Cheer not so loud:
There are some, remember you who sing,
Who can have no share in this triumphing;
   They are here in the crowd.
Their tears must start and their hearts must ache,
No! their dear ones died for Ireland's sake,
   They are brave, they are proud.
With you they mourned and with you rejoice,
Lift up the flag, then lift up each voice,
   And shout aloud.

Constance Markievicz being welcomed home to Dublin on her release in 1917.

The German Plot

In May 1918 a Vice-Regal proclamation was issued which asserted that Irish nationalists were conspiring with Germany. This was used to justify the rounding up of dozens of Sinn Féin figures and their deporting to internment camps in England. The 'plot' is believed to have been a stunt designed to provide the pretext for increased repression.

Text: Samuels Collection, TCD.
Air: 'The Shan Van Vocht', see p. 6.

Now boys I ask ye'r lave,
  Sez the Shan Van Vocht,
Whilst I sing a little stave,
  Sez the Shan Van Vocht,
'Tis about a German plot,
That we almost had forgot,
And 'twas in the one bright spot,
  Sez the Shan Van Vocht,

'Twas no plot of cabbage green,
  Sez the Shan Van Vocht,
Nor a German submarine,
  Sez the Shan Van Vocht,
It was started down in Clare,
By a man from God knows where,
So the people all declare,
  Sez the Shan Van Vocht.

Then Lloyd George got fits of pain,
  Sez the Shan Van Vocht,
And he dreamt about Sinn Féin,
  Sez the Shan Van Vocht,
Sez he, at last they're caught,
And I'll bag the bloomin' lot,
And I'll do it on the spot,
  Sez the Shan Van Vocht.

Then the 'G' men made a round,
  Sez the Shan Van Vocht,
And a lot of lads they found,
  Sez the Shan Van Vocht,
De Valera – Ireland's pride,
And Griffith true and tried,
And a hundred more beside,
  Sez the Shan Van Vocht.

So Lloyd George he hatched the plot,
  Sez the Shan Van Vocht,
And he bagged the blessed lot,
  Sez the Shan Van Vocht,
Then he put them into jail,
And of course he gave no bail,
But there's more in Granuaile,
  Sez the Shan Van Vocht.

Now we've heard of plots and schemes,
    Sez the Shan Van Vocht,
Of warnings and of dreams,
    Sez the Shan Van Vocht,
But the worst I now maintain,
Is a nightmare called Sinn Féin,
For it rises to your brain,
    Sez the Shan Van Vocht.

Those Sinn Féiners are a curse,
    Sez the Shan Van Vocht,
But the Volunteers are worse,
    Sez the Shan Van Vocht,
And my loyal heart it grieves,
For sure everyone believes,
That they've arms up their sleeves,
    Sez the Shan Van Vocht.

Very soon declares Lloyd George,
    Sez the Shan Van Vocht,
The details I'll disgorge,
    Sez the Shan Van Vocht,
Those plotters every one,
Had communion with the Hun,
And I'll prove it 'fore I'm done,
    Sez the Shan Van Vocht.

Whilst we're waiting for the plot,
    Sez the Shan Van Vocht,
We'll keep the 'G' men hot,
    Sez the Shan Van Vocht,
And the English press will see,
Whilst they talk of Liberty,
That Ireland must be free,
    Sez the Shan Van Vocht.

And whilst Lloyd George we'll rile,
    Sez the Shan Van Vocht,
Till he gives the boys a trial,
    Sez the Shan Van Vocht,
We'll keep digging at our plot,
Till all English rule shall rot,
In the only one bright spot,
    Sez the Shan Van Vocht.

Where's De Valera?

Maeve Cavanagh

Oh my name is Dame Brit - tan - nia, I'm the Mis - tress of the Seas,

My good old flag, the U - nion Jack, still floats u - pon the breeze,

And the on - ly man in all the world that e - ver makes me sneeze

Is a fel - low by the name of De Va - le - ra,

He split the Vo - lun - teers, and said the Ger - mans ought to win,

And that eve - ry - one who fought for me com - mit - ted mor - tal sin,

Now his crimes would take so long to tell, I ough - tn't to be - gin,

But I'll ask you where on earth is De Va - le - ra?

Text: Maeve Cavanagh Papers, National Library of Ireland.
   Air: 'Eileen Oge' or 'The Pride of Petravore'.

Oh my name is Dame Britannia, I'm the Mistress of the
    Seas,
My good old flag, the Union Jack, still floats upon the
    breeze
And the only man in all the world that ever makes me
    sneeze
Is a fellow by the name of De Valera.
He split the Volunteers, and said the Germans ought to
    win,
And that everyone who fought for me committed mortal
    sin –
Now his crimes would take so long to tell, I oughtn't to
    begin,
    But I'll ask you where on earth is De Valera?

Chorus
Oh where's De Valera? – He was seen in Mary's Lane,
And also in America, in Paris and in Spain,

534

We've searched in every village, every boat and every
    train,
    But we can't find a trace of De Valera.

Some years ago this Mr De Valera had the cheek
To take up arms against our Gracious King in Easter
    Week,
But I feel so cross about it I can scarcely bear to speak
    Of a ruffian like that fellow De Valera.
Our clever gunners managed quite a lot of shells to send
All over his positions down in Boland's and Ringsend –
Our Intelligence Department, though, they gave our men
    the bend
    That we hadn't dropped one shell on De Valera.

A friend of mine, a Mr Shortt, he found a German Plot,
The persons implicated were a very dangerous lot;
We arrested them and gaoled them, and we gave it to
    them hot –
    Need I say that they included De Valera?
One afternoon the Devil and his Angels came around,
They may have brought him through the air, or dragged
    him underground;
But that night in Lincoln Prison there was no-one to be
    found
    That would answer to the name of De Valera.

We sent the 'G' Division out on De Valera's track,
They quickly got a clue and brought us information
    back –
That a person seen in Dame Street, in the costume of a
    'WAAC',
    Was undoubtedly the missing De Valera.
The staff of Scotland Yard they also worked with might
    and main,
They say he's left the country in a special aeroplane,
And he's over with this uncle, fighting Irish Bulls in
    Spain,
    Still I don't believe we'll capture De Valera.

Chorus
Oh where's De Valera? He was seen in Mary's Lane,
And also in America, in Paris and in Spain;
We've searched in every village, every boat and every
    train,
    Won't you tell us – where the Devil's De Valera?

The German Plot

Seosamh Penros

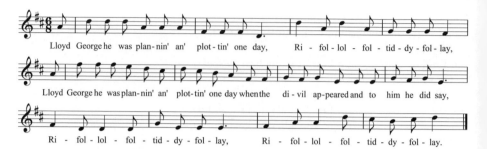

Lloyd George he was plan-nin' an' plot-tin' one day, Ri - fol-lol - fol - tid-dy-fol-lay,

Lloyd George he was plan-tin' an' plot-tin' one day when the di - vil ap-peared and to him he did say,

Ri - fol - lol - fol - tid - dy - fol - lay, Ri - fol - lol - fol - tid - dy - fol - lay.

Text: The comic Dublin publication *Irish Fun*, April 1919.
  Air: The intended air is clearly that of the ballad 'The Farmer's Cursed Wife' or 'The Women Are Worse than the Men'.

Lloyd George he was plannin' an' plottin' one day,
    Ri-fol-lol-fol-tiddy-fol-lay
Lloyd George he was plannin' an' plottin' one day
When the divil appeared and to him he did say,
    Ri-fol-lol-fol-tiddy-fol-lay,
    Ri-fol-lol-fol-tiddy-fol-lay.

'Sinn Féin is giving great trouble you say,
Well, I've a nice little plot to put 'Shinners' away.'

'Oh, that's very good of you, now, to be sure,'
Said the Wizard from Wales as he skipped round the
    flure.

Then they drank to John Bull and his beautiful jails –
The divil from hell and the divil from Wales.

The Oul' Boy then asked to have Carson sent in.
So up Neddy rambled, as ugly as sin.

The divil gave Ned a fraternal embrace.
To see them you'd swear they were from the same place.

They decided to say that they saw Kaiser Bill,
And he plottin' with 'Shinners' on Vinegar Hill.

And who do you think they gave charge of the plans?
Who but 'warrior' French – An 'Archangel from Mons!'

So this great German Plot they had ready full quick –
Manufactured by Georgie, by Ned and by Nick.

536

Whack Fol De Diddle
(New Version)

Joe Devlin's day is nearly past,
   Whack fol de diddle fol the dido day.
No more he'll sit for West Belfast,
   Whack fol de diddle fol the dido day.
The picture house has sealed his doom,
For felon-setters there is no room,
So we'll sweep him from his seat with a Sinn Féin
   broom,
   Whack fol de diddle fol the dido day.

Chorus
Whack fol de diddle fol the dido day,
Their empire is being swept away,
Then what will the traitors do for pay?
Whack fol de diddle fol the dido day.

'Tis said that Satan told Ananias,
   Whack fol de diddle fol the dido day.
Get out of hell, you are far too pious,
   Whack fol de diddle fol the dido day.
For you blush at the tales of the Dublin liar,
That lad who runs the 'Journal of the famed Sham
   Squire',
There's a special spot for him at the fire,
   Whack fol de diddle fol the dido day.

Didn't Viviani tell his friend J.D.,
   Whack fol de diddle fol the dido day.
In case of disruption in the B.O.E.,
   Whack fol de diddle fol the dido day.
Keep up your heart, don't be dismayed,
By Masonic influence I'll persuade
Lorcan to give you a job at your trade,
   Whack fol de diddle fol the dido day.

The political reign will soon terminate,
   Whack fol de diddle fol the dido day,
Of the Party of the 'No Far Distant Date',
   Whack fol de diddle fol the dido day.
Their wild cheering when the men were shot,
'Twas but the death-rattle of the lot,
In the grave with the empire let them rot,
   Whack fol de diddle fol the dido day.

The Sham Squire (verse 2) was Francis Higgins (1745–1802). He was the betrayer of Lord Edward Fitzgerald in 1798, and in 1784 he gained control of the nationalist newspaper *The Freeman's Journal* and turned it into a pro-government publication.

Viviani (verse 3) was René Viviani, the French Premier, and a Freemason. See p. 105 for a note on the BOE. J.D. Nugent was Viviani's friend, and a leading member of the Dublin Vigilance Committee, a reactionary body opposed to alcohol, 'dirty books' and other social evils. In *The Spark* of 9 May 1915 he is described as 'the originator of the "German Gold" canard, the man who never took part in any movement without first assuring himself that there was coin in the coffers, because "patriotism" which doesn't pay is only faction and crankery according to the great Hib. Nugent.'

Lorcan Sherlock was the nationalist Lord Mayor of Dublin from 1912–15.

Text: *New Songs, Ballads and Recitations*, Fergus O'Connor, n.d.
  Air: see p. 393.

The Wreck of the 'No Far Distant Date'

Jimmy Mulkerns 'The Rajah of Frongoch'

Before his involvement in the Rising and subsequent internment in Frongoch prison camp in Wales, the author had been an amateur entertainer. He wrote and produced theatrical shows while in Frongoch, dressing in oriental garb and adopting the persona of 'The Rajah of Frongoch'.

De Valera (line 10) is of 'Notts and Derby fame' possibly because his unit around Boland's Mills and Mount Street Bridge ambushed the Sherwood Foresters on their way into the city. That regiment is also known as the Nottinghamshire and Derbyshire Regiment.

The references to North Roscommon, South Longford, East Clare, Kilkenny and Armagh are meant to recall the by-elections that took place in those constituencies during February, May, July, and August of 1917, and February 1918. In the first four a Sinn Féin candidate defeated the Nationalist Party candidate. The South Armagh seat was won by the Nationalist.

The 'Man in Jail' (p. 539, line 1) was Joseph McGuinness, who was in Lewes Jail at the time, but secured his release through being elected to Parliament. See p. 403 for a song by McGuinness.

See p. 105 for a note on the expression 'no far distant date'.

Text: Samuels Collection, TCD.

It was the ship 'No Distant Date' that sailed Westminster Sea,
John Redmond stood upon the bridge with a glance quite angry,
And he shouted to Skipper Joe, 'There's submarines in sight,
And from their decks they all do fly the Orange, Green and White.
What shall we do to steer this barque away from danger clear?
Come Devlin here and tell me now why you do shake with fear.
Who is this pirate on the sea that dares to cross our track,
While up aloft from our topmast we fly the Union Jack?'
Have you not heard, responded Joe, that is the captain's name,
'Tis De Valera he is called, of Notts and Derby fame.
The crews upon his submarines, although it may seem queer,
They work for Freedom, and they scorn four hundred pounds a year.
Send word down to the stoke-hold, let your cry be – 'Full steam'.
Send a message to the people that we're bound for College Green,
That Home Rule's on the Statute Book, and when the war is won,
That England will be kind to us when she has smashed the Hun.
They've heard that yarn oft before, that tale you cannot tell.
Do you think the people are all fools? Quietly spoke Ginnell.
I'm sick of this old rotten barque. I'm going to sling my hook,
And leave behind catch-cry and cant about the Statute Book.
Look out – 'the first torpedo' – roars Dillon with a quake,
And it's labelled 'North Roscommon' as it rushes on its wake.
Too late! exclaims John Judas, they've got in the first blow.
There's many more to follow, says Larry from below.
Quick, quick to port, John Judas shouts, what madness pirates think!
That blows, no matter how well aimed, this Dreadnaught they can sink.
See, see! another comes! shouts John, it's aim, alas, too true,

It's labelled 'Up the Man in Jail' – South Longford is true
  Blue.
What shall we do, shouts Judas now, can we once more
  get back
To the hearts of men behind on shore to stop this huge
  attack.
What mean this super-dreadnaught now I notice on the sea
With decks all cleared for action, too, approaching steadily.
Come tell me, Nugent, what's her name? See! See! her guns
  do flare,
She's struck us too, says Modesty, with a shell made in East
  Clare.
Throw up the sponge, exclaimed Ginnell, and leave this
  doomed old barque,
The men behind such guns as these can never miss their
  mark.
Sinn Féin on every side assails; its power grows day by day.
Surrender to the people's call. From London stop away.
Another swift torpedo comes, it dashes o'er the wave,
From the submarine, Kilkenny, and all her crew so brave.
We must hold on, shouts Judas John, tho' things look
  black, no doubt,
Get Carson's men to load the guns and help to knock one
  out.
The guns are fired with slavish hate, then comes a loud
  hurrah,
The trick has worked, the captain shouts, we've sunk the
  craft – Armagh.
Alas! alas! shouts Judas John, our victory comes too late,
Already we are half submerged, the poor 'No Distant
  Date'.
The Sinn Féin navy men ashore, they work by night and
  day,
I know their power, alas, too well, I cannot face the fray.
Take to the boats, John Judas sobs, and leave this doomed
  old craft,
The Irish Party's days must end a-clinging to a raft.

. . . . . .

And here we leave them to their fate – this band of British
  slaves,
Soon! soon! the 'No Far Distant Date' will sink beneath the
  waves.

'The Man in Jail',
Joseph McGuinness.

That's the Stuff to Give 'im

The e - lec - tions her in Ire___ land have wor - ried John Bull sore,___

He'd like to have a lot of I - rish mem - bers on his floor.___

Four hun - dred quid a year for each he ea - si - ly can call,___

But the I - rish peo - ple shou - ted out "we won't have this at all!"___

Chorus

That's the stuff! That's the stuff! That's the stuff to give 'im!___

We will show, John Bull must go, for we can't for - give___ him.

E - ver more, from E - rin's shore, the ty - rant must be dri - ven,___

Shout a - gain,___ Up Sinn Féin! That's the stuff to give 'im!___

Text: Mansfield Library, University of Montana.

Air: 'That's the Stuff to Give 'Em', music hall song written in 1917 by Harry Freeman and George Grant.

The elections here in Ireland have worried John Bull sore,
He'd like to have a lot of Irish members on his floor,
Four hundred quid a year for each he easily can call,
But the Irish people shouted out 'we won't have this
    at all!'

Chorus

That's the stuff! That's the stuff! That's the stuff to give
    'im!
We will show John Bull must go, for we can't forgive 'im,
Ever more from Erin's shore the tyrant must be driven,
Shout again, Up Sinn Féin! That's the stuff to give 'im!

Lord French he had an army, a hundred thousand men,
He marched them up a great big hill but he marched them
    down again,
For the Germans were there first you know, old French he
    had to run,
Sure he thought he was in Dublin when he tried to smash
    the Hun.

Chorus
That's the stuff! That's the stuff! That's the stuff to give 'im!
Yanks stepped in, saved their skin, that is why they're livin',
Conscription here, they thought was near, but Ireland
    started jibbin'.
No blood tax! Try the Wacs, that's the stuff to give 'im!

Our boys in prison have been thrown away in Belfast town,
And branded there as criminals to try and keep them down,
But though in jail they did not fail to raise the barricade,
In spite of England's brutal laws the 'Soldier's Song' they
    played.

Chorus
That's the stuff! That's the stuff! That's the stuff to give 'im!
Ireland's cause 'gainst England's laws fought out in a
    prison,
Well to-day the world may say 'Ireland's sun has risen.'
'Short' or 'Long' the fight goes on, that's the stuff to give
    'im!

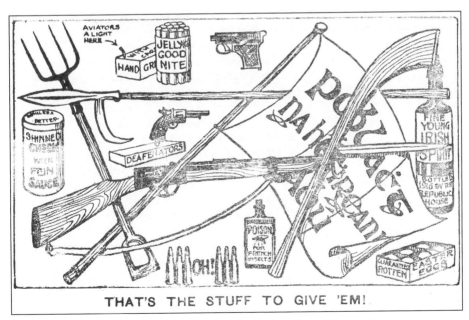

The postcard shown above was published by Sinn Féin *c.* 1918, and was probably inspired by this song.
The 'stuff' includes 'Jelly good nite', .303 rifle bullets, 'Poison for French insects', 'Deafenators', 'Shinned cheek with Fein sauce', 'Easter eggs, guaranteed rotten', and 'Fine young Irish spirit, bottled 1916 by the Republic House'.

The East Clare Election 1828–1917

Dermot O'Byrne

This poem contrasts the East Clare by-election of 1917 with the famous 1828 by-election which saw Daniel O'Connell elected to the constituency.

O'Connell was a committed pacifist who sought to recover civil rights for the majority Catholic population of Ireland through strictly non-violent means.

More controversially, although a native speaker of the Irish language himself, he regarded it as a worthless hindrance to economic advancement and encouraged his supporters to abandon it in favour of English.

He was rumoured to be so sexually promiscuous (see verse 5) that an extensive body of folklore grew up about his exploits, including a song which suggested that he was finding the traditional way so inefficient, he was considering the introduction of a new system of 'making babies by steam'.

Owen Roe O'Sullivan (1748–82), also celebrated as a noted rake, was a Gaelic poet, songs and tales of whose exploits are still performed in his native Sliabh Luachra and farther afield.

Text: Sir Arnold Bax, *A Dublin Ballad and Other Poems*, Candle Press, Dublin, 1918.

While in this day of victory
    We moil and sweat to plan aright
The Ireland that is to be,
    A Titan of the conquered night
Stays with us through the summer hours,
Pillared among the bogland flowers,
A huge unhappy shade that towers
    Between our ardours and the light.

We know you who you are, Old Dan,
    Our Liberator from our chains;
All freedom that your dream could span
    Flooded our clouded window-panes.
You hailed us from our prison-den
And scourged us towards the stars, and then
You beat us down to less than men
    And juggled with our helot brains.

You caged our valiant phantasies
    That used to see the sunset flames,
Trampled by such high masteries
    We shook with pride to speak their names;
You turned our narrowing gaze to scan
The world of church and party-man,
And drove our minds from Cruachan
    To the dark House of Lies on Thames.

You filched from us our ancient speech,
    Nurse of our laughter and our tears,
And bade us learn the yap and screech
    Of journalists and pamphleteers;
They whipped us with a wind of words
And we who dared a cloud of swords
Bowed down our wits to paper-lords
    And slept upon our rusty spears.

Aye, when our Sword of Light is swung,
    A blue flame in the zenith's blue,
Kerry may count the challenge flung
    From drunken lips by her old crew
Of shameful poets, nobler born
Than all your bastard-breathing scorn,
And Owen Roe O'Sullivan
    A better Irishman than you.

542

Yet you clove Ireland's darkest night,
  Despair before you and behind.
Could your resolve our sphinx aright,
  Or climb to read the Mother's mind?
Lie down and rest forgiven, old king,
Before your time – so poets sing –
Eagles have trailed a broken wing,
  And God himself had one eye blind!

Britannia's Appeal to East Cavan

Joseph Stanley

East Cavan, dear, I'm proud of you,
  Says the Grand Ould Dame Britannia.
I know you'll vote Red, White and Blue,
  Says the Grand Ould Dame Britannia.
You won't believe the Sinn Féin lies,
And you'll give Lloyd George a grand surprise,
He'll send Conscription in disguise,
  Says the Grand Ould Dame Britannia

Don't mind their talk of Easter Week,
  Says the Grand Ould Dame Britannia.
Don't listen when the Bishops speak,
  Says the Grand Ould Dame Britannia.
In Parliament there's a quiet nook,
Four hundred quid on a fishing hook,
Come on and see the Statute Book,
  Says the Grand Ould Dame Britannia

Come back to England, gra machree,
  Says the Grand Ould Dame Britannia.
On the Terrace there's a 'Home Rule Tea',
  Says the Grand Ould Dame Britannia.
We'll pulverize the Sinn Féin men,
And show you the grand old clock, Big Ben,
It'll play you 'A Nation Once Again',
  Says the Grand Ould Dame Britannia.

Send us the man from the 'Anglo-Celt',
  Says the Grand Ould Dame Britannia.
And we'll hit the priests an awful welt,
  Says the Grand Ould Dame Britannia.

Text: Samuels Collection, TCD.
Air: 'The Grand Oul' Dame
Britannia', see p. 235.

If you give Lloyd George another chance,
He'll send you – single fare – to France,
On the Conscript graves to sing and dance,
Says the Grand Ould Dame Britannia.

I Don't Mind If I Do

Jimmy Mulkerns 'The Rajah of Frongoch'

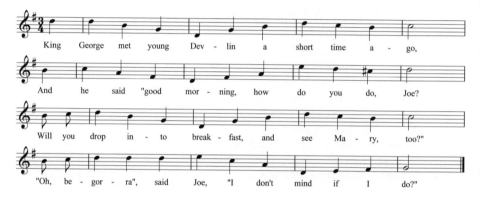

King George met young Dev - lin a short time a - go,
And he said "good mor - ning, how do you do, Joe?
Will you drop in - to break - fast, and see Ma - ry, too?"
"Oh, be - gor - ra", said Joe, "I don't mind if I do?"

Text: Samuels Collection, TCD.
 Music: 'Arranged by Joseph Stanley',
from sheet music in the Samuels Collection, TCD. The final verse here is
missing from the sheet music.

King George met young Devlin a short time ago,
And he said 'Good Morning, how do you do, Joe?
Will you drop into breakfast, and see Mary, too?'
'Oh, begorra,' said Joe, 'I don't mind if I do.'

To the Palace they rambled – T.P. he was there,
John Redmond he sat on a plush-covered chair.
'Will you all' said Queen Mary, 'have some Irish stew?'
And they roared in one voice, 'We don't mind if we do.'

'Sinn Féiners,' said George, 'are spoiling my plan,
De Valera, their leader, he seems a strong man.
Will you tell him his flag should be red, white and blue'.
'It's no use,' said T.P., 'he won't mind if we do.'

'Five counties in Ireland,' said Georgie, 'have gone
Away from that party that I dote upon.
Will you think out a plan to stop this rebel crew?'
'Oh, begorra,' said John, 'I don't mind if I do.'

'Behind prison walls they should all be,' said Joe.
'When you had them all in sure you let them all go,
To spread their sedition each county around,
And to knock out the men with the four hundred
     pound.'

'That's right,' said T.P., 'I agree with you there,
The rod on the rebels, oh Georgie, don't spare.
The whole world over sure they've knocked me flat,
I'm back from the States with a big empty hat.'

The flag of Sinn Féin everywhere it does fly,
And 'Down with the Party' is now Ireland's cry.
The Green, White and Orange, alas and alack,
Has taken the place of the old Union Jack.

'Recruiting,' said Mary, 'is now very low,
To the trenches in Flanders the Irish won't go.
Why not try conscription – oh John, what say you?'
'Oh begorra,' said John, 'there'll be hell if you do.'

Then the anti-air guns through the sky they did roar,
And the Zepps overhead sure they gave an encore.
'To the cellar,' said Georgie, 'for one hour or two.'
And they rushed, shouting out 'We don't mind if we do.'

Lloyd George's Convention

Patrick Hogan

All farces and frauds that attracted attention
Are cast in the shade by the latest Convention,
For there's nothing on earth like this 'Irish' Convention,
     The rickety step-son of Mr Lloyd George.

Chorus
Ach, Mr Lloyd George, there ain't any flies on you,
But somehow, avic, there are too many eyes on you,
Ireland is free from the Sea to the skies, on you,
     That's what is galling you, Mr Lloyd George.

They've taken a flat to start legislatin',
There's green on the benches – to match the oratin',

The Irish Convention was an assembly set up by David Lloyd-George, which met in Dublin from July 1917 to March 1918.
     Its mission was to provide a forum for all shades of opinion in Ireland to try and find an agreed way forward. The British government's decision in April 1918 to tie the introduction of Home Rule to the application of conscription in Ireland dealt a fatal blow to the hopes of the Convention succeeding.

Text: Samuels Collection, TCD.
     Air: 'Father O'Flynn', see p. 109.

An' a seven-day's licence Mahaffy has taken,
   'Twill help towards 'The Atmosphere', Mr Lloyd
      George.

With Duke in the chair – a man most impartial –
An' Mahon outside dictatin' Law Martial,
And all things surrounding luxurious, palatial,
   Who'd venture a protest 'gainst Mr Lloyd George.

If you want to drop in while the Club is debatin',
You just give the 'grip' and the token is taken
To see Joe himself, whose part is relatin'
   How breakfast is served up with Mr Lloyd George.

The cranks and the soreheads have left their seats empty,
In war time that's waste, for the grub-stakes are plenty,
In eating for Ireland, we're never left stinty
   When the cook and the butler is Mr Lloyd George.

I hear that each day they will pose 'fore the film,
With John on the bridge and Wee Joe at the helm,
Twice nightly, I'm told, but – 'Defence of the Realm' –
   The picture's arranged by Mr Lloyd George.

The cartoon on the right is from the comic magazine *Irish Fun* of October 1919.

It depicts an imagined conversation between the Censor and DORA (the Defence of the Realm Act):

Censor – 'Good-bye, Dora; I'm off. Here's my fountain pen. Whenever it runs dry use your bayonet.'
Dora – 'Tanks, my dear boy, many tanks.'

DORA REMAINS.

Ireland's Latest Flag Days

Some people say that Flag days are becoming quite a
  bore,
And stingy folk declare they don't want Flag Days any
  more,
But we're going to have some Flag Days that you never
  saw before,
  That will cause a sensation here in Ireland.

We're going to have a Flag Day to help each public
  house.
They're making such small profits don't blame them if
  they grouse,
So we must do something for them before they're down
  and out,
  To help the poor publicans of Ireland.

The police must have a Flag Day to show there's no
  dislike.
To every 'G' man we'll present a twenty guinea bike,
For you never know the minute they might go out on
  strike,
  Then what would become of us in Ireland.

We won't forget a Flag Day for Mr Lloyd George too,
To help the League of Nations and the cause of freedom
  true,
Tho' I've heard the London Conference is looking very
  blue,
  So we must do our bit for them in Ireland.

We'll have a special Flag Day to aid Mountjoy Hotel,
Where you get free board and lodging, tho' it often
    proves a 'cell'.
I spent my holidays there once, so easily can tell,
  'Tis the best boarding-house we have in Ireland.

We'll have a great big Flag Day to help this nation small,
And pin the flags with Wilson's Fourteen Points on one
  and all,
While for self-determination we'll continue still to call,
  Till we get the Republic here in Ireland.

Text: *The Granuaile Song Book*, The
Irish Supply Depot, Dublin, 1922.
  Prescribed air: 'We'll Crown De
Valera King of Ireland'.

The House That Jack Built

Tomás Ó hAmhlaidh

The 'Jack' of the title is John Redmond. 'Tay Pay' is T.P. O'Connor and 'the Mighty Atom' is Joe Devlin, two of Redmond's supporters.

Text: The comic Dublin publication *Irish Fun*, April 1918.

This is the House that Jack built,
This is the Party that fought and won,
And spoke and denounced the savage Hun,
To the great amusement of 'Irish Fun',
On the 'flure' of the House that Jack built.

This is the orator, Tay Pay,
Who went to beg money beyond the say,
And who holds an undisputed sway
Over the Party that fought and won,
And spoke and denounced the savage Hun,
To the great amusement of 'Irish Fun',
On the 'flure' of the House that Jack built.

This is the great and peerless one
Whom men have titled 'Honest John',
Who travelled afar in days bygone
The fight by Parnell made to shun,
Who hath stood recruiting platforms on,
And in lofty accents oft did prate
Of a certain No Far Distant Date,
And always and ever did obey
The behests of the orator, Tay Pay,
Who went to beg money beyond the say,
And who holds an undisputed sway
Over the Party that fought and won,
And spoke and denounced the savage Hun,
To the great amusement of 'Irish Fun',
On the 'flure' of the House that Jack built.

This is the Mighty Atom, Joe,
Who tried with his Board of Erin O,
Dissension in our land to sow,
Who bids us all stand to attention
And await the verdict of his Convention,
Who doth conspire with the peerless one
Whom men have titled 'Honest John',
Who hath stood recruiting platforms on,
And in lofty accents oft did prate
Of a certain No Far Distant Date,
And always and ever did obey
The behests of the orator, Tay Pay,
Who went to beg money beyond the say,
And who holds an undisputed sway

Over the Party that fought and won,
And spoke and denounced the savage Hun,
To the great amusement of 'Irish Fun',
On the 'flure' of the House that Jack built.

This is the coming General Election
That is giving the Party food for reflection,
That will for ever sweep away
Knaves like the orator, Tay Pay,
And show the world that Ireland's sons
Mean to get rid of her Honest Johns;
And the Mighty Atom they call Wee Joe
Will also have to pack and go.
They'll all lament at the doleful news
That they can no longer air their views
Where they fancied they had fought and won,
Where they warned and threatened the savage Hun,
To the great amusement of 'Irish Fun',
On the 'flure' of the House that Jack built.

Hold the Harvest 1918

Fanny Parnell (1848–1882)

Now, are you men, or are you kine, ye tillers of the soil?
Would you be free, or evermore the rich man's cattle, toil?
The shadow on the dial hangs, that points the fatal hour –
Now, *hold your own!* or, branded slaves, for ever cringe and cower.

The serpent's curse upon you lies – ye writhe within the dust,
Ye fill your mouths with beggar's swill, ye grovel for a crust:
Your lords have set their blood-stained heels upon your shameful
   heads,
Yet, they are kind – they leave you still their ditches for your beds!

Oh, by the God who made us all – the seignior and the serf –
Rise up! and swear this day to hold your own green Irish turf!
Rise up! and plant your feet as men where now you crawl as slaves,
And make your harvest fields your camps, or make of them your
   graves.

The birds of prey are hovering round, the vultures wheel and
   swoop –
They come, the coronetted ghouls! with drum beat and with troop –
They come to fatten on your flesh, your children's and your wives';
Ye die but once – hold fast your lands, and, if ye *can*, your lives.

Fanny Parnell was the sister of Charles Stewart Parnell, and was as radical, or more radical, than her brother on the subject of land reform. Along with her sister Anna she founded and ran The Ladies Land League, which functioned as an auxiliary organization to The Land League.

Under the title 'Hold The Harvest' (without the date) this poem was published in 1880 by Fanny Parnell and 'Addressed to the Irish farmers'. It is regularly referenced, but without being given in full; only the first three or four verses are usually quoted. In 2015 it was printed in full, probably for the first time in nearly a century, in Ruth Clinton's collection *This Fearless Maid*, published by the Howth Singing Circle.

Part of its fame rests on the oft-repeated assertion that Michael Davitt had

referred to it as 'The Mar-
seillaise of the Irish peas-
antry'.

The text is published here
because it was included,
under the above title, in J.J.
Walsh's songster *Victory
Song Book*, which was published in 1918. This was a
24-page booklet with 38
songs, showing Éamon de
Valera in military uniform,
and was intended to whip
up support for the Sinn Féin
candidates in the forthcoming General Election.

It was also published in
Vol. VII of the ten-volume
anthology *Irish Literature*,
edited by Justin McCarthy
MP and published in 1904
by John D. Morris, Philadelphia; and in J.J. O'Kelly's
Gill's Irish Reciter, which
appeared in several editions
between 1905 and 1929,
published by M.H. Gill,
Dublin.

Let go the trembling emigrant – not such as he ye need;
Let go the lucre-loving wretch that flies his land for greed;
Let not one coward stay to clog your manhood's waking power;
Let not one sordid churl pollute the Nation's natal hour.

Yes, let them go! – the caitiff rout, that shirk the struggle now –
The light that crowns your victory shall scorch each recreant brow,
And, in the annals of your race, black parallels in shame,
Shall stand, by traitor's and by spy's, the base *deserter's* name.

Three hundred years your crops have sprung, by murdered
    corpses fed –
Your butchered sires, your famished sires, for ghastly compost
    spread;
Their bones have fertilised your fields, their blood has fall'n like
    rain;
They died that ye might eat and live – God! have they died in vain?

The yellow corn starts blithely up; beneath it lies a grave –
Your father died in 'Forty-eight' – his life for yours he gave –
He died that you, his son, might learn there is no helper nigh
Except for him who, save in fight, has sworn HE WILL NOT DIE.

The hour has struck, Fate holds the dice, we stand with bated breath;
Now who shall have our harvest fair? – 'tis Life that plays with
    Death;
Now who shall have our Motherland? – 'tis Right that plays
    with Might;
The peasant's arms were weak indeed in such unequal fight!

But God is on the peasant's side, the God that loves the poor,
His angels stand with flaming swords on every mount and moor,
They guard the poor man's flocks and herds, they guard his
    ripening grain,
The robber sinks beneath their curse beside his ill-got gain.

O, pallid serfs! whose groans and prayers have wearied Heaven
    full long,
Look up! there is a Law above, beyond all legal wrong;
Rise up! the answer to your prayers shall come tornado-borne,
And ye shall hold your homesteads dear, and ye shall reap the corn.

But your own hands upraised to guard shall draw the answer down,
And bold and stern the deeds must be that oath and prayer shall
    crown;
God only fights for them who fight – now hush the useless moan,
And set your faces as a flint and swear to Hold Your Own!

The Oath of Allegiance, Boys

Oh, we're the sappy pledge-bounders, boys,
And though our policy founders, boys,
    We won't go on the shelf,
    We'll fight for our pelf,
Like true blue 'four-hundred-pounders', boys.

Text: Samuels Collection, TCD.
Air: 'The Young May Moon', see p. 281.

Chorus
For we've taken the oath of allegiance, boys,
We've promised to give our obedience, boys,
    To King George and his toffs,
    To the Cecils and Goughs,
Spawn of the hottest of regions, boys.

Oh, we did Dame Britain's recruitin', boys,
We stumped the Bright Spot highfalutin', boys;
    We spilled Ireland's blood
    In the Picardy mud,
For a wink when Lloyd George we're salutin', boys.

We went in red-hot for 'Partition', boys,
With Ned Carson we had a co'lition, boys;
    To let Ulster, 'get out'
    And Old Ireland to flout,
But Sinn Féin blew our scheme to perdition, boys.

We can flaunt 'mid the swank and the snobbery, boys,
We revel in wines and the strawberry, boys;
    When the Terrace is cool
    We jest at Home Rule,
And we centre our thoughts upon jobbery, boys.

We're out to put down revolution, boys,
We stand for the King's Constitution, boys;
    At Downing Street Dinner,
    Tay Pay, the ould sinner,
Will swallow the federal solution, boys.

From the 'flure of the House' to the garret, boys,
We'll shriek the 'Home Rule' like a parrot, boys;
    We can't stick the pace
    When rainbows they chase;
What we want is a whiff of the carrot, boys.

At Sologbeg the War Began

On 21 January 1919, the day the First
Dáil met in Dublin, two RIC men,
escorting gelignite from a quarry at
Soloheadbeg, near Tipperary town,
were ambushed and shot, and the
gelignite taken. This action is regarded
by many as the start of the Anglo-
Irish War, post-1916. Seán Hogan, a
participant at Soloheadbeg, was subsequently arrested and, while being escorted to Cork, on 12 May 1919, he
was rescued from his RIC guards, two
of whom, Wallace and Enright, were
shot dead in a ferocious gun battle at
Knocklong Station. Hogan was one
of the 'Big Four' prominent Tipperary
IRA personnel – Seán Treacy, Dan
Breen, Séamus Robinson and Seán
Hogan. [LM]
   'The Rag' in verse 5 is the village
of The Ragg, near Thurles in Co.
Tipperary.

   Text: Ernie O'Malley, *On Another
Man's Wound*, Anvil Books, Dublin,
1979.

At Sologbeg the war began,
And next was heard the song
Of the rescue of Seán Hogan
At the station of Knocklong.

Soon after Hunt, the bully, fell,
Races day in Thurles town.
It broke the hearts of peelers
For miles the country round.

From Thurles town to Galtees brow
All peelers turned pale
When the boys attacked the barracks
At the call of Graine Ua Uaile.

From hill to hill that winter's night
Did speed the rifle's ball;
We won at Rea and Hollyford
But failed at Drumbane Hall.

The Rag we need not mention,
There we lost a comrade true;
They may trample on his body,
But his spirits ne'er subdue.

By peelers' hands MacCarthy fell;
In sainted ground he sleeps,
'Neath the ancient walls of Holy Cross
Where Suir's bright water creeps.

All true men miss them sorely
And their death they do deplore,
Three hirelings for them suffered
In the groves of Lackamore.

We'll drink a health to every man
Who treads in death's pathway;
Drink up my boys, get ready,
'Tis the rising of the day.

The Station of Knocklong

The news has spread thro' Ire—— land and sprung from shore to shore,——
Of such a deed as li - ving man has e - ver—— heard be - fore;——
From out those guar - ded car - ria - ges, 'mid a pa - nic—— stri- cken—— throng,——
Sean Ho - gan he was res - cued at the sta - tion of Knock - long.——

The news had spread through Ireland
    And sprang from shore to shore,
Of such a deed no living man
    Had ever heard before;
From out those guarded carriages,
    Mid a panic-stricken throng,
Seán Hogan he was rescued
    At the station of Knocklong.

With a guard of four policemen
    And their prisoner minded well,
As that fatal train sped o'er the rails,
    Conveying him to his cell;
The prisoner then could scarce foretell
    Of hearts both brave and strong,
That were planning for his rescue
    At the station of Knocklong.

'Twas on a gloomy evening
    When at last the train pulled in.
It was halted for an hour or more
    By a few courageous men;
Then springing to the carriages,
    It did not take them long,
'Hands up or die' was the warning cry,
    At the station of Knocklong.

King George's pampered hirelings
    They shrivelled up with fear,
When they thought of how they'd placed in cells
    Full many a volunteer;
Now face to face with armed men,
    To escape how they did long,

Text and air: Patrick Galvin, *Irish Songs of Resistance*, Workers' Music Association, London, 1955.

But two of them met traitor's deaths
   At the station of Knocklong.

From Solohead to Limerick
   Such deeds as these were seen,
And the devil a tear was ever shed
   For Wallace or Rosegreen;
They did old England's dirty work
   But they did that work too long,
For the renegades were numbered
   At the station of Knocklong.

Now rise up, Mother Erin,
   And always be of cheer.
You ne'er shall die while by your side
   There stand such volunteers;
From Dingle Bay to Garryowen
   The cheers they'll echo long,
Of the rescue of Seán Hogan
   At the station of Knocklong.

God Save the Peelers

Sir Hamar Greenwood was the Chief
Secretary for Ireland during the Anglo-
Irish war, and provided political cover
for the brutal tactics of the Black and
Tans and Auxiliaries.

The 'Sinn Féin Courts' were established by Dáil Éireann in June 1920,
the first one being at Ballinrobe, Co.
Mayo.

Ian Macpherson was Greenwood's
predecessor as Chief Secretary.

Text: Mansfield Library, University
of Montana.
  Air: 'God Save Ireland', see p. 275.

Sez Greenwood, now, sez he,
Things in Ireland puzzle me,
   And the Peelers there seem up against bad times;
So I must make some big coups,
And send along more troops,
   To reinforce the Peelers fighting lines.

Chorus
God save the Peelers, they are hayroes,
   Down to Miltown-Malbay make a call.
And to Cork and Thurles too,
Then you'll find I'm speaking true,
   For the Peelers there are hayroes one and all.

Sinn Féin courts throughout the land
Sit and British courts are banned,
   The fact has made me weep salt tears of woe;
But I'll send some extra guns,
Bully-beef and Currant Buns
   To protect the loyal Peelers from the foe.

Poor McPherson got abuse,
But he was not much use.
    I have better cards than he had up me cuff;
I'll conscript the British race
And send them to fill this place,
    And I'll bring the W.A.A.C.s if these are not enough.

Freedom's Way

Ben O'Hickey
September 1919

I've trod the hillsides cold and bleak,
While my heart was filled with hate
For the canting knaves who rob the weak,
And fawn upon the great;
I've often prayed to God on high
That we our land might save,
...... Even tho' a host must die,
'Twere better than lives as slaves.

But 'tis no prayers, but work and deeds,
Can free our native land,
We are not cowards, we know our needs,
So let us together stand,
And strike but one more vengeful blow . . .
Give all that's ours to give,
And win or lose . . . what matter that,
We die that she may live!

Text: Ben O'Hickey, *From Prison Cells*,
The Elo Press, Dublin, 1935.

A copy of Sean Keating's 'Race of the Gael'
depicting Ben O'Hickey, Commander of the
IRA in Bansha, Co. Tipperary (left), with
Brigadier Ben Carty.

Ashtown Road

Wolf Stephens

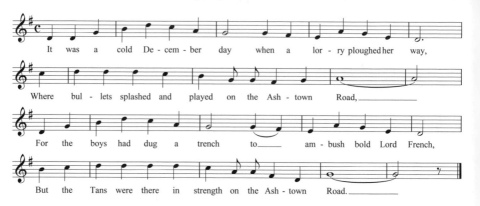

This ballad relates the story of Martin Savage, an officer of the Dublin Brigade of the IRA, who was killed in an ambush at Ashtown, Co. Dublin, on 19 December 1919. [LM]

Text: The first four verses are contained in Dominic Behan's *The Singing Irish*, Scott Solomon Productions Ltd, London, 1967. The final verse is from tradition.

Air: A ballad slip version of the song in the National Library of Ireland prescribes the air of 'The Snowy-Breasted Pearl' for this song (see p. 323). However here it is set to the air associated with John B. Keane's 'The Sive Song'.

It was a cold December day
When a lorry ploughed her way,
Where bullets splashed and played
    On the Ashtown Road.
For the boys had dug a trench
To ambush bold Lord French,
But the Tans were there in strength
    On the Ashtown Road.

There were lorries front and rear
Of the car where sat the Peer,
And he thought his end was near
    On the Ashtown Road.
To get at that living tool
Of England's hated rule
There was begun a duel
    On the Ashtown Road.

Though outnumbered ten to one
The fight it was soon on,
With their Parabellum guns
    On the Ashtown Road.
Though the British had the best
Of equipment and the rest,
Still we put them to the test
    On the Ashtown Road.

Martin Savage, unafraid
With gun and hand grenade,
Attacked them undismayed
    On the Ashtown Road.

But a bullet laid him low
From a rifle of the foe.
That's another debt we owe
    On the Ashtown Road.

But another day shall dawn
Like that cold December morn
When a martyr's name was born
    On the Ashtown Road.
We laid him in a grave
Where the willows sadly wave,
Oh! son of Erin brave
    Farewell to thee.

Pop Goes the Peeler

Cathal MacDubhghaill

Harcourt Street's a horrible place,
    Full of lanes and byeways;
Redmond should have minded himself,
    And kept to the highways.
It must have been a flapper that fired,
    'Twas easy to conceal her –
An automatic in her muff –
    And pop goes the Peeler.

Sergeant Dreelan's very depressed,
    All his friends are dying;
Every night his mammy will say
    'What has you crying?'

In his military service pension claim, Seán Hyde outlined his involvement in January 1920 in the successful plot to kill William Redmond, the assistant commissioner of the Royal Irish Constabulary. Redmond had been brought to Dublin from Belfast and charged by the authorities with tracking down Michael Collins.

While living quarters were being prepared for Redmond in Dublin Castle, he stayed at the Standard Hotel on Harcourt Street and was escorted to and from the Castle by two detectives. Hyde was sent to track his movements.

'On the Sunday morning I picked up Redmond at his hotel, had several

557

good looks at him from several angles, and also discovered his room was number 12. Furthermore I overheard him say he would be back for dinner.

I reported to Michael Collins at lunch and had a shooting party at my disposal that evening.

One thing and then another upset the actual shooting for a few days but eventually we got him at the door of 91 Harcourt Street on the Wednesday evening when on his way up to the Standard.'
– *The Irish Times*, 3 October 2014.

Sergeant Martin Dreelan was a member of the G Division of the DMP. Fergus Quinn and John Bruton were members of the same body.

A 'muff' (line 7) was a ladies' accoutrement made of fur or other warm material. Shaped into a cylinder, it was used to keep one's hands warm when abroad in cold weather, and could obviously serve to conceal a pistol.

Text: Maeve Cavanagh Papers, National Library of Ireland. In her statement to the Bureau of Military History, Cavanagh attributed it to her husband Cathal MacDubhghaill.

Air: the song is modelled on the popular song 'Pop goes the Weasel'.

Says he 'I'm not a dancer at all,
　　A jigger or a reeler,
And perhaps they want to make me step
　　To 'Pop goes the Peeler.'

Fergus Quinn is wasting away,
　　So is Sergeant Bruton;
Every day the two of them say
　　'Please stop the shooting.'
A burglar doesn't trouble them much,
　　A forger or a stealer,
The only thing that makes them jump
　　Is 'Pop goes the Peeler.'

The 'G' man has a terrible time,
　　He's living like a hermit;
If you want to fire at him now
　　You must get a permit;
You've got to put your 'stickyback' on,
　　To sign her and to seal her,
Before you may enjoy the sport
　　Of 'Pop goes the Peeler.'

Pop Goes the Peeler

On 23 June 1919 District Inspector Michael Hunt of the RIC, who was on duty at Thurles Races, was shot dead by two armed men.

Text: Ernie O'Malley Collection, New York University.

Racing day in Thurles town
There was great excitement
And Inspector Hunt was there
Seeking employment.

Everyone enjoying themselves
From Duke to cattle dealer.
When in the middle of the fun
'Pop goes the Peeler'.

Chorus:
Compensate the widow my boys.
That's the stuff to heal her,
But, laws, it is an awful thing
When, 'Pop goes the Peeler'.

Crowe's Bridge

It's— near Crowe's Bridge at I - nagh— a mo - nu - ment now stands,——

E— rec - ted by the peo—— ple as— done in o—— ther lands.—

In the me-mor - ry of— De—— vitt,— who led his gal— lant band,——

And took his stand at I - nagh— to free his na - tive land.

It's near Crowe's Bridge at Inagh
  A monument now stands,
Erected by the people
  As done in other lands.
In the memory of Devitt
  Who led his gallant band,
And took his stand at Inagh
  For to free his native land.

'Twas in February 1920,
  This gallant little band
Set out from Ennistymon
  And down across the land.
They moved along the countryside,
  As the eel moves through the sand,
And at Crowe's Bridge near Inagh
  They took their noble stand.

Ignatius now has posted them,
  They obey without a grouse.
Two men lay at the south side,
  Two more near Duggan's house.
Some local scouts were posted too,
  In case of a surprise.
Their one and only duty was
  To signal to the boys.

Thus on an Irish hillside
  The battle scene was laid
And as those soldiers waited,
  Silently they prayed
To ask their heavenly father
  To give them steady hand,

Martin Devitt and Ignatius O'Neill
were members of a Volunteer unit that
ambushed an RIC patrol near Inagh,
Co. Clare, in February 1920. Devitt
was killed in the encounter, and
O'Neill was injured.

Text: Tom Munnelly (ed.), *Local
Songs*, Ennistymon Festival of Tradi-
tional Singing, Ennistymon, 1990.
Air: 'The Home I Left Behind'.

And play their part in Inagh
   For to free their native land.

No sooner were they ready
   Than the signal was passed through,
That four English Peelers
   Were cycling into view.
The order 'load!' was given
   As those boys lay in a drain,
But Martin fires already,
   And again is taking aim.

But the Peelers do not like the lead,
   To battle they'd not go.
So their only alternative
   In a boghole to lie low.
But spoke brave Martin Devitt,
   'We soon will get them out,'
As they moved from their position
   From the wall that faces south.

They moved along inside the ditch
   And then they crossed the road,
When Martin stopped his comrades,
   Their rifles for to load.
They then moved up the hillside,
   Through furze and heather green,
Until they came to the fatal spot
   Where the monument now is seen.

The battle then it starts again
   As the boys lay in the drain.

A Flying Column of the Mid-Clare Brigade of the IRA.

But sniper Hughes has seen them,
    And shot Martin through the brain.
Ignatius his brave comrade
    Does not fear the English lead,
He goes to help poor Martin,
    But finds him to be dead.

As he kneels to say a silent prayer,
    Down by his comrade's side
The Peelers kept on firing
    But their shots were falling wide.
Their shots were fired at random,
    Some were low and some were high.
But sniper Hughes has fired again
    And shot him through the thigh.

Ignatius, weak from loss of blood,
    He could no longer stay,
So over to Jim Meaney's
    He quickly made his way.
There his wounds were washed and bandaged,
    Still his spirit light and gay,
'Listen lads, this wound is nothing,
    We will fight another day!'

The battle was scarcely over
    On the cold and tragic day,
When Martin's comrades came
    To take his body away.
But God's angels also came for
    That soul of Irish pride,
Who fought so bravely and so true,
    For Ireland's cause he died.

A Tale of the Mail

They were sorting out the letters at the G.P.O.
To send up to the Castle so it's right to let you know,
When instead of bags a lot of men came sliding down the chute,
And the weapons they held in their hands looked as if they
    could shoot.
The sorters were held up with the greatest of ability,
The staff in amazement were rooted to the floor.
They sorted the Mails with the greatest of agility.
While another lot with guns kept guard convenient to the door.

Text: Ernie O'Malley Collection,
New York University.
    Air: The intended air for this
piece is probably that of Percy
French's song 'Phil the Fluter's
Ball'.

Chorus:
With your whack fol di de ri tooral ooral addy O.
Whack fol di de ri torral ooral ay.
John Bull's in collapse and worn to a shadow O.
The way the boys in Dublin came and took the Mails away.

The Viceroy (poor old gentleman), he got some letters back,
Of course they were all censored and perhaps he'll get the sack,
What would we do without him, this thought it makes me sad,
Without him this poor country will start going to the bad.
With all his fine sogers and warlike activity,
With all his fine guns and his martial array,
To my mind it looks like martial stupidity,
So here's good luck to all the boys who got the Mails away

Battle of Mountjoy
April, 1920

In Mount-joy Gaol for Free-dom's right, our gal-lant lads put up a fight,
'Gainst Eng-land's power and Eng-land's might and con-quered in their hun-ger strike.
No ar-moured cars or guns had they, to help them on to win the day,
But a Will of Steel to pave the way and burst in twain the pri-son gate.

IRA prisoners in Mountjoy Jail staged a mass hunger strike in April 1920.

Text: Mansfield Library, University of Montana.
Air: 'Clare's Dragoons' or 'Viva La'.

In Mountjoy Gaol for Freedom's right,
Our gallant lads put up a fight,
'Gainst England's power and England's might
    And conquered in their hunger strike.
No armoured cars or guns had they,
To help them on to win the day,
But a Will of Steel to pave the way
    And burst in twain the prison gate.

Chorus
Shout hurrah! for Erin's right,
    Sing hurrah! our men are free,
They've conquered over England's might
    For fatherland and liberty.

For ten long days near death's abyss,
With bloodless lips and glazing eyes,
The tyrant still their right denies
    As soldiers fighting Erin's cause.
But hark! a voice that shakes the land,
The cause of Labour takes her stand,
All work and commerce now is banned
    Until we've set our captives free.

Two days 'down tools' our answer then,
The prison gates fly open once again,
Sing Oh! they're free, the gallant men,
    Ere death had claimed them for his own.
See England, futile is your reign,
Your armoured tanks and aeroplane,
While with us men like these remain
    Unconquered by your frightfulness.

The Old King's Inns
(June 1st, 1920)

Not far from Broad-stone station, in good old Dub-lin town,
The British troops on sentry stood and nursed their rifles brown.
Then this command "Hands up, now stand!" if you would save your skins,
For we're here to seize the rifles from the old King's Inns.
The British troops put up their hands and perhaps they didn't stare
As the "boys" removed the rifles to the motors waiting there,
And never yet such lads I met so nimble on their pins,
So simply they departed from the old King's Inns.

The King's Inns, at the top
of Henrietta Street in central
Dublin, was raided for arms
on 1 June 1920. Kevin Barry
was one of the Volunteers
who took part in the raid.

Text: The Ernie O'Malley
Collection, New York
University.
    Air: 'The Old Plaid Shawl'.

Not far from Broadstone station, in good old Dublin town,
The British troops on sentry stood and nursed their rifles brown.
Then this command 'Hands up, now stand!' if you would save
    your skins,
For we're here to seize the rifles from the Old King's Inns.

The British troops put up their hands and perhaps they didn't stare
As the 'boys' removed the rifles to the motors waiting there,
And never yet such lads I met so nimble on their pins.
So simply they departed from the Old King's Inns.

The Lewis guns and Maxims soon vanish out of sight
As like the moon o'er clouded in the middle of the night,
And when the people heard the news their faces wore broad grins,
And they cheered the flying motors from the Old King's Inns.

I've seen the heroes on the screen whom danger ne'er dismayed,
But the 'hold up' in the Temple here quite puts them in the shade.
So here's to every gallant heart whose courage victory wins,
Like the boys who seized the rifles from the Old King's Inns.

Where Did General Lucas Go?

'Twas over in Rathcormac near the town of sweet Fermoy,
They captured General Lucas and away with him did fly.
They said, "you are our prisoner, and this you've got to know,
You can't do Greenwood's dirty work where the Blarnes roses grow.

Text: Seán Moylan, *Seán
Moylan in his Own Words*,
Aubane Historical Society,
Milstreet, 2003.
    Air: 'Where the Blarney
Roses Grow'.

'Twas over in Rathcormac near the town of sweet Fermoy,
They captured General Lucas and away with him did fly.
They said, 'You are our prisoner, and this you've got to know
You can't do Greenwood's dirty work where the Blarney Roses
    grow.'

Chorus
Can anybody tell me where did General Lucas go?
He may be down in Mitchelstown or over in Mallow,
He's somewhere in the County Cork, but this I want to know,
Can anybody tell me where did General Lucas go?

'Twas on a Sunday morning out a-fishing he did go,
And when he had his fishing done he was caught by You Know Who!
They said, 'You'll have to come with us, or else down you will go,
For that's the way we'll treat you where the Blarney Roses grow.'

'There's good men down in Galway and the same in County Clare,
But the likes of those young Cork men you won't find anywhere.
They treated me so kindly, and if they'd only let me go
I'd promise to stop reprisals where the Blarney Roses grow.'

Now to conclude and finish, I hope it won't be long
Till we see old Ireland free again and the RIC men gone,
And when they free our prisoners and tell them they may go
We'll do the same for Lucas where the Blarney Roses grow.

A Song of Fermoy

Near the town of sweet Fermoy,
   Sez the Shan Van Voch
Once good fishing to enjoy,
   Sez the Shan Van Voch
A General strolled out,
But on the homeward route,
Was captured there about,
   Sez the Shan Van Voch.

Oh! it took me by surprise,
   Sez the Shan Van Voch,
Sure I thought it was all lies,
   Sez the Shan Van Voch,
Till I saw them hunting round,
Over hill and underground,
But no General was found,
   Sez the Shan Van Voch.

Oh! where has Lucas gone,
   Sez the Shan Van Voch,
(Sure no khaki had he on),
   Sez the Shan Van Voch,

Another song dealing with the same incident as the previous one.

Text: Mansfield Library, University of Montana.
   Air: 'The Shan Van Voch', see p. 7.

565

Och! it's more than I can tell,
But I hear he's doin' well,
In some big Sinn Féin hotel,
   Sez the Shan Van Voch.

Now a moral this will show,
   Sez the Shan Van Voch,
If a fishing you should go,
   Sez the Shan Van Voch,
Returning take a thought,
'Tis yourself that may be sought,
And like a fish be 'caught',
   Sez the Shan Van Voch.

The Walls of Derry
June, 1920

Shoo - ting, loo - ting, all de - fy - ing, bi - gots shou - ting, bul - lets fly - ing,
Car - son's lambs for blood are cry - ing in the town of Der - ry.
Eng - land helps them in their game, helps to fan the bi - got flame,
Thinks 'twill blac - ken E - rin's name, from the walls of Der - ry.

Text: Mansfield Library, University of Montana.
Air: 'The Rakes of Mallow'.

Shooting, looting, all defying,
Bigots shouting, bullets flying,
Carson's lambs for blood are crying,
   In the town of Derry.
England helps them in their game,
Helps to fan the bigot flame,
Thinks 'twill blacken Erin's name,
   From the walls of Derry.

Carson's German guns are pealing,
Snipers on the roofs are kneeling,
Timid folks with fright are reeling,
   In the town of Derry.
Who will stop the carnage now?
Or the Orange ruffians cow?

Making good Sir Edward's vow,
   'Neath the Walls of Derry.

Oh! Derry's crushed with blood and tears,
Oh! what can now allay her fears.
'Tis the Irish Volunteers,
   On the streets of Derry.
Scorning all sectarian strife,
Order keeping, saving life,
Peace shall come where blood was rife,
   'Neath the walls of Derry.

The Bold Black and Tan

Says Lloyd George to Macpherson: 'I'll give you the sack.
To uphold law and order you haven't the knack.
I'll send over Greenwood, a much stronger man,
And fill up Erin's Isle with the bold Black and Tan.'

He sent them all over to pillage and loot,
And burn down the houses the inmates to shoot.
'To re-conquer Ireland,' says he, 'is my plan,
With Macready and Co. and his bold Black and Tan.'

The town of Balbriggan they've burned to the ground,
While bullets like hailstones were whizzing around,
And women left homeless by this evil clan.
They've waged war on children, the bold Black and Tan.

From Dublin to Cork and from Trim to Mayo,
Lies a trail of destruction wherever they go.
With England to help and fierce passions to fan,
She must feel bloody proud of her bold Black and Tan.

Text: *Songs of the Irish Republic*,
Coiste Foillseacháin Náisiúnta,
Cork, 1962.
  Air: 'Brian O'Lynn'.

Ah, then not by the terrors of England's foul horde,
For ne'er could a nation be ruled by the sword,
For our country we'll have yet in spite of her plan
Or ten times the number of bold Black and Tan.

We defeated conscription in spite of their threats
And we're going to defeat old Lloyd George and his pets,
For Ireland and Freedom we're here to a man
And we'll humble the pride of the bold Black and Tan.

A Black and Tan, armed with a Lewis light machine gun, guarding a Dublin premises.

The Ambush at Rineen

'September 22nd 1920 is a date burned deeply into the history of West Clare. On that day the 4th Battalion of the Mid Clare Brigade of the IRA lay in ambush at Rineen Cross, about two miles out from Miltown Malbay on the Lahinch road. Their objective, to hold up an RIC lorry and relieve it of its arms, was at first thwarted when faulty signals resulted in the lorry passing through the waiting men, unscathed

Come all you gallant Irishmen, come listen for a while,
I'll sing to you the praises of the sons of Erin's Isle
'Tis of an awful, awful ambush I'd have you to beware
That happened in Rineen, in a spot in County Clare.

Our boys they waited patiently with an eye both sharp
    and keen,
They waited for these lorries to return to Rineen.

Their scout at once they sighted them, without the least
delay
And signalled to their comrades to get ready and prepare.

Their comrades they got ready without the least delay
And signalled to their scouts again to let them come
their way.
The Black and Tans they came along, in lorries, as you
know,
And met our boys upon the road which gave them a
heavy blow.

They fought upon the highway, man to man you know,
With shotguns and revolvers against armoured cars and
so;
The Black and Tans put up their hands, and the Peelers
too likewise
When they saw the determined faces upon our Irish
boys.

So now to conclude and finish, as I think 'tis nearly
time,
And all the gallant Irishmen together should unite.
Together should assemble and gather all you can,
And have another ambush soon, to fight the Black and
Tans!

and unaware of its lucky escape. The
men waited for the lorry to return and
this time it was attacked and the seven
RIC men aboard it were slain. Unknown
to the attackers, a Captain Lendrum,
RM, had been shot at Doughmore the
same day on his way to attend court in
Ennistymon.

Word was sent to the military forces
garrisoned in Ennistymon and ten or
twelve lorries with about one hundred
and fifty men aboard set out immediately from the barracks. On their way,
and to their mutual surprise, they came
upon the IRA at Rineen while they
were still engaged in removing the
arms from the RIC lorry. The IRA unit
managed to retreat in an exemplary
manner almost unbelievable in such
largely untrained men.

Only four minor wounds were inflicted on the IRA, but they left fourteen dead RIC and Black and Tans in
their wake. Miltown Malbay, Lahinch
and Ennistymon in particular suffered
severely in the savage reprisals that
followed. A monument now marks the
scene of the action in Rineen.

Originating in such harrowing
events, Tom Lenihan's song on the ambush is surprisingly jaunty. The air is a
rollicking variant of "The Wearing of
the Green".' – Tom Munnelly

Text: Tom Munnelly, *The Mount Callan
Garland – Songs from the Repertoire
of Tom Lenihan*, Comhairle Bhéaloideas
Éireann, Dublin, 1994.

Seán Treacy

We often heard our fathers tell
How in the Fenian times
The noblest of Tipperary's sons
Imprisoned spent their lives.

Those tales we can hear daily,
And the deeds of valiant men,
As the war goes on unceasingly
Through valley, hill and glen.

They searched for Seán at midnight;
His comrades with him slept.
Macready's murdering bloodhounds
In silence on them crept.

This is just one of several songs about
Seán Treacy. See p. 375 for Peadar
Kearney's tribute to him.

Seán Treacy from Solohead, Co,
Tipperary, a fearless and determined
fighter, was one of a number of
prominent and very active IRA men;
he was one of the 'Big Four' (Treacy,
Dan Breen, Séamus Robinson, Seán
Hogan) of the 3rd Tipperary Brigade.

Involved in a large number of
engagements in Tipperary and adjoining
counties, he also operated in Dublin,
carrying out intelligence work to elimi-
nate spies, with Michael Collins's
'Squad'. Huge effort was put by
British Intelligence into finding Treacy
and Breen, leading to a gunfight at Prof.
Carolan's house in Drumcondra, Dublin

on 12 October 1920. Carolan was murdered by the raiding party, five of whom were shot dead by Treacy and Breen, both of whom escaped, Breen being very badly wounded. Treacy was tracked down and shot in Talbot Street, Dublin, on 14 October 1920.

Sir Nevil Macready (verse 3) was the Commander-in-Chief of British Forces in Ireland, 1918–20. Smyth and White (verse 4) were two British Intelligence agents shot dead at the Drumcondra gunfight. Treacy is said to have been a crack shot. [LM]

Text: *Songs of the Irish Republic*, Coiste Foillseacháin Náisiúnta, Cork, 1962.

Our heroes fought as brave men should
    And made a gallant fight;
With bullet food they did conclude
    The lives of Smyth and White.

In a crowded Dublin street Seán died
    On a dim October day;
The story will be told with pride
    While men in Eirinn stay.

With trusty gun held in his hand,
    Two sleuth hounds he laid low;
'Twas well they knew the island through
    They had no braver foe.

When the British saw the battle
    They shook with fear and dread,
A machine gun then did rattle,
    And our hero bold lay dead.

Seán Treacy killed! Seán Treacy killed!
    Was borne along the breeze.
No bells were rung; no *caoin* was sung;
    He died for Ireland free.

While grass grows green in Eirinn,
    We'll think of you, brave Seán!
We'll sing your praise o'er hill and vale,
    When grief and gloom are gone.

And when the dawn of Freedom's sun
    Shines out on Erin's skies,
In our Gaelic tongue we'll tell our sons
    How brave Seán Treacy died.

The scene in Talbot Street after the shooting dead of Seán Treacy.

MacSwiney Taught Us How to Die

Fr. Francis P. Donnelly S.J. (1869–1959)

In fla- ming, fight, when man his man is fa— cing,— And down the line, ten thou-sand mad ly cheer,—

When through the veins the blood goes hot-ly cha— sing,— Then death, for - got - ten, lo-ses all its fear.—

But let the strife through months of an-guish leng_ then,— And all be si - lent save our lone-ly sigh,—

Be with us, God, our frigh-tened souls to streng then,— Twas so Mac - Swi - ney taught us how to die.—

In flaming fight, when man his man is facing,
    And down the line ten thousand madly cheer,
When through the veins the blood goes hotly chasing,
    Then death forgotten loses all its fear.
But let the strife through months of anguish lengthen,
    And all be silent save our lonely sigh,
Be with us, God, our frightened souls to strengthen –
    'Twas so MacSwiney taught us how to die.

This song extols the manner of Terence MacSwiney's death, which occurred on 25 October 1920, following a hunger strike of 74 days, and his courage and determination to resist despite the long agony of such a course of action.

See 'Shall my Soul Pass through Old Ireland', p. 360, for further information on Terence MacSwiney.

The funeral of Terence MacSwiney passing through the streets of London (courtesy Na Píobairí Uilleann). The pipers are (front, l-r): Harry Hough, un-named, M. Ring, Eoghan MacCarthy; (back, l-r): un-named, Sean Darmody, Arthur Hough.

In verse 2, first line, a reference is made to Barry: Kevin Barry was hanged on 1 November 1920 (see the following song), and in the second line of that verse Plunkett is referred to: Joseph Mary Plunkett, one of the leaders of the 1916 Easter Rising, was shot by British firing squad on 4 May 1916.

Dark Rosaleen (Róisín Dubh in Irish), in the second verse, is a poetic name for Ireland. [LM]

Text: *Songs of the Irish Republic*, Coiste Foillseacháin Náisiúnta, Cork, 1962.
Air: 'The Londonderry Air'.

Oh, all too swift was Barry's sacred scaffold,
  And swift the guns their gifts to Plunkett sped,
And hurried graves have often tyrants baffled,
  When Ireland calls to fame her patriot dead.
But here was one who clung to Death's embraces,
  Who, drop by drop, let all his life go by;
Dark Rosaleen, how gentle are thy graces!
  For thee he dared Death's longest death to die.

All chains are chains, tho' fashioned fair and golden,
  And Eire's race must never more be slaves,
The hearts of heroes all our hearts embolden,
  To win our freedom or to dig our graves.
Who nurtures now a spirit that is craven?
  Who fears to lift unshackled hands on high?
Who will not tread the shining path to Heaven?
  MacSwiney's there, who taught us how to die.

Kevin Barry

Kevin Barry, an eighteen-year-old medical student at Dublin's University College, was captured after an ambush on a British army supplies group at Monks Bakery, Church Street, Dublin, on 15 August 1920. His automatic pistol jammed and he sought refuge under a military lorry while trying to free the weapon. As the lorry drove off a woman shouted that there was someone under it. Opinions vary as to whether she was revealing his presence or was concerned for his safety.

Barry was tortured, court-martialled and hanged in Mountjoy Jail, Dublin, on 1 November 1920, the first execution since the Rising. His youth aroused widespread sympathy, and his contempt for his captors and dignified bearing going to his death were inspirational.

This song is known worldwide and has been popular within many freedom movements. The renowned American singer, Paul Robeson, has recorded it, Robeson having apparently learned it from Peadar O'Donnell, the Irish Socialist Republican. [LM]

Text: Donal O'Donovan, *Kevin Barry and His Time*, Glendale Press. Dublin, 1989. There are several other songs

In Mountjoy jail one Monday morning
  High upon the gallows tree,
Kevin Barry gave his young life
  For the cause of liberty.
Just a lad of eighteen summers,
  Still there's no one can deny,
As he walked to death that morning,
  He proudly held his head on high.

Chorus
Shoot me like an Irish soldier.
  Do not hang me like a dog,
For I fought to free old Ireland
  On that still September morn.
All around the little bakery
  Where we fought them hand to hand,
Shoot me like an Irish soldier,
  For I fought to free Ireland

Just before he faced the hangman,
  In his dreary prison cell,
British soldiers tortured Barry,
  Just because he would not tell.

The names of his brave comrades,
  And other things they wished to know.
Turn informer or we'll kill you,
  Kevin Barry answered 'No'.

Proudly standing to attention
  While he bade his last farewell
To his broken-hearted mother
  Whose grief no one can tell.
For the cause he proudly cherished
  This sad parting had to be,
Then to death walked softly smiling
  That old Ireland might be free.

Another martyr for old Ireland,
  Another murder for the crown,
Whose brutal laws may kill the Irish,
  But cannot keep their spirit down.
Lads like Barry are no cowards.
  From the foe they will not fly.
Lads like Barry will free Ireland,
  For her sake they'll live and die.

about Kevin Barry, by Constance
Markievicz, Brian O'Higgins,
Leo Maguire and many others.
  Air: 'Rolling Home to Bonnie
Scotland', see p. 330.

Kevin Barry in IRA uniform.

James Daly

The grey dawn had crept o'er the still-ness of mor-ning, the dew-drops they glis-tened like i - ci-cled breath,

The notes of the bu-gle had soun-ded its war-ning, a young Con-naught Ran-ger lay sen-tenced to death.

No cold bloo-ded mur-der had stained his pure con-science, he called as a wit-ness his Ma-ker on high,

He'd sim-ply been figh-ting for Ire-land's loved free-dom, ar-res-ted and tried, he was sen-tenced to die___

Chorus
Lay him a - way o'er the hill- side,___ a - long with the brave and the bold.___

In - scribe his name on the scroll of fame in let-ters of pu - rest gold.___

My con-science would ne - ver con - vict me,___ he said with his dy - ing breath.___

May God bless the cause_ of free- dom___ for which I am sen-tenced to death.

Private James Daly, from Westmeath, was one of a company of the Connaught Rangers, stationed in India, who mutinied in protest at the conduct of the British army in Ireland. The mutiny was quickly put down and fourteen men received death sentences. Daly was the only one to be executed, on 2 November 1920.

Like the song on p. 418, this is another case of a previously-existing song being made over to fit current events. In this case the original song was entitled 'Sentenced to Death', by W.C. Robey and Will H. Fox, and was published in 1891 in America. It is unclear who might be the subject of the original, but it probably refers to a 'young Irish soldier' in either the Union or Confederate army.

A different version, with the title 'Sentenced to Death', may be found in *The Fenian Song Book* (Irish Book Bureau, Dublin, *c*. 1940), where it is

The grey dawn has crept o'er the stillness of morning,
    The dew drops they glisten like icicled breath,
The notes of the bugle have sounded their warning,
    A young Connaught Ranger lay sentenced to death,
No cold-blooded murder had stained his pure conscience,
    He called as a witness his Maker on high,
He'd simply been fighting for Ireland's loved freedom,
    Arrested and tried, he was sentenced to die

Chorus:
Lay him away on the hillside,
    Along with the brave and the bold,
Inscribe his name on the scroll of fame
    In letters of purest gold,
My conscience would never convict me,
    He said with his dying breath,
May God bless the cause of freedom
    For which I am sentenced to death.

He thought of the love of his feeble old mother,
  He thought of the colleen so dear to his heart,
The sobs of affection, he scarcely could smother,
  Well knowing how soon from them both he must part.
He feared not to die though his heart was near broken,
  Twas simply remembrance of those he loved well,
His rosary he pressed to his heart as a token,
  The prayer cheered his soul in the felon's lone cell

To the dim barrack square, the doomed hero was hurried,
  In the grey of the dawn ere the sun rose on high,
With head held erect, undaunted, unworried,
  The gallant young soldier went proudly to die.
I blame not my comrades for doing their duty,
  Aim straight for my heart, were the last words he said,
Exposing his breast to the point of the rifles,
  The smoke cleared away, the young soldier lay dead

subtitled 'The Fate of a young Fenian in the British army'.

Text: Brendan Behan, *Confessions of an Irish Rebel*, Anvil Books, London, 1965.
  Air: From tradition.

The Scarriff Martyrs

The dreadful news through Ireland has spread from
  shore to shore
For such a deed no living man has ever heard before.
The deeds of Cromwell in his time I'm sure no worse
  could do
Than those Black and Tans who murdered those four
  youths in Killaloe.

Three of the four were on the run and searched for all
  around
Until with this brave Egan in Williamstown was found.
They asked him were the boys inside, to the rebels he
  proved true,
And because he would not sell the pass he was shot in
  Killaloe.

On the 16th of November, that day of sad renown,
They were sold and traced through Galway to that house
  in Williamstown.
They never got a fighting chance but were captured while
  asleep
And the way that they ill-treated them would cause your
  blood to creep.

On 16 November 1920 the Auxiliaries arrested three volunteers – Michael MacMahon, Martin Gildea and Alfie Rogers – along with Michael Egan, who had given them shelter.
  The four men were taken to Killaloe where they were tortured and murdered.

Text: John McLaughlin, *One Green Hill, Journeys Through Irish Songs*, Beyond the Pale Publications, Belfast, 2003.

They shackled them tight both hands and feet with twines they
    couldn't break
And they brought them down to Killaloe by steamer on the lake.
Without clergy, judge or jury on the bridge they shot them down
And their blood flowed with the Shannon convenient to the town.

With three days perseverance their bodies they let go.
At ten pm their funeral passed through Ogonnoloe.
They were kept in Scarriff chapel for two nights and a day,
Now in that house of rest they lie, kind people for them pray.

If you were at their funeral, it was a dreadful sight
To see the local clergy and they all dressed in white.
Such a sight of these four martyrs in one grave was never seen.
The died to save the flag they loved, the orange, white and green.

And now that they are dead and gone I hope in peace they'll rest,
Like all brave Irish heroes forever with the blessed.
The day will come when all will know who sold their lives away
Of young McMahon, Rodgers, brave Egan and Kildea.

The 'Cairo Gang' of British undercover agents. The assassinations of members of this group on the morning of
Sunday, 21 November 1921, were used as justification for the reprisals that took place later that day,
one of which is dealt with in the song on the following page.

Bloody Sunday

Joe O'Grady

In Croke Park one Sunday evening, nineteen-twenty was the year,
When the teams of Tipp. and Dublin on that green sward did
    appear,
One young Gael from Tipperary as he played our native game,
Was laid low by British bullets – Michael Hogan was his name.

Far away in Tipperary is a silent, lonely grave,
Far away in Tipperary he now rests among the brave,
Gaels like Hogan love their country, it was proved that fatal day,
When the mighty British Empire tried to smash the G.A.A.

Little did we know that evening when the teams came out to play,
That the murder gang of England to Croke Park were on their way,
Till an aeroplane it hovered o'er that silent, tranquil scene,
And sent down a hail of bullets on the crowd of Hill Sixteen.

Then the 'Tans' jumped from the lorries, drunken scruff of
    London town,
With their rifles at the ready, soon the gates were broken down,
As the people ran for shelter, they let go a murderous round,
And many a Gael lay dead, or dying, on Croke Park's historic
    ground.

The people's curse is on you, Greenwood, and your jail-bird
    'Black & Tans',
You will have to face our Maker with the blood upon your hands,
Of those inoffensive people, those whose lives you took away,
May their spirits ever haunt you, all the live long night and day.

Every year the Gaels assemble at the site of that sad scene,
And the Rosary is recited to our own Beloved Queen,
As our martyrs gather round her, in that holy place above,
There to rest with Her forever, the glorious Queen we Irish love.

God have mercy on Mick Hogan, Virgin Mary grasp his hand,
Fondly take him to your bosom, that young Gael from Ireland,
And the people who fell with him, in that murderous display,
May they rest in peace and glory, is our fervent prayer today.

But they failed to break the spirit, sure the proof is shown today,
When we gather in our thousands for to see the great Gaels play,
And in memory of our martyr is the famous Hogan Stand,
Where beneath they play The Anthem, those grand boys of Artane
    Band.

Text: Seán Reid Library,
Na Píobairí Uilleann,
Dublin.
    Air: 'Rolling Home
to Bonnie Scotland',
see p. 330.

577

Now the curse of poor old Ireland are Informers and Shoneens,
Those who crawl and pay allegiance to the British Kings and Queens,
They sell themselves for sport and pleasure, a rotten cowardly act to do,
Sure it's only slaves and traitors who will split their land in two.

But his name will live forever in that famous Hogan Stand,
And will never be forgotten by the Gaels of Ireland,
There are many still amongst us who survived that dreadful day,
When the mighty British Empire failed to smash the G.A.A.

Now you Gaels all over Ireland, when at Croke Park you attend,
Give a thought to Bloody Sunday and let this little prayer ascend,
It's not much that I am asking, just one Pater and Ave,
For all those the British murdered on that bleak November day.

In Tipperary So Far Away

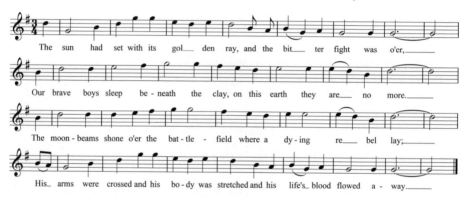

Text and air: Dick Hogan, *The Hogan
Collection*, Grand Parade Records,
Dublin, 2013.

The sun had set with its golden ray,
    And the bitter fight was o'er,
Our brave boys sleep beneath the clay,
    On this earth they are no more.
The moon-beams shone o'er the battlefield
    Where a dying rebel lay;
His arms were crossed and his body was stretched
    And his life's blood flowed away.

Our comrades in silent ambush laid,
    For the evening sky was clear,
Yet not one man was then afraid,
    Our brave boys knew no fear.
Few people in the city streets
    Had heard of that fierce affray,

Of that gallant youth whose home was set
    In Tipperary so far away.

There were none to weep for you, Sean Treacy, asthore!
    Or a keener to sing you praise,
To recite your deeds, like the Gaels of yore,
    As you we will never more see.
In that kingdom of love may your soul ever rest,
    Are the words that we fervently pray,
That we all meet above the old friends we loved best
    In Tipperary so far away.

A passing comrade soon heard him moan,
    As he wounded lay on the ground;
For this comrade knew well Sean was one of his own,
    As he warily looked all around.
'Lift me gently, comrade,' he cried,
    'For no longer on earth can I stay;
I shall never more roam to my own native home
    In Tipperary so far away.'

'A lock of my hair I implore you to take
    To my mother so dear to me.
Tell her 'tis down by the Liffey side,
    Where my mouldering bones do lay.
Tell her that here, in the battle of life,
    For the dawn of bright Freedom's Day,
I prayed for my home in the thick of the strife,
    In Tipperary so far away.'

'Tell her we fought for Granuaile,
    As our patriots did of yore,
For Ireland's cause that shall not fail,
    But shall win from shore to shore!
And heroes brave, our land to save,
    Shall sail o'er the ocean spray,
There's a vision of light before me tonight
    Of Tipperary so far away.'

The Soldiers of Ireland bore him on high,
    On their shoulders with solemn tread;
And many a heart, with tearful sigh
    Wept over our patriot dead.
In silence they lowered him in the grave,
    To rest till the reckoning day,
Sean Treacy, who died his home to save
    In Tipperary so far away.

The Boys of Kilmichael

Whilst we ho-nour in song and in sto - ry the mem-'ry of Pearse and Mac - Bride

Whose names are il - lu-mined in glo - ry with mar-tyrs who long since have died,

For - get not the boys of Kil - mi chael, those brave lads so gal-lant and true,

Who fought 'neath the green flag of E - rin and con-quered the Red, White and Blue.

The action referred to is the ambush, on 28 November 1920, by the Flying Column of the 3rd West Cork Brigade of the IRA, under the guerrilla leader Tom Barry.

The ambush took place in a remote mountainous location, between Dunmanway and Macroom, in West Cork. Two tenders of Auxiliaries were wiped out, with no survivors.

The Auxiliaries were an elite corps of mainly ex-military officers, with a fearsome reputation, hence the need to engage and defeat them as they were terrorizing and demoralizing the civilian population. This action was one of the most significant of the Anglo-Irish War. [LM]

Text: *Songs of the Irish Republic*, Coiste Foillseacháin Náisiúnta, Cork, 1962. Readers interested in a less restrained version should seek out Brendan Behan's recording, *Brendan Behan Sings Irish Folksongs and Ballads*, Spoken Arts SA760, 1960.

Air: 'Eoghan Cóir' or 'The Men of the West'.

Whilst we honour in song and in story
    The memory of Pearse and MacBride,
Whose names are illumined in glory
    With martyrs who long since have died,
Forget not the boys of Kilmichael,
    Those brave lads so gallant and true,
Who fought 'neath the green flag of Erin
    And conquered the Red, White and Blue.

Chorus
Then here's to the boys of Kilmichael
    Who feared not the might of the foe.
The day that they marched into battle
    They laid all the Black-and-Tans low.

On the twenty-eighth day of November,
    The Tans left the town of Macroom,
They were seated in two Crossley tenders
    Which led them right into their doom;
They were on the road to Kilmichael
    And never expected to stall,
They there met the boys of the column
    Who made a clean sweep of them all.

The sun in the west it was sinking,
    'Twas the eve of a cold winter's day,
When the Tans we were eagerly waiting
    Sailed into the spot where we lay;
And over the hills went the echo,
    The peal of the rifle and gun,
And the flames from their lorries gave tidings
    That the boys of the column had won.

The lorries were ours before twilight,
    And high over Dunmanway town
Our banners in triumph were waving
    To show that the Tans had gone down;
We gathered our rifles and bayonets
    And soon left the glen so obscure,
And never drew rein 'till we halted
    At the far-away camp of Glenure.

Mac and Shanahan

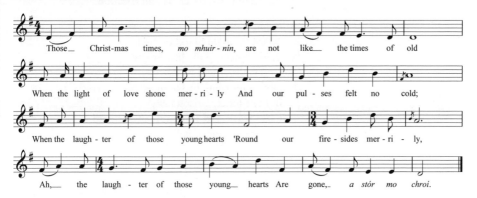

Those— Christ-mas times, *mo mhuir-nín,* are not like— the times of old

When the light of love shone mer-ri-ly And our pul-ses felt no cold;

When the laugh-ter of those young hearts 'Round our fire-sides mer-ri-ly,

Ah,— the laugh-ter of those young— hearts Are gone,— *a stór mo chroí.*

Those Christmas times, *mo mhuirnín,*
    Are not like the times of old
When the light of love shone merrily
    And our pulses felt no cold;
When the laughter of those young hearts
    Rang round our firesides merrily,
Ah, the laughter of those young hearts
    Are gone, *a stór mo chroí.*

It was on a dark December night
    Those bloodhounds found their way
To a dwelling house in Newtown,
    Not far from Doonbeg Bay.
It was there young Mac and Shanahan
    Were with irons firmly bound,
Placed in a lorry by Black and Tans
    And brought to Kilrush town.

There they were asked to give the names
    Of those, their comrades bold,
And told they'd get their liberty
    If their honour thus they sold.

In December 1920 the Black and Tans
arrested two young republicans,
Michael MacNamara and Willie
Shanahan, in Doonbeg, Co. Clare.
They took them to the barracks
at Kilrush where they tortured and
murdered them.

Text and air: Tom Munnelly, *The
Mount Callan Garland – Songs from
the Repertoire of Tom Lenihan,*
Comhairle Bhéaloideas Éireann,
Dublin, 1994.

This they refused defiantly
    And said they would rather gaze
On the cold dark gloom of a silent tomb
    Or seek a martyr's grave.

Next the priest was sent for,
    And, while those boys he blessed,
The rifles of the Black and Tans
    Pressed closely to their breast.
And before the priest departed
    He bade his last goodbye
And prayed that God might bring them safe
    Through Ireland's cross and triumph.

All night those boys prayed fervently
    To the Almighty God on high
To enable them to die like Pearse,
    Con Colbert and MacBride.
But when morning broke those boys awoke
    In their lonely prison cells
And the Black and Tans were in the yard
    Like devils out of hell.

While those boys were thinking deeply
    On their young days at home,
The Black and Tans with handcuffs and chains
    Came in the prison door.
They handcuffed, chained and brought them
    To a waiting bus outside
And shot them in the Ennis Road,
    Their brutal laws reviled.

It was then the news went like the wind
    That Miko Mac was laid low
And also Willie Shanahan,
    The pride of sweet Doughmore.
Their coffins wrapped in the tricolour flag,
    Side by side are laid to rest
In that lonely graveyard of Doonbeg
    With the noblest and the best.

Ah, they're dead today, those heroes,
    The pride of sweet West Clare.
All we can do for their poor souls
    Is to chant a silent prayer.
Sweet were their looks, soft were their smiles
    And were they to all,
And 'tis sad to say that those brave boys
    Met with such a sad downfall.

Johnston's Motor Car

Willie Gillespie (1883–1967)

Down by Brockagh Corner one morning I did stray,
When I met another rebel bold, who this to me did say:
I've orders from the Captain to assemble at Drumbar
But how are we to reach Dungloe without a motor car?

O Barney dear, be of good cheer and I'll tell you what we'll
    do.
The Black and Tans have plenty guns altho' we have but few.
We'll wire down to Stranorlar before we walk so far,
And we'll give the boys a jolly ride on Johnston's Motor
    Car.

When Johnston got the wire then he soon pulled on his shoes.
He says this case is urgent, there's little time to lose.
He wore a fancy castor hat and on his breast a star.
You could hear the din going through Glenfin of Johnston's
    Motor Car.

When he came to the Reelin Bridge, he met some rebels there.
He knew the game was up with him, and at them he did
    stare.
He said I've got a permit for travelling out so far.
You can keep your English permit, but we want your motor
    car.

What will my loyal comrades say when I get to Drumboe.
To say my car was commandeered by rebels from Dungloe.
We'll give you a receipt for her, it's signed by Captain
    Maher,
And when Ireland's free, then we will see to Johnston's
    Motor Car.

Text: *The National Comic Song Book*, Irish Book Bureau, Dublin, n.d.
  Air: From memory.

583

They put the car in motion, they filled it to the brim.
With guns and bayonets shining, while Johnston he did
    grin.
When Barney waved a Sinn Féin flag, she shot off like a
    star
And they gave three cheers for freedom and for
    Johnston's Motor Car.

When the loyal crew they heard the news, it grieved
    their hearts full sore.
They swore they'd have reprisals before they would give
    o'er.
In vain they searched through Glenties, the Rosses and
    Kilcar,
While the I.R.A. their flags displayed on Johnston's
    Motor Car.

Reprisals
W.B. Yeats

In this poem, written in November
1920, Yeats recalls his friend, the
aviator Robert Gregory who had died
during WWI, before addressing the
events taking place around Gregory's
old home. A nursing mother named
Eileen Quinn, a tenant of Coole Park,
had been shot and killed by an
Auxiliary, without reason, from a
passing lorry.

Text: Patrick Crotty (ed.), *The Penguin
Book of Irish Poetry*, Penguin Books,
London, 2010.

Some nineteen German planes, they say,
You had brought down before you died.
We called it a good death. Today
Can ghost or man be satisfied?
Although your last exciting year
Outweighed all other years, you said,
Though battle joy may be so dear
A memory, even to the dead,
It chases other thought away,
Yet rise from your Italian tomb,
Flit to Kiltartan cross and stay
Till certain second thoughts have come
Upon the cause you served, that we
Imagined such a fine affair:
Half-drunk or whole-mad soldiery
Are murdering your tenants there.
Men that revere your father yet
Are shot at on the open plain.
Where may new-married women sit
And suckle children now? Armed men
May murder them in passing by
Nor law nor parliament take heed.
Then close your ears with dust and lie
Among the other cheated dead.

The Dripsey Ambush

One Friday morning in January,
   The boys from far and near.
Assembled down in Godfrey's Cross,
   An ambush to prepare.
They were boys from Dripsey valley,
   And famed old Donoughmore,
All going to fight for Ireland
   Where the Dripsey river flows.

Long and patiently they waited,
   Tho' the day was bitter cold,
For little they knew that behind their backs,
   The ambush had been sold.
For a traitor dwelt amongst them,
   And this they did not know,
And the soldiers knew their hiding place,
   Where the Dripsey river flows.

At four o'clock the soldiers came,
   And they were well prepared,
With rifles and machine guns,
   They surrounded the volunteers.
But the bravest of them waited,
   To let their comrades go,
And they were shot and captured
   Where the Dripsey river flows.

God help those eight young gallant men,
   Now prisoners going away,
For they know that from these British dogs
   They will not get fair play.
God help their loving parents,
   For them the tears do flow,
And the Banshee now is wailing
   Where the Dripsey river flows.

And now my song is ended,
   But I have one word to say.
To hell with the Traitor
   Who gave the show away.
May every son of Cromwell
   Be banished from our shore,
And my God preserve the rebel boys,
   To strike another blow.

In January 1921 the IRA decided to ambush an army patrol which was known to follow a regular route from Macroom to Cork, passing on its way through the village of Dripsey.

The plan was known to a number of locals who were not supporters of the IRA and who passed on the details to the local priest, who informed the army. The priest also let the IRA know that their scheme had been compromised, but they disregarded this, believing that it was a ruse to get them to abandon the action.

When the moment arrived, the ambushers found that the army had deployed to outflank and encircle them. They made a good retreat but eight of their members were captured.

These were tried and sentenced to death, and in response the IRA took as hostages one of the locals who had passed on their plans, Mrs Lindsay, and her driver, threatening to kill them if their comrades were executed.

The captured IRA men were executed, and Mrs Lindsay and her driver were killed.

Text: *Songs and Recitations of Ireland, 1 – The Flag*, Coiste Foillseacháin Náisiúnta, Cork, n.d.

Upton Ambush

Many homes are filled with sorrow and with sadness
Many hearts are filled with anguish and with pain.
For old Ireland now she hangs her head in mourning,
For the men who fell at Upton for Sinn Féin.

The song recalls the ambush of the Cork to Bandon train, at Upton, Co. Cork, on 15 February 1921. The action, by the 3rd West Cork Brigade of the IRA, one of the most successful units of the Anglo-Irish War, was aimed at the Essex Regiment of the British army, a regiment based in Cork and outstandingly notorious for brutality, murder and torture.

The ambush, however, went badly wrong, due to incorrect information and the failure of scouts to report. The IRA unit fired on the coach where the Essex were expected to be, but instead they were interspersed among the civilian passengers throughout the entire train, and were more numerous than had been anticipated. Six civilians were killed and ten wounded in the resulting firefight, with two IRA dead and three wounded, one fatally, while the British suffered six wounded.

There is some licence taken in the song, as it is highly unlikely that the IRA would have contemplated close quarter use of bayonets. The guerrilla tactic of ambush and retreat into a 'safe area' in the surrounding countryside was the common practice.

The officer commanding the notorious Essex Regiment was the then Major Arthur Ernest Percival (1887-1966), later a Lieutenant-General, who in 1942 surrendered Singapore to the Japanese.

Major Montgomery, later Field-Marshal of WWII fame, also served as an intelligence officer at the same time as Percival, in Cork. [LM]

Text and air: Martin Shannon, *Ballads from the Jails and Streets of Ireland*, Red Hand Books, Dublin, 1966. The song is a parody of 'The Battleship Maine' published in 1898, which was itself a parody of 'The Banks of the Wabash'. The final verse is from the online archive of the songs of Seosamh Ó hÉanaigh (accessed 26 July 2015) at www.joeheaney.org/default.asp?contentID=929

Chorus
Let the moon shine tonight along the valley,
Where those men who fought for freedom now are laid.
May they rest in peace those men who died for Ireland,
And who fell at Upton Ambush for Sinn Féin.

Some were thinking of their mothers, wives and sweethearts,
More were thinking of their dear old Irish homes,
Did they think of how they drilled along the valley,
Or when they marched out from Cork City to their doom.

The morning cry rang out: 'Fix bayonets,'
And right gallantly, they fixed them for the fray,
Gallantly they fought and died for Ireland,
Around the lonely woods at Upton far away.

Some are sleeping 'neath the waters of Cork Harbour,
More are sleeping 'neath the good old Irish clay,
But their voices seem to cry out 'God save Ireland!'
From the lonely woods of Upton far away.

Brave Sons of Granuaile

'Twas in Cork Jail they shot them down, because they loved their land.

No crime was theirs, no motive base, no evil deeds they planned.

As gallant Irish Volunteers, when called they did not fail,

But proudly marched to death today, brave sons of Granuaile.

'Twas in Cork Jail they shot them down,
  Because they loved their land.
No crime was theirs, no motive base,
  No evil deeds they planned.
As gallant Irish Volunteers,
  When called they did not fail,
But proudly marched to death to-day,
  Brave sons of Granuaile.

Chorus
As gallant Irish Volunteers,
  When called they did not fail,
But proudly marched to death to-day,
  Brave sons of Granuaile.

Like school-boys on a holiday,
  They wait the fatal hour.
For England kills the captives
  Who fall into her power.
A last fond look, they stand erect,
  And face the bullets hail,
And show how Irishmen can die,
  Brave sons of Granuaile.

When lads like those can give their lives,
  The Cause is safe and sure,
"'Tis not to those who suffer most,
  But those who can endure.'
For these are brave MacSwiney's words,
  Who died in Brixton Gaol.
They've followed in his footsteps,
  Brave sons of Granuaile.

The sub-title to this song relates that it refers to Thomas O'Brien, Daniel O'Callaghan, John Lyons, Timothy McCarthy, John Allen, and Patrick O'Mahony, who were shot in Cork Jail, 28 February 1921.

Text: *The Granuaile Song Book*, The Irish Supply Depot, Dublin, 1922.
  Air: The prescribed air is 'Granuaile', which is probably the air here: 'A New Song Called Granuaile' from Colm O Lochlainn's *Irish Street Ballads*, At the Sign of the Three Candles, Dublin, 1939.

587

The Heroes of Selton Hill

John McDonald

On 11 March 1921, an IRA training camp, having been informed upon by a local doctor who had been in the British army, was surrounded by Auxiliaries on Selton Hill, near Ballinamore, Co. Leitrim.

Despite their courageous resistance, their position was finally overrun and the six members of the column killed, with one wounded man surviving by lying in the cold water of a drain.

The six who were killed were Commandant Seán Connolly, a Longford man who was a GHQ Organizer and Training Officer, and Volunteers Joseph O'Beirne, James J. Rynn, Michael Baxter, John J. O'Reilly and James J. O'Reilly.

In retribution, the unionist who had told the doctor of the location of the training camp was shot dead, while the doctor escaped to England. In the last verse, the word 'huns' is used in a derogatory way, to suggest barbarity and viciousness. The word is quite frequently used in songs of the 1916–21 period to describe the British troops, many of whom were indeed barbarous and vicious in their dealings with prisoners and the civilian population in Ireland. [LM]

Text: Martin Shannon, *Ballads from the Jails and Streets of Ireland*, Red Hand Books, Dublin, 1966.
    Air: The source notes that this ballad 'can be sung to the air of "The Croppy Boy".'

On the afternoon of a bleak March day
While machine guns on their thinned ranks play,
Overmatched, outnumbered, they stand at bay,
    Firm as the hills of Erin.

There is never a murmur, not thought of flight –
They deal blow for blow in the waning light,
Though their's an unequal, a hopeless fight,
    They fight for the honour of Erin.

No shelter there, 'twas the bare hillside
As volley to volley in rage replied.
They will die as their warrior fathers died,
    Nor haul down the flag of Erin.

'Lay down your arms!' Comes the proud reply;
'We know no master but One on high!'
'Surrender!' 'No; we are ready to die –
    To die as we lived for Erin.'

As the shades of evening around them close,
They sink, overpowered, girth round by foes.
From many a gash the red blood flows
    To moisten the soil of Erin.

There is never a prisoner! All are slain –
On the fallen flag there is never a stain –
That flag will float on the breeze again,
    Free as the winds of Erin.

Those soldiers of Erin sleep cold and low,
Yet we shed no tears, though we loved them so,
Their's a glorious death, with face to the foe,
    With sword in hand for Erin.

Their sorrowing comrades laid them to rest,
While many a wound upon face and breast,
Plainer than spoken words attest
    Their undying love for Erin.

And Leitrim is proud of her peerless sons,
Who died like heroes facing the guns,
Not yielding an inch to the English huns
    Of the sacred soil of Erin.

The Men of Barry's Column

When British terror failed to win
Allegiance from our people then,
The Black and Tans they were brought in,
	They thought they'd teach us manners;
Instead of teaching they were taught
A lesson which they dearly bought,
For when Kilmichael's day was fought
	Low was their bloody banner.

They sought to wipe the column out,
From East to West, from North to South,
'Till at Crossbarry's bloody rout
	They woke from their daydreaming.
Though ten to one they were that day,
Our boys were victors in the fray,
And over the hills we marched away
	With bagpipes merrily screaming.

The Essex brutes who tortured Hales,
They scoured the land to fill their jails,

Barry's Column was the Flying Column of the 3rd West Cork Brigade of the Irish Republican Army. One of the most successful guerilla units in the Anglo-Irish War, it was commanded by Tom Barry, a most able, determined and resourceful leader.

Kilmichael, verse 1, refers to the ambush where two Crossley tenders of Auxiliaries were wiped out on 28 November 1920 (see the song 'The Boys of Kilmichael', p. 578).

Crossbarry, verse 2, refers to the action there, when about 1200 British troops were defeated, with heavy losses, by Barry's column of about 110 men. Flor Begley played his warpipes during the action, after which the column retreated safely, with the British unwilling to pursue, in fear of further ambushes.

The Essex Regiment (verse 3), under Major Percival was, unlike most regular British army regiments, notorious for its brutality. The Hales referred to is Tom Hales, a captured IRA officer, who had his nails torn out with a pliers by these gentlemen.

589

Toureen, verse 3, was the site of a very successful ambush against the Essex Regiment, on 22 Oct 1920.

Rossa's town (verse 4), is Rosscarberry, where Jeremiah O'Donovan Rossa, the Fenian leader, was born. Roscarberry RIC barracks was captured and destroyed by Barry's Column on 30 March 1921. [LM]

Text: *Songs of the Irish Republic*, Coiste Foillseacháin Náisiúnta, Cork, 1962.
  Air: 'Follow Me Up to Carlow'.

Though their ugly deeds would pale
  The cheeks of Irish mothers.
Paid dearly for their deeds were they
When passing by Toureen one day,
We dearly made the Essex pay
  And well avenged our brothers.

When Barry saw the Tans efface
The spirit of his fighting race,
Right through his soul did madly chase
  His blood went boiling over.
He marched his men to Rossa's town
And burned that famous fortress down,
And never again will Britain's crown
  Her foothold there recover.

Chorus
So, piper, play a martial air
For the gallant boys who conquered there,
No merry tune to banish care,
  Or mournful, or solemn.
The grander tune of all was played
By the fighting squad of the Third Brigade,
Whose glorious deeds will never fade,
  The men of Barry's Column.

Flor Begley, 'The Piper of Crossbarry', can be seen in this picture of a Cork flying column.

The Piper of Crossbarry

Bryan Mac Mahon

The Pi-per of Cross-bar-ry, boys, he rose ere mor-ning tide.
He walked up to his cap-tain bold, his war-pipes laid a-side.
Says he "I'm through with pi-ping, I'll fight for li-ber-ty.
To-day, please God, we'll hold the sod and set old Ire-land free".

The Piper of Crossbarry, boys, he rose 'ere morning tide.
He walked up to his captain bold, his warpipes laid aside.
Says he – 'I'm through with piping, I'll fight for liberty,
Today, please God, we'll hold the sod and set old Ireland free.'

'Now, Piper boy,' the Captain said upon that fateful day,
'Today you'll stride between our lines and martial music play;
For when we hear our Irish pipes we'll strive for victory;
And maybe, at Crossbarry, we shall set old Ireland free.'

From Cork, Kinsale and Bandon town, from Ballincollig too,
The British poured two thousand men upon Tom Barry's few;
But when the sun was setting on that day of victory,
The Piper of Crossbarry, boys, had piped old Ireland free.

From break of dawn as day wore on, Crossbarry battle rolled,
For Irish guns and Irish sons had challenged England's hold.
And when the blazing lorries flamed to signal victory,
Hey! The men of old Crossbarry, boys, had set old Ireland free.

A health to brave Flor Begley, boys, who raised the chant of war,
He strode among the fighting men while his warpipes droned afar;
For the music of his warlike tunes it cowed the enemy,
'Twas the Piper of Crossbarry, boys, who piped old Ireland free.

Forget not those brave volunteers who fell on that bloody plain,
For them the piper raised a dirge to *caoin* above the slain,
And the banshee's sad lament was heard in the time of victory,
But the Piper of Crossbarry, boys, had piped old Ireland free.

This song recalls the major engagement at Crossbarry, when an encirclement of the 3rd West Cork Brigade Flying Column, under Tom Barry, was attempted. The British were heavily defeated and suffered substantial casualties in this, the largest engagement of the Anglo-Irish War. See 'The Men of Barry's Column', p. 589, for further details.

Flor Begley was the piper who marched and played his warpipes in the Haroldds's farmyard during the course of the engagement.

The word 'caoin' in the last verse is 'lament' – for the three IRA volunteers who died at Crossbarry, and in the second-last line the 'banshee' is the fairy woman who keens for the dead. [LM]

Text and air: Colm O Lochlainn, *More Irish Street Ballads*, At the Sign of the Three Candles, Dublin, 1965.

The Woodlands of Loughglynn

The sum-mer sun was_ sink-ing low be_ hind the wes-tern sky.

The lark's loud song was peal-ing sweet, but it brought no joy to me.

For the one I love is gone for aye, he left the ty-rant's den.

He_ fought till death and_ then he left the_ Wood-lands of Lough-glynn.

This street ballad commemorates Volunteers John Bergin and Stephen McDermott, two members of the IRA who were killed when their training camp was informed upon and raided by British troops in Loughglynn, Co. Roscommon, in 1921. [LM]

Text and air: Martin Shannon, *Ballads from the Jails and Streets of Ireland*, Red Hand Books, Dublin, 1966.

The summer sun was singing low
  Behind the western sky,
The lark's loud song was pealing sweet,
  But it brought no joy to me.
For the one I love is gone for aye,
  He left the tyrant's den.
He fought till death and then he left
  The Woodlands of Loughglynn.

He was a brave young Irishman,
  John Bergin was his name.
He belonged to Tipperary
  And from Nenagh town he came.
But now thank God that he is gone
  He's free from care and sin.
And he let them have his parting shot
  In the Woodlands of Loughglynn.

McDermott too, was brave and true
  From the plains of Ballingare.
He's missed at many a fireside
  By his friends both near and far.
He's missed at home in old Brackloon
  By his own dear kith and kin,
And his comrades true shall miss him, too,
  In the Woodlands of Loughglynn.

When our heroes brave were dying there,
  They called for a clergyman.
Let no one think they feared to face
  The English Black and Tan.
The clergy came and were in time,
  But as they said 'amen',

McDermott's soul was departing
    Through the Woodlands of Loughglynn.

Young Bergin said that he was proud
    To die for Ireland's cause.
The deed was done that should be done
    Against England's cruel laws.
Saying, 'Good-bye to Tipperary
    And to every dale and glen,
And to all my faithful comrades
    In the Woodlands of Loughglynn.

Take this message to our own brave boys
    And tell them we are dead.
Tell them to be of utmost cheer
    And to hold no drooping head.
To keep old brains a-using,
    To fight and not give in,
And be proud to die 'neath an Irish sky
    In the Woodlands of Loughglynn.'

These were the words our brave boys said
    As they died for Ireland's cause,
To free the land from Black and Tans
    And cruel alien laws.
Good-bye, old friends, fight side by side,
    Like gallant Irishmen.
So they closed their eyes and said good-bye
    To the Woodlands of Loughglynn.

The Dear Little Ambush

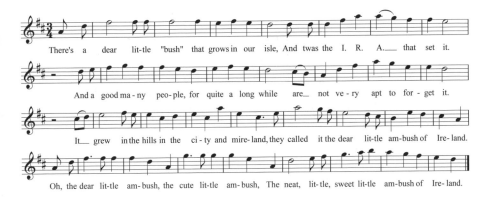

There's a dear lit-tle "bush" that grows in our isle, And twas the I. R. A.__ that set it.

And a good ma-ny peo-ple, for quite a long while are__ not ve-ry apt to for-get it.

It__ grew in the hills in the ci-ty and mire-land, they called it the dear lit-tle am-bush of Ire-land.

Oh, the dear lit-tle am-bush, the cute lit-tle am-bush, The neat, lit-tle, sweet lit-tle am-bush of Ire-land.

In May 1921 Éamonn de Valera convinced Dáil Éireann to abandon the military strategy that they had followed up to then (the hit-and-run tactics of a guerilla force against a regular army) in favour of a major action with a large number of men committed to it. The target was to be Custom House, which was the centre of Local Government in Ireland.

The attack took place on 25 May 1921. It was a propoganda success, but a military disaster. The IRA lost five killed and eighty captured. It was also a disaster for Irish historiography, as centuries of irreplacable records were lost when the IRA fired the building.

Text: The Donagh MacDonagh Song Collection. See http://songbook1.tripod.com/ (accessed 3 April 2015).

Air (see preceding page): The song is clearly modelled on the ballad 'The Dear Little Shamrock'.

There's a dear little 'bush' that grows in our Isle,
    And 'twas the I.R.A. that set it,
And a good many people for quite a long while
    Are not very apt to forget it.
It grew in the hills, in the cities and mireland,
And they called it the dear little ambush of Ireland!
    Oh, the dear little ambush, the cute little ambush,
The neat little, sweet little ambush of Ireland.

And in spite of everything John Bull could do,
    The 'bush' it grew bigger and bigger,
The boys were not daunted when lorries rushed through,
    They had always their hand on the trigger,
So it flourished in East, South and West in our Sireland,
And they called it the dear little ambush of Ireland.
    Oh, the dear little ambush, the cute little ambush,
The neat little, sweet little ambush of Ireland.

The 'bush' grew so big that in Dublin one day
    Was a sight made us all stare in wonder,
The Custom House, burning away on the quay,
    Where England kept notes of her plunder,
The Taxes and Records that kept down our Sireland,
They say have 'Gone West' in this ambush in Ireland.
    Oh, the dear little ambush, the cute little ambush,
The neat little, sweet little ambush of Ireland.

The Custom House, Dublin, burning after the attack by the IRA.

The West Mayo Brigade

You may talk of the brave men who fought, boys,
    For Ireland a nation once more.
There are some we are told died as martyrs
    While thousands in jail suffered sore.
Yet there's one that we all love and honour
    Though Munro said he was a bad boy,
For his country he fought like a hero,
    Brave, faithful, undaunted Kilroy.

Chorus
Here's to brave Michael Kilroy, boys,
    Who of bullets was never afraid,
He was always the last to retreat, boys,
    While commanding West Mayo Brigade.

In Kilmeena our boys fared out badly,
    Outnumbered by rifles and men.
Kilroy fought while his men they retired
    To safety's cover again.
Then he fired a last parting volley
    At his foes as he bade them goodbye
And he bitterly thought of his brave boys
    Who in death's cold embrace did now lie.

The whisper went round that in Skerdagh
    The rebels lay wounded and sore.
Munro being in charge of the foemen,
    Got word at the old barrack door.
And he said to his bold R.I.C. men,
    'Those rebels, being tired, will sleep.
Who'll volunteer now and we'll take them
    And into town drive them like sheep.'

Then Munro and his bold R.I.C. men
    Crept like robbers so silent they were.
The rebels worn out lay a-sleeping,
    Never dreaming that danger was near.
But hark! What's that sound at O'Malley's?
    Is it the noise of a gun?
Go, give the alarm to Skerdagh,
    We'll make history ere this day is done.

When Kilroy got his men all together,
    He sent some with the wounded away,
When the bullets began their sharp whistling

The Kilmeena ambush on 19 May 1921 was a major setback for the IRA in Mayo, as they lost thirteen men killed or wounded.

In a follow-up action a few days later the retreating column was attacked at the village of Skerdagh, where they fought off the army, and in early June they scored a major victory against the army at Carrowkennedy.

The leader of the column was Michael Kilroy (1884–1962) of Newport, who later became a Fianna Fáil TD.

Text: Ernie O'Malley Collection, New York University.

The foemen were soon held at bay.
The police got some stripes undesired
   And their hearts were not beating with joy,
For Munro got one in the shoulder,
   So give three ringing cheers for Kilroy.

Jim Browne got shot bravely fighting,
   All the others got safely away.
But Kilroy swore for Browne and Kilmeena
   The foemen would dearly pay.
Carrowkennedy soon told a story,
   The Saxon was beaten once more.
But Kilroy vows he won't be contented
   Till they're driven complete from our shore.

The Valley of Knockanure

Bryan MacMahon (1909–98)

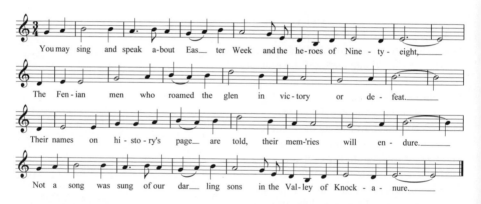

This is the best known of a number of songs relating the murder of unarmed members of the IRA, taken prisoner by Black and Tans, at Gortaglanna, near Knockanure, Co. Kerry, on 12 May 1921. The Tans, reputed to have been drunk, which was a common feature due to their wrecking and looting of shops and public houses, were seeking revenge for the burning of Listowel RIC barracks.

The dead IRA men were Jeremiah Lyons, Patrick Walsh and Patrick Dalton. Con Dee, though shot and wounded, ran for it and managed to escape. [LM]

You may sing and speak about Easter Week
   And the heroes of Ninety-eight.
Of the Fenian men who roamed the glen
   In victory or defeat.
Their names on history's page are told,
   Their memories will endure.
Not a song was sung of our darling sons
   In the Valley of Knockanure.

There was Walsh and Lyons and the Dalton boys,
   They were young and in their prime.
They rambled to a lonely spot
   Where the Black and Tans did hide.

The Republic bold they did uphold
　　Though outlawed on the moor,
And side by side they fought and died
　　In the Valley of Knockanure.

In Gortagleanna's lovely glen
　　Three gallant men took shade,
While in young wheat full soft and sweet
　　The summer's breezes played.
But 'twas not long till Lyons came on
　　Saying 'time's not mine nor yours';
But alas 'twas late and they met their fate
　　In the Valley of Knockanure.

'Twas on a neighbouring hillside
　　We listened with calm dismay.
In every house, in every town,
　　A maiden knelt to pray.
They're closing in around them now
　　With rifle fire so sure,
And Lyons is dead, and Dalton's down,
　　In the Valley of Knockanure.

They took them then beside a fence
　　To where the furze did bloom.
Like brothers so they faced the foe
　　To meet their dreadful doom.
When Dalton spoke, his voice it broke,
　　With a passion proud and pure.
'For our land we die as we face the sky,
　　In the Valley of Knockanure.'

But ere the guns could seal his fate
　　Con Dee had broken through.
With a prayer to God he spurned the sod
　　As against the hill he flew,
But the bullets tore his flesh in two
　　Yet he cried with calm dismay:
'Revenge I'll get for my comrades deaths
　　In the Valley of Knockanure.'

I met with Dalton's mother
　　And she to me did say:
'May God have mercy on his soul
　　Who died in the glen today.
Could I but kiss his cold, cold lips,
　　My aching heart 'twould cure,

Text: this song exists in several versions. The text here is the one declared to be MacMahon's original by the song collector Gabriel Fitzmaurice in his essay on the song on the Moyvane Village website www.moyvane.com/people/ gabriel-fitzmaurice/where-history-meets-poetry-the -valley-of-knockanure/ (accessed June 2015).

The version included by Dick Hogan in his recent publication *The Hogan Collection* contains many minor differences, and also the following sixth verse, not found in other versions:

And there they lay on the cold, cold clay
　　They were martyred for Ireland's cause,
While the cowardly clan of the Black and Tan
　　It showed them England's laws,
No more they'll feel the soft breeze steal
　　O'er the uplands so secure,
For the wild geese fly where our heroes lie
　　In the Valley of Knockanure.

Air: from memory.

The gravestone erected by Con Dee on the grave of his comrade Jerry Lyons.

597

And I'd gladly lay him down to rest
In the Valley of Knockanure.'

The summer sun is setting now
Behind the Feale and Lee.
The pale, pale moon is rising
Far out beyond Tralee.
The dismal stars and clouds afar
Are darkening o're the moor,
And the Banshee cried where our heroes died
In the Valley of Knockanure.

While Walsh and Lyons and Dalton
Are resting in the clay,
We have true men yet in Ireland
To man the gap today.
While grass is green in Ireland
Your memory will endure.
So God guard and keep the place you sleep
In the Valley of Knockanure.

A detachment of Black and Tans in a Tipperary village in 1921.

Roscommon Brigade

The bright dawn was peeping o'er Cloonsuck,
    And the valleys of Clonree,
When the clash of arms rang out in rage,
    The fight was for Ireland free.
For when Connaught raised the battle-cry,
    Our boys were never afraid;
They met foeman's steel, the cause must live,
    God bless Roscommon Brigade.

A June sunrise is a glorious sight,
    When peace lulls a western scene;
But one hour of battle changed Cloonsuck,
    They fell in their coats of Green.
The tyrants yelled: 'Come out murderers,'
    For blood, wicked plans they laid;
Ireland first, and the Green, White and Gold,
    Replied Roscommon Brigade.

For months 'on the run' o'er green hillsides,
    They fell for the flag that day,
Under Crown Forces' guns they held the cause,
    They fought 'till death in the fray.
Young Vaughan's command: 'To arms, my boys!'
    Undaunted they all obeyed;
And Act of Contrition, meet your God,
    Fight on, Roscommon Brigade.

Their heart's blood crimsoned the soft green sod,
    Roscommon may well feel proud;
The Shamrock was sprinkled there before,
    With blood from Volunteer shroud.
To right Ireland's wrongs, in penal days,
    With cannons fierce fusillade;
The West rang out the slogan call,
    Onward, Roscommon Brigade.

A Nation's glory – our martyred dead,
    Their blood was not shed in vain;
Vaughan and Shannon gave up their lives,
    To free old Ireland again.
'The West's awake, may God bless the Flag,'
    With their dying lips they prayed,
The Saxon foe by the Gael must go –
    Lead on, Roscommon Brigade!

On 22 June 1921 the RIC raided the home of the Vaughan family at Cloonsuck, where three Volunteers were billeted. Two of them, Ned Shanahan and John Vaughen, were killed, and Martin Ganley was captured.

The RIC commander, Sergeant James King, was assassinated in Castlerea the following month.

Text: *Second Album of Roscommon Verse*, The Roscommon Association, Dublin, 1983.

Commandant MacKeown

Seán Mac Eoin, aka 'the Blacksmith of Ballinalee', was the leader of a flying column in Longford. He was captured in March 1921 and sentenced to death for killing an RIC inspector.

He had gained a reputation for the chivalrous treatment of any prisoners that he had captured, and there were many appeals for clemency, which were rejected by General Macready, the British Commander-in-Chief.

He was eventually released when Michael Collins threatened to break off the negotiations over the Treaty if he was executed.

Text: *The Granuaile Song Book*, The Irish Supply Depot, Dublin, 1922.
Air: 'Rory O'More'.

There is joy in the heart of old Ireland to-day,
Because of a man who has well won his way,
For courage and daring, oh, he is the boy,
A son of old Ireland, her pride and her joy.
When surrounded by foes sure he fought to the last,
And never a thought on his own life he cast,
But vastly outnumbered and captured was he,
And brought into Dublin, court-martialled to be.
'You stand charged with murder,' the Judge sternly said.
'No! I fought for my country, for her sake I bled.
For Erin's fair honour, your charge I disown,
And I'll die for her sake,' said Commandant MacKeown.

'When your troops I captured, I treated them right,
As prisoners of war who had lost in the fight.
For myself all I ask as a soldier to die,
And with my dear comrades my body may lie.'
Then away to the prison the hero was borne,
P'rhaps to die on the scaffold some bright summer
   morn,
But the fates in their courses had taken a hand,
For a Truce was proclaimed all over the land.
Says England, 'We'll let all your prisoners free,
That all of you meet and make terms with me.
But one we will hold, and one man alone,
And that is one known as Commandant MacKeown.'

600

Then the men of Dáil Éireann said this will not do.
If you hold our Commandant your words are not true.
If a Truce is to hold, and if Peace is to be,
We demand that at once you MacKeown must set free.
For a while England hedged as often of yore,
But then showed she'd more sense than ever before.
The gaol gates are open, MacKeown is set free,
When the Conference meets with his comrades he'll be.
Then long may he reign to help the old Cause,
Till Erin has all her own freedom and laws,
For a little bird told me we'll soon have our own,
So long life and good luck to Commandant MacKeown.

The 'G' Man's Lament
Soliloquy on the Establishment of the Irish Republic

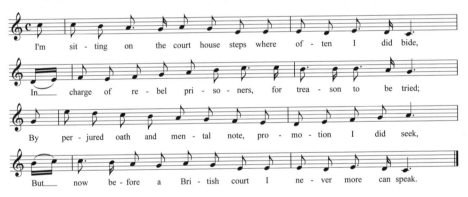

I'm sit - ting on the court house steps where of - ten I did bide,

In charge of re - bel pri - so - ners, for trea - son to be tried;

By per - jured oath and men - tal note, pro - mo - tion I did seek,

But now be - fore a Bri - tish court I ne - ver more can speak.

I'm sitting on the Court House steps where often I did bide,
In charge of Rebel prisoners, for treason to be tried;
By perjured oath and mental note promotion I did seek,
But now before a British court I never more can speak.

My occupation is all gone, I'll have to starve – or work,
A thought that makes my blood run cold, it only suits a Turk;
No shoneen Judge or Castle Hack the money now can pay,
O, I'm feeling sad and lonely here since Sinn Féin gained the day.

The place is little changed since when I kidnapped Murphy's boy,
A youngster of but sixteen years, I sent him to Mountjoy;
I gave him six long months in jail to make him understand
That it was treason when he sang 'The Felons of our Land'.

'G' men were the members of G Division of the RIC, the political section. 'Wacs' (verse 4) were members of the WAAC, the Women's Auxiliary Army Corps, established in 1917.

Text: *The Granuaile Song Book*, The Irish Supply Depot, Dublin, 1922.
Air: 'Lament of the Irish Emigrant' or 'I'm Sitting On the Stile, Mary'.

601

I'm going off to England now (or perhaps to Timbucktoo),
For since Erin a Republic framed I don't know what to do;
I must make tracks or join the Wacs to try and make a show,
But I'll keep my ears well cocked, bedad, no matter where I go.

The Riot
(Belfast, August 1921)
Tom Carnduff (1886–1956)

In June, July and August 1921, Belfast went through a period of intense violence. Sparked by IRA attacks on the RIC, anti-Catholic pogroms and sectarian warfare broke out, in which hundreds of Catholics were driven from their homes and jobs, scores were killed and hundreds of homes destroyed. The destruction and loss of life were likened to that experienced by Dublin during the 1916 Rising. The story of the time may be read in Alan Parkinson's *Belfast's Unholy War* (Four Courts Press, Dublin 2004).

Text: Tom Carnduff, *Songs of an Out-of-Work*, Quota Press, Belfast, 1932.

Peace reigns in Harkly Street!
People pass to and fro
On either side,
Women idle about the doors,
And chatter;
Children scamper up and down
In playful frolics,
Their shrill cries frighten
The very pigeons;
A milk cart rumbles by;
A fruit vendor cries his wares –
Life is so dull
In Harkly Street!

Crash!
A window-pane is shattered;
Women scream, and rush
Their children to safety;
Men scramble for shelter,
Crouch behind lamp-posts,
Squeeze into doorways;
For none can see
The 'gunman's' hidden post.

A solitary figure emerges
From an alley;
A revolver gleams –
Then a flash.
A man curls up in a doorway,
And groans.
A head peeps around the corner,
A rifle cracks,
And the solitary figure drops –
Blood dyes the flagstones
In Harkly Street!

Forms dart back and forth
At either end
O Harkly Street.
Rifles spit out
Their leaden messengers;
Revolvers bark;
The dull boom of a grenade
Verberates the air –
Hell has opened its floodgates
In Harkly Street!

A lad of tender years
Screams,
And is hurried away;
A passing woman coughs,
Leans wearily against the wall,
Lifts her hand
To wipe the blood
From her mouth –
Oh, it is horrible!
An armoured car
Swings into position;
The crackle of a Lewis gun
Is heard;
Bullets whine through the air,
Knocking chips out of the walls,
Crashing through window-panes,
Ricocheting off flagstones.

The street is deserted.
Not a human being
Is seen:
Just the black hulk
Of the car
With its grinning muzzle
Spewing lead.

People pass to and fro,
Matrons sit at their doors,
Knitting;
Men chat pleasantly
As they smoke;
Children's voices are raised
In boisterous enjoyment;
Youthful maids pass comment
On passing swains –
Life is so dull
In Harkly Street!

The Man from the Morning Post

There's a tear in my eye and the rea-son is why, I was ne'er in this coun-try be - fore,___ I___ came fee-ling glad__ but now I am sad since I lan-ded on E___ rin's shore;___ For__ ev' ry Jac - keen__ has cocked his cau - been and se - di - tion and trea-son they boast,___ This cur-sed Sinn Féin has quite turned their brain sez the man from the "Mor - ning Post".___

Chorus

I came to Ire - land smi- ling___ but__ now I'd like to cry,___ When I talk the "Hem- pire" they___ wink the o - ther eye.___ The Bol - she - viks are pou- ring___ in__ gold all round the coast,___ Since the day I came here__ I'm tremb-ling with fear sez the man from the "Mor - ning Post".___

Text: *The Granuaile Song Book*, The Irish Supply Depot, Dublin, 1922.
Air: 'When Irish Eyes Are Smiling'.

There's a tear in my eye and the reason is why,
   I was ne'er in this country before,
I came feeling glad, but now I am sad,
   Since I landed on Erin's shore;
For every Jackeen has cocked his caubeen,
   And sedition and treason they boast,
This cursed Sinn Féin has quite turned their brain
   Sez the man from the 'Morning Post'.

Chorus
I came to Ireland smiling but now I'd like to cry,
When I talk the 'Hempire' they wink the other eye,
The Bolsheviks are pouring in gold all round the coast,
Since the day I came here I'm trembling with fear
   Sez the man from the 'Morning Post'.

'Tis a terrible tale how they break out of jail,
   And kill all before them as well,
When they make their escape your life is not safe,
   But the worst part I've yet to tell,

604

They've bombs in galore hid under the floor,
    And of rifles and bayonets a host,
All purchased I'm told with Bolshevik gold
    Sez the man from the 'Morning Post'.

On truth I was bent, to Mounjoy I went,
    And asked all the warders up there,
How the 'Shinners' got out? They answered in doubt,
    And pointed up in the air.
There's a big aeroplane, controlled by Sinn Féin,
    That comes down in the night like a ghost,
And before you can cough, it has hopped them right off,
    Sez the man from the 'Morning Post'.

I'm now going home, away o'er the foam,
    To give my report to the 'Sub',
How the streets run in blood, in a regular flood,
    And you can't get a drink in a pub.
On the first morn in May, they struck work all day,
    And swore their employers they'd roast,
Sure I really believe they've got arms up their sleeve
    Sez the man from the 'Morning Post'.

Martial Law in Dublin

Dermot O'Byrne

Text: Edna C. Fitzhenry, *Nineteen-Sixteen Anthology*, Browne & Nolan Ltd, Dublin, 1935.

By day this sunlit citadel of death
    Flashes the arrogance of your bayonets,
Sharp biting gleams that sear our pride like teeth
    Of the old dragonish sowing that begets
Even today as dangerous a birth
    As ever bristled up from ancient earth.

Also by dusk we're home at your desire
    To meditate upon your iron might.
Fool, have you padlocks for our inner fire?
    Are there not long deep hours before the night
Flaming with signs of Her whose solemn eyes
    Make empty all your brutish mysteries?

The Ballad of the Volunteers

Sylvia Lynd

Text: *The Literary Digest*, New York, 23 April 1921, reprinted from the Manchester *Guardian*. It was reprinted in the Connolly Association's newspaper *Irish Democrat*, No. 476, October 1983, with the following comment: 'This fine song can be sung to the air of either 'Paddies Evermore' or 'The Low-Backed Car'. It was written in 1921 by Sylvia Lynd, wife of Robert Lynd, the distinguished author and member of Connolly's ISRP, who wrote the introduction to several of James Connolly's books.'

Oh, may the fields that hide the hare
   Hide well our hunted men,
As scattered rocks conceal the fox
   And smallest trees the wren.
As by the cart-wheel's crushing track
   The skylark knows no fears –
In vain, God grant, may England hunt
   The Irish Volunteers.

Oh, may the winter be a spring
   About them where they hide.
Oh, may by night the stars be bright
   Their silent feet to guide.
May streams with fish and boughs with fruit
   Be teeming through the years,
And every field a harvest yield
   To the Irish Volunteers.

For bloody-hearted are their foes
   And honour's path they spurn.
They take their pay, a pound a day,
   To torture, kill, and burn;
To rob the helpless and the poor,
   Rejoicing in their tears,
And mercy none is ever shown
   To the Irish Volunteers.

Oh, you that torture captive men,
   That hapless prisoners slay,
That shoot, or drown, or sack a town
   In a devil's holiday,
Can do but shame your country's name,
   While ours more bright appears –
From scoundrel bands of 'Black-and-Tans'
   God save the Volunteers.

It was such men as these that set
   America's flag on high.
It was such men that freed again
   Victorious Italy;
And Belgium fought the German foe
   In such a cause as theirs –
Then well we boast the fearless host,
   The Irish Volunteers.

Remember well the noble dead
    Who died to make men free.
In every land they make their stand
    For Ireland's liberty.
That cause has stood through pain and blood
    For seven hundred years –
So till Freedom's day we'll sing and say
    God bless the Volunteers!

The Men of the Bold I.R.A.

When you read of martyr and hero,
    Who suffered in dark Ninety-Eight,
'Gainst a far greater tyrant than Nero,
    How bitter and sad was their fate.
Then remember the men of to-day, boys,
    Who have fought for us all through the fray,
And died for the country they loved, boys,
    The men of the Bold I.R.A.

Chorus
Then here's to the Bold I.R.A., boys,
    Who have fought now for many a day,
When Ireland was shattered and bleeding,
    She looked to the Bold I.R.A.

When brute force was tried to subject us,
    And laws worse than ever before,
We looked to our men to protect us,
    When hearts had grown weary and sore.
O, the boys with revolver and rifle,
    They oft chased the foemen away,
And looked upon death as a trifle,
    The men of the Bold I.R.A.

And when if defeated in numbers,
    And suffered what nobody knows,
Or captured, tired out, as they slumbered,
    Small mercy they got from their foes.
The prison and scaffold have claimed them,
    For these who have died we shall pray,
The living that's with us, God spare them,
    The men of the Bold I.R.A.

Text: *The Granuaile Song Book*, The Irish Supply Depot, Dublin, 1922.
    Air: 'The Men of the West', see p. 580.

The Boys of Barr na Sráide

Sigerson Clifford

The town it climbs the moun-tain, and looks u-pon the sea.

And slee-ping time or wa-king, 'tis there I long to be.

To walk a-gain that kind-ly street, the place I grew a man,

And the boys of Barr-na Srái-de went hun-ting for the wran.

The hunting of the wren (in Irish *dreoilín*) is a seasonal custom in many parts of Ireland, taking place on St Stephen's Day, 26 December.

Barr na Sráide (literally 'the high part of the road') is a stretch of road on the upper side of the town of Cahersiveen, in Co. Kerry.

Text: Sigerson Clifford, *Ballads of a Bogman*, Mercier Press, Cork, 1986.

O the town it climbs the mountain, and looks upon the sea.
And sleeping time or waking 'tis there I long to be,
To walk again that kindly street, the place I grew a man,
And the boys of Barr na Sráide went hunting for the wran.

With cudgels stout we roamed about to hunt the droileen.
We looked for birds in every furze from Letter to Dooneen;
We sang for joy beneath the sky, life held no print or plan,
And we boys in Barr na Sráide, hunting for the wran.

And when the hills were bleeding and the rifles were aflame,
To the rebel homes of Kerry the Saxon stranger came,
But the men who dared the Auxies and beat the Black and Tan
Were the boys of Barr na Sráide hunting for the wran.

And here's a toast to them tonight, the lads who laughed with
    me,
By the groves of Carhan river or the slopes of Beenatee,
John Dawley and Batt Andy, and the Sheehans, Con and Dan,
And the boys of Barr na Sráide who hunted for the wran.

And now they toil on foreign soil, where they have gone their
    way
Deep in the heart of London town or over in Broadway.
And I am left to sing their deeds, and praise them while I can,
Those boys of Barr na Sráide who hunted for the wran.

And when the wheel of life runs down and peace comes over me,
O lay me down in that old town between the hills and sea,
I'll take my sleep in those green fields, the place my life began,
Where the boys of Barr na Sráide went hunting for the wran.

The Pig Push
Dedicated to Diarmuid Lynch,
Sinn Féin Food Controller
Cathal Mac Dubhghaill

I met a friend the other day and this is what he said:
'Sinn Féiners they are out again, the streets are running red.
The slaughter it was dreadful, thirty-four of them are killed;
I never in my life,' said he, 'saw blood so freely spilled.'
So, says I to him, 'Your dreadful tale, it fills me with dismay,
And have thirty-four Sinn Féiners bold in Dublin passed away?'
'No, it's pigs, you fool, that's killed,' says he, 'myself I saw
    it done,
'Twas Diarmuid Lynch that did the work, be the hokey, there
    was fun.'

Chorus
We'll have pig's cheek and pork chops enough for you and me;
There'll be rashers for our breakfast and some sausages for
    tea.

The boys they commandeered the pigs and drove them down
    the street.
Says they, 'The common Irish should have something nice to eat.'
And though all the pigs they kicked and squealed and
    struggled very hard,
They slaughtered all the thirty-four in the Corporation Yard.
Oh! the boys they worked like divils, there their lives were
    not insured,
And they sent the pigs to Donnelly's on motors, to be cured.
While the Peelers stood like fairies, or like dainty little elves,
But they moved no pigs at all until they moved away
    themselves.

Though the great Pig Push is over, other drives will come to
    pass;
We'll commandeer the 'G' men next, and then you'll see some
    gas!
When the pigs they squealed the other day they raised a
    dreadful din,
But they'll hear the 'G' division squeal as far off as Berlin.
Just imagine Johnny Barton chopped in hams and port steaks
    neat,
Sure his dainty little crubeens would be tasty things to eat,
And though we'd miss his features, if he ever had them spoiled,
His cheek is something dreadful, and I like to see it boiled.

This song relates an actual event when Diarmuid Lynch ordered that a shipment of pigs awaiting export to Britain be slaughtered and sold into the Irish market. Johnny Barton (verse 3) was a detective-sergeant in 'G' Division who was killed by Michael Collins's 'Squad' in November 1919.

Donnelly's (verse 2) was a slaughter-house and factory in Brown Street in Dublin's Liberties area. Up to the 1960s the classes in the nearby Weaver Square school were often conducted to the sound of the squealing of pigs as they were being killed.

Text: Samuels Collection, TCD.
Air: 'The Wearin' of the Green'.

The Gunman

Desmond Crean

Text: Desmond Crean, *Songs of an Old I.R.A. Man*, Frederick Press, Dublin, 1939.

The spoon that I supped of was silver,
    The comforts I had were of gold,
The parents who reared me were gentle,
    And kinder the more they grew old.
They pictured for me a great future,
    For I was their favourite son,
But the music of battle was kindled,
    And away went their son with a gun.

On a night with the moon hid by cloud-drifts
    The murder-gang's tender swept down,
And failing to find the men wanted,
    They burned all our homes to the ground.
When you list to the cry of the orphan,
    See the anguish of sweetheart and wife,
When your own mother's homestead is burning,
    Sure you don't care a damn for your life.

For months we had been on the mountains,
    A home for the men on the run,
To sleep in the clear open moonlight,
    To be waked by the glare of the sun.
From the mountain top seeing the burnings,
    We quickly descended below,
And quietly encircling the village,
    We ambushed the murderous foe.

When you make an attack on a barrack,
    Or ambush the Tans by surprise,
When you're chased like a hare o'er the mountains,
    And tracked by the enemy spies;
When for months you don't know what a meal means,
    When you're stupid and weary for sleep,
Why, the soul that would grant you a night's rest,
    You would lay the whole world at their feet!

I remember one night on the mountains,
    I had tramped weary miles through the day;
Our company surprised near a village,
    Fought a rearguard and all got away.
I had battled a mountainous snowstorm,
    Weak with hunger and numbed to the bone,
I saw when knee-deep in a snow-drift,
    The light of a mountaineer's home.

I doggedly fought my way onward,
    But hours seemed to pass till I came
To that heaven-sent haven of refuge,
    And staggered half-dead down the lane.
At the door in the gleam of the moonlight
    Stood a girleen of beautiful grace,
Who had eyes of a lustrous beauty
    And the sweetness of God in her face.

In whispers I told her my story –
    A much-wanted man on the run,
With the Black and Tans tracking his footsteps,
    And his only protector – a gun!
She instantly bade me a welcome
    To the cosy turf fire inside,
Loudly praising our struggle for freedom,
    And mourning the brave boys who died.

Her parents received me most kindly;
    They granted the refuge I sought,
Then I told of the murders and burnings,
    Of the many stiff battles we fought.
And when the news came o'er the mountains
    That the Tans on my track were around,
She found me a cave near the sea cliffs
    Where she knew that I couldn't be found.

When you're up there for months on the mountains,
    A cold cavern floor for your bed;
When they're offering a fortune to find you,
    Three hundred pounds, living or dead;
When one risks their life thus to save yours,
    Such an act is inspired from above,
No service in life can repay it,
    No mortal can show greater love.

I have now when the struggle is over
    All the comforts that mortal could crave,
Yet somehow I yearn for those mountains
    That hide in their vastness a cave.
There's a peacefulness there that's enchanting,
    There's a girleen of beautiful grace,
Who's enthroned in the heart of a gunman
    With the sweetness of God in her face.

Out On the Hills

Desmond Crean

Text: Desmond Crean, *Songs of an Old I.R.A. Man*, Frederick Press, Dublin, 1939.

Out on the hills in the dead of night
    In the fight for the land we love,
Out on the hills in the dead of night
    With the glow of God's moon above.
Pierced to the bone by the icy wind,
    Drenched with the pelting hail;
Famished for food, weary for rest,
    With Black and Tans on the trail.

Out on the hills in the dead of night
    After an ambush fight,
When Tans were shot – in an ambush trap,
    By the glow of the morning light;
With eyes keenly piercing the darkened night,
    With ears alert for the foe,
Who soon will return as reprisal to burn
    The snug little cabins below.

Out on the hills in the dead of night
    At the foot of a new made grave,
Saying a prayer in the moonlight there,
    For the soul of a comrade brave.
He had lived and he died, true, trusted and tried,
    With sorrow we laid him to rest,
And all eyes were dim as we prayed there for him,
    For the Tans had taken our best.

The Hill-Side Men

Dora Sigerson

Text: Dora Sigerson, *Poems of the Irish Rebellion 1916*, Maunsel and Company, Dublin, 1916.

Oh, were my heart a little dog
I'd call it to my side,
To hold it with a silken lead,
And would not be denied.

For, oh, it wandered far from me
By mountain, vale, and glen;
How glad it marched the weary miles
Amongst the hill-side men!

Ah, were my heart a singing bird
I would not let it free,
It dare not dream of sunrise skies,
Or chant of liberty.

For, ah! it sprang cloud high to sing
From mountain, vale, and fen,
When first it heard the secret drums,
The hearts of hill-side men.

My hopes are lost, my dreams are fled;
How lone are vale and fen!
My heart lies cold within the grave
That holds the hill-side men.

My Love Who Died for Ireland

The flowers again are budding, 'tis the springtime of the year,
And all around the woodlands the birds are singing clear,
While in loneliness and sorrow I kneel beside you here,
  My love who died in battle brave for Ireland.

O Heart the tears I shed for you – the tears that still I shed –
When first they told me that my Love was out there with the
    dead.
And yet, *mo croidhe*, I could not wish for you a holier bed,
  Than where you fell in battle brave for Ireland.

Mo croidhe, mo croidhe, I made no moan when forth from me
    you went,
Though many a day and many an hour in sorrow since I spent.
But Mary's Son was kind to me and courage to me lent,
  The day that you went forth to fight for Ireland.

I have waited in the boreen, dear, full many a time since then,
And have crooned my song of sorrow to the hawthorn and the
    whin.
The boreen where I met you – ah – we shall not meet again –
  The day that you went forth to fight for Ireland.

They have laid you in the valley where so nobly, dear, you died.
And ever since you left me my tears have not been dried.
But I know that up in heaven, dear, your soul is glorified,
  Because you fell in battle brave for Ireland.

Text: *The Granuaile Song
Book*, The Irish Supply Depot,
Dublin, 1922.

613

The Third West Cork Brigade

Text: *Songs and Recitations of Ireland,
2 – The Harp*, Coiste Foillseacháin
Náisiúnta, Cork, n.d.
  Air: The prescribed air is 'Easter
Week', probably 'The Memory of the
Dead', or 'Who Fears to Speak of '98',
see p. 88.

We'll raise our voices in Ireland's praise
  Glad are our hearts to-day,
For Ireland's sons have proved their worth
  In the good old IRA.
All parts fought well for Róisín Dubh
  But we a record made
In good old Cork, in famed West Cork,
  The Third West Cork Brigade.

At Newcestown we struck a blow
  For Ireland and Sinn Féin.
At Ballinhassig next we proved
  Our rights we would maintain.
The English foe we twice laid low,
  We faced them undismayed.
In good old Cork, in famed West Cork,
  The Third West Cork Brigade.

The Black and Tans to Ireland came
  To send us to our doom.
The doughtiest warriors sallied forth
  In lorries from Macroom.
But at Kilmichael's bloody fight
  Their conquering course was stayed
By good old Cork, by famed West Cork,
  The Third West Cork Brigade.

Then at Crossbarry's battlefield
  Our gallant boys saw red.
For ten to one the Saxon host
  Before our onslaught fled.
And o'er the hills we made our way
  Whilst our gallant piper played.
In good old Cork, in famed West Cork,
  The Third West Cork Brigade.

Rosscarbery's barrack strong and grim
  Next fell before our fire.
For Black and Tans and RIC
  We made a funeral pyre.
The echo of our fierce attack
  Was heard through glen and glade.
In good old Cork, in famed West Cork,
  The Third West Cork Brigade.

Our boys fought well in every fight,
 We need not call a name.
But Commandants Hales and Barry
 Are now well known to fame.
Napoleon-like they led us on
 With courage we obeyed,
In good old Cork, in famed West Cork,
 The Third West Cork Brigade.

But in our triumphs we shan't forget
 Our comrades brave who fell.
Some sleep to-day in nameless graves
 But soon their deeds will tell.
In grateful Ireland brave and free
 We'll have their names displayed,
In good old Cork, in famed West Cork,
 The Third West Cork Brigade.

Republican Soldiers' Song
With apologies to Peadar Ó Cearnaig

We'll sing a song of victories won
 With cheering rousing chorus
As round our blazing fires we throng
 The starry heavens o'er us
Some now are false to Erin's rights
But we'll not fail her in the fight
And in the silence of the night
 We'll chant a soldier's song.

See p. 429 for Peadar Kearney's original of the song.

Text: Samuels Collection, TCD.

Chorus
Soldiers are we who fought and bled for Ireland
 Some have gone to the land beyond the grave
Died to be free, No, No, our ancient sireland
 Shall not now become a willing slave
Tonight we man the Bearna Baogail
Against traitors stroke and Saxon steel
'Mid cannons roar and rifle peal
 We'll chant a soldier's song.

Pearse bravely faced the English squad
 The scaffold Barry mounted.
MacSwiney pined on alien sod
 No pain for Erin counted.

615

And we'll not now outrage our dead
Nor stain the flag for which they bled
But face the foe till he has fled
    And chant a soldier's song.

Sons of the Gael men of Granuaile
    The long-watched dawn is breaking
The serried ranks of Innisfail
    Great England's power is shaking
Our camp fires now are burning low
Again will come the Saxon foe
Get ready for the final blow
    And chant a soldier's song.

The Merry Ploughboy
Jeremiah Lynch

The reference to a Thompson gun in the chorus would date the song to the very end of the Anglo-Irish War, or perhaps it was written at a later date, as the Thompson sub-machine gun did not feature to any degree in the war. The Thompson, a US weapon, was reputedly tested by Tom Barry of the 3rd West Cork Brigade, and may

Well I am a merry ploughboy and I plough the fields by
    day
Till a sudden thought came through my mind that I
    should run away.
For I'm tired of this civilian life since the day that I was
    born,
So I'm off to join the I.R.A. and I'm off tomorrow morn.

Chorus

And we're off to Dublin in the green, in the green
Where the helmets glisten in the sun,
Where the bayonets flash and the rifles crash
To the echo of a Thompson gun

I'll leave behind me pick and me spade, I'll leave behind
  my plough,
I'll leave behind me horse and yoke, no more will I need
  them now.
And I'll leave behind my Mary, she's the girl that I adore,
And I wonder if she'll think of me when she hears the
  cannon roar.

And when the war is over and dear old Ireland's free,
I will take her to the church to wed and a rebel's wife
  she'll be.
Well some men fight for silver and some men fight for gold,
But the I.R.A. are fighting for the land that the Saxons stole.

have been first used in action against a troop train in Drumcondra, Dublin just prior to the Truce in July 1921.

The weapon, having a short range, would not have been very useful in the countryside, but might have been used to effect in street ambushes. The weapon became very popular in Prohibition-era America, being used by gangsters and law enforcement officers. The gun continued in use as a US infantry weapon until 1971.

Thompsons were used by the Official and Provisional IRA in the North of Ireland in the 1970s. [LM]

Text and air: From memory. It is somewhat ironical that this song is a makeover of an English song in praise of the British army – 'Hurrah for the Khaki and the Blue'.

Shanagolden

Sean McCarthy (1923–1990)

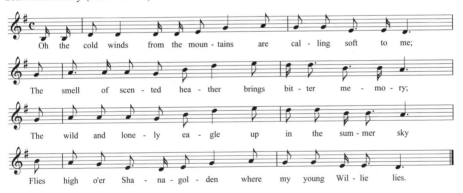

Oh the cold winds from the mountains are calling soft to me;
The smell of scented heather brings bitter memory;
The wild and lonely eagle up in the summer sky
Flies high o'er Shanagolden where my young Willie lies.

Do you remember darlin' we walked the moonlit road,
I held you in my arms love I would never let you go.
Our hands they were entwined, my love, all in the pale moonlight,
By the fields of Shanagolden on a lonely winter's night

Shanagolden is a Limerick village lying between Foynes and Newcastle West.

Text and air: 'Inishowen Song Project' at www.itma.ie.

617

Then came the call to arms love and the hills they were aflame.
Down from the silent mountains the Saxon strangers came.
I held you in my arms then, my young heart wild with fear,
By the fields of Shanagolden in the springtime of the year.

You fought them darling Willie all through the summer days.
I heard the rifles firing in the mountains far away.
I held you in my arms then, your blood ran free and bright,
And you died in Shanagolden on a lonely summer's night.

Oh but that was long ago my love and your son grows fine and tall.
These hills they are at peace again the Saxon strangers gone.
There's roses on your grave my love, there's an eagle in the sky
Flies high o'er Shanagolden where my young Willie lies.

Oh the cold winds from the mountains are calling soft to me.
The smell of scented heather brings bitter memory.
The wild and lonely eagle up in the summer sky
Flies high o'er Shanagolden where my young Willie lies.

Remembrance – A Kerry Column
Domhnall Ó Cathail

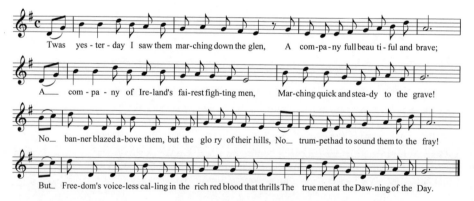

Twas yes-ter-day I saw them mar-ching down the glen, A com-pa-ny full beau ti-ful and brave;

A_ com-pa-ny of Ire-land's fai-rest figh-ting men, Mar-ching quick and stea-dy to the grave!

No_ ban-ner blazed a-bove them, but the glo ry of their hills, No_ trum-pet had to sound them to the fray!

But_ Free-dom's voice-less cal-ling in the rich red blood that thrills The true men at the Daw-ning of the Day.

This simple but poignant song idealizes the young men of a Kerry flying column, a mobile unit of guerrilla fighters. The flying columns were constantly on the move, seeking to engage the British forces in ambush conditions favourable to the column. The columns were fed and sheltered by the people and the local IRA units acted as scouts, guides, sentries and intelligence gatherers. The IRA did

'Twas yesterday I saw them matching down the glen,
    A company full beautiful and brave;
A company of Ireland's fairest fighting men –
    Marching quick and steady to the grave!
No banner blazed above them, but the glory of their hills,
    No trumpet had to sound them to the fray!
But Freedom's voiceless calling in the rich red blood that
    thrills
    The true men of the Dawning of the Day.

'Twas yesterday I blessed them on the road they'll march no more,
    For they're sleeping in the Sunset down below;
With their faces towards the Eastward, like the Chivalry of yore,
    To the eastward full of promise – and the foe.
But I'll keep them in my dreaming with a love that none shall say –
    That company full beautiful and brave –
And I'll see them as I saw them, laughing, yesterday,
    Marching quick and steady to the grave.

not have the armament, nor the training, to confront the British army in open, regular warfare.

As the Anglo-Irish War developed the ambush become very refined and effective, with the result that towards the middle of 1921, the British in West Cork would only move in units of about four hundred. The 'Dawning of the Day' at the end of verse 1 means the coming of freedom. [LM]

Text: Ballad sheet, National Library of Ireland.
    Air: 'The Road to the Isles'; the last four lines of each verse are repeated as a chorus.

White, Orange and Green

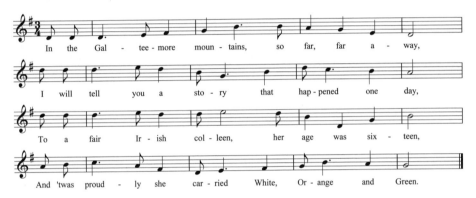

In the Galteemore mountains, so far, far away,
I will tell you the story that happened one day,
To a fair Irish colleen, her age was sixteen,
And 'twas proudly she carried White, Orange and Green.

A bold English bobby by chance passed that way,
Saying: 'Who is the maiden with the banner so gay?'
With a laugh and a sneer he jumped off his machine,
Determined to capture the flag of Sinn Féin.

'Will you give me that banner?' the bold bobby cried,
'Will you give me that banner, and do what is right?
Give me that banner and do not be mean,
For I must have that emblem, the flag of Sinn Féin.'

'You'll not get that banner,' the young maiden cried,
'Till your blood and my blood its colours have dyed.
I here have a rifle, and that's nothing mean,
And it's proudly I'll die for the flag of Sinn Féin.'

Text: *Songs and Recitations of Ireland, 2 – The Harp*, Coiste Foillseacháin Náisiúnta, Cork, 1968.
    Air: from memory.

The poor Peeler's face turned as white as the snow,
And he mounted his cycle and started to go,
Saying: 'What is the use, when a maid of sixteen
Would die for her colours, White, Orange and Green?'

That very same day in sweet Tipperary town,
That gallant young girl from the Galtees came down.
Her poor heart was torn with anguish and pain,
For that very same day Mickeen died for Sinn Féin.

Ye young men and maidens of Erin's green shore,
Raise a cheer for the maid from the proud Galteemore,
And keep on fighting the cause of Sinn Féin,
Till we make dear old Ireland a republic again.

Black and Tan

I am a man known as a Tan in Ire-land I'm mar - king time.

One pound a day is - n't bad pay for ma-king things hum— and shine.

And when the day-light is daw - ning, I sleep till ten in the mor - ning.

I'm for-e-ver cha - sing Shin ners.— I seek them eve - ry where.—

I came o - ver here for mo-ney and beer, and to ar - rest a Vo - lun - teer.

They are al - ways hi - ding— I've searched eve - ry wher—

I'm for-e-ver hunt - ing Shin ners— but they va - nish in thin air.—

A note in the source states: 'A version
of the song "I'm Forever Blowing
Bubbles" popular many years ago
ran somewhat as follows.'

Text: Ernie O'Malley Collection,
New York University.
Air: 'I'm Forever Blowing Bubbles'.

I am a man known as a Tan
In Ireland I'm marking time.
One pound a day isn't bad pay
For making things hum and shine,
And when the daylight is dawning
I sleep 'til ten in the morning.

Chorus

I'm forever chasing Shinners, I seek them everywhere.
I came over here for money and beer, and to arrest a Volunteer.
They are always hiding, I've searched everywhere.
I'm forever hunting Shinners. but they vanish in thin air.

Home-Sickness or The Sinn Féiner Abroad

After 'The Lake Isle of Innisfree,' with sincere apologies to
   Mr. W.B. Yeats
Evoe (E.V. Knox 1881–1971)

I will arise and go now to Galway or Tralee
   And burgle someone's house there and plan a moonlight raid;
Ten live rounds will I have there to shoot at the RIC
   And wear a mask in the bomb-loud glade.

And I shall have great fun there, for fun comes fairly fast,
   Bonfires in the purple heather and the barracks burning fine,
There midnight is a shindy and the noon is overcast
   And evening full of the feet of kine.

I will arise and go now, for always in my sleep
   There comes the sound of rifles and low moans on the shore;
I see the sudden ambush and hear the widows weep,
   And I like that kind of war.

E.V. Knox was a regular
contributor to, and eventually editor of the London
magazine *Punch*.

Text: *Punch, or the London
Charivari*, Vol. 158, 16
June 1920.

In the Hush of the Night

In the hush of the night when the curfew tolls
And the churchyards yawning upheave men's souls,
Hark! a rattle of wheels on the cobblestones
And heedless of churches and dead men's bones,
With an armoured car leading and massed in vans
Come the 'devil-may-cares' called the Black and Tans.

What are they after, why are they here
And at dead of night do they now appear?
They are here of set purpose for hunting down
Assassins defying the Empire's Crown,
To trace them out to the hidden lair
And shoot at sight when they find them there.

This anonymous piece is the work
of a member, or sympathizer, of the
Black and Tans. In attempting to
justify their behaviour it rather
confirms perceptions of them as an
out-of-control murder squad. The
reference in the second verse to
shooting on sight gives the game
away.

Text: Verses 1, 2, 4, and 5 were
printed in Francis J. Costello, *The
Irish Revolution and Its Aftermath
1916–1923*, Irish Academic Press,
2002, where they are annotated: 'Sir
John Anderson's Files, Irish Executive, C.O. 904/16B'. Verses 3 and 6
were discovered on the website

621

www.irishconstabulary.com
(accessed 26 December 2015).
    A note on the website says that
the text was discovered in the form
of a handwritten text in papers
relating to the Public Information
Branch, a propaganda section based
in Dublin Castle.

By lake or mountain or beetling cliff,
Whether roads be pleasant or climbing stiff,
Though storms surround them till day be done,
Through rain or snow or a grilling sun,
They'll comb out the places from shore to shore
Till law and order prevail once more.

They are after the cult that is called Sinn Féin
Which bears on its forehead the brand of Cain
And deludes young men into ghastly deeds
Whose expanding bullet the victim bleeds,
Whilst the widow's wail and the orphan's cry
Ascend to the throne of God on high.

They see these sights but the arm-chair men,
The newspaper critics who wield a pen
And speak of reprisals with bated breath,
What do they care for the victim's death?
But by God, to avenge him the job's a man's
And we'll see it through, say the Black and Tans.

On the Black and Tan mission of which we sing
We serve and acknowledge our Empire's King.
In loyalty ever all goodness grows
And disloyal men are the country's foes.
If the flame of rebellion the Sinn Féiner fans
He will meet with short shrift from the bold
    Black and Tans.

'Eroes
M.J. MacManus

Text: M.J. MacManus, *Dublin
Diversions*, Talbot Press, Dublin, 1928.

'Twere very pleasant fightin'
When we were on the run;
You simply climbed the 'illsides
An' took your bloomin' gun.
'Twas easier than whistlin' jigs,
With lots of fun an' fame,
An' the blarsted Tan was a gentleman
An' *always* played the game.
    (With a *tow-row-row*!)
    Don't believe it,
    I assure you
    It's an error!

An' we didn't half enjoy it
Goin' out on winter nights,
A-bombing of the lorries
An' looking out fer fights.
In Dublin's lanes and back streets
We simply *loved* to roam
An' pitied the pore chaps who were
A-sittin' safe at 'ome.
 (With a *tow-row-row*!)
 Don't believe it,
 I assure you
 It's an error!

So we're 'appy, 'opeful 'eroes,
An' we'd volunteer agen
To save the land that never
Forgets 'er fightin' men.
We'd find another rusty gun
An' go through blinkin' 'ell,
An' we wouldn't care just when or where
For Erin dear we fell.
 (With a *tow-row-row*!)
 Don't believe it,
 I assure you
 It's an error!

Often described as a Civil War era anti-Treaty patrol, it seems more likely that the picture below, taken in Grafton Street, Dublin, shows a scene during the lull between the cessation of hostilities with the British and the outbreak of the Civil War. In *The Kerryman* of 13 March 1937 it was captioned 'Party of IRA entering Dublin during the Treaty negotiations'. (Courtesy of South Dublin Libraries.)

The Irish Free State

I went to see David, to London to David. I went to see David and what did he do? He gave me a Free State, a nice little Free State, A Free State that's tied up in Red, White and Blue.

Text and air: Patrick Galvin, *Irish Songs of Resistance*, Workers' Music Association, London, 1955.

The air is the Welsh tune 'The Ash Grove'.

I went to see David, to London to David.
   I went to see David and what did he do?
He gave me a Free State, a nice little Free State,
   A Free State that's tied up with Red, White and Blue.

I brought it to Dublin to show to Dáil Eireann,
   I brought it to Dublin and what did they do?
They asked me what kind of a thing was a Free State,
   A Free State that's tied up with Red, White and Blue.

Three-quarters of Ireland a nation – I told them,
   Tied on to the Empire with Red, White and Blue;
And an oath they must swear to King George and Queen Mary,
   An oath they must swear to the son-in-law new.

I'm teaching them Irish and painting their boxes
   All over with green, sure what more can I do?
Yet they tell me they want just an Irish Republic
   Without any trimming of Red, White and Blue!

The 'Free Staters' Evening Prayer

Text: Ernie O'Malley Collection, New York University.

As the name of God does not appear, either in the 'Treaty' or the Constitution of the Irish 'Free State', while the name of the King is ever present in, and dominates both documents, it naturally follows that all 'Free' Staters will henceforth pray to the King.

The Prayer
Oh, Dear King George, I lay me down
To have a snooze beneath thy crown.
The lion and the unicorn

Will guard my soul until the morn.
Let thy grand fleet watch over me
And the other fish that are in the sea.
On the Union Jack my head shall rest,
The hangman's rope upon my breast.
The rope that strangled Barry's life
And took brave Traynor from his wife.
Ask Oliver Cromwell, hear my word,
And guard me with his gory sword.
Suffer no murdered babies' cry
Disturb me while in bed I lie.
And if 'tis pleasing unto thee,
Permit Queen Bess to flirt with me.
Have sweet Victoria, the 'Famine Queen',
Starve all Republicans, fat and lean.
I adore my King, I love my Queen,
I'll place the red above the green.
I love the little Prince of Wales,
I'll kneel and kiss his dear toenails.
I love the Lords, their big, flat feet,
The monocle, cane and gaiters neat.
I love the Barons and the Dukes,
The Knights and all the Royal Crooks.

All Royalty I now admire,
I want to be in your Empire.
Please crush Republicans, one and all,
Save us, our backs are to the wall.
And order Uncle Sam to take
His commerce off your Majesty's lake,
And ask Lloyd George, that saintly man,
To guard us with his Black and Tan.

I'll help you hold the Hindoos down
I'll help you sack each Irish town.
Irish Republicans I will kill,
And quicklime graves I'll gladly fill.
I'll help you gather in the loot,
And I 'won't hesitate to shoot'.
I'll use the torch and battering ram,
I'll help you conquer Uncle Sam.
I shall be faithful unto you,
Your kin and their successors too.
Forgive me now, my dearest King,
For the rebel songs I used to sing.
And grant unto me, though weak I am,
Eternal rest in Buckingham. – Amen

THE GLITTERING GATES

'The Glittering Gates', a cartoon by Arthur Booth from the magazine *Dublin Opinion* at the time of the Treaty negotiations. The gates are topped with the words 'Irish Free State' and the ladder down into the pit is captioned 'Immediate and terrible war.'

Griffith, Collins and de Valera are in conversation with Lloyd George:

St David Lloyd George: 'In you go.'
Arthur: 'Righto, it'll be heavenly.'
Michael: 'I'm a bit doubtful, but I'll try it for a while.'
Eamonn: 'I'll go below; it might be easier to get out!'

From '16 to '21
Patrick J. Fleming

Text: Leslie H. Daiken,
*Good-bye, Twilight – Songs
of the Struggle in Ireland,*
Lawrence & Wishart,
London, 1936.

It was the fight for independence in the year nineteen-sixteen
When Irish Volunteers came out to save Dark Rosaleen,
To save her from the cunning tricks of traitors, cowards, knaves,
To save their brother-Irishmen from ever being slaves.
And save her from the dying grip of an Empire almost done,
That began the glorious history of Sixteen to Twenty-one.

Ah, who among us can forget those glorious five years.
The men that fought, the brains that taught, the sorrows, joys and
    tears.
The cause for which they trudged each day, that dark and dreary
    road,
No turning to the right or left, no leaving down the load.
But on for Independence, spoke every voice and gun,
O Lord what men you gave us then – Sixteen to Twenty-one.

Pearse, Connolly, Ceannt, MacDermott, those leaders died with joy,
MacSweeney from Cork City, FitzGerald from Fermoy,
These noble minds were never changed by greedy wealth or fame,
But their principles were guided by the teachings of Sinn Féin.
And they shook the mighty Empire with their voice, their pen, their
    gun,
And the world applauded Ireland from Sixteen to Twenty-one.

But the cunning tyrant fooled them, when their fight was bravely won,
And he beat them at the table when he failed to with the gun,
And he tore their ranks asunder, with his greedy robber's hand,
And he tried 'divide and conquer' as a cure for Ireland.
And some weak-kneed Irish joined him, saying 'Freedom now is
    won' . . .
So ends the saddest chapter of Sixteen to Twenty-one.

But our country's still divided and our people still unfree,
And the stranger still is with us, for to make us bend the knee,
For to make us show submission as he did in ages past,
For to make us help that Empire which now is crumbling fast,
For to rob us of the birthright that our martyred brave have won
In the fight for Independence from Sixteen to Twenty-one.

Then let this be our slogan, let it sound o'er land and sea,
Ireland again united, Ireland forever free.
And the good God of Justice knowing our martyrs' sole request
Will help us in our struggle if we only do the rest.
If we stand again as those men stood till the fight at last is won
Then Ireland free shall bless the men of Sixteen to Twenty-one.

The Soldiers of '22
Brian O'Higgins

I sing no song of the long ago,
  Of the warriors staunch and bold,
Who bore their spears on the Irish hills
  In the golden days of old;
But I raise a rann for our own dear lads –
  The loyal, the brave and true
Who flung their lives in the *bearna baoghail* –
  The soldiers of '22.

When they heard the call of a cause laid low
  They sprang to their guns again,
And the pride of all was the first to fall,
  The glory of our fighting men.
In the days to come, when the pipe and drum
  You follow in the ways they knew,
When their praise you sing, let the echoes ring
  With the memory of Cathal Brugha.

Brave Liam Lynch on the mountainside
  Fell a victim to the foe,
And Dinny Lacey for Ireland died
  In the Glen of Aherlow.
Neil Boyle and Quinn from the North came down
  To stand with the faithful few,
And we'll sing their praise in the Freedom days
  'Mong the heroes of '22.

Some fell in the proud red rush of war,
  And some by the treacherous blow,
Like the martyrs four in Dublin town,
  And their comrades in Dromboe.
And a hundred more in the barrack squares,
  And by lonely roadsides, too –
Without fear they died and we speak with pride
  Of the Martyrs of '22.

They were true to the Right, they fought the good fight,
  And they rest in the peace of God.
Lift up your hearts, O brave young men,
  And march in the ways they trod!
The cause still calls that called to them,
  And the task will be only through
When freedom comes to the land that we loved
  By the soldiers of '22.

The Irish words 'bearna baoghail' in the first verse (meaning 'gap of danger') are a poetic expression for 'battle' or 'combat'.

Text: *Songs and Recitations of Ireland, 1 – The Flag*, Coiste Foillseacháin Náisiúnta, Cork, 1971.
  Air: 'The Foggy Dew', see p. 404.

The Road at my Door
W.B. Yeats

This poem forms the fifth section of Yeats's 'Meditations in Time of Civil War', written in 1922 and published in *The Tower* in 1923.

Text: W.B. Yeats, *The Poems*, Everyman, London, 1992.

An affable Irregular,
A heavily-built Falstaffian man,
Comes cracking jokes of civil war
As though to die by gunshot were
The finest play under the sun.

A brown Lieutenant and his men,
Half dressed in national uniform,
Stand at my door, and I complain
Of the foul weather, hail and rain,
A pear-tree broken by the storm.

I count those feathered balls of soot
The moor-hen guides upon the stream,
To silence the envy in my thought;
And turn towards my chamber, caught
In the cold snows of a dream.

The Night Darrell Figgis Lost His Whiskers
A.J.B.

In June 1922 Darrell Figgis, a supporter of the Treaty, was assaulted in his home by a group of anti-Treatyites including Robert Briscoe. They released him after shaving off his luxuriant beard.

Text: Samuels Collection, TCD.

Darrell Figgis by Estella Solomons.

Now, Mr Darrell Figgis had a beard of lovely red,
'Twas just before Election time as he was going to bed;
When some chaps come along to him and unto Darrell said:
    'We've come sir, to commandeer your whiskers.'

Chorus
More power to your whiskers sir, this will be our refrain.
Which brought you in three thousand votes – you really
    can't complain,
And the bands all started playing 'A Nation Once Again',
    The night Darrell Figgis lost his whiskers.

Now, Darrell's lovely whiskers had not been trimmed for years,
They brought along big scissors and a pair of garden shears,
And the job was such a tough one that the barber was in tears,
    The night Darrell Figgis lost his whiskers.

But the loss of Darrell's whiskers won't make us sad or sore,
They'll grow again, and blow again as in the days of yore,
Sure the Treaty and the Free State was made safe for evermore,
    The night that Darrell Figgis lost his whiskers.

628

Irish History
(Recommended for use in the junior classes of our Elementary National Schools)
M.J. MacManus

The Danes came over the eastern sea
And they gave us fire and sword,
And they tried to make us bend a knee
To heathen gods abhorred.
But Brian called on another God
On a hill by Clontarf's shore,
And the Northmen fled through a sea blood-red
From those dauntless men of yore.
    Those dauntless, invincible men,
    Those glorious men of yore.

Cromwell came and praised the Lord,
For the Irish babes he burned,
And a fateful coin was spun at Boyne
When to craven James we turned.
But the Wild Geese flew with a drooping wing
To battle-fields afar.
And so we became with a doubtful fame
The wandering race we are.
    The wandering race, the nomad race,
    The far-flung race we are.

To Killala Bay the Frenchmen came
To teach us a trick or two,
But we were only a pawn in the game
And they left – for Waterloo.
And Wolfe Tone sleeps in Bodenstown
And Emmet God knows where.
And so we became in Liberty's name
The innocent fools we were.
    The innocent fools, the chivalrous fools,
    The absolute fools we were.

Armageddon broke in fire and smoke
And a sea of blood and tears,
And Suvla Bay holds the whitened bones
Of Dublin's Fusiliers.
But Belgium kept its frontier line
Whilst Pearse and Plunkett fell,
And the Tans came down on village and town
To make an Irish hell.
    The gentle Tans, the gallant Tans,
    The Tans who gave us hell.

The remains of Robert Emmet (verse 3) sleep 'God knows where' because after his execution in 1803 his body was buried in a secret location. Despite several investigations, its location has never been determined. See note p. 443.

Text: M.J. MacManus, *Dublin Diversions*, Talbot Press, Dublin, 1928.

629

The Four Courts blazed to a sudden flame
(And Churchill lost his frown)
And the very stones cried out our shame
In the streets of Dublin town.
And the hope we hoped and the dream we dreamed
Sank like a dying star,
And so we became in Freedom's name
The absolute mugs we are.
>   The absolute mugs, cantankerous mugs,
>   Hysterical mugs we are.

A Four Courts Ditty
A.J.B.

Rory (verse 2) was Rory O'Connor, one of the leaders of the forces opposed to the Anglo-Irish Treaty, who occupied the Four Courts in Dublin in April 1922.

They were attacked by the forces of the (pro-Treaty) Provisional Government in late June, using field guns loaned by the British.

Text: Samuels Collection, TCD.
Air: 'Whack fol the diddle', see
p. 393.

The Four Courts has been shelled and shocked,
>   Whack-fol-the-diddle-lol-the-di-do-day,
For the Free State Party won't be mocked,
>   Whack-fol-the-diddle-lol-the-di-do-day,
With bould Mick Collins to the front,
But Dublin's borne the battle's brunt.
Five million pounds! O it's a stunt,
>   Whack-fol-the-diddle-lol-the-di-do-day,

Chorus
Whack-fol-the-diddle-lol-the-di-do-day,
See the Four Courts on the Quay,
What did Mr Churchill say?
Whack-fol-the-diddle-lol-the-di-do-day,

The Army is Mick's joy and pride,
>   Whack-fol-the-diddle-lol-the-di-do-day,
And England the big guns they supplied,
>   Whack-fol-the-diddle-lol-the-di-do-day,
No wonder that the Four Courts fell,
Stone walls won't stand 'gainst shot and shell.
But I heard that Rory gave them – well,
>   Whack-fol-the-diddle-lol-the-di-do-day,

From the Four Courts to the GPO,
>   Whack-fol-the-diddle-lol-the-di-do-day,
The armoured cars rush to and fro,
>   Whack-fol-the-diddle-lol-the-di-do-day,
They're painted green – a lovely hue,
But pr'haps it should be Red, White and Blue.
For further news – try GHQ.
>   Whack-fol-the-diddle-lol-the-di-do-day.

When England Gave the Orders

Text: Samuels Collection, TCD.

England gave the orders,
    And England gave the guns,
And Michael dressed the boys in green,
    And took my gallant sons,
And spilled their blood out on the grass,
    To please the English Huns.
For England gave the orders,
    And England gave the guns.

England blew the bugle,
    And threw the gauntlet down,
And Michael sent the boys in green
    To level Dublin town.
For the blood of Irish martyrs
    Must deck the British Crown.

England pealed the trumpet,
    And England gave the steel,
And Michael dressed the boys in green,
    And bade the guns to peal.
For Irish blood is goodly fare
    To dress an English meal.

England gave the watchword,
    And England gave the sign,
And Michael told the boys in green
    To take that son of mine;
For there is need of broken hearts
    In England's proud design.

England gave the orders,
    And England gave the lead,
And Michael raised the battle cry
    While children wept for bread.
For England must be undisturbed
    While we watch with our dead.

England gave the orders,
    And gave the cannon, too;
And Michael sent the boys in green
    To conquer Cathal Brugha.
For England's bloody vengeance
    Must be satisfied anew,
For England gave the orders,
    And gave the cannon, too.

The Battle of the Four Courts
A Visitor's Impression
(A.J.B., Dublin)

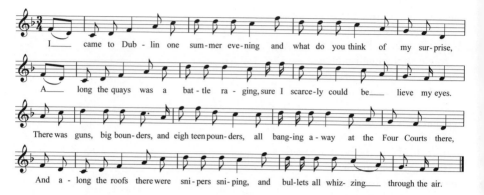

I   came to Dub - lin one sum - mer eve - ning and what do you think of my sur - prise,

A   long the quays was a bat - tle ra - ging, sure I scarce - ly could be lieve my eyes.

There was guns, big boun - ders, and eigh teen poun - ders, all bang - ing a - way at the Four Courts there,

And a - long the roofs there were sni - pers sni - ping, and bul - lets all whiz - zing through the air.

Text: Samuels Collection, TCD.
Air: 'Muldoon, The Solid Man'.

I came to Dublin one Summer evening,
    And what do you think of my surprise,
Along the quays was a battle raging,
    Sure I scarcely could believe my eyes.
There was guns, big bounders, and eighteen pounders,
    All banging away at the Four Courts there,
And along the roofs there were snipers sniping,
    And bullets all whizzing through the air.

Ah, now, sez I, have the English soldiers
    Come back again to old Erin's shore,
And I thinking it was all over,
    And the British departed for evermore.
'O, begor, it's not,' sez a Dublin Jackeen.
    ''Tis a scrap on their own they are having now,
And upon my honour, 'tis Rory O'Connor,
    Is blamed for the starting of all the row.'

He's in the Four Courts, its walls defending,
    And much I admire his brave cry.
But the Free Staters to him some shells are sending,
    Where they got them all sure it puzzles me.
Then I looked again, and God bless my eyesight
    There were armoured cars all painted green,
And soldiers dressed in a colour likewise,
    And above them waved the flag, Sinn Féin.

Well I stopped the week, till the fight was over,
    (You see I could not well get away),
But the Four Courts fell on a Friday morning,
    And I'm sure there'll be a quare oul bill to pay.

Provisional Government Troops shelling the Four Courts from the corner of Bridge Street.

Sure I've seen the ruins out in France and Belgium,
    And the battle fronts in far off Belgrade,
But the ruins I saw in dear old Dublin,
    Completely puts them all in the shade.

A Dublin Battle Ditty
June–July 1922
A.J.B.

O, Churchill dear, and did you hear the news from Dublin
    town,
They've listened to your good advice and blown the Four
    Courts down,
And likewise with O'Connell Street, the like I've never seen,
An' guns (the best), as per request, and lorries painted green.

Text: Samuels Collection, TCD.
    Air: 'The Wearin' o' the Green', see p. 246.

633

Sure I met with Dick Mulcahy an' he took me by the the hand,
Sez he, how goes it 'cross the town, how does the Gresham stand?
These rebels want a lesson, we cannot stand their cheek,
So we'll finish what the British started here in Easter week.

Then Michael Collins came along an' unto me did say,
The guns were most effective in their work along the quay,
Sure I'm out for law and order like Greenwood was of yore,
For Churchill has just asked me, come and take my place, asthore.

Then along came Arthur Griffith (whom I had not seen of late).
I asked him how was everything with the new Free Irish State,
Och, sez he, it's not a Free State, but an awful state I'm in,
To make good all this damage, O, where will we get the tin.

Then I bid them all Good Evening! for the dusk was drawing nigh,
It wasn't safe to be around when shots begin to fly.
But this much I'll remember if I live to see the day,
Next time elections come around I'll vote the other way.

The Four Courts burning after the explosion of munitions that had been placed in The Record Office.
Thousands of documents, relating to centuries of Ireland's history, were destroyed in the fire.

Cathal Brugha

In Dublin's fair city, the sun it was sinking
  Our I.R.A. assembled, the fight to resume.
Marshalled by the Commandant, Old Ireland's greatest
    defender
  And our Easter Week survivor, the dauntless Cathal
    Brugha.

Chorus
May God rest the soul of our brave undaunted soldier,
  To his land and his comrades 'till death he proved
    true.
And may God bless the brave lads who followed in his
    footsteps,
  But remember, 'No Surrender' were the dying words
    of Brugha.

The fight it was raging, the roofs they were blazing,
  The cannons were pealing, every aim sad and true.
His comrades raised the white flag, to save their brave
    leader,
  Far more prized than their own, was the dear life of
    Brugha.

He cried: 'Boys no white flag shall ever wave above me,
  I'll make my dash for freedom and fighting I'll go
    through.'
Then dashing through their cordons, the deadly bullets
    hitting him,
  What a vict'ry for the Free State, three hundred
    shooting Brugha.

Bleeding and dying lay Ireland's defender,
  No earthly aid could save him for his wounds were
    old and new.
He left this world on Friday, the same day as Our
    Saviour,
  And to join the Irish martyrs, went the soul of
    Cathal Brugha.

His body lies in Dublin, in a cold and silent grave,
  But forever in old Ireland, his memory shall be new.
Nor foreign gold could buy him, no foe could ever
    change him,
  What a model for Old Ireland was the life of Cathal
    Brugha.

In July 1922 Cathal Brugha was in
command of anti-Treaty forces that
had occupied buildings in upper
O'Connell Street in Dublin. These
were attacked by Free State forces,
forcing their evacuation. However,
Brugha, leading a rearguard action,
refused to surrender and was shot as
he approached the surrounding
troops, with a pistol in his hand.

Text: *Songs of the Irish Republic*,
Coiste Foillseacháin Náisiúnta,
Cork, 1975.
  Air: 'The Tri-Coloured Ribbon',
see p. 379.

Cathal Brugha

The Ballad of Michael Collins

Donagh MacDonagh

Text: The Donagh MacDonagh Song Collection. See http://songbook1.tripod.com/ (accessed 3 April 2015). Air: 'Lord Lovell'.

Mick Collins he cursed as soldiers curse
And he drank as soldiers drink,
And he fought the fight that soldiers fight
And then he sat down to think, think, think,
And then he sat down to think.

Now where are you going, Mick Collins? they said,
Now where are you going? said they.
I am going to Cork to settle this war
That is leading this country astray – stray – stray,
That is leading this country astray.

Then take a convoy of lorries, they said,
And a Crossley-tender so fast
And a scout to search for Republican men
Who will ambush you as you go past, past, past,
Who will ambush you as you go past.

A scout and a lorry behind,
And a Crossley-tender between,
They sheltered him safely to Cork it is true
But returning they weren't any screen, screen, screen,
But returning they weren't any screen.

There were six men waiting at Beál-na-Blath
Well furnished with rifles and lead,
Oh who is the officer fallen and pale?
'Tis Mick Collins that no one wished dead, dead, dead,
'Tis Mick Collins that no one wished dead.

They took him up and carried him home
And he lies in a Soldier's plot,
And men who fought each other deplore
The hour that Mick Collins was shot, shot, shot,
The hour that Mick Collins was shot.

Michael Collins

636

The Simple Violence of the Gun
Donagh MacDonagh

The simple violence of the gun
Solved problems of '21,
But '22 demanded thought
Years of action had not bought.

The blindfolded figure with the scales
Turned her back and filled the gaols;
Right and wrong had equal weight,
Poised above Dublin Castle gate.

Some sold for the immediate good
Imperious dictates of the blood;
Others could not forget an oath
The scales hung equally for both.

The Four Courts taken, shelled and burned,
Proved what diplomats have learned,
That the divided race is ruled
By those whom centuries have schooled.

Seen from a pinnacle of time
All that violence is but mime,
The issue simple – liberty
Or a prolonged dependency –

An issue simple as the choice
Between the grim, deterrent voice
And that which urged man to be free,
Un-fruiting the forbidden tree.

Text: Ernie O'Malley Collection,
New York University.

The Chieftain
Michael Collins 1890–1922
Padraic Colum

A woman said, 'He would sit there,
Listening to songs, my mother's sheaf,
And he would charm her to regain
Songs out of note for fifty years,
(Did he remember the old songs?)
For he was of the mould of men
Who had renown in her young days,
The champions of cross-roads and fields.'

Text: Padraic Colum, *Irish Elegies*,
The Dolmen Press, Dublin, 1961.

637

(His head as like the head upon
A coin when coins were minted well,
An athlete passing from the games
To take his place in citadel.)

'But once I saw a sadness come
Upon his face, and that was strange –
The song she sang had less of fret
Than all the rest – A Milking Song,
(Did he remember the old songs?)
A girl's lilt as she drew streams
Into her pail at evening fall.
But you would think some great defeat
Was in his mind as she sang on.'

(Some man whom Plutarch tells about
Heard in the cadence of a song
The breaking of a thread, and knew
The hold he had was not for long.)

'Only that once. All other times
He was at ease. The open door
Might show no danger lay across
That young man's path as he sat there,
Listening to songs of the old time
When songs were secret in their hope.
(Did he remember the old songs?)'

(A strategist, he left behind
Pursuit each day and thwarted death
To plan campaign would leave no name
To field nor to a shrine a wreath.)

But she had seen upon his face
Something that danger could not cause
Nor could she guess: the fateful glimpse
On instant opened to the man
Summoned by history. He will know
While someone outside lilts the words
That have no fret, that he must choose
Between what forceful men will name
Desertion, but that he'll conceive
As action to bring fruitful peace
And see (it could be) rifle raised
Against deserter who had led.

(Who breaks into a history breaks
Into an ambush, frenzy-set,
Where comrades turn to foes, and they
The clasp of comradeship forget.)

'Did he remember the old songs?'
She asks where requiem leads us on
By quays, through streets, to burial-ground.
I answer from my parching mind,
'His powers made him prodigy,
But old devotions kept him close
To what was ours; he'd not forget
Threshold and hearthstone and old songs.
The requiem made for divers men
Is history; his music was
The thing that happened, as said Finn.'
'No one is left on Ireland's ground
To hear that music,' she intoned,
'Since Michael Collins walks no more.'

(The citadel he entered in
Without procession or acclaim
And brought a history to an end,
Setting his name 'gainst Norman name.)

Mournful Lines on the Death of General Michael Collins

Come listen ye true men to my simple rhyme,
For it tells of a young man cut off in his prime,
A soldier and a statesman who laid down the law,
And who died by the roadside in lone Béal na Blá.

When barely sixteen he to England crossed o'er,
To work as a boy clerk in a Government store,
But the Volunteers' summons he could not disobey,
So to Dublin he came back to join in the fray.

Text and air: Colm O Lochlainn, *More Irish Street Ballads*, At the Sign of the Three Candles, Dublin, 1965.
Air: 'Lovely Willie'.

At Larkfield near Kimmage he joined the brave band
Of exiles returning to free their dear land.
By drilling and training by night and by day,
With rifle and bayonet they learned the hard way.

At Easter nineteen sixteen when Pearse called them out,
The 'Lambs' of old Larkfield rose up with a shout,
And in the Post Office they nobly did show
How a handful of heroes could outface the foe.

To Stafford and Frongoch transported they were,
And as prisoners of England they soon made a stir.
Released before Christmas and home once again,
He banded old comrades together to train.

Dáil Éireann assembled our rights to proclaim,
Suppressed by the English, you'd think it a shame
How Ireland's best and bravest were harried and torn
From the arms of their loved ones and children new-
      born.

For years Mick eluded their soldiers and spies,
For he was master of clever disguise.
With the Custom House blazing she found 'twas no use,
And soon Mother England had to ask for a Truce.

For the Treaty he wrung from Lloyd George and his
      train,
He steadfastly pleaded in the Dáil but in vain.
De Valera and his die-hards they forced Civil War
And Mick Collins was ambushed in lone Béal na Blá.

Oh! when will our young men the sad lesson learn,
That brother on brother they never should turn.
Alas! that a split in our ranks we e'er saw,
Or Mick Collins stretched lifeless in lone Béal na Blá.

Oh! long will old Ireland be seeking in vain
Ere she find a new ruler to match the man slain.
A true son of Gráinne, the name long will shine
Of gallant Mick Collins, cut off in his prime.

The Laughing Boy
Brendan Behan (1923–1964)

'Twas on an Au-gust mor-ning, all in the daw-ning hours,____

I went to take the war-ming air all in the Mouth of Flowers.____

And there I saw a mai____ den, and mourn-ful was her cry,____

"Ah, what will mend my bro-ken heart? I've lost my Laugh-ing Boy."____

'Twas on an August morning, all in the dawning hours,
I went to take the warming air, all in the Mouth of
    Flowers,
And there I saw a maiden, and mournful was her cry,
'Ah what will mend my broken heart, I've lost
    my Laughing Boy.'

So strong, so wild and brave he was, I'll mourn his loss
    too sore,
When thinking that I'll hear the laugh or spinging step
    no more.
Ah, cure the times and sad the loss my heart to crucify,
That an Irish son with a rebel gun shot down
    my Laughing Boy.

Oh had he died by Pearse's side or in the GPO,
Killed by an English bullet from the rifle of the foe,
Or forcibly fed while Ashe lay dead in the dungeons of
    Mountjoy,
I'd have cried with pride for the way he died,
    my own dear Laughing Boy.

My princely love, can ageless love do more than tell to
    you,
Go raibh maith agat for all you tried to do,
For all you did, and would have done, my enemies to
    destroy,
I'll mourn your name and praise your fame, forever,
    my Laughing Boy.

This song is a lament for Michael Collins. The phrase in the first line, 'mouth of flowers', is a mis-translation, probably the result of folk etymology, of the Irish name of the place where Collins was ambushed and shot dead, Béal na Blá.

Text and air: This song was performed by Brendan Behan on the LP recording *Brendan Behan Sings Irish Folksongs and Ballads*, Spoken Arts SA760, 1960.

641

The Battle of the Bower

Ned Buckley (1880–1954)

The following verses are descriptive of an engagement
in September 1922, when Free State soldiers were
ambushed by Irregulars at 'The Bower', between
Rathmore and Killarney

The term 'irregular' in the subtitle was
a propagandist term, regarded as
derogatory, for the Republicans in the
Civil War.
   Piaras Béaslaí (1881–1965), the
Free State director of communications,
issued a directive: 'Free State troops
are to be referred to as the 'National
Army', the 'Irish Army', or just
'troops'. The Anti-Treaty side are to be
called 'Irregulars' and are not to be referred to as 'Republicans', 'IRA',
'forces', or 'troops', nor are the ranks
of their officers allowed to be given.
No letters about the treatment of Anti-
Treaty prisoners are to be published.
The words 'attacked, commandeered
and arrested' as used to describe their
actions are to be replaced by, 'fired at,
seized and kidnapped'.' [LM]

Text: Brendan Clifford and Jack Lane
(eds.), *Ned Buckley's Poems*, Aubane
Historical Society, Aubane, 1987.

You may talk about Thermopylae
   Or of the Bridge of Rome;
You may mention wars of foreign lands
   Or battles fought at home;
But from the days of the Crusades,
   Until this present hour
There ne'er was such a rattle as
   The Battle of The Bower.

The people who were list'ning thought
   That all the world was dead.
There was such noise of machine guns
   And such discharge of lead.
No horse nor man could pass that road,
   With either meal or flour.
No pigs were fed the day they fought
   The Battle of The Bower.

Men who let the Republic 'up'
   Fought men who 'let it down',
And men who held the country
   Shot at men who held the town.
They fought the Black and Tan until
   They said they'd smashed his power,
And now they fought each other at
   The Battle of The Bower.

Some people say that both sides won,
   Some say none won at all;
And each side swears that they saw scores
   Of th' other side to fall.
But one thing's true, that bullets flew
   In a dark and deadly shower,
Though none were killed or wounded, at
   The Battle of The Bower.

For miles around that fighting ground
   Men did no work that day,
But when they met at night-time,

To each other they did say,
The Devil a peace we'll ever have
   Till something come and scour
This land of such as those who fought
   The Battle of The Bower.

The Leggings and the Bandoliers
Charlie Gilmore

When I was a little lad
   Across the hills from Blessington,
We shared what little wealth we had
   With those who still kept fighting on.

For some had little time to live
   When trusted pens had signed away
A name it was not theirs to give
   And turned a bright dawn back to grey.

The borrowed guns in Dublin town
   Scribbled across the clouds at night,
And battered Rory's ramparts down
   Where still the few stood up to fight.

I only knew them as 'the boys'
   Who straggled, weary, through the glen,
And helped me with my broken toys
   And milked the cows. But they were men.

I found them sleeping in the hay,
   I did not ask them who they were,
And in the fields they worked, or lay,
   They went and came like mountain air.

Strange singing reached my straining ears
   As the late firelight, flickering, shone
On leggings and on bandoliers . . .
   And in the morning they were gone.

And every day through Ballycross
   Mulcahy's mercenaries came;
And many a wall has now its cross
   To mark a loss in Ireland's name.

Text: Charlie Gilmore, *The Leggings and the Bandoliers*, Repsol Publications, Dublin, 1976.

643

And then, when Ireland's name was lost
    And ever strong and stronger grew
Their ranks, like green waves current-tossed,
    And fewer still the few.

'That Lady' called, and said: 'Here, love,
    Just take these few things to the boys;
You're strong, and know the hills above,
    And, in your climbing make no noise!'

I knew that lady's face so well
    It seems to dwell in candle-light;
I waited 'til the evening bell,
    And climbed . . . by Seskin, to the right . . .

By stream-wet marl below the rath
    I crossed by log and weathered stone,
A sheep stepped stiffly from my path
    I had no fear to be alone.

An otter streamed a silver wake,
    A rabbit thumped and nightjars churred;
And in the fern beyond the brake
    A brown stoat chirruped like a bird.

Dew-webs of spiders, whin-to-whin,
    I broke on many a rabbit-track;
And almost heard them start to spin
    Another web behind my back.

Foxglove and bracken through the stones
    Wove this year's green with brown of last;
And squirrels searched among the bones
    Of seeded cones from banquets past.

I felt the larches' fringes sway
    Where darkly lay the pine above,
And through deep carpets, brown and grey,
    A golden ray of sunlight wove.

Pale gleam of fungus under trees,
    Sharp scent of heather and wild thyme;
Pine-needles sharpened in the breeze . . .
    And hoof-tracks, deep in stagnant slime.

I passed a red buck and his does,
    And came into the 'little' glen
And felt the path between my toes,
    Without my shoes . . . and counted ten!

A woodcock chirped, on sentry-go,
    A raven croaked a mile away
By Coolakay, and watched, below
    Some movement of the dying day.

My ears, to still small voices tuned,
    Heard sighing tunes among the pine;
And through my mind ran sleepsongs crooned –
    That grew into a throbbing whine.

Were snipe still drumming in the sky?
    I close my eyes and held my breath
And prayed while death was passing by
    The little path my toes beneath . . .

A car-lamp swept a field near Balnagee;
    And high on Maulin sounded clear
    The whistle of a startled deer
That showed me, sure as eye could see,
    Where to expect them to appear . . .

Above Bahana; by the birch?
    Before their lorries turned the hill
And roared away towards Kilakee
And Dublin on their deadly search;
    And once again the night was still.

The little voices all were hushed,
    No whisper stirred on land or sea;
Only the bracken-fronds I crushed
    Seemed louder than they used to be.

Pale gold and silver washed the West;
    And quiet slept the mountain breeze . . .
I eased across a heather-crest
    And crouched among the rowan trees.

Warped through grey rock and hostile air
    Steel-grey their tortured sinews stood;
And writhing fingers touched my hair
    With clotted berries, red as blood.

645

Gaunt, giant knuckles ridged the capes
   With weathered rock like whitened bone,
I strained to see which shadowed shapes
   Were sentinels of flesh . . . or stone.

And, straining, glimpsed a sheen of swords
   Where water stirred among the stones;
And water echoed back the words
   Of men long dust among their bones . . .

Many the names the echoes gave:
   'The Man from God Knows Where' and Tone...
And volleys by a prison grave
   Where generations stood alone.

And many a man who got his death;
   And many a good man not yet dead,
McDonnell to Elizabeth
   Echoed... 'My Son Hath Many a Head!'

And Connolly and Lalor spoke;
   And Jemmy Hope and Michael Dwyer
Who fanned a forge to rive the yoke
   When ashes woke to flickering fire.

And Robert Emmet's shade was there,
   And many an unknown, pitchcapped skull
Spoke; echoing through the shuddering air,
   To Liam Mellowes' fierce 'Ní thoil'.

Winds waved their words away like smoke
   Through ghosts of men and ghosts of trees;
And the last line of Ireland broke
   As froth amid contending seas.

And women came like Granuaile
   Or gentle with the grace of steel,
Who bowed to kneel beside a gaol
   For men who thought it hard to kneel.

Silent as monuments they stood
   Where turf, and seed and springing shoots
Were oak-trees old before the flood...
   Stark shapes among their whitening roots.

And through slim pikes... or Fenian spears?
   Or rushes...? small winds whine and die
And by my side... or down the years?
   A pibroch... or a plover? cried.

For I was weary from the climb
   And ancient legends hazed my sight,
And folded back the page of Time
   And held the closing doors of Night.

And far, beyond the granite sills
   Where Lackandarragh struggles high,
Retreating regiments of hills
   Marched, silent, to a silent sky.

And silence filled the valleys deep,
   And silent sang the streams below;
The silent sentry seemed to sleep,
   I loosed my load, and left it so.

All night I slept among the ling;
   But through my dreams a clamour ran
And great dogs chased before a king
   Great deer... that lived when Time began.

And, though I wakened in the dawn
   And searched from there to Glenmacnass;
From Ummera to Mullacleevaun
   No shoe but mine had bent the grass.

So do not ask me who they were
   Or had I slept among the Sidhe;
For still the Fianna gather there
   In empty air, about Knockree.

And still ... whenever dewdrops shine
   Or shadows climb a sunwashed wall,
Or brown leaves fall among the pine
   As mountain echoes, wavering fall.

Or when the geese are on the wing
   And clothes hang frozen on the line,
And axes in the forest ring ...
   Or when a hand is clasped in mine.

When sheepdogs whine, or plovers call
  Or tassels in the larches swing;
Or when a horse moves in its stall,
  Or when the gorse is gold in Spring.

Or when the dawnlight rises grey
  And hints of day creep down the glen;
I see again the heather sway
  Across the way of weary men.

Their legends lengthen down the years
  To spread across the turning earth,
And touch the shafts of taller spears
  Where new life stirs to laggard birth.

They come again through forty years
  When tired feet stumble by my door;
The leggings and the bandoliers
  Of boys who cross the glen no more.

Their passing stirred a little breeze
  Among the dead leaves crisply curled;
But sap still rises in the trees
  And tempests roar around the world.

The Ballad of the Tinker's Son

Sigerson Clifford

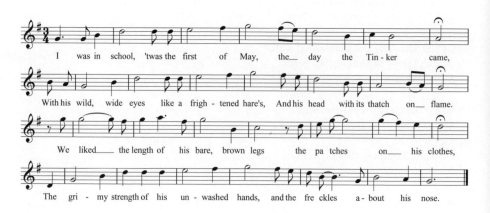

I was in school, 'twas the first of May, the day the Tin-ker came,
With his wild, wide eyes like a frigh-tened hare's, And his head with its thatch on flame.
We liked the length of his bare, brown legs the pa tches on his clothes,
The gri-my strength of his un-washed hands, and the fre ckles a-bout his nose.

I was in school, 'twas the first of May,
    The day the tinker came,
With his wild wide eyes like a frightened hare's,
    And his head with its thatch on flame.

We liked the length of his bare brown legs,
    The patches upon his clothes,
The grimy strength of his unwashed hands
    And the freckles about his nose.

The master polished his rimless specs
    And he stared at him hard and long,
Then he stood him up on a shakey bench
    And called on him for a song.

The tinker boy looked at our laughing lips,
    Then with a voice like a timid bird's
He followed the master's bidding
    And these are his singing words.

'My father was jailed for sheep-stealing,
    My mother is black as a witch,
My sister off-ran with the Sheridan clan
    And my brother's dead-drunk in a ditch.

'O, Tralee jail would kill the devil,
    But Tralee jail won't kill my da,
I'll mend ye a kettle for one-and-fourpence
    And bring home porter to my ma.'

He bowed his head as the schoolhouse shook
    With the cheers of everyone,
Then the master made me share my desk
    With the raggedy tinker's son.

The days dragged by and he sat down there,
    His brown eyes still afraid,
He heard the scholars' drowsy hum
    And, turning to me, he said . . .

'Now what would I want with X and Y
    And I singing the crooked towns,
Or showing a drunken farmer
    The making of silver crowns?

Text: Sigerson Clifford, *Ballads of a Bogman*, Mercier Press, Cork, 1986.
    Air: This air was created for the song by Tim Dennehy, who can be heard singing it on his CD *Between the Mountains and the Sea*.

'And will Euclid teach me to light a fire
  Of green twigs in the rain,
Or how to twist a pheasant's neck
  So it will not shout with pain?

'And what would I want with ancient verse
  Or the meaning of Latin words,
When all the poetry I'll ever need
  Rings the throats of the singing birds?'

But he stayed at school and his flowering
  mind
  Grew quick as a swooping hawk;
Then came a day when we said goodbye
  To the master who smelt of chalk.

He went to the life of ribbon roads
  And the lore of the tinker bands;
They chained my bones to an office stool
  And my soul to a clock's cold hands.

But I often thought of my tinker friend
  And I cursed the smirking luck
That didn't make me a tinker man
  Fighting the road to Puck.

With a red-haired wife and a piebald horse,
  And a splendid caravan,
Roving the roads with Cartys and Wards,
  The O'Briens or the Coffey clans.

The years went by and the Trouble came,
  And I found myself again
Back where I whittled the worn desks,
  With the mountains and the rain.

They put a trench-coat on my back,
  And in my hands a gun,
And up in the hills with the fighting men
  I found the tinker's son.

And there on the slopes of the Kerry hills
  Our love grew still more strong,
And we watched the wrens on the yellow
  whins
  Spill their thimblefuls of song.

Then came a truce and I shook his hand,
  For a while our fighting done;
But I never spoke a word again
  To the red-haired tinker's son . . .

'Tis many a year since he went away
  And over the roads the vans
Wheel gaily to horse and cattle fairs
  With the O'Briens and the Coffey clans.

The tinker's son should be back again
  With the roads and the life he knew,
But I put a bullet through his brain
  In nineteen-twenty-two.

Cosgrave's Ould Shebeen
With apologies to the author of
'Shanahan's Ould Shebeen'

'Shanahan's Auld Shebeen', by Gerald
Brenan, appeared in *The New York
Times* in the late nineteenth century
and inspired several parodies.

  Text: Samuels Collection, TCD.

This is the tale our President told
As he sat in his chair with his feet so cold –
Told with a sigh and perchance a tear,
As he thought of the days when he dosed the beer;

Told as he gazed on the walls near by,
Expecting each moment a bullet to fly,
Where a rough little print in a frame between
Showed a picture of Burca's ould shebeen.

I'm tasting my mother's whiskey,
But somehow 'tis not the same;
Though 'tis paid for by the Free State,
And I lap it up in shame.
My Free State servant brings it,
And I always drink it 'nate',
Being cooped up here for ever –
It's a 'Free' but an awful 'State'.
Look at them all around me,
They'd fill your heart with gloom,
Like restless slugs in torment,
They crawl from room to room.
There's Blythe stuck under the table,
Shivering in every limb;
With O'Higgins, the would-be statesman,
Nephew of England's Tim;
There's Johneen there in the corner;
Milroy with his voice so loud;
Gorey the Kilkenny dungman –
Oh, God! they're an awful crowd!
Whilst Mulcahy's funeral speeches
Are the devil and all to stand –
Ho, soldier! three more bottles
Of me mother's favourite brand!

Hush! Here comes His Grace's carriage,
There'll be trouble by and by –
Soldier, quick with them bottles!
For I'm feeling powerful dry.
I've got to meet the Archbishop –
I'm a Republican now no more;
But, ochone! those were the good times –
To think of them makes me sore.
When I'd gentlemen around me
And comrades tried and true –
Boland, Childers and Barton,
De Valera and Cathal Brugha –
The memory comes like the Banshee
Myself and my job between,
And I long to be back at the counter
Of me mother's ould shebeen.

Whose face is that at the window?
Whose voice is that in wind?
Is it the murdered prisoners,
Or is there worse behind?
Oh! what is that awful shadow
That comes in the dawn so grey,
With outstretched hand to greet me?
My God! it is Castlereagh!
And see! there are others behind him
With terror I'm stricken through!
Sadleir! Keogh and Higgins!
McNally and Carey, too!
Away ye sprites of darkness!
From my fevered vision flee!
You come to the wrong department –
It's Mulcahy you want – not me!

I'll leave this terrible dungeon –
It's the foulest ever seen –
Let me end my days as potboy
In my mother's ould shebeen.

The Felons of Our Land

M. MacG.

This is a parody of a song
with the same title by
Arthur M. Forrester, which
was published in 1891.
This song looks back to the
Rising and the leaders'
graves in Arbour Hill
prison, but also mentions
some of those who per-
sisted in armed action into
the 1930s.

Text: Leslie H. Daiken,
*Good-bye, Twilight – Songs
of the Struggle in Ireland*,
Lawrence & Wishart,
London, 1936.
Air: 'The Felons of Our
Land', see p. 354.

Fill up once more the same old toast we drank some years ago;
The shadow of each Fenian ghost is close beside we know.
As we rise up with eyes bedimmed to drink to that brave band,
Who lie in lonely Arbour Hill – Brave Felons of Our Land.

We feel the blast from yonder glen – the breath of frosty dells;
What must they feel, these naked men, in dreary dungeon cells?
The bearded man, the beardless boy abused by ruffian hand,
In Arbour Hill, and lone Mountjoy – Brave Felons of Our Land.

Then drink to these brave Gilmore boys, the bravest of the brave;
Then drink to our brave exile chief – Frank Beirne o'er the wave,
To Con Realy, and Sean Hogan, and others of that band,
To our Leitrim Chief O'Farrell – Brave Felons of Our Land.

Then shall they lie in dungeon cells abused by cruel foes
Held by a viler type of man than England's vilest yeos?

No: o'er the land the peoples's voice like waves across the sand
With sweeping force has said 'Release those Felons of Our Land.'

Thank God the land has heroes still to dare the tyrant host,
In prison cell or on the hill where e'er they're needed most.
And till the dawn of freedom's glow shines out so proud and grand
Our country's cause is safe we know with Felons of Our Land.

The Boys from County Cork

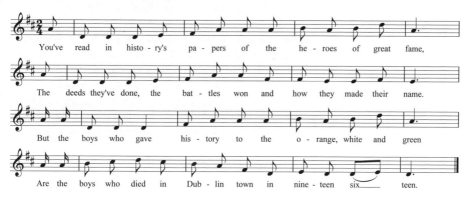

You've read in history's papers of the heroes of great fame,
The deeds they've done, the battles won, and how they made their name;
But the boys who gave history to the orange, white and green
Are the boys who died in Dublin town in 1916.

Text and air: James N. Healy, *Ballads from the Pubs of Ireland*, Mercier Press, Cork, 1965.

Chorus
There were some of the boys from Kerry, some of the boys from Clare,
From Dublin, Wicklow, Donegal, and boys from old Kildare.
There were boys from the land beyond the seas from Boston and
    New York
But the boys who bate the Black and Tans were the boys from
    County Cork.

Cork gave us MacSwiney, a hero he did die,
Wicklow gave us Michael Dwyer in the days so long gone by,
Dublin gave us Padraic Pearse, MacBride and Cathal Brugha,
And America De Valera for to lead ould Ireland through.

We seem to be divided, I really don't know why,
We've a glorious list of martyrs, who for Ireland did die;
Now why not get together and join in unity
The North, the South, the East and West will set ould Ireland free.

The First Cork Brigade

Text: A composite of different versions in traditional use.
Air: 'The Battle Hymn of the Republic', see p. 94.

When John Bull sent his gunmen to shoot McCurtain down,
He thought Sinn Féin was dead and gone in this old Rebel
    town.
He thought he had us to the wall but we were not afraid,
'No Surrender' is the war cry of the First Cork Brigade.

Chorus
Glory, Glory to old Ireland,
Glory, Glory to our sireland,
Glory, Glory to the men who fought and died,
No surrender! Is the war cry of the First Cork Brigade.

The Staters came from Dublin all equipped with British guns,
They thought Sinn Féin and Rebel Cork would soon be on the run.
But ere they got to Mallow they were seriously delayed
By the fighting tenth battalion of the First Cork Brigade.

We bombed them in the Abbey, we bombed them in the Glen,
We bombed them up at Dillon's Cross, they bombed us back again.
We bombed them in the 'Wessie' and we bombed them in the Parade,
And we gave them who began it in the First Cork Brigade.

We have no shiny gaiters and no Sam Brown belts to show
But we're able to defend ourselves no matter where we go.
We're out for a Republic and to Hell with the Free State,
'No Surrender' is the war cry of the First Cork Brigade.

The Hills of Sweet Mayo

It was on a sum— mer's eve - ning as I ram - bled from my home,—
U - pon the banks of a sil - v'ry stream I care - less - ly did roam,—
I chanced to hear— a fair young maid as the tears from her eyes did flow,—
'Twas for the loss of her own true love on the hills of sweet Ma - yo.—

It was on a summer's evening as I rambled from my home,
Upon the banks of a silv'ry stream I carelessly did roam,
I chanced to hear a fair young maid as the tears from her
    eyes did flow,
'Twas for the loss of her own true love on the hills of sweet
    Mayo.

Late last night I heard the news that nearly broke my heart,
When a bounty boy came from the hills and said that you
    must part,
Part from your own love Willie that loved you long ago,
He's wounded, deadly wounded, on the hills of sweet Mayo.

Forget about your Bolshie boy and come along with me,
We'll both go off together and 'tis happy we will be,
For what's the use of mourning now for one who's lying
    low
With death's cold dew upon his brow on the hills of sweet
    Mayo

My own true love was a rebel bold; he loved sweet liberty,
He fought in 1916 to set old Ireland free,
He fought for Ireland's freedom and never feared the foe,
But 'twas Free State guns that shot my love on the hills of
    sweet Mayo.

There is one request I ask of you and grant it to me please,
It is not much to ask of you but 'twould set my mind at
    ease.
Have pity on a fair young maid who knows not where to
    go
And come with her to find her love on the hills of sweet
    Mayo.

We started out together her true love for to find,
Two days and nights we searched for him with sad
    thoughts on our mind,
Till at last we came to a silent spot and the tears began to
    flow,
It was there she found her true love dead on the hills of
    sweet Mayo.

My own true love was a rebel bold who loved sweet liberty,
He fought in 1916 to set old Ireland free.
He fought for Ireland's freedom and never feared the foe,
But 'twas Free State guns that shot my love on the hills of
    sweet Mayo.

The song relates the quest of a young woman for her lover, shot dead in action. This version is from the Civil War, as is clear from the reference to Free State guns shooting her lover.

The term 'Bolshie boy' in verse 3 notes the fact that in some areas the Republicans in the Civil War period were sometimes called Bolshies (Bolsheviks). Another such reference can be found in the song on p. 604.

While it would be incorrect, in retrospect, to attribute a very radical stance to the Republicans, this term Bolshie points to some realization that the Republicans offered, at least in theory, a somewhat more radical view of the state and society. The areas in which the Republicans were more strongly supported were the poorer areas of the country, whereas in the more prosperous areas, the Roman Catholic hierarchy, business and finance supported the Free State.

The first organization to oppose the Anglo-Irish Treaty of 1921 was the Communist Party of Ireland. [LM]

Text: Liam McNulty.
  Air: 'The Hills of Glenswilly' or 'The Homes of Donegal'.

The Lay of Oliver Gogarty

William Dawson

Come___ all ye bould Free Sta - ters now and lis - ten to my lay,___

And pay a close___ at - ten - tion please to what I've got to say.___

For 'tis the tale of a win - ter's night in last De - cem - ber drear___

When O - li - ver St John Go - gar - ty swam down the Sal - mon Weir.

Senator Oliver St John Gogarty, a supporter of the Provisional Government, was kidnapped and threatened with death by anti-Treatyites in January 1923. He was brought to a spot near the River Liffey at Islandbridge, where he begged for a moment to pray. Kneeling on the riverbank, he suddenly dived into the water, swam to the other side and escaped his captors. While making his escape he vowed that if he lived he would present a pair of swans to the river.

The picture on the opposite page shows this promise being kept the following year, as the swans are released into the river at the Trinity College Boat Club. Along with Gogarty are W.B. Yeats and William Cosgrave.

The swans in the picture were apparently added by the photographic studio, as the real ones left the location the moment they were released.

The constant repetition, in full, of Gogarty's name has led to the suggestion that he wrote the song himself. He was quite adept at comic verse and was at ease in the language register of the street ballad.

Text and air: Colm O Lochlainn, *More Irish Street Ballads*, At the Sign of the Three Candles, Dublin, 1965.

Come all ye bould Free Staters now and listen to my lay,
And pay a close attention please to what I've got to say.
For 'tis the tale of a winter's night in last December drear
When Oliver St John Gogarty swam down the Salmon Weir.

As Oliver St John Gogarty one night sat in his home
A-writin' of prescriptions or composin' of a poem,
Up rolled a gorgeous Rolls-Royce car and out a lady jumped
And at Oliver St John Gogarty's hall-door she loudly thumped.

'O! Oliver St John Gogarty,' said she, 'Now please come quick
For in a house some miles away a man lies mighty sick.'
Yet Oliver St John Gogarty to her made no reply,
But with a dextrous facial twist he gently closed one eye.

'O! Oliver St John Gogarty, come let yourself be led.'
Cried a couple of masked ruffians puttin' guns up to his head.
'I'm with you, boys,' cried he, 'but first, give me my big fur coat
And also let me have a scarf – my special care's the throat.'

They shoved him in the Rolls-Royce car and swiftly sped away,
What route they followed Oliver St John Gogarty can't say,
But they reached a house at Island Bridge and locked him in a room,
And said, 'Oliver St John Gogarty, prepare to meet your doom.'

Said he, 'Give me some minutes first to settle my affairs,
And let me have some moments' grace to say my last night's prayers.'
To this appeal his brutal guard was unable to say nay,
He was so amazed that Oliver St John Gogarty could pray.

Oliver St John Gogarty releases the swans on the Liffey in 1924 (http://comeheretome.com/).

Said Oliver St John Gogarty, 'My coat I beg you hold.'
The half-bewildered scoundrel then did as he was told.
Before he twigged the game was up, the coat was round his head
And Oliver St John Gogarty into the night had fled.

The rain came down like bullets, and the bullets fell like rain,
As Oliver St John Gogarty the river bank did gain,
He plunged into the ragin' tide and swum with courage bold,
Like brave Horatius long ago in the fabled days of old.

Then landin' he proceeded through the famous Phoenix Park,
The night was bitter cold and what was worse, extremely dark,
But Oliver St John Gogarty to this paid no regard,
Till he found himself a target for our gallant Civic Guard.

Cried Oliver St John Gogarty, 'A Senator am I,
The rebels I've tricked, the Liffey I've swum, and sorra the word's a lie.'
As they clad and fed that hero bold, said the sergeant with a wink,
'Faith, then Oliver St John Gogarty, ye've too much bounce to sink.'

Air: A different version of 'The Homes of Donegal', also used for the previous song.

657

The Drumboe Martyrs

Michael McGinley (1852–1940)

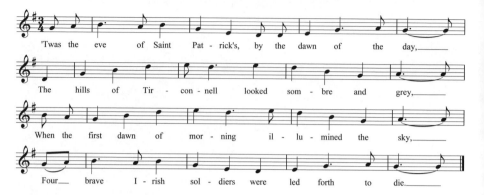

'Twas the eve of Saint Pat - rick's, by the dawn of the day,_

The hills of Tir - con - nell looked som - bre and grey,_

When the first dawn of mor - ning il - lu - mined the sky,_

Four_ brave I - rish sol - diers were led forth to die._

This song remembers the execution by the Free State army of four Republican soldiers, in Drumboe Castle, near Letterkenny, Co. Donegal, on 14 March 1923. Three of those shot were from Kerry and had been sent to the north to organize.

Charlie Daly was sent in May 1921 and Timothy O'Sullivan and Daniel Enright went there in January 1922. Seán Larkin was from Magherafelt, Co. Derry and joined Charlie Daly's column as most of his, Larkin's, unit had taken the Free State side. Daly's column operated in west Donegal, an area where the people were poor and so it was difficult for a column to operate.

During a sweep of the area in November 1922, Daly and members of his column, including the three who were subsequently shot with him, were captured near Errigal. The four were sentenced to death by court martial on 16 January 1923, but, as was common, the death sentences were often not immediately carried out. It was Free State practice to re-frain from carrying out the sentence and hold the prisoners as 'hostages' against any Republican activity in the area concerned.

Controversy surrounds the incident, as to whether in fact it was a Republican action, in which a Free State officer was shot dead, and as a result of which the four prisoners were executed. It has been suggested that, as the Republican resistance was worn down and was on the verge of collapse, Free State soldiers engaged in 'actions' to give the impression that they were still required as a threat to

'Twas the feast of St Patrick
  By the dawn of the day;
The hills of Tirconaill
  Stood sombre and gray;
When the first light of morning
  Illumined the sky,
Four brave Irish soldiers
  Were led forth to die.

Three left their loved homes
  In Kerry's green vales,
And one came from Derry
  To fight for the Gaels,
But instead of true friends
  They met traitors and foe,
And un-coffined were laid
  In the woods of Drumboe.

Four Republican soldiers
  Were dragged from their cells
Where for months they had suffered
  Wild torments like hell's.
No mercy was asked
  From their pitiless foe
And no mercy was shown
  By the thugs at Drumboe.

The church bells rang out
  In the clear morning air
To summon the faithful
  To penance and prayer,

When a crash from the woodlands
    Struck terror and woe –
'Twas the death knell of Daly,
    Shot dead at Drumboe.

Let Tirconaill ne'er boast
    Of her honour or fame;
All the waters of Finn
    Could not wash out the shame;
But while the Finn and the Swilly
    Continue to flow,
The stain will remain on
    The woods of Drumboe.

the Free State still existed. In a time of difficulty in finding employment in the civilian field the continuation of military employment was preferable to unemployment.

Daly, Enright, O'Sullivan and Larkin were shot six weeks before the end of the Civil War, when in fact the war had been lost by the Republicans. Tirconaill (Tír Chonaill) is another name for the Donegal area, and the Finn and the Swilly are two rivers in Co. Donegal. [LM]

Text and air: Liam McNulty.

Churchill's Green and Tans

Hurrah! Hurrah for freedom boys, our liberty is won,
We'll reap the golden harvest like the eagles in the sun.
We'll rob and steal and plunder, and stick to all we can,
For we are the boys can play the game, we're
    Churchill's Green and Tans,
We're Churchill's Green and Tans.

We've got the gold from England. We've got her
    gallant sons,
We're got her tanks, her aeroplanes. We've got her
    mighty guns.
We'll hunt the true Republicans and rope them to a
    man,
We'll rule the land as Cromwell did. We're Churchill's
    Green and Tans,
We're Churchill's Green and Tans.

We've Wellington Mulcahy and Bonaparte MacKeon,
Joe Sweeny and McGoldrick and McGuirk from Innis
    Owen.
We have the far famed Houston, tho' he wouldn't face
    Lehane.
But he flogged the boys at Glenty with his roaring
    Green and Tans,
His roaring Green and Tans.

Text: Ernie O'Malley Collection, New York University.

659

Then here's to Merry England, boys, long may she rule
    the waves,
Long may she send her dollars while we grind our
    brother slaves.
We're got the clergy at our back and the Bishops to a man.
But the Pope hasn't sent his blessing yet to Churchill's
    Green and Tans,
To Churchill's Green and Tans.

Then fill your glass with whiskey boys and drink to Liberty,
We'll raise blue Hell with shot and shell from the centre
    to the sea.
We'll fill our graves and churchyards, and torture all we
    can,
For we are the boys can play the game, we're Churchill's
    Green and Tans,
We're Churchill's Green and Tans.

1923

Brian O'Higgins

During the Irish Civil War, the Free State government executed 77 anti-Treaty IRA members, in an effort to compel the opponents of the Treaty to call off their armed resistance.

Text: Brian O'Higgins, *The Voice of Banba*, Dublin, 1931.

Seventy-eight of mine, said Ireland,
    Walking the dismal road of death,
Avowed their faith in a tortured sireland,
    Called my name with their latest breath;
Lifted their hearts to God above them –
    Hearts as pure as the mountain snow –
Prayed for the faithful ones who love them,
    But never quailed at the tyrant's blow.

Killed in my name! My best! My dearest!
    In the lonely fields, in the barrack squares.
Surely, O God of Love, thou hearest
    An outraged sireland's heart-wrung prayers!
Surely for their sake Thou wilt send me
    A host of soldiers to set me free!
O God of Battles! do Thou befriend me,
    For I have been loyal and true to Thee.

Seventy-eight of mine are sleeping
    Under the sod for love of me;
I have placed them in God's good keeping
    As my pledge for the glorious day to be,
When men shall spring from the down-trod masses

And march with a manly stride once more,
To fight in the streets and the hillside passes
    Till the night of thralldom and shame is o'er.

Mellows, McKelvey, Barrett, O'Connor,
    Childers, Brugha and my martyrs all,
Shall gather my soldiers for Ireland's honour,
    Shall send through the land my olden call;
My sons shall answer that brave reveille,
    And heedless of sorrow, of strife and pain,
Bring freedom and peace to hill and valley –
    The true revenge for my soldiers slain.

Take It Down from the Mast
Lines written by a Republican Soldier in 1923

James Ryan

Take It down from the mast Irish traitors,
    'Tis the flag we Republicans claim.
It can never be owned by Free Staters
    Who shed nothing upon it but shame.

Then leave it to those who are willing,
    To uphold it in war or in peace,
Those men who intend to do killing
    Until England's tyranny cease.

Take it down from the mast to remember,
    Your comrades who fell in the fight,
Those brave men who'd never surrender
    To John Bull, that big tyrant of might.

Text: Leslie H. Daiken, *Good-bye, Twilight
– Songs of the Struggle in Ireland,*
Lawrence & Wishart, London, 1936.
    Air: A version of the American folk-song
'The Red River Valley'.

661

The flag which to these men spelled freedom
    From a foe that is centuries old;
Looking back on the past we can see them
    Defending the green, white and gold.

I saw it in all the bright glory
    When first it was flung to the wind,
When of freedom they told us the story
    That no other nation could find,

When of martyrs their blood often freed us
    Till a traitor to England had sold
The land that now sorely doth need us
    To fight for the green, white and gold.

Take it down for its cause you have scorned
    To make permanent o'er us the Crown,
You who linked yourselves up with the foemen
    The tricolor then to pull down.

'Tis we and no other can claim it
    For to-day joined as one we stand, bold,
To fight England combined with Free Staters
    In defence of the green, white and gold.

New Year, 1923

Joseph Campbell (1879–1944)

Text: Austin Clarke (ed.), *Poems of Joseph Campbell*, Allen Figgis, Dublin, 1963.

Lying awake at midnight in the prison,
I heard a sudden crash of chiming bells,
Bronze bass and silver tenor, tone on tone.
– 'The church,' thought I, 'rings in another year.'
Then through the jangled bells the wail of horns
(Ship's sirens blowing from the river walls)
Smote, like a trumpet blast in sea-born 'Tristan'.
– 'Commerce,' thought I, 'rings in another year.'
And, as if stricken with the night's wild fever,
The prison shook in peals of Fenian cheers;
Mugs rattled, chambers clanked, old songs were sung.
– 'The Law,' thought I, 'rings in another year.'
Ear-surfeited, I turned to sleep; but sleep
Fled fearfully before a Thompson gun
Making new music at the prison gate.
– 'War,' pondered I, 'rings in another year!'

Chesspieces
Joseph Campbell

It was a time of trouble – executions,
Dearth, searches, nightly firing, balked escapes –
And I sat silent, while my cellmate figured
Ruy Lopez' Gambit from the 'Praxis'. Silence
Best fitted with our mood: we seldom spoke.
'I have a thought,' he said, tilting his stool.
'We prisoners are so many pieces taken,
Swept from the chessboard, only used again
When a new game is started.' 'There's that hope,'
I said, 'the hope of being used again.
Some day of strength, when ploughs are out in March,
The Dogs of Fionn will slip their iron chains,
And, heedless of torn wounds and failing wind,
Will run the old grey Wolf to death at last.'
He smiled. 'I like the image. My fat Kings,
And painted Queens, and purple-cassocked Bishops
Are tame, indeed, beside your angry Dogs!'

Text: Austin Clarke (ed.), *Poems of Joseph Campbell*, Allen Figgis, Dublin, 1963.

The Isle of Innisfree
1924
Brian O'Higgins

I will arise and go now, and go to Innisfree,
   (If 'twere *Inis Fraoigh* now, I wouldn't know its name)
And in my hut of wattles I'll be spooning with the Shee,
   (Don't make it *Sidhe*, dear printer, for it wouldn't be the same).

And in the Celtic twilight, I'll destroy the A B C
   Of *Is* and *Tá* and other things I'd dearly love to ban;
For *Caitlín Ní Uallacháin* is different, do you see?
   To Cathleen, the daughter of Houlihan.

The language of the Senate there shall fall upon my ear
   (I'll purchase me an aerial when my pension cheque is paid)
And with my own right hand I'll draw Three-Sixty Quid a year,
   To keep the Pot of Broth a-boil in the W.B.-loud glad.

And when the vulgar Gaelic Tongue is dead as Finn McCool,
   (Don't print it *Fionn MacCumhaill*, or 'twill baffle W.B.)
I'll teach Yeatsonian Irish, in a purely Pagan School,
   To keep the home fires burning in the Isle of Innisfree.

W.B. Yeats was appointed to the Senate of the Irish Free State in 1922. This poem is a satirical parody of his 'Lake Isle of Innisfree'.

Text: Brian O'Higgins, *The Voice of Banba,* Dublin, 1931.

Free State
1925
Eileen Shanahan (1901–79)

Text: Gerald Dawe (ed.), *Earth Voices Whispering, An Anthology of Irish War Poetry 1914-1945,* Blackstaff Press, Belfast, 2008.

O Ireland once as Rosaleen
   Your woes were heard across the sea
But now assuaged, we've lost a queen
   And found instead a bourgeoisie.

Clery's Van

This song was 'Given to Ernie O'Malley by Patrick Donnelly, 3 Carrol Terrace, Philsboro, Dublin' according to a note in the O'Malley Collection in New York University.

Jack Keogh, an opponent of the Treaty, rejected the 'dump arms' order of 1923 and continued to oppose the Free State government in arms near his home place of Ballinasloe. He was captured and imprisoned in 1924, and subsequently transferred to Dundrum Asylum, from where he was helped to escape in 1926 through the ploy described in this song.

Text: Ernie O'Malley Collection, New York University.

Now comrades come and listen till I tell you one and all
The news the birds are singing from Cork to Donegal,
From Dublin to the Wicklow Hills they have it to a man
How a daring Galway rebel escaped in Clery's Van.

His comrades sat in council throughout a long May night,
And swore they'd gain his liberty or wage a bloody fight.
Said the leader giving orders, 'Let each man bring a gun.
We'll take him from the tyrant's grasp and send him on
   the run.'

On a Dublin street they met next day, all present to a
   man,
And motor-cars being rather scarce they held up Clery's
   Van.
They drove up to the massive gates, the entrance to
   Dundrum,
And told the gate officials from Clery's they had come.

The gate man bade them welcome saying 'I'll open wide
   the door,'
But Clery's men with 45's I've never seen before;
They drove up to the building in a free and easy way
Wishing all the Warders a pleasant time of day.

One man said, 'The grounds are nice, and blooming are
   the flowers.'
Another said, 'I do believe those men are some of ours.'
'Is that Jack Keogh,' he shouted. Said Keogh, 'The very
   man.
Three days I have been waiting for the boys with Clery's
   Van!'

The Song of the Legion of the Rear-Guard
The New Rallying Song of the Republic
Inspired by President De Valera

Written and composed in Hore Park Camp by Jack O'Sheehan

Lu-rid the mor-ning with flame and shot and shell, Now ral-ly Ire-land the sons who love you well.

Pledged they'll de-fend you through death or pri-son cell, Wait for the Sol-diers of the Rear - Guard.

Up the Re-pub-lic! they raise their bat-tle cry. Pearse, Clarke, Mac-Der-mott will pray for them on high.

Ea-ger and rea-dy for love of you to die, Proud march the Sol-diers of the Rear - Guard.

Chorus

Le-gion of the Rear___ Guard, ans-wering Ire-land's call.

Hark, their mar-tial tramp is heard from Cork to Do-ne-gal.

Tone and Em-mett guide___ you, though your task be hard.

De Va-le-ra leads you, Sol-diers of the Le-gion of the Rear - Guard.

Lurid the morning with flame and shot and shell,
Now rally, Ireland, the sons who love you well.
Pledged they'll defend you though death or prison cell,
    Wait for the soldiers of the Rear-Guard.
Up the Republic! They raise their battle cry.
Pearse, Clarke, MacDermott will pray for them on high.
Eager and ready for love of you to die,
    Proud march the Soldiers of the Rear-Guard.

Chorus
Legion of the Rear-Guard, answering Ireland's call,
Hark! their martial tramp is heard from Cork to Donegal.
Tone and Emmet guide you. Though your task be hard
    De Valera leads you! Soldiers of the Legion of the Rear-
    Guard.

Street, hillside, valley, – they send their sons along.
Plough, office, workshop, – a score of thousands strong.

Text: The Samuels Collection, TCD.
Air: Sheet music published by The
Emton Press, Dublin, 1924.

665

Spirit of Brian! They come with joyous song.
  Fearless, the Soldiers of the Rear-Guard.
Cork, Kerry, Wexford, Tipperary, Clare.
Galway to Dublin – Tirconaill to Kildare.
None shall be missing – all Ireland shall be there.
  True Gaels, the Soldiers of the Rear-Guard.

Crimsoned the roadside, the prison-wall, the cave.
Proof of their valour. Go, sleep in peace, ye brave!
Comrades, tread lightly. You're near a hero's grave.
  There lies a Soldier of the Rear-Guard.
Shell-shattered fortress and shot-scarred barricade
Trumpet the story of the gallant fight they made.
Weary, outnumbered, undaunted, undismayed.
  God bless the Soldiers of the Rear-Guard.

Oh Lord Above!

As noted on p. xvii, songs in praise, or defence, of the pro-Treaty side of the Civil War are all but non-existent. All except this little rhyme, which I'm told was current in certain Dublin households decades after the end of the Civil War!

Oh Lord above,
  Send down a dove
With beak as sharp as razors
  To cut the throats
  Of the the dirty louts
That shot our brave Free Staters!

Bibliography — Poetry & Song

Materials for this collection were sourced in the following libraries and publications:

LIBRARIES & GALLERIES

Trinity College, Dublin

National Library of Ireland

New York University

University of Montana

Ward Irish Music Archives
    Milwaukee

Brown University Library

Brother Allen Library

University College Dublin

An Chartlann Mhíleata/The Military Archives, Irish Defence Forces

The British Library

The Crawford Gallery, Cork

Dublin City Library and Archives

The Irish Traditional Music Archive, Dublin

Na Píobairí Uilleann, Dublin

The Royal Irish Academy

The Samuels Collection of Printed Ephemera

Maeve Cavanagh Papers
Papers of Éamonn and Áine Ceannt

The Ernie O'Malley Papers

Mansfield Library, Archives and Special Collections

Sheet Music Collection

Anne S.K. Brown Military Collection

Éamonn Ceannt Papers

PUBLICATIONS

Anonymous – *1916 Song Book*, The (Dublin, n.d.)

— *1916 Song Book*, The (Additional Songs) (Dublin, n.d.)

— *Ballads and Marching Songs of Ireland* (Dublin, n.d.)

— *Barricade Song Sheet* (Dublin, n.d.)

— *Connolly Souvenir* (Dublin, 1919)

— *De Valera Song Book, The* (Limerick, n.d.)

— *Fenian Song Book, The* (Dublin, *c.* 1940)

— *Flag of Freedom Song Sheet, The* (Dublin, n.d.)

— *Granuaile Song Book, The* (Dublin, 1922)

— *Grave and Gay Song Book* (*c.* 1940)

— *Green Flag Song Book, The* (London, n.d.)

— *In Dublin City in 1913* (Dublin, 1988)

— *Irish Fireside Songs, No. 9, Patriots' Treasury* (Dublin, n.d.)

— *Irish Fun* (Dublin, 1918–19)

— *Irish Popular Song Sheet, The* (n.d.)

— *Irish Soldier's Song Book, The* (Dublin, n.d.)

— *Irish Songs of Resistance, Vol 2* (n.d.)

— *IWW Songs to Fan the Flames of Discontent* (Chicago, 1973)

— *Literary Digest* (New York, 23 April 1921)

— *Marching Songs of Ireland* (Dublin, n.d.)

— *Marching Songs of Ireland, No. 1* (Dublin, n.d.)

— *Marching Songs of Ireland, No. 2* (Dublin, n.d.)

— *Marching Songs of Ireland, Number Three* (Dublin, n.d.)

— *Marching Songs of the Irish Volunteers, The* (London, n.d.)

— *National Comic Song Book, The* (Dublin, n.d.)

— *New Songs, Ballads and Recitations* (n.d.)

— *Old "Come-all-Ye's"* (Derry, n.d.)

— *Orange Standard* (Glasgow, n.d.)

— *Parnell's Land League Songster* (New York, 1889)

— *Poems and Songs of Easter Week* (n.d.)

— *Poets of 1916, The, With Life and Notes* (Dublin, n.d.)

— *Rallying Songs, No. 2* (Dublin, n.d.)

— *Rallying Songs, No. three* (Dublin, n.d.)
— *Rebels who fought and died for Ireland, The* (n.d.)
— *Second Album of Roscommon Verse* (Dublin, 1983)
— *Soldiers Song Book, The* (Dublin, n.d.)
— *Songs and Ballads of Dublin* (n.d.)
— *Songs and Recitations of Ireland, 1, The Flag* (Cork, 1971)
— *Songs and Recitations of Ireland, 2, The Harp* (Cork, 1968)
— *Songs and Recitations of Ireland, 3, The Easter Lily* (Cork, 1976)
— *Songs and Recitations of Ireland, 4, The Tara Brooch* (Cork, 1972)
— *Songs and Recitations of Ireland, 5, The Wild Geese* (Cork, 1978)
— *Songs of a Kerry Ballad Singer* (n.d.)
— *Songs of Battle* (Dublin, 1916)
— *Songs of Freedom* (London, 1893)
— *Songs of Resistance 1968–2001*, Fourth Enlarged Edition (Dublin, 2001)
— *Songs of the Irish Republic* (Cork, 1962)
— *Songs of the Irish Republic* (Cork, 1975)
— *Songs of the Irish Republic* (n.d.)
— *Songs of the Workers* (Dublin, 1975)
— *Songs of the Workers' Republic* (n.d.)
— *Songs the Soldiers and Sailors Sing* (New York, 1918)
— *Spirit of The Nation* (Dublin, 1845)
— *Treoir* 42.1 (Dublin, 2010)
— *Tri-Colour Song Book, The* (Dublin, n.d.)
— *Walton's Treasury of Irish Songs and Ballads* (Dublin, 1947)
— *Walton's New Treasury of Irish Songs and Ballads, Vol. 1* (Dublin, 1968)
— *Walton's 132 Best Irish Songs and Ballads* (Dublin, n.d.)

Arthur, Max, *When This Bloody War Is Over* (London, 2001)
Ashraf, Mary (ed.), *Political Verse and Song from Britain and Ireland* (London, 1975)

Barry, Dan (ed.), *The Tricolour* (Cork, 1976)
Bax, Sir Arnold, *A Dublin Ballad and Other Poems* (Dublin, 1918)
Béaslaí, Piaras (ed.), *Songs, Ballads and Recitations by Famous Irishmen – Arthur Griffith* (Dublin, n.d.)
Beauchamp, Joan, *Poems of Revolt* (London, 1924)
Behan, Brendan, *Confessions of an Irish Rebel* (London, 1965)
Behan, Dominic, *The Singing Irish* (London, 1967)
— *Ireland Sings* (London, 1973)
Berresford Ellis, P. (ed.), *James Connolly Selected Writings* (1973)
Boas, Frederick S., *Songs of Ulster and Balliol* (London, 1917)
Bolger, Dermot (ed.), *16 on 16 – Irish Writers on the Easter Rising* (Dublin, 1988)
Bond, Patrick, 'Irish Songs' in *Irish Democrat*, No. 476 (London, October 1983)
Boyd, Andrew, *Jim Connell, Author of The Red Flag* (2001)
Brayton, Teresa, *Songs of the Dawn and Irish Ditties* (New York, 1913)
— *The Flame of Ireland* (New York, 1926)
Brearton, Fran, *The Great War in Irish Poetry* (Oxford, 2000)
Breathnach, Fr Pádruig, *Songs of the Gael, First Series* (Dublin 1922)
Breathnach, S.S., *Victory Song Book* (Dublin, 1920)
Brown, S.J., *Poetry of Irish History* (Dublin, 1927)
Browne, P. (ed.), *Collected Works of Pádraic H. Pearse* (Dublin, 1917)
— *Aftermath of Easter Week* (Dublin, 1917)

Callahan, Mat (ed.), *Songs of Freedom, The James Connolly Songbook* (Oakland, CA., 2013)
Callan, Patrick, 'The Political War Ballads of Sean O'Casey, 1916–18' in *Irish University Review*, Vol. 13, No. 2 (Dublin, 1983)
Carberry, Ethna, *The Four Winds of Eirinn* (Dublin, 1906)
— *We Sang for Ireland, Poems of Ethna Carberry, Seumas MacManus and Alice Milligan* (Dublin, 1950)
Carnduff, Tom, *Songs of an Out-of-Work* (Belfast, 1932)
Cavanagh, Maeve, *Sheaves of Revolt* (Dublin, 1914)
— *A Voice of Insurgency* (Dublin, 1916)
— *Soul and Clay* (Dublin, 1917)
Chesterton, G.K., *Utopia of Usurers and Other Essays* (New York, 1917)
Clarke, Austin (ed.), *Poems of Joseph Campbell* (Dublin, 1963)
Clarke, George Herbert (ed.), *A Treasury of War Poetry* (London, 1917)
Clarke, R. Dardis (ed.), *Austin Clarke Collected Poems* (Manchester, 2008)

Clarke, Thomas J., *Glimpses of an Irish Felon's Life* (Dublin, 1922)
Cleary, Thomas S., *Songs of the Irish Land War* (Dublin, 1888)
Clifford, Brendan and Jack Lane (eds.), *Ned Buckley's Poems* (Aubane, 1987)
Clifford, Sigerson, *Ballads of a Bogman* (Cork, 1986)
Clinton, Ruth, *This Fearless Maid* (Dublin 2015)
Clune, Anne (ed.), *Dear Far-Voiced Veteran, Essays in Honour of Tom Munnelly* (Clare, 2007)
Collins, Mal, Dave Harker, and Geoff White (eds.), *Big Red Songbook* (London, 1977)
Colum, Padraic, *The Road Round Ireland* (New York, 1926)
— *Irish Elegies* (Dublin, 1961)
— *Broad-Sheet Ballads* (Dublin, n.d.)
Colum, Padraic and Edward J. O'Brien (eds.), *Poems of the Irish Revolutionary Brotherhood* (Boston, 1916)
Connell, Jim, *Red Flag Rhymes* (Huddersfield, 1900?)
Connell, Joseph A.E. Jnr., *Dublin in Rebellion, A Directory 1913–1923* (Dublin, 2009)
Connolly, James (ed.), *The Worker's Republic* (Dublin, 1915–16)
— *Songs of Freedom by Irish Authors* (New York, 1907)
— *The Legacy and Songs of Freedom* (Dublin, 1918)
— *The Dying Socialist To His Son! (A Legacy) and Other Verses* (Sydney, 1918)
— *James Connolly Songbook, The* (Cork, 1972)
— *The James Connolly Songbook* (Cork, n.d.)
— *James Connolly Songbook, The* (Dublin, n.d.)
Considine, J.S., *Ná Bac Leis* (Ballykinlar, 1921)
Coogan, Tim Pat, *Who Fears to Speak?, Ballads of Irish Freedom* (Dublin, 1985)
Costello, Francis J., *The Irish Revolution and its Aftermath 1916-1923* (Sallins, 2002)
Cox, Eleanor R., *A Hosting of Heroes and Other Poems* (Dublin, 1911)
Crean, Desmond, *Songs of an Old I.R.A. Man* (Dublin, 1939)
Cronin, Seán, *Kevin Barry* (Cork, 1965)
Crotty, Patrick (ed.), *The Penguin Book of Irish Poetry* (London, 2010)
Crowley, Jimmy, *Jimmy Crowley's Irish Song Book* (Cork, 1986)
— *Songs from the Beautiful City, The Cork Urban Ballads* (Cork, 2015)
Curry, James, *Artist of the Revolution, The Cartoons of Ernest Kavanagh* (Cork, 2012)
Curtayne, Alice (ed.), *The Complete Poems of Francis Ledwidge* (London, 1974)
Cusack, Niall, 'An Cor Tuathail' in *Irish Political Review, 21.2* (Dublin, 2006)

Daiken, Leslie H., *Good-Bye, Twilight, Songs of the Struggle in Ireland* (London, 1936)
Dallas, Karl, *The Cruel Wars* (London, 1972)
Daly, Mrs de Burgh, *Percy French, Prose, Poems and Parodies* (Dublin, 1929)
Daly, Raymond and Derek Warfield, *Celtic and Ireland in Song and Story* (Kildare, 2008)
Dawe, Gerald (ed.), *Earth Voices Whispering, An Anthology of Irish War Poetry 1914–1945* (Belfast, 2008)
de Brún, Pádraig, *1916* (Dublin, n.d.)
de Burca, Seamus, *The Soldier's Song* (Dublin, 1957)
Donnelly, Francis P., *Shepherd My Thoughts, The Verses of Francis P. Donnelly* (New York, 1918)
Duggan, G.C., *The Watchers on Gallipoli* (Dublin, 1921)
Dungan, Myles, *Irish Voices from the Great War* (Dublin, 2014)
Dunn, Hubert, *The Minstrel Boy, Francis Ledwidge and the Literature of his time* (Ireland, 2006)
Dunsany, Lord, *The Complete Poems of Francis Ledwidge* (London, 1919)
— *Fifty Poems* (London, 1929)
— *War Poems* (London, 1941)
Dworkin, Dennis (ed.), *Ireland and Britain, 1798–1922: An Anthology of Sources* (Indianapolis, 2012)

Earhart, Will and Edward B. Birge (eds.), *Songs of Stephen Foster* (Pittsburgh, 1955)
Erskine, John (ed.), *Contemporary War Poems* (New York, 1914)
Ewer, W.N., *Five Souls* (London, 1916)

Fagles, Robert (Trans.), *The Odyssey* (New York, 1996)
Fahy, Francis A., *The Ould Plaid Shawl and Other Songs* (Dublin, 1949)
Faolain, Turlough, *Blood on the Harp* (New York, 1983)
Fitzgerald, John, *Legends, Ballads & Songs of the Lee* (Cork, 1862)
Fitzhenry, Edna C., *Nineteen-Sixteen Anthology* (Dublin, 1935)
— *Nineteen-Sixteen, An Anthology, Golden Jubilee Edition* (Dublin, 1966)
Fitzmaurice, Gabriel (ed.), Between the Hills and the Sea, Songs and Ballads of Kerry (Ballyheigue, 1991)
Fitzwilliam, Edward, *Songs and Poems* (Boston, 1906)
Forrester, Arthur M., *An Irish Crazy-Quilt* (Boston, 1891)
Forrester, Ellen and Arthur M., *Songs of the Rising Nation* (Glasgow, 1869)
Fox, R.M., *Rebel Irishwomen* (Dublin, 1935)

Galvin, Patrick, *Irish Songs of Resistance* (New York, 1962)
Gavin, William, *Flights of Fancy* (Dublin, 1939)
Gilmore, Charlie, *The Leggings and the Bandoliers* (Dublin, 1976)
Gioti, Labrini, *The Foggy Dew: Processes of change in an Irish Rebel song* (n.d.)
Gogan, Robert, *50 Great Irish Fighting Songs* (Dublin, 2005)
Golden, Peter, *Ballads of Rebellion* (New York, 1914)
— *The Voice of Ireland* (New York, 1916)
Gore-Booth, Eva, *The Perilous Light* (London, 1915)
— *Poems of Eva Gore-Booth* (London, 1929)
Graves, C.L., *The Blarney Ballads* (London, 1893)
Greaves, C. Desmond, *The Easter Rising in Song & Ballad* (London, 1980)
Gregory, Padric (ed.), *The Poems of John Francis MacEntee* (Dublin, 1917)
— *Ireland: A Song of Hope and Other Poems* (Dublin, 1917)
— *Ulster Songs and Ballads* (Dublin, *c.* 1918)
Gregory, Lady, *The Kiltartan History Book* (London, 1926)
Gwynn, Stephen and T.M. Kettle, *Battle Songs for the Irish Brigades* (Dublin, 1915)

Hand, John, *Irish Street Ballads* (Dublin, 1976)
Harte, Frank, *Songs of Dublin* (Cork, 1993)
Haughey, Jim, *The First World War in Irish Poetry* (New Jersey, 2002)
Healy, James N., *Ballads from the Pubs of Ireland* (Cork, 1965)
— *Percy French and His Songs* (Cork, 1966)
Hewitt, John & Frank Ormsby, *The Collected Poems of John Hewitt* (Belfast, 1991)
Hoagland, Kathleen, *1000 Years of Irish Poetry* (New York, 1947)
Hogan, Dick, *The Hogan Collection* (Dublin, 2013)
Hogan, Robert (ed.), *Feathers from the Green Crow – Sean O'Casey 1905–1925* (Columbia, 1962)
Hone, Joseph, *W.B. Yeats, 1865–1939* (New York, 1943)
Huntington, Gale (ed.), *Sam Henry's Songs of the People* (Athens, GA, 1990)

Jeffrey, Keith, *Ireland and the Great War* (Cambridge, 2000)
Johnson, Lionel, *Poetical Works of Lionel Johnson* (London, 1917)
Jolliffe, Maureen, *The Third Book of Irish Ballads* (Cork, 1970)
Joy, Maurice (ed.), *The Irish Rebellion of 1916 and its Martyrs* (New York, 1916)
Joyce, James, *Ulysses* (Paris, 1922)
— *Poems and Shorter Writings* (London, 1991)
— *Poems and Exiles* (London, 1992)

Kauatt, William H., *The Anglo-Irish War 1916–1921, a People's War* (Westport, Ct., 1999)
Kavana, Ron, *Irish Ways: Story of Ireland in Song, Music & Poetry* (London, 2007)
Keebaugh, Aaron C., *Irish Music and Home-Rule Politics, 1800–1922* (Florida, 2011)
Kelly, A.A., *Pillars of the House, An Anthology of Verse by Irish Women from 1690 to the Present* (Dublin, 1987)
Kelly, R.J., *Volunteer Verses* (Dublin, 1914)
— *Popular and Patriotic Poetry* (Dublin, n.d.)
Kendall, Tim (ed.), *Poetry of the First World War, An Anthology* (Oxford, 2013)
Kettle, Tom, *Poems & Parodies* (Dublin, 1916)
Kipling, Rudyard, *Rudyard Kipling's Verse* (Garden City, NY, 1922)
Klaus, Gustav, *Strong Words, Brave Deeds – The Poetry, Life and Times of Thomas O'Brien, Volunteer in the Spanish Civil War* (Dublin, 1994)
Kleinrichert, Denise, *Republican Internment and the Prison Ship Argenta 1922* (Dublin, 2001)
Krause, David (ed.), *The Letters of Sean O'Casey 1959–64, Vol. IV* (Washington, D.C., 1992)

Lane, Jack and Brendan Clifford (eds.), *A North Cork Anthology* (Millstreet, 1993)
Letts, W.M., *Hallow-e'en and Poems of the War* (New York, 1916)
— *Patriotic Pieces from the Great War* (Philapelphia, 1918)
Lighter, Jonathan, *The Best Antiwar Song Ever Written – Occasional Papers in Folklore, Number One* (New Jersey, 2012)
Loftus, Richard J., *Nationalism in Modern Anglo-Irish Poetry* (Madison and Milwaukee, 1964)
Longley, Michael (ed.), *Poets of the Great War – Robert Graves* (London, 2013)
Lowery, Robert G., 'Sean O'Casey: A Letter, A Song, and an Article' in *Sean O'Casey Review, Vol. 5, No. 2* (New York, 1979)

MacDonagh, Donagh, 'Ballads of Nineteen-Sixteen', *The Bell*, Vol. 2, No. 1, April 1941 (Dublin, 1941)
— *Poems from Ireland* (Dublin, 1946)
— *A Warning to Conquerors* (Pennsylvania, 1968)

— *Ballads with Music* (Dublin, n.d.)
— *The Donagh MacDonagh Song Collection* (http://songbook1.tripod.com)
MacDonagh, Thomas, *The Golden Joy* (Dublin, 1906)
— *Songs of Myself* (Dublin, 1910)
— *Lyrical Poems* (Dublin, 1913)
— *The Poetical Works of Thomas MacDonagh* (London, 1919)
MacGabhann, Liam, *Rags, Robes and Rebels* (Dublin, n.d.)
Macgill, Patrick, *Soldier Songs* (New York, 1917)
Mackey, Herbert O. (ed.), *The Crime Against Europe, Writings and Poems of Roger Casement* (Dublin, 1966)
MacMahon, Bryan, *Seachtar fear Seacht Lá* (Dublin, 1966)
MacManus, M.J., *Dublin Diversions* (Dublin, 1928)
MacQuaile, Brendan, *March Away My Brothers* (Dublin, 2011)
MacSuibhne, Toirdhealbhach, *Battle-Cries* (1918)
MacSwiney, Terence, *The Music of Freedom* (Cork, 1907)
MacThormaid, Brendan Mary, *Deathless Glory* (Dublin, 1966)
Maguire, Leo, *The Faithful and the Few* (Dublin, 1959)
Malins, Edward, *Yeats and the Easter Rising* (Dublin, 1965)
Maynard, Theodore, *Poems by Theodore Maynard* (Toronto, 1919)
McCabe, Eugene and Michael Davitt, *Padraic Pearse, Selected Poems* (Dublin, 2001)
McCall, P.J., *In The Shadow of Saint Patrick's* (Dublin, 1976)
McCarthy, Sean, *Ballads by Sean McCarthy* (Dublin, n.d.)
— *The Songs of Sean McCarthy* (Listowel, 1973)
McCollum, L.C., *History and Rhymes of the Lost Battalion* (Columbus, Ohio, 1919)
McCracken, Donal P., *Forgotten Protest, Ireland and the Anglo-Boer War* (Belfast, 2003)
McCurry, Samuel S., *The Ballads of Ballytumulty* (Belfast, n.d.)
McDonnell, John, *Songs of Struggle and Protest* (2008)
McEvansoneya, Philip, 'Insider on the Outside: Thomas Ryan PPRHA' in *Irish Arts Review*, Vol. 13 (Dublin, 1997)
McHugh, Roger, *Dublin 1916* (New York, 1966)
McLaughlin, John, *One Green Hill, Journeys Through Irish Songs* (Belfast, 2003)
Mitchell, Pat, *The Dance Music of Willie Clancy* (Dublin, 1976)
— *The Dance Music of Seamus Ennis* (Dublin, 2007)
Moulden, John, *Songs of the People, Part 1* (Belfast, 1979)
— *The Printed Ballad in Ireland* (Unpublished Thesis, 2006)
Moylan, Seán, *Seán Moylan in His Own Words* (Millstreet, 2003)
Moylan, Terry, *The Age of Revolution, 1776–1815 in the Irish Song Tradition* (Dublin, 1998)
— *Johnny O'Leary of Sliabh Luachra, Dance Music from the Cork-Kerry Border* (2nd edn Dublin, 2014)
Mulcahy, Michael and Marie Fitzgibbon, *The Voice of the People, Songs and History of Ireland* (Dublin, 1982)
Mulgan, John (ed.), *Poems of Freedom* (London, 1938)
Mulkerns, Jimmy, *Topical Ditties* (Dublin, n.d.)
Munnelly, Tom (ed.), *Local Songs* (Ennistymon, 1990)
— *The Mount Callan Garland, Songs from the Repertoire of Tom Lenihan* (Dublin, 1994)
— *The Singing Will Never Be Done* (Clare, 2014)

Nettleingham, Frederick Thomas, *Tommy's Tunes, A Comprehensive Collection of Soldiers' Songs, Marching Melodies, Rude Rhymes, and Popular Parodies* (London, 1917)
— *More Tommy's Tunes, An Additional Collection of Soldiers' Songs, Marching Melodies, Rude Rhymes, and Popular Parodies, Composed, Collected, and Arranged on Active Service with the B.E.F.* (London, 1918)
Ní Chathain, Nóra, *The Heart of Ballinascreen* (Dublin, 1926)
Ní Chinnéide, Veronica, 'The Sources of Moore's Melodies' in *The Journal of the Royal Society of Antiquaries of Ireland* , Vol. LXXXIX, pt. II (Dublin, 1959)
Nicoll, Sir William Robertson, 'The Twenty Best War Poems' in *The War Illustrated,* Vol. 3, No. 71 (London, 1915)
Novick, Ben, *Conceiving Revolution, Irish Nationalist Propaganda during the First World War* (Dublin, 2001)

Ó Braonain, Cathaoir (ed.), *Poets of the Insurrection* (Dublin, 1918)
O'Brien, Patrick "Rocky Mountain", *Birth and Adoption* (New York, 1904)
O'Casey, Sean, *Songs of the Wren, New Series, No. 1* (Dublin, n.d.)
— *Songs of the Wren, New Series, No. 2* (Dublin, n.d.)
— *More Wren Songs* (Dublin, n.d.)
— *Windfalls* (London, 1934)
O Cearnaigh, Peadar, *Camp-Fire Songs* (Dublin, n.d.)
Ó Cillín, Seán P., *Ballads of Co. Clare* (1850–1976) (Galway, 1976)
O'Connor, Frank, *Kings, Lords and Commons* (Dublin, 1959)
O'Connor, Ulick, *Brendan* (New Jersey, 1971)
— *Life Styles* (Dublin, 1973)
O'Donovan, Donal, *Kevin Barry and His Time* (Dublin, 1989)

Ó Dubhda, Seán (eag.), Duanaire Duibhneach (Dublin, 1933)
Ó Dubhghaill, M., Insurrection Fires at Eastertide (Cork, 1966)
O'Hagan, Thomas, The Collected Poems of Thomas O'Hagan (Toronto, 1922)
O'Hanlon, Terence, The Minstrel of Erinn (Dublin, 1930)
O'Hickey, Ben, From Prison Cells (Dublin, 1935)
O'Higgins, Brian, The Voice of Banba (Dublin, 1931)
— My Songs and Myself, The Wolfe Tone Annual, 1949 (Dublin, 1949)
— 1916 Before and After, The Wolfe Tone Annual 1950 (Dublin, 1950)
O'Kelly, J.J. (ed.), Gill's Irish Reciter (Dublin, 1907)
Ó Laoi, Tomás, Pádraig Mac Piarais, Éireannaigh Stairiúla (Dublin, n.d.)
O Lochlainn, Colm, Irish Street Ballads (Dublin, 1939)
— More Irish Street Ballads (Dublin, 1965)
O'Malley, Ernie, On Another Man's Wound (Dublin, 1979)
O'Neill, Nathalie, A Poet's Revolution: Rhetorical Violence, Irish Nationalism, and the Easter Rising
    (Montreal, 2013)
O'Reilly, Stephen, Spirit Flowers (Dublin, 1923)
O'Riordan, Manus, 'Seán O'Casey's Songs Against Sommery' in Irish Political Review, 22.11 (Dublin, 2007)
O'Sullivan, Seumas, Requiem and Other Poems (Dublin, 1917)
— Dublin Poems (New York, 1946)

Palmer, Roy, What A Lovely War, British Soldiers' Songs from the Boer War to the Present Day (London, 1990)
Parry, Gertrude (ed.), Some Poems of Roger Casement (Dublin, 1918)
Pearse, Pádraic, Collected Works of Pádraic H. Pearse, Songs of the Irish Rebels, etc. (Dublin, n.d.)
Plunkett, Edward, The Complete Poems of Francis Ledwidge (London, 1919)
— Fifty Poems (London, 1929)
— War Poems (London, 1941)
Plunkett, Geraldine (ed.), The Poems of Joseph Mary Plunkett (Dublin, 1916)
Plunkett, Joseph Mary, The Circle and the Sword (Dublin 1911)
Powell, Anne, The Fierce Light, The Battle of the Somme, Prose and Poetry (Gloucestershire, 2006)

Russell, George, New Songs (Dublin, 1904)
— Collected Poems (London, 1919)
— Imaginations and Reveries (Dublin, 1921)
Ryan, Desmond (ed.), The 1916 Poets (Westport, Conn., 1963)

Sartin, Paul, The Last Post Song Book, Volume 1, 1914 (Bristol, 2014)
Saunders, Norah & A.A. Kelly, Joseph Campbell, Poet & Nationalist 1879–1944 (Dublin, 1988)
Service, Robert W., Rhymes of a Red Cross Man (New York, 1916)
Shannon, Martin, Ballads from the Jails and Streets of Ireland (Dublin, 1966)
Sheehy Skeffington, Hanna, British Militarism As I have Known It (New York, n.d.)
Sigerson, Dora, Poems of the Irish Rebellion 1916 (Dublin, 1916)
Sigerson, George, The Poets and Poetry of Munster (Dublin, 1860)
Simpson, John E., Unreliable Sources: How the Twentieth Century was Reported (London, 2011)
Siúbhalach, Réilthin, Rebel Songs (n.d.)
Skinnider, Margaret, Doing My Bit For Ireland (New York, 1917)
Stallsworthy, Jon, Anthem for Doomed Youth (London, 2002)
Stephens, James, Green Branches (Dublin, 1917)
— Collected Poems (London, 1926)

Tunney, Paddy, The Stone Fiddle (Dublin, 1979)
— Where Songs Do Thunder (Belfast, 1991)

Van Wienen, Mark W., Partisans and Poets, The Political Work of American Poetry in the Great War
    (Cambridge, 1997)
Varian, Ralph, The Harp of Erin (Dublin, 1869)

Waters, Fiona, A Corner of a Foreign Field (Hertfordshire, 2007)
Watkins, Glenn, Proof Through the Night, Music and the Great War (Berkeley, 2003)
Watson, Sir William, Ireland Unfreed, Poems of 1921 (London, 1921)
Wright, Robin, Poems of Protest (London, 1966)

Yeats, W.B., The Poems (London, 1992)

Zimmermann, Georges-Denis, Songs of Irish Rebellion (Dublin, 1967)

Bibliography — History

There is a vast range of publications covering Irish history for the years 1913–23, and before and after those dates. The list below is merely a fraction of what is available dealing with personalities, events, regional and local conflict and happenings, and other aspects of the period.

As many of the personalities involved in Irish struggle from pre-1916 continued to be prominent until after the end of the Irish Civil War, the biographies and memoirs in this bibliography may cover a longer period of the struggle than that in which they are listed. Also, some of the books with general titles cover the entire period pre-1916 to the Civil War and the following years. [LM]

1913–1916

Barton, Brian, *From Behind a Closed Door, Secret Court Martial Records of the 1916 Easter Rising* (Belfast, 2002)
Bateson, Ray, *They Died by Pearse's Side* (Dublin, 2010)
Brennan Whitmore, W.J., *With the Irish in Frongoch* (Cork, 2013)
Clarke, Anne, *Unlikely Rebels – The Gifford Girls and the Fight for Irish Freedom* (Cork, 2011)
Coogan, Tim Pat, *1916: The Easter Rising* (London, 2001)
Githens-Mazar, Jonathan, *Myths and Memories of the Easter Rising, Cultural and Political Nationalism in Ireland* (Dublin, 2006)
Kiberd, Declan, *1916 Rebellion Handbook* (Dublin, 1998)
McGarry, Fearghal, *The Rising, Ireland: Easter 1916* (Oxford, 2010)
O'Connor, John, *1916 Proclamation* (Cork, 2001)
O'Farrell, Mick, *1916: What the People Saw* (Cork, 2013)
O'Mahony, Sean, *Frongoch, University of Revolution* (Dublin, 1987)
Ryan, Annie, Witnesses, *Inside the Easter Rising* (Dublin, 2005)
Townshend, Charles, *Easter 1916, The Irish Rebellion* (London, 2006)
Yeates, Pádraig, *Lockout Dublin 1913* (Dublin, 2001)

1916 Personalities

Collins, Lorcan, *James Connolly* (Dublin, 2012)
Dwyer, T. Ryle, *Thomas MacDonagh* (Dublin, 2014)
Feeney, Brian, *Seán MacDiarmada* (Dublin, 2014)
Gallagher, Mary, *Eamonn Ceannt* (Dublin, 2014)
Gibney, John, *Sean Heuston* (Dublin, 2013)
Haverty, Anne, *Constance Markievicz: Irish Revolutionary* (Dublin 2016)
Henry, William, *Éamonn Ceannt; Supreme Sacrifice* (Cork, 2005)
— *John MacBride* (Dublin, 2015)
Hughes, Brian, *Michael Mallin* (Dublin, 2012)
Kostick, Conor, *Michael O'Hanrahan* (Dublin, 2015)
Litton, Helen, *Edward Daly* (Dublin, 2013)
— *Thomas Clarke* (Dublin, 2014)
Mitchell, Angus, *Casement* (London, 2003)
— *Roger Casement* (Dublin, 2013)
Ní Ghairbhí, Róisín, *Willie Pearse* (Dublin, 2015)
Ó Brolcháin, Honor, *Joseph Plunkett* (Dublin, 2012)
O'Callaghan, John, *Con Colbert* (Dublin, 2015)
O'Donnell, Ruan, *Patrick Pearse* (Dublin, 2015)
O'Rahilly, Aodogan, *The O'Rahilly, A Secret History of the Rebellion of 1916* (Dublin, 2016)
Pearse, Pádraig, *Coming Revolution: Political Writings of Patrick Pearse* (Cork, 2013)
Ryan, Meda, *Thomas Kent* (Dublin, 2015)

Anglo-Irish War 1918–1921

Barry, Tom, *Guerrilla Days in Ireland* (Cork, 2013)
Campbell, Fergus, *Land and Revolution, Nationalist Politics in the West of Ireland 1891–1921* (Oxford, 2005)
Deasy, Liam, *Towards Ireland Free* (Cork, 1987)

Doherty, Gabriel (ed.), *With the IRA in the Fight for Freedom, 1919 to the Truce* (Cork, 2010)
Dwyer, T. Ryle, *The Squad: The Intelligence Operations of Michael Collins* (Cork, 2005)
Ferriter, Diarmuid, *A Nation and Not a Rabble, The Irish Revolution 1913–1923* (London, 2015)
Gallagher, Frank, *The Four Glorious Years* (Dublin, 2005)
Hannigan, Dave, *Terence MacSwiney, The Hunger Strike that Rocked an Empire* (Dublin, 2010)
Hopkinson, Michael, *The Irish War of Independence* (Dublin, 2004)
Killeen, Richard, *A Short History of the Irish Revolution 1912 to 1927* (Dublin, 2007)
Lawlor, Damian, *Na Fianna Éireann and the Irish Revolution, 1909 to 1923* (Offaly, 2009)
Lawlor, Pearse, *The Burnings 1920* (Cork, 2009)
Macardle, Dorothy, *The Irish Republic* (Dublin, 1999)
Matthews, Ann, *Renegades: Irish Republican Women 1900–1922* (Cork, 2011)
McCarthy, Cal, *Cumann na mBan and the Irish Revolution* (Cork, 2007)
McMahon, Sean, *Rebel Ireland: Easter Rising to Civil War* (Cork, 2001)
Morrison, George, *Revolutionary Ireland, A Photographic Record* (Dublin, 2014)
Ó Ruairc, Pádraig Óg, *Revolution, A Photographic History of Revolutionary Ireland 1913–1923* (Cork, 2011)
O'Farrell, Padraic, *Who's Who in the Irish War of Independence 1916-1921* (Dublin, 1997)
O'Malley, Ernie, *On Another Man's Wound* (Cork, 2002)
— *Raids and Rallies* (Cork, 2011)
O'Donoghue, Florence, *IRA Jail breaks 1918–1921* (Cork, 2010)
Ryan, Annie, *Comrades, Inside the War of Independence* (Dublin, 2007)
Tobin, Fergal, *The Irish Revolution, An Illustrated History 1912–1925* (Dublin, 2013)
Townshend, Charles, *The Republic, The Fight for Irish Independence* (London, 2014)

Regional Accounts

Borgonovo, John, *Spies, Informers, and the Anti-Sinn Féin Society: The Intelligence War in Cork City, 1920–1921* (Dublin, 2006)
Durney, James, *War of Independence in Kildare* (Cork, 2013)
Dwyer, T. Ryle, *Tans, Terror and Troubles, Kerry's Real Fighting Story 1913–1923* (Cork, 2001)
Gillis, Liz, *Revolution in Dublin, A Photographic History 1913–1923* (Cork, 2013)
Hart, Peter, *The I.R.A. at War 1916–1923* (Oxford, 2005)
Hegarty, Kathleen, *They Put the Flag a-Flyin', The Roscommon Volunteers 1916–1923* (Newberg, 2005)
Henry, William, *Blood for Blood: The Black and Tan War in Galway* (Cork, 2013)
Joy, Sinéad, *The IRA in Kerry 1916–1921* (Cork, 2005)
Lynch, Robert, *The Northern IRA and the Early Years of Partition* (Dublin, 2006)
Murphy, Jeremiah, *When Youth Was Mine* (Dublin, 1998)
Ó Conchubhair, Brian (ed.), *Dublin's Fighting Story 1916–1921* (Cork, 2010)
— *Kerry's Fighting Story 1916–1921* (Cork, 2009)
— *Limerick's Fighting Story 1916–1921* (Cork, 2009)
— *Rebel Cork's Fighting Story 1916–1921* (Cork, 2009)
Ó Duibhir, Liam, *Donegal Awakening: Donegal & War of Independence* (Cork, 2009)
Ó Ruairc, Pádraig Óg, *Blood on the Banner, The Republican Struggle in Clare* (Cork, 2009)
Ó Suilleabháin, Míchéal, *Where Mountainy Men have Sown, War and Peace in Rebel Cork in the Turbulent Years 1916–1921* (Cork, 2013)
O'Callaghan, Michael, *For Ireland and Freedom: Roscommon 1917–1921* (Cork, 2013)
O'Reilly, Terence, *Rebel Heart, George Lennon, Flying Column Commander* (Cork, 2009)
O'Shea, Brendan and Gerry White, *Baptised in Blood: Illustrated History of the Cork Brigade* (Cork, 2001)
— *Burning of Cork* (Cork, 2006)
Parkinson, Alan F., *Belfast's Unholy War: The Troubles of the 1920s* (Dublin, 2004)
Price, Dominic, *The Flame and the Candle, War in Mayo 1919-1924* (Cork, 2012)
Sheehan, William, *Fighting for Dublin, The British Battle for Dublin 1919–1921* (Cork, 2008)
Yeates, Pádraig, *A City in Civil War Dublin 1921–4* (Dublin, 2015)
— *A City in Turmoil, Dublin 1919–1921* (Dublin, 2015)
— *A City in Wartime, Dublin 1914–18* (Dublin, 2012)

Personalities and Memoirs

Ambrose, Joe, *Dan Breen and the IRA* (Cork, 2006)
— *Seán Treacy and the Tan War* (Cork, 2007)
Breen, Dan, *My Fight for Irish Freedom* (Cork, 1993)
Carroll, Aideen, *Seán Moylan, Rebel Leader* (Cork, 2010)
Desmond Greaves, C., *Liam Mellows and the Irish Revolution* (London, 2004)
Ferriter, Diarmaid, *Judging DEV, A Reassessment of the Life and Legacy of Eamon de Valera* (Dublin, 2007)
Fitzpatrick, David, *Harry Boland's Irish Revolution* (Cork, 2004)

Griffith, Kenneth and Timothy O'Grady, *Ireland's Unfinished Revolution, an oral history* (Boulder, 1999)
MacCurtain, Fionnuala, *Remember it's for Ireland: Family Memoir of Tomás MacCurtain* (Cork, 2008)
Maher, Jim, *Harry Boland, A Biography* (Cork, 1999)
Neligan, David, *The Spy in the Castle* (London, 1968)
Ó Duigneáin, Prionnsíos, *Linda Kearns, A Revolutionary Irish Woman* (Manorhamilton, 2002)
O'Donoghue, Florence, *No Other Law, The Story of Liam Lynch and the Irish Republican Army, 1916–1923* (Dublin, 1954)
O'Donovan, Donal, *Kevin Barry and His Time* (Dublin, 1989)
O'Malley, Cormac K.H., *The Men Will Talk to Me, Galway Interviews by Ernie O'Malley* (Cork, 2013)
— *The Men Will Talk to Me, Kerry Interviews by Ernie O'Malley* (Cork, 2012)
O'Reilly, Terence, *Rebel Heart – George Lennon* (Cork, 2010)
Ryan, Meda, *Liam Lynch, The Real Chief* (Cork, 1986)
Ryan, Meda, *Tom Barry* (Cork, 2005)
Walsh, Margaret, *Sam Maguire* (Cork, 2003)
Wilkinson, Burke, *The Zeal of the Convert* (New York, 1985)

The Civil War

de Burca, Padraig, *Free State or Republic?* (Dublin, 2003)
Deasy, Liam, *Brother Against Brother* (Cork, 1998)
Dwyer, T. Ryle, *Big Fellow, Long Fellow; A Joint Biography of Collins and de Valera* (Dublin, 1998)
— *I Signed My Death Warrant, Michael Collins and the Treaty* (Cork, 2006)
— *Michael Collins and the Civil War* (Cork, 2012)
— *Michael Collins, The Man Who Won the War* (Cork, 1994)
English, Richard and Cormac O'Malley, *Prisoners, The Civil War Letters of Ernie O'Malley* (Dublin, 1991)
Hopkinson, Michael, *Green Against Green, The Irish Civil War* (Dublin, 1988)
MacDowell, Vincent, *Michael Collins and the Brotherhood* (Dublin, 1997)
MacEoin, Uinseann, *Survivors* (Dublin, 1980)
MacEoin, Uinseann, *The IRA in the Twilight Years 1923–1948* (Dublin, 1997)
Mulcahy, Risteárd, *Richard Mulcahy (1886–1971) A Family Memoir* (Dublin, 1999)
Neeson, Eoin, *The Irish Civil War 1922–1923* (Dublin, 1989)
Ó Cuinneagáin, Mícheál, *On the Arm of Time* (Donegal, 1992)
Ó Drisceoil, Donal, *Peadar O'Donnell* (Cork, 2001)
O'Donnell, Peadar, *The Gates Flew Open* (Cork, 1965)
— *There Will Be Another Day* (Dublin, 1963)
O'Malley, Cormac K.H., *No Surrender Here, The Civil War Papers of Ernie O'Malley, 1922–1924* (Dublin, 2007)
O'Malley, Ernie, *The Singing Flame* (Cork, 2012)
Pat Coogan, Tim, *Michael Collins, The Path to Freedom, Articles & Speeches by Michael Collins* (Cork, 2011)
Regan, John M., *The Irish Counter-Revolution 1921–1936* (Dublin, 2001)
Younger, Carlton, *Ireland's Civil War* (New York, 1979)

Regional Accounts

Borgonovo, John, *The Battle for Cork, July–August 1922* (Cork, 2012)
Doyle, Tom, *The Civil War in Kerry* (Cork, 2009)
— *The Summer Campaign in Kerry* (Cork, 2010)
Durney, James, *The Civil War in Kildare* (Cork, 2011)
Gillis, Liz, *The Fall of Dublin* (Cork, 2011)
Harrington, Michael, *The Munster Republic, The Civil War in North Cork* (Cork, 2010)
Harrington, Niall C., *Kerry Landing, August 1922* (Dublin, 1995)
Mac Suain, Séamus, *County Wexford's Civil War* (Wexford, 1995)
Macardle, Dorothy, *Tragedies of Kerry* (Dublin, 2004)
Murphy, Seán and Síle, *The Comeraghs 'Gunfire & Civil War' The Stories of the Deise Brigade IRA, 1914–1924* (Clonmel, n.d.)
Ó Gadhra, Nollaig, *Civil War in Connacht 1922–1923* (Cork, 1999)
Ó Ruairc, Pádraig Óg, *The Battle for Limerick City* (Cork, 2010)
O'Callaghan, John, *The Battle for Kilmallock* (Cork, 2012)

Index of Titles and *Tune Titles*

Index of First Lines

683

Index of Authors

689

General Index